Strategies of Social Research

3rd Edition

Strategies of Social Research

3rd Edition

Herman W Smith

University of Missouri—St. Louis

Publisher	TED BUCHHOLZ
Acquisitions Editor	CHRIS KLEIN
Production Manager	ANNETTE DUDLEY WIGGINS
Text Designer	CALIBER
Cover Designer	GUY JACOBS
Design, Editorial, and Production Service	CALIBER

LIBRARY OF CONGRESS CATALOGING-IN-PUBLICATION DATA

Smith, H.W (Herman W), 1943–
    Strategies of social research: the methodological imagination/
Herman W Smith.—3rd ed.
      p.   cm.
    Includes bibliographical references and index.
    ISBN 0-03-023077-2
    1. Sociology—Research. 2. Sociology—Methodology. I. Title.
HM48.S55   1991
301'.072—dc20   91-6617
                                            CIP

ISBN: 0-03-023077-2

Address for Editorial Correspondence
Holt, Rinehart and Winston, Inc., 301 Commerce Street, Suite 3700,
Fort Worth, TX 76102

Address for Orders
Holt, Rinehart and Winston, Inc. 6277 Sea Harbor Drive, Orlando, FL 32887
1-800-782-4479 or 1-800-433-0001 (in Florida)

Printed in the United States of America

1 2 3 4   0 1 6   9 8 7 6 5 4 3 2 1

Holt, Rinehart and Winston, Inc.
The Dryden Press
Saunders College Publishing

To the Interlibrary Loan Staff at UM–St. Louis who have, for over 20 years, brought the libraries of the whole world to my feet. None of my books or research could ever have been accomplished without this staff's faithful, but often thankless, efforts in my behalf. If this book is *DIGNA QUAE LEGANTUR* (worthy of being read), it is largely due to their help.

Preface to Third Edition

When I first started to prepare this revision, I was surprised by the number of extraordinary changes that had taken place in social science research methods. The second edition of this book was finished a decade ago, just before the personal computer made its meteoric influence. Many of the advances in research methods are directly related to the degree to which personal computers have affected both mathematical computations and qualitative notekeeping. Available with this text are sets of both IBM-PC and Apple II-compatible software. I hope instructors and students will take advantage of this software. The Instructor's Manual provides hints on efficient use of this software for classroom demonstration, laboratory use, and individualized homework. The CLEAR software series—available in both MS–DOS and Apple II format—was originally intended for Introductory Sociology students but is well-suited for hands-on demonstration of basic methodological principles and problems: sampling, operationalization, reliability, validity, measurement and scaling, ethical issues, and simple statistical computation and interpretation, to name only a few. The SOCIALSCENE/SOCIALTREND disk (MS–DOS compatible only) includes a subset of National Opinion Research Center survey files. This disk takes most of the normal pain and misery out of teaching data management and analysis. If you have access to personal computers, why spend hours teaching clumsy, expensive mainframe-based packages when you can have students doing similar analysis on a PC in half an hour? The point of software ought to be to ease the burden of learning and teaching methods—not increase it.

Research methods texts generally emphasize either knowledge-production or knowledge-consumption. Because most research methods courses are taught in either one semester or quarter, I think it is unrealistic to do a good job at teaching the complete production of new knowledge. Over the course of 20 years of teaching, I find that few social science research methods students go into research-oriented Masters or PhD programs. Furthermore, most of our students are Administration of Justice, Nursing, and Social Work majors who need to learn to evaluate and apply social scientific information. It is also unrealistic to expect to teach students a simple set of how-to-do-it principles for doing quality research in one semester or quarter. As practitioners, we know that quality research of any type typically takes years from inception to publication. Consequently, this book is aimed at those instructors interested in producing smarter consumers of knowledge. Therefore, new features in this text are the inclusion of *key terms* and *study guide questions* for each chapter and a glossary in the end matter. It makes sense to make sure beginning students understand the fundamental language and logic of methodology before allowing them to try their hand at actual research.

A unique feature of this text is the inclusion of some complete Citation Classics© from the Institute of Scientific Information (ISI). On a weekly basis, the ISI produces useful analyses of the most cited articles in all scientific fields. Those which have an unusually high rate of citations and long citation history become the focus of particular issues of *Current Contents.* These short, one-page articles give insightful, and oftentimes entertaining, behind-the-scenes looks at the way in which truly classic research was accomplished.

The third edition is written using an example-based approach as opposed to a principle-based approach. I have pretested all the materials in this text on my own students, who are for the most part first-generation college students at a typical commuter urban university, as well as most of the chapters on one group of Japanese students with English as a second language. Also, a colleague tested all chapters in the third edition alongside a leading competitor in a research methods course in a prison-extension undergraduate-degree program. The students in that program expressed a preference for the present text because of the many contemporary examples.

Contemporary research methods consist of a great variety of methods. Each of those methods can be likened to special tools on the master carpenter's workbench: In essence, each tool performs specialized functions and is most appropriate only in limited circumstances. Most introductory research texts overemphasize survey research at the expense of other equally useful tools. By contrast, this text emphasizes the value of using a variety of methods depending on the circumstances. Just as it is inefficient to use a hammer when a screwdriver is more appropriate, some methods are more efficient than other methods for doing particular types of research. I believe students can profit greatly from an introduction to the major methods, rather than specializing in one before they understand the variety of tools at their disposal.

I have ordered chapters according to the logic of how good research is done. Certain chapters are best read in their numbered order. All of the first five chapters ought to be read in order. Chapter 1 presents an overview of the role of theory in research: the ideal versus actual research process; and issues of Truth and Beauty that affect how scientists judge scientific results. Chapter 2 presents the basics of library research to: (1) increase awareness of what research has already been done on any particular topic; (2) indicate the larger context of particular studies; (3) aid the process of theory-building; and (4) facilitate prevention of the "rediscovery of the wheel." Chapter 3 explains the "building blocks" of science: concepts, variables, hypotheses, and theories. It gives: (1) examples of the various types of variable scales; (2) advice on how to create stronger scales; (3) counsel on the logic of deducing causation; and (4) rules for building more testable theories. Chapter 4 introduces fundamental concepts of measuring variables, hypotheses, and theories: (1) creation of specific measures of variables; (2) testing for the reliability of those measures; (3) the logic behind demonstrating whether those measures actually measure what they are intended to measure; and (4) techniques for judging whether the findings are valid or are due to alternative explanations. Chapter 5 discusses the advantages and disadvantages of particular sampling techniques for representing populations. In sum, these first five chapters explain the fundamentals of research that crosscut any particular technique for producing data and the standards by which we judge the quality of all data.

It is also wise to read Chapter 6 in order for several reasons. First, this chapter acquaints the student with all of the generic research designs used in social science. Second, it reviews and reemphasizes the threats to validity introduced in Chapter 4. Third, it provides a firm basis for comparison of experimental, quasi-experimental, and nonexperimental methods. Fourth, it communicates the steps involved in doing true experiments in the social sciences.

The instructor may treat the order of presentation of Chapters 7 through 14 somewhat more loosely. Chapters 7 and 8 make a natural pair because both chapters explain methods for studying what people *say* they do or feel; the former chapter focuses on the particular types of attitude scales, rules for forming them, and their strengths and weaknesses. The latter details advantages and disadvantages of survey research, as well as techniques for insuring high quality survey data. Chapters 9 through 12 focus more upon what people *actually do*. Chapter 9 concentrates on the various tools available for systematizing what people do. The broad area encompassed by field research is explained in Chapter 10. The increasingly popular methods of historical methods by non-historians are the focus of Chapter 11.

If the instructor is pressed for time, Chapters 12 and 13 make fairly natural cuts. However, simulations and computer modeling are quickly becoming powerful tools for studying complex social processes beyond the purview of traditional experimental methods, so the choice of cutting this chapter is not so easy as one might first imagine. Furthermore, there are numerous representative software examples available (some of which I mention in Chapter 12) that provide entertaining as well as instructive introductions to modeling and that require minimal preparation on the part of the instructor. Because evaluation research has become a growth area for nonacademics with strong research methods backgrounds, Chapter 13 may be particularly interesting for more professionally oriented students because of the practical importance of evaluation research in social work, administration of justice, and other such programs.

Chapter 14 serves two purposes. First, it shows how each method has relatively narrow utility and, therefore, needs the supplementation of other methods. Second, it explores the use of combinations of methods; studies over time, investigators, and place; and testing of alternative theories. In a sense, this chapter is a summary for the preceding seven chapters.

Part III explains the basics of later stages of research when it turns from the collection to the analysis and presentation of data. The quality of modern data management and statistics programs used by microcomputers is vastly superior to, and more efficient than, earlier mainframe ones. Chapter 15 details easy step-by-step procedures for introducing students to the joys of electronic data management. MYSTAT© and SOCIALTREND/SOCIALSCENE© diskettes are invaluable aids for demonstrating these techniques to students in a very short time span. Chapter 16 is intended as a primer for the use of basic statistics—not as a substitute for a good statistics course. In particular, Chapter 5 (sampling), 16, and 17 are based on statistics, the details of which are beyond the scope of this text. However, all of these chapters provide the essential logic necessary for understanding these statistics without burdening the student with the need for taking a course in statistics.

Because the SOCIALTREND/SOCIALSCENE© diskette comes with large sets of actual social science data, students can get an efficient, intuitive, hands-on feel for particular statistics without having to master tedious computations. Similarly, Chapter 17 is intended only as an introduction to the logic of more complex data analysis and not to the drudgery of computation. Of course, the same diskettes useful in Chapter 16 are useful here, too. However, for a basic introduction to the logic of multivariate analysis, I would recommend the instructor purchase and use one of the already prepared demonstrations put out by Cognitive Development, Inc. known widely as SHOWCASE©. The actual statistics underlying these methods are best left to a special course in social statistics. As for social change analysis, the SOCIALTREND© program included with this text provides highly useful examples. I would also recommend that the student read Appendix C on the proper display of data during this final sequence of any methods course. Also, many of the CLEAR© demonstrations introduce fundamentals of statistical analysis in an interesting, student-paced way. I have indicated some ways in the Instructor's Manual and in the text itself in which each of the software packages can be profitably introduced into the reading of individual chapters and used as simple laboratory assignments.

The remaining two appendices are more freely placed in a course on research methods. Appendix A summarizes information on the importance of ethical considerations in research. Appendix B focuses on writing in the social sciences. I personally prefer to have students read it early in the course because few of them come prepared with good communication skills.

There is a traditional split among those of us who teach research methods over the proper sequencing of methods and statistics courses. Contemporary methods depend very heavily on an understanding of basic statistics. In particular, understanding of the logic of the Pearson's correlation coefficient is extremely helpful in understanding theory building, reliability, and validity; and statistics are helpful for understanding sampling techniques, survey research, experimentation, and computer simulations. I have tried to bridge this gap by giving some minimal aids to understanding statistics in appropriate places. Nevertheless, this text is not intended to be a replacement for a statistics text.

I have combined the subject index with a glossary of basic research methodology terminology as a student aid. This ought to increase the use of the subject index for cross-reference purposes, as well as provide more efficient explanation of important concepts. From the instructor's standpoint, the test bank and suggested assignments sections of the Instructor's Manual ought to ease the burden of evaluating student progress. Although I have also included suggested research projects, I would encourage instructors to consider less burdensome tasks that focus on understanding of the concepts and techniques, rather than attempting to make students into researchers in a semester.

Herm Smith
Visiting Fulbright Professor
Tohoku University
Sendai, Japan

Acknowledgements

I am grateful most of all to my wife, Mary Burrows, who took up the odious task of critiquing the entire manuscript from the point of view of a novice reader. She was extremely helpful in making sure the text is clear and readable. The text revisions also profited from help from numerous colleagues and students. My host professor, Micheo Umino at Tohoku University in Sendai, Japan, closely read nearly half of the chapters for translation in his methods classes during my 1989 Fulbright grant there. This reading and translation proved greatly beneficial for pretesting much of the text. Cindy Stern, while teaching courses in Research Methods through my university, read all chapters and offered valuable improvements in clarity. Clare Coffey, a librarian with the Memphis Public Library system, aided me in constructing the chapter materials on library research. Genevieve Owens and Sandy Snell of my own university's reference section help trace down numerous references through their on-line computer searches. Several of my colleagues critiqued specific chapters within their specialties: Mike Stein (field research); Cindy Stern (almost all chapters); Harry Bash (theory; historic research); Fred Springer (evaluation research); David Heise (simulation and modeling); and Ron Denowitz (the final three chapters on quantitative techniques). Additionally, several undergraduate students gave me valuable feedback on close to all of the chapters—Jerry Boone, Roscoe Truitt, and William Poole. Finally, Georgeanna Tryban of Indiana State University and Ed Brent of the University of Missouri-Columbia read and critiqued the final draft copy. Although I take responsibility for any errors or misunderstanding left remaining, all of the above persons gave freely of their time to helping stamp out editorial gremlins that like to subvert the educational process, for which I am extremely grateful.

Contents

2

Using Libraries to Start Research   39

3

Formulating the Research Problem   68

4

Operationalization, Reliability, and Validity   92

5

Sampling: The Search for Typicality   132

PART II

THE PRODUCTION OF DATA   173

6

Experiments: Variations and Approximations   175

7

Scaling Subjective Phenomena   216

8

Surveys: Use and Misuse   244

9

Systematizing Observations   292

10

Strategies of Field Research   320

11

The Historic Imagination and Method   366

9

Systematizing Observations   292

10

Strategies of Field Research   320

11

The Historic Imagination and Method   366

12

Simulation and Modeling   407

13

Evaluation Research   447

14

Triangulation: The Necessity for Multimethod Approaches   482

PART ■■■

ANALYSIS AND PRESENTATION OF DATA   515

15

Data Management   517

16

Fundamentals of Data Analysis   532

17

Further Analytic Techniques   563

APPENDIX A

APPENDIX B

APPENDIX C

APPENDIX D

MYSTAT®: An Instructural Version of SYSTAT   655

PART

I

Introduction to Social Research

CHAPTER

1

An Introduction to the Scientific Process

Writing without good research is a peril.[1]

Key Terms

Analogy	Reification
Big science	Research method
Deduction	Science
Explanation	Scientific anomaly
Falsification	Scientific revolution
Hypothesis	Serendipity
Induction	Skepticism
Invisible college	Spurious association
Metaphor	Tautology
Operationalization	Theoretical abstraction
Paradigm	Theoretical scope
Parsimony	Theory
Prediction	Verification

[1]Attributed to Confucius.

Study Guide Questions

1. How does the word "theory" differ in lay and scientific usage?

2. Why is theory important to research?

3. Give a short description and explanation of Poincaré's five principles of doing science.

4. What are the roles of logical induction and logical deduction in science?

5. According to Kuhn, how do paradigms influence research?

6. Compare Kuhn's and Wallace's views of the scientific process. Which seems more reasonable? Why?

7. What are the roles of accident and intuition in science?

8. Why should the neophyte researcher abide by the rules of the scientific method?

9. What is the difference between belief and thinking?

10. Why do we say that science proceeds by falsification rather than verification?

11. Why is skepticism important to the scientific process?

12. Briefly discuss the importance of scope and abstractness in theory.

13. How do metaphors and analogies affect scientific understanding?

14. In what ways do scientific and ordinary language differ?

15. What attributes of science contribute to an aesthetic sense of beauty and ugliness? Why?

16. Give several examples of tautologies. Why are tautologies poor means of communication?

17. In what ways is theory always implicated in research?

"Science" as a word came to us from the Latin *scientia,* which meant knowledge, as opposed to belief or opinion. Over time the word "science" has come to denote particular branches of knowledge and ways of knowing. The social sciences are among these.

   Research methods provide ways to organize scientific inquiries into knowledge. Without adhering to the rules and principles of research, we run the danger of producing ideas and information unrelated to each other or to reality. Theory is necessary to research so that we do not create piles of disjointed facts with no apparent rhyme or reason. Method aids us in our choice of facts. Not all facts are created equal. Some facts are more important than others, and therefore, choosing the more important ones becomes an important task.

After all, we cannot know everything. We are forced to be selective because there isn't time to see everything. The average person is selective because of the norms of culture rather than for any well-thought-out reason. For example, American norms coerce us into *not* paying attention to certain facts, such as how others smell or feel. Also, our culture emphasizes that what we say is more important than what we do, although psychological research into deceit demonstrates that what we do is at least as important as what we say. Because our culture stresses individualism, most individuals' perceptions are selective at that level. However, sociological theory stresses the fundamental importance of groups and organizations to being human.

We can solve the problem of the burden of an infinite number of potentially observable facts in a number of ways. First of all, we could allow the pure caprice of our curiosity to determine our choice. But to do so would imply that all facts are equally important. Because all facts are *not* equally important, we need methods or rules for ranking the importance of facts. In science, we have both norms and facts, but we need theory to think clearly about them. Some useful points to consider for thinking clearly about scientific facts follow (Poincaré 1921).

1. The more general a fact, the more meaningful it is.

We know general facts in part by how often the facts keep appearing, in part by how much they explain, and in part by how many other facts may be subsumed under their umbrella. The scope of description, understanding, explanation, or prediction is important: The greater the scope, the more valuable the fact. For example, humans are capable of making over 270,000 discrete gestures, and they have created over 15,000 adjectival labels for describing individuals. Because social scientists find such huge numbers cumbersome, they search for means of bringing order to such near infinities of facts by reducing them to a manageable number with broad application. They ask such questions as the following: How many emotions are fundamental to all humans? What kinds of principles might bring order to the range of human gestures? For example, Morgan and Heise (1988) extracted 99 emotional labels from the thousands that exist, and then simplified them into two dimensions. One dimension discriminated positive emotions—liveliness extremes ranging from calmness to excitation. By contrast, two dimensions ordered negative emotions—liveliness and power. The negative emotions of disappointment, sorrow, and regret all clustered under perceptions of low liveliness and high power; envy, jealousy, and mortification were perceived as connoting medium levels of liveliness and power; and brokenheartedness, self-pity, depression, and dejection clustered under low levels of liveliness and power. Much of the effort of science is expended toward producing more general facts. Whereas the specific labels of "jealousy" and "envy" do denote different emotions, to focus only on their uniqueness would be to lose sight of where each fits into the general pattern of all emotions. This is because general patterns have wider application in society as a whole and across individual societies. Scientists are ultimately interested in more general patterns and relationships, rather than specific elements that make up those patterns.

2. *Simpler facts are likely to have greater generalizability.*

Poincaré suggests that those facts that are likely to reappear again and again are those with true simplicity. It is important to distinguish between true simplicity and what might appear to represent simplicity. If it only *seems* simple, then the fact's actual complexity makes its elements indistinguishable. Therefore, in the truly simple case, we will meet this single fact again many times, whereas in the apparently simple but actually complex case, the illusory simplicity is probably due to *non*random occurrence of facts together.

Although there are many types of emotions and attitudes, social psychologists like Morgan and Heise have long known that they are all orderable according to three dimensions: liveliness, powerfulness, and goodness. The fact that social scientists find these three dimensions across a wide variety of societies implies that all humans react fundamentally the same way in similar situations. Although differences exist between humans of differing races and nationalities, such differences often mask underlying similarities and simplicities.

Where are these simple facts? How does the scientist locate them? Poincaré's answer was:

3. *The simple facts are most likely to be found in the infinitely small and infinitely large extremes.*

Figuratively speaking, all scientists use microscopes to study the infinitely small and telescopes to study the infinitely great. Morgan and Heise looked at relatively microscopic behaviors of individuals' emotions.

At the other extreme, sociologists traditionally refer to a more macroscopic concept or characteristic, such as a whole culture or social structure. Consider the seemingly individualistic and highly private act of taking one's own life: Although a psychologist might turn to examining microscopic aspects of individuals—their attitudes, dispositions, or method of child rearing—sociologists since Emile Durkheim have known of powerful macroscopic causes of suicide reflective of social structures. Characteristics of groups often explain surprisingly high amounts of seemingly individualistic behavior. Durkheim noted the powerful and socially integrative functions of Roman Catholicism, compared to Protestantism, in preventing suicides. Such social climates are exterior to individuals but exert terrific force on them. A list of suicide rates per 100,000 population for 1980 by state shows an apparently complex pattern, with New Jersey at the low end with 7.4 and Nevada at the top with 22.9. However, the macroscopically trained social scientist can bring much order to understanding the close to 300% variation in state suicide rates by considering such social-structural variables as percent of Roman Catholics in the population and ratio of men to women (men are more likely to commit suicide than women). Nevada has an oversupply of men and few Roman Catholics, whereas New Jersey has an oversupply of women and the second highest percentage of Roman Catholics per 1,000 (53) in the United States. Although suicide appears on the surface to be a classic microscopic and individualistic act, social scientists contribute to our understanding of suicide by focusing on macroscopic causes that are not so apparent to the untrained mind.

4. ***Once you have found a generalizable pattern, look carefully at the exceptions.***

Exceptions can be instructive. This rule helps us to recognize likenesses hidden under apparent divergences. The researcher asks: How do exceptions overturn our established rule? What is it about these exceptions that gives our rule the greatest possibility of failing? By understanding these more blatant exceptions to our simple fact, we often discover that the characteristics that seemed discordant at first actually share simple resemblances.

Durkheim's work on suicide suggested that divorced persons ought to have higher suicide rates than married persons because divorce separates individuals from the socially integrative power of the family. Divorce rates in Nevada are exceptionally high compared to the rest of the United States. Therefore, we might expect Nevadans to have exceptionally high suicide rates. However, Nevada's divorce (and suicide) rates are grossly influenced by Californians, who often come to Nevada to gamble, divorce, marry, redivorce, and remarry. Any true test of Nevadan divorce, marriage, or suicide rates ought to take these facts into account.

However, it is not the facts but the *relationships* between facts that result in this universal harmony. Therefore, another point to consider is:

5. ***Look for the relationships between facts.***

The scientist comes to recognize scientific facts *because* of their relationships. The choosing of facts that contribute to some order is similar to the artist choosing from the features of a topic those that perfect the picture and give it character and life. It is this harmony that gives value to certain facts, both in science and art. Of little value are the actual suicide rates per 100,000 population of states: New Jersey at 7.4, Massachusetts at 8.2, Missouri at 11.9, or New Mexico at 17.4. Those facts are trivial and mundane. However, the *relation* of Roman Catholic and sex composition to suicide rates condenses and orders specific suicide rates and allows us to see harmony or order between facts. The constant effort in science is to search for economy of thought and effort in explanation and description.

The Ideal Scientific Process

So far I have written mostly about the observation of interesting facts and their relationships. I have also noted that those facts that are most interesting are those that lead to empirical generalizations. Ultimately, empirical generalizations interest the scientist when they can be used to formulate theories and hypotheses. Figure 1-1 gives some simplified notions of the ideal process.

Scientists use the terms "theory" and "hypothesis" much more strictly than do laypersons. In the strict sense, a *hypothesis* describes the relationship between at least two variables such that we can say, "As x increases, y increases (or decreases)." A scientific hypothesis must derive from some theory. Likewise, the term *theory* should be reserved for referring to the systematic relationships between two or more hypotheses. These are minimal definitions because mature theories and hypotheses often relate more than two hypotheses and variables. However, in any case, scientists do not use "theory" or "hypothesis" in the way laypersons do to mean a simple personal opinion or belief.

Theories are abstraction; they exist only in our minds. We cannot touch, see, taste, smell, or hear a theory. Theories exist to organize and order information for description, causation, or prediction. Of course, some theories are better at description, causative analysis, or prediction than others. Theories are not just for scientists either. (There are more and less efficient theories concerning how to use a can opener!) Scientists often use the processes of logical induction and deduction shown in Figure 1-1 to improve theories.

Logical induction begins with specific observations from which one determines a general principle. Prior to Durkheim's late-nineteenth-century work on the causes of suicide, numerous governments had published data showing astoundingly stable rates of suicides, homicides, diseases, and so on; areas in England that had high rates of mortalities due to lung diseases at one point in time were likely to have high rates at another point in time; and those that had low rates one year had low rates in other years. From these very specific empirical particulars, social scientists induced that suicides were not simply caused by private decisions of individuals to take their own lives. More positively, they induced that general social processes must be at work, creating these inequities between geographic areas, because they detected associations between different statistical maps they had drawn. For example, they noted that individuals living away from the intense smog of London had fewer deaths attributable to lung disease than those in the smoggiest sections of the city.

Such general conclusions set the stage for the first sociological theories. Durkheim, in his classic work on suicide published in 1897, argued that (a) social disorganization leads to social pathologies, and (b) lack of moral integration leads to social pathologies. Now, no one can really see such abstractions as "social disorganization," "lack of moral integration," or "social pathologies." These concepts provide means for classifying some phenomenon into particular categories—for using logical induction to move from very specific observations to more general principles of explanation.

Logical deduction is the reverse process of using general principles to derive specific testable hypotheses. For example, Durkheim's theory that social disorganization leads to social pathologies led him to deduce the following tangible hypothesis: The more immigrants in a particular geographic locale, the higher the suicide rates of that area. Immigration and suicide rates, unlike social disorganization and social pathologies, are observable. Immigration

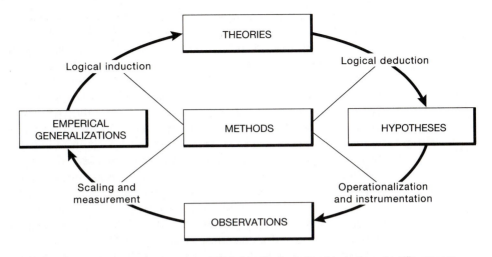

Figure 1-1.   Principle components and their idealized relationship in the scientific process.

Source: Reprinted with permission from Walter L. Wallace, editor, SOCIOLOGICAL THEORY: AN INTRODUCTION (New York: Aldine Gruyber) copyright © 1969 by Walter L. Wallace.

rates serve as an indicator of social disorganization because immigrants are most often uprooted from their habitual social relations. Suicide rates provide the same function for lack of moral integration. At this stage of his research, Durkheim worked from a generality back to particular data. That is, he used a tangible hypothesis to predict what his data should look like. Logical deduction starts from theory to make predictions; the predictions tell the scientist what the data should look like if the deduction has merit. Durkheim's mind worked something like this: If social disorganization causes suicide rates and if immigration rates measure social disorganization, then I ought to observe higher suicide rates in geographic areas with higher immigration rates.

Social science uses these two types of logic to obtain generalized understanding of variations in social phenomena. Ultimately the scientific process is oriented toward both deriving *specific* predictions based on general principles and ordering specific facts under general principles. This involves both inductive and deductive processes.

The third stage in this ideal process, noted in Figure 1-1, involves operationalization of these concrete indicators. An *operationalization* is the precise means of measurement. In Durkheim's classic study, he relied on official statistics to measure suicide. Clearly, official statistics have problems that may influence the measurement process necessary to the testing of the hypothesis. For example, a medical doctor is often reluctant to list a possible suicide as a suicide case; embarrassed loved ones may attempt to hide the cause of death from the authorities. How the researcher operationalizes the hypothesis may have great bearing on the outcome. It is important for a scientist to detail as explicitly as possible the ways in which he or she operationalized a study so that other scientists may judge how accurately and adequately those operationalizations test the study hypotheses. Because operationalization is so crucial in any science, one-third of Chapter 4 is devoted to a discussion of it.

Again, referring back to Figure 1-1, systematic observation of how a particular operationalization behaves under study may then lead the researcher to improve the observational method through scaling and other refinements in measurement. A good proportion of scientific effort goes into the attempt to improve and purify our measurements. For example, Whitney Pope (1976) reanalyzed Durkheim's classic study of suicide. In the process, he refined Durkheim's conception of modernization with a scale that included measures of (1) the percent of the population who lived in urban areas, (2) the miles of railroad per 1,000 square miles of area, and (3) the proportion of the labor force not employed in agriculture. This refined measure produces an astounding statistical association of 0.93 (very close to the upper limit of 1.0 for a correlation) between modernization and suicide, as Durkheim predicted it would (Stark 1987): The more modernization, the more suicide.

Most of the chapters in this text center around better means of making observations. Later chapters in this text focus on the bottom half of the research process (scaling, measurement, operationalization, and instrumentation) as outlined in Figure 1-1. The rest of this chapter and Chapter 4 center around the top half of that figure.

The cycle shown in Figure 1-1 is a true never-ending story; it is a cycle without start or finish. In the case of Durkheim's theory, sociologists (Pope 1976; Stark 1987) have continued to make empirical generalizations that have led to questioning parts of Durkheim's classic theory of suicide. For instance, because Stark's data for Latin America, Canada, and Europe all show a weaker relationship between the percentage of populations who are Roman Catholic and suicide than the relationship between the percentage who claim to be non-Catholic and suicide, scholars conclude that Durkheim's original Roman Catholic hypothesis was defective and needs modification to emphasize the socially integrative effects of religions in general rather than just Roman Catholicism.

Scientific Process in Practice

Thomas Kuhn (1970:62–65) described a disturbing psychologic experiment conducted during the 1940s. Two psychologists (Bruner & Postman 1949) gave subjects a glimpse of playing cards one at a time and asked the subjects to name the cards. The psychologists had designed a few of the cards to be freakish; for example, one was a red six of spades and another was a black queen of diamonds. When the subjects saw the cards for only a split second, they did not notice the anomalies. They would say unhesitantly, "six of spades" or "six of hearts." However, as the psychologists displayed the cards for longer intervals, the subjects hesitated because they became aware of something odd without being able to put their finger on it. A subject might say something like, "That's odd. I think I saw a red border around a black heart." With even longer intervals for the display of cards, most subjects would see the altered cards and accurately describe what they had seen. Other subjects were not able to make the mental shift and experienced true mental disorientation. One subject might say, "I can't remember what a spade looks like any more!" Another might say, "That suit doesn't look like anything I'd recognize."

According to Kuhn, this experiment offers some intriguing insights into the human psyche of scientists as well as laypersons. Although science has built-in checks and balances to aid the discovery of the truths that are formalized in Wallace's (1971) model shown in Figure 1-1, Kuhn proposed that scientists are human too. Rather than follow a strictly mechanical method of doing research, Kuhn suggested that human propensities lead scientists to practice science in ways that may be at variance with Wallace's ideal.

Paradigms and Science

Although Wallace (1971) does not explicitly say so, the assumption that knowledge flows freely from place to place underlies Figure 1-1. In other words, people—including scientists—making important decisions *are supposed to have more or less the same body of information.* His model takes for granted a free market of ideas: Ideas become the common property of the scientific world once information is made public. Science rises like a building, brick by brick. According to Kuhn, however, this view of science is *normal science,* which works best when a well-defined discipline awaits the resolution of a well-defined problem.

The history of ideas is not so neat. Many new ideas are only understood at first by a few insiders. Some insiders may even act as gatekeepers to keep out new ideas that threaten theories currently in vogue, rather than sticking to the accepted practice of using induction, deduction, operationalization, and scaling to test new ideas. Normal science presumes a straightforward, routine accumulation of scientific knowledge. It does not allow for new ideas and theories or unacceptable practices and methods.

In Kuhn's view of the scientific process, groups of scientists possess different paradigms. Although Kuhn used numerous definitions of a paradigm, I believe that *paradigm* can be thought of best as a special type of intellectual puzzle. As a metaphor, consider for a moment how a jigsaw-puzzle freak goes about putting a picture puzzle together. The efficient puzzle aficionado probably operates by a number of rules: Look for all the pieces that appear to have straight edges and put them in one pile, separate out pieces by colors and patterns and shapes, and so on. Usually one works from the assumption that all the pieces are from the same puzzle. It may even appear that some pieces fit together that do not really belong there, which may become apparent only after other parts of the puzzle are put together.

Similarly, different scientific communities share specific constellations of beliefs, values, and techniques for deciding which questions are interesting, how one should break down an interesting question into solvable parts, and how to interpret the relationships of those parts to the answers. Psychologists are most interested in personalities, motivation, and individuals; sociologists are more interested in bureaucracies, institutions, groups, and roles. Each discipline has a relatively narrow conceptualization of which questions should be of interest. An article accepted for publication in a top sociological journal normally would not be acceptable in a top psychological journal, and vice versa, because of the different paradigms by which each discipline works.

Kuhn observed that new scientific paradigms may (1) represent radically new conceptualizations of a phenomenon, (2) suggest new research strategies or methodological procedures for gathering empirical evidence to support or deny the paradigm, (3) offer new problems for solution, and (4) explain phenomena that previous paradigms are unable to explain.

Consider Durkheim's classic study of suicide to understand what Kuhn is saying. The moral statisticians of the early nineteenth century were puzzled by suicide rates. They started out with the assumption that suicide rates were among the most individualistic and private of behaviors. However, as they mapped the rates of various incidences, they discovered that the rates were not only highly variable across geographic locations, but that rates in any one area were quite stable over time. These two pieces of information were incompatible with their individualistic paradigms. If suicide rates are purely individualistic, they ought to occur randomly in space and time. Clearly, this was not the case. Durkheim's work almost a century later proposed a more sociological paradigm: He suggested a radically new way of approaching the causes of suicide, new strategies of testing his reconceptualization, and new sociological questions for future generations of sociologists.

Anomalies in Science

Scientists respect most puzzles that have long-standing credibility in the scientific community. The puzzles that the classic thinkers like Durkheim gave us are ones with such pedigrees: These are problems with testable solutions. It is dangerous to waste time on the untestable. Members of all scientific disciplines draw invisible lines and say, "Beyond this line we cannot go because that problem is untestable, a waste of time, or out of our province." As future generations of scientists continue work on pedigreed puzzles in the spirit of Wallace's (1971) ideal, mapped out in Figure 1-1, they are bound to come across observations that are incompatible with their hypotheses—ones that not only are not deducible from established theories, but that contradict the accepted approach. Scientists in such situations are likely to act like the picture-puzzle addict who finds what appears to be a part of another puzzle because of its incompatible colors; that is, they disregard those parts as anomalies.

Scientists experience similar anguish and confusion when they experience incongruities in nature. Inevitably, scientists run studies that lead a sheltered existence from reality. They prefer studies with the expected answer, but the real world eventually intrudes. Scientists will try to ignore the unexpected when someone says, "Gee, what about this little fluff here?" For example, one of the classic questions in social psychology is "How do attitudes influence behavior?" The most accepted theory maintains that attitudes affect behavior indirectly through intentions (Fishbein 1980). However, there are some anomalous studies indicating that attitudes may at times directly influence behavior.

The tried and true response is "Oh, it's experimental error, don't worry about it." Some feel compelled to pretend the anomalies are nothing too startling. Furthermore, the idea that "something is funny here" may be simply from setting an instrument dial wrong, rather than from an actual anomaly. After all, because anomalies interrupt the normal flow of scientific work, it becomes easier to disregard an anomaly as a simple mistake or accident (Star & Gerson 1986). The scientist is caught in a dilemma that ideally resolves itself when the scientist "scrutinizes the purported anomaly with a sharp and critical eye, determined to detect fraud, illusion, or some commonplace cause while still hoping against hope that the phenomenon will withstand his scrutiny and turn out to be the world-shaking prodigy that it seems" (Quine 1987:6).

However, the metaphor of a puzzle may break down here. After all, the colors of a puzzle are more tangible than the facts with which a scientist has to work. Two scientists may not see the same implication of the same fact; what appears anomalous to one researcher, may not be to another. Star and Gerson (1986) point out that there are different types of anomalies. Some may be simple mistakes and accidents that depend only on eventual rectification of the problem. Other anomalies may be artifacts of the methods of science that can be corrected with better study designs or improved instruments. Others might be due to fraud. If the event is not defined as out of line, work goes on as usual. If it is defined as out of line, scientists simply may continue to believe that better study design or improved instrumentation will eventually iron out the problem.

Scientists have several options when faced with anomalies: They can (1) introduce additional hypotheses after the fact to account for the strange findings, (2) live without changing the theory, or (3) refine and modify the theory. Kuhn's position is that scientists will attempt to live without changing the theory as long as possible. But because no paradigm can fit all the facts, they may attempt to tinker with it rather than radically change. This is very much the course that social scientists tried to take with Durkheim's original theory of suicide.

Because scientists believe scattered anomalies are not important, they rarely examine anomalies systematically. After all, they fit into no known scientific puzzle, and they can appear to be both insignificant in number and random events. However, over greater periods of time, some anomalies may grow to proportions that can no longer be ignored. Like the tale of the emperor who had no clothes, eventually a "young Turk" will challenge the faith of the masses by pointing to this body of anomalies. In the case of Durkheim's classic explanation of suicide, who would challenge such a pedigreed theory? It would be outrageous for a young research assistant to point out defects in the master's original paradigm. It has taken over three-quarters of a century for researchers to build up enough anomalies to be forced to recognize that while Durkheim's theory holds up in general, parts of it are clearly defective.

Furthermore, traditional scientific disciplines brainwash their students with a specific curriculum under the guise of "academic suitability." The field must have a name, people must receive doctorates in it, and jobs must be available with this kind of speciality, or the field does not exist. Scientists get enough grant money to pay for laboratory equipment and the salaries of research assistants. These assistants are graduate students who piggyback on the major professor's grant. The grant pays for photocopying, travel to meetings, and summer salaries. To cut oneself off from the grant is to cut oneself off from more than just finances: It is to cut oneself off from scientific respectability, from accepted intellectual puzzles, from authorized publication outlets, and from respected peers. All of these factors act as conservative elements slowing change in science.

The problem is that scientists are not immune to human frailties. One human frailty is to transmute loyalty to an intellectual ideal into political attachment to institutions supposed to embody that ideal. Scientists are reluctant to betray a scientific institution even when it engages in the suppression of scientific truth. Anomalous work is hard to get published: Rejection letters from a journal editor mean the work is unfit for publication. Although peer review is not supposed to be a matter of taste, the gatekeepers of science can keep anomalous work from being printed. How we know what we know is a matter of much concern and debate. Scientists' faith in observation and experimentation has deepened to the point of tolerating little that is contrary to accepted dogma. In science, it is easy to overlook the fact that some of what we find depends on what we seek.

Crisis and Revolution in Science

As a scientific paradigm matures and elaborates, relatively insignificant artifacts tend to become proportionately more significant. As the number and significance of anomalies grow, "young Turks" may start looking in the trash cans of science to see if what they are observing is not an exception but perhaps more widespread than the "old guard" gatekeepers suspect. This is not the theoretician's approach—it is the naturalist's. The naturalist says to forget the theory and look at the data. The naturalist induces by asking, "What kinds of useful theory does an anomaly suggest?" Rather than evolve in a "normal" fashion, science may undergo a revolution.

New sciences or disciplines begin when someone challenges a fundamental rule: Suppose space were curved instead of flat, as Euclid proposed. Or in sociology: Perhaps not *all* religions protect individuals from suicide as Durkheim thought; maybe it is only those religions that have medium levels of social integration of individuals, as Pescosolido and Georgianna (1989) proposed in their reconceptualization of Durkheim's work. Pescosolido and Georgianna found that religions that were extremely high in social integration (the social cults) and those very low (cults of the individual) had very high suicide rates compared to organized religions with more moderate levels of social ties. This newer work changes the focus of explanation from religious affiliation to social-network affiliation.

At the very least, changes in the fundamental rules by which scientists propose to work create problems over how we can know the truth. Much as environmental groups or religious cults are dependent upon their supporters for survival and growth, so are scientists. Interests of powerful scientific groups play a part in opening, closing, and shaping the direction of research fields. Einstein is reputed to have said that his theories of relativity would not be accepted until the older generation of scientists had all died off. Max Plank is often quoted (1949:33–34) as saying that "new scientific truth does not triumph by convincing its opponents and making them see the light, but rather because its opponents eventually die, and a new generation grows up that is familiar with it." During the heat of the rapid accumulation of anomalies and the induction of radical explanations for them, each side of a scientific controversy talks past the other side, invoking the authority of their own paradigm like any two persons heatedly discussing opposing points of view. As Kuhn puts it (1970:23), "Communication across the revolutionary divide is inevitably partial."

However, Cohen (1985) gives repeated examples of revolutionary scientists who witnessed the conversion of their opponents. Revolutionary ideas necessitate rethinking of fundamental beliefs, the recasting of perspective, and the switching of allegiances from long-held, cherished ideas. Kuhn (1970) used the metaphor of religious conversion to describe this process in science. One of the clearest examples of scientific conversion is shown in the correspondence between Darwin and biologists of his day. Drawing on this correspondence, Cohen (1985:469–470) shows the gradual conversion of famous opponents of Darwin's theory of natural selection. Such opponents found hard to swallow the role of chance for strict causality implied by Darwin's theory. Interestingly, some of these detractors used the metaphor of religious conversion by referring to the "old pagan goddess, Chance." Eventually, however, Darwin and his followers won over the majority of skeptics among the old guard biologists.

From such data, Kuhn (1970) concluded that in the final analysis a consensus takes shape among scientists about which innovations and which contributions have been most influential in the shaping of the new dominant paradigm. Work returns to normal as the new revolutionary paradigm takes root and science again becomes normalized.

Cohen scoured the annals of discovery for years looking for scientists who had declared their own work to be "revolutions" over the past four centuries. All told, he found just 16 (not all of which were true revolutions). Only a few of the scientists responsible for those revolutions are well known to us and deserving of the term: for example, Copernicus, Charles Darwin, Albert Einstein, James Watson (for his work on the structure of DNA), and Alfred Wegener (for the now accepted earth-science theory of continental drift.). Each case verifies Kuhn's point that as converts switch allegiance to revolutionary paradigms, a scientific field will cycle back to normal science, once again, awaiting the inevitable new onslaught of anomalies that will eventually call it into question just as a previous onslaught gave birth to it. The corrective factor in this drive for dominance is truth and beauty, as I shall describe in detail later. A new paradigm comes to be accepted because its adherents perceive that it embodies the characteristics of great natural truths better than other paradigms; it clarifies what was obscure; and it adds greatly to previous knowledge. The new paradigm also expresses scientific conceptions of beauty because it simplifies what was perceived previously as intricate, even though it will not explain everything.

Accidents and Intuition

Although Wallace's (1971) idealization of the scientific process is partially corrected by Kuhn's (1970) conceptualization of paradigms and scientific revolutions, Kuhn's theory does not allow for as much serendipity as actually exists in science. *Serendipity* has come to mean looking for one thing but finding another. As it happens, scientific history is filled with serendipitous findings: Many of the modern wonder drugs of pharmacy were discovered unexpectedly, and the initial discovery of superconducting materials by physicists in 1987 was not predicted by any then-existing theory.

Such historic examples of scientific accident, intuition, and serendipity have led some scientists to point out that other acceptable approaches to doing scientific research do exist. Albert Szent-Gyorgyi (1972), a famous biologist, makes a useful distinction between scientific Apollonians and Dionysians. The majority of scientists described in Figure 1-1 would be Apollonians. The *Apollonian* clearly sees the future lines of research, whereas the *Dionysian* knows only the *direction* in which he or she wants to go out into the unknown. Szent-Gyorgyi makes it clear that Dionysians are *not* unsystematic in their observations. Indeed, the Dionysian use of "intuition" probably involves both conscious and subconscious reasoning, only the end product of which becomes fully conscious. The Dionysian researcher, therefore, usually needs to make theory and methods more *explicitly* systematic.

In the first section of this chapter, I argue for the researcher, *particularly the neophyte,* to be relatively choosy about which kinds of facts he or she will look at or for. One of the best reasons for this is that it is what distinguishes the true expert from the masses: The true expert knows when to break the rules. *The neophyte must learn the rules of the scientific method well before considering violating them.*

However, when one is looking for new sources of explanation, Borgatta (1961:433) argues that one should explicitly throw in "the kitchen sink, the garbage pail, or whatever else is available that has not been looked at yet." This is precisely what happened in the case of the new superconductivity materials. Physicists grossly widened the types and amounts of materials they considered after the initial discovery. But scientists have faith that variation in any phenomenon is not random. Very quickly, physicists established theory to explain their discoveries for the purpose of predicting where they should look next. Social scientists are no different in the logic of their approach. Serendipitous findings eventually lead to theory if they prove worthwhile.

Ray Mack tells a story (1969:54) of a conversation he once had with a doctoral candidate at a professional convention. The candidate said he had just started to work on his dissertation. Mack asked him what he planned to study. The fellow said that he did not know but he was going to use a sophisticated technique called analysis of covariance. To quote from Mack: "Such enthusiasm for tools as opposed to products reminds one of a little boy hard at work with hammer, nails and wood, uncertain of what he is building." Once again, we have an example of the tendency to put the cart before the horse.

The basic principle underlying these tales is this: To speak of doing research without a theoretical basis is naive. There is always theory *implicit,* if not explicit, in all research. Therefore, it is better to make the theory explicit. The selection and use of a particular measurement technique implicitly expresses the researcher's assumptions about the nature of the phenomenon investigated, and the technique should be chosen carefully. For example, the one-time-only use of a questionnaire implicitly means the phenomenon it measures will be measured in a static way. One-time questionnaires are an extremely poor means of measuring phenomena undergoing change. If the researcher has theoretical reason for believing the phenomena he or she is studying is undergoing some change of importance to the study, then a corresponding methodological decision should be made to use a more appropriate technique than a one-time questionnaire.

Of course, theories and paradigms do not solve all problems of research. Rosalyn S. Yalow, the 1977 Nobel laureate in physiology, states (1979) that grant proposals are "inherently dishonest" because "few established investigators whose contributions are highly original and imaginative can spell out . . . detailed plans for a three- or a five-year period." If the investigator can do so, then "he does not expect to make a discovery; in fact, that mind-set can keep him from recognizing a discovery."

There is an old saying that a discovery is an accident finding a prepared mind. "Prepared mind" is the key phrase. As I stated earlier, there is always theory implicit, if not explicit, in the research process. But, unfortunately for many scientists, not every theory is as successful as another theory for explaining a particular phenomenon. Paradoxically, although paradigms provide sets of assumptions by which the scientist interprets experience, they are so much a part of our subconscious that it is difficult for anyone to step back and seriously question or challenge their inadequacies. Therefore, Kuhn spoke of the "blinding function" of paradigms. This blinding mechanism is useful to the extent that it prevents the scientist from wasting time on "trivia" while centering attention on "sensible problem areas." Unfortunately, rather than reevaluate a paradigm when data do not fit, the researcher most often rejects or misperceives the conflicting data, as Kuhn has shown.

Because of the potential pitfalls of any paradigm, scientists have developed criteria to minimize the faulty accumulation of knowledge. First, scientists are committed to search constantly for better means of making observations. Second, those observations must be made public so that any properly trained observer could replicate them. Third, those observations must fit into some theory that consistently and logically accounts for what has been observed. Fourth, that theory must have observable consequences from which it must be possible to make predictions that can be verified by observation.

These same criteria operate in the social-science community. We cannot, in other words, look upon any scientific product as simply systematic analysis of raw sensations. Therefore, no matter how intuitive a scientist may claim his or her research to be, the very scientific paradigms or conceptualizations he or she has (1) act as a screen through which only those aspects of experience that are consistent with the paradigm are filtered, and (2) set limits to the scientific questions he or she might ask.

Yet it would be a mistake to react negatively to paradigms. Commitments to paradigms, as pointed out earlier, are necessary to the formulation and expression of scientific problems. In fact, the scientist may actually use these two "limitations" to advantage in scientific discovery. Useful paradigms, as you shall discover in the Truth and Beauty sections below, have lead to a wealth of interesting discoveries.

Not all interesting science comes from laboring under the banner of a particular theory or paradigm. Unjust as it may seem, some scientists may happen to do the right thing at the right time in the right place and do it well. The end result is that, by accident, a researcher may clean out a whole problem. But the chances of such accidents are small. Sociologists who study Nobel Prize–winners have long noted that the winning discoveries are not random events. Nobel Prize–winners beget Nobel Prize–winners. If you ask Nobel Prize–winners how they happened onto a particular problem area, the chances are great they will say they were fortunate enough to study under the tutelage of other Nobel Prize–winners, who taught them primarily what the important questions were in their field. In spite of the hype about accidents and intuition, surprise and serendipity, Nobel prizes do not go to unknowns (Zuckerman 1977: 188).

Individual versus Group Effort

Price (1986) notes that of all the individual scientists who have ever lived, 80% to 90% are alive now. It is not so much the sheer exponential growth in the size of science—an estimated five orders of magnitude in three centuries—as the logistic character of that growth that calls for special notice. So Price (1986) goes further by emphasizing that science goes well beyond the individual scientists; increasingly, groups of scientists have become important to scientific advancement. Price uses the metaphor of "invisible colleges" to denote some of these social relations so important to science.

An *invisible college* denotes the informal collectives of closely interacting scientists, generally limited to a size "that can be handled by interpersonal relationships." Invisible colleges are significant social and cognitive formations that advance the research frontiers of science beyond the physical universities and research laboratories to which scientists are formally attached. Scientists send each other data for replication of each other's work. Several microbiologists separated by an ocean will send a suspected HIV-like (AIDS) virus they have cultured to examine and work with. Sociologists send copies of their raw data on diskettes to fellow scientists who wish to try a new method of analysis.

Scientists send preprints of their latest manuscripts to each other to scrutinize, criticize, or improve. Groups of scientists communicate regularly by modem across international borders using established noncommercial computer networks such as BITNET (Because It's Time Network). At regular intervals, scientists meet at agreed-upon locations to exchange information on important advancements in their specialities.

Little seen by laypersons (therefore, the term "invisible"), these collegial relations are absolutely crucial to modern science. In fact, they probably always have been. "If we can see further than previous scientists, it's because we are like the pygmies who can stand on the shoulders of the giants" is a well-known metaphor that Robert Merton (1965) traced back in various forms to the prehistory of science. Social scientists keep returning to read the early classics by Weber, Durkheim, Simmel, and Marx. Such theorists laid the broad frameworks by which our specialities have advanced. They were not always right nor did they solve all of our problems, but they continue to point us in the right direction. To use another metaphor, each scientist has a private constellation of intellectual parents, and the classic theorists are our intellectual parents. They nurture our intellectual development; even though we may attempt to break with them and go our own independent way, we eventually find ourselves returning to listen to their wisdom.

Another important aspect of the social nature of the scientific process is the mentor-protégé system. The mentor-protégé exchange process is one in which research assistants help with laboratory work or tedious calculations. The professor gives assistants shares of grant money and bits of publication credit. Furthermore, a good mentor helps his or her students choose problems that are both manageable and fruitful. If the relationship prospers, the professor's influence helps the protégé find employment. Often their names will be forever linked. Out of these symbiotic relationships are born seminars in specific subjects, centers of specialized studies, textbooks in a particular field, and journals.

Price (1986) coined another metaphor important to our understanding of the inherently social nature of science: the distinction between little and *big science*. Science started out basically as an amateur affair requiring very little financial investment: a few beakers, pieces of wire, paper and pencils, and so on. But work on the atomic bomb during the 1930s and 1940s radically changed science. Massive financial support by the federal government became crucial in physics for the first time. Scientists increasingly became full-time employees of research laboratories.

The preceding half century has borne witness to the development of big science outside as well as inside physics. While it is still possible for individual scientists to design and carry out inexpensive but important research without outside support (witness the recent flurry of research on superconductivity experiments all the way down to the high-school level), big science is now firmly established in all scientific disciplines. Some research has become so expensive and requires such large numbers of scientists working in collaboration that big science has become internationalized: Physicists and politicians in Europe collaborate by building and sharing only one huge atom smasher; the quest to unravel the genetic code is so overwhelming financially and scientifically that biologists worldwide coordinate work across international boundaries (biologists in different countries will likely focus on different portions of the genetic strand to speed up the process); and sociologists in Japan, Poland, and the United States collaborate in the coordination of cross-national verification of the effects of type of work on personality.

Social science, therefore, is no exception to this trend: Vital organizations such as the National Opinion Research Center (NORC) and the Institute for Social and Political Research (ISPR) have outgrown the funds and staffs that the Universities of Chicago and Michigan initially gave in their support. Social scientists increasingly find the need for huge financial support and large research teams for large-scale studies at both national and international levels.

The modes of collaboration of contemporary science have become global in nature. World networks of scientific literature and research exist now that were undreamed of half a century ago. Patterns of research citations are less bound to colleagues of one's own nationality. Nonacademic research centers forge close links to strong academic departments, postgraduate fellowships may be used across many national borders, and international networks of scientists exist for handpicking the best and brightest of young scientists. The way scientific ideas spread becomes as important as the way they originate.

Of course, not all ideas are equal. Invisible colleges of scientists regulate the worth of ideas through their conceptions of truth, beauty, and justice. Justice is the main topic of Appendix A, in which I consider ethics, and truth and beauty are covered below.

Truth

We often say, "I believe that x is true," "I believe the earth is round," "I believe that gravity exists," and so on. To state a belief is to state that we believe something is true. But beliefs (and their cousins, feelings) are dispositions: Either something is true or it is false. In this sense, believing (and feeling) is not thinking. *To believe something does not necessarily require thinking. Thinking is an activity; believing is not.* As Quine (1987:18) puts it: "We could tire ourselves out thinking, if we put our mind to it, but believing takes no toll. We sit and think, but do we sit and believe?" Science ideally is not about belief but thinking. Scientists may come to believe something, but science at its best is about methods of thinking.

We think in order to know. "But what counts as knowing something? First one must believe it. Second, it must be true. Knowledge is true belief. However . . . not all true belief is knowledge. If something is believed for the wrong reason but just happens to be true, it does not qualify as knowledge" (Quine 1987:108). Although we often speak of two types of knowledge—knowing *how,* as in skiing and typing, and knowing *that*—we are primarily concerned with the latter. Therefore, knowledge denotes *justified* true belief. Science provides methods for justifying the truth of some, but not all, beliefs.

Strictly speaking, the beliefs in which science is most interested are those related through theories that explain or predict, rather than simply describe. It is true that a physicist may believe that a particular combination of materials gives higher superconductivity than a previous combination, a microbiologist that a particular drug is more effective than another in meliorating the effects of a malignant organism, or a sociologist that married folks are less susceptible to suicide than singles. However, the beliefs that ultimately interest scientists are of a higher level of importance. Think of an individual who, upon retiring for bed one night, says, "Everything I've said today is true." Ignoring the veracity of this statement, such a statement must have precedence over everything else that individual said that day. Scientists are interested in more general statements that have logical precedence over lower-level statements of truth.

Falsification and Verification

Science is ultimately concerned with the truth of theories. A good portion of scientific effort is concerned with formulating research problems that are testable. If one cannot adequately test a theory for falsehoods or truths, scientists will either lose interest in the problem or attempt to reformulate it so that it is testable. The ideal scientist invents hypotheses to represent theory and then makes every effort to falsify them by devising cunning experiments. Durkheim started out with a theory of suicide that rested on the abstractions of "moral and social integration." These are ideas that one cannot see, smell, taste, hear, or feel. They require less abstract representation to render them testable. Durkheim (and a host of other sociologists since) provided more tangible tests by setting up numerous predictable hypotheses: Social integration might be represented by the percent of persons who have never moved because more stable areas ought to be more socially integrated than ones that are more transient in character. More transient populations ought to have higher suicide rates than more immobile populations. If true, this hypothesis ought to hold regardless of the geographic region, culture, or time period.

Durkheim, being a good scientist, never said, "It is proven that lack of social integration causes suicides." Such statements as "It is proven that . . ." are beliefs. Scientists are interested more in thinking how to assess such statements through clever tests. Therefore, Durkheim tested his hypotheses in numerous Western European countries. The model he followed may seem strange to the nonscientist: It is a model that rests on disproof. *The idea is to think how to disprove one's theory by setting it up against good tests of the theory.* The more such attempts to assess the hypotheses that subsequently pass this test, the more confidence the scientist gains in the hypotheses (and its mother theory). *But a theory is never proven.* The scientist knows that he or she simply may not have performed the crucial test of the theory. Durkheim knew that just because higher suicides were associated with his indicators of lack of social integration in the late nineteenth century, this in no way proved they would continue to be associated in the future. Of course, Durkheim believed they would, but belief is not adequate in science. Instead, thinking how to substantiate one's beliefs is the objective.

Finke and Stark (1988) give a contemporary example of why we must continually challenge beliefs. Ever since Durkheim, sociologists and clergy have believed that religious participation is weaker in cities because competition between religious bodies weakens faith. But Finke and Stark show that these beliefs are myths. As with any marketplace, these researchers demonstrate from a unique set of American census data collected in 1906 that urbanites are more likely to actively participate in religion than rural people and that religious pluralism increases levels of religious activity and participation. They were able to *disprove* past beliefs about the alleged evils of religious pluralism.

By reasoning, scientists often claim that something must or must not exist: They may never have seen something, but *with the proper evidence,* their claim is sufficient. Physicists have never seen a charm or a quark, but their belief is substantiated by hundreds of person-years of thinking and experimentation to back up that belief. Similarly, no sociologists need ever to have seen a "group" or "group cohesion." We infer such abstractions through thought, experiments, and studies. We try never to take our abstractions so seriously that we *reify* them: that is, to come to mistake them for reality.

The strategy of falsification aids the scientist's attempt to guard against untruths. The formal goal of science is not to verify, but to falsify one's hypothesis. That is, because the scientist realizes the impossibility of proving the hypothesis in a theory, the scientist does the next best thing—disproving alternative hypotheses. The logic of the scientific attitude is that the more alternative hypotheses for some phenomenon that the scientist disproves, the more likely the remaining hypothesis is correct.

Formally, falsification involves setting up what is termed a null hypothesis. A *null hypothesis* is an alternative hypothesis to the one under consideration; it is the negation of one's hypothesis. Consider the hypothesis, "The higher the geographic mobility, the higher the suicide rate." At the simplest level, the null hypothesis for this includes at least two possibilities: (1) There is no relationship between geographic mobility and suicide rate; or (2) the higher the geographic mobility, the lower the suicide rate.

When the null hypothesis can be rejected, the scientist feels more comfortable that the original, alternative hypothesis is correct. Because there is an infinity of null hypotheses, however, the scientist never really directly proves the truth of a hypothesis. As an analogy, think of the cowboy who claimed to be the fastest gun in the West. For every gunslinger (alternative hypothesis!) the cowboy meets whom he outdraws, his confidence in being the fastest gunslinger increases. However, it is always possible that he simply hasn't met stiff-enough competition or that some unborn cowboy will eventually prove even quicker at the draw. Proof of hypotheses and theories should be treated like the "fastest gunslinger." Ideally, the scientist attempts to match the hypothesis or theory with the best possible competing hypotheses or theories with an attitude of "May the best one win," although the scientist certainly places bets on a particular favorite with good reason.

The conduct of science through the process of falsification-in-the-name-of-verification often leads not so much from answer to specific answer, as it does along converging successions of questions. It is a matter of the often-subtle but sometimes critical distinction between fact and hypothesis. Assumptions are occasionally found masquerading as established fact, as in Finke and Stark's (1988) aforementioned study of religious pluralism where assumption masqueraded as fact for nearly a century.

It is well to keep the scientist's goal of "falsification" separate from the unethical connotation of "fraudulent." Ideally, there is little profit in cheating in science *over the long run* because of the methods of falsification to which the scientist adheres. On the one hand, the unscrupulous scientist may escape detection by falsifying an insignificant finding, but there will be no reward. (Scientists do not get their reward from salary increases so much as from citations of their work from admiring colleagues.) The unprincipled scientist may falsify an important finding, but then it most likely will form the basis for subsequent experiments and become exposed. One of the beautiful features of the scientific method is that it is ideally self-correcting. If the data, hypothesis, or theory are important, another laboratory will repeat them, and any discrepancies will become evident.

Skepticism

Underlying the goal of falsification in science is the burden of skepticism. Skepticism is nothing very esoteric. We are all skeptical at times. When we buy a used car we might say, "Would you buy a used car from that person?!" rather than, "He looks like an honest sort of fellow. I'm sure I should take whatever offer he proposes." The stereotype of the used-car buyer is an individual who kicks the tires, looks under the hood, and asks, "Do you mind if my mechanic looks at this first?" The reason is quite simple: Blind faith is likely to lead to paying a heavy price later.

Skepticism is an elementary tool in science for the purpose of setting us free. In science, the problem is keeping the need for scrutiny of all hypotheses in balance with the need for a great openness to new ideas. To be purely skeptical is to be unopen to free ideas, whereas to be unquestioningly open to new ideas is to be unskeptical. Scientists work in a climate of tension, therefore, between skepticism and receptiveness.

In science, the resolution of this tension is satisfied through a rule: Those who make claims out of the ordinary have an obligation to demonstrate their contention before skeptics, under controlled conditions. The burden of proof is on them, not on those who might be dubious. Extraordinary claims are too important to think about carelessly. It is not that extraordinary conclusions are necessarily wrong; more to the point, they are not yet known to be correct. The scientific community requires demonstrations to support extraordinary claims.

Ideally, scientists operate by stringent rules of the game for demonstrating claims, and skepticism is at the top of the list of rules. The reasons for this posture can be readily observed by focusing on scientific communities that do not hold as rigidly to it as others. Yoder (1987) examined the reasons for disproportionately large numbers of Nobel prizes going to American scientists and virtually none to the Japanese. He interviewed Susumu Tonegawa, the 1987 Nobel laureate in medicine, who has been an outspoken critic of the consensus-system of research in Japan. Tonegawa flatly states that he could never have done his Nobel-Prize–winning work in Japan. Young Japanese scientists must consciously *accept* authority and social convention; promotions are based on age rather than ability in Japan; and young researchers end up doing routine chores for senior researchers and professors who have worked their way up through the strict hierarchy. Free scientific discussion—which risks being skeptical of other scientists' work—is relatively unknown in Japanese as compared to American science. The result is that the brightest Japanese scientists, such as Tonegawa, leave for places like the United States where the free market of ideas is more routinely accepted by their peers.

Scientists ideally end up challenging "what everybody knows," but "what everybody knows" may be more dangerous than what scientists discover. Social scientists long accepted the belief that the lower-middle class supported Hitler's rise to power in forming Nazi Germany. Such a belief has important policy implications for individuals interested in preserving world peace and order. Hamilton (1982) refuted this view. Electoral data for 14 German cities indicated no distinctive lower-middle-class vote in any case. Hamilton was able to reject decisively the lower-middle-class hypothesis along with the hypothesis that lower-middle-class anti-Semitism created Nazism. The more likely reason for the rise of Hitler to power was the economic crisis felt most strongly by the small Protestant farmers who did demonstrate strong anti-Semitism and fears of Marxism, and who lacked organizational power in the more traditional party system.

Only proper respect for skepticism brings advances in knowledge such as Hamilton's. To refute a theory may seem like a small advance to the nonscientist, but science works over the long run, not the short. To refute a theory at least tells the scientist where not to look any more, and that is no small achievement in the final analysis. The cycle of skepticism now picks up to challenge Hamilton's work for the purpose of refining further our understanding of important causal events.

Scope and Abstraction

Theoretical *scope* pertains to the universality of the theory. Universality makes the difference between the beautiful and the useful. It means that different systems behave identically. It is more satisfying to have explanations for the operation of an entire social system rather than the specific components of that system. It would be more satisfying to have explanations of bureaucracy, urbanization, or industrialization rather than just of *federal* bureaucracies, *Western* urbanization, or *twentieth-century* industrialization.

The general rule is that the wider the theoretical scope of the theory tested, the more varied the data needed to test the theory. Wallace (1971:107) notes that "theories of great scope . . . are more apt to be induced from prior theories of lesser scope than to spring full-blown from abstract speculation."

Theoretical *level of abstraction* concerns how concrete one's theories are—the more concretely grounded in actual observations, the less abstract the theory. Because more abstract theories are more distant from concrete observations, they cannot be tested as directly as less abstract theories. Thus, the more abstract the theory, the greater the reliance on theoretical assumptions. Theories of higher abstraction, therefore, increase the difficulty of linking measured indicators to the abstract concepts. Additionally, more abstract theories allow the researcher a wide range of specific indicators from which to choose. Because specific indicators can test only over a narrow range, more abstract theories require more indicators to give adequate tests.

Scope and level of abstraction are related, but not synonymous, concepts: "Although an increase in level of abstraction implies an increase in scope, an increase in scope does not necessarily imply an increase in level of abstraction" (Wallace 1971:110). If we increase the level of abstraction from that of friendship networks to status networks, we must increase the level of scope because status implies a wider variety of situations than friendship. However, if we were studying status among factory workers and decide to expand our scope to status among blue-collar workers, no increase in abstraction is necessary.

We ultimately desire theories of greater abstractness just as we desire theories of greater scope. The reason for this is that the greater the variety of events for which our theories account, the greater the informational value of our propositions. It would be more informative to have propositions dealing with "bureaucratic hierarchy" or "family role bargaining" than with "political-party jobs" or "husbands."

Scope and abstraction have been the subjects of much debate and controversy in the social sciences. Merton (1967) has challenged the beliefs of those who wish for an all-encompassing theory of social life. He warns against both extremes: Low-level abstractions are limited in what they can explain and high-level abstractions explain everything (and therefore nothing). Merton urges us to seek "theories of the middle-range"—to build upon our special theories in all their lack of splendor. We should, he argues, consolidate these low-level assertions into more general formulations through logical inductions, rather than work from general to more specific theories through logical deduction. Glazer and Strauss (1967) echo Merton by calling for empirically "grounded" theory obtained from social research. Crane (1972) suggests that at least one of the Mertonian extremes of theory distortion, low-level assertions, are typical of the early preparadigmatic stages of scientific disciplines. In her research, middle-range studies involving hypothesis-testing are typical of more mature stages.

Theoretical Structure

Truth in science is largely a search for causal relationships. A maxim of causality is that something cannot be the cause of something else unless it occurs prior to the effect. The well-known positive correlation between homicides and crowded housing conditions provides an excellent example. Logically, crowded housing conditions must come before homicides; it makes little sense to assume that homicides cause crowded housing conditions, in part because the time order is illogical. Furthermore, for causality to exist, two variables must covary: As one variable increases, the other variable must increase (or decrease) in a predictable fashion. If changes in one variable cannot be predicted from changes in another, then neither variable can be a direct cause of the other.

However, correlation offers no substantiation to the claim of causation. The Presidential Commission on Pornography mentioned a strong, positive association between *Playboy* magazine readership rates and the rape rate. This association is fictitious: It is a result of the fact that young men read *Playboy* and young men live in greater numbers in areas where one finds high rates of rape. When this fact is accounted for, the original relationship drops to insignificant levels. So, at the lowest levels of theoretical structure are single relationships between two variables. Because such relationships may prove to be spurious, much of science is spent trying to demonstrate that the introduction of some third variable has no influence on the original relationship so that the researcher may say with greater confidence that the original two-variable relationship is a real one.

Ultimately, however, theory is more than the gathering of information on separate two-variable relationships. Some of the most interesting theories propose numerous causes of some phenomenon, or numerous effects of some causal variable. For example, Finke and Stark (1988) determine three direct *causes* of increases in the religious-services attendance of in the United States: (1) the amount of religious diversity in an area, (2) recruitment through Sunday schools, and (3) increases in population growth. By contrast, Shepelak (1987) notes three *results* of family income. The three effects of higher incomes she researched are that advantaged individuals will be more likely than disadvantaged individuals (1) to attribute their own socioeconomic standing to their own effort, (2) to have more positive self-evaluations, and (3) to believe their rewards to be fair and just.

Slightly more complex yet are chains of causal relationships of the form "A causes B causes C." In Shepelak's aforementioned research, she posited several chains. In one, high family income leads to high self-evaluations, which in turn lead to the belief that one has been equitably paid. Ultimately, scientists are interested in even more complex theoretical structures, to the extent that they explain more than the simpler ones. For example, in Finke and Stark's (1988:46) explanation of adherence to religion, their final theory posits the causal structure shown in Figure 1-2, in which four variables (religious diversity, percent Roman Catholic, population growth, and Sunday schools) directly

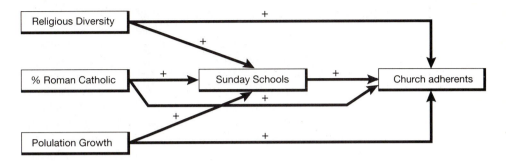

Figure 1-2.   Path diagram for the model of the 1906 religious economy.

Source: Adapted from Finke & Stark (1988: 46)

affect adherence to churches and three variables indirectly affect adherence to churches through Sunday schools.

Complex multivariate structures of the type proposed by Finke and Stark are not the end to the complexity possible or desirable in science. Many causal variables in science interact in strange but important ways. I shall treat interaction at greater length in Chapters 4, 6, 16, 17, and Appendix C. For the moment, consider a nonsocial example because of its familiarity to the average layperson. Many prescription drugs will help a sick person get well, but some of those drugs will interact with each other in ways that—if taken in combination—can easily be lethal. Similarly, many social variables behave in combination quite differently from the ways in which we know they behave singularly.

Metaphor and Analogy

The complex and strange behavior predicted by many causal structures often sends the scientist scampering about for ways to understand that are based on past experiences. One primary method of understanding is the metaphor. Metaphor refers to a particular set of linguistic processes whereby aspects of one object are "carried over" or transferred to another object, so that one speaks of the second object as if it were the first.

Simple examples include "the brain is a computer," "the human body is a machine," or "man is a wolf." Metaphor is related to simile, in which one employs the term "like" or "as" to emphasize the transference, as in "society works like an organism." It is also related to analogy. The *Oxford English Dictionary* states that analogy is "presumptive reasoning based upon the assumption that if things have some similar attributes, their other attributes are similar."

Scientists often use metaphor as a bridge between new and old theories and as a way to explain causality. For example, Darwin employed the metaphor of evolution as a "tree of descent," which was a significant departure from the "ladder of life" metaphor used by earlier theorists, who represented life as a single, unbroken chain of organisms from the lower to higher forms of life. Darwin's representation was a radical departure from this paradigm because it showed a branching diagram indicating gradual diversification among numerous independent lineages.

One of the most persistently useful metaphors in science are "maps." Many areas of science use the metaphors of "atlas," "universe of discourse," and "charts" of accumulated knowledge. Indeed, the use of "discoverers" in science often employs the imagery of the exploration of changes in our worlds of knowledge, the advances and alterations in the way knowledge is represented, or the mapping of the relationship of various elements and relationships that, without benefit of the mapping metaphor, seem confusing and separate.

The danger is that metaphor may be allegorically transformed into myth or fantasy. Studies of persuasion started with "hypodermic" or "bullet" images of a *passive, gullible public* that was easily manipulated by the masters of persuasion: Hitler or Franklin D. Roosevelt, for example. Modern students of persuasion have found these images inaccurate; recent studies emphasize the *active* information-processing capacity of the human mind in the interpretation of persuasive messages. Metaphors are powerful constituents of causal expression only so long as their use is governed by realistic standards of precision. Danger arises when individuals start taking the metaphor literally. All metaphors break down somewhere.

Explanation and Prediction

Theories in science have two functions: (1) *to explain* how things have worked in the past, and (2) *to predict* how those things will work in the future. Ultimately we are interested in combining explanation with prediction. It would be scientifically satisfying to say that we have a theory of bureaucratic organization that goes beyond explaining twentieth-century bureaucracy by predicting twenty-first-century bureaucracy. In the final analysis, we are not interested in simply describing phenomena. Although it is useful to know where poverty or crime is most entrenched, we would like to predict what causes and diminishes poverty or crime.

As the editor of *Science* magazine (Koshland 1987:727) states it:

Diagnosis of infectious disease is an area in which experts are almost invariably successful and nonexperts do not know where to begin. Why not test parole boards with case histories of known criminals and ask them to predict courses of conduct of these known parolees? Their predictions could then be compared with the actual outcomes to generate a "predictive quotient," much as batting averages in baseball are computed to evaluate competence. Cost estimators for public projects, psychiatric experts who commit mental patients, legal experts who predict trial outcomes, and transportation experts who predict usage of public transportation systems are a few of the categories that instantly spring to mind for similar treatment. The day might come when one could look on the wall of a physician's office and see the predictive quotient of the ability to diagnose illness. Judges seeking office might have to produce their predictive quotients on cases in which they gave "good risks" suspended sentences or drunken drivers one more chance.

This may seem utopian, but it is both feasible and appropriate for the scientific society to evaluate those who claim to be experts. Science has advanced by a sequence of confrontation of facts: hypothesis, prediction, verification. The predictive criterion is as important to social science as to any science. Although prediction is still relatively rare in the social sciences, social scientists have long been interested in predicting criminal behavior, divorce, marital happiness, and other social phenomena. Consider the following insight prediction that W. G. Sumner made almost a century ago (cited in Sorokin 1956:17):

> The great foe of democracy now and in the near future is plutocracy (government by the rich). Every year that passes brings out this antagonism more distinctly. It is to be the social war of the twentieth century. In that war militarism, expansion and imperialism will all favor plutocracy. In the first place, war and expansion and imperialism will favor jobbery (corruption in public office), both in the dependencies and at home. In the second place, they will take away the attention of the people from what the plutocrats are doing. In the third place, they will cause large expenditures of the people's money, the return for which will not go into the treasury, but into the hands of a few schemers. In the fourth place, they will call for a large public debt and taxes, and these things especially tend to make men unequal, because any social burdens bear more heavily on the weak than the strong, and so make the weak weaker and the strong stronger.

This is sociological prediction at its best, and it is rare.

Theoretical Language

Scientific language differs from ordinary everyday language. Everyday English is often ambiguous. The words of everyday language are susceptible to more than one meaning. For example, does the word "American" refer to North Americans, South Americans, middle-class Americans, or American Indians? Scientists work toward the goal of improving the precision of language so that individual scientists working in the same area can be more confident that they are studying the same phenomena.

Everyday language is also culture-bound. Many words do not readily translate across cultures. The Japanese word *amai* has caused considerable consternation among psychiatrists and sociologists because it translates into English as "indulgent" with respect to child rearing. The problem is that the word "indulgent" has a negative connotation in English lacking in the Japanese. Similarly, the word *shibui* translates as "astringent"; although this has an undesirable connotation for most Americans, "shibui" has a pleasant sense of cultured refinement in Japanese.

One of the most important tasks before scientists is the careful reworking of verbal (as opposed to mathematical) theories to make them less culturebound. Blalock (1968:27) suggested that the major part of this task will consist "of classifying concepts, eliminating or consolidating variables, translating existing verbal theories into common languages, searching the literature for propositions, and looking for implicit assumptions connecting the major propositions in important theoretical works." This task is no less important today than it was when Blalock first wrote it. Chapter 3 will consider some practical rules that aid the formulation of theoretical language for research applications.

Lenski (1988) offers insights on how scientists strive to rework verbal theories through his discussion of falsifiable theories. First, it is impossible to advance any science without defining key variables in unambiguous ways. Second, the scientist must define the *relationships* among and between variables unambiguously. Without such clear specifications, critics cannot identify the theory's limitations, and authors can "hide confused or mistaken views behind verbal smoke screens" (Lenski 1988:167). Later chapters will explain methods for clearly stating and measuring variables and variable relationships.

Beauty

Truth is the dominant intellectual pursuit of science; truth is ultimately knowable through results. However, in science, there is also an aesthetic force in which elegance counts almost as much as results do. Scientists do not admire money or brute force; they admire the clever mind and ingenuity. Relations among results matter more than many incongruous facts. The difference is one of pleasure over an entirely assembled puzzle or an orderly, connected group of facts compared to a disorderly pile of either. Better yet, the difference is in the pleasure of more efficient means of piecing the puzzle together over inefficient or ineffectual means. Just as the puzzle aficionado knows ingenious ways to speed up the puzzle-solving process, the beauty of a scientific theory emanates from its ability to efficiently and effectively organize myriad facts and hypotheses. Given two different theories explaining some phenomenon, scientists will evaluate them primarily in terms of parsimony: If both theories appear to perform equally well at prediction or explanation, the one with the most austere form will be preferred and accepted as more beautiful.

Parsimony

Although most scientific definitions of parsimony refer to it as the simplification of theory, I prefer not to define it that way because the goal of parsimony is not to simplify for simplicity's sake or to make a theory simple-minded. Furthermore, simple theoretical statements are notorious for leading to complex implications. *Rather, the principle of parsimony states the logic that the scientist assume no more causes or forces than are necessary to account for all the facts.* In practice, this means that when faced with two theories with equal explanatory value, the scientist should choose the simpler one. It makes no sense for the scientist to seek an explanation of ten causes of some phenomenon if one with nine causes works as well.

Parsimony does *not* imply that scientists prefer facts, hypotheses, or theories that are easy to understand. Sometimes we must face the fact that a situation is so complex that we cannot extract the causes immediately and devise simple solutions. Dominant theories in science may be parsimonious but they are, unfortunately for the layperson, not easily understandable. Similarly, social-science theories strain toward parsimony but run counter to intuitively simple theories. Criminologists, for example, find that crime appears to be a multidimensional phenomenon.

On the other hand, the expert scientist knows when to break the rule of parsimony. Just as physicists have learned much by positing what would happen if a frictionless machine could exist, social scientists also have their own equivalents. The simplest model of father-to-son occupational mobility presumes perfect independence—that is, the social scientist should not be able to predict what occupation the son will have just by knowing the father's occupation. However, this model has been repeatedly found to be too simplistic for describing the observed data. The most parsimonious explanation of the observed weak dependence of a son's occupation on that of father needs observations of the effects of a number of possible causes: inheritance of the father's occupation (as often happens in farming), such barriers to occupational mobility as union quotas, birth into particular social classes, and such achieved status effects as education at the bare minimum. The social scientist chooses between models with various combinations of such effects by observing the smallest number of explanations needed without losing descriptive accuracy. In a sense, then, the scientist does not really break the rule of parsimony in research. In effect, the most parsimonious model, the perfectly independent father-to-son mobility model, becomes the null hypothesis, which is easily rejected in favor of more complex models.

"Preparadigmatic" (Kuhn 1970) refers to the early stages of a new scientific field when there are as yet no generally agreed-upon theories. Preparadigmatic areas of science do not allow for the consensus necessary to show how to achieve parsimony, much less whether or not it exists. Specialists in intergenerational mobility, criminal careers, or social and moral integration deal with huge amounts of well-known data and hypotheses, and therefore, they have come to recognize more parsimonious explanations. Other areas of research without well-established paradigms require more data and more imaginative alternative hypotheses and theories to work toward parsimony of explanation.

Twice Nobel laureate Linus Pauling has asserted that the trick to coming up with good ideas is to think of a great many ideas and then simply get rid of the bad ones. But it is not always so simple as Pauling would have it. Theories that make long-term predictions cannot be so easily tested. For example, a Harvard–Yale study (Bennett & Bloom 1985), well reported by the popular press, predicts that white, college-educated, currently single, 30-year-old American women have just a 20% chance of ever marrying. It further predicts that single white American women at age 35 have a mere 5% chance; at age 40, the odds dropped to a minuscule 1.3%. For single black American women over 30, the prospects were considered even dimmer. Compare this with a Census Bureau study (Moorman 1987) that projected a 58% to 68% chance of getting married for white, college-educated, single, 30-year-old women, and a 17% to 23% chance at age 40.

The differences in the projections do not lie in the data: The same data are publicly available. Instead, it depends on the theory underlying the projections. The Bennett and Bloom study used a complicated mathematical model to project future marriage rates of college-educated women who are now in their thirties; for example, the researchers tracked the rates of those women when they were younger and found that for each year past the peak marriage age of about 26, the rates declined. They then projected that the rates would continue to fall each year as the women became older. By contrast, Census Bureau researchers simply used marriage certificates and other population data from 1978 and 1979 to determine the total marriage rate of women in their thirties. They assumed this rate would not change in the future; that is, the Census Bureau assumed that marriage rates of 1978 will hold true for the next half century, and sociologists know that is incorrect. Many demographers feel both studies are only partially correct. The assumptions of the Census Bureau's methodology are overly simplistic and those of the Bennett and Bloom model may be too complicated. It will take another two decades to adequately test the two theories.

To test for parsimony, scientists must presume also that their measurements and data are adequate to the task. However, "noise" (which refers to anything that causes inaccuracy in measurement) hampers measurement and corrupts data: Scientists rarely have perfect, direct measures with which to work. Social scientists observe humans who know they are being measured and may change their behavior in response to that measurement, and scientists use imperfect, indirect measures because more direct measures may not exist. Much of the task before any scientist, therefore, concerns thinking about how to improve the measurement process to rid tests of "noise" that confounds tests of the adequacy of theories.

Many of the other methods used by social scientists to help choose the most parsimonious explanation are beyond the scope of this chapter. Such methods generally require statistical knowledge. Chapters 15 through 17 will provide some of the rudiments of the logic of such statistical tests for parsimony.

Tautology

If parsimony is the epitome of beauty in science, then tautology is the model of ugliness. From its original meaning of "to say the same thing," philosophers and scientists have expanded the definition to denote the absurdity of the repetition of a statement as its own reason, or the meaninglessness of the identification of cause and effect. At the lowest level of tautologies, it is silly (but much practiced) to say, "It is so because it is so," "Boys will be boys," or "A rose is a rose is a rose." No less silly, but slightly more difficult to pick up, are banalities such as, "When people are out of work, unemployment results," "The business of America is business," "Where you are is where the world is today," and "The cause of the steady development of Puritanism was the Puritan fostering of individualism." All of these are of the generic type of tautology: "P" is "P."

More subtle yet is the "P" and "Q" are "P" type of tautology: "Tomorrow is another day," "All babies are young," "All radical revolutionary change is violent," or "Our past has gone into history." A third common form of tautology is an assertion that something is either "P" or not "P." Machiavelli's classic work *The Prince* (1989) is replete with such tautologies: "The nobles are to be considered in two different manners; that is, they are either to be ruled so as to make them entirely dependent on your fortunes, or else not" (p. 37). The "or else not" makes this sentence tautological.

Tautologies can send intellect into tailspins; we keep walking in circles, arriving at the same point again and again. One particularly insidious form of such tailspins is the "everything else" tautology because it defies description: "Something is bound to happen," "He's not as young as he used to be," and "It's impossible to find anything that is successfully hidden." Hall of Fame–catcher Yogi Berra may deserve the tailspin-award-of-the-century for his numerous contributions to tautology-land, including "You can observe a lot just by watching," "You've got to be very careful if you don't know where you are going because you might not get there," and "It ain't over 'til it's over." Tilly (1984:51) gives an excellent example of how easy it is to slide into such a tailspin with this example: ". . . all we need is to define disorder as a certain kind of differentiation and to define order as the absence of disorder."

Some individuals might insist that tautologies are not always bad practice. It may be true that tautologies, when used skillfully, make for good political rhetoric, but they are not good practice in science. Science requires problems of the sort that can be resolved by empirical research, and tautologies fail this test.

Although causal statements may be cited that appear to be tautological because of their circularity—Homans' (1950) famous statements that "Liking *leads to* friendship" and "Friendship *leads to* liking" are such statements—there is a world of difference between the two. After all, Homans did not say that liking *is* friendship or that friendship *is the same as* liking. Science is filled with other good examples of variable relationships that predict causality in both directions without making the mistake of *equating* each phenomenon.

The Inescapability of Theory in Research

Theory is always implicated in the research process. The facts do *not* speak for themselves. We cannot ignore theory—we can only choose among alternative theories.

Theory involves determination of which data are relevant, the social situations for which the data are to be collected, what the data mean, and what the observational contexts for collecting data are. Unfortunately, some researchers do not make their theory explicit. One of the first lessons the novice scientist must learn is that he or she brings implicit theoretical biases into the research situation: the problem selected for study, the manner chosen to study those problems, and the idiosyncratic observations made. No matter how ex post facto (after the fact) the conclusions drawn from the data, the methodological procedures followed will have a great effect on the theoretical or practical conclusions drawn from the data. Consequently one major purpose of later chapters will be to clarify the theoretical limitations and advantages of various research methods.

Ultimately, science is biased in favor of theorists rather than methodologists. Physicists do not remember the nineteenth-century experimentalists; they remember Einstein, the Great Theorist who organized the sundry physical facts collecting dust in disorganized minds of lesser physicists. Similarly, sociologists do not acclaim the moral statisticians of the nineteenth century whose data collection set the stage for sociologists. Rather, we remember Durkheim because he gave us the theory to organize those social data. The fact of the matter is that although researchers and theorists exist in a symbiotic relationship, the theorist is more esteemed. Gleick (1987:125) states it beautifully:

> Theorists conduct experiments with their brains. Experimenters have to use their hands, too. Theorists are thinkers, experimenters are craftsmen. The theorist needs no accomplice. The experimenter has to muster graduate students, cajole machinists, flatter lab assistants. The theorist operates in a pristine place free of noise, of vibration, of dirt. The experimenter develops an intimacy with matter as a sculptor does with clay, battling it, shaping it, and engaging it. The theorist invents his companions, as a naïve Romeo imagined his ideal Juliet. The experimenter's lovers sweat, complain, and fart. . . . [but] *ultimately prestige accumulates on the theorist's side of the table.* [italics added for emphasis]

Theory can add to the truth and beauty of science in ways that no isolated set of data, no matter how convincing or how much is accumulated, can ever accomplish. In the long run, theory wins over method because theory aids the organization of facts, whereas method simply shows the discovery of facts. The research techniques explained in this text are simply no substitute for good theory.

This discussion of theory brings us full circle back to paradigms. I have noted that scientific paradigms act as filters for our experiences and as limitations to the scientific questions we can ask. It would be a mistake to assume theories and paradigms are "good" and "bad," or "right" and "wrong." No paradigm or theory is ever a completely accurate representation of social reality. Some paradigms and theories, however, give more insights into a particular phenomenon than do others. The utility of any paradigm or theory is a function of its efficacy of (1) prediction, (2) explanatory power, and (3) productivity in generating new theory. Few theories or paradigms measure up in terms of all of these three criteria. Nevertheless, they are the goals toward which scientists aim.

Summary

Science is a series of methods for knowing, rather than simply believing or opining; it is an attempt to learn, using research methods, how and why things fit together. Because not all facts are created equal, the scientist needs rules for deciding what to study. Poincaré provides five basic rules for aiding the scientist in making such decisions: (1) search for more general facts; (2) choose those facts that seem simple; (3) seek simple facts in the infinitely small and the infinitely great; (4) establish regularities before turning to the exceptions to the rules; and (5) choose the facts that contribute the most to the harmonious ordering of facts.

The brilliant German artist-scientist Goethe (pronounced Ger-ta), who lived at the turn of the nineteenth century, wrote that the public has a right to expect from anyone who might give us the history of any science, information on how that science's phenomena were gradually known. Such a right is demanding because scientists are trained to do what they do, rather than ruminate over how they do it. Understanding how scientists do what they do requires that scientists patiently open their files, search their memories, debate one another, and suggest ways of thinking about their occupation. Happily, scientists have increasingly done just that for such historians of science as Kuhn (1970) and Cohen (1985), and our understanding of the process of how science is accomplished is therefore all the more informed. The result has been an understanding of science as a dynamic—even revolutionary—social process of knowing and discovering, rather than a finished product.

Wallace (1971) has delineated the formal system of science in its ideal form; his system emphasizes the interplay between methods, theories, hypotheses, observations, and empirical generalizations. Theories are abstractions—that is, ideas in the scientist's head concerning how to organize the empirical generalizations he or she observes. A good theory should produce many logically deduced hypotheses. If a theory is correct, it should produce hypotheses that are supported through observation. Hypotheses in science refer to relationships between sets of variables such that as one variable increases, another variable should increase or decrease. The process of observing instances that confirm or disconfirm hypotheses requires some means of precisely and explicitly measuring the variables in the hypothesis so that any other trained scientist can replicate the work. Observations in turn often profit from scaling and measurement: Improvements and refinements in observations are made by combining the observations into facts that have greater empirical generalizability. From such empirical generalizations, the cycle continues back to theory through logical induction, the use of specific observations of relationships between variables to make further refinements in theory.

Although Wallace's picture describes the routines of science, it does not describe some of the nonroutine activities introduced through chance, human error, anomalies, or the social structure of science. Kuhn's work more adequately describes some of these features. In Kuhn's work, scientists are viewed through the type of intellectual puzzles, known as paradigms, that interest them. A paradigm is a sort of super-theory that orients the scientist toward conceptualizing a phenomenon in a particular way, it suggests certain strategies as more correct or efficient for solving the puzzle, and it offers means for explaining the phenomenon.

However, because no paradigm can explain everything, scientists are bound to uncover anomalies, or facts that do not fit into their puzzles. The human response to an anomaly is to try to ignore it as long as possible. However, as anomalies multiply, it becomes more difficult to exclude them. Scientists eventually find it necessary to deal with noise by improving their methods and instruments to cut down on artifacts of the measurement process, defining the anomalies as fraudulent or unimportant, or reconceptualizing their theory to account for the anomalies.

If the anomalies pile up, they can cause a crisis in science. The more anomalies that accumulate and that scientists recognize, the more likely a revolution will eventually take place that overthrows the accepted paradigm. The controversy over which paradigm is ultimately the winner comes through accumulation of authority—that is, the extent to which the evidence is better assembled and organized by the new paradigm.

Accidents do occur in science. A scientist may be in the right place at the right time, or do the right thing without plan. Science is filled with serendipitous findings: unexpected leads that pan out, but that no theory predicted. Some scientists are more intuitive in their approach than others, too. On the one hand, there are Apollonian styles of research, that have clearly developed futures, as is true of more normal science; on the other hand, there are Dionysian styles, which only have a particular direction in mind. Another way of visualizing these distinctions is to think of saltshaker versus shotgun approaches. The Apollonian style is more saltshaker-like in its approach; the Dionysian is more shotgun-like. Although shotgun styles may lead to new, unexpected findings, the neophyte researcher should first learn to be more choosy. The neophyte needs to learn well the rules of science before attempting to break them. Furthermore, accidents in science are not as random as they might appear on the surface. To recognize the significance of an accident takes a prepared mind.

Another important feature of science is the growing importance of group effort. Individually, scientists may have their own constellation of intellectual parents. They may each have their own picture of the landscape of ideas, with each picture limited in its own way. However, scientists, even the Galileos and Einsteins, do not work in isolation from their colleagues and other scientists.

Scientists' ties to other scientists through "invisible colleges" or informal collectives of closely interacting scientists are important to scientific advancement. Scientists do not work in isolation. Another component is "big science." Increasingly, science cannot be done without substantial federal funding or international cooperation.

The worth of scientific ideas is judged through truth and beauty. The methods of science are about methods of thinking. Knowledge denotes justified true belief. The beliefs of science are special because they are beliefs of explanation or prediction rather than mere description. Much scientific effort goes into formulating research problems that can be tested for their truth value. In its ideal form, science involves invention of hypotheses to represent theory and then invention of means of attempting to disprove—not prove—those hypotheses. The logic is simple: If the hypothesis stands up to the attempt to disprove it, the scientist has increased faith in its veracity. Scientists, then, do not say they have proven something, but rather that they have not disproven it. This is analogous to American law, in which the point is not to prove innocence but lack of guilt.

One of the engines of falsification is the null hypothesis. The null hypothesis is the opposite of the scientist's hypothesis. If the scientist can disprove the null hypothesis, then faith in the true value of the hypothesis is increased. However, because there are an infinity of alternative hypotheses to the scientist's actual hypothesis that are impossible to test, the scientist can never be sure all competing evidence to claims of the actual hypothesis have been tested adequately.

An outcome of this strategy of falsification is that it aids the scientist's attempt to guard against reification, the mistaking of theoretical abstraction for reality. Another outcome is the ultimate self-correcting feature of science: The scientific method is based on repeating other scientists' work in order to search for discrepancies. Underlying this search is the skeptical posture. Science is caught in a tension between the need to scrutinize all hypothesis and the need for a great openness to new ideas.

Truth in science is a search for theories of greater scope and abstraction. The reason is that such theories account for a greater variety of events and therefore have greater informational value. Greater scope and abstraction are signs of more mature stages of theories. The search for truth in science also involves a search for causal relationships. At the lowest levels, this means the pursuit of two-variable relationships. But because the world is complex, scientists attempt to piece together multiple causes, multiple effects, and chains of causation.

The complexity of the world around us is often more easily understood through metaphor and simile. Metaphor is a device that can accommodate everyday language to the causal structure of the world. The danger is in transforming metaphor into either myth or literalness.

The truth or falsity of scientific theories is known in two ways: first, by how much does the theory explain, and second, by how well does it predict the future. Ultimately, scientists want theories that both explain and predict well. Because everyday language is imprecise, it is normally ill-suited to this process. A good part of science, therefore, concerns the reworking of verbal theories.

Scientists first pursue truth through results of their efforts. However, some theories express results more elegantly. Scientists know beauty through the harmony of results, the efficiency of certain theories for organizing facts, and the effects of theories for explaining anomalous results. The word "parsimony" expresses the ideal of scientific beauty. Parsimony refers to the logic that no more causes or forces be used to account for the facts than are necessary. If two theories appear to explain a set of facts equally well, the rule of parsimony suggests settling on the theory that is more economical in explanations.

Tautologies are, by contrast, the model of ugliness in science. Tautology refers to the absurdity of the repetition of a statement as its own reason, or the meaningless identification of cause and effect. A tautology is like the dog chasing its tail—it keeps going in circles, arriving at the same point again and again.

All research involves theory. A first lesson is for the researcher to make explicit the theory underlying the research process. Each research method, as you will discover in later chapters, has theoretical limitations and advantages. In the long run, theory wins over method because theory aids the organization of facts, while method simply allows the discovery of facts. The utility of any theory or paradigm is judged in terms of how well it predicts, explains, and generates new leads.

CHAPTER

2

Using Libraries to Start Research

*I knew that my destiny would be to read,
to dream, well, perhaps to write, but that
was not essential. And I always thought of
paradise as a library, not as a garden.*[1]

Key Terms

Abstract

Bibliography

Boolean search

Card catalog

Citation

Index

Interlibrary loan

Keyword search

Literature review

Note taking

On-line catalogue

On-line database search

Primary source

Ready-reference

Reference source

Secondary source

Serial

Snowball sampling

Thesaurus

[1]Translation of part of Jorge Luis Borges' "Poem of the Gifts," written in irony after he became blind.

Study Guide Questions

1. Why are literature reviews important to research?

2. Discuss four means of producing state-of-the-art literature reviews.

3. What are the major advantages and disadvantages of quoting from primary versus secondary sources?

4. What are the necessary steps for conducting successful library research?

5. Compare the main sources of ready-reference information. What are their limitations and advantages?

6. What are the two primary means of library organization, how are they different, and how do those differences affect library searches?

7. How does government-document organization differ from traditional library organization, and how do these differences affect library research?

8. How does most quality library research differ from ready-reference research?

9. What differences in research strategy must you consider when using books versus serial articles?

10. What strategies are most effective in using indexes and abstracts in literature reviews?

11. When is it most appropriate to consult with a reference librarian? Least appropriate?

12. What are the advantages and disadvantages of using on-line cataloguing in literature reviews?

It is valuable for both scientists and consumers to be able to conduct efficient reviews of existing literature through library research. Most people have at one time or another done a variety of literature reviews—a book review, an English literature review, or a review of some specialty topic such as a CD player. Likewise, scientists need to know what research has already been done so as not to reinvent the wheel. A literature review will also help in the formation of theoretical problems through the discovery of what other scientists have already accomplished toward solving a particular problem. Additionally, a comprehensive literature review helps identify important problems, refine ideas, map out alternative means of doing research, and understand the results of others' efforts in their larger context. Research involves more than testing one's own ideas. The serious researcher must establish where his or her own ideas fit into the "genealogy" of established scholarship: that is, these ideas extend, modify, support, or challenge the work of other researchers. Each of the resources I consider in this section are fundamental to doing good research.

However, even if you never plan to do scholarly work, as a consumer of information you should consider this an important chapter. All of us need to be able to judge information from misinformation, and useful information from the unuseful. The worth of any information can only be judged in reference to other information. When buying a car it is useful to have comparative information on prices, likelihood of repair, costs of repairs, and so on. Similarly, in judging the value of reports on topics such as ozone-layer depletion or AIDS, the consumer needs to be aware of other studies in the field to judge the importance, credibility, and utility of "new information." The consumer of information can make valid judgments only after reviewing a report within the context of other similar reports.

Furthermore, it is important that the consumer distinguish between *primary sources* and secondary (etc.) sources of information. In general, the most accurate sources of information are primary, or original, sources. Typically, academic journals publish only original research. *Secondary sources* are those that cite from primary sources. Textbooks, encyclopedias, handbooks, annual reviews, newspaper articles, and television reports typically quote or cite from original research or writing. These may be helpful in orienting the researcher to a particular topic. However, the problem with secondary sources is that the reader does not know how accurately a quote or citation reflects the original. Because a secondary source may inaccurately reflect the original, it is important to read primary sources. If you quote only from secondary sources, your report becomes a tertiary source and may perpetuate errors found in secondary sources.

The goal of this section is to get the apprentice moving in the proper direction: to give basic information on good notetaking skills; how libraries are organized; what sources are available in a good research library; how to locate particular resources concerning previous research on a specific topic; and when to consult a reference librarian.

Consider the following steps for successful library research before beginning a review of the literature:

1. Choosing a clearly defined topic;
2. Understanding how the library works;
3. Making reference searches;
4. Identifying appropriate sources through reading and notetaking skills;
5. Organizing notes and double-checking all references for accuracy and completeness;
6. Writing the first draft quickly to get your ideas down early;
7. Rewriting for clarity, accuracy, and completeness; and
8. Preparing the final manuscript.

This chapter focuses on Steps 2 and 3. Step 1 can make or break your research, so approach this very seriously and discuss your topic at length with your instructor to be sure it is appropriate. The most common downfall among novices is to choose too broad a topic and get bogged down in details. Assuming you have established a clearly focused topic, the next goal is understanding the library and how to use its resources most effectively.

Good Note Taking and Literature Reviews

Maintaining a file in which one records "ideas, personal notes, excerpts from books, bibliographic items, and outlines of projects" (Mills 1959:198) is essential to good research. Keep manila file folders for each subject of interest. As file material accumulates, subdivide any particular file into a number of topical areas; files on abortion might be subdivided into such subtopics as religion, husband-notification laws, rape, incest, and repeat abortions. As subdivided files become larger, continue to subdivide them.

C. Wright Mills (1959:196–206) also recommends using such files as a sort of research journal that includes both the most undeveloped and most finished of one's ideas. In his own files, he included such diverse resources as snatches of conversations overheard, dreams, ideas produced through systematic review of his research problems, and plans. Mills further suggested hunches and possible research designs to test those hunches, restatements of various authors' arguments, reasons, and arguments for accepting or refuting particular arguments, and definitions of key concepts and logical relationships between these key concepts. Become a heavy consumer of that famous American product—the little Post-it™ note pad. Keep these little stick-um pads close by in case you have a brain storm. Remember the dictum, "If you don't write it down when you think of it, you'll forget it."

In addition to these types of materials, the researcher should add systematic library research. This primarily involves library *topical* catalog searches and searches of journal abstracts such as *Sociological Abstracts*. By using a list of possible synonyms for (and other sources of potential research on) an area of interest, the researcher systematically checks the topical index and journal abstracts for leads to research on the subject of interest. Any leads that pan out are checked for other references to the subject, which in turn are checked for useful references, and so on until all possible leads to further references appear to be exhausted through "snowball sampling." The purpose of this review is to clarify what research has already been accomplished. Quite often, the researcher starts off with only a hunch, guess, or impression. The literature review aids the ultimate goal of shaping such vague ideas into testable hypotheses. It also should give the researcher a clear view of what procedures and results others have already produced.

Ideally, the researcher produces a state-of-the-art literature review that answers two questions: (1) What is known? (2) How was this knowledge produced? To accomplish these tasks, the researcher must depend for the most part on primary sources (actual research reports) rather than secondary sources (one researcher's reports concerning the research of others). Remember that secondary sources are a useful means of quickly finding out what research exists, but they are no substitute for actually reading the primary sources.

Notetaking skills are highly important in building a good research file. The summary and abstract for each article become important to quickly sifting out the irrelevant from relevant research. For those studies that appear relevant, the researcher then proceeds to reading the entire text. Rather than take verbatim notes, it is most efficient to record selectively only the ideas central to the chosen topic in one's own words. Notes taken down in one's own words force one to be selective, to critically evaluate, and to synthesize large bodies of material. It is worthwhile taking care to make accurate and legible notes rather than assume that one can recopy and fill in blanks later on. Chasing down poorly copied references only takes more time in the long run. Because many social-science journals use the American Psychological Association (or related) style, you will want to make sure you have accurately recorded the author, title of article, name of periodical, volume number, pages, and date of publication for serial articles; and author, title, city and state of publication, publisher, and pages of books from which notes were taken.

Of course, some articles will be so important that more extensive reading and note taking is required. Photocopying these aids accuracy at the expense of critical selectivity. Make sure you note the complete source (as mentioned above) so that you do not have to retrace this step at a later date. Even with these sources, you will want to underline and choose more important ideas judiciously.

Part of the researcher's selection should be based on recency: As a general rule, read and note the most current research first because it is most likely to be state-of-the-art. The majority of the references should normally have dates from the previous five years. Just like bread, research becomes stale as it ages. In high growth areas of any science, it is not hard to follow this five-year rule. If the researcher finds that certain types of research appear to have fewer and fewer publications over the past five years, that is often a good sign that other researchers are losing interest in the area or that barriers to new discoveries exist. Many times a loss of interest is due to the unproductive nature of particular lines of research, so the review process is a good way to be come sensitive to "hot" and "cold" areas of research.

After the completion of an exhaustive literature review, the researcher's task shifts from library research to structuring the growing file into testable research questions. Many researchers suggest that one of the best ways to aid the process of structuring the research file is to rearrange the filing system. Indeed, Mills (1959) goes so far as to suggest seriously that the researcher dump all the file contents haphazardly on the floor and then start from scratch in re-sorting the contents. The reason for this is that it is a (drastic) means of discovering chance combinations of various ideas and notes. In terms familiar from Chapter 1, this process helps loosen viewpoints by shifting the researcher's perspective to hitherto-unrelated phenomena.

Another, less drastic method of achieving potentially valuable shifts in understanding is to work with the opposite of the phenomenon being studied: normalcy in the case of deviance, competition in the case of cooperation. The idea is to compare and contrast material in the search for what makes them similar or different. Still another useful measure is to keep the files in a computer system, which allows for easy search-and-find routines, indexing, and synonym checking.

Part of the reason for the above exercises is to keep the researcher from becoming committed too early to a particular way of thinking. Becker (1986b:135) notes the mistake of starting by using a particular approach, as when an individual says, "I think I'll use Durkheim." The classic literature is always important: It is a source of fundamental hunches, ideas, and hypotheses. However, the classic thinkers were not necessarily correct, and to adhere to them unthinkingly is to treat their work more as part of a religious sect than science. Classic thinkers are good for a starting point, but it is important to see how others have contributed to the same subject since then. The world has moved on since Durkheim, Weber, and Marx.

Science is a cumulative process and a good part of that process is generated through "invisible colleges" as discussed in Chapter 1. When researchers ask other scientists to list their information sources, they often note that informal personal contact—conferences, meetings, telephone contacts, letters, simple requests of professors expert in an area, and so on—is essential. These "invisible colleges" help get research going and help it along, but they are no substitute for exhaustive library research because no set of individuals knows everything about a particular subject. "Invisible college" networks can get the researcher going, but they can neither choose nor narrow a topic for the individual researcher. Such networks help form the nucleus for expanding the researcher's search through the snowballing techniques I described in the last section. Consider your professors, friends, and fellow students as part of your own "invisible college." Each of these sources may help you more clearly focus your topic through discussion.

"Ready-Reference" Information

For short, quick answers to basic questions, the researcher may turn to standard reference works: dictionaries, encyclopedias, almanacs, yearbooks, and the like. However, these reference works have known limitations that all novice users must learn to recognize. The function of this section is to introduce all types of basic information sources and to discuss the limitations of each.

Dictionaries

Many varieties of dictionaries exist. At the one extreme are general dictionaries of the English language. Because modern languages are living, growing entities, no dictionary can do all things for all people. For practical purposes, three dictionaries of the English language stand out in scholarship.

First, the *Great Oxford English Dictionary* (OED) is noted for etymology, the tracing of the history of words. It gives some 2 million supporting quotations for over 500,000 words to show word origins; for example, its unabridged sixteen volumes list over twenty full pages of variations on the word "set." The recent computerization of the OED on compact disks keeps it more abreast of current English than in the past. For example, neither "AIDS" nor "black hole" was included in the last version.

Second, the unabridged *Webster's Third New International Dictionary of the English Language* includes some 450,000 words that its publisher frequently revises with new words and new definitions. (Note that just because a dictionary uses the word "Webster's" in the title, does not mean it is an authentic *G. & C. Merriam Company Webster's* dictionary. The name "Webster's" is not copyrightable.) Its advantages include quotations to aid understanding of usage, authoritative definitions, and inclusiveness. Its disadvantages include the assumption that everyday use is proper use of words, complicated symbols for pronunciation, and lack of information on whether a word is acceptable in writing or speech.

The *Random House Dictionary of the English Language* is also an acceptable dictionary, but it has far fewer entries. It includes 260,000 words, only about 60% of the Webster's unabridged. It excels in *prescriptive* use of language—that is, when to use a word or how to use a word. By contrast, Webster's and the OED serve more *descriptive* functions—the listing of the meanings of particular words.

Other dictionaries may give you acceptable spellings, syllabications, or pronunciations but do not have the scope or authoritativeness of these English dictionaries. If you are looking for evaluations of dictionaries for home or office use, your reference librarian is likely to have a copy of Kister's *Dictionary Buying Guide* available for comparison of the advantages and disadvantages of each: currentness of definitions, writing level, usage, authority, format, and spelling. The problem is the trade-off between comprehensiveness and the user's willingness to lift a big volume. Brevity has forced too many compromises in definitions over the years of evolution of dictionary style.

Nevertheless, no *general* dictionary is likely to list current scientific usages. Most reference sections in academic libraries carry specialized dictionaries that are useful to understanding current social science words: for example, Abercrombie, Hill, and Turner's (1988) *The Penguin Dictionary of Sociology* and Stang and Wrightsman's (1981) *Dictionary of Social Behavior and Social Research Methods*. Other specialized dictionaries are often useful to scholars—biographical dictionaries, dictionaries of synonyms and antonyms or of abbreviations, and bilingual foreign-language dictionaries. Again, these are generally available in reference sections of most academic libraries.

Encyclopedias

The general purpose of an encyclopedia today is to capsulize and organize accumulated knowledge alphabetically by subject; but for scholarly purposes, encyclopedias are rarely very useful. The reasons, given by Barzun & Graff (1970:80), are "(1) scholarship is always ahead of any but a newly published encyclopedia; (2) the size and scope of an encyclopedia make error or ambiguity more likely than in a book; and (3) revisions and additions introduce discrepancies." Therefore, no one should blindly use any encyclopedia. Use it mainly for quick reference and confirmation of minor dates, titles, or place-names or subjects for which you know absolutely nothing.

The *New Encyclopaedia Britannica* stands out as the most up-to-date and authoritative of English encyclopedias. It is buttressed with scholarly bibliographies that offer springboards into deeper understanding of subjects, and it is strong in science and humanities subjects. As with dictionaries, Kister authors an *Encyclopedia Buying Guide*, which provides useful materials on age level, indexing, illustrations, and other important considerations in using and buying an encyclopedia.

Many specialized encyclopedias exist in the sciences. Two noteworthy ones that are likely to be in any academic library are the *International Encyclopedia of the Social Sciences* and the *Encyclopedia of Crime and Justice*. However, be wary of the *International Encyclopedia of the Social Sciences* because it is out of date (1968); for example, it includes none of the advances in statistical analysis mentioned in Chapter 17 and none of the many advances in measurement of such important social variables as stratification.

Because encyclopedias go out of date so quickly, most scientific disciplines encourage and support a variety of specialized handbooks, annual-review series, and the like. For example, two important serials in the social sciences are the *Annual Review of Sociology* and the *Sociological Methodology* series. The former series publishes narrowly defined reviews of currently important areas in sociology by experts on family violence, observational techniques, and so on. The latter publishes mostly quantitative breakthroughs in statistical analysis.

Handbooks

There are also many topic-specific handbooks that are more current than encyclopedias but that serve much the same function. Some examples are Binstock and Shanas' (1985) *Handbook of Aging and the Social Sciences,* Brewer and Wright's (1979) *Sex Research: Bibliographies from the Institute for Sex Research,* Treiman and Robinson's (1981) *Research in Social Stratification and Mobility,* and Lindsey and Aronson's (1985) *Handbook of Social Psychology.* Although these are more current than many other sources, they have the disadvantage of being written by and for other scholars with similar interests— and vocabularies! These handbooks usually assume that the user understands the methods and logic of particular disciplines, and they may not have subject indexes, further limiting their use.

Statistical Sources

Another important source of ready-reference answers are almanacs, yearbooks, and statistical abstracts. Four important statistical sourcebooks in the social sciences are (1) *American Statistical Index: A Comprehensive Guide and Index to the Statistical Publications of the U.S. Government,* 1973– (ASI); (2) *Statistical Reference Index: A Selective Guide to American Statistical Publications (from Sources Other than the U.S. Government)* 1980– (SRI); (3) *Statistical Abstract of the United States*, 1879–; and (4) *Sourcebook of Criminal Justice Statistics— 1985*. Once again, almost every academic library is likely to have these in their social-science or reference sections. However, even some academic libraries find the ASI and SRI too expensive to purchase. Most other fact books and almanacs draw from the first and third of these sources because they have the authority and resources of the U.S. Government behind them. You should keep in mind that many "facts" presented in privately published almanacs and year-books are misinformation, out-of-date, or trivial, whereas other facts come from less-expensive government sources. Also keep in mind that facts by them-selves have no real importance in science. Science is not about the trivial pursuit of collecting individual facts, but rather it concerns the means of orga-nizing data to explain and predict. A particular scientist may work for 20 or more years on a particular problem. The simple question of why a citizen pulls one lever and not another when voting is puzzle enough to keep many political scientists busy for decades.

Many atlases and gazetteers also give useful statistical information in vi-sual form. However, you should always check the date of publication and the authority of the publisher. The National Geographic Society and Rand McNally are both known for quality atlases. Both usually include indexes to aid digging out information.

All of the sources listed so far—dictionaries, encyclopedias, handbooks, and statistical sources—are ways to get at some types of information relatively fast, but each of these sources lacks depth. At some point the user must turn to books and journals in the search for deeper information.

Newspapers and Other Mass Media

Newspapers and magazines often summarize research and provide quick sources of information. However, the reader should be particularly wary of scientific reporting in newspapers and other popular mass media. These sources of information usually "write down" for an audience with at most an eighth-grade education and, in the process, may easily distort or exaggerate scientific claims. Such sources do not carry standards of scientific caution that good researchers maintain. Remember that most research-journal editorial boards practice peer review for the purpose of insuring high-quality reporting. The popular press reports of "cold fusion" in early 1989 provide a good example of the differences between journal and mass-media reporting. The scientists involved in the early release of "cold fusion" findings later stated that they were quite sorry their reports were prematurely reported in nontraditional outlets. Similarly, social scientists often find that the popular press is more interested in sensationalistic reporting of their published or nonpublished work than in accurately reflecting its content.

Libraries and the Organization of Knowledge

Because knowledge is power, the heart of any university is the library. However, to the uninitiated, a library is a black hole. Information is useful only if one can get it; and to get it, one has to know how to extract the information that is needed. One of the consequences of the fact that over 90% of all scientists who have ever lived are now living is an explosion of information—about 100,000 scientific and technical periodicals, which publish over 2 million articles each year, and a tenfold increase in book titles in the United States in the last 20 years (Katz 1982a:29). The information explosion has created a great demand for the reference librarian. The reference librarian is trained to organize data and information for library users and to be aware of information sources and the probabilities of successful search strategies. Without the reference librarian, we would be in a position similar to looking for a needle in a haystack.

The rate at which information is accumulating is astounding, and many fear that the information explosion is a crumbling edifice that will engulf us all before we control it. Although it is the reference librarian's role to stop that from happening, none of us can expect the reference librarian to do for libraries, knowledge, or science what the originators of McDonald's did for cuisine. In spite of the general public's appetite for quickie information, no reference librarian should be expected to do the scientist's (or student's) actual work. Library users should treat the reference librarian as someone who can put them on the right road and treat the information they wish to find as nuggets of gold that must be painstakingly searched and mined. Just as the geologist methodically searches for particular minerals in particular places, the reference librarian has methods for efficiently organizing information and searching for particular nuggets of information. However, all students and scholars, like good geologists, must learn to be self-reliant and do the mining themselves.

The relationship between reference librarians and scientists is symbiotic. Individuals specialize in particular subjects in part to become efficient. Scientists specialize in creating new information; reference librarians specialize in organizing and retrieving information. Although scholars should, and generally do, become fairly proficient at knowing how to search particular, specialized bodies of knowledge, they often profit from collaboration with information specialists. Librarians can help the researcher make connections between ideas and sources, and can help them become selective and critical about those sources. Scientists need to learn how to cope with increasingly rich information environments—that is, learn how to monitor, select, acquire, synthesize, use, and disseminate scientific and technical information relevant to their needs. However, reference desks are often busy places. The user will progress more swiftly if he or she learns how to do some basic work learning fundamental facts about how information is organized and deposited in libraries. Many users may want only to obtain information rather than learn how to find that information. However, the user who knows how to find basic information enables librarians to concentrate on finding more difficult, obscure information.

Reference Questions

Regardless of the user's skills at exploiting library and information resources, at some point even the typically self-reliant user must consider asking a reference librarian where to find particular scholarly materials. The most common complaint of reference librarians is that their patrons do not ask specific-enough questions for finding specific citations, books, or other materials. The patron normally has only a vague notion of what he or she wants and does not express it well enough to locate needed information, or asks a question that leads to either too much information or too little.

The problem is one of retrieving specific data or specific documents, but as Katz (1982a:16) states, "The most common complaint heard among reference librarians about their work is that few people know how to ask reference questions." For this reason, librarians learn how to conduct reference interviews with their patrons, the basic format of which is: How much material do you want on the subject? Do you want difficult or elementary material? Do you have time for gathering the information? Do you need material in a particular form?

The user may think that all that is necessary is to determine what he or she needs and then communicate this process to the reference librarian. However, the reference librarian and user usually end up negotiating because the reference librarian is unlikely to fully understand the initial question. The question most likely needs refinement, supplemental clues, and translation into a form that the reference librarian knows how to pursue. The reference librarian will redefine most questions so as to help enumerate the concepts that need searching, organize them into particular search strategies, and guide the user in conducting the actual search.

Even experienced reference-desk users are likely to find they need help to redefine what they thought were clear requests. A set of ten commandments for library users (Gardner & Zelevansky 1975:26) gives tongue-in-cheek, but sage, advice to the library user:

I.   Thou shalt be prepared with a valid, logical and/or reasonable query and not an inchoate (imperfectly formed) question, without form and void.

II. Thou shalt request all information in the beginning.

III. Thou shalt be honest and true with thy librarian in revelation of what thou seekest, much as thou wouldst not hold back symptoms from thy physician.

IV. Thou shalt exhibit the patience of Job in waiting at the librarian's desk (or at the other end of the telephone) so that when the answer to thy query is divined, the search shall not have been in vain.

V.   Thou shalt express thine appreciation of labor well done by thy librarian through written testimony to his/her supervisor.

VI. Thou shalt not designate the "Source," but rather utter clearly that which is sought.

VII. Thou shalt not require thy librarian accountable for that which is not yet published.

VIII. Thou shalt not require thy librarian to interpret data in chapter and verse.

IX. Thou shalt not scorn a wise referral, for surely any sage counsel cannot lead thee far astray and may indeed bear fruit.

X.   Thou shalt not steal.

Library Classification Systems

Almost all libraries use one of two general systems for classifying books, journals, and other materials. Over one-hundred years ago, Melvil Dewey invented the *Dewey Decimal classification system* as a means of coping with the burgeoning information explosion of his day. If the library assigns fixed numbers in the hundreds to the books, the system is the Dewey system. For example, the social sciences have numbers ranging between 300 and 399. The logic of the Dewey system is to place a number after a decimal to represent subdivisions into specialities. For example:

323.4   Civil rights

323.44   Freedom of action

323.6   Citizenship

The beauty of this system is that no one need memorize all of the numbers, just a logical pattern. Therefore, if you recall that all the social sciences use the generic 300 listing, it is easier to associate 301 with sociology and 330 with economics titles. Nevertheless, the Dewey system does not accommodate specialized subjects well. Larger, more research-oriented libraries therefore prefer the Library of Congress method.

The *Library of Congress classification system* matches the logic of the Dewey system, but it allows for more expansion. This system uses one (or more) of 21 letters before a number. For example, all the social sciences are located under H. By using combinations of letters, the library user may easily locate subfields. Sociology titles are located under HM, Psychology (not a social science) under BF, and psychiatry under RC. By adding a few numbers, librarians classify even more specialized knowledge; the user can go to any library using this system and quickly locate the major sociology journals under HM1 or titles on "social science—authorship" under H91.

Because of the logic of organization that librarians have devised, the user can get a fairly good sense of the size of any particular scholarly subdivision by canvassing particular classifications of interest that will be shelf-companions in any library. Catalogers are often faced with very tough decisions about classification, and unfortunately, a journal or book cannot be in two places at once! Therefore, catalogers may assign call numbers to books and periodicals that then become strange bedfellows indeed. The journal *Agricultural History* is assigned a call letter sympathetic to scholars interested in soil chemistry rather than to rural historians, but may be cross-referenced in the card catalog. *The problem is that because much of knowledge crosses disciplinary borders, scholars need to learn where related fields of speciality are shelved.* Nevertheless, the merits of both the Dewey and the Library of Congress systems are that they make accessible the vast majority of particular knowledge to the user with only the most rudimentary of experience in any particular library.

The Card Catalog

Most libraries have two types of card-catalog systems: one for books and another for serials (journals and other publications that are published on a regular basis). Even if the library has switched over to a computerized system without actual files of paper cards, it is worthwhile to understand the traditional card-catalog system because computerized terminal systems are still based on the original card-catalog filing system.

Books may be filed in numerous ways, by author (and coauthor), corporate author (if not an individual), title, and subject matter. Clearly, the easiest way to find a book is to search by author or title. However, such methods presume the user knows the author's name or the book's title. As long as the user knows how to spell properly (which is not always an easy task for proper names) and can use alphabetized files, author and title searches are relatively easy. Katz (1982b:89–90) gives discouraging information on author and title searches. He notes that 77% of errors in locating a reference cited in a scientific journal result from misspelling of authors' surnames and the omission of their first and middle initials. In another study, he cites 15% of scholarly references had at least one citation error. The morals should be clear: Take extreme care in spelling during searches and be skeptical of the care others took.

Figure 2-1 illustrates typical cataloging information in an author card-catalog system for Howard S. Becker and his colleagues' classic book, *Boys in White.* Librarians stress the need for uniformity throughout all card-cataloging so users will universally recognize all the elements that make up the record. The first element in this figure shows the author; if it was from a title catalog, the first element would have been the title. Following the author heading is the body of the entry. The body includes the actual title, an edition statement, place of publication, publisher, date of publication, and physical description (illustrative details, number of pages, size of book). A second paragraph typ-

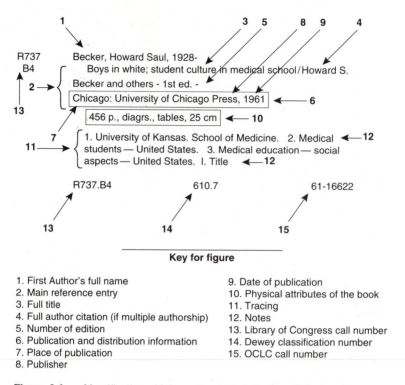

Figure 2-1.   Identification of information included on a catalog card.

ically includes such tracing materials as subject headings. Finally, call-number information is listed at the bottom of the card and in the upper-left-hand corner of the card.

On-line catalogs unfortunately take a variety of forms as librarians experiment with which form is most understandable to users. Most so far have chosen to display the records in a form that resembles that found on a catalog card. Figure 2-2 is an example of the display used in the University of Missouri libraries system. The top line (*a*) ("2. Loc") gives the location (TJL = Thomas Jefferson Library) with a Library of Congress call number of R737.B4. One of the most common mistakes in using large university library systems is not to note which library houses a particular source; for example, the University of Illinois at Urbana-Champaign has over 38 libraries on campus—if you look for a particular call number in the right section of the wrong library you may not find it! The second line lists the name of the author (*b*) and date of the author's birth (and death when applicable) (*c*). The next information is the title and subtitle of the book (*d*), followed by the author's name again. The reason for the duplication of the author's name is twofold. First, if the author had a literary name, as in Samuel Clemens' pseudonym "Mark Twain," the pseudonym would have been given on line two and the legal name later. In such ways, the user can look up cross-references under "see" and "see also" indexings, as used in the indexes in this text. Next is the publisher's information (*e*) followed

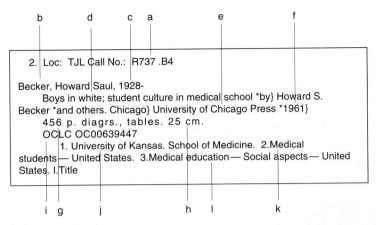

Figure 2-2. One example of on-line computer catalog information.

by the date of publication (*f*); the number of pages (*g*); and the size of the book stated in height (*h*). Some cataloging systems do not provide the next piece of information—the OCLC (On-line Computer Library Center) number (*i*)—which is important to librarians who wish to order particular books from other libraries, but this number is basically irrelevant for the researcher. The last three pieces of information are highly important to the user who wishes to locate other works written in the same general area. The user interested in medical students or social aspects of medical education in the United States now knows several subject headings (*j, k, l*) under which other similar works may be indexed as well as the "R737" portion of the Library of Congress call number R737.B4, under which similar subjects are likely to exist.

The same uniform information about a publication is indexed by author, title, and subjects. The notion of using the cataloging information on a record to locate similar records is *extremely* important. Using these indexes efficiently requires learning to take notes in a systematic manner. I prefer 3″ x 5″ cards, but any format will do as long as each sheet is the same size because using different sizes leads to the loss of smaller ones. For later organizational purposes, it is better to use a separate page (front and back) for each individual entry. Then copy all relevant information from the card or other source at the top in a uniform manner: author's name, call number, title, publisher, date of publication, and subject indexes. Sloppy note taking makes for very inefficient scholarship. Any researcher can tell you horror stories about trying to track down an incomplete reference after the fact. Also, if you take quotations from your source, note the page number for the same reason.

In the majority of cases the novice researcher probably has little idea who the key researchers are or what the major book titles are in a particular area. Rather than search author indexes, the researcher may wish to search subjects and titles. However, although Katz (1982b:82) states that over 50% of catalog and index searches use subject indexes, these indexes are quite difficult to use by inexperienced users. The problem of "noise" in subject searches makes only half of layperson searches effective, compared to 70% to 80% of librarian searches (Katz 1982b:83). Therefore, the novice should not hesitate to ask the reference librarian for guidance.

Most of the reason for ineffective searches hinges on the user's searching only under one subject heading. A user with an interest in social-stratification theories would be better off to look under "social inequality," "stratification, social," or perhaps even "inequality, social" rather than "middle class" or "social class." Certainly, looking under "theory" would be of no help. The user of subject catalogs must "form the habit of imagining synonyms and possible permutations of terms" (Barzun & Graff 1970:59). This suggests at least two reasons for ineffective searches by users: (1) less than satisfactory subject headings, and (2) lack of familiarity with subject-heading systems used by particular library systems. However, other reasons for ineffective searches include users who have little idea of what they are looking for, who may have found what they are looking for but do not recognize it, or who have not considered alternative approaches.

One alternative approach experts use, which few novices seem to consider, is to use a *snowball sampling method*. For example, if you can locate one or two key books, you can usually use those books to locate others by (1) noting the citations in those sources and then locating these citations to provide additional citations, (2) noting the subject-heading information provided either on the copyright page of the book or at the bottom of the catalog card, and (3) then searching under that specific subject listing in the subject catalog.

Serials

Libraries catalog magazines, journals, and newspapers in the same way as books but include detailed information on which issues the library holds. With the advent of computerized library systems, this information is increasingly found by using a computer. Figure 2-3 represents typical computer-screen information for the official journal of the American Sociological Association. Note that the first line gives the library location (TJL = Thomas Jefferson Library) and the Library of Congress system call number HM1.A7. Line two states that the first volume of this journal was published in 1936, and the third line that the last bound volume is number 52 in 1987. In many libraries, this implies that the 1988 issues are either out at the bindery or in the library's current periodical reading area. Lines five through eleven give other important information: the place that the *American Sociological Review* (ASR) was first published (Albany, New York); that it includes illustrations (v. ill.); that it is 26 centimeters in bound form, comes out bimonthly, and has an acronym (ASR); that it is the official journal of the American Sociological Society, which changed its name around 1959 to the American Sociological Association; that volumes from 1936 until 1949 carried the directory of members; and information on which information services index it and for which years particular indexes exist. (The ISBN, OCLC, and ISSN information concerns only library staff who need to catalog and reference the ASR.) This information is followed by subject-heading information for users who wish to look up broader subject searches.

FULL DISPLAY

```
2. Loc:  TJL   Call No.:  HM1 .A75
   Vols:  v.1-    Dates:  1936-
   Last bound volume: 52, 1987.
   Current issues in CP/M.
```

- -
American sociological review. v. 1- Feb. 1936- Albany, N.Y.
*etc.} American Sociological Association *etc.}
      v. ill. 26 cm. bimonthly.
      Other title: ASR
      Official journal of the American Sociological Society, 1936-59?;
of the American Sociological Association, 1960?-
      Vols. for   -1949 include the Association's Directory.
      Indexed by: Public affairs information service
      Indexed by: Social sciences and humanities index 0037-7899
      Indexed by: International index
      Indexes: Vols. 1-20, 1936-55. 1 v.; Vols. 1-25, 1936-60. 1 v.;
Vols. 26-30, 1961-65. 1 v.

      ISBN MUAAA03008
      OCLC OC01480848
      ISSN 0003-1224
        1.Social systems—Research—Periodicals.   2.Sociology—
Research—Periodicals. I. American Sociological Association. II.
American Sociological Association. Directory. III. Title: ASR
        37-010449

   (LHDISPL)
   TYPE p for PREVIOUS screen   n for NEW search
      l to LIST more holdings
   TYPE CHOICE & PRESS ENTER :
```

- - - - - - - - - - - - - - - - - - - - - - - - - - - - - - -

**Figure 2-3.**    On-line serials information.

It is important to read and understand all of the above card information to locate efficiently which part of which library holds any particular volume of a periodical. Because some libraries may hold incomplete sets of any particular periodical, many reference desks have special reference books available to inform the user of the closest library that holds a particular volume of a periodical. Periodicals have become so expensive in recent years that many research libraries now cooperate to avoid duplicate holdings of some periodicals. For example, libraries in the state of Missouri produce the Missouri Union Listing of Serial Publications so that scholars can track down libraries in the state that carry less well-known or more specialized serials.

# Government Sources

The United States Government is the world's largest publisher, and it publishes a wealth of information of use to the social sciences. Katz (1982a:353–354)
```

classifies government documents as "(1) records of government administration; (2) research documents for specialists, including a considerable number of statistics and data of value to science and business; and (3) popular sources of information." Only the latter category is of little interest to most social scientists. Social scientists depend heavily on government statistics; homicide rates, infant mortality rates, unemployment figures, child-abuse data, and disease-specific rates of mortality by geographic area are only a sample of the gold mine of information in the U.S. Government document collections.

The U.S. Goverment has designated certain libraries as official repositories for the purpose of making most of its documents available for general distribution. The problem is that the organization and cataloging of government documents is confusing to all but trained reference librarians. Because the information in government-document collections can be rewarding, it is well worth the library user's time to consult with a reference librarian concerning various government documents. Katz (1982a: 354—356) gives suggestions on published guides to government documents. One basic guide is by Morehead (1983) and is revised about every four years. Morehead discusses the methods of acquisition, organization, and selection of government documents in nontechnical language.

To use government documents, the user must know which government (or which of its components) authored it. Government documents are normally not listed by individual authors but rather by corporate authorship: country (United States), state (Missouri), city (St. Louis), or some other official unit (U.S. Bureau of the Census, National Science Foundation, National Institute of Mental Health, etc.). Another problem is that most people ask for government documents by their popular name (the Pornography Commission report, the Coleman report, the Kerner Commission report) whereas documents are listed only under their official name. For this reason, the *Monthly Catalog of United States Government Publications* now indexes by most popular and all official names. Reference librarians use these indexes to locate the unique Superintendent of Document number that accompanies every document. This number is necessary for the librarian to learn where a document is located because the government system differs from the Dewey and Library of Congress numbering systems.

Government-document librarians in official repositories organize documents using the specialized *Federal Depository Library System*. Federal documents in these large repositories are housed in special collections under Superintendent of Document classification categories. All Department of Commerce holdings are housed together. Because the Bureau of the Census is part of the Department of Commerce, the user will normally find its publications in the same location. However, some librarians organize according to their own system because they argue that more popular documents that are housed next to highly specialized documents limit the use of the more popular ones. Only a trained reference librarian, therefore, is likely to get the user quickly to the appropriate document.

State and local documents collections are generally even more difficult to use because there is no official-standard system for controlling them and because some people do not view them as important as federal sources. Increasingly, this situation is changing for the better as librarians, users, and state and local officials understand the value of creating centers of information on population growth, demographic patterns, economic and social forecasts, and the like. Numerous states now have official state data centers, planning and budgeting departments, health departments, and so on that collect valuable social-science information on such topics as abortions, housing starts, new lead-poisoning cases, and AIDS-related deaths. The Library of Congress puts out a *State Publications Index* that may aid the user interested in an incomplete but valuable bibliography of state publications.

Abstracting and Indexing Guides and Resources

Academic libraries carry a wide range of indexing and abstracting sources that cover journals and other periodicals. Larger libraries may carry several hundred different periodical indexes and abstracts. To use these sources requires patience on the part of the user, but the benefits that can be reaped are immense. The problem is that there is no standard method of indexing and abstraction and no consistency of subject headings across indexes. The user must learn to adapt to the index by learning its own system and by thinking in synonyms and antonyms.

Journal indexing requires looking up journal titles, searching for specific volumes, issues, and pages of journals, and so forth. The most common mistake for the novice is to look up *article* titles. The problem is that a particular journal may come out several times a year and include between 10 and 20 articles by different authors. For example, suppose you wanted to locate a copy of the following article from this text's references:

Bridges, W.P., & Villemez, W.J. (1986) Informal hiring and income in the labor market. *American Sociological Review,* 51, 574–582.

You would first want to find out where the *American Sociological Review* is located in your library. Then you would want to search through the set of volumes for volume 51 published in 1986. Finally, you would want to locate pages 574 through 582 in that volume. You could *not* look up this article either through its authors or its title.

The natural place to start a literature review in the social sciences is the *Social Science Index;* this quarterly index covers over 265 journals in anthropology, economics, environmental science, geography, law and criminology, political science, psychology, public administration, and sociology by author and subject. The name index is difficult to use because it presumes you know the name of one or more authorities. The user who becomes deeply involved in social-science research needs to learn to use this index. However, remember that this (and any other) index simply describes articles; they do not evaluate their worth. Social scientists do not consider all journals of equal importance. For example, sociologists typically rank articles in the *American Journal of Sociology* (AJS) and *American Sociological Review* (ASR) at the top, with *Social*

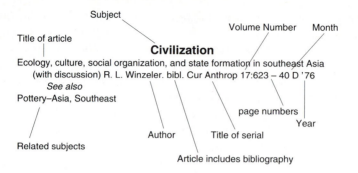

Figure 2-4. An example of a typical subject entry.

Forces and *The Sociological Quarterly* next, and with other journals somewhat below these in quality.

Examples of subject headings found in typical social-science indexes are child study, cities and towns, divorce, family, social change, United States—foreign population, and violence. A typical subject entry and accompanying information are shown in Figure 2-4. Notice how much information is packed into this subject index. The experienced user knows that by checking pages 623 through 640 of the December 1976 issue of *Current Anthropology* that Winzeler has not only published a particular article relating to civilization, but that (a) he includes a bibliography that is likely to give further references, and (b) that another possible synonym for subject searches is "Pottery—Asia, Southeast."

The author index is similar to the subject index except that the author's name rather than the subject's is given in bold. For example, from the same 1977 issue of *Social Science Index*, I have drawn the following two citations:

Ash, Robert

Aspects of timing in child development. bibl Child Develop 47:622–6 S '76

Infant state and stimulation. Develop Psychol 12:569–70 N '76

Robert Ash is listed as author of two articles in 1976. The first listing was published in the Spring 1976 issue of volume 47 of *Child Development* on pages 622 through 626, and it includes a bibliography. The second is listed as a short two-page note published in *Developmental Psychology* in November 1976 in volume 12 on pages 569 through 570.

Most indexes are organized much like the *Social Sciences Index,* so that once the user has learned to use one, it is relatively easy to learn to use others. The user must learn to utilize the brief subject-index headings and be able to follow the order of the subject headings, subheadings, and subdivisions. Learning the index's method of abbreviation is also important; especially for journal titles. Most indexes include a guide to abbreviations on front matter (acknowledgement, preface, etc.) for user reference. The user must also learn to check for "see" and "see also" cross-references in addition to the ones the user might have chosen.

Once the user has located appropriate references, he or she would be wise to write down all information on a separate index card. This means copying the name of the periodical, the date of publication, page numbers, and the name of the index in which the reference was located, as well as its date and where the user found it. The same format should be used on all cards. Although this may seem superfluous, experienced researchers know how hard it is to relocate materials that they have not documented carefully. Also, the same format on all cards aids alphabetizing or otherwise organizing them.

There are many other indexes and abstracts in which the social-science user may most profitably search for current material. The most important ones in sociology are the American Sociological Association's 15-year-old *Cumulative Index of Sociology Journals, Science Citation Index, Population Index, Current Contents: Social and Behavioral Sciences,* and *Social Science Citation Index*. For example, the ASA's *Cumulative Index* covers all the association's sponsored journals plus *The American Journal of Sociology* and *Social Forces*. Because most individuals may only recall particular articles vaguely (or incorrectly) or not read particular journals, such indexes may save huge amounts of time.

Abstracts are even more important than simple indexes because they provide one crucial piece of information lacking in simple indexes: a short (often less than 200-word) synopsis of the article. Because a title or subject does not tell the user such important information as size of sample, type of method used, or findings, *Sociological Abstracts, Psychological Abstracts, Sociology of Education Abstracts, Sage Race Relations Abstracts, Sage Family Studies Abstracts, Social Planning, Policy and Development Abstracts, Inventory of Marriage and Family Literature*, and *Dissertation Abstracts* are invaluable sources. Most first-time users find them hard to use because citations are often arranged in a complex fashion. I suggest that the first-time user consult with a reference librarian or professor in the speciality who is familiar with a particular system first. However, once the user has learned a particular system of abstracting, whole worlds of knowledge open up quickly.

Citation Indexing

The Institute for Scientific Information (ISI) (see boxed inserts in Chapters 3, 4, and 7 for examples of some of their important work) provides an expensive but highly useful type of indexing called citation indexing. Citation indexing reports alphabetical lists by author of papers cited in published articles. The ISI provides quarterly indexes of three types: a citation index, a source index, and a "permuterm" subject index. Their source index provides standard bibliographic information on individual articles written in a particular time period, their permuterm subject index classifies each of these articles by significant words used in each article's title, and the citation index lists by author or by referenced articles.

Citation indexing is important because it graphically depicts scientific networks by quantifying who cites whom. Any scientific article or author published at any time and cited during a particular year will have an accompanying bibliographic list of authors, books, articles, reports, and the like who cited the article or author. The user may then create a snowball sample of citations in a particular area by looking up each new list of citations ad infinitum. If you know that Peter Blau is an expert on bureaucracies, you could look his name up in *Social Science Citation Index* to start tracing a collegial network of like-minded experts.

More importantly, whereas most indexes may take over a year to produce information, citation indexing is rapid because the compiler simply has to key in the author, title, and full citation in a machine-readable form. I used the ISI's *Science Citation Index* to locate most of the work on randomization explained in Chapter 5. Because I knew several important names of statisticians doing pathfinding work in probability (Diaconis & Efron), I went to the current *Science Citation Index*'s Citation Index and looked up their names in each of the quarterly editions of 1986 and 1987, searching for references to their work. Citation indexes are the fastest way to locate recently published work because they are generally at least a year ahead of *Sociological Abstracts* and *Psychological Abstracts,* but they do have two clear disadvantages: (1) The print in these indexes practically requires a magnifying glass to read, and (2) the abbreviations can be positively confusing. Presently, citation indexing on-line is easier to read and more understandable than the bound hard-copy version.

There are many other indexing and abstracting sources in an academic library. Because not all of these sources are equally trustworthy, it is wise to stick mostly with the respected ones cited. Two widely available books on the subject to which the interested reader might refer for more in-depth information are Aby's (1987) *Sociology: A Guide to Reference and Information Sources* and McMillan and Kennedy's (1981) *Library Research Guide to Sociology.*

Interlibrary Loans

No library holds everything that every user wants. The cost of books and periodicals has far outstripped library budgets over the past several decades. As a result, many libraries belong to cooperative local, state, regional, national, or international networks built upon joint agreements to avoid the expense of duplication of rarely used materials, to encourage reciprocal borrowing and lending of materials, and to allow for greater freedom of access to information. The computer has truly revolutionized library cooperation. One expert (Evans 1979:12) concludes: "On-line library networking now seems to be emerging as a specialty in its own right, which requires knowledge of, and draws from, library and information science, computing, telecommunications, information technology, economics, marketing, business, public service administration, and the behavioral sciences."

Two bibliographic service networks stand out: OCLC (On-line Computer Library Center), with over 2,000 members, and the more selective RLIN (Research Libraries Information Network), with less than 100 members. These networks provide a variety of important services to member-libraries, including shared cataloging, reference searches, and interlibrary loan. From the standpoint of the user, the result is simple enough. A librarian who wants to know basic information about a book or periodical types a query on a computer terminal, the computer searches its files, and then displays answers to the query on a screen or in printed form. The result is extremely efficient processing of interlibrary loans.

Many libraries belong to small networks as well. For example, the entire four-campus system of the University of Missouri has all holdings available online accessible to any user via computer terminal. It is possible to access computer catalogs via a home-based personal computer using a modem dial-up to find holdings available in the network system.

Most academic libraries supply their own preliminary interlibrary-loan forms to users at the reference desk or at a special interlibrary loan department. Although some restrictions do apply—for example, to rare books—the librarian is normally happy to help the user borrow the necessary book or periodical from other institutions. If the material cannot be borrowed, it is usually possible to microfilm or photocopy the relevant portions, subject to the rules of copyright.

Computers and On-Line Searches

By 1989, two-thirds of academic libraries had replaced card catalogs with computer-based public-access catalogs for searching holdings. Although many library users voice the opinion that these systems are inferior to card catalogs, these electronic systems, when used properly, are superior to any card catalog for information retrieval. Rice (1988) has delineated some of the superiorities of on-line systems under the headings of (a) holism and (b) serendipity.

Holism refers to the ability to see many cards at one time. In the traditional card catalog, the user may quickly thumb through a number of cards to get a quick sense of how many books a particular author has written or how many titles are listed under a particular subject. Most on-line systems actually allow the user to see a number of titles at a glance, along with a count of titles found that the user would otherwise have to look at individually and painstakingly count up. For example, refer to Figure 2-5, which lists 7 total holdings for Howard S. Becker. If the user wishes to delve more deeply into any one title, he or she may then type in the line number to get more title-specific information. With larger searches, the user simply enters "d" for down or "u" for up, to scroll through the remaining titles.

Serendipity refers to "the ability to somehow stumble onto relevant citations or relevant items" (Rice 1988:139). Some researchers praise the card catalog and open stack system because they claim it allows them to stumble across materials of which they were previously unaware. But on-line-systems designers studied the habits of users in developing these new technologies. Because subject searches account for over half of all catalog use, these de-

FULL DISPLAY

1. Art worlds / Becker, Howard Saul, c1982.
    Loc: TJL   Call No.: NX180.S6 B42 1982
2. Boys in white; student culture in medical school Becker, Howard
   Saul, *1961}
    Loc: TJL   Call No.: R737 .B4
3. Campus power struggle. Becker, Howard Saul, *1970} (Trans-action
   books TA-1)
    Loc: EDUC   Call No.: LA229 .B36
4. Culture and civility in San Francisco. Becker, Howard Saul, *1971}
    Loc: TJL   Call No.: F869.S35 B4
5. Doing things together : selected papers / Becker, Howard Saul,
   c1986.
    Loc: TJL   Call No.: HM51 .B387 1986
6. Exploring society photographically / c1981.
    Loc: TJL   Call No.: TR820.5 .E94 1981
7. Institutions and the person; papers presented to Everett C.

------------------------------------ (BIMPREV)

TYPE line no. for more complete display   **n**   for NEW search
      d to scan DOWN display   **u** to scan UP display
      r to REVISE search   **p** for PREVIOUS AUTHOR list
TYPE CHOICE & PRESS ENTER :

Figure 2-5.   An example of an author search.

signers have built keyword searching for meaningful, standardized, and the-saurus-based terms into each on-line record. The result is that "serendipity is . . . more possible on-line than it is through card systems . . . [because of] a much larger database of authority files and cross-reference information" (Rice 1988:139). In fact, the on-line problem is more one of needing to narrow the search result by filtering out less-relevant items.

Surveys indicate that users prefer on-line catalogs to card catalogs once they master them. They no longer need to move between different card files, although once they have call numbers they still have to run around the library looking for materials. Users may print out copies of the holdings for their own records, thus at least partially circumventing the problem of incomplete references caused by the lazy hand. They may even check to see when a title is due back if it is checked out. They can use an on-line system to do any of the types of searches previously depicted—title keyword, author, corporate/governmental, subject browse, or official subject term—or searches not possible in card catalogs, such as series or call-number browse searches. Figure 2–6 shows a typical on-line search menu. Although such menus are not standardized across libraries, they make going between different libraries relatively easy if the user takes the time to read the entire menu the first time. For example, in Figure 2-6 the menu instructs the user to type in "a" for an author search and then press the "enter" key. A new screen then appears asking the user to type in the author's name. The only difference between this system and the one used by another major university in St. Louis—Washington University—is that the user there types "a =" followed by the author's name.

The *Boolean search* is a particularly useful strategy for efficiently locating some materials. The Boolean search allows the user to search for two things at once—two authors, an author and a subject, or whatever. The operator "OR"

LUMIN MASTER SEARCH MENU

h = HOW TO LOGOFF OF LUMIN

TITLE SEARCH:
   t = title keyword search

AUTHOR SEARCHES:
   a = author search - (personal and corporate/governmental bodies)
   k = corporate/governmental bodies keyword term search

SUBJECT SEARCHES:
   s = subject browse search - (use if unsure of heading)
   o = official subject term search - (use if sure of heading)

OTHER SEARCHES:
   w = series searches
   b = boolean searches
   c = call number browse search
   q = quick-facts about the library and LUMIN

(SRCHSTZ)
TYPE THE LETTER FOR YOUR SEARCH CHOICE & PRESS ENTER :

Figure 2-6. An on-line search screen.

may be used to ask for more material. Perhaps the user knows both the subject area and the name of a particular expert in that area. Then the use of the "OR" command can locate any titles with a particular subject matter *as well as* a particular author. The "AND" operator is useful for narrowing a broad number of titles. "Social change" and "deviant behavior" are too broad to be of much use in subject searches. However, connecting both topics with an "AND" operator would narrow the search to only those titles dealing with both topics. The final operator used is "NOT," and this may also be helpful in winnowing searches. "Bureaucracies" is a broad category that might be narrowed by adding the command "NOT federal."

On-line databases

"On-line" refers to direct communication with a computer. A "database" is a machine-readable record on which indexes, abstracts, catalogs, or other data are stored. By 1988, 95% of all academic-health science and university-research libraries, 60% of college libraries, and 35% of public libraries offered on-line database searches. Both computer catalog and on-line database searches employ Boolean-search strategies. These databases are not a luxury; they are a crucial component of research and education in the information society. It is possible to do more in-depth searches on-line in a fraction of the time of a manual search because a computer can now read a quarter of a million bits of information in a second.

However, computer searches require skills, study, and training beyond that of most general library users. The odds are against a do-it-your-selfer mastering the complexities of on-line database searches. In fact, because this technology is relatively new, not all librarians have the necessary skills to do on-line bibliographic searches efficiently.

Numerous commercial vendors offer computerized databases. The two largest and most useful vendors for the general library user are Bibliographic Retrieval Services (BRS) and Lockheed Information Systems's DIALOG. The costs of these services continues to increase. In 1988, some private systems cost as much as $185 for each hour that the user is connected to the system. Although these costs may seem high, an *efficient* on-line search rarely takes more than a few minutes of connect-time.

Furthermore, the same compact disks that offer 75 minutes of unsurpassed Beethoven now provide 600 megabytes of database at relatively low cost. In 1988, Sociological Abstracts Inc. started offering all abstracts from over 1500 serials on compact disks since 1974 updated biannually for an annual subscription fee of less than $2,000. Because there is no connect-time, telecommunications, or per-search charges and such CDs can be used with any IBM-PC compatible with a CD-ROM drive, these new technologies are increasingly competitive means of bibliographic searching. ($2,000 is the equivalent of just over four days of continuous connect time at $15 per hour on traditional on-line systems.) By using CD-ROM disks, some database vendors think they can reasonably reduce costs to as little as 75 cents per hour on microcomputers by the early 1990s. However, the interested user should realize that these databases are not as complete as traditional ones used by professional librarians; they still require knowledge of specialized thesauri and vocabulary to be used efficiently.

Keywords

Regardless of the reduction in cost of doing bibliographic searches, few users will want to do them on their own because of the special skills required. Compiling a list of keywords and their synonyms that describe the topic of the search is a demanding task. It is not all that useful to know the official subject headings prescribed by the Library of Congress. Because database searches are highly language-dependent, reputable database vendors compile thesauri of descriptors. Knowing how to use these thesauri is a highly technical and complex operation that only a few reference librarians master.

To do a bibliographic search, the searcher must clarify sometimes badly expressed questions. To say one is interested in "abortions" will lead literally to hundreds of thousands of articles. Clarifying the search to "human abortions" will narrow the search to less than one-third of the original. Limiting the search further to "research since 1980" and "social aspects of" with a Boolean "AND" operator will produce thousands of titles, which is still far too many. One must make more discriminating choices: Which database or bases should be searched—ones that reference law journals, sociological articles, medical studies, or psychology experiments? What are the most likely search elements—subject, author, title, or keywords from abstracts? If keywords are used, how can the search be delimited without losing important articles? An intimate knowledge of the terms available in the vendor's thesauri becomes crucial to picking adequate synonyms.

Even if the user has carefully put together a detailed description of databases, subjects, synonyms, delimitors, etc. for the librarian to use, most professional bibliographic searchers have learned from experience that the user must schedule an appointment in advance for doing the actual search interactively. A surprising number of references may turn up under a given heading. For example, in doing a search for "triangulation" or "multimethods" for Chapter 14, a librarian colleague uncovered 62 references since 1980. Through negotiation the second search was limited to sociological abstracts only, and elicited a more manageable 13 references. Similarly, at $185 dollars per hour, making the mistake of listing and printing numerous references can become quite costly. Once a library science student searching the abortion literature started with "wom" because "woman," "women," and "womb" all begin with those three letters. Two pages into the listing there appeared "wombat"—shades of the sorcerer's apprentice!—so it was decided that it would be a costly mistake to continue with this strategy, but help was needed to stop the machine's relentless listing of words from womc to womz. Happily, this is not a mistake that an experienced searcher would make!

Researchers do get anxious to conduct their own searches (Garson 1986; L. Smith 1988). Virtually every major bibliographic database is now available electronically. Therefore, the scholar well versed in a particular field is likely to want to try bibliographic searches without the aid of a librarian. As Garson (1986:69) states "direct searches . . . result in greater control, deeper searches, and the capture of fewer unwanted citations." As long as the scholar knows what he or she wants, Garson is correct. However, in the hands of the inexperienced, bibliographic searches can end up with an expensive sorcerer's apprentice experience of not knowing how to start or when to stop.

Artificial-Intelligence Library Systems

OCLC (On-line Computer Library Center) and Carnegie Mellon Library are working in partnership toward building an electronic library that will bring to any user's desk all the information needed for research projects. The computer capabilities already exist for this project. The core is an "artificial intelligence" (see Chapter 12) program called a "reference assistant" for which much of the work has been accomplished already. The goal is a program that will help users locate information even if they do not know which of the system's databases to search. Besides offering a working electronic library of over 17 million records, the researchers are studying how users use information so the system can become self-supporting and independent of already heavily burdened reference desks. By the mid-1990s, the average user ought to be able to locate most any scholarly information by telephone without leaving home or office.

Summary

The information explosion of the twentieth century has created a need for humans to control information rather than be engulfed by it. Librarians are concerned with management of information. How librarians manage information, therefore, becomes central to efficient use of information. Whether one is a producer or consumer of information, it becomes imperative to learn how to use and assess it.

Most libraries in the United States conform to one of two general means of organizing information: the Dewey Decimal classification system, which is preferred by many smaller libraries, or the Library of Congress classification system, which is predominant in larger libraries. Either system amounts to a mapping system that can aid the user find materials in any library with a similar system efficiently. The principle underlying both systems is to organize similar topics under the similar call numbers.

Standard reference works—dictionaries, encyclopedias, and the like—are usually located near each other. Because not all reference works are equally comprehensive, easy-to-use, or accurate, it is important to learn which ones scholars consider most worthwhile to consult, their limitations, and how to efficiently use them. However, no general dictionary can keep abreast of current scientific usages. Librarians can point out more specialized dictionaries for scientific usage.

Encyclopedias cannot keep current of the knowledge explosion either. Scientists rarely use encyclopedias for anything other than confirmation of minor points. Even specialized encyclopedias quickly become out-of-date. The rapidity of accumulated knowledge along with the need for organized reviews of special areas of science, has lead scientists to publish special annual review series and topic-specific handbooks that are more current than encyclopedias.

Another source of short, quick answers are almanacs, yearbooks, and statistical abstracts, atlases, and gazetteers. Keep in mind that much of the information in such sources are ill-informed, trivial, or out-of-date. As with dictionaries and encyclopedias, these sources lack depth. Because the most informed sources of knowledge are found in books and journals, the user must learn how to search for deeper information.

Librarians cross-catalog books by author, coauthor, corporate author, title, and subject matter. The easiest way to search library catalogs is by author or title. However, because the user may not have that information or may have incorrect information, over half of all searches in libraries are done by subject. Successful subject searches require much patience, forethought, and planning: consideration of synonyms and antonyms; understanding and use of specialized thesauri; and other alternatives to classification.

Journals are often cataloged in different ways from books because journals are published on a long-term bases. Therefore, locating journal articles requires more knowledge than locating books: exact volume of articles, year of publication, and, in some cases, microfilm or microfiche information.

Even more challenging to use are government sources. Because social scientists depend on government statistics, the organization of government documents collections is important to much research. Government documents are listed by corporate authorship: country, department, state, city, or other official unit titles. The quickest way to understand how a particular library organizes government documents is to ask a reference librarian.

Indexes and abstracts are the key to locating most articles published in particular specialties. The first place to start in the social sciences is the *Social Science Index*. It cross-references articles in over 260 journals by title, subject, author, bibliographic sources, title of series, volume number, page numbers, month and year of publication, and related subjects. The user must learn the brief subject indexing and abbreviation systems to use indexes efficiently. Abstracts are even more important than indexes because they also include short synopses of articles. Abstracts normally give hints as to sample size, type of method employed, theory tested, and new key subject headings to search. The unique numbering system of many abstracts requires some aid from a reference librarian for first-time users.

Reference librarians are also good sources of information. However, to use them effectively, the user must learn to ask specific enough questions on what material is needed, reading difficulty, and time limits on material usefulness. Finding particular esoteric materials is a reference librarian's specialty, which requires patience, planning, and negotiation between librarian and user.

The knowledge explosion makes it improbable that any library will carry every book or article that users desire. Increasingly, therefore, users turn to the interlibrary loan department. Interlibrary loan networks provide a variety of important services to member-libraries that users find increasingly necessary and convenient to use: shared cataloging, reference searches, and interlibrary loans. These services have done much for standardization of information cataloging and retrieval across all libraries. Such standardization makes information searches easier and quicker.

The information revolution has necessitated computerization of cataloging. A side benefit of computerization is superior information-retrieval using on-line terminals rather than older card catalogs. On-line cataloging allows users to use the computer to search millions of cards for specific authors, titles, or subjects in seconds. In effect, without ever leaving a computer terminal, the user may rummage through untold numbers of items, increasing serendipitous findings. Also, major indexing and abstracting services now stored in computer-readable form allow users to more efficiently search for particular authors, citations, and subjects than previously possible through older manual processes. At present, such on-line indexes and abstracts require the aid of reference librarians, but the day is not far off when the typical user can effectively conduct such searches on his or her own.

CHAPTER

3

Formulating the Research Problem

It is much more exciting not to catch a big fish than not to catch a little fish.[1]

Key Terms

Association (statistical)

Cardinal scale

Causation

Concept

Dependent variable

Dummy variable

Hypothesis

Independent variable

Necessary condition

Nominal classification

Ordinal scale

Probability scale

Ratio scale

Reliability

Replication

Sensitizing concept

Sufficient condition

Testable questions

Theory

Variable

Variable relationship

[1]Attributed to Nobel Prize–winner Albert Szent-Gyorgyi, on the practice of taking on only large scientific questions.

Study Guide Questions

1. How do the terms "hypothesis" and "theory" differ in usage between laypersons and scientists?

2. What are the differences between a concept and a variable? How do researchers construct variables out of concepts?

3. Illustrate the differences between different types of scales through definition and example.

4. Discuss the relationship between scaling and theory; include information on the trend toward more quantitative scales.

5. How do social scientists create stronger scale types?

6. What are non-cardinal-based variables, and why do scientists discourage their use?

7. What means aid the formation of testable hypotheses?

8. Discuss the merits and demerits of natural and mathematical languages for describing variable relationships.

9. What logical conditions must take place for causation to exist?

10. What are the most typical fallacies of causation, and how can they best be avoided?

11. Why is variable association only a necessary but not sufficient condition for causation?

Webster's Third New International Dictionary defines theory as "the coherent set of hypothetical, conceptual, and pragmatic principles forming the general frame of reference for a field of inquiry." Several words in this definition need highlighting. First, "coherent set" implies more than one or two statements; that is, it is not sufficient in science to call such a Durkheimian hypothesis as "the higher the social integration, the less the suicide rate" a theory. A theory implies a number of such statements that fit together into a larger whole. Second, the word "principles" refers to laws of nature rather than to definitions, static abstractions, symbolic constructions, summaries of known facts, concepts, or descriptive statements. The following are *not* examples of theoretical principles: "all social systems have identifiable status hierarchies," "the probability that a male in the United States will enter the same occupation as his father is 0.10 if his father is (or was) a laborer," and "job turnover is high in restaurants." While such descriptive statements interest scientists, ultimately, the scientist wishes to go beyond mere descriptive statements to construct hypotheses or propositions. Strictly speaking, a scientific theory is a set of *interrelated* hypotheses or propositions concerning a phenomenon or set of phenomenon.

A *scientific hypothesis* consists of *two or more* variables linked by some relationship. For instance: "If the rate of succession (changes in membership) in an organization is constant, then an increase in formalization of the organizational size will be followed by an increase in formalization of the organizational structure and procedures." Or: "The lower the rate of job turnover in a work group, the higher the work productivity." Notice that the *variables* "rate of succession" and "rate of job turnover" differ from the *concepts* of "succession" and "job turnover." By explicating that, these concepts may vary.

Principles of Theory Construction

Theory construction is a complex process usually learned over a number of years under the tutelage of a respected scientist in one's own field. The principles presented in this chapter are designed to introduce how scientific theories are developed. The student should come away with an understanding of how scientists develop and revise scientific theories. This chapter section expresses this development and revision process through nine rules:

1. *Search for variable measurements with the most quantitative characteristics available.*
2. *Progressively develop and refine variables through beginning with low-scope assertions but ending with wide-scope assertions that are logically based on assertions of low scope.*
3. *Make the variable's scale properties explicit by stating all of the variable's mutually exclusive and totally inclusive categories by degree.*
4. *Describe the means used to sort observations into variable categories in sufficient detail so that others can evaluate and replicate the methods.*
5. *Always consider the alternative variable names that might be more appropriate for a given set of operations and the alternative operations which might be more appropriate for a given variable name.*
6. *Treat variables without cardinal-scale base as basically arbitrary and relatively meaningless.*
7. *Form habits of formally analyzing variables through their relationships.*
8. *Link two or more formal propositions through a shared independent or dependent variable where possible.*
9. *Link variables using acceptable scientific conventions.*

Constructing Variables from Concepts

A concept, *by definition*, is a classification of some phenomenon, which may or may not be a variable. A *variable* is a particular type of concept, namely, a classification into two or more mutually exclusive and totally inclusive categories that explicitly undergoes change in degree. Although "Protestant," "Catholic," "Jew," and "other religions" provide mutually exclusive and totally inclusive classifications of the concept of "religion," they *cannot* be ordered by degree of "religiousness." While it is true that social scientists often use such nonvarying concepts in their work, they find such concepts ultimately nonsatisfying. In fact, scientists who use such concepts in their work usually assume some implicit ordering of the classifications. In his classic work on suicide, Durkheim assumed that he was imperfectly measuring more socially integrative religiosity as he moved from the Protestant to the Catholic to the Jewish faiths; we now know he was wrong in this assumption.

The following are general rules of constructing theory.

Rule 1: Search for variable measurements with the most quantitative characteristics available.

The history of any science shows a gradual paradigmatic shift toward variable concepts with more quantitative characteristics. The reasons for this are that the precision and scope of any theory increase with more quantitatively measured variables. Many astute observers have noted that the difference between the "hard" and "soft" sciences comes down to the number of decimal points to which theories make accurate predictions or explanations. All sciences participate in a trend toward more quantitatively measured variables. The early stages of the physics of light were based on such primitive concepts as blue, yellow, and red; over time, physicists developed more quantitative measures of colors based on their wavelength.

The point to remember is that precise quantitative measurement is more critical in testing theory than any allegedly intrinsic qualitative characteristic of whatever one observes. A qualitative concept is a nominal classification of types of things that can only be differentiated as alike or unalike. Naming is an act of enumeration and identification of concepts that is extremely important for any science. Nevertheless, the act of naming in and of itself does not denote variation.

On the other hand, a quantitative variable can be differentiated by degrees or levels of continuous connections. The researcher should work at learning to translate from qualitative concepts into quantitative variables. "Population" is a concept. To state that the population of the United States in 1990 is about 240 million is to make a static description of little scientific interest. While it is true that we could compare national variations in population, such comparisons are not explicit in the notion of "population." "Population density" presumes a more interesting concept of variation. We gain precision of variation by measuring "population density per square mile" and even more precision by measuring "population density per square mile of habitable land."

Types of Measurement

Duncan (1984) has enumerated, in increasing order of interest to scientists, five types of measurement: nominal classification, ordinal scaling, cardinal scaling, ratio scaling, and probability scaling.

The least interesting way of measurement is what Stevens (1975) inappropriately called nominal scaling. It is better to speak of this as nominal classification (rather than nominal scaling) because, by definition, a scale must be a quantifiable graduated measurement laying off dimensions or distances in ascending or descending order.

Nominal classification encompasses the identification and differentiation of some phenomenon such that any number may be arbitrarily substituted for any other number. Our lives are teeming with nominal classifications: the "numbering" of athletic uniforms, social security numbers, vehicular model numbers, etc. Social scientists often use nominal categories to assign names to social phenomena: sex, race, and religious categories are notable examples. Social scientists refer to such categories as "yes/no" and "male/female" as *dummy variables* reflecting this lack of quantification. For example, researchers often categorize sex by assigning a "0" for males and a "1" for females, or—because it is arbitrary—"1" for males and "0" for females. Such assignment of numbers is a completely arbitrary convention that is necessary for some types of sophisticated computerized statistical analyses. (The word "dummy" is an unfortunate choice because dichotomized nominal classifications can be highly useful in statistical analysis.)

Nominally classified numbers (except dummy variables) cannot be meaningfully used in most forms of mathematical manipulations because the numbers are arbitrarily defined. A nominal classification simply states that two or more things are alike or unalike. Merely naming an object does *not* aid its measurement. Nominal concepts are relatively uninteresting in science because they deny the precision of variation that may exist. To say that one received "a grade" or "no grade" is not as meaningful as to say that one received a "high" or "low" grade. Still more precise would be to say that one received an "A", "B", "C", "D", or "F"; and even more precise might be to give a percentage of correct answers on a test.

Scientists prefer to work with quantitative scale properties where possible although it is not always possible to transform concepts into quantitative variables immediately. In research situations where empirical evidence is lacking, it may only be possible to use "sensitizing concepts"—that is, to use qualitative variables that refer only to *what* will be observed as opposed to the more quantitative variables that refer to *how* it will be observed. During the early history of AIDS, the sensitizing concept was only that a group of persons were dying of some previously unrecognized illness. As research progressed biologists were able to identify specific AIDS-related retroviruses common to all patients. Identification of these retroviruses was necessary for progress in treatment and avoidance of AIDS. Similarly, the problem of "homelessness" in the United States started out as a vague concept with which social scientists grappled for ways of observing and measuring. As social scientists found ways to more adequately measure "homelessness," they recognized that it included groups of Americans not traditionally thought of as homeless: mothers and their young children. However, becoming sensitive to a social problem such as homelessness does not answer the more interesting scientific problem of what causes homelessness. Science cannot depend on sensitizing concepts for long without retarding the growth of cumulative knowledge.

Somewhat better than a nominal classification is the ordinal scale. *An ordinal scale allows for the rank ordering of some phenomena in terms of fixed greater or lesser amounts.* Once again, our life is rife with ordinally scaled classifications. Many clothing labels carry an implicit ordering of sizes XL, L, M, S, or XS that imply XL > L > M > S > XS. The fact that buyers are unwilling to buy shoes with out trying them on is a sign that sizes are only ordinal; although one might wear a "size 12," it could be necessary to try on new pairs of 11s, 11 and 1/2s, 12s, and even 13s sometimes because a size 12 does not really mean 12 inches, simply that a size 12 is larger than a size 11 for a particular brand. The moral of this example is that one should not trust that a number necessarily gives standard information. The Food and Drug Administration likewise "grades" meats according to ordinal scales that give rough measures of fat content.

Ordinal scales also find many current uses in the social sciences. Researchers often ask individuals to rank order foods, places of residences, types of vehicles, and so on from most to least preferred. IQ tests produce a numeric score that is ordinal. Ranking of social classes into "upper," "middle," and "lower" or other finer ranks is also ordinal. When Durkheim measured religion with Protestant, Catholic, and Jewish nominal classifications he was actually, upon closer examination of his work, proposing a crude, ordinal, measure of the amount, or degree of, religious dogma in each religion.

The problem with ordinal scales is that they do not allow the determination of how much greater or less one category or ranking is than another. Within Grade A meats is a wide variation of fatty marbling. The difference between pairs of size 11 and 12 shoes may not be the same difference as that between pairs of size 12 and 13 shoes. The difference between "strongly agree" and "agree" on an attitude scale may not be equal to the difference between "agree" and "slightly agree" in spite of the fact that a researcher codes "strongly agree" = 1, "agree" = 2, "slightly agree" =3, etc., as if that numeric assignment gives such conclusions. Numbering does not make it so; numbering in ordinal scales implies only that the phenomena so numbered has a particular order.

Cardinal scales[2], *in contrast to ordinal scales, are those that employ the "natural" or fundamental numbers 1, 2, 3, . . . n. Cardinal scales are used to answer the question: How many?* Any time one is interested in aggregates, cardinal numbers become important. Census counts of people, televisions, radios, and so on give prime examples of this common system of measurement.

[2]Some social researchers mistakenly refer to this type of scaling as "interval" scaling after Stevens' (1975) original terminology. See Duncan (1984) for the reasons "interval" scaling is incorrect and misleading.

Cardinal scaling is essential because it (1) offers natural units which cannot be altered without changing the meaning of the numbers; (2) has an absolute zero point which allows for meaningful comparisons across numbers; and (3) allows for the most variety of meaningful mathematical transformations of all numeric systems. For example, a population of 10,000 is exactly twice that of a population of 5,000.

One should keep in mind that a cardinal scale may lose its cardinality if the data are grouped or collapsed into more convenient categories. In individual sports heats, it may be the actual time (with true intervals) that wins, but once the heats are ranked into first, second, third, etc., the ordered data become ordinal. Similarly, social scientists often collapse such variables as family income that have true cardinal features into "more convenient" ordinal categories such as less than $15,000, $15,000 to $20,000, and "over $20,000." The new categories may be easy to view but they lose the cardinality of the original data.

As fundamental as cardinal scaling is, it does not solve all of the problems of scientific theory and measurement. The next two chapters consider some of the problems that crop up in measurement of particular phenomena and the role of theory to better understand the usefulness of other scaling methods. The story of scaling is inextricably intertwined with theory as well as the construction of reliable and valid instruments. To use a cardinal scale in measuring size of cities or bureaucracies is important not because it is a technological achievement, but because theories of cities and bureaucracies predict that size makes a difference. By contrast, it makes no difference to know that an individual of age 70 is twice as old as one of age 35 unless the researcher has theoretical reason for using such a specific cardinal measurement. Scientists invented each of the remaining scalar types for good theoretical reasons; not for the sake of quantification.

A ratio scale is based on the relationship between two quantities. Although censuses are based on simple counts, social scientists have long recognized that cardinal-based counts are highly misleading when each population has a different base. To know that one nation had 50 homicides and another nation had 300 during the same year would be highly misleading if the latter nation had a population six times that of the former. In such a case, the rate of homicides would be precisely the same. Social scientists, therefore, use standardized denominators for particular social phenomenon to make more valid comparisons. Because homicides are relatively rare, the rate of homicides is found by taking the count of homicides divided by the population in which the homicides occurred and then multiplying by 100,000. Because births occur much more frequently than homicides, the multiplier is standardly set at 1,000. However, because only women between the ages of 15 and 45 are likely to be fertile, more specific measures of fertility rates are necessary to make more valid comparisons. Social scientists often use *cohorts* (more narrowly defined age and sex groupings) for making even more exact fertility rate comparisons. Compare the Costa Rican fertility rates for women in the different age groups below. You can see that women in their early twenties were much more fertile than women in their late thirties. Also, you can readily understand how rapidly

Costa Rican fertility declined for specific cohorts of women. Furthermore, because some nations have much greater percentages of young, fertile women than other nations, this type of measure contributes to much more exact comparisons across nations.

| Year | *Live Births Per 1,000 Women in the Age Group* | |
	20–24 years	*35–39 years*
1960	357	223
1970	239	144
1976	207	86

A similar necessity calls for improving measures of males and females in a society. Because males and females are disproportionately spread throughout various ages and locales—there are 106 male babies born to every 100 female babies in the United States, but by age 65, the ratio can be as low as 70 men per 100 women because women live longer. These ratios can also differ dramatically by region. A much larger percentage of men than women are attracted to rural and frontier locales as opposed to urban areas—so that social scientists divide the number of males by females and multiply the outcome by 100. This gives a ratio of males per 100 females.

Ratio measures, therefore, have the advantage of standardizing comparisons across different categories. Whatever the category used, the denominator will be set at 100, 1,000, etc., so that as the ratio measure increases all researchers know that implies a greater relative number for the numerator compared to the denominator, and a smaller ratio implies a smaller numerator compared to the denominator.

Still, the reason for creating ratio measures does not hinge on technique but theory. Social scientists invented the sex ratio because of existing theory. Guttentag and Secord (1983) organized their sex ratio theory around the propositions that societies with shortages of women would treat women with greater deference and respect, while societies with shortages of men would lead to less deference and respect for women. South and Messner (1987) in one of many interesting tests of Guttentag and Secord's theory needed to produce still other ratio measures to test their hypotheses that relative undersupplies of women should be reflected in significantly increased ratios of women committing criminal offenses and increased police protection of women from homicide victimization. South and Messner invented ratio measures of female-to-male theft-offending rates and of female-to-male homicide victimization to test this hypothesis. By using ratio scales of the form,

$$\frac{\text{number of women committing a particular crime}}{\text{100 men committing the same crime}}$$

they found that relative undersupplies of women in the larger community did indeed lead to (a) greater female offending rates per 100 male offenders, and that (b) higher ratios of female to male homicide victims did lead to larger police forces.

A close relative of the ratio scale is the probability scale. *A probability scale is quite different from cardinal scales because probability presumes only the likelihood that a phenomenon exists while cardinal scales measure actual existence.* Science is replete with probability measures because we can rarely directly measure phenomena. Obviously either: it is raining or is not; a woman is pregnant or she is not; a cadaver was a homicide case or it was not. However, scientists can not predict on which day it will rain, which woman will become pregnant, or which person will become a homicide victim. Therefore, scientists have invented probabilistic means for measuring how likely it is that it will rain, a particular group of women will become pregnant under different conditions, or persons in different situations are likely to be victimized.

There are a variety of other theory-based scaling inventions that scientists routinely employ. Among them are mathematical transformations based on logarithms, differences, and powers of cardinal numbers. Scaling by any method is always based on assumptions that need conceptual justification. Taking the log of an ordinal variable does not magically make it into a true log. Scientists give particular care to scaling with the knowledge of a tension between their desire to employ more rigorous scales tempered by the knowledge that theory, and not method, ultimately limits how they measure any phenomenon.

Creating stronger scale types

Social scientists spend much time trying to create variables with stronger quantitative properties. Hage (1972:16–28) explicates five techniques of searching for and creating quantitative variables out of qualitative concepts. First, the researcher can search for *implied dimensions underlying* qualitative concepts. For example, the concept of "social group" implies a number of more quantitative dimensions (Campbell 1958): degrees of proximity, similarity, perceived common fate, and perceived spatial pattern.

Second, one can often create new variables by comparing conceptual *synonyms* or *analogies* in a search for *more abstract* synonyms or analogies. A good place to start looking for synonyms is in a thesaurus. For example, Roget's Thesaurus lists six different categories of meaning for "similarity": identity, sameness, uniformity, agreement, equivalence, and comparison.

Third, one can search the literature for *exceptions* to a hypothesis or *rarely occurring associations* between phenomena. In their classic work on perceived similarity of rewards and costs in small groups, Thibaut and Kelly (1959) formulated a principle that two persons would have a more stable relationship if they both perceived the other person had a similar high reward-to-cost ratio. However, they found some interesting exceptions to their principle: individuals who perceived a low reward-to-cost ratio and individuals who perceived great inequity in their own versus their partner's reward-to-cost ratio who nevertheless appeared to have a stable relationship. In this case, because of these exceptions, Thibaut and Kelly found it necessary to formulate another principle: Two persons also made comparisons of the reward-to-cost relationship in their own case with alternative relationships. Only if they perceived they could get a "better deal" in another relationship were they likely to leave their present relationship.

The fourth method is to compare diverse conceptual contents to discover new variables. Rather than just study perceived similarity of rewards to costs in dyads (two-person group), the researcher might wish to compare dyads to triads (three-person groups) and larger groups. For example, triads have known differences in similarity-dissimilarity of power that lead to coalitions of two against one. Similarly, studies of larger size groups have led to an array of interesting variables that cannot be found in dyads and triads such as hierarchy, status orders, etc.

In such ways, the researcher may create useful variability. Scientists learn much more through studying variability than nonvariability. When AIDS researchers became excited in 1988 with the discovery of new strains of HIV, it was because they could learn much more by studying slightly different strains of the same virus. Similarly, sociologists learn more about social variables when they can study areas with variations in amounts of each. To discover that some areas have three times the homicide rate of other areas piques interest in why those areas differ; lack of variability decreases interest because individuals then assume a phenomenon is "naturally given."

Fifth, researchers profit from ordering concepts from more to less abstract. "Group similarity" is much more abstract than the related concepts of "similarity of rewards to costs," " value similarity," or "similarity in dress." Scientists typically find it necessary to use less abstract concepts in the initial stages of research to aid in the development of more concrete measurement.

Variables of lesser scope are more specific to particular situations and more directly observable. Therefore, they are more easily testable than variables of greater scope, but those of lesser scope have less generalizability. Variables of lesser scope find their primary use as observable indicators of variables of greater scope. This leads to the second rule of theory construction:

Rule 2:   Progressively develop and refine variables through beginning with low-scope assertions but ending with widescope assertions that are logically based on assertions of low scope.

The process for adhering to this second rule is threefold. First, the researcher compiles a list of low-scope assertions that should be related according to theory. Durkheim's classic study of suicide starts with a large number of assertions of low scope: Married persons are less likely to commit suicide than unmarried persons, and Protestants are more likely to commit suicide than Catholics.

Second, taking those low-level assertions that receive empirical verification, the researcher asks what, if anything, these assertions have in common. What, for example, might Protestants and unmarried persons have in common?

Durkheim felt that each of these categories of individuals were more likely to be anomic (or normless) than Catholics—he was wrong!—or marrieds.

Third, having isolated a potential variable as a candidate for an explanation of wider scope, the researcher attempts to set up a variety of situations with which to test hypotheses. Durkheim asked: If it is true that anomie (lack of norms) is a more parsimonious explanation of suicide, what other variables of low scope could be used to test this hypothesis? He reasoned that because urbanization was associated with anomie, data should show that more urbanized countries such as France have higher suicide rates than low-urbanized countries like Ireland.

Note that because there are an infinity of tests of any theory that *scientists can never prove a theory.* Even if Durkheim's theory stood up in his day and age (which it did not completely), there is no way to know if it stands up today without retesting the theory. The goal of science is more modest than proof; it is to lend credibility to a theory through a barrage of tests that, if they hold up, lend support to that theory, or at least do not disconfirm it.

A third rule is proposed by Davis (1970:17).

Rule 3: **Make the variable's scale properties explicit by stating all of the variable's mutually exclusive and totally inclusive categories by degree.**

With some variables, such as income expressed in dollars, it is relatively easy to conceptualize all categories. Unfortunately, social scientists often use conceptualizations such as "role conflict," "social change," or "bureaucratic structure" without necessarily explicating the categories. A good habit is to state the *intensities* of role conflict, *amounts* of social change, or number of *levels* of bureaucratic structure, and so on.

Mutually exclusive categories refers to categories that do not overlap. For example, it would be inappropriate to code income as "less than $5,000 a year," "$5,000 to $9,999," and so on. Rather, the researcher will code it as "less than $5,000," "$5,000 to $9,999" with a rule for rounding off when necessary. Totally inclusive categories refer to a complete cataloguing of all categories. It would not be appropriate to start coding income at $5,000 to $10,000 because that system misses those individuals making less than $5,000.

Sometimes it is impossible to avoid overlapping categories. In Japan, many people claim two or three (Buddhism, Confuciousism, Shintoism) religions so that it is impossible to separate individual Japanese out into each religion. Because the Japanese themselves do not make such exclusive distinctions, it is acceptable to "double-" or "triple"-count them. As a matter of fact, in such areas as Kyoto, close to 300% of the population claim religions through this method of counting overlapping memberships, versus areas like Hokkaido which show close to 100%. Such a measure becomes an interesting means of tapping into traditionalism, as those areas with higher religious percentages tend to be more traditional. Also, in survey research, individuals often are allowed to chose more than one answer to particular questions. Nevertheless, the novice researcher will find such research much more difficult to analyze and, therefore, should be shy of overcomplicating the analytic task. However, in cases where such complications do exist, they should be explicitly stated.

Other scientists cannot properly assess the scale's numerosity without explicit accounting of how the phenomenon was measured, hence, Rule 4, as follows.

Rule 4: Describe the means used to sort observations into variable categories in sufficient detail so that others can evaluate and replicate the methods.

"Personality disintegration" and "schizophrenia" provide good examples of poorly operationalized variables (Szasz 1987) that are, unfortunately, currently still in much use by social scientists. Replication by other scientists is a generally accepted step toward credibility in research. If others cannot replicate the measures (poor reliability), it follows—as Chapter 4 demonstrates—that validity must also be low.

As a model example of this rule, consider for a moment the belief that capital punishment ought to negatively affect homicides. Stack (1987) found such a relationship for publicized executions and homicide rates. More to the point, however, for criminologists is how Stack measured each variable. Operationalizing homicide rates was fairly straightforward and easy to replicate. Stack used data on monthly homicide counts from the U.S. Public Health Service's *Vital Statistics of the United States* for 1952 through 1984. He then reports standardizing these figures using monthly population estimates from the U.S. Bureau of Labor Statistics. His rates refer to homicides per 100,000 population 16 years and older because this is the population most at risk.

More difficult was Stack's measurement of a list of nationally publicized executions. First, Stack (1987:534) searched *Facts on File* under "crime, executions, death penalty, hangings, (and) capital punishment" for the same three decades and located 28 executions. He notes that he excluded several because "they involved executions in foreign countries or because they involved rape as opposed to murder." He then verified these executions by checking the *New York Times Index* and *New York Times Personal Names Index*. Only 16 of the execution stories fulfilled this verification criteria. Finally, he created "an aggregate execution story dummy variable" where "1 = a month with a publicized execution story and where 0 = a month without such a story." To allow stories appearing late in the month to show effects in the following month, Stack coded stories occurring after the 23rd of the month as affecting the next month by coding the next month with a "1."

Although some researchers disagree with Stack's methods, what is important here is that he gives enough information with which to quibble. The point is that his research specifies the operations *in sufficient detail* for others to evaluate the validity of the measurements. This raises yet a fifth rule (Davis 1970:17).

Rule 5: **Always consider the alternative variable names that might be more appropriate for a given set of operations and the alternative operations which might be more appropriate for a given variable name.**

To avoid the fallacies of improper measurement, the researcher must be highly critical of the methods which presumably measure particular variables. The more abstract or higher the scope of the variable, the more cautious the researcher should be in presuming it is measuring what he or she purports to measure. Age is of such low-level abstraction that it is less necessary to consider the question "What is your age?" as tapping variables other than "age" by contrast to Stark's (1987) measurement of "good-old-boy" culture with ownership of a pickup truck. Ironically, pickup truck ownership turns out to be an excellent indirect means of "good-old-boy" culture while the age question itself is not a "pure" measure of age. It is useful to remember that *no* measure is ever perfect. Many individuals round off their ages to the nearest 0 or 5, such as 25, 30, or 35. Some means of measuring, however, are better than other means of measuring any particular phenomenon. The idea then, is to get the best means of measuring any particular variable.

The more abstract the variable, the more consideration that the researcher should give to alternative measures. Chapter 7 will be partially concerned with the question of alternatives to single measurements of variables.

The sixth rule is one of the most often misunderstood rules.

Rule 6: **Treat variables without cardinal-scale base as basically arbitrary and relatively meaningless.**

The major problem with nominal classfications and ordinal variables is that they lack a natural zero point. Thus, noncardinal, one-variable distributions are arbitrary because they have *no intrinsic lower boundary*. Although they may be *descriptive* on a low information level: "Group A had a low rate of productivity," the problem is that such one-variable statements are used to imply two-variable assertions—logically false assertions of an *explanatory-predictive* nature. Yet statements of that form are virtually meaningless without a *comparison* with some other group or time, unless they are based on a natural cardinal scale. The statement "Group A had a low rate of productivity" demands a comparison with at least one other group. Furthermore, it suggests a question: Why does group A have a low rate of productivity?

Ironically, most of social science's more sophisticated variables have noncardinal bases: IQ, anomie, personality integration, social stratification, and racial heterogeneity. Although the distributions of *single* variables like racial heterogeneity are meaningless *in and of themselves,* when one measure *relationships* of such variables ("the more racially heterogeneous a city, the more likely minority groups will be integrated into their communities"), the variables can be meaningful even though they may lack cardinal scale qualities. Thus, Rule 7 follows.

Rule 7: **Form habits of formally analyzing variables through their relationships.**

Constructing Hypotheses from Variables

Rule 7 forms the backbone of true scientific theory. Scientists do not measure variables for measurement's sake. Rather, they seek to explain variation in particular variables known as dependent variables. A *dependent variable* is a variable for which the researcher asserts the variation is an effect of some other variable (or variables) known as an independent variable. (If you need a mnemonic, use the metaphor of a dependent variable as a "child" forced to change.) An *independent variable* is a variable that the researcher presumes causes change. (Again, the metaphor of independent variable as the "adult" forcing change may help you remember the definition.)

At the simplest level, Rule 7 states that the researcher specify a causal relationship between an independent variable and a dependent variable of the generic form "a change in the independent variable produces a change in the dependent variable." For example, the classic Durkheimian hypotheses suggests that lack of social integration produces social pathology. Scientists strive to specify their hypotheses so that the relationship between the independent variable and dependent variable is clearly stated. It is not enough to say that two variables are "related." How two variables are related matters greatly.

A basic means for specifying the relationship is to predict the direction of change. In the above example, the relationship between lack of social integration and social pathology is a *positive* one: the *greater* the social disintegration, the *greater* the social pathology. A *positive relationship* may take one of two forms: (1) As x increases, y increases; or (2) as x decreases, y decreases. Richardson (1988:214) specifies the following hypotheses in this positive form: Increased interpersonal trust leads to higher personal self-esteem. A *negative relationship* also takes one of two forms: (1) As x increases, y decreases; or (2) as x decreases, y increases. Richardson also researched a negative hypotheses known as the principle of least interest: Greater amounts of individual interest in the relationship cause that individual to have less power in that relationship.

James Davis (1970:2) warns that "It is often the case that pages of introductory discussion and definitions of variables yield only a sentence or two where the author 'actually says something'—where (the author) asserts a relationship between two variables." Because scientific hypotheses are the backbones of theory, the reader oftentimes ends up translating pages of argument into testable hypotheses. Remembering that theoretical arguments must always be clearly specified, consider a classic, but less than explicit, discussion of secrecy and power in extramarital affairs. Richardson (1988:212) states that "because (the man) is married, the (extramarital) relationship's time constraints are affected by his marital obligations. When time constraints exist and when energy is invested to achieve a rendezvous, positive expectations rise."

Implicit in Richardson's enlightening discussion are many interesting hypotheses that need clearer explication. In this case it is useful to consider two clearer specifications. Richardson's quote suggests at least three hypotheses: (1) the stronger the man's perceptions of his marital obligations, the more time constraints he feels on his outside relationships; (2) the greater the constraints on the married man's time, the more positive expectations the unmarried women has for the extramarital relationship; and (3) the more energy the married man invests in the extramarital relationship, the more positive expectations the unmarried woman has for the extramarital relationship. Understanding that the "positive expectations" refer to the unmarried woman and not the married man requires reading the argument surrounding the original quotation. Clearer specification of Richardson's hypotheses aids generation of other hypotheses because we can now substitute "unmarried woman's" for "man's" in the first hypothesis, and "married man" for "unmarried woman" in the remaining hypotheses to judge whether or not these alternatives actually fit into Richardson's surrounding argument.

Conventional Language versus Mathematical Hypotheses

Natural languages such as English are poor at describing variables; they are even poorer at expressing variable relationships. The problem is that scientific hypotheses can be connected by a multitude of "If so . . . then so" solutions.

The most simple theoretical statements are the "either-or" type (which usually contain some form of the verb "to be"), such as: "If person A likes person B and B dislikes C, person A will dislike person C" or "All societies are stratified." Such statements are limited to only one "If so . . . then so" statement. Continuous theoretical statements of the form "the greater the dislike person A has for person B and the greater liking person B has for person C, then the greater the tendency for person A to dislike person C" present a more intricate web of "If so . . . then so" statements, but they are still too simple compared with a mathematically formalized statement that can deal with situations where not only several causes converge on a single effect, but also where the causes and effects all interact with each other, such as the equation for the "ideal gas" that reads

$$PV = RT$$

where P is the pressure, V the volume, T the temperature, and R is a constant for all gases. Scientists prefer theoretical statements that have the greater degree of continuousness and preciseness in specifying "If so . . . then so" solutions. Obviously, however, such preferred theoretical statements require at least cardinal-scale based variables.

Sociologists have come late to discover such formalized relationships. Jasso (1978) has used empirical work on perceived judgments about the fairness or unfairness of income earnings to derive a Law of Justice Evaluation. He points out that earlier research into this question suggested that "judging oneself overpaid produces guilt and judging oneself underpaid produces anger" (p. 1,399), but because we previously lacked precise measures of how much injustice people feel, we were unable to test adequately the responses of persons to each kind of injustice. His work has indicated that our justice evaluations are a logarithmic function of the ratio of actual amounts to just amounts of socially distributed goods:

$$\text{justice evaluation} = \ln \frac{\text{actual amount of goods}}{\text{just amount of goods}}$$

(Note that in mathematics, the dependent variable is always placed to the left of the equality sign.) Ultimately, we prefer such formalized statements because they give us unambiguous claims, which make them more easily subject to falsification-verification due to their more elegant preciseness of statement and are more easily replicable.

Davis (1970:19) points out that the sentence-verb-object structure of conventional languages makes it difficult to describe *mutual* relationships. Likewise, Hage (1972:35) illustrates how verbal theoretical statements containing some form of the verb "to be" also cannot connect variables with constants, powers, and coefficients. Homans' (1950) propositions that "liking tends to lead to more interaction" and "more interaction tends to lead to more liking" are not easily expressed in a single clause. Also, as I have noted, the strength of variable relationships is usually extremely inexact as in the use of "tends to" above. Finally, "strong," "mild," or "weak" do not specify relationships as well as mathematical indicators.

Deducing Causation

Although the goal of hypothesis formation is the expression of causal relationships, it is wise to remember how scientists logically deduce causal ordering and some associated fallacies of causality. Remember first that nonscientists are too ready to perceive causality; humans are biased to perceive causality when it does not exist. (Chapter 4 in H. Smith [1987] summarizes much of the evidence.) Scientists use various logical and statistical tools for encouraging caution in attributing causality that are worthwhile understanding. This section covers some logical means of deducing causality or its lack; Chapters 16 and 17 covers statistical means.

There are two logical conditions for causation to take place. A causal explanation explains the occurrence of an event by reference to at least one antecedent that makes its occurrence probable. *The first condition, then, is that the assumed cause must come first in time. The second condition is that there must be a one-to-one relationship between the independent variable and the dependent variable such that if a change occurs in the independent variable a corresponding change must occur in the dependent variable.* The problem is *which* antecedent out of the infinity of antecedents is the cause. Although scientists cannot rule out all possibilities, they can logically rule out numerous ones by considering various fallacies of causation (Fischer 1970:164–186).

First, the fallacy that if event *B* happened after event *A*, it happened because of event *A*. In a clever test of this overperception of causality, Michotte

(1963) designed animated films in which two squares moved about the screen. In one particularly interesting sequence, two squares moved in the same direction followed by leading square stopping, the following square then stopped up against the leading one, and the leading square then moved away from the first. Subjects perceived a causal relationship between the movements of the two squares; they used such comments as the following square "hitting," "pushing," "chasing" or "causing" the second square, or the the leading square "fleeing from" the first.

A similar error is the belief that the full moon causes deviant behavior because a full moon happens to occur before *some* crimes. Criminologists believe that if there is an association between the moon's cycle and criminal behavior, it is not necessary to posit anything mysterious about "effects" of the moon. Rather, criminals prefer light (most crimes, contrary to popular belief, take place during daylight hours), which the reflection of the full moon at night gives. *When one event occurs before another, it is wise to consider other variables that might more parsimoniously explain the association.*

Second, the fallacy of mistaking statistical association for causation. Statistics texts invariably warn against this error. The classic example is the association between number of storks' nests and the number of human births in various parts of northern Europe. Storks do not bring babies, as the association suggests. The association is fallacious; it is due to other variables which correlate with these two variables: Human population increase creates a demand in building construction, and more buildings produce more places for storks to nest.

Association is a necessary but not sufficient condition for causation, but lack of association is sufficient to show lack of causation. (A *necessary condition* refers to a state of affairs that must exist for another state to exist. A *sufficient condition* is a state that assures the existence of another state.) Very high associations exist between the number of crimes and number of officers of the law in the United States, but this is an artifact of the fact that large numbers of both occur in large metropolitan areas. When researchers control for size of population, this association disappears. Thus, in spite of the initial high association, the number of officers of the law is neither a necessary nor sufficient condition for high crime rates, and high crime rates do not cause increases in officers of the law. Again, the presidential pornography commission unethically cited a strong positive association between reading *Playboy* magazine and rape as evidence of the harmful effects of reading girlie magazines even though the commission footnoted that the association disappears when controlled for areas that have a large number of male residents. The reason for the spurious association is the fact that males read Playboy and areas with high rape rates have large proportions of adult, single male households. These examples suggest that individuals should consider alternative explanations for the existence of an association other than a simple, direct causal one.

More embarrassing is the fallacy of putting the effect before the cause. If an event *A* occurred before event *B*, event *B* cannot have caused event *A*. In science cause and effect must be separated in time no matter how slight, and the cause must have occurred first. There is a strong positive association between overcrowded households and poverty, but it would be illogical to say that overcrowding causes poverty because the time sequence is wrong. Individuals live in overcrowded conditions because they are poor, not the reverse.

Finally, a major mistake is to assume that a causal relationship is all-or-nothing; that a cause is both a necessary and a sufficient condition of an effect. More accurately, an "effect" probably has numerous causes. As you will see later in this chapter in Figure 3-2, the "causes" of crime are multiple. No one cause is a sufficient condition in and of itself.

Constructing Theories from Hypotheses

Although hypotheses are the backbones of theories, logically related hypotheses organized into theories are the heart of science. As with overinterpretation of causality, humans are also too willing to stop at single explanations. This implies yet another fallacy: the fallacy of reductionism, or the reducing of the complex to the simple. When asked to explain why some event occurred, humans normally give one likely explanation without due consideration of others. The world is much more complex than this. Scientific explanation most often indicates multiple causes and effects. *One* formal hypothesis is not enough to make a scientific theory. A theory must be composed of at least two related propositions: the dependent *or* independent variable must be shared by at least two hypotheses, leading to the eighth rule:

> **Rule 8:   Link two or more formal propositions through a shared independent or dependent variable where possible.**

A classic example of such practice is seen in Durkheim's classic work on suicide once again. The dependent variable in the following special theory is shared by each of the following hypotheses:

1. Married persons are less likely than unmarried persons to commit suicide.
2. Married persons with children are less likely than married persons without children to commit suicide.

From these types of concrete relational observations, Durkheim inductively produced a number of more abstract formal hypotheses that make up a theory such as:

1. Suicide rates vary inversely with the degree of group cohesion.
2. Suicide rates vary positively with the degree of individualism.

From such a theory, it is then possible to deduce a number of testable statements. *These testable statements set true theory apart from simple opinion* because one can have an untestable opinion or an opinion that one does not wish to test. (Scientists do not believe in letting sleeping dogmas lie!) Therefore, scientists wishing to test Durkheim's theory would look for indicators of greater and lesser degrees of group cohesion and individualism and test whether or not they behave as he predicted they should. As one example, because areas with higher population turnover should be an indicator of lack of group cohesion, social scientists test the hypothesis that high population turnover associates positively with suicide rates.

Because the world of cause and effect is multidimensional and complex, it helps to analyze variable relationships formally and to summarize such relationships through relational diagrams. Rule 8 can be strongly implemented by the use of various conventions summarized in the last rule.

Rule 9: **Link variables using the following conventions: (a) If a set of independent variables is correlated without an assertion of causality, link the set with a curved solid line that has arrows at both ends; (b) Where there is an assertion of causality, draw an arrow from the independent to the dependent variable; (c) Show the direction of the relationship by placing a "(+)" next to line if the relationship is positive and a "(−)" if it is negative; and (d) Use multiple diagrams for "conditional" variables (where the relationship depends on the level or type of some independent variable.**

Figures 3-1 and 3-2 illustrate the use of these conventions. First, Figure 3-1 depicts suspected causal influences on criminal homicide (Williams & Flewelling 1988). Originally, Williams and Flewelling hypothesized a fifth independent variable—violent (Southern) cultural orientation—which their data disconfirmed so I have trimmed it from their original model. Rule 9 (a) is demonstrated in the hypothesized noncausal association between social disintegration and resource deprivation. That is, Williams and Flewelling hypothesize that social disintegration and resource deprivation are positively associated without any necessary causal link; or, if a causal link exists, it is bidirectional. Williams and Flewelling also hypothesize four negative causal relationships and

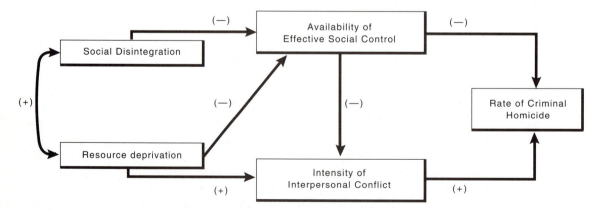

Figure 3-1. A simplified model of social production of criminal homicide.

Source: Adapted from Williams and Flewelling (1988: 426)

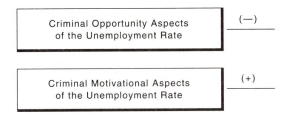

Actual criminal effects, depending on type of criminal aspects

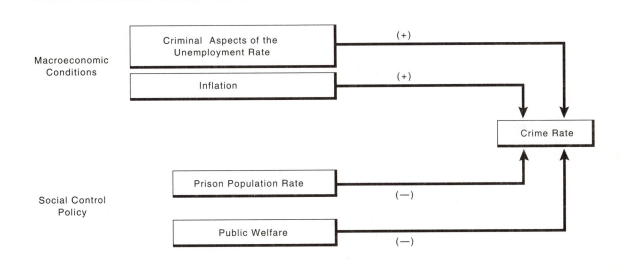

Originally postulated casual effects

Figure 3-2. A simplified model of some macroeconomic and social policy influences on changes in the rate of victim-target crimes.

Source: Adapted from Devine, Sheley, & Smith (1988: 409)

two positive causal relationships shown in Figure 3–1. Beyond these six direct causal relationships, this figure hypothesizes several important indirect causal links. Social disintegration does not directly cause criminal homicide in this model; rather, it operates indirectly through availability of effective social control and intensity of interpersonal conflict. Also, Resource deprivation indirectly influences the rate of criminal homicide through availability of effective social control and intensity of interpersonal conflict. (You should be able to verify three separate paths through which resource deprivation indirectly affects the rate of criminal homicide and two indirect paths through which social disintegration affects the rate of criminal homicide).

Figure 3-2 demonstrates the need for Rule 9(d). Quite often social scientists find that apparently similar variables do not measure the same phenomenon because each variable shows a different relationship to other variables.

Devine, Sheley, and Smith (1988:409) visualized the effects of two macro-economic conditions and two social control policy variables on the general crime rate as shown in Figure 3-2 with a positive relationship between the unemployment rate and the crime rate. However, curiously, a careful reading of their article indicates a much more complex effect of unemployment *depending on the type of crime*. Some studies Devine et al. cite indicate a negative relationship, others a positive relationship, and at least one, no relationship. Devine et al. argue that the motivational aspects of unemployment ought to have a positive effect on crime and that the criminal opportunity aspects of unemployment ought to have a negative effect. Although they do not state it clearly, they presume that motivational aspects outweighs opportunity aspects because their model lists only a positive relationship between the unemployment rate and the crime rate. However, when Devine et al.. tested their model on different types of crime, they found different relationships for different types of crime, indicating that their model is still too simplified. Nevertheless, Devine et al. postulate a *testable* model of three negative influences and two positive influences on the crime rate.

Not all social scientists are as explicit as Devine et al. (1988) or Williams and Flewelling (1988) in setting up testable models. In many cases a researcher will quite sloppily explicate variable relationships, and this results in considerable ambiguity as to how to relate the variables. Herein lies much of the necessity for restating theory in terms of formalized variable relationships because through such analysis it is possible to expose flaws or gaps in the work's theory and methods. This is particularly true when social scientists combine two or more related variable relationships into a theory. In such theories the researcher can test for logical consistency of variable relationships through the several deductive methods I mentioned in Chapter 1. Such theories make clearer parsimony or its lack also. For example, Figure 3-1 is more parsimonious than Williams and Flewelling's original formalization through cutting out a nonexistent relationship after the fact.

Box 3-1   *A Citation Classic on Generating Theory*

William J. Goode (1963) *World Revolution and Family Patterns*. Glencoe, IL: Free Press.

World Revolution and Family Patterns analyzed the relationships between social structure and family patterns as they have changed over roughly the past century in China, Japan, India, Arabic Islam, Sub-Sahara Africa, and the Western nations. Its findings are thus historical and cross-national, and they suggest directions of change in the future. [*The Social Science Citation Index* (SSCI) indicates that this paper has been cited in over 540 publications.]

Had I understood what I was attempting, I would not have begun the task. I started with modest goals and was gradually drawn into larger ones. Along with other prominent sociologists who had been students at the University of Texas—my classmates C. Wright Mills, Kingsley Davis, Logan Wilson, and Marion J. Levy—I was invited in 1958 to give a lecture in honor of Warner E. Gettys and took the occasion to summarize the complex set of broad changes in the family. I then believed I was only codifying some ideas and data that were fairly obvious but scattered in the research literature. However, some colleagues challenged my unpretentious paper, and I set about amassing further proof. Each time I reached a new synthesis, I found other skeptics—for of course I continued to hit upon new findings and to expand upon my coverage of both history and nations.

Eventually, I had collected demographic data on a dozen or more nations (e.g., Russia, whose quantitative research was too poor to be used). I had read books and articles in six foreign languages (seven, if one adds the one Afrikaans book I read), found a treasure of data from the 1950s, probably translated by the CIA in that period of China-watching, and cajoled hundreds of tables from foreign scholars (especially those in governmental statistical bureaus), which I could not have obtained at Columbia University where I was working. Thus, in successive revisions and expansions of my inquiry, I had come to include much of the world's population over the last century.

What has been the fate of the book's findings? First, none of its main trends have been *reversed* (a revised edition, bringing some findings up-to-date has appeared in Italian under the title *Famiglia e Transformazioni Sociali*). Second, some were confirmed faster than I had supposed possible (e.g., the age of women at marriage in some countries where that age had been very low). Third, my general hypothesis that in some modernizing countries the divorce rate would fall and then rise applies to several countries (Taiwan, China, some Arab nations; will Malaysia follow?) Fourth, some contemporary patterns are at time carelessly described as "traditional" (contrary to my analysis), but they are structurally in accord with my expectations (e.g., the three-generational household is still fairly common in Japan, but it is no longer the *elders'* household).

Most important are the evaluations that others have been making, as witness the citations, and there is an interesting irony in this frequency. My guess is that there is a substantial *under*count in the number of citations the *Index* reports, since the book seems to be noted in a high percentage of family texts and research monographs that touch on family change cross-nationally in this and European countries. Why so many citations in this literature? (I do not think that it is because the book won the MacIver Prize.)

My answer is a hunch without any quantitative basis. I feel that the book became one of those "standard" works that are useful for introducing a known, broad, theoretical framework in which new *contrary* findings acquire some weight. ("Goode says the joint family is disappearing, but I have just completed a study in Mahaliburipan, and at least 10% of households still claim to be joint.") Or, a more pointed challenge may be offered, noting that I was in error about how fast the change would come. ("Goode implies the *Onako-do-San* will diminish in importance, but the go-between is still common in Japanese marriage.")

All such citations, even when they correct my errors, are a kind of flattery, as was the comment by a reviewer in a major anthropology journal that the work should have been done by an anthropologist. That in the social sciences one can still be cited and chided many years after publication testifies to the complexities and difficulties we face in arriving at final answers to our larger questions. In this field, we are still trying to answer such a question: What are the relationships between social structure and family patterns over time?

Source: Current Content, January 26, 1987, p. 14.

Summary

The first step in creating testable research is to learn how to construct variables from concepts. This means searching for the most quantitative characteristics available for measuring a variable. Although the identification of concepts is important, merely naming an object does not aid its measurement. Ultimately, scientists learn more from studying variation in any phenomenon. Variable expressions contain more information than simple concepts. At the simplest level of scaling are ordinal scales that give rank indications of "more" or "less." Scientists prefer cardinal-scale based measures that determine how much greater or less. They prefer a natural zero point, meaningful units of measures, and meaningful mathematical transformations of their numeric systems. Ratio-based variables permit standardized comparisons across different categories and expression of the relationship between two quantities. Probability scales express likelihood of existence or nonexistence. Other theory-based scaling inventions employ logarithms, differences, and powers of cardinal numbers.

Scientists strive to develop and refine variables of higher scope progressively. During this process the scientist conceptualizes the scale properties as explicitly as possible into mutually exclusive and totally inclusive categories. The point is to describe variable categories in sufficient detail that other scientists can evaluate and replicate the work. Because of the goal of achieving variables of wider scope, scientists consider alternative variable names that might be more appropriate as well as more appropriate means of measuring a variable.

Scientific analysis uses variables in hypotheses, and variables make sense only through their relationships to each other as dependent (effects) or independent (causal) variables. At the most fundamental level, this means that the researcher must specify how and why a dependent variable increases or decreases as an independent variable increases (or decreases). Because natural languages are only crude means of explicating hypotheses, scientists strive to quantify variable relationships.

In early stages of their research, scientists use logical means to deduce causal relationships. First, unless one variable comes before the other in time sequence, it cannot logically be an independent variable. Second, a change in one variable must produce an associated change in the other; the two variables must be correlated or associated. These two rules aid ruling out many but not all possible causal statements. Just because an event happened after another event does not mean the first event caused the second. Association is only a necessary but not a sufficient condition for causality. Because humans are too ready to perceive causality, scientists and logicians continue to develop means of treating associations between any two variables with proper skepticism.

Scientists organize hypotheses into theories. Although laypersons are comfortable with stopping with single explanations, scientists attempt to develop multiple cause and effect explanations of phenomena. To set theory apart from opinion, the theory must also produce testable or falsifiable predictions. Because of the complexity of causal relationships, scientists also find it useful to map out the relationships between variables with conventions for visualizing multicausality.

CHAPTER

4

Operationalization, Reliability, and Validity

When a scientist doesn't know the answer to a problem, he is ignorant. When he has a hunch as to what the result is, he is uncertain. And when he is pretty darn sure of what the result is going to be, he is in some doubt.[1]

When you cannot measure, your knowledge is meager and unsatisfactory.[2]

Key Terms

Blind-experimental condition	History effect
Concurrent validity	Interaction effect
Construct validity	Inter-item correlation reliability
Content validity	Maturation effect
False-negative error	Multiple (alternate) forms validity
False-positive error	Operationalization

[1]Attributed to Lee A. DuBridge.
[2]Attributed to Lord Kelvin.

Phenomenology

Placebo

Predictive validity

Reactive effect

Reliability

Replication

Split-half reliability

Statistical regression

Test-retest reliability

Validity

Study Guide Questions

1. Why is operationalization crucial to science? Give two examples as part of your explanation.

2. Explain the basic differences between, and the relations between, reliability and validity.

3. What are the comparative advantages and disadvantages of the four ways of measuring reliability?

4. How do scale length and item reliability influence scale reliabililty?

5. What are crucial differences between validity of measurement and validity of findings?

6. What differences exist in using content validity, predictive validity, concurrent validity, and construct validity? What are the main advantages and disadvantages of each?

7. Why do researchers distinguish between internal and external validity? What does each concept measure?

8. Among the seven types of internal validity factors, which does randomization help guard against invalidity? Why? What other means does the researcher have for aiding internal validity?

9. What are the differences between history and maturation effects?

10. How do testing, reactive effects of testing, and reactive effects of data-collection arrangements differ?

11. What is the difference between false-negative and false-positive errors? Why does the danger of both errors always exist in research?

12. How does replication aid the balancing of statistical conclusion validity?

13. What are double-blind and triple-blind experiments? What purposes do they serve?

Social and behavioral research has two fundamental philosophical traditions. The one which has been the dominant one is known as positivist empiricism. *Positivistic empiricism* maintains that there is an objective, external reality that humans can understand through thought and nonsensual intuition. By contrast, there is a smaller, but significantly persuasive, group of scholars who argue for a phenomenological point of view. *Phenomenology* holds that humans cannot know reality, but rather, humans construct reality by virtue of what goes on inside their minds. Phenomenologists maintain that it is impossible to know an object external to the self without considering how the mind influences perceptions of the outside world.

Most probably positivists and phenomenologists are both right; the external world is *really* there, but is influenced by what humans *want* to see and what they *expect* to see. There is a large body of research that suggests phenomenologists are at least partly correct. Because personal beliefs, feelings, and thoughts do have powerful influences on the ways in which humans perceive the world external to themselves, research methodology is greatly concerned with developing *independent* checks on reality. This chapter explains three intertwined independent checks on reality that lie at the heart of science: operationalization, reliability, and validity.

Most of us hate new jargon, but "operationalization" is not really new, although most nonscientists are unfamiliar with it. According to the Oxford Dictionary, its scientific meaning traces back to everyday usage in the fourteenth century: Chaucer used it to refer to the performance of something of a practical or mechanical nature. Scientists have extended his use of the term "operationalization" when they speak about measuring the evidence for or against some theory. Operationalization, therefore, is a bridge between research methods and theory because to compare evidence with theory requires that the researcher measure the ingredients—the propositions, concepts, or categories—of some theory. It also requires that the researcher be skeptical; a consideration of operationalization, reliability, and validity demonstrates specific means by which reputable researchers practice skepticism.

Operationalization

There are two fundamental types of knowing: awareness of objects known through (1) personal sensual experience, and (2) the use of nonpersonal, empirical evidence and rational thought. The branch of philosophy known as phenomenology is highly concerned with the former; *phenomenology* assumes that only the former type of awareness is possible, while positivistic science assumes the latter is possible.

As scientists understand the term science in its modern sense, it has come to be defined as the enterprise of gaining knowledge of natural phenomena through continually testing one's theories *against empirical evidence*. The process of agreeing upon acceptable means of measuring some phenomena is a crucial component of the process of scientific explanation and prediction. For such scientific ingredients as weight or speed, it is clear what to measure, but what would you measure if you wanted to understand violent criminal behavior, political confrontations, or social empowerment? Somehow we would have to design a series of actual operations that yield suitable measurements—that is, we must operationalize the variables in our theories.

Scientists and nonscientists alike do this all the time, whether or not they consciously think about it. For example, in everyday life, children argue over such things as whether or not one piece of cake is larger than another piece. One child says the one piece of cake is larger than another, and the other says it is not. To settle the argument, their mother might operationalize "larger" by weighing the two pieces. Suppose she finds that one piece weighs 3 grams and the other weighs 3.5 grams; the mother has settled the argument through the operation of applying a numeric weighing system.

A second example comes from practical chemistry. Those of us concerned with dieting wish to know how sweet various foods are or how many calories they contain. These are problems that scientists could not accurately solve until the eighteenth century, when chemists figured out how to measure the components of matter. To solve this problem, chemists tinkered for decades with such methods as measuring the weight or the light particular substances absorb. Eventually, chemists found a highly accurate but complex method of measuring sweetness. First, they treat a glucose solution with an enzyme that liberates hydrogen peroxide. They then add another enzyme to a combination of the hydrogen peroxide and a substance called dianisidine; the resulting reaction turns the substance brown. Finally, chemists measure the intensity of the brown color with an instrument called a spectrophotometer. The deflection of the needle on the spectrophotometer dial points to a number that provides an *operational definition of sweetness*.

Social scientists study phenomenon that are even more challenging to operationalize. We cannot fit criminal behavior or homelessness into a test tube; nor can we precisely control all the variables that might influence those phenomena—as can the chemist interested in sweetness. Nevertheless, we can still use genuinely scientific tests of our theories. It is important to human survival that we continue taking up the challenge of understanding how to reduce international tensions, alleviate individual frustrations, or alter escalating trends in crime rates.

My third example comes from sociohistorical research during the 1980s on operationalizing crime rates. Most of the popular literature on variations in crime rates has emphasized the actual incidence of crime behavior through crimes reported to the police. However, as social scientists have struggled with how to measure crime rates, they have discovered that variations in official crime rates may be more a function of changes in governmental legislation and police behavior. Therefore, social scientists have mulled over the question: How can we measure the relationship between the social organization of policing and arrest practices? Monkkonen (1981) devised a good first approximation by examining arrest records in 23 American cities from 1890 to 1920. In brief, he asserted that beginning in 1890, municipal police forces shifted from a predominant concern with public order offenses (operationalized as drunkenness, disorderly conduct, and vagrancy charges) to an emphasis on the prevention and control of more serious crimes against persons (operationalized as homicide) and property (operationalized as robbery); that is, Monkkonen suggests that policing changed from controlling a *class of people* to preventing and controlling certain *classes of crime*.

Monkkonen's work provided an excellent and provocative start for two reasons. First, his use of time series analysis to explicitly test policing is open to replication in other settings. Second, his explanatory framework is open to reformulation. However, Boritch and Hagan (1987) proposed alternative operationalizations based on careful reasoning that his "tests of a shift from a class-control to a crime-control model of policing rests on an operational definition of public order offenses that includes too little, and an operational definition of crime that includes too much" (p. 309).

Boritch and Hagan's theory starts by assuming that the major change in police roles from the eighteenth to the twentieth century was not a shift to crime control but rather a change in the form of class control. To demonstrate their alternative, they had to reconceptualize crime and crime control. Monkkonen had focused narrowly on police behavior and labeled crime. Boritch and Hagan argued that Monkkonen's operationalization—by accentuating arrests for drunkenness, disorderly conduct, and vagrancy—seriously underestimates such class-related crimes as prostitution, gambling, liquor law violations, Lord's day violations, and narcotic law violations.

Accordingly, Boritch and Hagan broadened the operationalization of class-control crime to include more types of crime in a fairer test of Monkkonen's thesis. They also recategorized these class-related crimes into three different public-order offenses: (1) drunkenness, disorderly conduct, and vagrancy; (2) public morality offenses; and (3) breaches of city bylaws. Similarly, although Monkkonen had used only per capita homicide arrest rates as a measure of the level of interpersonal violence, Boritch and Hagan contend that because homicide occurs relatively infrequently, a more comprehensive operationalization should include robbery, rape, attempted murder, and assault. Boritch and Hagan expanded their final operationalization of crime to comprise general categories of persons and property, including total arrests per 100,000 population for homicide, manslaughter, attempted murder, assault, rape, robbery, theft, burglary, trespassing, arson, and fraud—minus drunkenness and vagrancy arrests.

Boritch and Hagan's meticulous operationalizations over time indicated that—in the case of Toronto over the 100 years from 1860 to 1959—public-order arrests fell from roughly 7,000 (per 100,000 population) to 3,500, while crime arrests fell from 3,000 to just over 1,000. Furthermore, they compared their time-series data with the minutes of City Council meetings, minutes of the Board of Police Commissioners meetings, the daily Order Books of the police force, and other materials in the Toronto Police Museum Archives. Their comparison of these qualitative operationalizations with the quantitative arrest records indicates that although the Toronto police embraced the rhetoric and ideology of crime control, their arrest practices continued to show a strong class-control focus.

In short, all scientists have to solve the task of operationalizing their intuitive concepts. Ultimately, we are not satisfied with the imprecision of "more or less." Sometimes, our measurements are indirect but precise, as in the case of astronomers who use knowledge of the Doppler effect to measure the speed of the expansion of the universe by measuring shifts in color. Other times, we are forced, by existing technology or lack of theory concerning how best to measure some phenomena, to resort to more direct but less precise methods.

Everybody seems to have an opinion on the matter, and many ridicule the triviality of what scientists write and do, but the fact is that much of the "triviality" of science is found in the banal but critical routine of operationalization. While Americans insist that we are losing our technological edge to other nations, scientist-educators have produced disturbingly accurate measures of investment of time in teaching that are highly correlated with mathematical and verbal achievement test differences between nations. Stevenson, Lee, and Stigler (1986) found a pattern of relative lack of investment in teaching in America. By the time of high-school graduation, American students have spent four years less time in classrooms than their Japanese counterparts—who have far less vacation time. The investment in teaching time showed also at finer levels: American first-graders spent 18% less time in academic activities in the classroom than Japanese children; by the fifth-grade, this difference had increased to 30% less time.

In the final analysis, Stevenson and his associates computed startling differences between the American children's and Japanese children's behavior. On average, American children received only 6.3 hours a week educational instruction from their teachers, compared to 12 hours a week for Japanese children. For fifth-graders, American mothers estimated that their children spent an average of 14 minutes a day on homework, while Japanese mothers estimated 37 minutes. Also, they found that American teachers actually spend much more time than Japanese teachers giving directions than imparting information. These figures show up clearly in achievement tests: The mathematical performance of American high-school graduates on standardized mathematics test was much inferior to Japanese high-school graduates; the highest scoring American student did not do as well on either numeric or word-mathematical problems as the lowest scoring Japanese student.

The higher the quality of the operationalizations, the more confidence the researcher has in those operationalizations. Judging data quality encompasses three important questions. The first question has already been introduced: By what means, or operations, can the researcher show that the data correspond to whatever it is that those data are meant to represent? Second, how reliable is that operation? Third, how valid is that operation? The researcher must deal satisfactorily with each question before the scientific community will accept the study results. In the formative years, the data-collection methods social analysts used were primarily unsystematic. Increasingly, social analysis depends on more systematic data-collection procedures. In large part, this is because certain types of systematic data-collection procedures lead toward higher quality data.

Reliability

Reliability and validity are important concepts that the lay public often misunderstand. To understand the way a scientist uses them, first consider the following example from everyday life. Let us assume that you ask two friends for directions to the bookstore from your classroom, and one friend says "Walk east two blocks," and the other say "Walk west two blocks." Because you do not yet know where the bookstore is, all you really know is that their responses—using each as a separate measure of direction—are different, and therefore unreliable. *Reliability implies that you obtain the same responses on different measures.* Similarly, if just one of your friends, on two different occasions, gives different directions to the bookstore from the same location, a scientist would call the set of directions unreliable.

Although consistency of measurement is necessary to good scientific practice, it is not sufficient; validity of measurement is also necessary. A friend who is highly reliable at giving directions may, in a constant state of disorientation, mix up east and west so that he always says "Go east!" when he means "Go west!" Although he gives reliable directions, they are invalid directions. *Validity concerns whether or not a measurement really represents that which it is suppose to measure.* Just because a person gives reliable directions therefore does not mean they are valid directions. In the case of the friend who reliably gives incorrect directions (although they are completely invalid), because you can verify the degree of bias and its consistency in his directions, you could turn this knowledge into a completely valid measure by simply going east whenever he said "west" or vice versa. (However, more often than not, reliability is a matter of degree so that the relationship of reliability to validity is more complex.)

Researchers pose the question of reliability as: *Will the same methods used by different persons produce the same results?* In other words, reliability refers to *consistency* between independent measurements of the same phenomenon. Data quality clearly demands highly reliable measures. A minimal requirement for any science is that it yield consistent measurements confirmable by independent observers—that it be independently replicable.

Some methods tend to produce unreliable data. Field research methods are so demanding that trained ethnographers often produce partial descriptive accounts that are difficult to compare. In fact, Agar (1986:15) states flatly that "an item of folklore holds that anthropologists are (in)famous at granting agencies for proposing one study and returning with another." This is due in part to the enormous amount of information from which a fieldworker must chose.

Paradoxically, of the methods at our disposal, field research is normally the most valid way of gaining insight into meaning and symbolism.

This problem of increasing the reliability of scientific data is a problem throughout all sciences. For example, Paul Cleary (1987), a Harvard School of Public Health researcher, states that of 9,000 persons who tested positive on available AIDS screening tests, only 1,200 would show up positive on a second, confirmatory test. One would do better at guessing! However, by giving two different tests—both the ELISA and Western blot tests—the reliability can be increased to 90% over two testing periods.

Although it is rare for researchers to obtain perfect reliability between independent measurements, sometimes social scientific research does significantly better than this. Alwin (1986) reanalyzed classic work on the influence of religion in Detroit done three decades earlier by Lenski. He found less than 1% difference in the way he and Lenski independently coded the same data. Also, well-constructed observational forms used by trained observers often reveal agreement in up to 97 out of 100 cases. Anderson and Silver (1987) discovered very high agreement between Soviet emigrant spouses on objective measures of household material status in the U.S.S.R. (0.95 correlation for amount of housing space), but low agreement on more subjective items (correlation of 0.77 between rating oneself as religious and one's spouse's rating of oneself as religious).

There are four ways to test measurement reliability: test-retest, multiple forms, split-half, and average intercorrelation techniques. In *test-retest reliability,* we take two measurements on the same population with the same instrument at different times. The higher the agreement between these measurements, the higher we judge the reliability of our measurement. Social scientists often use a correlation coefficient or some other measure of association as a measure of agreement for two sets of interval-level measurements. Correlation coefficients approaching 1.0 indicate high reliability, those approaching 0.0 indicate complete lack of reliability, and those approaching -1.0 indicate two variables that reliably measure polar opposites.

Test-retest reliability has one major drawback: The first application of the measurement may affect responses on the second administration. This is particularly likely the closer the application of each measurement. Therefore, the shorter the period between test and retest, the more chance participants may wish to appear consistent and their memory may cause spuriously high reliability. On the other hand, the longer the period between test and retest, the more chance that *actual* change in the phenomenon will produce a spuriously low reliability coefficient. For this reason, scientists say that test-retest procedures measure reliability only in terms of *stability* of findings.

Second, we may simultaneously administer *multiple (alternate) forms* of identical measuring devices to the same sample. A researcher interested in "group cohesion" might use two measures: first, a measure of the individual members' attraction to a group; second, a measure of prestige gains from group membership. Again, a high association between measures is a criteria for high reliability. Researchers say that multiple-forms measures of reliability provide a measure of *equivalence* of forms. Therefore, low associations between

Box 4-1 *A Citation Classic on Operationalization and Validity*

Rochel Gelman (1969) Conservation acquisition: a problem of learning to attend to relevant attributes. *Journal of Experimental Child Psychology*, 7, 167-87. [*The Social Science Citation Index* (SSCI) indicates that this paper has been cited in over 150 publications.]

This *Citation Classic* was based on my dissertation. How I came to do one of the first studies showing it is possible to train children who fail Piaget's conservation task is less than a noble tale. I was gearing up to do a multidimensional scaling study of how adults respond to music. It would not have been an easy study to do, and I wasn't sure I would learn anything musicians did not already know. I began to get cold feet and allowed myself to get talked into a brief skiing trip to Mammoth, California, but I took a bit of work along—a copy of Flavell's *The Development of Psychology of Jean Piaget*.

The choice of book may seem odd. I had resisted the fact that developmental topics interested me most because I did not like being told that women fared better in this area. So throughout graduate school I did two lines of work in parallel, one in what is now called cognitive psychology, one in developmental psychology. The two lines came together while I was lying in a hospital bed with a broken leg and with nothing else to read but Flavell's book. As I read and reread it, the work I was doing on the role of attention in learning kept coming to mind. Its juxtaposition alongside my thoughts of Piaget led me to the idea that I might succeed in teaching children to conserve quantity if I adopted the methods of those who treated learning as a function of the ability to attend to relevant attributes or dimensions in a display.

The translation of the attention argument into a Piagetian training study involved thinking of the standard conservation stimuli as two complexes of relevant and irrelevant dimensions. The relevant dimension was the quantity, e.g., the liquid in two identical containers; the irrelevant dimensions were the height, width, size, color, etc., of the containers. Given that the irrelevant and relevant dimensions are redundant to start, probability favors attention to one or more irrelevant dimensions. Since Harlow could teach monkeys to ignore irrelevant dimensions and respond to the odd stimulus of three, I thought it reasonable to try to adapt his learning-set method to teaching five-year-olds.

I could not rush out and work with children. I had a cast on, and they attended more to the fact I had no shoe on my left foot than to my questions about same or different number or length—my trinket reinforcers notwithstanding. With time to think, I realized that children needed to see how different transformations varied the relevant and irrelevant dimensions—even though Harlow did not let monkeys watch him set up the within-problem trials.

The young children in my experimental group responded quickly to the training; they also applied what they learned on follow-up tests of conservation. More importantly, they could justify their answers and, when given a post-test six months later, continued to conserve. I had at least met some of the Piagetian transfer criteria.

My effort to publish the work introduced me to the world of conflicting reviews. The journal editor would accept the manuscript if I could deal with the "enclosed reviews." One reviewer as much as said I could not have done what I said I had done and would know this had I cited comparable studies. Worse yet, I could not have read any Piaget, either in the original or as presented in Flavell's book on Piaget. The other encouraged publication and asked me to try to explain the robustness of the transfer effects, especially the explanation data. It was signed by John Flavell! I shipped the reviews off to Tom Trabasso and Wendell Jeffrey, the cochairmen of my dissertation, who explained that the article had not been rejected—quite the contrary.

It wasn't until 1982 that I published another conservation training study. I reasoned that the children in the first one caught on too quickly if they really lacked underlying structures to interpret the environment I was presenting them; they had to have known more about quantity. I turned my efforts to studying what preschool children do know about quantity—and to other domains.

Source: Current Content, January 26, 1987, p. 14.

---

alternative forms might be due to the forms simply not being equivalent rather than to low reliability.

Third, in the *split-half technique* we randomly split the measurements (where possible) in half. Assume we wish to measure the reliability of a 20-statement attitude scale. We could form two separate scales of ten items each by flipping a coin for each item: If the coin turned up heads we would assign that item to one subscale, and if it turned up tails to the other subscale. Because we randomized (without any particular pattern) item assignment to each subscale, we may treat each half as an alternate form of the same scale. The easiest means of finding split-half reliability involves the use of elementary statistics: It requires the researcher to measure the variation in *differences* between measurements of the two half-tests (S^2_d) and the variation in total (unsplit test) scores (S^2_T).

Then, the split-half-formula r_{tt} reads:

$$r_{tt} = 1 - \frac{S^2_d}{S^2_T}$$

Box 4–2 provides an example of how researchers compute this split-half formula.

Fourth, the *average inter-item correlation* technique correlates each item in a scale against every other item, and obtains the *average* intercorrelation for the entire set of correlations or associations. In the following matrix are listed sets of hypothetical Pearson's correlations between four scale items:

	1	2	3	4
1	—	0.8	0.5	0.4
2	—	—	0.9	0.6
3	—	—	—	0.7
4	—	—	—	—

For example, the correlation between items 1 and 3 is 0.5, and between items 3 and 4 is 0.7. The average interitem correlation measure of reliability for these items is

---

Box 4-2 *Finding Split Half Reliability*

Assume we have four respondents who took a ten-statement attitude scale and their answers were ranked from 1 = strongly agree to 5 = strongly disagree:

Respondent 1: 4, 5, 3, 5, 2, 5, 3, 1, 5, 2
Respondent 2: 4, 4, 1, 2, 2, 3, 1, 4, 3, 4
Respondent 3: 1, 5, 5, 3, 4, 2, 2, 2, 3, 1
Respondent 4: 4, 5, 4, 4, 1, 4, 5, 1, 1, 3

Step 1: Use a coin to randomize the items into two halves. Then sum the first half and last half of each respondent's items.

Respondent 1	Respondent 2	Respondent 3	Respondent 4
5	4	1	4
3	2	3	5
5	4	4	1
2	2	2	4
5	3	2	5
20	15	12	19
1	4	5	4
3	1	5	4
5	3	1	3
2	1	3	1
4	4	2	1
15	13	16	13
35	28	28	32

Step 2: Subtract second half from first half subtotals to find the differences between halves and find the mean of these differences (μd). (Ignore negative signs [treat as absolutes].)

$$\mu d = \frac{[20 - 15] + [15 - 13] + [12 - 16] + [19 - 13]}{4}$$

$$= \frac{5 + 2 + 4 + 6}{4} = 4.25$$

Step 3: Find the variance of these differences, $\sigma^2 d$ [To calculate the variance of these differences, follow the following steps. From each difference (5,2,4,6 in the above example) subtract the mean of the differences (4.25) and square the resulting numbers. Add all the squared numbers together and divide by N (in this case 4).]

$$S^2 d = \frac{[5 - 4.25]^2 + [2 - 4.25]^2 + [4 - 4.25]^2 + [6 - 4.25]^2}{4}$$

$$= \frac{0.5625 + 4.84 + 0.0625 + 3.0625}{4} = 2.19$$

Step 4: Find the mean and variance for the total scores (μt and βt^2). (To find the mean for the total scores, take the total of both column halves and divide by N. To find the variance of the total scores follow the same steps used in step 3 above, but use the total score of both column halves times the mean from step 4.)

$$\mu t = \frac{35 + 28 + 28 + 32}{4} = 30.75$$

$$S^2t = \frac{[35 - 30.75]^2 + [28 - 30.75]^2 + [28 - 30.75]^2 + [35 - 30.75]^2}{4}$$

$$= 8.69$$

Step 5: Substitute your figures for σ^2d
and σ^2t
in the formula

$$r_{tt} = 1 - \frac{\sigma^2_d}{\sigma^2_T} \text{ and solve.}$$

$$r_{tt} = 1 - \frac{2.19}{8.69} = 0.75.$$

Step 6: Interpret your answer such that + 1 equals a perfectly reliable measure and 0 equals total lack of reliability. Therefore, a 0.75 coefficient, in this case, indicates a relatively strong measure of reliability.

$$\frac{0.8 + 0.5 + 0.4 + 0.9 + 0.6 + 0.7}{6}$$

or 0.65.

This procedure provides the most stable index of reliability. But because it requires a great deal of computation with large numbers of scale items, most researchers find it most efficient to use computer software to perform the actual calculations. It makes sense that reliable items should be highly associated. If they were not, there would be no grounds for combining them into an overall score, because they would measure different concepts. Items with low or negative associations, by contrast, should logically be excluded from the scale.

Another procedure for which computer programs exist is to take each of the possible $n-1$ items from the n items in the scale and compute all correlations between each $n-1$ subscale combination. The arithmetic mean of the resulting set of correlations also provides a quite suitable estimate of reliability, because it measures how much each item subtracts from the total test score. For example, if there are 4 items in the scale, the research might take each of the 3 ($n-1$) subscale combination (1,2,3; 1,2,4; 1,3,4; and 2,3,4), sum each combination, run correlations between each of these subscale sums, and then compute the average correlation coefficient. As an example, in the following hypothetical subscale correlations

	1,2,3	1,2,4	1,3,4	2,3,4
1,2,3	—	0.7	0.8	0.8
1,2,4	—	—	0.9	0.9
1,3,4	—	—	—	0.7
2,3,4	—	—	—	—

the researcher would again find the mean of the subscale combinations:

$$\frac{0.7 + 0.8 + 0.8 + 0.9 + 0.9 + 0.7}{6}$$

which is 0.80.

One particularly important influence on reliability is scale length. (A scale is *two or more* indicators of some phenomenon that the researcher combines in some fashion to produce a single measure. Longer scales give higher reliability, as evidenced by Figure 4–1 where $\rho_{xx'}$ [read as "the rho sub x to x-prime correlation"] stands for the *average* reliability coefficient for an item initially before the researcher added other scores to it to form a scale; $\rho_{x_n x'_n}$ stands for the reliability coefficient for the scale formed from those items; x stands for the first measurement; x' for the second measurement; and n for the number of scale items.)

This figure demonstrates two important points concerning the relationship of reliability to number of scale items. First, it shows that the more items (n) added to the scale, the higher the reliability ($\rho_{xx'}$). Second, the first several items added contribute more heavily to reliability than items added later. Thus,

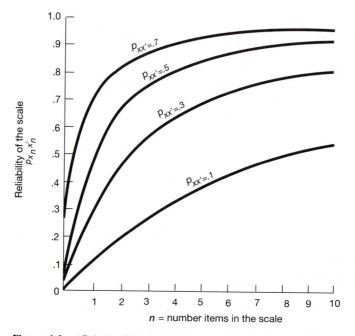

Figure 4-1.   Relationship of reliability to number of scale items.
Source: Adapted from Bohrnstedt (1970:87)

after a point (eight to ten items) any additionally added scale items will contribute almost insignificantly to raising the reliability.

You should verify that the researcher can usually obtain fairly reliable measures with scales of only eight to ten items. Look at the $\rho_{xx'} = 0.7$ line in Figure 4–1. Note that it flattens out with a high reliability of approximately 0.9 with seven or more scale items. That is, although each item averages 0.7 reliability, the second item adds only 0.1 reliability to the first item, the combination of the second through seventh item adds only a total of 0.2 to the reliability coefficient, and any further items are simply redundant because they add nothing at all. Next, look at the $\rho_{xx'} = 0.1$ line which has by far the worst average reliabilities. The first two items each contribute approximately 0.1 reliability to the total scale reliability in this case, but by interpolating beyond 10 items we can visualize that the total scale reliability will never do much better than 0.55. Any item beyond the tenth adds insignificantly to the total scale score, so we can conclude that further items are superfluous.

In spite of these clear relationships, it is surprising to note how many researchers remain ignorant of the scale length-reliability relationship. Some researchers blissfully create scales of 40 or more items, and then impose those unnecessarily lengthy scales on some sample of subjects. A far better practice would be to (1) do a pretest of a large set of scale items on a small sample of subjects; (2) check the inter-item correlations between each item and the total scale; and then (3) select only the eight to ten items with the highest inter-item correlations for the actual study. This practice saves the researcher unnecessary time and costs: Lengthy scales take more time to administer and more paper on which to print the scales. Furthermore, unnecessarily long scales are likely to produce boredom in the respondents which may decrease scale reliability.

Why does this relationship between scale length and reliability hold in general? *Any* measurement has idiosyncratic sources of error. The use of income as a measure of socioeconomic status (SES) has such peculiar problems as including $100,000 salaried Mafia members in the upper class. With every item added to the scale, we may expect item-specific errors to decrease because item-specific errors normally cancel each other out. Each measure taps factors irrelevant to whatever the researcher is measuring, but because these irrelevant components should be spread randomly across items and because all items share a common focus, the total set of measures should provide a purer measure of the phenomenon under study than any single measure. *Generally speaking, low reliability is due to random errors. If errors are biased— that is, consistently of a particular type—we then question the validity of our measurements.*

Remember that it is possible to have very reliable data that have low validity. The undergraduate grade-point average has high reliability: If several researchers jotted down G.P.A.s from university registrar records, we could predict only a few random errors in their work and, therefore, high reliability. However, there is a mass of cumulative evidence demonstrating that undergraduate G.P.A. has extremely poor validity in the prediction of postbaccalaureate income, job prestige, or success in professional school. Furthermore, when researchers (Wylie 1979) ask students to write down their own G.P.A.s, they find a slight bias to round up the G.P.A.s in the student's favor; this is, strictly speaking, a problem of validity, because the errors are not random.

Validity of Measurements

Validity is defined as the *degree to which the researcher has measured* what he or she set out to measure. Alternatively, we can think of validity and invalidity as the truth or falsity of the researcher's hypotheses. Consider the infamous exchange (Carroll 1960:268–269) between Alice and Humpty Dumpty which cuts to the meat of validity of our operationalizations by questioning the calling of things by their right, or valid, names:

> "There's glory for you!"
> "I don't know what you means by 'glory,'" Alice said.
> "Humpty Dumpty smiled contemptuously. "Of course you don't—till I tell you. I meant, 'there's a nice knock-down argument.'"
> "But 'glory' doesn't mean a 'nice knock-down argument,'" Alice objected.
> "When I use a word," Humpty Dumpty said, in rather a scornful tone, "it means just what I choose it to mean—neither more nor less."
> "The question is," said Alice, "whether you can make words mean so many different things."

Reputable scientists are not willing to accept the naive positions that words can mean so many different things: *Validity of measurements can be defined simply as calling things by their right names.* In the rest of this chapter section we consider assessment of the validity of measurements which concerns the question: *How do researchers create more valid operationalizations?* In the next section we shall consider the *validity of findings which goes a step beyond those operationalizations to consider how the actual findings are affected by rival, alternative explanations.* The researcher has an obligation to assess research findings in terms of both types of validity problems because validity criteria are too often conventional and arbitrary.

Although operationalization of measures is a fundamental first step in research, an easy trap awaits the researcher who is not skeptical of the validity of his or her operationalizations. Hubert Blalock (1968:11) most eloquently summarizes the dangers of such naive operationalism when he states:

> Let us admit, with the critics of operationalism, that perhaps it is unwise at this point—when research techniques are quite crude—to become overly rigid by tying down a theoretically defined concept to a particular operation. If we associate the term "prejudice" with a specific paper-and-pencil attitude test, then we run the risk either of adding new concepts to our already vastly overly complicated theoretical language or of losing the flexibility required of a science in its infancy.

Multiple operationalizations (see Chapter 14 on triangulation for more details) is one important corrective for naive single methodological operations. Briefly, just as combining a number of different indices into a single index aids reliability, the use of multiple operations most likely reduces the influence of invalid "noise" inherent in different operations. Also, there are several strategies of investigating and improving the *validity of measurement* that conscientious researchers employ: content validity, criterion-related validity, and construct validity.

Content Validity of Measurement

This type—sometimes referred to as "face validity"—refers to the degree to which a measurement represents a particular concept. That is, the researcher asks the question: Is my measure appropriate to the content area claimed for the measure? For example, if you were interested in operationalizing the American public's knowledge of the meanings of particular words, on the face of it, it would not seem appropriate to ask them how to spell those words. Just because a person can spell a word does not mean that person knows what the word means. By contrast, if you were interested in assessing attitudes toward minorities, a battery of questions concerning equal employment, integrated housing, affirmative action, school busing, intermarriage, and social-welfare programs might represent a valid sampling of minority-group attitude content.

Content validity is the most primitive form of testing for validity, because it normally arises from a simple social consensus on what defines a particular content area. But there are many areas of research where even the experts disagree or lack concrete definitions or operationalizations. For example, studies of equity and inequity indicate a lack of consensus among the public. Some people define equity as equality and would divide rewards equally; some others would divide wealth according to each person's needs; still others perceive granting rewards according to abilities; and yet another group of persons would use the principle of reward proportional to effort expended.

The problem with content validity is finding means of insuring representativeness of each shade of meaning. The following procedures promote this process. First, the researcher lays out the most important and obvious meanings so as to *exhaust* all meanings of the concept. Second, the researcher then further subdivides those dimensions if they do not appear to represent a single dimension. For example, powerlessness may be subdivided into political, economic, and familial powerlessness. The general rule is that the more refined the subareas, the easier operationalization becomes. Third, each stratum or substratum should have *no fewer* than seven to ten items to capture various shades of meaning; this also adds to higher reliability as you have seen from Figure 4-1. Fourth, quite often items the researcher selects do not behave as anticipated (for example, scale items which have negative correlations with each other) and have to be rejected, leaving a smaller (and, therefore, less reliable) scale. If the researcher discovers items that appear to tap more than one dimension or items that appear not to tap the wanted dimension, he or she ought to eliminate them.

Criterion-Related Validity of Measurement

Researchers measure this type of validity by correlating the operation with some direct measure of the operation's characteristics. There are two types of criterion-related validity: concurrent and predictive. *Predictive validity* associates the operationalization with *some variable* of theoretical interest; the higher the association, the better the prediction. Predictive validity has a long history in sociology. Dodd (1947) proposed criteria that are as appropriate today as a half-century ago, when he stated that survey organizations (p. 111)

> should make studies of their survey results, correlating them against criteria (such as elections, censuses, government statistics, larger samples, friends' samples, and other independent measures of behavior or conditions which check on assertions, etc.) whenever possible and publish the correlations. Accurate predicting is the final test of validity.

Accordingly, we would predict that individuals who state a belief in equity according to a rule of effort expended, would feel injustice if they were rewarded according to some other rule.

Paradoxically, sometimes researchers find little relationship between predictive and content validity. A survey question such as "Do you intend to keep smoking or do you intend to quit smoking?" may seem to have high content validity for smoking behavior yet be a very poor predictor of actual smoking or quitting. Social psychologists interested in predicting behavior from attitudes or behavior intentions often uncover such enigmatic findings. Alexander and Rudd (1984) noted that the widely used Machiavellian attitude scales actually do not do as well as one would expect at predicting willingness and facility at interpersonal manipulation in spite of the fact that they do have high content validity in testing for cynical acceptance of the idea that the "ends justify the means." Similarly, although asking couples to estimate the number of children they expect to have has intuitive appeal as a measure of completed fertility, it consistently produces predictions substantially below actual completed fertility (Hendershot & Placek 1981). Ideally, researchers prefer measures with both predictive and content validity.

The second criterion-related validity variation is termed *concurrent validity*. Here, the researcher locates *known groups* or *judges*—as opposed to *variables* in predictive validity—who experts agree are defined as high or low on the variable in question. Let us suppose we had an attitude scale designed to measure religious conservatism. We could assume that if it really measures religious conservatism, Jehovah's Witnesses should score high on the measure, while Unitarians should score relatively low. As another example, consider demonstrating the concurrent validity of a measure of bureaucratization where expert judges concurred that the Roman Catholic Church was more bureaucratized than the Southern Baptist Church. In this case, the data should agree with those judgments.

Construct Validity of Measurement

Researchers evaluate construct validity through determining the degree to which certain explanatory concepts (known as constructs) account for performance on the measurement. In other words, researchers do studies of construct validity to confirm the conceptual relationships underlying some theory. Each of the other two types of validation procedures may be based on a simple single judgment or theoretical association, but construct validation is always based on multiple measures or theoretical predictions. However, although the instrument may either confirm or deny the hypotheses predicted from a theory based on constructs, negative evidence can result either from a lack of construct validity or an incorrect theory.

The classic paper outlining the logic of construct validity (Campbell & Fiske 1959) argues that a measurement of some construct should not correlate too highly with measures of different constructs. If there really are five dimensions to alienation, each should *not* be associated too highly with the others. On the other hand, *different* measures of the *same* construct should be associated fairly highly. For example, if we had two different measurements of religious conservativism, they should correlate relatively highly. But each of those scales should not correlate with average rainfall. Campbell and Fiske named these procedures discriminant and convergent validation. *Convergent validation* refers to the idea that when measurements correlate highly with each other, they may be measuring the *same* rather than different constructs. By contrast, with *discriminant validation* we reason that if the measurements correlate lowly or negatively, they may be measuring a *different* rather than the same construct.

Dawes and Smith (1985:542) reanalyzed research in which four clinical psychologists independently ranked patients on four traits (social adjustment, ego strength, intelligence, and dependency), using four operationalizations (MMPI, Rorschach, Wechsler, and vocational history). The average correlation between different judges ranking patients on different traits was so low (0.08) that they judged a lack of convergent validation; that is, the low correlations signify that each operationalization measures different constructs. In a sense, Campbell and Fiske proposed a compelling method for systematically comparing correlation coefficients. Although other researchers (Dawes & Smith 1985) have explained improved methods of showing convergent and discriminant validation, the logic of these more complex methods traces back to the simplicity of logic of the Campbell and Fiske technique.

The various methods of validation are not mutually exclusive. The reputable researcher attempts to use as many of them as possible, because each provides some unique information. Generally speaking, the more of these strategies the researcher uses, the more valid his or her operationalizations.

Box 4-3   *Measuring Association between Two Variables*

If you have access to an Apple II-DOS or MS-DOS personal computer and CLEAR 3, this is a good time to put this text down and play with the CLEAR 3 assignment which teaches the logic of measuring and interpreting association between two variables. If you don't have such access, this box insert will give you a shorter introduction to computation and interpretation of an easy measure of association known as Spearman's rho. In either case, the concepts of association and correlation between variables is fundamental to understanding theory building and testing, reliability, and validity.

Any measure of association or correlation exists to measure objectively the relationship between two variables with one number. Usually, *correlation* refers to relationships that do depend on cardinal data, and *association* refers to the relationship between two variables that depend on nominal or ordinal data. Spearman's rho is a measure of association that uses ordinally ranked data. The researcher compares the two data sets for rank, subtracts the differences in rankings, squares the differences in rankings, and sums those squared differences. For example, consider the following two individuals's rankings of the quality of five wines:

Wine	Person A's Ranking	Person B's Ranking	Rank Diff	Squared Diff
A	1	3	-2	4
B	2	2	0	0
C	3	1	2	4
D	4	5	-1	1
E	5	4	1	1
			SUM =	10

The formula for Spearman's rho is:

$$p = \frac{6*(\text{Sum of Squared Differences})}{N*(N*N-1)}$$

where N equals the number of cases—five in this case. Therefore, rho is equal to (6*10) divided by 5 (5*4) or 0.60. If the rankings are perfectly matched, rho will equal $+1.0$; if they are perfectly opposite of each other, it will equal -1.0; and a 0 indicates no rank pattern. In this case, the 0.60 suggests a moderately similar pattern of ranking between the two individuals.

A measure of association or correlation is not the same as a percentage. In the example shown, only 1 of the 5 rankings, or 20%, are the same. This is quite different from the rho of 0.60, which measures a moderate agreement in the two individuals' rankings in this case. The interpretation of correlations is similar but depends on a different formula to arrive at a single, interpretable number.

Validity of Findings

Although a researcher may use a valid operationalization, the process of validity nevertheless obligates him or her to consider another problem: the problem of validity of study findings. That is, even if one uses valid operationalizations of particular variables, there are a number of ways in which the researcher may interpret the relationship between those variables. Science operates very much like an infinitely long baseball season in which each hypothesis, or finding, is in competition with every other hypothesis or finding. As in baseball, the only way for finding the strongest hypothesis is to pit it against every other possible hypothesis in a series of contests. Through these contests, science has a number of rules for deciding which hypothesis is the strongest or whether one hypothesis is a "rain out" and must be replayed.

Validity of findings concerns methods for ruling out plausible, rival interpretations of findings. Cook and Campbell (1979) list and discuss the following major known problems in the validity of findings:

A. Internal Validity
    1. History
    2. Maturation
    3. Testing
    4. Instrumentation
    5. Selection
    6. Mortality
    7. Interaction Effects
B. Statistical Conclusion Validity
    8. Statistical Regression
    9. Low Statistical Power
    10. Violated Assumptions of Statistical Tests
    11. Fishing Error Rate Problems
C. External Validity
    12. Reactive Effects of Testing
    13. Differential Selection-Independent Variable Interaction
    14. Reactive Effects of Data Collection Arrangements
    15. Multiple Independent Variable Interference
    16. Irrelevant Responsiveness of Measures
    17. Irrelevant Replicability of Independent Variables

These sources of invalidity may cause problems of interpretation in particular research settings. They offer plausible, rival interpretations to the researcher's findings if they are left unaccounted for in the study design. Jumping to conclusions makes it easy to overlook evidence that does not fit a preconceived theory. To exclude rival hypotheses, scientists use a logical process of elimination. Researchers find it necessary to search for clues that might narrow the field of potentially rival hypotheses or interpretations. Remember that poor validity is caused by *biased* or *nonrandom* errors; if the researcher leaves these factors unaccounted for in the study design, potentially nonrandom sources of error may confuse the usefulness of study findings, just as not pitting two baseball teams against each other leaves open the question of which is the better team.

Internal Validity

Internal validity concerns the question: Did the research methods used make a difference in the specific results; that is, would a different method have produced different results? If the researcher can reasonably answer "yes" to this question, then the findings may be invalid. In other words, internal validity refers to the confidence with which we can draw *cause-and-effect conclusions from the research results* (Aronson, Brewer, & Carlsmith 1985:477). There are at least seven major causes of internal validity problems.

1. History

Typically, scientists assert causal relationships in which they state how one (or more) independent variable affects one (or more) dependent variable. Over the time span of data collection, many events—in addition to the study's independent student variable—can change. The history factor refers to the possibility that any one of these events—rather than the originally hypothetized independent variable—might have caused observed changes in the dependent variable. For example, Briggs (1987) articulated three major contributions to the rapid growth of the U. S. labor force from 1975 through 1985: unprecedented numbers of women who have entered the labor market, the maturing of the post-World War II "baby boom" population cohort, and the acceleration in the number of immigrants coming to the United States. However, though Briggs' case is a good one, the many other variables that have changed over the same period cannot be ruled out in his study. Briggs's study failed to account for important changes in demand for particular types of jobs; for example, the increasing trend toward a service-based economy, occupations oriented toward the creation and use of information, and high technology. Furthermore, as in other countries, international markets increasingly influence employment patterns in the United States.

The reason Briggs' study cannot rule out alternative explanations for the growth of employment has to do with the nonexperimental type of study he employed. The effects of history can only be ruled out when the research design permits the logical elimination of all stimuli extraneous to the study variables. *Only the true experimental designs explained in Chapter 6 allow for such logical rejection.* Another way of describing history effects is to view history as effecting as all those possible independent variables (causes) *other than* the one(s) for which one wishes to study the effects on some dependent variable(s). The most logical way of excluding such extraneous variables is to set up the study in such a way that the researcher (1) randomly divides some group into two subgroups so that they are almost exactly alike in every respect at the start of the study, and then (2) the researcher randomly introduces an independent (treatment) variable to one group (the experimental or treatment group) but not the other.

The logic behind this two-stage experimental procedure is crucial in understanding history effects. Because both subgroups were randomly created, they started out equivalent in all respects—including the likelihood that they had, on average, encountered the *same historical experiences.* That is, any differences between the two groups can logically *not* have been due to the study participants' having experienced different histories. In fact, adolescent and adult black male unemployment rates were so exceptional that Briggs was forced to concede that a whole subclass of people exist outside the normal labor market who have not participated in its unprecedented growth. This particular group has had an entirely different historical experience outside the traditional labor market that Briggs' analysis must leave unexplained.

Of course, most social research cannot control for such alternative events, explanations, and analyses. For example, in Briggs' study labor force changes involve an indeterminately large number of macro-forces that encompass mass populations. Controlling for all potential alternative hypotheses in such naturalistic studies is necessarily an impossible task. (It is not completely impossible: In Chapter 17, I shall introduce analytic techniques upon which researchers capitalize, to logically demonstrate the illogic of some alternative explanations.)

2. Maturation

Whereas history effects are particular macro-events that are external to the study sample or population, maturation effects include relatively micro-changes in the internal conditions of the sample or population that are independent of the study's independent and dependent variables. Studies that involve lengthy spans of data collection (child development, historical fluctuations in national unemployment rates) are particularly susceptible to such maturation effects as growing older, more tired, or less interested. At the macro-level, even national populations grow old: the age structure of the industrialized countries is fast becoming top heavy with dependents over age 65. Such profound maturational changes must have momentous influences on the structure of national labor markets, social security systems, etc.

Maturation can present problems even in one-shot surveys. For example, a woman answering questions on "what is most important" to her might well respond "food," if she were hungry. Interviews conducted with a study population just before lunch or dinner could present significant biases toward thoughts of food. Notice that unlike history, maturation effects are *not* a function of specific historical events.

As with the ruling out of history effects, usually the only way we can rule out maturation effects is by random assignment of members of the population into true experimental conditions. For example, if we randomly assigned 100 seventh-graders to two groups, one group of which will receive special phonetic reading training while the other will receive only normal reading assignments, maturational effects cannot logically explain any improvements in scores—for example, just as many girls and boys at various stages of puberty ought to have been randomized into each of the two groups. Similarly, if we randomly assigned individuals to groups in order to study the effects of various types of training on leadership emergence, each group—regardless of treatment—would begin with just as many individuals who are likely to be bored or satisfied with the group assignment.

3. Testing

We speak of testing effects when we ask the question: Does the prior measurement used affect the study participants? Any time participants suspect or know they are being observed, experimented with, or tested, there is the chance the measurement process will modify their behavior. One of the primary criticisms leveled against the classic Masters and Johnson sex research has been precisely that the participants' knowledge of experimentation might have modified or eliminated their normal sexual behaviors during the study. Similarly, A. C. Nielsen ratings of television audiences have known testing effects: Some people, swayed by a "halo effect," will claim they had watched a highbrow series like "National Geographic Special," when they actually watched lowbrow professional wrestling.

However, other factors may yield testing effects other than awareness of testing: Any measurement not a part of the participants' normal environment may be considered a testing effect. Therefore, tests, experiments, and observations are *not* reactive per se. If a researcher wished to observe the effects of teaching style on student test scores with a multiple-choice test measuring student score changes, she could administer such test without fear of uncharacteristic effects of testing—assuming such kinds of testing are a normal part of that school's environment.

4. Instrumentation

When the researcher may attribute changes in the dependent variable to spurious changes in the measurement or testing process, we speak of instrumentation effects. Interviewers or observers who become increasingly sloppy, fatigued, or more competent and experienced may artificially alter study results. The U. S. Bureau of the Census finds that new interviewers consistently count slightly more respondents as unemployed than do more experienced interviewers. Because one respondent represents approximately 25,000 persons in their surveys, high interviewer turnover could lead to grossly inflated unemployment figures. Similarly, during 1987, the A. C. Nielsen Co. changed its rating system for television audience listening from a handwritten diary-based method to a hand-held device that records what viewers watch and who is watching. The new method led to serious discrepancies in measurement: The new method indicates huge drops in children's Saturday morning cartoon viewing (Kneale & Barnes 1987)—as much as 62% less. Rather than a "declining audience," the change in measurement may have caused pseudochanges in audience ratings. Unfortunately, because A. C. Nielsen Co. did not do a comparative study of both methods before instituting the new method, we will never know the true answer.

We regard instrumentation changes as a special case of maturation problems; the maturation of the researcher or research instrument causes them, rather than the maturation of the study participant. In the just-mentioned A. C. Nielsen Co. ratings study, rather than the change in audience ratings being due to instrumentation change per se, the drop in ratings may be due to children being lazy button pushers—a true maturational effect. The problem is that because we have no means of comparing results of the new and old methods, no accurate judgment can be ascertained.

Some types of research produce greater likelihood of instrumentation effects than others: Field researchers undergo known changes in roles that may grossly affect their ability to collect data. By contrast, highly structured interviews administered by well-trained personnel are much less open to such changes in instrumentation as in tone of voice, research roles, or change of question wording. Researchers often utilize equipment (electronic eyes, cameras, camcorders) that fail or fatigue, producing "instrument decay." The fatiguing of a battery-operated lap-top computer used to time the length of some observed behavior would exemplify this problem.

5. Selection

A biased, or nonrandom, selection of participants or units of analysis may also contribute to bogus interpretations of findings. Interviewers (when given the choice) are more likely to select houses on corner lots (which are usually more expensive) and, therefore, oversample wealthier households. Similarly, if the researcher allows individuals to self-select themselves into or out of a particular study, highly skewed results normally result. For example, concerned social scientists have objected to Hite's (1987) allowing women to self-select themselves into her study of the "war between the sexes." Less than 4% of the questionnaires Hite distributed were returned to her. Based on those questionnaires, she has outrageously contended that she has fairly represented all American women's opinions and behaviors—in spite of the fact that her results indicate 75% of married women have at some time carried on affairs outside of marriage, an amount three times larger than more carefully constructed samples have ever indicated. Similarly, two epidemiologists (Eron 1988:7), after a five-year study of 2,300 women between the ages of 45 and 60, found that only 3% of them expressed regret during or after menopause about their physical changes, including normal hot flashes, cold sweats, and menstrual irregularities; and that the majority of the women expressed relief from the concerns of pregnancy, contraception, and menstruation. These findings directly contradict the samples of women seen by physicians. Physicians assume they see most women, when actually they see less than one-fourth of women undergoing menopause.

Randomization is the key to overcoming unrepresentative selection of sub-jects. Particularly when the researcher wishes to compare groups, it is impor-tant to insure that participants are randomly assigned to groups rather than haphazardly selected, differentially recruited, or self-selected. Otherwise, dif-ferences between groups on the dependent variable may be due to unrepresen-tative selection procedures rather than the independent variable. Imagine if the A. C. Nielsen Co. ratings were based on completely self-selected groups of couch potatoes: Television watching ratings would be based on motivations to participate or to push certain types of television programming, or unknown individual habits and traits which would easily confound study results.

6. Mortality

Any time *nonrandom* subsets of units of analysis or participants drop out of the study, these "mortality" rates rather than actual effects of the independent variable may account for differences in the dependent variables. In interview-ing persons drawn randomly in their studies of monthly unemployment, the U. S. Bureau of the Census recognizes that unmarried black males between the ages of 18 and 25 make up a significantly transient and unemployment-prone group. Therefore, the loss of high numbers of these participants in the final study means that the actual unemployment figure is significantly higher than lack of this knowledge would indicate.

Initial equivalence between groups is not enough; the researcher must maintain equivalence throughout the study. Often, a researcher may start with initially equivalent groups only to discover that participants later self-select themselves out of the study. Imagine a true experiment dealing with AIDS drug testing. Suppose the participants in the experiment volunteered on the basis of the possibility that they might benefit from experimental drugs. After they had been randomly assigned to research groups (placebo versus actual experimen-tal drug), let us assume that somehow the placebos learned they will not receive the experimental drug, and therefore, many of them find excuses for discontinuing their participation. This turn of events would mean the two groups had not been exposed to the same selection procedures and invalidate the procedures. Winklestein, Samuel, Padian, Wiley, Lang, Anderson and Levy (1987:687) believe some such scenario may have influenced their own study of the reduction of HIV transmission in San Francisco.

By the same token, the experimenter should not remove participants from any experimental treatment *after* they have been assigned to a particular condition. Researchers may permissibly weed out participants from the initial pool only *prior* to random experimental assignment. Weeding out after random treatment assignment presents potential hazards of creating nonequivalent comparison groups.

Differential mortality rates may take other, more subtle, forms. It is not uncommon for trained observers to begin coding various aspects of ongoing interaction, only to lose data because the participants leave the field of obser-vation during the coding or because the participants turn away from the ob-server so that the observer can no longer observe particular measures (facial

expressions). Likewise, interviewers often encounter situations where they obtain the interview but lose particular information in patterned, nonrandom ways (income information losses may be greater at higher SES levels).

7. Internal validity interaction effects

Some types of particularly insidious internal validity problems are those in which history, maturation, etc. work in combination to produce spurious results. In the aforementioned A. C. Nielsen Co. change of method for measuring television audience viewing, the drop in ratings may have been due to either maturation or instrumentation effects. However, the more likely cause is some strange composite of the two threats to validity. I believe this because different types of instrumentation are likely to have different individual response sets; the handwritten diary technique which viewers only updated every three weeks is particularly prone to maturational problems of forgetting while the hand-held meter approach is vulnerable to lazy button pushing. In another example, consider a scenario in which, unbeknownst to the researcher, one out of two groups of student volunteers has had more past history in taking aptitude tests. This history-differential selection *combination* might make the comparison of each group's answers to attitude scales or aptitude tests less genuine.

The social sciences are replete with studies based on nonrandom samples of units that have these types of interaction problems. Most of the effects of different mental institutions, psychiatric methods, prisoner rehabilitation, etc., are explainable in terms of a combination of prestigious institutions selecting out inmates, patients, or whatever, that have a better chance—a maturation effect—of success. The results of such selection-maturation procedures will lead to artificially inflated success rates of more prestigeful institutions or methods and spuriously deflated success rates of less prestigeful ones. In this vein, Cook and Campbell (1979) point out that causal comparison rates of job training corps members with those who do not receive such training are biased against showing an advantage to the training because those selected are chosen on the grounds of excellent prospects of success.

Statistical Conclusion Validity

This problem refers to the possibility of the researcher drawing false conclusions when asking the question: Are the presumed independent and dependent variables associated or correlated? Statistical conclusion validity faces the researcher with three problems: (1) Whether the study is statistically sensitive enough to make a reasonable statement about the relationship between variables; (2) If the study is sensitive enough, whether the evidence supports covariation between the presumed cause and effect; and (3) If that evidence does exist, how to measure the *strength* of covariation between the variables.

Fluctuations in measures, sampling units, or repeated or equivalent measures give results that differ from those which would have occurred without such fluctuations. Researchers typically use statistical tests of significance to assess the chance that they can accept, or reject, their data as fluctuating from its true value. There are two possible errors in such tests:

Type I or "false-negative" error: Rejecting a decision that is actually true.
Type II or "false-positive" error: Accepting a decision that is actually false.

The accompanying figure demonstrates the dilemma. Normally, a researcher working with a sample estimates the probability that the null hypothesis (the inverse of the hypothesis in question) is true or false, using the area under the normal curve. Suppose the researcher's estimate suggests that the null hypothesis is likely to be true in less than 5 out of 100 samples—as depicted with the estimate "a" shown below, under the darkened area of less than 5% chance. However, because the researcher is working with a sample, the percentage in the actual population may be different. Suppose the actual chance falls somewhere in the white area—outside of the 5% chance level. In such a case, the researcher has been mislead to accept as true the actual hypothesis (because the null hypothesis has been rejected), when in fact the actual hypothesis should have been rejected. This is a false positive error. By contrast, if the significance level indicated for the null hypothesis was located at "b," while the actual significance level for the population was "a", the researcher would misleadingly have committed a false negative error.

These two types of errors are found throughout science. The congressional Office of Technology Assessment reported in 1987 that among persons at low-risk, nine out of ten people who test positive for AIDS would not really be infected with the virus—that is an alarmingly high false-positive rate. The public naively trusts medical lab tests as infallible, though many known sources of error exist: Doctors who take sloppy cultures, patients who have eaten foods or taken drugs that cancel out whatever is being disease-tested, sloppy lab work, machines that lose their calibration, chemicals that lose their potency, human specimens that inadvertently get switched, and misread test results.

Similarly, psychiatrists have a poor record of predicting violent behaviors. They are only correct about 25% of the time, and the majority of their errors are false positives, which are due to their fear of turning loose someone who might go on to assault or kill. However, by using a scale of four risk factors (conviction for violent crime, history of violent crime, measurable neu-

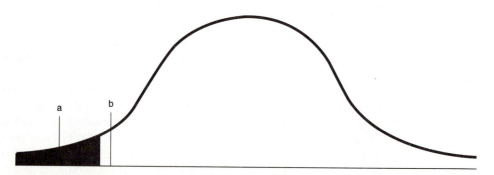

Figure 4-2. The dilemma of commiting false-positive and false-negative errors.

rologic abnormality, and family environment that included a broken home, child abuse, or a parent's substance abuse), researchers have been able to improve this to 70% correct predictions with 24 percent false positives and 6% false negative cases (Greenberg 1987). If you have access to a PC that can use the CLEAR 10 assignment, this would be a good place to pause and review the issue of false-positive and false-negative cases in prisoner-release studies.

Finally, the use of the polygraph as a means of catching liars has become a huge industry, in spite of much data questioning the number of false positives that it produces. Government and industry perform over a half-million lie detector tests each year on workers in America yet Ekman's (1985) careful review of liar detector studies indicates that close to 10% of those tests are false positives—individuals who are judged liars but actually told the truth. Public insensitivity to all of these types of statistically invalid conclusions leads to a serious problem with persons who are incarcerated due to misdiagnosis, or lose jobs, family support, etc. because of false accusations based on misunderstanding of important statistical logic.

Researchers must continually ask whether there are properly balanced risks of *both* Type I (false negative) and Type II (false positive) errors, for, paradoxically, as one decreases, the danger of committing the other error increases. Reputable research does not include hypotheses based on intuition but rather based on formal, objective, communicable, and reproducible statistical procedures. The plausibility of the risk can be assessed with standard statistical procedures. Whenever researchers adopt a particular level of significance (.05 or 5 out of 100 chances) in any test of statistical significance, in effect they accept a certain risk for *both* Type I and Type II errors. In the .05 case, they set a relatively low risk of rejecting a true hypothesis and a relatively high risk of accepting a false hypothesis.

It is always necessary to consider carefully how serious the consequences of each type of error are for a particular circumstance. In a study of social work practice effectiveness, assume the traditional practice proved to be 50% effective, and researchers wish to assess a new social work practice. Clearly, the new practice should be "significantly" better than 50% effective because the practical cost of switching over to the new practice would be high compared to retaining the existing old practice. But how much better should the new practice be to protect against an *erroneous* decision that the new practice is superior to the old? If the probability of the new practice working were 0.52, then its use would lead to the benefit of only two persons among each 50 who would not have benefited without it. By contrast, a probability of 0.65 for the practice's effectiveness, would lead to the benefit of 30% more people than the old practice.

On the surface, the 65% effective study might seem to warrant the adoption of the new practice. However, *no study ever proves a hypothesis—it merely adds plausibility to it.* Therefore, if you recommend adoption of the new method, you may actually be recommending a practice as more effective when it actually is not (Type I error). On the other hand, you do not want to reject as ineffective a practice that is more effective than the old practice. Therefore, you must consider which error is more important. Assuming you consider both errors to be equally serious, you could set the rejection probability for the practice near that point where it makes no difference whether the new practice is adopted or not (0.50 in this example). In sum, statistical conclusion validity, unlike the other internal validity problems, is *always* present—if you get rid of Type I (II) errors, you have then to deal with Type II (I) errors.

Too many people expect single studies to settle all issues once and for all. Replication, however, is generic and indispensable to all science; in fact, it is more important to the social sciences where we lack the experimental rigor found in the physical sciences. Therefore, *replications are an important component in challenging the potential statistical conclusion validity of study results.* Replications as well as tests of significance help answer the question: What *chance* is there that the difference was found by chance? There are four important sources of statistical conclusion validity: statistical regression, low statistical power, violated assumptions of statistical tests, and fishing error rate problems.

8. Statistical regression

Statistical regression refers to a fact well-known among statisticians that quantitative measurements taken at two points in time are subject to misinterpretation if participants were either initially selected or are compared on the basis of *extremity* of their scores (extremely overweight, extremely short, upper 10% of all IQ scores, low in authoritarianism, or social areas with high crime rates).

Francis Galton (1885) coined the term statistical regression in a study of the relationship between parents and their offspring's heights. He noted that children of tall parents were typically shorter than their parents and short parents' children were taller on average than their parents. Therefore, he suggested that if one did not know about the regression fallacy, it would be easy to mistakenly conclude that succeeding generations produce children who are closer to the average population height. This is a false conclusion because it is an artifact of the selection of extreme cases. That is, an examination of cases closer to the mean would show that parents of average height are likely to have children whose heights are further away from the mean.

Similarly, unsophisticated analysts often conclude, after looking at data on IQ of the offspring of bright parents, that we are producing a generation with mediocre IQs. However, if these analysts were to work in reverse and reflect on the IQs of the *parents* of very bright offspring, they would note the extremely bright children, who, on the average, had parents with IQs closer to the mean!

What produces these pseudoeffects? Regression effects are caused by effects of either scale reliability, or natural regression effects, or both in combination. *Natural regression effects* is a phrase statisticians use to denote regression stemming from some equilibrating factor(s) found in nature. Researchers regard this type of regression effect as an actual, true, or substantive change. Natural regression effects are probably due in part to the effects of "ceilings" and "floors" to measurement variation. Extremely heavy people usually weigh less at a second weighing while extremely light people weigh more at a second weighing than they did at the first weighing because any species has natural limits to its survival. Extremely heavy or light body weights are not healthy and, if continued, will produce death or disease; bodies have natural feedback mechanisms that, when they function properly, work toward restoring an optimum level of equilibrium.

Regression may also be an artifact of poor reliability: The more unreliable the measure—the more pseudoeffects or pseudochange—the more regression will confound results. This is not a problem with weight because we have good reason to assume a weight scale gives essentially true scores. However, when social scientists work with social or behavioral scales where measurement error is likely to be present, we expect regression as a matter of consequence; the more the measurement error, the greater the regression effects: some persons' scores artificially approach the mean on second readings due to poor reliability.

Poor reliability can be seen as due to unbiased error, while poor validity can be seen as due to biased error. When the error is biased—in this case, regression toward the mean—the problem is a validity problem. Chance fluctuation is unbiased error—that is, chance errors cancel each other out because they are due strictly to random factors—and, therefore, is a reliability problem.

Sometimes regression effects do not equalize out because of a combination of natural causes and reliability effects. The measurements in Figure 4–3 represent a typical pretest-posttest IQ score pattern: Extreme scores change more than do less extreme scores. We believe there are two reasons for this clearly biased pattern. First, natural ceiling and floor effects prevent IQ from going beyond some natural (or even arbitrary) boundary point. For example, an IQ of 40 has the *theoretical* possibility of falling only 40 points or rising over 160 points upon retest. The more extreme the score the more built-in bias against a score changing equally in either direction. But, second, more extreme scores also probably contain more measurement error. Campbell and Stanley (1963:11) express this phenomenon through the statement that

> in a sense, the typical extremely high scorer has had unusually good "luck" (large positive error) and the extremely low scorer bad luck (large negative error). Luck is capricious, however, so on a posttest we expect the high scorers to decline somewhat on the average, the low scorers to improve their relative position. (The same logic holds if one begins with the posttest scores and works back to the pretest.)

Research by the Triple Nine Society and the International Society for Philosophical Inquiry have suggested that the popular standard IQ tests do not accurately measure IQ above the "gifted" threshold of 130. Their results indicate that mere speed of thought alone only allows test takers to race through the trivia but does not guarantee results when the questions are deep and difficult. They have developed more "mind-crushing" tests for the gifted that few people dare to try (Primoff 1987). It may be that more extreme scores of any type need

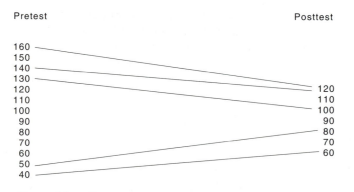

Figure 4-3. Regression scatter of posttest scores from pretest scores and vice versa.

special instrumentation: After all, you wouldn't use a normal human weight scale to measure an elephant's!

However, because regression toward the mean is so common, regression *away* from the mean takes on theoretical importance. For instance, ghetto children bused to superior schools might show regression away from the mean as a result of two forces. First, the more challenging environment might stimulate children with above-average IQ; second, the same environment might prove too challenging for those with below-normal IQs who might give up trying to keep up with the faster-paced learning.

It is difficult to control for the effects of regression. Usually, the researcher controls by multiplying the time one measurement by that measure's test-retest reliability coefficient. However, when extreme scores are less reliable than scores closer to the mean, this procedure will produce corrections that are too conservative for more extreme scores. If the researcher is fortunate to have a meaningful control group available for comparison, he or she may subtract its regression effects from the experimental group's score changes. Then the researcher may logically attribute any score changes remaining to natural regression change. However, this procedure is restricted to true experimental designs (see Chapter 6), where participants are *randomly* assigned to experimental and control groups.

There are many research settings where researchers are unable to randomize by reason of factors beyond their influence—for example, administrators may limit the study to use of particular work groups, classes, or individuals. In such cases researchers need to take special precautions in comparing change scores. Statisticians never recommend *matching procedures*—after-the-fact creation of pseudo-control groups through some such criteria as similar scores on one or more variables (age, sex, race, aggression index). Matching procedures potentially confound the design with *differential* regression effects: The more imperfectly matched the groups, the greater the differential regression. Regression artifacts are one of the most recurrent forms of research self-deception for *any* data collected over time that have variability. If you move along the time dimension of any time series graph and pick the "highest (or lowest) point so far," you will note that the next point will, on the average, be lower (or higher)—that is, *nearer* the general trend.

9. Low statistical power

Some statistical tests are more sensitive than others to detection of significant differences. Other major sources of this problem, besides insensitive and inappropriate statistical tests are sample size and the level of statistical significance accepted. Small sample size and particularly low levels of statistical significance tend to increase type II errors. Some researchers wish to perform statistical tests on extremely small samples that would very unlikely reach statistical significance. One researcher wanted to test experimental contact lens products on ten patients—but that would most likely be far too few to show statistical significance.

On the other hand, samples that are extremely large will lead to statistical significance overkill. If you are testing for significant differences in samples of tens of thousands you will come up with trivial differences as "significant." Cohen (1977) and Kraemer and Thiemann (1987) give valuable information on the extent to which particular tests and sample sizes differ in power, which is sometimes called *robustness*.

The issue of planning an analysis that gives alternative hypotheses a reasonable chance of being supported is a highly important but often overlooked issue that depends on three factors: (1) the critical effect size (in standardized form) that would convince scientists that a relationship exists; (2) the power of the test the scientist uses; and (3) the size of the sample. Factors one and three are relatively straightforward: The larger the effect size or size of the sample, the more likely a hypothesis will be supported. However, for these two factors the scientist still needs to know how large an effect size or sample size. Factor two is less obvious to persons without much statistical training. Nevertheless, an important concept to remember is that some statistical tests are more robust or powerful than others for supporting and rejecting hypotheses. For example, Spearman's rho is roughly 90% as effective as Pearson's r for measuring association. Advanced statistics becomes an important tools, therefore, in deciding which statistical test is most appropriate as well as robust.

10. Violated assumptions of statistical tests

Every statistical test is based on known statistical assumptions. Many tests require that groups being compared have similar variances. Robustness of any statistical test has to do with which of these assumptions can be violated without significant losses of sensitivity or power of the test. Cohen (1977) is one of the numerous standard statistical references available to the researcher who wishes to check how robust his or her tests are. Violating assumptions that lower the robustness of statistical tests is simply another form of statistical accounting's GIGO (garbage in, garbage out) rule. Statistical tests that are inappropriately used give garbage results that can mislead an unsophisticated public.

11. Fishing error rate problems

In a worst case scenario of a classic scientific "fishing" expedition one researcher reportedly tested 3,963 hypotheses in a single study. We could expect at the 0.05 level, 160 of those hypothesis to be judged statistically significant by chance alone. That is, we can expect 1 out of 20 hypotheses to be statistically significant at the 0.05 level without being theoretically significant. These types of considerations are important so that we do not falsely conclude that covariation exists when it actually does not exist (Type I error).

The best corrective to fishing error rate problems is to stop haphazardly "fishing." The analogy is appropriate. Some 90% of all fish are reportedly caught by 10% of persons who fish. Like the person fishing who haphazardly casts for fish, the naive researcher who dregs every nook and cranny of the data for statistical significance wastes time. Properly knit theory, like a good fishing net, will let the insignificant catches through but aid finding the real catches.

External Validity

External validity concerns a different sort of question still: How generalizable are the results? How representative of, or generalizable to, particular populations, settings, independent variables, and dependent variables is the study? It is possible to have high internal and statistical conclusion validity yet have low external validity. The internal rigor may be such that the researcher can rule out rival causal explanations while the study results are still low in breadth of generalizability.

12. Reactive effects of measurement

Most often, novices confuse reactive effects of measurement with testing effects. The difference between the two is important to understand. Testing effects pertain to problems of internal validity which involve cause-and-effect concerns; it refers to whether or not the measurement process has modified or otherwise affected the participant's behavior or attitudes. Reactive effects of measurement refers to problems of external validity, asking how broadly applicable the results of the study are; that is, it questions how the process of measurement may *change* that which the researcher is measuring. In other words, while testing effects refer to participant changes occurring *only* during the measurement process, reactivity refers to the possibility of *relatively permanent* changes caused by the measurement process that decrease its comparative utility.

One of the classic cases of such measurement-process induced change is the ongoing U. S. National Health Survey. Investigators have found that this survey increases the health of the sample population *compared* to the population of the United States because participants receive a free medical examination that gives them knowledge of health problems of which they were not previously aware. Such participants are likely to see a physician for correction of health problems uncovered by the free medical examination—an act they would have been much less likely to have performed had they not participated in the survey.

Testing effects are much more ephemeral than reactive effects. While it is true that an individual may *temporarily* change some behavior or attitude in an experimental situation that is out of the ordinary, reactive effects are much more permanent and serious. A police officer who knows she is being observed as part of a research project might only temporarily change her behavior during the course of observation, and then revert back to more normal behavior at the end of observation—an example of a testing effect. By contrast, a questionnaire that contains questions about problems relatively remote from the participant's previous experience or concerns (international nuclear proliferation pacts, inter-nation acid-rain negotiations, worldwide deforestation) that seems innocuous to the researcher but that activates some individuals to start researching the topic or to join an activist group they would not have otherwise joined, produces a reactive effect of measurement. Any later reinterviews of such individuals would indicate an increase in sophistication of answers or behavior that is not generalizable to the population at large.

13. Differential selection-independent variable interaction

This fact suggests that samples differentially selected from the group to which the researcher wishes to compare them may be unrepresentative of that group. This is particularly true with volunteer participants. The only way to overcome this problem is through random sampling. Winkelstein et al. (1987:687) skeptically questioned the generalizability of their own HIV (AIDS) transmission study results because (1) study subjects at high risk of testing positive may have participated in their study in disproportionately smaller rates than those of low risk and (2) members of the cohort who engaged in high-risk behavior might have become infected early in the epidemic leaving only low-risk persons available for infection during the study. These researchers wisely caution that either or both of these possibilities might interact with the independent variable (HIV transmission)—grossly distorting actual infection estimates (the dependent variable).

14. Reactive effects of data-collection arrangements

These types of reactive effects are *short-lived* in the sense that they apply to changes that are *in effect only during the data collection*. They are thus similar to what methodologists call testing effects, but they refer to a different question because they refer to the attempt to *generalize* from the participant population to some wider population. Knowledge of exposure to particular data-collection instruments may lead to change of study behavior in contrast to normal behavior. Many of these spurious effects are based on participants having geared their responses to match their *perceptions* of researcher expectations—even though the researcher may not state his or her intentions. For example, experimental participants in marijuana studies acted differently under conditions of knowing they smoked pot than not knowing, simply because they expected to act and feel particular ways when stoned or not stoned (Smith 1978). If they thought they were smoking pot but it was a placebo, they still "acted" stoned.

The only way to control for such effects is to use *double-blind* techniques in which neither the observer or the participant know who receives what treatment or placebo (or better yet make it triple-blind so that even the researcher doesn't know). Placebo comes from the Latin *placebo* meaning to please or be acceptable. In the eighteenth century, physicians adopted it as an euphemism meaning any medicine meant to please more than benefit the patient—the proverbial sugar pill. Researchers have broadened the meaning to include any innocuous treatment that can serve as a control, because participants believe they are receiving a real treatment when in fact they are not.

The importance of double-blind techniques is clearly demonstrated in an article on wine critics who sample 20 English wines and condemned them as "flat, dull, dead, foul, acidic, sulphuous, and nasty" (Fialka 1987: 10) A producer of the wines challenged the critics to a blind taste test: 10 English wines against 10 world-class wines. When a jury of English wine experts selected the dozen they like best, half turned out to be English.

15. Multiple independent variable interference

Whenever the independent variable is *repeatedly* and *continuously* introduced into the research setting, there is likelihood that observed effects will differ from settings with *single* introductions of the independent variable. The simplest experimental research situation is one in which some group receives a one-shot treatment. It would be hazardous to presume that the results of one-shot treatments could be extended to multiple-treatment situations. To understand the logic, consider the person who tries smoking cigarettes only once versus someone who is a pack-a-day smoker. We would expect the pack-a-day smoker to develop health problems (emphysema, lung cancer) that the once-in-a-lifetime smoker would not. Similarly, a one-ounce drink of scotch a day ought to have quite different effects on your liver than a bottle of scotch a day. Social experiments or programs in which participants receive multiple treatments (monthly unemployment checks, weekly psychiatric visits, etc.) ought likewise have quite different generalizations than single treatments (one-shot lump-sum payment, single psychiatric examination).

Multiple treatment interference may also refer to situations in which the participant receives *combinations* of an independent variable in a study group. A researcher interested in the effects of "drugs" might look at the combined effects of marijuana and alcohol. But it would be unwise to generalize from that setting to settings where marijuana and alcohol were used separately. After all, this use of multiple independent variable interference is a *check* for interaction effects. Just as two drugs that may separately benefit the patient may in combination kill him, the effects of multiple social independent variables may not be additive. On the one hand, sometimes multiple variables interact in complex ways. Drinking and driving is as likely a likely cause of automobile accidents and deaths as is driving late at night. However, statistics show that individuals who drink alcohol and then drive between the hours of two and four A.M., greatly multiply their chances of dying in automobile accidents.

On the other hand, sometimes multiple treatment effects are relatively additive. Kruttschnitt, Ward, and Sheble (1987) established that a "double-dose" of violence—being an abused youth who also witnessed spousal violence—increased the odds almost twofold of criminal offense, compared to those who had only experienced one of the the two for the 109 male youths in their sample. Whatever the case, as researchers have become more sophisticated, they have no longer taken the effects of multiple treatments for granted.

16. Irrelevant responsiveness of measures

All measures have immaterial components. This is the problem of generalizing from an imperfect measure to whatever the researcher is ostensibly measuring. The various imperfections in any measure may cause spurious generalizations. The objective is to reduce these irrelevancies to manageable levels. For example, data based on union records consistently indicate 3% to 5% more union members than survey-based data collected by the government (Farber 1987). That may not seem like much, but implies that survey-based data lose from 15% to 20% of the actual union membership, or that union rolls are inflated by a similar amount. In either case, that is a substantial portion of union membership, the loss of which might substantially change generalizations about the effects of union membership.

As a second example, Benbow and Stanley (1983) have piloted a long-term project on the "math gap" between the sexes that has produced controversial findings, in part, because of the way they have operationalized their variables. They concluded that parental attitudes do not account for sex differences in mathematics ability, based on *children's perceptions* of their parent's attitudes. A more direct test of actual parental attitudes might have lead to a quite different conclusion.

Benbow and Stanley have long maintained that the math gap is due to real genetic differences rather than social explanations, based on the fact that they continue to fail to produce family correlates of these differences, and because such differences show up most markedly at puberty. However, other components of children's social environment might well produce differences in valuation of mathematics: Some suggested alternative measures might be studies of how students spend their spare time (how much difference there is between boys and girls in such behavioral activities as reading popular magazines, listening to pop music [with lyrics that inculcate values]), how math teachers respond differentially to boy and girl students, and examination of normal conversations of each sex for content (things versus relationships, styles, cars, etc.). Cars, for example, have many quantifiable specifications; hair and clothing styles have very few.

17. Irrelevant replicability of independent variables

Just as *measures* are complex (multidimensional), constructs that are subject to irrelevant effects, *variables* of research interest, are typically multidimensional. Therefore, replications of variables may fail to include the dimension(s) actually responsible for the effects. Turning the question on its head, to what could the original study's independent variable(s) actually be generalized to include if it failed later replication attempts?

Kemper (1987) has done exemplary checks on cross-disciplinary replications of primary human emotions. His checks of work based in evolutionary, neural, psychoanalytic, facial expression, empirical classification, and developmental approaches all support that some emotions are replicable across humans regardless of how the variables are measured. His work further supports the existence of multiple emotional dimensions: Fear, anger, and sadness are primary emotions that turn up in each type of approach. However, secondary emotions appear only in some types of studies: Anticipation, astonishment, resignation, tension, and appetite are among them.

More importantly, his work illustrates why emotions are often not replicated by different types of studies. Beyond the primary emotions, he demonstrates that emotions are socially constructed through the attachment of social definitions, labels, and meanings to different conditions of interaction and social organization. For example, Kemper argues that guilt results from a felt sense of using excess power against another; and shame occurs only upon realization that one has acted in a manner that belies one's status. His research demonstrates the extent to which the effects of particularly independent variables cannot be replicated; primary emotions are replicable best by physiological responses, and secondary emotions by social situations.

The history of the social sciences is replete with examples of studies that lack validity because the researcher failed to take the above 17 plausible rival alternative hypotheses into account. If we had to make a choice between each type, we would probably pick those high in internal validity because we can make do with low generalizability of findings, but we are not ultimately satisfied with research that is internally open to alternative explanations or interpretations.

The Relationship Between Reliability and Validity

Novice researchers also often ask which problem—reliability or validity—is more important to solve. In considering the worth of a particular measurement, validity is a more important criterion than reliability. As we have seen, we can have high reliability, and yet still have low or no validity. Recall the simple example at the beginning of this chapter with a person who is always disoriented and tells you to "go west" to find the library when in fact the library is east. Such a person may give highly reliable but completely invalid directions.

Lord and Novick (1968:72) demonstrated how validity and reliability are related: The validity of a measure can *never exceed* the square root of its reliability. Therefore, reliability limits validity. If one has a measure with low reliability, a statistical correlation of 0.49 that measure can never correlate greater than 0.70 with some other variable. Again, assume a split-half test estimate of reliability of 0.64; the validity estimate *cannot exceed* 0.80. Therefore, although reliability and validity are related, if one cannot reliably measure a variable, one cannot measure that variable with any assurance of validity.

Do not, however, be misled by this reliability-validity formula. It is *not* true that the square root of a reliability coefficient determines the validity of a measure. In the first place, we never know the actual reliability of a measure— only its estimate. Second, the square root of the reliability is a correlation between the measurement and whatever that measurement is measuring. Whatever it actually measures may or may not be what one wants to measure. Remember, once again, the example of the disoriented direction giver. Such a person might give completely invalid directions all the time even though the directions are completely "reliable" in the scientific sense of giving the same misdirections all the time.

Summary

This chapter introduces three critical concepts to aid fuller understanding of the skeptical attitude in science: operationalization, reliability, and validity. Operationalization is a concrete mechanism for joining theory and methods. It is the vehicle by which the researcher demonstrates precisely how he or she measured study variables. This demonstration is crucial from the point of view of the scientific audience. Other scientists need to know how their fellow scientists measure particular phenomena, so they themselves can replicate it or so they can better understand its limitations and work toward better reformulations. The words "more or less" are ultimately unacceptable to scientists: If it can't be measured, it doesn't exist. Most advances in science come from the boring, tedious, routine of discovering more exacting means of measuring specific concepts.

Strictly speaking, reliability refers to unbiased or random error while validity refers to biased or nonrandom error. That is, measures of reliability error ought to produce such symmetrical distributions as we see in the normal, bell-shaped distribution. Similarly, the distribution of validity errors are more skewed in shape.

Reliability concerns the problem of how consistently the researcher obtains the same response each time the researcher measures a variable. High reliability is a minimal condition of scientific measurement. Researchers measure reliability in four different ways. First, they take a test and retest measurement of stability with the same instrument and compare the pattern of results with a correlation coefficient. Second, they may administer multiple forms of the same construct, and again compare the association between scores. Third, scientists may split a number of items into two halves by some method of randomization, and compare the results with a measure of association. Fourth, there are two more complex inter-item correlation techniques: First, one can correlate each item in a scale against every other item and obtain the average intercorrelation for the entire set. Second, one can systematically subtract out each item from the total scale, and take the correlations between the n -1 item subscales and the total scale scores. Although these last two methods are mathematically more complex, computer programs have reduced this complexity, and they provide the most stable indexes of reliability.

Reliability is related to the number of items used in the measurement processes. As a general rule of thumb, no more than ten items in a scale will produce the highest reliability obtainable. Furthermore, even single items of low reliability when added into a scale of eight to ten items can produce acceptable levels of reliability. This is because the irrelevant components of each item normally cancel out other ones.

Although consistency of measurement is important to science, it does not insure validity—whether or not the measurement really represents that which it is suppose to measure. One may have highly reliable data that do not measure what they should measure. The first step in scientific checks on validity is the validity of the measurements. Scientists wish to check their measurements for "noise"; they do this through employing the techniques of content validity, criterion-related validity, and construct validity.

Content, or face, validity is the weakest of all three techniques because it is based on nonempirical, or nontheoretically linked, checks. The researcher simply asks: Is my operationalization appropriate for measuring the claimed construct? The problem is that content validity rarely exhausts all representative operationalizations of a particular construct. Criterion-related validity consists of two techniques, each linked to specific theories: Predictive validity, which is based on finding variables of theoretical interest that anticipate specific high associations with the operational instrument; and concurrent validity, which uses experts to judge known groups as high or low on the construct in question. The final type of validity of measurement check is the most complex: construct validity. It is based on a theoretical pattern of associations among numerous variables. The logic of construct validity is that different measures of the same construct should be highly associated, while those measures that measure different constructs should have low association.

Researchers also scrutinize studies for the threats to the validity of study findings through examination of internal validity, statistical conclusion validity, and external validity. Internal validity stresses the search for threats to drawing specific cause-and-effect conclusions. Such threats include historical events outside of the independent and dependent variable that are not adequately controlled, such internal maturational events as growing hungry, tired, etc., that may be confounded with causal findings, subject knowledge that they are being tested, inadvertent changes in the calibration of measurements, biased selection of units of analysis, participant drop-out rates, and complex interactions between these variables.

Statistical conclusion validity stresses how adequately specific statistical techniques measure the cause-and-effect relationships. It is particularly affected by the need to balance trade-offs between two types of errors: rejecting a decision that is actually true (false negative decision), and accepting a decision that is actually false (false positive). Statistical conclusion validity is affected particularly by the number of replications, sizes of samples, and robustness of specific statistics when the assumptions are violated, and atheoretical "fishing" for relationships in the data. One specifically problematic type of statistical conclusion validity is statistical regression toward the mean, in which extreme scores are pulled toward the average score on later measurements producing such specious conclusion as tall persons give birth to short ones, etc.

External validity deals with the generalizability or representativeness of study results. Specific threats to external validity include: long-term reactive measurements, interactions between the independent variable and differential selection of subjects that distort findings, short-term reactivity of data collection methods, treating the effects of single introductions of the independent variable as if multiple treatments would produce the same results, irrelevant components of multidimensional measurements that lead to spurious conclusions, and multidimensional variables in which not all dimensions are completely measured.

Of the two concepts, validity is ultimately more important than reliability. We have no use for an operationalization that does not measure what it is suppose to measure regardless of how reliably we can measure it. The two concepts are related so that if we have an adequate measure of reliability we can take its square root which produces the highest limits of validity that are obtainable using that operationalization.

CHAPTER

5

Sampling: The Search for Typicality

In chemistry or physics, there is often no problem of finding [the pure case]. When the chemist wants to establish a proposition about sulphur, he can use any lump of chemically pure sulphur (provided its crystalline structure is irrelevant to the experiment) and treat it as a true and pure representative of sulphur. If a social scientist wants to study the Norwegian voter, it would simplify research enormously if he could find the pure voter, the one person who would be the representative of all Norwegian voters, so that all that was necessary would be to ask him or watch his behavior. At present, the belief in the possibility of finding [the pure case], on the individual or collective level of analysis, seems to have disappeared completely from social research.[1]

Key Terms

Biased sampling	Cluster sampling
Bootstrap sampling	Confidence limit
Central limit theorem	Expert choice sampling

[1]Johan Galtung, *Theory and Methods of Social Research* (New York: Columbia University Press, 1967:16).

General universe

Haphazard sampling

Heterogeneous sampling

Homogeneous sampling

Jacknife sampling

Multistage sampling

Probability proportionate to size (PPS)

Probability sampling

Primary sampling unit (PSU)

Purposive sampling

Quota sampling

Randomness

Rare element sampling

Sampling frame

Simple random sampling (s.r.s.)

Snowball sampling

Strategic informant sampling

Stratified sampling

Structural sampling

Systematic sampling

Time sample

Tolerance limits

Working Universe

Study Guide Questions

1. What are the major advantages of using samples rather than whole populations in research?

2. Why is it important to distinguish between general and working universes in sampling?

3. Briefly explain differences among the five types of interactive samples and their uses.

4. How has the concept of randomness changed due to research by statisticians and physicists? How does this change affect operationalizing probability sampling?

5. When is it most appropriate to use a probability sample? A purposive sample?

6. Briefly describe each of the following types of purposive samples, and explain an advantage of each: Haphazard, homogeneous, rare element, heterogeneous, structural, strategic informant, and expert choice samples.

7. How does the central limits theorem influence our faith in the precision of our sample results?

8. Explain the differences between tolerance limits and confidence limits in accessing sample precision.

9. How does sampling with replacement differ from sampling without replacement?

10. **Why is systematic sampling less likely to be random than simple random sampling?**

11. **Explain the different trade-offs involved in using cluster versus stratified sampling.**

12. **Why is cluster sampling a particularly tricky type of operation?**

13. **When do researchers prefer to use cluster or stratified sampling over simple random sampling? Why do they sometime combine them into a stratified cluster?**

14. **What is the purpose of using some primary sampling units as self-representing and others as non-self-representing?**

15. **Explain the Probability Proportionate to Size (PPS) strategy.**

16. **What is the relationships of size of sample and size of universe to sampling precision? How do they differ from everyday conceptions?**

17. **How does (a) frequency of occurrence of the phenomenon of interest in a working universe and (b) number of variables to be analyzed affect sample size?**

Everyone has had some experience in sampling, whether intentionally or not. If you have ever tasted one grape from a bunch or sipped a little wine, you've been engaged in a sampling process. *Sampling* is a procedure by which we infer the characteristics of some group of objects (a population) through experience with less than all possible elements of that group of objects (a sample). Because the researcher samples less than all objects, he or she must take special care that the *numbers* and *kinds* of objects in the sample sufficiently represent the total population. Otherwise, the researcher cannot make sound generalizations about the population. In terms familiar from Chapter 4, this means that sampling procedures are a means of developing good external validity. Certainly, how we select our data influences the degree to which we may make generalizations from it. This chapter discusses means by which we may objectify and specify sample selection procedures that permit generalizations from our data.

Advantages of Sampling

Why should we be interested in sampling? Why not take complete counts in our research? In brief, sampling usually permits the researcher to cut costs, reduce work-force requirements, gather information more quickly, and obtain more comprehensive data, because our populations are typically large and spread out. Take the case of a researcher interested in analyzing the content of the "Peanuts" comic strip for reflections of changing societal norms and values. If the analyst used all of the Peanuts strips, the amount of material to cover would be enormous, given the fact that the strip has appeared in the newspaper over a quarter century 365 days a year. If the analyst could devise some means of accurately representing the entire Peanuts strip with a smaller set of the daily output, he or she could save time and money. In addition, there are obvious advantages to sampling, when the researcher can estimate how accurately the sample represents the complete population. Some sampling methods make such estimates possible.

Finally, although it may seem particularly paradoxical on first reflection, some samples actually give *better* estimates of the complete count than would a survey of every possible case. The U.S. Census Bureau has long emphasized that its ten-year population census is in many ways less accurate than its ongoing sample research, if only because the population census involves the use of large numbers of relatively inexperienced interviewers. Such a mammoth project normally produces more nonsampling (mechanical and clerical) errors than sampling errors, due to the relatively massive amounts of data the Census Bureau must process. Thus, a carefully designed sample survey may contribute more reliable data than a survey of an entire population simply, because researchers can control certain sources of error much more effectively when they examine a relatively small number of cases.

General Universes, Working Universes, and Samples

Given the advantages of sampling, good sampling is still not feasible without some clear conception of *what* the researcher is sampling. The researcher can partially eliminate such problems through clear construction of three notions (Sjoberg & Nett 1968:130) known as the "general universe," "working universe," and "sample." The *general universe* is the abstract, theoretical population to which the researcher wishes to generalize study findings; it is the ideal. The *working universe* is the *concrete* operationalization of that general universe; it is a practical approximation of the ideal general universe. In practice, survey researchers and statisticians refer to the working universe in probability sampling by the term sampling frame; the *sampling frame* is the concrete list of sampling units from which a probability sample is selected. Therefore, a sampling frame is not as general as the term working universe because a sampling frame working universe is only one kind of working universe. The *sample* is some portion of the working unit that the researcher draws.

All scientists grapple with this problem. For example, because chemists rarely find general universes of pure chemical elements, they attempt to purify some amount of raw chemical material from which they will sample for laboratory tests. Similarly, experimental psychologists have carefully bred a population of white mice that share a known set of genetic materials. These mice are used worldwide even though they do not mirror the impurities of all mice (the general population), because of their known characteristics. When social scientists construct a working universe, they strive for this same goal: They strive to create working universes (or in the case of probability samples, sampling frames) that have well-known characteristics, so that their scientific critics may judge how adequately representative (pure) their samples are.

The researcher draws the actual sample not from some abstract general universe but rather from a tangible working universe. Therefore, it is imperative that the working universe represent the general universe as closely as possible. Figure 5–1 visualizes four ideal typical kinds of general universe and working universe relations. Of the four, the working universe (termed "b") in Example 1 better operationalizes the general universe (termed "a") than the other examples: Its area coverage is greater and has no false positive cases— ones that are inaccurately attributed as members of the universe (unshaded areas of b in examples 2, 3, and 4). Pollsters interested in attitudes of the general American public (the general universe) toward various topics might decide to use all working phone numbers with an American area code as their working universe. Because some 98% of American households now have a phone, random-digit dialing methods could be used to select a sample from that working universe, and that working universe would closely approximate the general universe of the general American public.

More likely, such a working universe would be closer to that diagrammed

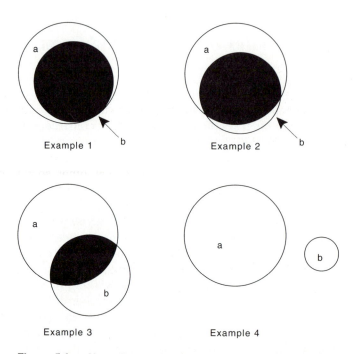

Figure 5-1.   Venn diagram representations of four hypothetical general universes (a) and working universes (b). The shaded areas represent those areas shared by both the general and working universes.

in Example 2, if only because some few people with American phone numbers would not be American citizens and therefore would not belong in the general universe. In both Examples 1 and 2, the majority of cases from which the researcher wants ideally to sample are included in the working universe. Because it is unlikely that any working universe will include all cases to which the researcher wishes to generalize, these two examples give good approximations. However, many of the subjects that social scientists wish to study are not so easily approximated; for example, working universes for the study of AIDS are (at the time of this writing) appallingly inaccurate. A social scientist interested in the behavioral aspects of how this disease spreads would wish to have an accurate working universe of AIDS cases from which to sample. The large number of false positive and false negative cases, using current testing methods in conjunction with the large population of untested individuals, would most likely lead to a working universe something like that shown in Example 3: one in which a large part of the working universe cases belong to the general universe (shaded area of b), whereas a large part do not (unshaded area of b).

The worst-case scenario would be those approximating Example 4. In this case, the working universe shares nothing in common with the general universe. Perhaps the clearest example of such working universes are scientific hoaxes like the infamous bones of Piltdown Man. In this case researchers were falsely led to believe for several decades that they had a sample of a working universe of bones from the "missing link" in the evolution of humans. In reality, the bone were doctored animal bones. Eventually, as more accurate working-universe approximations to general universes become known to, available to, and used by scientists, it becomes harder to dupe other researchers with such hoaxes.

Social scientists expend much time and effort in the process of attempting to operationalize their working universes so that they closely mirror some general universe of scientific merit. The reason is that if the working universe provides a poor approximation, then the best sampling methods in the world will not be able to overcome this Achilles' heel of operationalization. In fact, most social scientists bend over backwards to describe how they operationalized a particular working universe so that other social scientists may more easily replicate their work. The classic work on the American academic labor market by Caplow and McGee (1958) exemplifies this process. They operationalized this general universe by creating a working universe from lists of assistant, associate, and full professors in nine major American universities whose employment terminated between June 30, 1954 and July 1, 1956. However, they knew that these types of lists did not perfectly replicate the general universe of the total academic labor market because (Caplow & McGee 1958:24–25).

> In most institutions, records of departed professors are kept very indifferently. . . . (E)rrors were not uncommon. . . . A case was included if it involved an assistant professor replaced by an instructor, but not if it involved an instructor replaced by an assistant professor. If the vacancy occurred between the specified dates, the case would be included even if no replacement had been made at the time of the interview.

Notice how Caplow and McGee's operationalization of the academic marketplace is *specified* and *qualified* in the above quotation. They painstakingly pointed out the means by which they obtained their list of academic vacancies, so that the reader may judge the *adequacy* of their generalizations to all academic vacancies.

This working versus general universe distinction is important, because researchers rarely have opportunities to sample directly from general universes. Suppose a researcher wishes to sample from all known "small groups." This researcher must operationalize "small" and "groups." Is the group small if it has seven members? Ten? Twelve? Is a "crowd" considered a group? What is the difference between an "aggregate" and a "group" of four persons? And where do you find representative "small groups"?

Even when a researcher draws a sample from a much more concrete phenomenon such as a human population, the general and working universes still do not usually coincide completely. Since 1940, the U.S. Bureau of the Census has measured monthly national unemployment rates. The Census Bureau has operationalized "unemployment" in many different ways; each method gives a somewhat different picture of unemployment. For instance, is a college sophomore who claims to be looking for a summer job unemployed? What about the high-school basketball player who says she's looking for a part-time job after school but does not have the time for such a job right now because of basketball practice? Such questions should not be taken lightly. In a survey such as the Census Bureau's unemployment survey, each person sampled represents approximately 25,000 others. Therefore, slight changes in definition—working-universe operationalization—may lead to radically different unemployment rates.

Even if a working universe cannot be empirically demonstrated to represent a general universe, social scientists often are willing to generalize. The reason is that, as in Galtung's opening chapter quote, scientists are often not skeptical enough: They may implicitly or explicitly assume that the phenomena that they study are stable over time and space. Good scientific work does not make such assumptions. Unfortunately, researchers sometimes fail to concern themselves with questions about the working-universe representativeness of their general universes. The number of studies carried out on college sophomores, *as if* they were representative of all homo sapiens, attests to this fact. Researchers have an obligation to *demonstrate* the typicality of a particular working universe.

This demonstration brings us back full circle to the relation of theory to research. The kind of working universe employed reflects theoretical assumptions of the researcher. The Census Bureau definition of unemployment states that to be counted as unemployed, a person must have *actively* been looking for work during the week prior to the interview. Yet it is well-known that there are many communities (West Virginia coal towns) and occupations (teaching positions are available only at certain times of the year) where there is gross joblessness with no jobs to search out actively. Also, the census counts "part-timers" (who may want full-time jobs and are "underemployed") as "employed." As a consequence, the Census Bureau's operational universe does not adequately include certain types of unemployment phenomena.

Samples in Search of Universes

Neophyte researchers commonly "sample" without an explicit rationale as to *what* universe it is they are trying to represent. When this occurs, the resulting sample is usually biased, that is, nonrepresentative, because of an unknown universe. Perhaps the greatest problem in using such samples is that unconscious selection procedures control the selection process. There are studies demonstrating that subjects asked to sample "randomly" from a universe of pebbles will *unconsciously* pick biased selections—some pick smoother pebbles, others pick larger pebbles, and some choose particularly colored pebbles. Indeed, this tendency for people to have particular unconscious response biases is so well-known to professional sampling experts that most respectable survey research organizations do not allow their interviewers to make *any* sampling decisions.

The problem of samples with questionable generalizations is not limited just to nonrandom samples. We could very easily sample from a college student population at random. However, we may still have little idea as to how generalizable that college student working universe is to some more general universe of all adults. Are crime rates, food-stamp usage, or drug-use behaviors among American college youth generalizable to American working-class youth, Japanese college students, or Middle Eastern hijackers? Simply because one has an accessible working universe from which to sample does not settle the question: "Generalizable to what?" The only way researchers can normally settle this question is through replications of a study across time and cultures. Similarities and differences in several samples may show the boundaries of the general universe; replication similarities show universe inclusion while differences show universe exclusions.

Neophyte researchers are not the only ones who make the mistake of drawing samples from unclearly delimited universes; professional social scientists make this error more often than might be realized simply because many of our general universes are extremely abstract. Bureaucracies, industrialized societies, and groups are intangibles in the sense that one cannot touch, smell, hear, taste, or see them. Other general universes are hidden from view, making them relatively inaccessible to the researcher—unwed mothers, illicit drug users, and AIDS carriers. There are many classic studies based on one, or just a few, such social phenomena. Researchers have often cited Peter Blau's (1964) case study of an Internal Revenue Service office as illustrating typical bureaucratic processes, and yet it is possible that it typifies a somewhat more narrow general universe such as American federal bureaucracy.

However, it is particularly perplexing when writers make such claims from samples that are particularly suspect. Such is the case in Shere Hite's (1987) publicly acclaimed book, *Women and Love*. Because she used a particularly large sample of 4,500 women to represent all American women, many lay people might be impressed. But her sampling methods were highly suspect. She passed out over 200,000 questionnaires through various women's groups she contacted. Because only slightly more than 2% of her working universe—

which is already suspect because we have no idea how representative of all American women it is—returned her questionnaires, we are left with the strong suspicion that women self-selected themselves in and out of her study. The problem is: Who do her questionnaires represent?

Any regular reader of letters to editors might sense that she had a huge oversample of unhappy people who felt driven to put their emotions on paper. Indeed, Hite claims that over 70% of married American women have had an extramarital affair, while numerous less-suspect samples have shown such a situation to occur at no more than a third of that rate. The problem with Hite's work is quite typical in the United States: Local television and radio stations, and, on occasion, national television networks have used such suspect sampling methods. However, the results of such sampling techniques are not generalizable to any known population because of the self-selection bias of the sampling procedure; that is, the only persons included in the survey are those who choose to participate.

Universes in Search of Samples

One of the ironic twists to social and behavioral research is that we have a large number of theoretically interesting general universes that are *relatively* abstract or inaccessible from a sampling viewpoint. Most of these types of universes are what researchers call relational or interactive. Denzin (1970:89–91) distinguishes among five types of interactive samples: encounters, dyadic structures, social groups, social organizations, and communities or entire societies.

An *encounter* is the most transitory of social relationships because it has no prior- or afterlife. An encounter, according to Denzin (1970:90), "lasts only as long as persons are in each other's symbolic and physical presence." Joint action, interpersonal coordination, and coorientation of behavior are minimal or lacking in an encounter. Therefore, examples of encounters cover a broad spectrum of social events such as cocktail-party interaction, conversations with a hitchhiker in a moving automobile, playing bridge, an airplane hijacking, singles-bar interaction, or behavior in a radar speed trap. For those individuals interested in pursuing encounter studies, suggested readings would include Erving Goffman (1974), Humphrys (1970), and Stein (1989).

Encounters present particularly difficult problems of location of working universe units from which to sample because of their situational nature. Denzin (1970:93) offers a unique solution to the problem which has some merit: Empirically locate and enumerate the potential situations for interaction, then draw a sample of those situations at a rate proportionate to the probability that an encounter occurs within them.

A *dyadic structure* is a two-person group that shares a common role-set. Such a role-set might include husband-wife, work supervisor-subordinate, colleague-colleague, or friend-friend. Dyadic structures, by way of contrast to encounters, exist outside of the partners' physical copresence. Researchers often use the *snowball technique* of sampling to study dyads. In the snowball technique, the researcher asks individuals to list those persons with role relationships of particular interest (employer-employee, husband-wife), their addresses, and their specific role relationships to the respondent. This technique is then continued with those persons suggested by the researcher's first wave of respondents, second wave, and so on, until the the researcher exhausts new dyads from which to sample.

It is important that the researcher who claims interest in dyadic universes study the dyad itself, and not just one of the participants. Often researchers incorrectly make inferences to the whole dyad from the study of one of the participants; methodologists term this type of incorrect inference: the *fallacy of the wrong level of analysis.* Specifically, this procedure potentially confuses prescribed role norms, actual role behavior, and the participant's *perceptions* of each. A wealth of information demonstrates empirical differences between each component. For instance, if an interviewer questions members of the complete marital dyad separately, researchers often find that each partner has grossly different perceptions about how often they actually have sexual intercourse or when they last fought. Ambert (1988) confirmed the importance of dyadic sampling when she reported from such sampling methods that divorced parents have much more similar perceptions of each other's behavior and attitudes than divorced couples without children. Without sampling the entire dyad, she would not have been able to report such findings.

Sociologists characterize *social groups* by interaction between three or more individuals. Researchers often study social groups in terms of such characteristics as cohesion or stratification, or they may break groups down into dyads or encounters. Because researchers may analyze social groups by their focal activity, their places of interaction, and the nature of involvement among participants, we can often use these indicators for isolating a working universe from which to sample. Such social groups as sea kayaking clubs, Meals on Wheels, P.T.A.s, and Red Cross volunteers are easily identified because of the more visible organizations that support them—specialty sports stores, airports, and so on. Because families typically live in a household, it is not usually difficult to sample families.

In a cleverly constructed convenience sampling method, Davies and Kandel (1981) analyzed adolescent-parent-best school friend triads; they reported how this method enabled them to reveal how much more influence parents have on adolescent educational plans than do peers. The sample of families of homeless persons and alcoholics that Bahr and Caplow studied (see Caplow 1983) was more systematic yet. They derived a list of homeless people and alcoholics by randomly sampling households. They then interviewed members of the family; in the process, they discovered the need to weight their derivative sample by number of children in the family to compensate for the fact that families with *n* children had *m* opportunities for representation in their sample. Had they not weighed their sample accordingly, they would have artificially mislead their readers to conclude family size was associated with both homelessness and alcoholism. Therefore, obtaining a viable working-universe list from which to sample may not always prove difficult.

Social scientists define *social organizations* as any group composed of large numbers of persons who share specified goals, structured by an internal division of labor, formalized by specified sets of interactions and social controls, and with a legitimated territory for existence. Social organizations, including bureaucracies, are identified relatively easily. This may partially account for why they have drawn much empirical attention from social scientists.

Some of the more interesting analyses of social organizations have shown how the various social levels within the organizations relate to each other, how different organizations cooperate and conflict, and how organizations impinge on individuals. For instance, Granberg (1982) reported on the political conflicts between pro-choice (Missouri Citizens for Life) and pro-life (Abortion Rights Alliance) organizations; and Moure and Sugimoto (1986) challenged myths which depict Japan as a relatively conflict-free and homogeneous society by focusing research attention on such phenomena as work group-company relationships in Japanese industry and stratification systems in industry.

Communities present particular problems as sampling concepts because neighborhoods and communities exist only through consensually imposed definitions rather than clearly demarcated geographical boundaries. Neighborhood boundaries are based on arbitrary, cognitively differentiated, and consensually agreed-upon symbols, rather than actual physical, ethnic, homogeneous, or economic barriers.

Studies of social organizations, communities, and entire societies share common problems: (1) access to data; (2) characterizations on several levels or processes of analysis; and (3) relating of different levels of analysis. The problem of access to data always exists, but it presents itself in unique form in any relational study. The refusal of an organizational officer to give the researcher access, in itself, is not much different from an interview refusal by an individual. In both instances, it is probably the case that motivations for refusal are similar. But at an organizational level of analysis or higher, one has access problems that structural cross-pressures create. Field researchers have long noted that when management gives investigative access to researchers, the rank-and-file workers often become suspicious and refuse to cooperate. Prior or perceived commitments to particular levels of an organization may make access to other levels difficult or impossible. Organizations may consist of a multitude of levels—some unions and companies are stratified into tens of units. The number of possible samples necessary to fairly depict any organization, community, or total society, then, is enormous. The result of ignoring these problems may lead to serious sampling bias.

Ignoring the analysis of relations between different levels may lead to what is termed the fallacy of the wrong level of analysis. For example, how can we say that a particular economic climate characterizes the United States? Certainly, such a climate does not affect all citizens alike—stock-market brokers, federal regulators, and nonstockholders surely have little in common. When the researcher is involved in these more macro-levels of analysis such as total societies, they must take precaution to sample from the various organizational levels. Each of the above relational types of analysis defines the core of social science. However, neophyte researchers are likely to underutilize each type because of their abstract character. Sampling practitioners who fail to pay attention to the problems presented by each of these relational levels of analysis, risk reducing society to just an aggregate psychology—the fallacy of the wrong level of analysis once more.

Many social researchers pay too much attention to easily accessible populations: college students, lower-class individuals, prisoners, and the mentally ill. Easy access does not insure relevance; indeed, easy access generally cuts down on relevance, because such populations are more homogeneous than populations which include both easily accessible and practically unapproachable subjects. The best test of any theory requires samples with great variability or heterogeneity.

The Meaning of "Randomness"

One of the trickiest concepts in science is that of randomness. Scientists have made heroic attempts to define randomness but the concept remains elusive. Paradoxically, the more scientists have researched randomness, the more they have realized that nature is much less random than they previously believed. Books on probability do not even try to define it, just as geometry books lack definition of the concept of a point; to do otherwise would be similar to taking a geometric point apart to see what's inside.

However, because the concept of randomness touches on all aspects of life, its definition is important. For example, in 1970, the U.S. government carried out a draft lottery. To make the drawing fair, the planners decided to have officials pick birthdays out of an urn. They placed 365 capsules—each with a birthdate inside— in an urn, and then mechanically shook up the urn for several hours. After they considered the capsules properly mixed, they chose capsules one by one from the urn. Although the planners used standard procedures for randomizing the date, a few statisticians were struck by the apparent nonrandomness of the final drawing: Officials tended to draw birthdays in December first, those in November next, then those in October, and so on.

A Stanford University statistician—his interested piqued by the apparent lack of randomness—investigated the government planners' methods (Diaconis 1986). He discovered that the reason the draft lottery drawing was not random, was that the planners put the capsules in the urn in a definite pattern: the planners first entered the January birthdays which promptly fell to the bottom; they then put the February capsules in next, and those capsules ended on top of the January birthdays. Last of all, the planners entered the December capsules. Although the federal planners turned the urn for several hours before the drawing, it turned out that it takes much longer than they thought to properly mix up the contents of the urn.

Another example of the uses and abuses of randomness is the generation of random numbers by computers. Computer-generated random numbers are a mainstay of scientific computations. Scientists from every scientific discipline use millions of such numbers every day. But Diaconis (1986) states flatly that these numbers are not really random because computers generate these numbers according to fixed recipes. Although they pass certain tests for randomness—a high number follows a lower one as often as a lower number follows a higher one—their intrinsic lack of randomness troubles many investigators (Marsaglia 1984). Marsaglia generated numbers using *all* the standard random-number generating programs and found that all of them failed simple tests of randomness; for example, tests that half of all the numbers ought to be odd and half even. His results impelled computer programmers to write new software that generates random numbers, so that they pass Marsaglia's tests. Collins (1987) has since successfully tested five modern complex random-number generators against Marsaglia's twelve stringent tests that even run on personal computers. However, he believes that in all likelihood statisticians will someday devise other simple randomness tests that these new random-number generators will fail. Such generators must pass increasingly more sophisticated tests for randomness to provide acceptable results.

If Marsaglia is correct, scientists should be worried, because we will end up with misleading results if we continue to be naive about computer-generated numbers. Scientific conceptions often depend on robotlike, nonthinking assumptions about chance. When those assumptions are fundamentally unsound, scientific conclusions become meaningless. For example, Friedman (1986) asserts that the use of probability models in large-scale models of the economy is out of control. The use of these models by economists and government officials has become an industry in itself. However, Friedman makes a good case that many of these scientists and government officials naively make incorrect use of standard assumptions about sampling probability to make all sorts of unsound predictions—from the rate of inflation to the rate of depletion of the nation's energy resources.

As is true of scientific advancement, the clearest, simplest questions and examples aided the breakthrough to the question: What does it mean to be random? Another statistician, Brad Efron, provided Diaconis (1986) with a key image and a crucial question. Efron asked Diaconis to imagine a wall painted with 10-foot wide black and white stripes. He observed that if Diaconis threw a dart at the wall, it would be easy to decide beforehand whether the dart would land on a black or a white strip; that is, there is nothing random about this decision. Next, Efron asked Diaconis to consider shrinking the wall until each stripe was only 1/10th of an inch wide. We can now agree that where the dart will land—on black or white—is uncertain or random. Efron asked: "Can you make a theory of that?"

Diaconis followed Efron's example by returning to one of the clearest and simplest examples of randomness: coin tossing. Most of us have an image of coin tossing as fundamentally random. However, Diaconis and Engel (1986) demonstrated that coin tossing is not random but depends instead on simple physics. They showed this with a graph on which they plotted velocity on the *x*-axis and spin on the *y*-axis. A point on their graph represented the initial conditions for a coin toss. Their graph indicated that tiny differences in initial conditions result in a final outcome of the regions of heads or tails. As with the black-and-white striped wall image, as these regions get closer and closer together (imagine heads and tails on a dime as closer regions than on a nickel), the initial conditions get farther and farther from the origin of the graph. Both graphically and mathematically, Diaconis and Engel showed that coin tossing is almost random—you would have to toss a perfectly balanced coin millions of times to see any bias caused by tiny changes in the initial conditions.

In a similar manner, Diaconis and Engel analyzed roulette, the rolling of dice, and card shuffling. Each had its own long story and for each the results were roughly similar: If you look hard enough, things are not as random as everyone assumes. For example, they observed cutoff points after which a phenomenon that is not random at all becomes nearly so: If cards are shuffled five or fewer times, they simply are not randomly mixed, but after seven or eight shuffles, they suddenly mix well. Similarly, spinning capsules in an urn for several hours does not result in proper mixing, but the capsules will mix suddenly after a much longer period of time that depends on the number of capsules and the velocity of urn spin. These examples are allowing Diaconis to build a theory (1986) that allows him to come to terms with his results.

Diaconis points to two competing views of randomness in the scientific community. The first view is what he terms the frequentist view. A *frequentist,* if asked what it means to say a coin tossing is random, will respond—based on faith in the law of large numbers—that if you flip a coin often enough, it will come up heads half the time and tails half the time. But this definition is not satisfactory to Diaconis, because he observes that people often misperceive randomness in situations where there is no chance of *repeating* the process over and over; people speak about the chance of a Mideast war in the next year, although we cannot even *repeat* things once in that case.

The other standard notion of randomness is the subjectivist view. A *subjectivist* believes that coins do not have probabilities; people have probabilities. That is, this view asserts that probability is a measure of someone's belief in an outcome, as evidenced by such bald statements as: "For me, it's random." Ironically, Diaconis' work demonstrates that, as more and more data accumulate (for example, the more often a coin is tossed), a frequentist and subjectivist will gravitate toward the same belief. He says that the data collected from such essentially objective chance devices as spinning wheels, spinning urns, and flipping coins simply swamp their initial positions.

Diaconis proposes a theory of randomness that combines both views. He accomplishes this by searching for empirical answers to three important questions: How much uncertainty exists in the initial conditions? How quickly—after how many iterations (computational repetitions) or trials—is a little bit of uncertainty in the initial conditions magnified? How close is the system to random after a certain number of iterations? This new conception of randomness is not a simple one, but if randomness were simple, it would not have remained undefined for so long in standard probability texts. Diaconis demonstrates how one can use these questions quantitatively to show the degree of randomness in standard examples of chance phenomena.

The user of random-sampling techniques who does not ask these types of questions risks naively misapplying random sampling. Randomness is a matter of degree, and can only be approached through more careful application than the unthinking use of traditional sampling statistics suggest: The misapplication of random sampling leads to biased samples.

Types of Sampling Strategies

This section introduces the various types of samples social scientists use. As stated previously, if the researcher wishes his or her samples to *typify* some specified universe, then it should be representative. Different types of sampling strategies characterize particular universes with different degrees of accuracy. Although scientists prefer to use the most accurate sampling technique available, this is not always possible. The general rule is to use the sampling technique that best represents the working universe within the financial means available. Accuracy and cost are the key determinants of the type of sample the researcher prefers.

The difference between a biased and unbiased sample is an important one. A *biased sample* is one in which the working universe is not accurately or fairly represented. At the other extreme are samples that we say are *relatively nonbiased* because they closely typify the working universe. Biased and unbiased samples are polar types: It is impossible to draw a completely unbiased sample that does not sample the whole universe (making it, by definition, no longer a sample because the sample must always be smaller than the universe from which it is drawn). The danger of a biased sample is that it may misrepresent the working universe.

The statistician's use of the term "bias" conveys no value judgments as to how "good" a sample is. Often, an expert statistician correctly introduces particularly forms of bias into the sampling procedures. Such distortion requires that the statistician know where the bias is *and* that he or she has omitted no part of the working universe. In other words, the researcher may *purposely* induce sampling bias if he or she corrects for the distortion in the *analysis*; it is for *unwitting* bias that the researcher must be on guard, because then there is no way to know what manner or degree of distortion is present.

Although I will discuss some variations, there are two basic types of samples: purposive and probability. The difference between each type centers on *how* elements are selected, rather than on *which* elements are selected. As a general rule, purposive samples are liable to introduce unwitting bias whereas the bias in probability samples is known. Researchers prefer probability samples over purposive samples if they have a relatively adequately operationalized working universe from which to sample as well as adequate financial resources and time. Therefore, purposive samples are better than no sample at all (or a sample of convenience drawn without any purpose), but their use is at best second fiddle to that of probability samples.

Statisticians strictly define a *probability* sample as any sample where every unit has a chance of selection that is different from 0% or 100%, and that chance is a *known* probability. If the researcher has a list of 100 dyads, then every dyad has a known probability of selection of 1/100th. The researcher must draw at least 1 dyad (or else each dyad would have no chance of selection) and no more than 99 dyads (or else each dyad would have 100% chance of selection). To satisfy the conditions of a probability sample, the researcher must have a complete enumeration of units in the working universe. Unfortunately, this not always possible; a researcher interested in studying the effects of AIDS on the victims' family lives would find it impossible to obtain anything approaching a complete listing of AIDS victims or their families. In this case, the researcher would have to draw some kind of purposive sample.

A *purposive* sample lacks at least one of the characteristics of a probability sample; a purposive sample has units with a known selection chance equal to 0% or 100% or, as is much more likely, where the chance of selection is *unknown*. The main difficulty with purposive samples is that the researcher can rarely know how closely a purposive sample represents some working universe. By contrast, a statistician can measure representation through estimating sampling bias in a probability sample.

Purposive Sampling Strategies

There are several generic methods of purposive sampling: haphazard, homogeneous, rare element, heterogeneous, structural, strategic informant, and expert choice samples. In this section, each type of purposive sample is presented, as are primary variations of each.

Haphazard samples

These are the least purposive of any sampling technique, because they are simply samples of convenience that fortuitously present themselves for study. In fact, some researchers call them convenience samples. Volunteers form fortuitous sampling elements because the researcher does not usually know how volunteers may differ from nonvolunteers. Samples of items from the past are usually also fortuitous because of selective decay and selective retention. Stone grave markers decay more slowly than those made of wood; therefore, genealogists are more likely to sample graves of wealthier persons. While such sciences as physics and chemistry can afford to care little about the representativeness of their specimens, archeology, history, and other social sciences are often forced to draw conclusions about the past from whatever items fortuitously come to hand.

Homogenous samples

This type of sample depends on a relatively narrow range of some theoretical variable. Homogeneous samples are of two types: (1) extreme case samples represent only the boundaries of variable values, and (2) rare element samples which represent (or overrepresent) variable values of low frequencies. Purposive use of theory ought to determine the use of either type of homogeneous sample. Researchers interested in discovering the boundaries of human action or institutions ought to consider *extreme case sampling*. A researcher interested in stress and group cohesion seeking might study stress-seeking groups: white-water kayaking clubs, high-altitude mountaineering teams, or skydiving teams. Similarly, a researcher interested in creativity and intelligence might study those select college students that receive National Merit Scholarships,

Nobel prizewinners, members of Mensa (a group that admits only persons with an IQ over 135), or the select group of professional writers who are admitted to the annual Iowa Writer's Conference at one extreme and Army Alpha Test rejects or brain-damaged stroke victims at the other extreme. Any extreme case-based study acts as a quasi-experimental control over certain variations in the data because sampling units that might otherwise obscure observations are by definition excluded. However, extreme case samples are subject to the validity problem of regression toward the mean discussed in Chapter 4.

There are many types of phenomena so rare that a *rare elements sample* is the most efficient sampling design in time and cost. To name only a few: professed American atheists, survivors of mechanical heart transplants, hemophiliacs, teenagers over 16 living in Manhattan who have a driver's license, and religious communes. The cost of drawing random samples of such phenomena may be virtually incalculable. The researcher interested in these phenomena might better draw a rare elements sample: a known associations of atheists, a county public health list of hemophiliacs, or a locatable commune.

Some researchers refer to rare element sampling as deviant case sampling. "Deviant" is an unfortunately value-laden term because what is "deviant" or "normal" is relative in time and space. Certain types of behavior that Americans label "psychotic" are accepted as normal and valued in other cultures. Also, people often confuse "deviant" behavior with atypical, unapproved behavior: Many Americans do not perceive widespread federal tax evasion, such pervasive acts of white-collar crime as stealing company pencils, or the several-billion-dollars-per-year industry of purchasing "adult" home videos, as deviant or criminal. Finally, most people associate the word "deviant" with individuals, whereas it may apply to any unit of analysis. Therefore, the term "rare elements" sampling is preferable to "deviant case" sampling.

Heterogeneous samples

These types of samples are divisible into (1) representative samples, and (2) quota samples. Although homogeneous samples concentrate only on the narrow extremes of any given phenomena, heterogeneous samples consider the broadest possible spectrum of any particular variable. A researcher interested in the spectrum of excitement seeking might seek a variety of data: extremely boring, repetitive jobs on automobile assembly lines; mildly boring classroom lectures; mildly stimulating games of poker; quite stimulating intermediate-slope skiing, and extremely hair-raising white-water descents of unknown, steep rivers. The point of such sampling design is to create samples that are relatively representative of an entire continuum.

Quota samples are a special case of representative samples in which the variable representation is made *proportionate* to the working universe. The researcher would have no need to use a representative sample if he or she had an available known working universe. Because excitement-seeking behavior has a working universe that has no known proportions from which to draw, a non-quota type sample is the only viable option in that case. However, sometimes the researcher has information on the proportions of particular age, sex, or occupation groups within a working universe. In such cases, researchers might sample specific representative proportions of particular kinds of units. If a particular union consisted of 2% blacks and 21% women, the researcher might instruct his interviewers to seek out those percentages of each group for interviewing.

Although quota sampling insures proportionate heterogeneity of the sample, it has major drawbacks. First, sampling on more than three variables is prohibitively complex because the researcher must multiply the number of variables by the number of variable values. For example, if a union was represented by three races (white, black, and Hispanic), both sexes, and three levels of seniority, the researcher would have to select $3 \times 2 \times 3 = 18$ categories of quotas. Second, the freedom to choose which units to fill these quotas, makes nonrandom biases likely. In the earlier years of survey sampling, researchers frequently employed quota sampling because it does provide some assurance of representativeness with low cost. However, survey statisticians discovered that interviewers *over*sampled such units as houses on corner lots which, because they tend to be more expensive than non-corner lots, led to over-representation of more affluent households. The advent of cost-effective random-sampling methods has made this type of purposive sampling method into a dinosaur because it is rare that the researcher would have enough information to know proportions of units that he or she needs to chose without having a list (a known working universe) from which those proportions came.

Structural samples

Unlike the previously defined purposive samples, these are selected because of such specific *relational properties* as positions in a dominance hierarchy, communication chains, or social networks. Smith (1987: 377–412) presents an extensive review of this burgeoning area of research. Because relational units rarely exist as working universe listings available for sampling, the researcher with an interest in social structure usually ends up using some form of the previously mentioned purposive samples. Because valid working-universe listings of such social structural phenomena rarely exist, researchers in this important area depend most heavily on a *diversity* of convenient samples to add strength to their findings. The logic is simple: If a diverse set of samples from unknown universes produces the same or similar findings, confidence in those findings increases.

Strategic informant samples

One particularly interesting variant of heterogeneous and structural samples is strategic informant sampling. Social researchers have long recognized that knowledge, power, and other social resources are unequally distributed across social organizations, communities, and total societies. Researchers often wish to locate persons who have the most information about a social system or one of its components. Many researchers seek out persons occupying leadership roles to obtain an organizational picture from "the top down"; they use informants of lower rank to more fully comprehend the view from "the bottom up." Sometimes deviant or marginal (from the organization's point of view) informants provide distinctively strategic observations about the system's workings.

Two subtypes of strategic informant samples are (1) snowball sampling, and (2) expert choice samples. In *snowball sampling*, the researcher builds up a sample of a special population by asking an initial set of informants to supply names of other potential sample members. The researcher continues to ask each successive wave of informants who else they might recommend until he or she exhausts all possibilities through repetition of the names on the sampling list. For instance, members of deaf populations, political elites, medical specialists, and foreign expatriates often know about each other while outsiders would not likely have such information.

Expert choice sampling depends on judgments of an expert(s) to choose "typical" individuals, "representative" cities, or to postulate the parent universe of a sample that the researcher has already taken. The main problems are that experts often hold differing views on the best way to choose representative specimens, or to decide which are the most representative. These problems also brings us full circle to the dilemma presented in this chapter's opening quote: Quite often there is no valid pure case. After all, sampling seeks to represent the diversity of individuals and societies.

The major checks on the researcher's data quality in all types of purposive sampling are the repetitiveness and consistency of observations. The only times a researcher knows when to stop sampling purposively are when (1) researchers have reckoned with inconsistencies in the data, (2) they obtain repetitious data, or (3) the data form a coherent whole. Purposive sampling is strongest in the characterization of social *forms* or *types* and weakest in the characterization of actual *distributions* along a continuum. For example, purposive sampling techniques often lead a researcher to classifications of types of deviants, criminals, leadership styles, or social relationships, but they do not produce strong characterizations of the percentage of a population that engage in a particular type of deviance, criminal behavior, or whatever.

Probability Sampling Techniques

Many purists among the scientific community refer to probability sampling as the only "true" sampling method. As you have already seen, there are numerous cases, however, where it is impossible to employ probability sampling. Nevertheless, where feasible, researchers prefer probability samples, because they are the only sampling procedures by which we can accurately estimate how precisely a sample represents a working universe. To draw a probability sample the researcher must have an accurate up-to-date *sampling frame*: a list or file of all the units in the working universe. *In probability sampling, the sampling frame is the working universe.* Without such a frame, probability sampling is impossible. (Some types of probability samples, to be noted shortly, require more than just a simple list or file.) The sampling frame is virtually synonomous with the working universe, but is much more precise. Because a sampling frame uses an actual list of units, it become relatively easy to judge how accurately it represents the general universe. Therefore, it becomes easier to approximate the general universe. As a result, probability sampling experts can often produce sampling frames that are remarkably similar to the general universe, drastically reducing one major source of error in sampling: general universe-working universe (sampling frame) discrepancies. The result is that, in the hands of experts, probability sampling often leads to the type of relationship between the general universe, working universe, and sample described in Figure 5–2. This largely reduces the problem of representativeness to similarity between the sample and the working universe.

Types of Sampling Precision

Precision is a measure of sampling reliability; it refers to the degree to which the sample approximates the estimate, which the researcher would have obtained from a 100% count of the working universe if the researcher had employed identical data collection methods. Probability samples have an advantage over purposive samples, in that they allow the researcher the opportunity to stipulate the degree of precision he or she desires from the sample estimate *in advance* of sampling. This opportunity is exceedingly important because the degree of precision depends on the *use* to which researchers put their data. For example, most political candidates and ballots win by very narrow margins. A candidate who leads an opponent 51% to 49% in polling results with 3% sampling error is engaged in a contest that is actually too close to call. This is because this sampling error shows that the "true" (actual universe) value for the leading candidate most likely falls between 51% ± 3% (or 48% to 54%), while the opponent's true value in similar fashion most likely ranges from 46% to 52%. Obviously, the actual universe value might be 52% to 48% in favor of the opponent.

By contrast, if your city council members held a referendum for a new

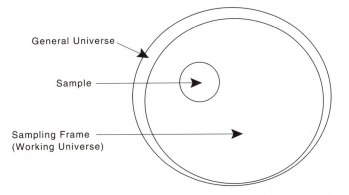

Figure 5-2.   Venn diagram of the ideal sample-sampling frame-general universe relationships.

city charter, with a probability sample that allowed for 5% sampling error and found that 60% of the eligible voters favored it, they could feel quite comfortable that the proposed charter would gain a simple majority. If sample size is held constant, the further away from 50% the percentage of a universe having a certain characteristic is, the larger the tolerable sampling error. The sampling expert can and does help set these types of sampling error rates for the client before actually drawing the sample. In fact, the sampling error rate a client is willing to tolerate is an important piece of business because, as a general rule, the lower the sampling error, the higher the client's costs.

The statistician's faith in a knowable sampling error is grounded in a powerful theorem known as the central limit theorem. The *central limit theorem* starts with the idea that one can infer the unknown population mean μ (the Greek letter mu) and its standard deviation σ (sigma)—regardless of the shape of the distribution—*if one repeatedly draws large enough simple random samples of size N*. Statisticians can demonstrate that the sample means will lean toward a normal bell-shaped distribution with mean μ and standard error $\frac{\sigma}{\sqrt{N}}$. In fact, the larger the N the better the normal bell-shaped curve will approximate the population distribution. Given a large enough number of samples, most estimates of the population mean will fall close to the actual mean value, and only a relative few will be poor approximations. For example, the researcher might poll three samples of 1,000 respondents concerning their approval of a city charter referendum giving the following results:

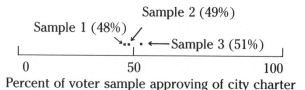

Percent of voter sample approving of city charter

In the three hypothetical samples above, one estimates 48% voter approval; the second, 49%; and the third, 51%. according to the central limits theorem, if we were to continue drawing samples of voter approval, with a large enough sample, the estimates would become distributed as evidenced by Figure 5–3. A conservative estimate of "enough" sample means is 100, although a sample of 30 sample means will normally give a good approximation. In other words, the sample estimates of the mean would become distributed around the actual population mean. Then the researcher, knowing the standard deviation, can estimate that slightly over 68% of the estimates will be within one standard deviation of the true value, and slightly over 95% within two standard deviations. Therefore, when researchers estimate a 95% confidence level, they are referring to approximately two standard deviations, and so on.

The actual number of samples needed to estimate μ cannot be known, because it depends on the amount of variation in the variable. The greater the variation (the more heterogeneous), the larger the sample size needed for accurately estimating the population mean.

Although spoken of as if sampling precision has only one component, in actuality, it consists of two very important components known as tolerance limits and confidence limits. *Tolerance limits* are the degree of variation in

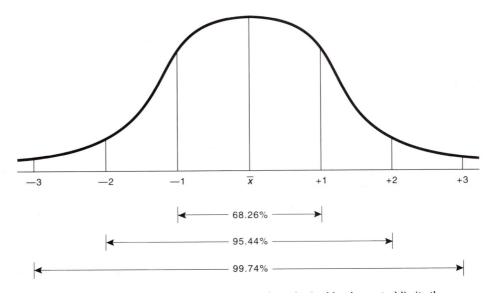

Figure 5-3.   Normal distribution of sample means hypothesized by the central limits theorem.

precision that a researcher (or client) will willingly bear. A political incumbent who is neck and neck with a challenger may accept the increased costs of lower tolerance limits. Similarly, the unemployment rate is such a vital indicator of modern democracies that governments accept the costs of low-tolerance errors. (Because each person they sample represents 25,000 other individuals, even one more person who claims unemployment in their sample has a substantial effect on their population estimates.)

Confidence limits specify the risks or betting odds for a particular tolerance limit. It is a probability of a probability; that is, it estimates the probability that the tolerance limit is correct. Clients might willingly tolerate only 3% error in 99 out of 100 samples, but they would certainly have more confidence in odds of 997 out of 1000 samples, because the betting odds of 997 to 3 are better than 990 to 10. Of course, finances impede researchers from drawing all 100 or 1,000 samples. Nevertheless, statisticians use their knowledge of probability to gain confidence. Anyone sophisticated in such games of chance as poker or bridge will recognize why statisticians are confident: One is always limited to such probability statements. If one's bridge hand is void of clubs and hearts, it is *almost* assured that someone else is also void in particular suits, but there is always a slim, *computable* chance that that is not true. One of the paradoxes of sampling error is that the computation of confidence and tolerance limits do *not* depend on the size of the *universe* being sampled; rather they depend on the size and type of the probability *sample*.

Types of Sampling and Precision

Before a sampling expert decides on the type of probability sample, he or she must have access to important types of information about the working universe. First of all, the number of units in the working universe may be *finite* (limited in number) or *infinite* (indefinitely large). The researcher may sample a finite universe as if it were infinite. If you selected a sample of marbles from a universe of 100 marbles by laying each marble aside, you would be sampling without replacement, which is equivalent to sampling from a finite universe. By contrast, if after every draw you replace the marble, you have the equivalent of sampling from an infinite universe. This is because each marble you draw will be replaced, giving each an indefinite number of possible draws.

Traditionally, statisticians have had to know enough information about the working universe to set up a sampling frame from which they can draw units in one or the other manner, because sampling with and without replacement require different formulae for calculating sampling error. In fact, the formula for sampling without replacement is considerably more complex. However, Efron (1987), over the preceding decade, has now worked out new computational methods for working backward from a sample or samples to estimate the parameters of an unknown working universe. In essence, he suggests drawing a large number of samples (perhaps as high as 100) from the original sample, and computes the average (mean) value of those sample means with the original—what he terms the *bootstrap method*. Or one computes a similarly high number of samples by taking one case at a time out of the original sample, and computing the mean of these $n-1$ samples—what he calls the *jacknife method*. Both methods require so many computations that they are only feasible when computed with a powerful computer. But the logic of both methods is simple. Estimating population parameters from n samples, each with a different set of $n-1$ cases (in the jacknife) or n minus some constant number of cases (in the bootstrap), gives an estimate of the sample units without the influence of particular cases that may unduly influence the original sample estimates (termed outliers). For example, because outliers (unusual cases) in samples have a magnetic effect on the population estimates, if those unusual cases are unduly represented in the original sample, the estimates of the true population values may be unreasonably skewed. Therefore, these powerful computations methods give a measure of how robust (stable) the original estimates were from observed variations in the bootstrap or jacknife estimates.

Systematic Sampling

This is one of the simplest, most direct and least expensive sampling methods. It consists of taking every nth unit after a randomly chosen starting unit equal or less than n. For example, say you have a sampling frame in the form of a list of 20 dwelling units on a block of which you wish to sample every fourth one. You could choose randomly—preferably by some fairly valid means such as the throw of a die—a number between 1 and 6 for a six-sided die, and thereon choose every fourth dwelling unit. If "3" came up as your starting unit, this would be:

1 2 ③ 4 5 6 ⑦ 8 9 10 ⑪ 12 13 14 ⑮ 16 17 18 ⑲ 20

Many survey statisticians claim this method produces pseudorandom selection, because every unit chosen after the first is statistically dependent on the first unit selected. The only case in which it would lead to valid random selection is the unlikely case where the working universe units had previously been thoroughly mixed or shuffled. The danger of sytematically sampling from a nonrandomly mixed working universe is in hitting a *cycle*: unusual properties associated with similarly numbered units. For instance, imagine a housing development with 7 houses to each side of every block. With a random start of 2 and a selection interval of 7, corner lots would be undersampled. Unfortunately, many social events such as unemployment and marriage rates are cyclical. Also, many lists have built-in cycles (such as some pupil records that alternately register boys and girls or a list maintained by the Small Business Administration that lists small businesses in order of their employment size).

Sometimes, to decrease the likelihood of hitting a periodic cycle, a researcher unfamiliar with a particular sampling frame will divide it into equal parts and take different random starts and selection intervals for each part. Of course, one could also do this according to some stratification principle as in the previously mentioned Small Business Administration frame where one could draw different systematic samples for differently sized businesses. Previous to the introduction of simple, inexpensive, and reliable computerized methods of generating random numbers, researchers frequently used this method. (However, as you should deduce from the next section, the trade-off danger of hitting nonrandom cycles in systematic sampling no longer justifies the simplicity of this method compared to the combined power and simplicity of simple random sampling.)

Simple Random Sampling

This method (known also by its abbreviation s.r.s.) is the classic form of probability sampling because all other forms are variations on its procedures. The definition of simple random sampling is a sample from a working universe in which every unit, whether sampled or not, has the same chance of selection. Note that, strictly speaking, sampling without replacement does not satisfy this requirement because units not drawn have more chance of selection. If you started out with 100 marbles and drew one, the probability on the first draw was 1/100th of selecting that marble, the second draw 1/99th, and so on. Happily, there are statistical correction formulae for those using simple random sampling without replacement (Kish 1965), so that this is not an insurmountable problem.

Simple random sampling requires statistical independence of the units from which the researcher samples—that is, the drawing of each unit must not depend on the drawing of any other unit (as in tossing of a coin where each toss is independent of every other toss). To insure independence of draws, statisticians recommend the use of some type of mechanical means of sampling. For instance, suppose we have a sampling frame available that lists 5,000 child-abuse cases that the local court system handled during the past year. We wish to draw a simple random sample of 100 of those cases. With the following 5-line Basic computer program:

```
SAVE IRANDOM
REPEAT 100
      LET A = 1
      LET B = 5000
LET I = A + INT(URAN * (B − A + 1))
```

Drawing the following set of random numbers, using the uniform random number generator provided by Systat™ on my Macintosh Plus™ in less than five seconds:

2642 3195 2152 2416 4711 2757 1673 338 4977 4532 3235 1211 512 0998
2877 1066 4595 3695 4038 219 32 1629 319 3431 269 4804 1188 4627
2549 753 749 3494 1991 3171 543 1004 4509 637 5000 2806 2452 331
1481 2609 457 3437 2655 1078 1627 2739 2765 3740 4765 3343 3302 1741
2669 3482 1597 1499 585 928 1242 952 1068 2340 750 440 4940 4707
2601 3609 2196 2905 2076 4144 2448 3387 2410 2328 3886 3001 2014 4763
1695 4363 4645 3014 214 22 2628 490 813 2075 1918 4840 3498 346
4986 152

We could now easily draw our sample of 100 cases. For example, the first number in this series, 2,642, represents the 2,642nd case, the next number represents the 3,195th case and so on. We would continue in like manner until we had drawn all 100 cases whose order of appearance on the court docket matched our 100 numbers. However, the reader ought to check that the random-number generating software he or she uses satisfies current knowledge of probability discussed earlier because many older statistical packages use computational methods that are not up-to-date. Also, remember that many statistics books offer fixed tables of random numbers that are based on out-of-date methods. The statistical package used provides two random number generators, modeled after the previously mentioned suggestions made by Marsaglia (1984), concerning more accurate methods of drawing random numbers.

When the researcher uses methods such as have been demonstrated, there is always the chance that a randomly generated number will appear more than once. Whether or not the researcher ignores the same number appearing more than once depends on whether sampling is with or without replacement. Without replacement, the researcher ignores duplicate numbers on later occasions. With replacement, the researcher doubly weights those numbers that appear twice, and so on. Experience shows the nonrandomness of picking numbers out of one's head or drawing slips of numbered papers from a bowl. For example, studies of numbers chosen in lotteries demonstrate people very infrequently pick numbers starting with zeros. Therefore, such mechanical means as computer-generated random numbers, dice, etc, are much preferable to the biases inherent in human choices.

Simple random sampling is based on an assumption of equality of units that very often is incorrect or may lead to misleading results. Democracy presumes a notion of equality that emphasizes "one person, one vote" but the opinions and actions of all persons and groups do not carry equal weight: Some persons have much more influence on persuading others, and the actions of some groups consistently overrules those of other groups. For example, the National Rifle Association—with less than 1% of the American population among its membership—is one of the most powerful special interest lobbying groups in the nation's capital; it consistently has had success in overruling national public opinion on gun control legislation. The assumptions underlying simple random sampling easily lead to underrepresentation of such powerful legislative forces.

Furthermore, simple random sampling may easily miss types of individuals or groups that occur infrequently: hemophiliacs, large metropolitan areas, or fledgling religious sects. For these types of reasons, simple random sampling is not used as commonly as one might suspect. Instead, the researcher may use information about individuals, groups, organizations, or whatever type of unit to draw even more accurate samples through some variation of two more sophisticated techniques: stratified and cluster samples.

Stratified Sampling

This type of sampling involves at least two stages. First, the researcher divides the working universe into homogeneous subparts technically known as "strata": A list of people might allow for division into men and women; a list of cities might be ordered by size of population. Second, the researcher then draws a series of random samples; one from each strata. This type of sampling is a probability sample because it is possible for the researcher to know the probability of selection of every unit. In other words, probability sampling does not require that all units have the *same* known probabilities. Sampling theory only requires that units *within* a particular stratum have the same probability of selection. For instance, if you were sampling from a mechanical engineering classroom list of 100 students stratified by sex, and 10% of the students were women, then you might chose a 1-in-2 sample from the strata of women and a 1-in-9 sample from the strata of men. Because you know the probability of selection, when it came time to interpret data for the five female and nine male students, you could easily weight the responses of the different sexes accordingly.

Sometimes the researcher is wise to sample disproportionately from different strata. In the previous example, because women are disproportionately underrepresented in engineering programs the researcher may need to oversample them, just to make sure he or she has collected enough analyzable cases. By contrast, the Bureau of the Census monthly, *Current Population Survey*, samples all cities over one million population and takes proportionately smaller sample fractions of cities of smaller size to give proper weight to such variables of interest as unemployment. The reason is that larger cities are so much more likely than smaller cities to influence the unemployment rate.

If you were interested in sampling crime statistics to test for the effects of size of urban population, it would be foolish to take a simple random sample, because that method would treat the selection of New York City's 14 million population equivalently to Red Bud, Illinois' 3,000 citizens. The researcher can easily stratify cities by their size: populations of more than one million; 500,001 to 1 million; 100,001 to 500,000; 25,001 to 100,000; and less than 25,001. Within each strata, the researcher could proceed to take simple random samples of crime statistics. Intuitively, one would correctly expect a better estimate from a stratified than a simple random sample because the built-in sampling heterogeneity insures against a lopsided (homogeneous) simple random sample.

Stratified sampling presupposes that the researcher already has existing knowledge of the working universe that he or she can utilize; for example, the number of bureaucratic levels in an organization and lists of bureaucratic functionaries at each level. However, simply because a sampling frame has clearly delineated strata does not mean those strata are theoretically relevant: *To be useful, the strata must be grounded in theory.* In the hypothetical example of the crime rates and size of city, it seems unreasonable to stratify on some variable unrelated directly to size of city such as the city's proportion of research and development firms because it would be expected that such a variable would have no relation to either size of city, or crime rates. The better the researcher's theoretical judgment in defining the strata, the higher the precision for any given size sample. On the other hand, the researcher may have difficulty obtaining a list that identifies the elements of each stratum.

It has been previously stated that the researcher can obtain the same level of precision with a smaller sample if he or she used stratified rather than simple random sampling. Table 5–1 demonstrates the effects of these types of sampling methods on sample size. For the same level of confidence (99 out of 100 samples) and tolerance (2% error) limits the researcher needs approximately 18% (175/963) of the units in a simple random sample if he or she uses a stratified sampling technique in this instance. You can easily see here the power of stratified sampling compared to simple random sampling because the costs of simple random sampling are less than one-fifth as much to gather data at the same levels of tolerance and confidence limits. Stratified samples nor-

Table 5-1 *Size of Samples for 98% Precision for Average Base Pay in the 10,000 employee Microwidget Industry, 99 Samples in 100*

Employee Status Sampling	Simple Random Sampling*	Stratified
Division Chiefs	—	12
Section Chiefs	—	14
Salespersons	—	33
Personnel Officers	—	26
Line Foremen	—	36
Machinists	—	10
Line Assemblers	—	10
TOTAL	963	175

Source: Slonin (1960:78) There are no numbers under the simple random sampling column because that column does not use strata from which to sample.

mally yield more precise estimates than simple random samples of the same size, provided the strata actually turn out to be more internally homogeneous that the population.

Cluster Sampling

In this type of sampling, the researcher samples from units chosen because of close spatial proximity such as counties. From these relatively small geographic areas, the researcher either samples all, or a subdivision, of the units within those designated spatial areas. Some examples of kinds of clusters are counties, blocks, or households for the U.S. population; colleges for undergraduate students; industrial parks or plants for manufacturing firms; and hospitals for heart-transplant patients. Whenever the sampling frame for a large, geographically spread-out working universe does not list all the elements separately, but only clusters with counts of elements for each cluster (for example, census counts by counties), cluster sampling is most appropriate.

Of all the types of sampling discussed, without question cluster sampling presents researchers with the most challenging and complex tasks. Specifically, the researcher must satisfy five criteria to use cluster sampling. First, each cluster must be well defined. Second, each unit must belong to one and only one cluster. Third, the researcher must have a reasonable estimate of the number of units in each cluster. Fourth, clusters must be sufficiently small to make cost savings over other types of sampling possible. Fifth, because clustering causes increases in known types of sampling error, researchers employ specialized sampling experts who choose the clusters so as to minimize the sampling error. These last two problems call for the expertise of survey samplers who know how to solve the particularly complex statistical formulae used in cluster sampling. The calculations for such measurements are complex enough that statisticians have designed computer programs that routinize the sampling errors for estimates based on such complex sample designs.

By contrast to stratified sampling, which gives more precise estimates than simple random samples, cluster samples usually give less precise estimates than simple random samples of the same size, because social areas tend toward homogeneity. Why then should the researcher ever use cluster sampling? The reason is that it cuts research costs and time. It would be simpler and cheaper to randomly select some 50 city blocks averaging 20 households each for enumeration rather than randomly select 1,000 households spread over an entire city. Therefore, other things being equal, although simple random sampling is more precise, cluster sampling is more efficient in time and cost.

Stratified Cluster Sampling

Because different clusters are most often unequal in number of units, researchers often utilize this hybrid form of stratified and cluster sampling in which they first order clusters by some strata, and sample clusters from each strata. This is particularly appropriate when there are a few clusters with extremely large populations. If a country has two counties with over a million population and the rest are under 100,000 population, it would make more sense sampling separately from two strata based on cluster size rather than chance losing the two largest counties through random selection from all clusters.

In contrast to stratified sampling, the most precise results in cluster samples are obtained when each cluster is as *heterogeneous* as the population from which the sample is drawn. Unfortunately, this is a rare outcome because social areas tend toward homogeneity—people usually live with or near people like themselves; similar businesses normally group together. The criteria for effective stratified sampling are just the reverse—strata should be as internally homogeneous as possible, but strata should differ from each other as much as possible. Because stratified and cluster sampling have contrary trade-offs, statisticians often use them in combination as a means of counterbalancing their costs and benefits.

Multistage Sampling

Several of the sampling strategies discussed employ at least two stages. As sampling experts have become more sophisticated, they have recommended the use of even more stages. Usually these designs combine various types of sampling methods to take advantage of the positive features of each. In studying the American higher educational system, one could profitably: (1) set up strata (prestige or size of institution) each of which included several clusters (such institutional divisions as schools within universities); (2) select clusters from each stratum; (3) draw a cluster sample (departments) within the first clusters; and, finally, (4) draw simple random samples of college professors within those subunits.

In actual practice, sampling experts recommend that multistage sampling designs utilize cluster sampling. Imagine a listing of all counties in the United States stratified according to size of population. Within each list, many survey organizations sample from the stratified clusters of counties as a first stage. In the second stage, they sample clusters of city blocks. Within these sampling units, they draw a simple random sample of dwelling units that they term primary sampling units.

Figure 5–4 represents an approximation to the monthly unemployment survey methods employed by the U.S. Bureau of the Census. Statisticians first organized the 3,141 counties, county equivalents (i.e., parishes in Louisiana), and independent cities (i.e., St. Louis City) into 600 strata of roughly 330,000 population each called Primary Sampling Units (PSUs). The most important characteristics that the Bureau of the Census statisticians use to define the homogeneity of PSU strata are: MSA (Metropolitan Statistical Area) status or not; rate of population change; percentage of population living in urban area; percentage of population employed in manufacturing; principal industries; average per capita value of retail trade; and proportion of population with race

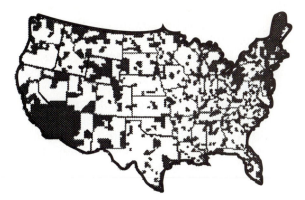

Stage 1: Identifying Primary Sampling Units (shown in black).

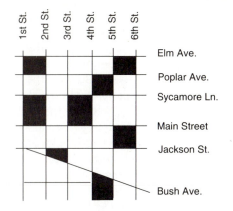

Stage 2: Identify clusters (city blocks in this case) and select a sample (shown in black)

Stage 3: Make a list of households in each block; then select a simple random sample of households from this list (shown in example with boxed enclosures).

1. 101 Elm
2. 103 Elm
3. 105 Elm
4. 107 Elm
5. 109 Elm
6. 111 Elm
7. 113 Elm
8. 115 Elm
9. 501 Elm
10. 503 Elm
11. 505 Elm
12. 507 Elm
13. 509 Elm
14. 511 Elm
15. 513 Elm
16. 515 Elm

17. 1000 First Street
18. 1002 First Street
19. 1004 First Street
20. 1006 First Street
21. 1008 First Street
22. 12 Bush Avenue
23. 14 Bush Avenue
24. 16 Bush Avenue
25. 18 Bush Avenue
•
•
•
98.1368 Jackson Avenue

Figure 5-4. Multistage sampling techniques.

not reported as white. The MSA status is particular important in the decision: Except in special cases, all PSUs with population greater than about 250,000 population in 1970 are termed "self-representing" (SR) PSU's because these PSU's do not need to be redefined. Non–SR PSU's are combined with other PSU's with similar characteristics so that they have populations varying between 321,000 and 357,000 population.

Statisticians divide SR and non–SR PSU's into separate stratum. Roughly 400 PSU's have SR status and these are insured a place in the sample through assignment of a probability of 1 of selection. The reason for this is simple: Such county-equivalent units as the Borough of Manhattan or the City of Los Angeles have such large and heterogeneous subpopulations that their loss from the sample would result in highly skewed population estimates. The remaining 200-odd PSU's are chosen through simple random selection methods.

In the second stage, the statistician faces the tricky issue of identifying subunits of each PSU from which to sample. The normal procedure is to identify distinct clusters such as blocks of housing units. The statistician then draws a random sample of city blocks. Finally, within the third stage, the researcher must then list all housing units, and draw a final sample of housing units from which to interview individuals. The reason these stages are so tricky has to do with the risks to sampling error caused by drawing unrepresentative samples of city blocks and housing units.

Recall that cluster sampling allows efficiency at the price of less accurate sampling. Because clusters tend to be homogeneous, the statistician risks drawing blocks and housing units within blocks that are more homogeneous than the actual population. On the surface, the solution to this problem would appear to be to draw more blocks and more housing units within blocks. However, remember that the sample size is fixed, limiting the practical number of blocks and housing units. Theoretically, one can chose more blocks and less housing units from those blocks, or less blocks and more housing units from those blocks. Because experience demonstrates that divergent clusters composed of similar units is more likely than similar clusters composed of diverse units, statisticians normally opt for choosing many more strata with fewer units than the reverse. Their rule of thumb within a given sample size is to maximize the number of clusters and minimize the number of units in each cluster.

Cluster sampling has another tricky issue: The varying sizes of clusters affects the change of any particular unit being chosen disproportionately. For example, the far west area of St. Louis County has under 1,000 persons per square mile, while University City on the central eastern fringe of the county has close to 56,000 persons per square mile. To deal with this problem, statisticians employ probability proportionate to size (PPS) sampling. *Probability proportionate to size* sampling takes into account the varying sizes of clusters. The statistician wishes to select a city block according to its size. For example, a highly dense city block with 1,000 households ought to have five times the chance of selection as a block with 200 households. (However, within each block, the statistician choses the same number of households so that each household always has the same chance of selection.)

The PPS strategy, therefore, calculates probability of selection as a three-stage process. First, multiply the number of elements in the population times the number of clusters to find the probability of a cluster being selected. Second, divide the sample size for each cluster by the number of total units in that cluster to find the probability of any unit being selected. Third, multiply the first answer by the second to find the probability of any particular unit being selected. To illustrate, assume we wish to draw a 1,000-household sample from a city of 100,000 households with 5,000 blocks. If we chose to draw this one-in-one-hundred sample by picking four households from each of 250 blocks, the probability of selecting each block would be: 250 sample blocks $\times$ (20 households on the average block / 100,000 households in the city), or 0.05. Then, we find the second-stage probability of any household being selected from an average block: $4 / 20 = 0.2$. Finally, by multiplying .05 times 0.2 we verify that that overall probability of selection is 0.01. Regardless of size of blocks, the probability will always be 0.01, because the number of households is the numerator in the first stage of computations and the denominator in the second, therefore canceling out the effect of cluster size. For example, in a more dense block of the same city with an average of 50 households per block, we would arrive at the same conclusion: $250 \times (50/100,000) \times (4/50) = 0.01$.

In practice, PPS is never this simple because the statistician does not know the actual number of households in each block. However, the statistician's toolbox contains clever solutions to the problem beyond the scope of this book (Kish 1987). Many social elements form natural clusters, in which case the utility of cluster sampling is most obvious: army platoons, school classrooms, churches, or bureaucratic departments. Although cluster sampling requires the most skilled sampling arts, when it is used properly it does produce reliable sampling estimates with considerable savings in time and money.

Size and Precision of Probability Samples

The desired size of any sample depends on the degree of precision desired, the variability of the data sampled, and the type of sampling employed, the effects of which have already been discussed. Several graphs in this section are used to more clearly illustrate how the researcher's desire for a certain amount of precision, size of the working universe, and frequency of occurrence of specific variables of interest influence the decision to draw a sample of a specific size. Figure 5–5 elucidates the relationship of number of sampling units needed with different tolerance (2% and 1%) and confidence limits (99 to 1; 997 to 3) to size of the working universe. It may appear paradoxical, but the figure clearly demonstrates that as the working universe increases in size, the sample size remains remarkably constant for 98% precision. Note that if we double the size of our working universe from 10,000 to 20,000 units, we need only add 60 sampling units to maintain 1% tolerance limits in 997 out of 1,000 samples! It is when the universe is very large, that we normally expect relatively precise results from relative miniscule samples. In any universe of over 10,000 population, approximately 1,200 sample units produce less than 1% sampling error in 997 out of 1,000 samples drawn! Therefore, we see that once we deal with universes larger than 10,000 we need only have slightly more than 1,100 sample units to gain this level of precision.

The reason for this apparent paradox is found in the complete formula for the standard error, which includes the sampling fraction (f) in addition to the standard deviation and sample size:

$$\text{S.E.} = \left(\frac{\sigma}{\sqrt{\overline{N}}}\right)\left(\sqrt{\frac{(1\text{-}f)}{1}}\right)$$

This formula demonstrates that for very large populations, a very small sample size is adequate for population estimates. When the sample represents only a small proportion of the population, then f will approach zero, so that the multiplier $\left(\sqrt{\frac{(1\text{-}f)}{1}}\right)$ approaches $\sqrt{1}$, or 1, which can be dropped from the formula. For example, in a sample of 1000 individuals from the United States pop-

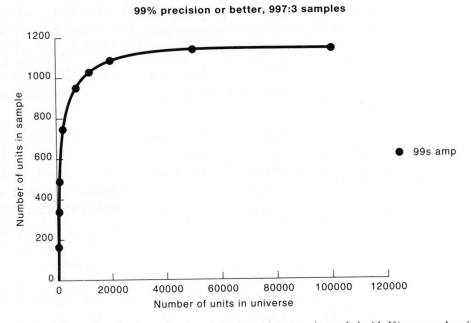

Figure 5-5a. Size of universe by size of simple random sample needed with 1% error or less in 997 out of 1000 samples.

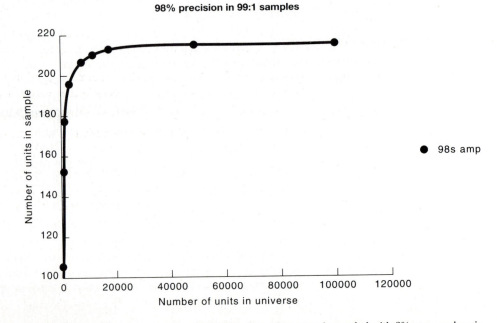

Figure 5-5b. Size of universe by size of simple random sample needed with 2% error or less in 99 out of 100 samples.

ulation of 240,000, f becomes a nearly trivial 0.004. By contrast, a sample of 1000 from a city of 10,000 gives a relatively large f of 0.1.

Figure 5-5b shows the same pattern as does Figure 5-5a for the reasons just given. Looking at Figure 5-5a you can see that with universes of over 10,000 units, the number of units needed in the sample for 1% error in 997 out of 1000 samples *stabilizes at just below 1200* cases. Similarly, looking at Figure 5–5b you can verify that with a universe of 200 units you need over half (a sample of 105) to obtain no more than 2% error in 99 out of 100 samples. However, with working universes of over 10,000 units, the number of sample units needed to attain the same levels of precision rapidly *stabilizes at just over 200 units*—actually at about 217 units, which is only 0.2% of a working universe of 100,000. These figures demonstrate that size of sample is largely irrelevant to precision of results, while size of universe is crucial to precision. It also helps explain why the prediction of presidential election outcomes has become remarkably accurate after as little as 2% of the vote has been cast.

A comparison of Figures 5-5 a and b also exhibits the effects of different levels of precision on sample size. Note that, for example, to increase precision from 98% in 99 out of 100 samples to 99% precision in 997 out of 1,000 samples, for a universe of 10,000, requires almost five times as large a sample, while the same increase in precision for a universe of 500 would require over twice as large a sample. However, these results apply only to estimates from the entire sample. Many times the researcher wishes to estimate how large some fraction of the working universe is.

Sampling Very Rare or Very Common Phenomena

When the researcher is interested in such relatively rare phenomena as Americans who speak Japanese or people who have been victimized by criminals, many times special care must be taken to draw samples with particular confidence and tolerance limits. Table 5-2 indicates that such rare phenomena would require very large shotgun-like random samples to detect. For example, because far less than 1% of the American population speak fluent Japanese, from the 1% column in Table 5-2, we can deduce that nearly the entire population would have to be randomly canvassed to discover who claims such fluency. That would be a ridiculously expensive venture; we would be far better off to sample from lists of colleges and universities that offer Japanese courses or the current directory of the Association of Asian Scholars, Inc. to find such information. Likewise, Nelson's (1980) work on multiple crime victimization indicates that the number of victimizations decreases exponentially: No more than 0.006% of the American businesses reported more than two burglaries in the 1975. Once again, the 1% column of Table 5–2 informs us that a random sampling technique of all businesses would be unconscionably costly. We would be better off sampling from Uniform FBI reports to gather this type of data.

Sometimes, of course, the researcher has no recourse but to take huge potshot samples. In recent research on abortions a large sample (1 in 7 of

Table 5-2   Sample Size by Percentage of Occurrence of Working Universe with 5% Error in 95 out of 100 Samples. (Error not to exceed 5% in 95 out of 100 Samples.)*

Number of Samples in Universe	Size of Sample Needed to Yield Error of 5% or Less in 95 out of 100 Samples, if Percentage of Occurrence Is:												
	1%	5%	10%	20%	30%	40%	50%	60%	70%	80%	90%	95%	99%
50	50	50	50	50	50	49	49	48	47	45	39	32	12
100	100	100	100	99	98	96	94	92	87	80	64	45	14
200	200	199	198	194	190	184	178	168	154	132	93	58	15
500	499	492	485	465	440	415	380	337	285	218	128	70	16
1,000	994	967	940	860	790	700	610	507	398	278	146	75	16
2,000	1,975	1,872	1,760	1,520	1,300	1,080	880	678	496	323	158	78	16
5,000	4,841	4,270	3,700	2,800	2,100	1,600	1,200	851	582	357	166	80	16
10,000	9,384	7,449	5,800	3,900	2,700	1,900	1,400	930	618	370	168	81	16

Source: Slonim (1960:78). Copyright © 1960, by Morris James Slonim. Reprinted by permission of Simon and Schuster, a Division of Gulf & Western Corporation.

*It is important to recognize that the 5% error limit specified here refers to *relative* rather than *absolute* percentage error. For example, if the percentage of occurrence is 20%, a 5% relative error limit would signify that our range of tolerance is 20% ± 5% of 20%, or 20% ± 1%. If we were concerned with a 5% absolute error (20% + 5%) our table of sample sizes would be entirely different from the one above.

68,000 abortions) produced only 50-odd cases of rape victims out of a sample of some 6,500 cases (Smith 1990). Although this is a highly inefficient means of sampling rare events, it proved the only viable way to do it in this case. Had the data been computer coded, it would have been more efficient to do use a computer to search for all known rape cases in the file and then draw a random sample from all those located by the computer.

Similarly, look at the rightmost column of Table 5-2. Some types of data occur so frequently that only miniscule samples are needed with 5% error in 95 out of 100 samples. For example, close to 99% of Americans claim they believe in God. In a city of 10,000 citizens, you would need no more than a sample of 16 people to demonstrate the triviality of sampling in this case.

The Effect of Number of Variables in Tabular Analysis

Much of the time in social research, we are interested in more than one variable because we are interested in variable relationships. When we wish to display the relationship between two or more variables with tables, we will want to insure that enough cases have been sampled for analysis. If we believe we need a minimum of 20 cases per cell and we will be using only two variables (religion, social class) per table with an average of four values per variable (Protestant, Catholic, Jewish, other; upper, middle, working, lower class), we will need at least 320 cases ($20 \times 4 \times 4$). In some cases, this multiplicative formulation will not insure enough cases because of highly skewed variable distributions. For example, Jews make up such a miniscule part of most American cities that 320 cases would not lead to more than a few Jews in the total analysis. Therefore, the researcher interested in rarely occurring phenomenon often has to ask these types of questions before drawing a sample if he or she is not to end up with too few cases. Sometimes the researcher, not having *any* idea about the value distributions of the variables, will select a small presample of units in a rapid, inexpensive manner and use the information from this sample as a basis for determining the size needed for the sample. Sudman (1976) gives mathematical formulae for computing sample size more exactly in such cases.

Time Samples

As you have seen, typical samples involve the selection of elements spread across *space*. However, there are often advantages to sampling elements across time. First, implicit in sampling across space at one point in time is the assumption that time is "typical" of all time periods. However, that simply is not always the case: Unemployment and church attendance are examples of phenomena that vary considerably with the season; such catastrophes as war and famine may have enormous influence on births, deaths, and mortality. Second, it follows that time sampling may yield data about variations between periods, estimates of seasonal and secular trends, and the effects of catastrophes.

Third, we can sometimes ingeniously get probability samples of a universe which are otherwise obtainable only through purposive sampling. A researcher interested in crosswalk-sign violation behavior might randomly select cross-walk signs for observation as a first stage, then randomly pick times to watch for violations. By weighting for unobserved times, he or she can estimate the size of his or her unknown universe.

Event Sampling

Another important type of sampling employed by social scientists is event sampling. The sampling of representative events is one of the most troublesome tasks. Observational research, field research, and historical sociology, are scholarly areas where researchers constantly grapple with the nagging question of how best to draw representative events for analysis. Event sampling is handled separately in Chapters 9, 10, and 11 because these forms of data often call for quite different methods and techniques than sampling of individuals, classrooms, factories, or other units focused on in this chapter. For example, historians have long grappled with "Croce's problem" (named after the great Classical Greecian historian), in which (1) only a limited body of data exists such as tombstones that have survived the ravages of time, or (2) over-whelming amounts exists such as field researchers normally encounter in their studies. Happily, modern statistical methods aid in solving these two problems as you shall discover in later chapters.

Summary

The variety of persons and social life make observation of total universes of many phenomena difficult, if not impossible. Furthermore, even if the re-searcher could observe all cases of any social category, the cost and time savings of observing a small, representative sample of those objects would diminish the need to observe all objects. Sampling methodology is concerned with drawing sufficiently large numbers and kinds of objects for representing whole universes of objects with minimum costs of time and money. To achieve this goal, the researcher must have a clear conception of *what* he or she is sampling.

To achieve this goal, the researcher needs to start out with a clear con-ceptualization of the abstract, theoretical universe to which the study results can be generalized—what I have termed the general universe. Next, the re-searcher must concretely operationalize that general universe with some method of deciding what group of objects from which to sample—the working universe. The ideal is to find some tangible working universe that closely matches the characteristics of the abstract general, or theoretical, universe. Finally, the researcher must operationalize the method of sampling from that working universe. The nature of the working universe and theoretical considerations largely control the type of sampling that the conscientious researcher finally selects. Seriously committed researchers engage in clearly conceptualizing each of these three stages; they continue to ask themselves such question as: What universe am I trying to represent? How can I best approximate the theoretical universe to which I wish to generalize? In what ways do my general and working universes differ, and how might those differences affect my results? How representative of my working universe is my sample, and how might its nonrepresentative features affect my results? To what are my results generalizable?

Social and behavioral researchers are interested in many things besides individuals; for example, they study dyads that dissolve through divorce, relatively short encounters between strangers, the effects of such social groups as political interest groups, organizations like bureaucracies, and even whole communities and societies. The relatively abstract nature of many interesting social phenomena creates special challenges to the researcher interested in representative sampling. One of the most important challenges is to avoid the fallacy of the wrong level of analysis, where the researcher assumes that information collected at one level of abstraction holds for other levels. For example, a common mistake is to assume that an individual's perceptions of his or her marriage describes that marriage when reality may more likely approximate the classic Japanese story of *Rashomon*, in which each party in the relationship has their own version of reality. As social researchers have become more knowledgeable, they have increasingly recommended the need for data on levels of abstraction beyond the individual level.

Another challenge to the researcher interested in sampling is the elusive concept of randomization. Although modern sampling theory is based on this concept, researchers have only recently discovered how wrong their previous conceptions of randomness were; many longstanding computer programs used for generating random numbers fail simple tests of randomness. Similarly, statisticians have shown that such intuitively chance-based methods of randomization as coin tossing, roulette, dice rolling, and card shuffling depend on a complex of non-chance-based physical factors that need attention to use them for making sound probabilistic predictions. Although current theories of probability have become much more complex as a result of this new knowledge, the happy result is better understanding of chance, randomness, and chaos which, in turn, has led to much better methods of probability sampling. Sampling experts now have better questions such as: how much uncertainty exists in the initial conditions; how quickly is that uncertainty magnified; and how close are the results to true randomness? Such questions have helped the practicing researcher to draw better samples with more confidence in their representativeness.

Statisticians term the lack of representativeness in the comparison of samples and working universes as "bias." The two generic types of samples—purposive and probability—differ in terms of how to measure bias. Researchers who use purposive samples cannot measure the actual amount of bias inherent in their samples. They can only judge the likelihood of sampling bias, by drawing a number of samples from different working universes and comparing their results for differences and likenesses; from this, they can infer whether or not their samples are adequate. As early as the 1930s, statisticians recognized that they could not rely on purposive sampling techniques to produce either "representativeness" in general or a rational basis for statistical inference.

By contrast, probability samples have two built-in measures of bias which allow a researcher to know before he or she actually samples how representative the sample will be: tolerance and confidence limits. The tolerance limit is the actual amount of error the researcher is willing to accept; the amount of error one is willing to tolerate depends on what one is researching. If one is interested in a hotly contested election between two candidates who are neck-and-neck, then the researcher or client can afford less error in the results than in a race which appears to be lopsided. By contrast, confidence limits deal with the betting odds for a particular tolerance limit. Therefore, a researcher might tolerate 1% error in 3 out of 100 samples. Paradoxically, these two measures of sampling bias or precision depend more on the size and type of probability sample than on the size of the universe.

The best samples provide three types of information. First, they provide means of determining an adequate number of units from which to sample. Second, each unit has a known probability of inclusion in the sample. Third, the amount of sampling precision can be specified with known tolerance and confidence limits so that the researcher can determine the degree of confidence that he or she can place in population estimates.

A wide variety of sampling techniques have been discussed in this chapter. Hopefully, you have come to understand why the ideal sampling technique is some form of probability sampling. The cardinal rule is to attempt to leave as much to chance as possible so that personal bias does not contaminate the sample selection. Nevertheless, because a multitude of factors mitigate against the employment of probability samples in many cases, alternatives to probability sampling are presented that sampling experts call purposive sampling techniques. Figure 5–6 summarizes the major sampling strategies.

Although the researcher must decide on the type of sampling method, ultimately more practical matters of time and cost constrain the type of sampling. If one is interested in sampling responses to naturally occurring disasters, time factors may mitigate against a completely random sample because there may not be enough time to set up a proper sampling frame. Further, cost is especially important because researchers do have limited resources.

Monetary considerations may dictate against or for particular sampling techniques. Cost and precision are the most important considerations in sampling. Unfortunately, they are directly related—one cannot achieve higher precision without more cost. Therefore, financial resources may well determine whether one's research can just be exploratory or whether it can consist of hypotheses and theory testing.

The mass media bombards us daily with "scientific data." By now you should be able to ask a number of important questions about the quality of sampling of that data.

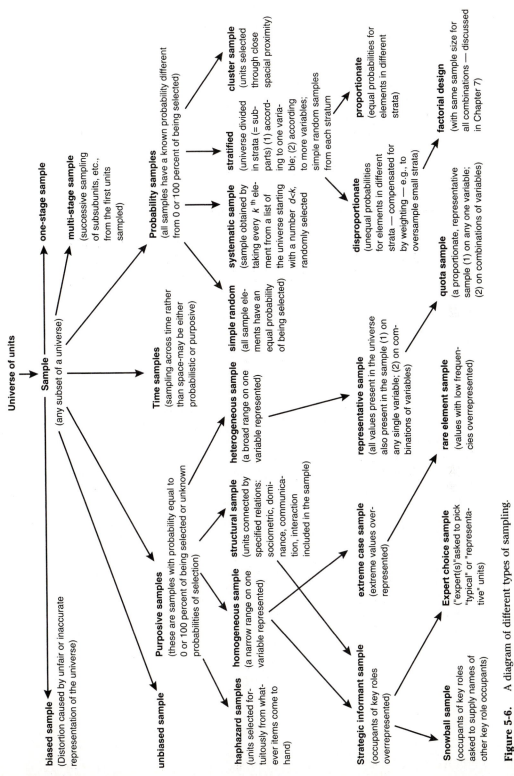

Figure 5-6. A diagram of different types of sampling.

Source: Adapted from Galtung (1967:56).

1. What was the general universe?
2. What was the working universe or sampling frame?
3. How was the sampling carried out and supervised?
4. Was there a probability sampling model? If not, why not? If so, what kind?
5. Did the sampling frame cover the universe?
6. What was the nonresponse rate (see Chapter 8)?
7. What was the estimate of sample precision?
8. Was the sample size adequate to meet the objectives?
9. Are possible biasing effects acknowledged?

If you cannot find answers to these questions, you will find it impossible to evaluate the sampling design. It is wise to be skeptical of any research that does not give you adequate information to evaluate these questions.

PART II

The Production of Data

C H A P T E R

6

Experiments:
Variations and
Approximations

All empirical proof is ultimately tied to the logic of the experiment, while the experiment focuses on the issue of control. . . . [Sociologists] try to introduce control at another level, in actually differentiating an experimental group from a control group. Here physical control is possible, although exceedingly difficult. Man is reluctant enough to be designated merely a statistical means to another's ends, whatever category he is assigned. . . . But again, the more thoroughly such control can be introduced, the closer one can approximate the canon of the logic of proof common to the community that is science. . . . Sociologists, then, are faced with decisions involving how much pressure to exert to bring individuals into their samples and the degree to which they should accept responsibility for changing or denying change to them. They must make this choice knowing that, other things being equal, increased control will enhance the validity of their conclusions.[1]

[1]Friedrichs R. (1970). *A Sociology of Sociology* New York: Free Press, pp. 169–171.

Key Terms

Additive effect

Blind treatment

Control group

Cross-sectional survey

Experimental debriefing

Experimental realism

Factorial design

Interactive effect

Internal analysis

Interrupted time-series design

Main effect

Matching

Multiple time-series design

Nonequivalent control group design

Nonexperimental design

Placebo

Pretest

Mundane realism

Posttest

Quasi-experimental design

Randomization

Separate-sample pretest-posttest design

Solomon four-group design

Statistical interaction

Treatment group

Treatment variable

Study Guide Questions

1. What general differences exist in experimental, quasi-experimental, and nonexperimental methods for inducing causality? Why?

2. How do additive effects differ from interactive ones? What kind of experiments can be used to test for each? Why?

3. What are the advantages and disadvantages of experiments over quasi- and nonexperiments?

4. Outline the four basic stages to planning and conducting experiments.

5. Discuss current ethical issues of use of deception in experimentation.

6. What are the basic requirements for a classic experimental design? What is the purpose of those requirements; that is, what sources of validity do those requirements control?

7. How does the term "randomization" differ in experiments compared to "random sampling"? Compared to "internal analysis"?

8. **Why is randomization superior to matching?**

9. **Why do some researchers forego pretesting in classical experiments?**

10. **Compare the types of information for which the Solomon four-group design and factorial designs are used.**

11. **In what ways are experimental methods weak in external validity? What strategies may aid stronger external validity in experiments?**

12. **Contrast experimental and mundane realism in experiments.**

13. **Compare the advantages and disadvantages of the interrupted time-series design, multiple time-series design, nonequivalent control group design, separate-sample pretest-posttest design, and separate-sample pretest-posttest control group design.**

14. **Compare one-shot cross-sectional, correlational, one-group pretest-posttest, and static-group comparison designs. Why are these types of studies weaker for making causal inferences than experimental and quasi-experimental ones?**

As Robert Friedrichs (1970) notes in the quote at the beginning of this chapter, social science methodology strives to meet the ideals of the true experiment. You shall see in this chapter that for a number of practical and ethical reasons, the researcher cannot always utilize rigorous experiment control.

Why are scientists so concerned with the experimental ideal? Scientists are interested in the *problem of causality*. Scientists wish to discover means of both predicting and describing the effects that certain variables they label "independent variables" have on other variables known as "dependent variables." The experimental method is the only method that *directly* concerns itself with the question of causality, which is not the same as saying it *proves* causality. Science is *not* in the business of proving or accepting hypotheses; rather, its task is rejecting or disproving hypotheses. This is not a trite difference. It means that science can only discard hypotheses. By discarding one or more hypotheses, we add slightly higher status to the multitude of undisproved hypotheses. There is a tale about Thomas Edison's thousands of unsuccessful attempts to make the first light bulb that may make this point clearer. The anecdote relates that someone asked him whether all of his failures discouraged him. He purportedly replied to the effect that it was not discouraging because his experiments at least rejected some thousands of implausible means of producing a light bulb, and therefore, he was that much closer to the truth.

Even strict experimental methods are open to rival or alternative explanations. However, the more alternative hypotheses disproved, the more confidence a scientist has in the original hypothesis. The main advantage of the experimental method is that it *minimizes* the effects of extraneous (alternative or rival) hypotheses that might confound the results. In Chapter 4, internal validity is defined as a concern with the drawing of cause-and-effect conclusions from research results. True experimental methods, by this definition, have the highest internal validity of any method.

The main scientific problem with the experimental method, as with all methods, is the problem of external validity: the problem of how generalizable the results are. Are the findings that with college students conformity increases with lower self-esteem generalizable to any other populations? Even if these conformity findings are generalizable, the extent of generalizability may still be in question due to the nature of most experimental methods. That is, we find in social science that various dependent variables usually have multiple causes. One of the weaknesses of experimentation is that usually the experimentalist can study at best only a few independent variables and one dependent variable at a time. But in real life, single causes rarely exist. Many experiments lack external validity due to the fact that, while experimentally accounting for extraneous variables, they do not account for variation in terms of the way events occur in the real world.

Consider an assumption found to underlie much experimental work: the assumption that multiple independent causes of some event are additive. Researchers wish to test whether the effects of two or more independent variables are additive—independent of each other—or work in some strange interactive combination. Sometimes the effects of two or more independent variables are additive; at other times, they are interactive.

The problem of understanding the multiple causes of the massive migration of Mexicans to the United States has become of national concern. Massey (1987) demonstrated that migration is a process affected by such houshold characteristics as land ownership, business ownership, and home ownership; such personal characteristics as sex, age, schooling, and type of worker skills; and such migrant characteristics as a father who has migrated; and personal experience in the United States. When Massey estimated migration probabilities for an average 25-year-old Mexican migrant farm worker with three years of schooling, an owned home, and no previous experience in the United States, he discovered a clear *nonadditive* effect of Mexican land and business ownership. The probabilities of migration for Mexicans who owned *both* land *and* businesses in Mexico was absolutely zero. The range of probabilities for those who owned land and *no* businesses ranged from 0.001 (one in a thousand) to 0.004. If the individual owned a Mexican business but *no* land, the probabilities ranged from 0.006 to 0.034 that he or she would migrate. Finally, Mexicans *without any* form of land or business ownership had migration probabilities, ranging from 0.056 to 0.273. If land and business ownership were additive variables, this last set of probabilities should have ranged from 0.007 to 0.038. We know this by adding up the effects of land only (0.001 to 0.004) with businesses only ((0.006 to 0.034) that gives us a possible range of:

$$0.001 + 0.006 = 0.007$$
$$0.004 + 0.034 = 0.038$$

compared to the actual range of 0.056 to 0.27 for Mexicans without either form of property to impede them from immigrating. That is, the effects of lacking both forms of property is roughly 7 (0.27/0.038 = 7.1) to 8 (0.056/.007 = 8) times greater than the effect of lacking either property or land. If they were additive, it would tell us that these two independent variables were independent of each other. However, we can clearly see their combined effect is much stronger than simply additive. Clearly, lack of business or land ownership alone have relatively paltry effects on migration patterns, compared to the combined interactive effects.

Contrary to the additive assumption underlying much research, social scientists regularly discover variables, when considered in tandem, that have complex *interactive (nonadditive) effects*. Because, in nature, we can rarely assume that only one independent variable influences some particular dependent variable, the validity of experiments with single independent variables will generally have less external validity than multiple independent variable experiments. Unfortunately, experimenters rarely perform multiple independent-variable experiments in the social and behavioral sciences because of their costliness.

The increased costs of such experiments is due to the fact that each additional independent variable added to the experiment multiplies the number of experimental groups needed by the number of categories of each group. For example, a common social experiment involves the assignment of an easy task to some groups and a difficult task to others. The easy and difficult tasks may be subdivided into those that have only one task and those that are divisible into a number of tasks. So far, we have a need for four experimental categories. If we added the category of sex of group members into all-male, all-female, and mixed-sex groups, we would need twelve experimental categories. The addition of one more variable—groups of three or five persons—would call for 24 experimental categories. You can see that the experimental categories quickly expand, dramatically increasing costs.

Why Experiment?

Nonscientists often look upon experiments, particularly laboratory experiments, with a great amount of skepticism and disdain over the relationship between "real life" and the experiment. Such individuals perceive that experiments are superficial and artificial creations of real-life scenarios. While a poorly designed laboratory experiment may not create realistic and relevant social situations, *social scientists have often demonstrated that their experiments are so realistic that ethical social scientists refuse to conduct those same experiments again.*

Experiments who employed the classic set of Asch conformity experiments asked individuals to make judgments of length of the following types of lines:

A _____

B _____

Although any person with normal vision and intelligence can tell that line B is the longer, the Asch experiments had added a demonic twist to the judgment process. Unbeknownst to the participants in the experiment, each was the only individual in a group who was a true subject. The others were paid confederates who would state that line A was longer. Some individuals became quite upset at their apparent inability to judge length correctly (by group standards). Psychologists stopped performing Asch-type experiments because of the quite real psychological discomfort they produced.

In another classic study, Haney, Banks, and Zimbardo (1973) randomized normal college students from Stanford University into a group of "prisoners" and "guards." This mock-prison experiment quickly degenerated into a pathological state in which mock prison guards invaded the mock-prisoners' privacy, oppressed the prisoner-students, and harassed them with constant surveillance. The researchers aborted the planned 15-week study after three weeks because of its gruesome simulation of prison life.

A second objection to experimentation relates to the experimental creation process: Experiments are often extremely difficult to design and, once designed, time-consuming to carry through to completion. As Aronson and Carlsmith (1968) point out,

> Typically a single person must be seen for an hour or two by an experimenter and one or more assistants or confederates. Frequently the experimenter goes to elaborate lengths to set the stage, motivate the subject, and, on occasion, to deceive him. After expending all of this time and effort, the investigator may obtain a single datum, perhaps something as simple as a "yes" or "no" response.

Given all the trouble an experiment normally takes, why not simply observe actual social behavior or survey attitudes and behaviors? The fundamental weakness of any nonexperimental study is its inability to specify cause and effect. One can find correlations galore between variables in nonexperimental science, but correlation alone never proves causation. *The experiment is the only method where the researcher can unambiguously attribute a change in one (the dependent) variable to another (the treatment or independent) variable.* Furthermore, the true experiment provides "the opportunity to vary the treatment in a systematic manner, thus allowing for the isolation and precise specification of important differences" (Aronson & Carlsmith 1968:9).

True Experimental Designs

Many individuals use the term "experiment" much too loosely. The original meaning of an experiment is quite broadly defined as anything someone experiences or observes. Even the esteemed Oxford Dictionary does not adequately define the experiment as it pertains to the sciences, instead calling it "a tentative procedure" or "a means to ascertain or establish by trial (a fact, the existence of some thing)." The true experiment in the social and behavioral sciences is anything but tentative; and although it uses trials, those trials establish not fact but causality.

The goal of true experimentation is to vary the relevant independent variables while eliminating the effects of other variables. The basic designs treated in this section are the only research designs that currently satisfy this goal. Students often mistakenly believe that experiments are defined by the place in which researchers often perform them: the laboratory. However, this is not true. Experiments may be easier to run in a laboratory, but experimentalists have run numerous true experiments in classrooms, military camps, prisons, and other natural (that is, outside the laboratory) settings.

There are two keys to the proper definition of true experimentation: The first is randomization of the individuals, groups, organizations, or whatever unit that the experimentalist uses; the second is random assignment of some experimental treatment to some of those randomized units, and lack of such assignment to the rest. Each of the following true experimental designs has those two elements. We can place experimental, quasi-experimental, and non-experimental designs on a continuum of more to less control over the independent and dependent variables. Randomization gives the researcher the most powerful means of controlling such variables.

Planning and Conducting Experiments

This section presents the conception of concrete experiments, from operationalization of the original hypothesis in experimental form through postexperimental procedures. As Aronson and Carlsmith (1968:37) state, "ideas—even interesting ones—are cheap in social psychology. The important and difficult feat involves translating a conceptual notion into a tight, workable, credible, meaningful set of experimental operations." Aronson, Brewer, and Carlsmith (1985) point out that experimentation involves four stages: (1) setting the stage for the experiment, (2) constructing the independent variable, (3) measuring the dependent variable, and (4) planning the postexperimental follow-up. This section discusses each stage in turn.

Setting the stage

Although William Shakespeare said "All the world's a stage," we all recognize that some stagings appear more realistic than others. Just as professional acting companies generally produce more realistic settings than amateur ones, some experimental settings appear more realistic than other ones. Particularly in the case of laboratory experiments, experimentalists recognize the necessity of designing credible experimental stagings because their subjects are intelligent, inquiring individuals.

The analogy to theatrical staging is an apt one. Few successful experiments involve hastily or ill-thought-out designs. Generally, experimenters will spend considerable time and effort setting up the experimental stage to mirror some aspect of everyday life. The experimenter will consider appropriate props; plausible scenarios, introductions, and exits; rehearsals; and "scripts" or "cover stories" with well-thought-out lines that the experimenter will commit to memory. The classic Haney et al. (1973) mock-prison experiment employed such props as prisoner uniforms with numbered identification, guard uniforms, beat sticks, badges, and rooms with jail-bars; and the opening scenarios included reading of "prisoner's rights and obligations."

Because the design of convincing experimental stages consumes much thought, time, and money, once experimenters have designed a sensible, plausible staging, they often continue to use it with only slight variations for decades. The work of Joseph Berger at Stanford (see a summary in Berger, Rosenholtz, & Zelditch 1980) stands out as a classic case of an experimenter who, after designing a clever experimental staging for the effects of status expectations, has continued not only to employ similar designs over three decades now, but has turned out numerous PhD students who also continue to use the same experimental setting as Berger. Briefly, Berger designed a bogus test called "Contrast Sensitive" that purportedly measures a hypothetical new "ability." In actuality, after taking this bogus test, the experimenter randomly informs participants that they are either high or low in Contrast Sensitivity. In later stages of the experiment, the experimenter tells the participants that they will work on a group task with clear success and failure indicators. Again, in reality, the experimenter randomly assigns them a bogus success rate.

Because of the complexity of each part of the experiment, participants have no way to evaluate Berger's test and success scores other than their apparent plausibility. Decades of research with this design attest to how seriously experimental participants take it. Former participants state that they took seriously the assigned high and low performance expectations: They believe that if they were assigned a higher Contrast Sensitivity score than their partner, "My score is higher than his, so if we disagree, I must be right and he must be wrong. If we are to succeed at this group task, therefore, I need to stick to my position." Berger's test insures the two subjects will be in constant disagreement over how to resolve their disagreement. The simplicity of Berger's staging is quite appealing; it allows for easy replication and variation. In the process, it has continued to produce a wealth of interesting theory concerning such sources of status as age, sex, race, physical attractiveness, objective competence, signs of dominance, and socioemotional behaviors.

Sociologists may have an advantage over psychologists in staging experiments because participants are all too ready to read psychological—but not sociological meaning—into experiments. In Berger et al.'s (1980) case, for example, participants mislead themselves into to thinking in terms of their own "ability" rather than the social context or structure built into Berger's design of interpersonal conflict. Participants in social experiments focus on individuals as individuals; they rarely consider such important factors as size of group, inherent conflict or cooperation, group interdependence, coalition formation, structures of rewards and costs, and degree of individual centrality in groups. For this reason, a small but significant number of sociologists such as Berger have found ingenuous means of studying group structures and processes with experiments.

Aronson et al. (1985) assert that many experiments involve deception; however, this deception may be less necessary in social experiments than psychological experiments for the reasons stated above. That is, in the Western world, we are so conditioned to look for individual causation that we rarely consider causes due to social context. In effect, participants deceive themselves—rather than social experimenters deceiving participants—when participants fail to consider social causation. As more evidence of this, consider the long line of research started by the late Robert Emerson at the University of Washington. As with Joseph Berger's work, Emerson pioneered experimental studies of power distribution and social network connections that his former colleagues and students continue (see Yamagishi, Gillmore, & Cook 1988 for an example).

The standard design in this Emersonian style of experimentation is to be honest, at the *individual* level, with student recruits: The experimenter tells them the experiment concerns an interest in money as a motive for taking part in an experiment. (This is true: In fact, recruits make between $15 and $30 dollars in trading.) The experimenter gives all volunteers a brief orientation in which they learn how to operate a computer terminal to make their individual financial transactions. However, at the *interactive* level, subjects have only partial information. They know only how many resources their partners receive after each trade; they never know the actual profit their partners made, nor do they know the actual experimental constraints on exchange opportunities that the experimenter controls.

The Emersonian and Bergerian experimental designs illustrate my point: Volunteers find individual-level aspects of experiments so salient that they normally disregard the social structural variables that experimenters design. Therefore, sociologists rarely need worry about volunteers "soc'ing out" an experiment as psychologists need worry about their subjects "psyching out" theirs.

Operationalizing the independent (or treatment) variable

The experimenter, in the conceptualization of the independent variable, must first ask what specific dimension(s) exists for the independent variable (experimental treatment). Part of this question concerns the dimension of the *possible variation* inherent in the variable. If the researcher is interested in the effects of power, then he or she should determine operationally how to *manipulate* both low and high amounts of power. In the Yamagishi et al. (1988) experiments, power was manipulated through control of the number and quality of individuals to whom one passed information or from whom one received information. This is because distance from a point of connection affects local scarcity of particular resources, and because individuals with alternative sources of a scarce resource have more alternatives (power) than those without alternatives. Because social connections beyond the computer terminal were transparent to volunteers, they had no idea that some volunteers had more alternative sources of resources than others or that some individuals were further down the chain of resource distributions.

It is important that the experimenter randomize which participants receive the treatment(s), as was true in the Yamagishi et al. experiments. While this may sound obvious, one does not have to search far in the literature to find examples of experiments that are not true experiments. Christie and Geis' (1970) book, *Studies in Machiavellianism*, speaks of eleven "experiments," none of which randomizes the treatment or independent variable. (In fairness to Christie and Geis, they never intended to show causal, but rather only correlational, relationships through these eleven *studies*.) Nevertheless, many researchers confuse readers with the use of the word "experiment" when they should use "study," because the experiment implies direct knowledge of causality while other types of research do not.

The pseudorandomization pitfalls (Aronson & Carlsmith 1968:40–42) are: (1) measuring the independent variable—for example Machiavellianism—and then looking at what happens to low and high Machiavellians under laboratory conditions; (2) allowing participants to assign themselves to the experimental conditions, as when Christie and Geis (1970:212) allowed participants to choose whose responses in an experimental group they wished to try to guess; and (3) the most subtle form of nonrandomization assignment of participants which occurs in experiments where the researcher randomly assigns participants to experimental treatments, yet the researcher finds his or her independent variable has not been powerful enough to discriminate dependent variable effects.

Then the researcher performs an *internal analysis* of the data by separating participants into two groups (those upon whom the manipulation seemed to work and those upon whom it did not) to check for the success of the treatment manipulation. Obviously, this is not random assignment, although one often has to read the experimental procedures closely to find out that a particular researcher used internal analysis. The most proper use of internal analysis would be in pilot-testing stages where the researcher is attempting to uncover the variable operationalization that sufficiently discriminates the behavior desired of participants in each experimental treatment.

The second question the researcher should ask of any operationalization concerns how to best present the experimental treatment(s), so that it has maximum impact on subjects. Most experimenters would agree that tasks that have a high amount of experimental realism and are motivationally engaging are preferred in terms of their impact on participants, as compared to having only a simple set of instructions read to the participant (a mistake often made by neophyte experimenters).

A third question concerns how "to prevent subjects from realizing the effect this variable is supposed to have on [their] behavior" (Aronson & Carlsmith 1968:42). Participants may act as "good" or "bad" subjects if they can guess "appropriate" behavior. Experimenters prefer events that participants cannot connect with the experiment: Christie's use of participants as "experimenters" when actually these persons are actually subjects; network connections that computer terminal hookups make transparent (Yamagishi et al. 1988) ; or an "accident" such as in Darley and Bateson's classic (1973) study of altruism. In this last experiment, Princeton Theological seminarians who served as participants delivered an "important" message across campus. There were two treatment conditions: one in which the message should be delivered "immediately" and another in which delivery time was not mentioned. On the way across campus, the experimenters tested the participants' good Samaritanism by passing over the spot where a confederate was lying, appearing to be badly hurt and bleeding. Seminarians in the immediate-delivery condition generally passed quickly by the victim while those in the no hurry condition stopped.

In the presentation of the experimental treatment, the experimenter wants to be reasonably sure to standardize participants' understanding of instructions. Because participants may differ in their need for comprehensive instructions, Aronson and Carlsmith (1968:48) recommend that in the interests of replicability, the experimenter keep a record of exactly what the experimenter said to each. Note that this recommendation seemingly contradicts Wiggins' (1968) stated belief in the need for standardized experimental treatments. Yet, we can see that there is often a conflict between standardizing experimental treatment and standardizing the participant's perception of that treatment. Obviously, the participant's *perception* is what we usually wish to standardize in such cases of conflict. Pilot tests are critical in assessing the adequacy and convincingness of any such experimental treatment.

Operationalizing the dependent variable

Aronson and Carlsmith (1968:56) state that

> it should be clear to the reader that the greater the degree of commitment demanded of the subject by the independent variable, the more confidence we can have in our experiment. For example, we would have a great deal of confidence that an experiment really involves antecedents of aggression if the experimenter reports that an experimental treatment induced more subjects to punch him in the nose (or even to volunteer to "meet him outside") than a control group. We would have far less confidence if the experimental treatment resulted in a higher rating of perceived feelings of aggression as measured by a questionnaire.

Therefore, the question of whether to measure the dependent variable by questionnaire, interview, or behavioral measures should hinge on the nature of the independent variable's strength. Due to the reactivity possible from the participant's knowledge of being tested, disguised or unsuspicious measures are an advantage. We have more confidence in a study of attitude change of prejudice against blacks by Rokeach and Cochrane (1972) in which the National Association for the Advancement of Colored Peoples (NAACP) sent letters asking for contributions at periods ranging from several months to a year after the experiment, than in a simple paper-and-pencil study of prejudice.

As previously indicated, it is wise to try to eliminate participant awareness of treatment conditions and dependent variable measurements—what is termed *blind treatments*. However, it is also important to keep the measurers unaware of the specific experimental treatments each participant is in and their hypothetical effects—known as *double-blind conditions*. Further safeguards include *triple-blind conditions* in which subjects, measurer, and experimenter do not know to what treatment each subject has been assigned. The reason is that the measurers or experimenter may unwittingly communicate his or her own biases.

Planning the postexperimental follow-up

All too often participants label the experimenter, at worst, an "academic imperialist" and, at best, an "ingratiating person." We sometimes forget that the volunteers in our research have done us a large favor by submitting their valuable time and energy in our behalf. Often, we show a double standard toward, and ingratitude for, their services by our willingness to do almost anything to obtain their services; then, once the experiment is finished, we leave them without any benefits or explanations.

We should be building a more positive image of ourselves through post-research explanations to our participants about how the data have benefited us (and hopefully our participants) in other ways than helping some college professor gain tenure through obscure publication. Such simple practices as sending a personal "thank you" note to respondents and participants help increase positive attitudes toward future research. Second, where potential benefits to participants (findings of "interest") are apparent, or asked for in return for the participant's services, a short summary of key findings without jargon not only helps to build understanding about the value of social science among the lay public, but also helps gain more secure sources of future research populations. Indeed, by contrast, researchers have found it increasingly difficult to research certain populations because of lay perceptions that researchers have "milked" them without offering any return for their own investment of time and energy.

In the case of the postexperimental interview, the volunteer needs more than just a full explanation of the experiment. The experimenter will want to determine, through a postexperimental interview, the participant's reaction to the experiment and will probe to see if the experimental procedures worked, and if they work, how the participant perceived them. The experimenter should gradually draw out any deception in the experiment, so that the participant has a good understanding of what the experiment did and why he or she did it. One of the most useful techniques is to ask the participant how the experiment could be made more credible, pleasant, and so on. This procedure may actually help improve the experiment, as well as giving the researcher cues as to whether he or she must spend more time in undoing harm done by experimental procedures. Finally, in concluding the postexperimental debriefing, the experimenter should attempt to convince the participant not to reveal experimental procedures to anyone.

Ethical considerations and deception

The position stressed in Appendix A is that the scientist must be concerned with the physical health and mental well-being of participants. Therefore, the researcher has an obligation to avoid any deceptive or other measures that cause discomfort whenever possible. Experimenters have no special privilege to extract data under false pretenses nor to expose individuals to physically or psychologically damaging situations.

There is a constant tension between experimental impact and control; the experimenter ends up sacrificing one for more of the other. It, therefore, is usually necessary to compromise. In other words, one may have to give up some impact of experimental treatment (less anxiety-provoking initiation rites) and, therefore, some control over participants rather than giving up the idea of experimentation (in this instance, the area of initiation rites). Experimenters can usually discard extreme experimental treatments and devious cover stories without seriously biasing experimental results.

Of course, "blind" experimental treatments and placebo controls are also deceptive devices that the experimentalist may consider foregoing. In blind-treatments, the experimenters should consider informing volunteers that he or she will employ treatments in which the volunteers do not know what treatment (if at all) they received. Fortunately, many experiments pose no such ethical questions. In many experiments the experimenter unquestionably preserves the safety of the participants safeguarding their dignity and privacy. Regardless of the ethical implications, the experimenter must always balance the extent to which new knowledge may benefit all concerned parties against the ethical implications of the experiment.

Classic Experimental Designs

The classic experimental design, often known as the pretest-posttest control group design, takes the following form:

Time 1	Time 2	Time 3	Time 4
Randomization of units* into:			
Group 1	Pretest(0_1)	Experimental treatment(X)	Posttest(0_2)
Group 2	Pretest(0_3)	No treatment	Posttest(0_4)

*Units may be individuals, groups, even nations. In actuality, there are many more than one unit randomly assigned to "Group 1" and "Group 2."

The classic experiment randomizes units into two subsamples: one which will receive the experimental treatment (Group 1, above) and a control group (Group 2) which does not receive the experimental treatment. Randomization of units into two groups makes both subsamples as nearly alike as is possible in the originally condition before pretesting. To insure that both groups are initially equivalent, the experimenter measures similarity of the two groups on the dependent variable during the pretest. After pretesting, the experimenter introduces the presumed causal factor (independent or "treatment" variable) into the experimental subsample, but withholds it from the control subsample. At some later date the experimenter takes posttest measurements or observations of the dependent variable. The experimenter then compares changes in the two subsamples according to differences in pretest minus posttest scores.

$$0_1 - 0_2 = d_{E(xperimental)}$$
$$0_3 - 0_4 = d_{C(ontrol)}$$

If the subsample differences (d_E and d_C) are significantly different, the experimenter infers that the experimental treatment is the cause of the difference. When the experimenter has rigorously followed the procedures outlined above, he or she can rule out most of the threats to internal validity presented in Chapter 4 as rival explanations of the experimental difference. It is important that you understand why. Assuming the researcher pretested and posttested the experimental and control groups at the same times, one can rule out history as an explanation of the differences because any historical events that affected d_E would also have had to have affected d_C.

A note on randomization as a procedure in experimental methods is crucial because of its widely misunderstood nature and functions in experimental control. Randomization is based on the employment of strategies using chance or probability. Researchers randomize to eliminate as much systematic bias or error (threats to validity of their findings) as feasible. Another way of stating this principle more positively is to say that they wish to achieve as much preexperimental equivalence (*not* equality) of groups as possible. Each participant should have an equal chance to be in any condition of the study. If the groups are preexperimentally equivalent, only the experimental treatment can logically explain any differences between the experimental and control groups. This is because randomizing subjects into each group fairly insures that equivalent numbers of participants in each condition will become bored with the experiment, try to "psych it out," or be of the same age, race or sex.

Of course, there is a small probability that any given randomization of units into experimental treatment or control groups can give inaccurate representations of each other. If you play any game of cards, you know the chance of randomly drawing five cards from the same suit is possible but infinitesimally small; the odds are also slim of drawing nonequivalent experimental and control groups in experiments. However, the only means of obtaining similar experimental and control groups is through randomization. Furthermore, the researcher will normally have some measure (the pretest) of how accurately each group actually mirrors the other through observations or measurements taken prior to the introduction of the experimental variable. If these pretest scores (0_1 and 0_3) are similar, the experimenter gains confidence that the subsamples indeed start out equivalently on the dependent variable. If the scores are dissimilar, then the experimenter must either consider the experiment invalid and scrap it or take the differences into consideration when interpreting results.

A second issue in randomization has to do with *matching* procedures. Some researchers, due either to lacking the experimental control needed to randomize or to ignoring randomization, match units on the dependent variable (they might insure that the same number of lower-class participants were in each group if they wanted to study class status as a variable). The researcher who matches units should—at the very least—randomly assign each pair of matched participants to the experimental and control conditions through the tossing of a coin or some equivalent procedure. Matching does reduce alternative explanations through the little control introduced through matching over one (or more) variables. Nevertheless, matching cannot control for all of the relevant factors that may influence the experimental results in the way that randomization would. Although matching procedures may often have to be substituted for randomization, keep in mind that the research design will no longer be a true experiment.

How does the researcher go about randomizing units into each subsample? One of the best ways would be to assign each unit an arbitrary number (1, 2, 3, . . . n). Then, with a random number generator built into many currently available personal computers, one could draw those 1 to n numbers. As they were drawn, the first would go into the treatment group, the second into the control group, and so on, alternately, until one had placed all numbers in one or the other pool. Another variation would be to use the random number generator to assign arbitrary numbers to each unit. Those units with even numbers would go in one group, and those with odd numbers would go in the other. Whatever the method, it is important that the experimenter not use human judgment in the selection process. The best means of insuring randomness is to use a modern random-number generator.

A few years ago Smith (1985) was interested in the improvement of observational accuracy. This is an important area of research in part because of the use of witnesses in court rooms. Students in Introductory to Sociology sections were randomized into experimental and control groups. As a pretest, all participants viewed a videotape and then took a written test to determine how accurately they had observed what people said, what people did, and how people looked on the videotape. The following week, experimental participants were given special instructions in making more accurate observations—which were not given to control participants. During the third week, the participants took the observational accuracy test, previously used as a pretest, now as a posttest. The results indicated the treatment had a small positive effect, in that experimental participants did slightly better on posttesting than did control participants.

Contrast our confidence in the causes of the above observational accuracy treatment with a nonexperimental method used to treat bulimia in female patients (Bower 1987). Bulimics are individuals who have episodes of binge-eating, accompanied by feelings that the binges are abnormal and cannot be controlled. Depression and anguish, as well as induced vomiting, often follow a binge. Some bulimics employ extreme diets, constant exercise, or laxatives to lose weight. Rather than randomize bulimic patients into normal control and experimental groups, a psychiatrist, David B. Herzog, (as Bower reports) assigned each bulimic patient her own treatment plan which included individual, group, and family psychotherapy, antidepressant medication, and nutritional counseling. Based on pre- and posttreatment interviews with patients, Herzog concluded that 22% of the patients did not improve after 18 months of treatment.

The Herzog study is a classic case of experimental ignorance typical of persons not trained in experimental logic. Without randomization into the standard treatment and control groups beforehand, we are left with no effective comparison group—the control group. If 22% of the patients did not improve with treatment, we are left wondering what percentage would not have improved with no treatment at all. If 22% of a true control group had not improved, then his combination of methods would be completely ineffective— but we will never know. Herzog's shotgun approach to giving patients a little of every possible therapy also gives us no means of evaluating any one of them nor of the potential interaction effects of the combined variables. Ironically, Bower reports that Herzog's research group has been funded by the National Institute of Mental Health to conduct a similar study of 225 women with eating disorders, including 125 bulimics, over five years. Of course, you should know by now that an increase in sample size will not improve the quality of this research study; we will still be left wondering how to disentangle the effects of multiple variables and to what we should compare the patient histories.

Posttest-Only Control Group Designs

While researchers utilize the classic experimental design in most true experiments, some researchers forego the pretesting of control and experimental groups, which produces the following design:

Time 1	*Time 2*	*Time 3*
Randomization of units into:		
Group 1	Experimental treatment (X)	Posttest(0_1)
Group 2	No treatment	Posttest(0_2)

Even though the posttest-only control group design controls for initial similarity of the experimental and control groups through randomization, it cannot provide evidence supporting equality of each group *prior* to introduction of the experimental treatment because it has no pretest evidence to support the assertion that the two groups start out with similar dependent variable distributions.

Many experimenters agree that there is no substitute for the information supplied by pretest measurements, even though the posttest-only control group design removes the same internal validity factors as the classic experiment. This general agreement may well be ill advised because in many cases pretests *change* participants in unwanted ways through what are termed testing effects and reactive effects (see Chapter 4). For example, researchers (Smith 1983) interested in observational accuracy invariably find that when the researcher pretests experiment participants for observational skills that they perform much better than unpretested subjects upon posttesting. Pretesting apparently makes participants more sophisticated on later tests. Therefore, experimentalists no longer recommend pretests in this type of research. Ironically, social and behavioral scientists have found it troublesome to wean themselves of preexperimental measurements, while most physical and biological experimenters trust randomization by foregoing pretesting.

Isen and Simmonds (1978) creatively used the posttest-only design to demonstrate how good mood can facilitate everyday helping behavior. As an inducement of good mood they *randomly* "planted" a dime (the treatment) in the coin returns of public telephones. They then observed the individuals who next used the public telephones. As the individuals left the booths, they approached the individuals and requested help in filling out a questionnaire on the individual's mood. Comparisons of participants who had found a dime versus those who had not showed significant differences in willingness to help the experimenter and elevation in the individuals' self-reported moods, as predicted. Note also how the Isen and Simmonds experiment illustrates how true experimentation can take place in naturalistic settings rather than just in laboratory environments.

Solomon Four-Group Designs

This design combines the classical and posttest-only designs:

Time 1	Time 2	Time 3	Time 4
Randomization of units into:			
Group 1	Pretest(0_1)	Experimental treatment(X)	Posttest(0_2)
Group 2	Pretest(0_3)	No treatment	Posttest(0_4)
Group 3	No pretest	Experimental treatment(X)	Posttest(0_5)
Group 4	No pretest	No treatment	Posttest(0_6)

Experimenters use it primarily to determine (and thus control for) any reactive effects of testing (pretest measurement or observation). By comparing the 0_6–0_3 difference with the 0_4–0_3 difference, the experimenter determines whether there were pretest effects. If the difference between these two differences is not statistically significant, the researcher concludes that there were no pretest effects, and vice versa.

The Solomon four-group design has a second advantage over the classical and posttest-only designs: It increases generalizability of results through the fact that the effect of the experimental treatment has four independent replications: 0_2–0_1, 0_2–0_4, 0_5–0_6, 0_5–0_3. The reason is that, even with randomization, the scores from the posttest-only and classical designs are subject to unstable fluctuations, caused by the same chance factors that occur when a card player

receives an improbably skewed distribution. Therefore, if these four comparisons are in agreement, the agreement increases the strength of inference that
the effects are not a quirk of chance. In fact, this is the design Smith (1985)
used to test for reactive effects of observational accuracy tests. In that study,
not only pretest and posttest effects of observational accuracy tests but also
pretest-posttest interaction effects were demonstrated.

Because of the fact that the experimenter needs twice as many participants and groups as in the other two types of experimental designs, it is an
expensive venture. Therefore, few researchers use this design unless they suspect reactive effects of pretesting. However, because replication is such an
essential component of science, experimenters ought to consider it more often
than they do.

Factorial Designs and Statistical Interaction

In each of the experimental designs illustrated so far, note that there are two
essential requirements: (1) control over assignment of the independent variable, and (2) randomization of the effects of extraneous variables that might
otherwise confound the results. Factorial designs elaborate on the *number* of
experimental and control samples. There are two reasons for elaboration: First,
the experimenter is usually ignorant which, out of the infinite possible independent variables, may ultimately prove to be the most important; second, the
experimenter usually has no knowledge that any one independent variable will
exert its effects independently of all others. Therefore, factorial designs set up
each possible combination of two or more independent variables in classical or
posttest-only form. For example, a classical factorial design with two independent variables (X_1, X_2) would look like this:

Time 1	*Time 2*	*Time 3*	*Time 4*
Randomization into:			
Group 1	Pretest(0_1)	X_1, X_2 treatment	Posttest(0_2)
Group 2	Pretest(0_3)	X_1, treatment	Posttest(0_4)
Group 3	Pretest(0_5)	X_2, treatment	Posttest(0_6)
Group 4	Pretest(0_7)	No treatment	Posttest(0_8)

If the factorial design uses classic experimental pretests, the experimenter might find it convenient to "nest" a Solomon four-group design into the
factorial design to account for any pretesting effects. There is nothing really
mysterious about factorial designs and their analysis. They are simply a *group*
of classical (or posttest-only) experimental designs that employ at least two
independent variables and take into account the effects of all combinations of
the independent variables.

To understand independent variable interaction consider this common warning on Contact®: "Do not use this product if you are taking another medication containing phenlypropanolamine. Avoid alcoholic beverages while taking this product." Most of you know that two drugs that may be safe and even beneficial when taken separately, may kill you if taken together. This is what is commonly called an interactive effect. If the effects of two drugs were additive and separately beneficial, they ought to be doubly beneficial in tandem—but the fact that they are not doubly beneficial is a sign that something in the combination works against the merits of each drug taken singly. When the researcher observes an interactive by-product, he or she knows that the combined variable effects must be due to some truly new causal process outside the independent effects of each independent variable.

This logic holds in all research. Consider for a moment the Massey (1987) study of Mexican migration. Although it is a nonexperimental design, Massey found that the effects of one independent variable (ownership of land) had a probability of 0.008 of keeping Mexicans from migrants to the United States, and another (ownership of a business) had a probability of 0.920 of keeping them from migrating. If those effects were additive, we would expect that those Mexicans who owned both land and businesses would have a sum of $0.008 + 0.920 = 0.928$ probability of remaining in Mexico. However, the observed combined effects was much stronger: the probability was 0.998 of remaining in Mexico. Apparently, the combination of these two variables interacts to make Mexicans with both land and a business particularly unmovable. Furthermore, ownership of land was 115 times as powerful a deterrent to migration as was ownership of a business.

Because Massey could not randomize Mexicans into those who owned or did not own businesses and land, there is always the possibility of other alternative causal explanations that he could not account for in his research design. By contrast, a factorial design, where it is possible to use one, gives strong evidence against any alternative explanations of study results. The reason is that factorial designs start out with individuals randomized into four (or more) equivalent groups at the start. Therefore, any differences between groups must be due to the independent variables or some combination of them.

A factorial design is particularly suited for manipulating more than one variable to show such independent (called *main*) effects and combined (called *interactive*) effects. Often times those interactive effects are interesting and unusual in themselves. To get a feel for interactive versus additive effects, it is useful to diagram them as stereotypically illustrated in Figure 6–1.

The rules of thumb for recognizing interaction and additive effects from graphs are: If the lines are parallel, there are two main additive effects, as shown in Figure 6–1a. (If one line lies on top the other, then only one main effect exists.) If the posttest score lines intersect, cross, converge, or are not parallel as in parts (b) and (c) of Figure 6–1, then an interaction effect exists. Figure 6–1b indicates a weak interaction effect because the two lines diverge only slightly, while Figure 6–1c shows a strong interaction effect with both lines almost at right angles to each other.

However, this graphing technique is actually rather crude because it leads one to look for only main effects or interaction effects. In reality, many

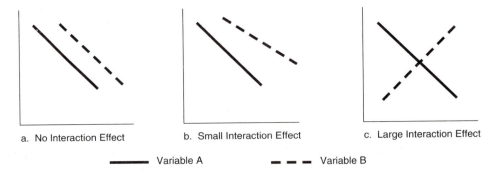

a. No Interaction Effect   b. Small Interaction Effect   c. Large Interaction Effect

———— Variable A   — — — Variable B

Figure 6-1.   Stereotypic interaction and noninteraction effects.

social science theories predict both main and interaction effects. Fishbein's (1980) model of the determinants of behavior predicts main effects of attitudes toward the behavior and norms as well as an interactive effect of the relative importance of the attitudinal and normative components.

Similarly, Heise's (1979) earliest model of attitude change and stability predicted that our evaluation of some individual who acts in some way toward some other person includes two main effects and one interaction effect. The strongest effect on our impressions, it predicts, is the main effect of the behavior followed by the main effect of our original impressions concerning the actor. However, it also predicts a significant effect of an interaction between the actor's behavior and whomever the object of action was. Intuitively, this makes sense. Consider the way you feel toward the object in the following two sentences:

The judge sentenced the burglar.
The judge sentenced the lawyer.

Certainly we feel different about situations in which persons of respect are sentenced versus persons of disrespect. In fact, Smith-Lovin (1979) carried out a complex three-variable factorial design that confirmed numerous interaction effects predicted by Heise's work. And Smith-Lovin and Heise's (1988) ongoing work now demonstrates a very complex set of 12 main and 22 interaction effects mirroring the complexity of human behavior and social organization.

Interaction effects are so important in science that you should pay attention to one last example. Consider the following attempt to use a factorial design to improve on the bulimic study which was criticized earlier. Suppose we wished to test the effects of an antidepressant medication and nutritional counseling on bulimia sufferers. We could easily set up the two-by-two factorial design. We would randomize the clinic patients into one of the four cells so that one-fourth would serve as controls by receiving no actual treatment—we could, in fact, given them the infamous placebo "sugar pill" treatment. Another fourth of the patients would receive true antidepressant medication; the third quarter would partake in counseling on proper nutrition and dieting; and the final group would receive both nutritional counseling and antidepressant medication.

We could then monitor our patients over some time period for specific measures of relapse: induced vomiting, feelings of depression or anguish, extreme diets, constant exercise, or use of laxatives to lose weight. In Figure 6–2 are some purely hypothetical numbers to allow us to test for main and interactive effects. If we look at differences in each cell of row and column raw scores, we often find rather complicated effects of each variable singly and in combination. For example, nutritional counseling singly has a hypothetical desirable main effect of decreasing episodes of induced vomiting from 36 to 30 times over the 18–month period—a decrease of six episodes, or 16.6%, of this undesirable behavior. The hypothetical main effect of antidepressant medication is greater—a raw score decrease from 36 to 21 equals a 15–episode reduction, or 41.7%. If the joint effects of nutritional counseling and antidepressant medication were additive, the bottom-right cell should have a score of 15 + 6 = 21 episodes, or a 58.3% drop in induced vomiting. However, the combined effect drop was much less than the effect of either treatment—from 36 to 31 episodes, or a 13.9% drop. Because a purely additive outcome would have produced a 58.3% drop but the actual combined drop was only one-fourth of that, this indicates a clear statistical interaction. Anytime the researcher discovers such interaction effects the results send a warning that the combined effects must have a different underlying causal structure than that of each variable singly.

The logic of two-variable interaction effects can be extended to any number of variables, but the number of effects and subjects that the researcher must examine increase rapidly. For example, in our hypothetical bulimia study, we might study the results of three main effects by adding a psychiatric treatment group to the nutritional counseling and antidepressant medication groups. This would mean that we also must examine three tables for two-way interaction effects: nutritional counseling with antidepressant drugs, nutritional counseling with psychiatric treatment, and antidepressant drugs with psychiatric treatment. Then, we need to examine a third three-way interaction table

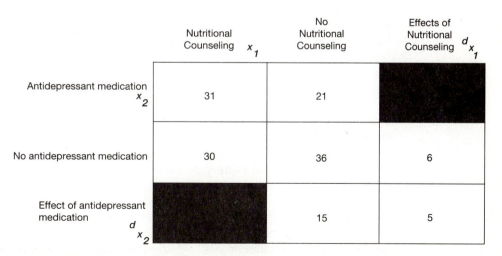

Figure 6-2.   Hypothetical analysis of joint effects of two experimental treatments.

for all three treatment variables. This is why it was stated earlier that researchers rarely do factorial designs with more than two or three treatments; the number of subjects and subanalysis needed quickly make factorial designs expensive and complicated. Nevertheless, because interaction effects are so common in the real world, the factorial design is a necessary tool in the scientist's workshop.

Problems of External Validity

The goal of science is to generalize findings to diverse populations and times. Such classic experiments as the Asch conformity experiments—with judgments of two lines of different lengths—show clearly the effects of group pressures to conform, but nevertheless raise questions of generalizability: Would we find the same results in another society and among non-college students in the United States? Would other types of tasks or measures of conformity produce similar results? Unfortunately, many experiments have well-known disadvantages or limitations to complete generalizability such as: problems of generalizability due to experimenter, participant, treatment, and measurement characteristics.

Experimenter characteristics

Wiggins (1968:401) summarizes a number of studies demonstrating that the experimenter's disposition, behavior, and such statuses as sex or age affect experimental participants. The participant's perceptions of the experimenter's statuses, behaviors, or attitudes may produce an experimenter-modeling effect consistent with the researcher's expectations or hypotheses. On the other hand, the experimenter's hypotheses may orient him or her to perceive the behavior of participants as consistent with the experimenter's hypotheses or even cause actual change in participants. In a classic demonstration of this phenomenon, Rosenthal (1966) had participants perform experimenter roles with Norway rats. Rosenthal told these "experimenters" that specified rats were "smarter" than other rats, even though he had randomly designated rats as "smart" or "dumb." His results supported the notion that the "experimenters'" preconceptions affected the rats' behavior in a way consistent with their expectations.

Fortunately, there are several ways to minimize experimenter effects, although it is nearly impossible to eliminate them. One can minimize the involvement of the experimenter through: (1) use of instructions to participants explaining that the experimenter prefers that they behave "normally"; (2) use of a naive substitute experimenter; (3) observer "blindness" as to which group (experimental or control) is being measured; and (4) populations of experimenters from which one randomly samples for each experimental condition. The first of these means is the least reliable because it makes salient certain aspects of the experimenter's role that may unduly influence his or her behavior. In fact, by telling individuals to disregard particular information, the experimenter is drawing attention to it. For example, when mock jurists in experiments are ordered to ignore testimony, they ignore the order (Allen 1988)! The fourth is expensive. The middle two are the most useful and most used because "blindness" is the only way to insure that the experimenter cannot unintentionally influence results. Double- and triple-blind experiments are relatively inexpensive and highly reliable means of controlling for potential experimenter and participant influences.

Participant characteristics

There are two problems in terms of participants: participant *selection* and *mortality*. Selection problems concern motivations for volunteering and cooperating in an experiment and participants' beliefs concerning laboratory experimentation. Many experiments rely on "volunteers" from college classrooms. The experimenter may motivate participation on such a basis through grades or monetary remuneration. Whatever the source of participation motivation, it is clear that some motivations may affect the participants to volunteer or cooperate. Although the researcher can control for the internal validity problem of participant selection through randomization, he or she cannot control for external validity (or generalizability) through randomization because people who volunteer or cooperate are mostly likely different from those who do not, regardless of whether they end up in a treatment or control group.

Second, the participant's beliefs concerning the experimental procedures and hypotheses are particularly plausible sources of experimental invalidity. While there are many different types of participant beliefs that can act as sources of experimental invalidity, one of the more critical types concerns beliefs about what the experiment is attempting to test. At least two factors may motivate an individual to "psych out" the experimenter: a desire to be a "good" participant by acting as one thinks the experimenter wants one to act, or an attempt by the participant to throw off the study results by acting in a manner contrary to that which the participant believes the experimenter wants.

One way of controlling for such variations between participants is to have a control group simulate (role play) the experimental group through pretending to be confronted with the independent variable. The experimenter may then assume that the independent variable causes between-group variation. However, there are no assurances that this will produce valid results.

Wiggins (1968:409) suggests that the experimenter educate the participants into the role of "good" participants through teaching them the value of the scientific approach and the value of behaving naturally. On the other hand, it might be necessary—in the cases of participants who the researcher suspects might use experimental deception, or who have too much trust in the experimenter—to point out one-way mirrors, observers, and other ostensibly deceptive devices or such artificial procedures as a practice shock. However, unless all participants are given the same treatment, the researcher risks defeating comparability of treatment and control groups.

The best way to control for participant characteristics is to design experiments where the participant is not aware of being in an experiment. If the participant is not aware of it, and the experimental setting seems natural, the participant will act normally as a matter of course. Christie and Geis (1970) pioneered several such experiments in which they asked participants to be "experimenters," when in actuality Christie and Geis were still experimenting on the participants. Similarly, one could easily design nonlaboratory experiments in which participants assumed the experimenters to be newscasters from a fictitious local radio station. Aronson and Carlsmith (1968:22) refer to this problem of participant characteristics as the problem of *experimental realism*—that is, the extent to which the experiment is realistic to participants, involves them, and forces them to take it seriously.

Treatment characteristics

In contrast to experimental realism is *mundane realism*: Whether or not the events that occur in the experimental setting are part of the realm of everyday experiences. Just because a participant finds the experiment personally engaging does not do much, if anything, for the experiment's external validity. Stanley Milgram (1963) suggests that participants who administered what they thought to be severe electric shocks to other participants did so, in part, because they perceived that the victim had voluntarily submitted to shock treatment. Therefore, while participants might think of severely shocking another person in real life as antisocial behavior, their perceptions of voluntary participation may or may not have liberalized their interpersonal behavior in the experiment.

Wiggins (1968:412–413) suggests that to achieve situational equivalence, or mundane realism, the experimenter would have to set up settings such that (1) participants do not perceive that all other participants have volunteered; (2) they are not aware that they are participating in an experiment; (3) they perceive the experimental task as related to some activity with which they have familiarity; (4) they meet with consequences similar to those they experience in ordinary situations; and (5) experimental ecological arrangements (seating arrangements, communication networks) are similar to everyday ecological arrangements. Often, to fulfill these requirements, only particular population settings and tasks would qualify for experimental manipulation. For instance, the experimenter might well conduct family decision-making experiments by using participants drawn from populations of persons with appropriate familial statuses, with the experiments conducted in living-room type settings while the participants engaged in such "normal" decisional processes as buying a set of encyclopedias.

Measurement characteristics

Observations, questionnaires, and interviews are commonly used in experimentation as measuring instruments. Observers and interviewers are particularly subject to changes in instrumentation—they learn, in the process of observing or interviewing, how to make different measurements, and their temporary motives (hunger, fatigue) may change the measurements. To the extent that they unwittingly make measurement changes during pretests and post-tests, they contribute to instrumental invalidity.

Measuring instruments, even if they are reliable, may be reactive; their use may cause changes in the participant's behavior. For instance, one-way mirrors, cameras, and observers may all cause the participant to act atypically. Second, exposure to the instrument in a pretest may affect later exposure during posttest because the participant's awareness of the pretest measurement process may make him or her more sophisticated or experienced in similar, later situations.

The time of measurement is also a potentially misleading variable. One may measure for effects of treatment before they have time to take; experimenters term these "sleeper effects" because they are well-known in research. Also, the experimenter may measure for effects of treatments after they have already waned, thus hiding the actual short-term effect. Kelly and McGrath (1988) explain how to strengthen findings through paying more attention to temporal factors.

Previously mentioned was the criteria of "blindness" to experimental conditions for participants. It is always wise to have experimental observers and interviewers "blind" as to the participant's experimental treatment status for similar reasons. Experimenters wish the measurer to be unaware of the type (or lack) of treatment administered, because such knowledge might influence the measurement process. Experimenters term experiments in which both participant and measurer are unaware of the participant's treatment status *double-blind*. Occasionally experimenters are also "blinded" to participant treatment conditions through the use of an outside party administering treatment, in which case the experiment is *triple-blind*. The more blind conditions, the less the possibility of extraneous human factors confounding experimental results.

The ideal social experiment would involve the administration of *convincing placebos* to control groups, just as medical experimentation often requires administration of "sugar pills" that, to the participant, appear to be the experimental drug received in the experimental condition. Convincing placebos restrict variation in participant responses, and they help better insure "blindness" of the experimental conditions; but their deceptive nature raises ethical issues.

Quasi-Experimental Field Methods

The true experiment may offer the most control in data collection, but nevertheless it has a number of inherent weaknesses as does any method: Experimenters may view participants as passive objects to manipulate; they may distort manipulations; or tear fragmentary bits of behavior from their natural context. There is also the problem of participants being aware that they are part of an experiment. Also, larger social groups, organizations, and processes often do not adapt well to the confines of controlled experimental conditions. Consequently, many social scientists have shunned the confines of the strict experiment for studies that only approximate experimental methods. What the researcher loses in control over variable manipulation and internal validity may be gained back in quasi-experimental field studies through less artificiality, reactivity, and deception, and gains in external validity from using more naturally occurring variables and participant populations.

Quasi-experimental studies differ in several important respects from true experiments. Although true experiments may often introduce treatment conditions that are unfamiliar to participants, quasi-experiments often can (and should) make more subtle modifications or interventions not as disruptive (unfamiliar) to the participants. However, such studies may raise ethical considerations concerning the deception of large numbers of individuals who are not aware that they are part of an experiment. In more generic terms, the researcher using quasi-experimental methods can control the *when* and *to whom* of *measurement*.

Unlike true experiments, however, there usually is little control over the *when* and *to whom* of *exposure* (randomization exposure) (Campbell & Stanley 1963:34). Occasionally, the field experiment may have full experimental control, as was true in the already mentioned (Darley & Bateson 1973) study of good Samaritanism among seminarians. The researcher should always chose the best research designs, where feasible. Therefore, if a naturalistic field study can be done with true experimental controls, the researcher will exercise more control over interpretation of findings, because the investigator can reject more plausible rival hypotheses. In the following discussion of types of quasi-experimental designs, we shall start with weak designs and proceed to a discussion of stronger designs.

The Interrupted Time-Series Designs

The generic form of the time-series study is as follows:

$$0_1 \; 0_2 \; 0_3 \; 0_4 \; X \; 0_5 \; 0_6 \; 0_7 \; 0_8$$

In between the periodic measurement of some group or set of individuals, 0_1 to 0_8, the treatment (X) occurs. The researcher assumes that any discontinuity in recorded measurements is an indicator of the effects of the treatment. History effects provide the most obvious weakness of this design because it has no randomized control group with which to compare its measurements. Therefore, the analyst has no means of knowing if the discontinuity is real or an artifact of the time periods chosen; or if it is real whether a control group's measurements would look similar or different.

The interrupted time-series data design is extremely common but by far the weakest of the quasi-experimental designs. I have graphed the well-known decline in U.S. union membership from 1973 to 1985 in Figure 6–3 to illustrate this point. As you can see, with the exception of 1978–1979, it has declined

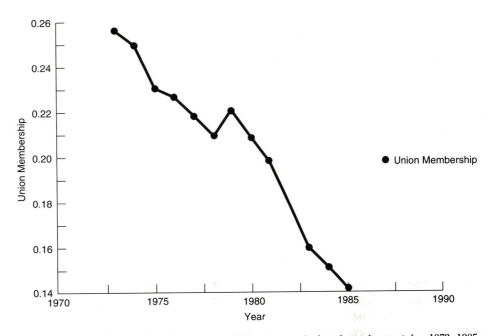

Figure 6-3.   Union membership as a fraction of nonagricultural employment for 1973–1985 based on U. S. Government current population survey data.

consistently since the early 1960s. Because the Democratic Party is traditionally union-backed and the Republican Party is employer-backed, we can test the difference made in 1981 with a change of both presidential and congressional control from Democratic to Republican. The data clearly do not support such a hypothesis: The slope of the pre–1981 decline is consistent with that of post–1981. However, because we have no group to serve as a control, we really have no idea what actually has generated this decline.

Farber (1987) insists that this well-known decline is due to increases in employer resistance to unionization, foreign competition, and new competition from deregulated industries. Each of these hypotheses is essentially untestable. First, data on employer resistance do not exist. Second, even if we compared data on union membership in other countries, they would be essentially meaningless. Unions in Japan are not interorganizational as is the Union of Auto Workers (UAW) for all auto makers in the United States, but are specific to each corporation. This creates interorganizational competition between Japanese unions that has no comparable form in the United States. Also, Farber says that interindustrial competition hurts unionization in the United States, but we might ask if that is true why it has had the opposite effect in Japan. Third, we would have to look for union data separated by regulated and deregulated industries in the United States. Even if we found such data, we could not be sure that some other factors—particularly historical—did not produce any difference we might find between each type of industry.

Figure 6–4 provides another example of an interrupted time-series de-

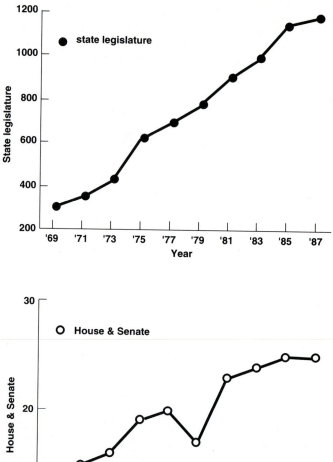

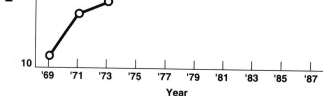

Figure 6-4.   Number of women serving (a) in state legislatures and (b) in the U.S. House and Senate.

sign. This one shows steady increases in number of women serving in state legislatures and the U. S. House and Senate. I picked this data because the selection of Rep. Geraldine Ferraro's vice-presidential candidacy during the 1980 presidential campaign influenced numerous political commentators to state that her candidacy would open the doors for more political officeholders among women. If this were the case, we should expect the post–1980 slopes to be steeper than for the pre–1980 slopes. However, we see that the slope of the number of women serving in state legislatures has continued to climb at a remarkably steady rate. The second graph for the U.S. House and Senate produces a less clear trend in part because the numbers are much smaller—there are only 335 seats that can be filled; and although the 235 house seats are up for election every two years, only one-third of the 100 senate seats are up for election at any two-year interval. Both of the subgraphs in Figure 6–4 are remarkably consistent in trends compared to many graphs of interrupted time-series data such as will be shown in the next section.

Multiple Time-Series Designs

Where it is possible to provide a comparison group (though *without* randomization of treatment), the researcher should use the multiple time-series design to give some indication of comparative, shared historical trends.

NOT RANDOMIZED INTO:	
Treatment Group	$0_1\ 0_2\ 0_3\ 0_4\ X\ 0_5\ 0_6\ 0_7\ 0_8$
Comparison Group	$0_1\ 0_2\ 0_3\ 0_4\quad 0_5\ 0_6\ 0_7\ 0_8$

Campbell and Stanley (1963) provide a classic illustration of the multiple interrupted-time-series design in their study of the effects of the 1955 Connecticut crackdown on speeding by comparing time-series data on traffic deaths before and after the crackdown. They point out many problems in looking at *only* the continuously graphed Connecticut data (if the graph had consisted only of the connected black dots) shown in Figure 6–5. While the data seem supportive of the crackdown's effect, other events could have caused the pattern; 1955 might have been a particularly wet or snowy year resulting in more dangerous than normal driving conditions and more accidents, because there is not much difference between 1951–1954 and 1957–1959 data. Obviously, other measures like randomly taken movies of highway traffic speeds and weather conditions would help in further clarifying the effects of the Connecticut reform.

Therefore, Campbell (1969) provided comparative fatality figures for four states bordering on Connecticut that provide some controls over weather conditions and other historical factors. (See Figure 6–5.) Without the control state data, it would be easy to conclude wrongly that the Connecticut crackdown did have an effect. But with the control state data, the analyst cannot be so sure: Control state data show a general decline over the entire period that, when the Connecticut data is smoothed, is not that dissimilar.

Jennings (1978) provides another interesting example of the multiple time-series design. He compared the effects of a group called Samaritan (which offers counseling and help to potential suicides in British and Welsh towns) on suicide rates in England and Wales. He noted that between 1963 and 1973, the suicide rates in these two countries fell from 12 per 100,000 to 8 per 100,000, which was unique for all of Europe. However, comparison of towns that had a Samaritan branch with those that did not showed no appreciable difference in

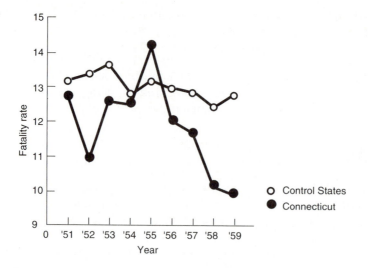

Figure 6-5. Control series design comparing Connecticut fatalities with those of four comparable states.

Source: D. Campbell, Reforms as experiments. *American Psychologist,* 24:409–429. Copyright © 1969 by the American Psychological Association. Reprinted by permission.

suicide rates between the two groups of towns throughout the period. Further analysis showed two likely reasons for the reduced suicide rates, unrelated to Samaritan influence: (1) reduced carbon-monoxide levels in the gas provided to homes, and (2) improved medical and psychiatric services. This study illustrates quite clearly the reasons for the need for multiple time-series analysis as a means of reducing alternative rival explanations missing from those in the interrupted time-series design.

Nonequivalent Control Group Designs

The nonequivalent control group design is one of the most widespread field experiment designs; it has equivalence to the classical design, except for the crucial factor of the researcher's inability to randomize subjects into treatments.

	Time 1	*Time 2*	*Time 3*	*Time 4*
Nonrandomized	Group 1	Pretest	Experimental treatment	Posttest
Nonrandomized	Group 2	Pretest	No treatment	Posttest

Because it lacks randomization, it is inadequate for ruling out such plausible internal validity rival hypotheses as history, maturation, testing, selection, mortality, and internal validity interaction effects. Nevertheless, because it is often impossible to randomize social behavior and institutions, the nonequivalent control group design does at least give some control, because the researcher at least knows that one group definitively received the experimental treatment while the other did not. The major problem for this type of design, therefore, is: How similar were the experimental and control groups at the time of recruitment? Pretest scores give some indication of the similarity of each group so that the more similar the test scores, the more internal validity we can assume. Compare the following two examples by this criteria of pretest score similarity. In the first one, the researcher was unable to pretest; while in the second, the investigators did have pretest measurements available.

Payne (1978) studied the cross-national diffusion effects of Canadian television viewers' attitudes and cognitions with this design. He attempted to overcome the problem of self-selection by isolating a small area of north central Minnesota that, because of its geographic location, was able to receive Canadian but not U. S. TV signals. (Remember that this was the pre-satellite dish era!) Then he compared this sample with areas that received U.S. TV only, and those receiving both Canadian and U.S. TV signals (which showed significant national differences on such issues as taxes, energy, and peace). In this quasi-experiment, Payne intervened in the *what* of treatment (Canadian only, U.S. only, or both types of TV). He had no control over the *when* of treatment (when viewers watched TV) nor over randomizing viewers into one of the three treatments. The differences he found could have been due to differences in when Canadians and Americans watched TV rather than differences in which TV programs they watched.

The second example had a pretest, giving us somewhat more confidence in the study results. The Center for Disease Control Vietnamese Experience Study group (1987) reported on a comparison of the effects of combat service in Vietnam in which they used enlistment in infantry, armor, artillery, or combat engineering units, and mental and intelligence tests as pretest scores to match 9,324 Vietnam Conflict combat veterans with 8,989 combat unit veterans who served in such places as North Korea, West Germany, and the United States during the same period of time. They reported a 45% higher death rate among Vietnam combat veterans in the five years after discharge. In addition, the Vietnam group had 72% more suicides, 93% more automobile fatalities, and 69% more poisoning deaths, mostly from drug overdoses.

The CDC researchers would like to conclude that excess stress endured while stationed in a hostile fire zone leads to excess mortality after the war, because past studies of World War II and the Korean Conflict survivors support the CDC Vietnamese Experience Study. These studies also indicate persistent elevation of drug-related deaths among combat survivors. A similar study of Australian survivors of Vietnam combat service again arrived at similar conclusions, according to the CDC report. However, the type of study does not support their conclusions. Although combat stress might have caused posttraumatic stress, the researchers cannot rule out a wealth of rival hypotheses. We are left with such nagging questions as: Did a peculiar virus in Vietnam or exposure to Agent Orange lead to behavior problems? Your guess is as good as the study group's. Only a truly randomized prospective experiment could uncover links between posttraumatic stress and eventual death rates.

Separate-Sample Pretest-Posttest Designs

This design is obviously similar to both the nonequivalent control group design and the classical design:

	Time 1	Time 2	Time 3	Time 4
Randomization into:				
Group 1		Pretest	*Probably* no experimental treatment	No Posttest
Group 2		No pretest	Experimental treatment	Posttest

This design is especially useful in studying *large* social units. For instance, the Icelandic government asked Payne and Peake (1977) to study the effects of the introduction of television in Iceland. Because TV signals cannot travel long distances, and satellite technology did not then exist, they found it possible to choose randomly which cities would receive the experimental treatment (TV stations). Payne and Peake pretested the non-TV station control group population for knowledge of such things as world and local affairs. After the introduction of TV stations to other areas, they posttested the treatment population for effects of TV. This procedure neatly avoided testing effects and reactive effects of testing because only the control group received the pretest and only the treatment group received the posttest.

The only major flaw in this design was the uncertainty as to whether certain members of the control group had exposure to the treatment variable. For instance, it might be possible for certain individuals to move between pretest and posttest from one city with a TV station to one without a station or vice versa. Or it is possible that individuals in a TV-station-less city might build a powerful enough receiver to gain access to signals from a distant city. Either way, the study illustrates that a control group may be "contaminated" fairly easily, confounding quasi-experimental results. Nevertheless, this design provides more assurance of high *external* validity than any other experimental or quasi-experimental method.

Separate-Sample Pretest-Posttest Control Group Designs

Campbell and Stanley (1963:55) suggested an expensive amendment to the separate-sample pretest-posttest design that considerably strengthens control over internal and external validity. The amendment is represented by the addition of two control treatments.

The total four-group design is known as the *separate-sample pretest-posttest control group* design. The beauty of this addition is that randomization creates equivalence at two levels not achieved in the former design alone. That is, in addition to Groups 1 and 2 being equivalent at Time 1 due to randomization, Groups 1 and 3 are similar at Time 2 (pretest) and Groups 2 and 4 are

Time 1	Time 2	Time 3	Time 4
Randomization into:			
Group 1	Pretest	*Probably* no experimental treatment	No Posttest
Group 2	No pretest	Experimental treatment	Posttest
Group 3	Pretest	No treatment	No Posttest
Group 4	No pretest	No treatment	Posttest

similar at Time 4 (posttest), with the crucial exception of Group 2's exposure to the independent (treatment) variable. An important consequence of these similarities and differences is that this design is the only design discussed in this chapter that satisfies all internal validity factors as well as some external validity factors. By contrast, a design with Groups 1 and 2 alone does not deal with important invalidity threats discussed in Chapter 4.

Nonexperimental Designs

In everyday life, scientists are unable to randomize individuals into different groups. Therefore, by comparison to true and quasi-experimental designs, the majority of study designs used in the social and behavioral sciences are necessarily deficient for causal explanation. The remaining six chapters dealing with the production of data rely heavily on these more primitive nonexperimental designs. Keep this fact in mind as you study Chapters 7 through 14. Although each of the methods has its place in the repertoire of social methods, they each suffer from an inability to produce strict causal explanations. In this section, three generic nonexperimental designs are presented, from least to most useful in reducing rival explanations, that are implicit in the methods presented in Chapters 7 through 14. When using the methods in those chapters, social scientists prefer to supplement their use with a nonexperimental design that most helps reduce rival explanations.

One-Shot Studies

The most frequent design in the social sciences is the *one-time* or *cross-sectional* survey; it is also the design with the least scientific value. The one-shot study may be represented by

Possible introduction of treatment variable (X)	Posttest

At the worst extreme are one-shot case studies of single instances of some phenomenon. However, when such case studies do not have explicit cases of comparison, we are left wondering whether the treatment or independent variable had actually occurred; and if it had occurred, we wonder what would have happened if the treatment had not been present. Most of the "evidence" supporting astrology and parapsychology has been of this type. Such studies usually give specific observations about particular events without comparable attention given to other, potentially nonconfirmable data. Figure 6–6 may shed some light on this logic. A case study of such infamous "seers" as Jean Dixon usually focuses on category *A*. It gives only details that support the possibility that the "seer" (*I*) has been able to make correct predictions about future events (*D*). Implicit in such discussions is the untested assumption that a nonseer (NOT *I*) could *not* do as well as the seer (cell *B* compared with cell *A*), but would end up with mostly nonsuccessful predictions (cell *D*). Further, the nonskeptic assumes that the seer would make fewer incorrect decisions (cell *C* compared to cell *A*) than by chance alone.

Likewise, psychoanalytic methods typically focus on Cell *A* (the effects of psychoanalysis on patient recovery rates) without proper attention to *comparative* recovery rates under nonpsychoanalytic means (cells *B* and *D*) or psychoanalytic recidivism rates (cell *C*). The point is that single-case studies (regardless of the fine detail collected) do not have adequate reference points or benchmarks for ruling out rival causal explanations. The minimum scientific requirement calls for at least one comparison with a case that did not receive the treatment variable.

Somewhat better than one-shot case studies are *one-shot correlational studies*. Most survey research falls under this heading. Nevertheless, regardless of sophistication of correlational analysis, correlation is only a necessary, not a sufficient, condition for causality. Indeed, correlational studies may be extremely misleading. One-shot correlational studies invariably show a direct relationship between age and prejudice: As one increases, the other increases. Only when the researcher accounts for education (older generations have less education) does it become apparent that aging does not cause prejudice. One-

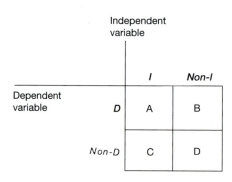

Figure 6-6.   A simplified two-variable, four-fold property space.

shot correlational studies (which make up over 60% of social science research) too easily involve confounding of the independent and dependent variables. As a result, researchers using one-shot correlational studies must be particularly careful not to fall into the trap of confounding independent and dependent variables.

For this reason, researchers who use correlational data turn to the special types of statistical analysis explained in Chapter 16. Although no statistical tool can replace randomization in causal analysis, the researcher finds such tools indispensable for helping to reduce the myraid of rival explanations in correlational data. Much of the recent advancement in statistical analysis in sociology has been directed toward improving causal analysis through what is called ordinary least squares regression. Because many of our variables are difficult or impossible to manipulate in truly experimental ways (age, sex, race), we often find it necessary to manipulate them statistically—as in the example of education, age, and prejudice above. The goal is the same in any case: We try to control as many rival alternative explanations for our data as possible given the data that are practical to collect.

Even so, even regression analysis will not necessarily overcome the problems of correlational analysis. Jones and Moberg's (1988) study well illustrates this problem. These investigators did a shotgun correlational analysis of 26 possible indicators of junior- and senior-high-school students use of smokeless (chewing) tobacco. Their analysis showed only two indicators (Caucasians and children living with both parents) with standardized regression coefficients of chewing tobacco use over 0.20. (Standardized regression weights are similar to correlations but they are better because they control for the effects of all other independent variables in the study, and their size shows the proportion of variation in the dependent variable that they explain.) Furthermore, the 26 "best" regression weights in their study explained only 24.6% of the total variance in smokeless tobacco use among teenagers. Essentially, this means that 75.4% of the total variance was unexplained. In spite of the fact that they used a noncausal means of analysis on one-shot correlational data that produced 24 of 26 insignificant standardized regression weights, Jones and Moberg absurdly concluded (p. 62) that "Substance use and abuse of legal and illegal drugs by adolescents have been shown to follow a progressive pattern in linear order of first use. . . . Smokeless tobacco may be considered a part of this behavior syndrome."

One-Group Pretest-Posttest Designs

Slightly better than the one-shot study is the following procedure:

Time 1	Time 2	Time 3
Pretest	Treatment variable	Posttest

Methodologists recommend this design only when *no better design is available* because it lacks a representative control group by which the researcher can make the necessary comparisons for eliminating rival alternative explanations. It is nevertheless better than one-shot correlational studies because the pretest-posttest measurement at least allows for a clear time order sequence—a necessary but not sufficient condition of causality.

Freedman, Carroll, and Hannan (1983) illustrate this in their study of organizational death rates. They researched the question of whether new organizations are more likely than old organizations to die by comparing organizational death rates in national labor unions, semiconductor electronics manufacturers, and newspaper publishing companies. As it turned out, each type of organization had quite different rates of dissolution for the same ages of each organization: Semiconductor companies were the most likely to die and unions the least likely.

These differences in death rates were so large that it became clear that age alone could not explain the disparities. Freedman et al. tried to introduce other controls into their analysis but found that they could not eliminate age disparities in death rates completely although they did find that size of organization was another likely factor in the organizational death rates. We can trace many of the problems in their study to the lack of randomization; organizations may die not only due to internal processes but due to environmental pressures; and they may die not only because of disbanding but because of mergers. Without randomization, it would be impossible to separate out these and other potential rival explanation of the observed organizational death rates.

Static-Group Comparison Designs

This design can be visualized as:

Time 1	Time 2	Time 3
Group 1	Treatment variable (X)	Posttest
Group 2	No treatment	Posttest

As you can see, this is similar to the posttest only experimental design, with the crucial deletion of randomized treatment and control groups. This lack of randomization is its Achilles' heel. That is, how participants are selected into comparison groups and how they select them out of the study or a comparison group are grave cause for concern in interpreting differences found between the groups. The nagging question is: Are such differences, or lack of them, due to actual differences or simply to the haphazard nature of each group's formation?

Most such static-group comparison groups studies use matching as an approximation to randomization. For example, Lehman, Wortman, and Williams (1987) became interested in the traumatic effects of sudden, unexpected loss of a spouse because it is the number-one killer of persons under age 45 in the United States—claiming approximately 150,000 victims annually. They used Michigan state records to locate every motor fatality in Wayne County, Michigan between 1976 and 1979. They then located potential subjects for two studies and asked for interviews in 1983. In the first study, they selected 39 bereaved individuals and matched 39 nonbereaved individuals for sex, age, income, education, and number and ages of children. The second study selected 41 pairs of bereaved parents and 41 matched pairs of nonbereaved parents.

After six to eight years had passed since the traumatic death, nearly all the bereaved subjects in both studies said the deceased continued to occupy their thoughts and conversations. Often these thoughts that produced hurt and pain in bereaved respondents yielded poorer performance as indicated by measures of general psychological functioning than matched comparisons. Lehman et al. concluded that lasting distress is a common response to sudden death of a loved one. However, they also noted that about half of the bereaved persons they tried to contact had either died or refused to participate in their study, and that most of those that consented to interviews were women. We can see the potential problems of history, maturation, and subject selection and mortality to which their study is left open, as in any static-group comparison design.

Similarly, my favorite case of misplaced causal attribution from the static-group only control group design comes from studies of the effects of "Type A" personality on heart disease. The earliest studies compared men who had had heart attacks with those who had not, and concluded that those who were classified as Type "A"—generally ambitious, time-conscious, aggressive, and inwardly hostile workaholics—were more likely to have experienced heart attacks than those they classified as Type "B," who were easygoing by nature. Ragland and Brand's (1988) replication of these earlier studies came out with the opposite conclusion: That Type "A" personality made one more resistant to heart disease. By now you should be able to identify plausible reasons for the inconsistency: None of the men were randomized into the Type A or B groups, the study directors of both studies were not blind to each group, and the studies were done after the fact. In standard terms employed since Chapter 4, these studies lacked crucial means of ruling out history, maturation, testing, interaction of testing and independent variable, and other crucial internal and external validity factors.

The reasons why standard statistical methods of testing for causality do not always solve problems of causal analysis have become clear to methodologists only recently. Methodologists have long known that simple statistical regression analysis assumes one-way causation when, in fact, many causal situations are reciprocal in nature with A causing B and B causing A in return. Also, statisticians have demonstrated that errors in measuring independent and dependent variables can serious distort causal interpretations. More recently, however, Lieberson (1985) and Achen (1987) have pointed to two other serious problems: selectivity and censoring. (Selectivity has been discussed at length in Chapter 4.)

Simple regression analysis (sometimes referred to as OLS, for "ordinary least squares regression") yields misleading results when subjects choose their own levels of treatment, known as *selectivity*. Social scientists have collected a wealth of evidence that subjects who choose "treatment" differ from subjects who choose "control group" in ways that we cannot measure. These unmeasurable differences invalidate the OLS assumptions that the independent variables are uncorrelated with the unmeasured term. Achen (1987) illustrates this problem by referring to the theory that one measured variable—social class—influences the choice between private and public schools but does not influence mathematics achievement. He then suggests an interesting and plausible scenario in which some unmeasured variable which is correlated with social class—parental assessment of prospects for son's or daughter's success—affects both school selection and mathematics grades. That is, if parents pay the money for private education only if they think their children will do well in school, then the observed higher achievement of children from private schools might reflect students' unmeasured potential and not anything intrinsic to the private school treatment itself. In this way, Achen shows how OLS will make it appear as though social class affected mathematics achievement while underestimating the true effects of private schools.

The problem arises because at least two independent variables—social class and the type of school—are correlated with inaccurate variable measurements in the achievement equation. Worse yet, Achen demonstrates that none of the usual statistical indicators will show any signs of trouble. The general principle is: controlling for variables that affect selection but not the outcome itself exacerbates the inherent problems of selectivity. Therefore, researchers who add control variables to their regression equations can actually come to a conclusion opposite to the correct one.

The second problem Achen discusses is *censoring*: when subjects are absent from the field of observation altogether. This is equivalent to subject mortality, as described in Chapter 4. For example, consider the hypothesis that severity of crime predict rearrest or that severity of crime positively effects rearrest. These are actually impossible hypotheses to test under law enforcement systems that detain suspects while they are awaiting trial, because such suspects have no chance of being rearrested during their detention. In fact, law enforcement systems usually release only "good risks" during pretrial periods. Achen points out that a "good risk" release system *assumes* that serious offenders (rapes, murders) must be detained because they are more likely to commit new crimes than petty offenders (larceny), when in fact they may be less likely. The researcher needs a statistical control for the severity-release correlation that is unavailable under the detention system which amounts to a censoring problem. He demonstrates that without the introduction of such a statistical control, the researcher may wrongly conclude either that severity of crime does not predict rearrest or that more severe crimes lead to lower rearrest records. Whatever the case, we conclude that modern statistical methods do not completely solve the problem of causal inference.

Summary

Experimental methods provide the models against which we measure the validity of causal relationships. Yet, we have seen that, for ethical and pragmatic reasons, we must often relax experimental rigors. The issues of experimental *control* and *impact* provide crucial focal points in the design of research. True experimental methods are the most direct and sure means of disentangling causal effects from rival explanations because they have higher internal validity than other methods.

On the other hand, experimental methods have more problems with external validity than other methods. It takes much care and thought to design a true experiment with high generalizability in the everyday world. This is, in part, due to the multiple number of causes that exist in the normal everyday life. Many everyday occurrences have multiple causes that may not be additive but interactive. Although such experimental designs as the Solomon-four group design and factorial designs directly handle multiple causal analysis, such designs are expensive and complex. Nevertheless, social scientist have often demonstrated that true experiments are realistic and economical ways of gathering social explanations.

In the social and behavioral sciences, the term "experiment" is reserved for studies in which the researcher randomizes the participants into at least two groups. The reason is that the groups must start out exactly equivalent before the introduction of the treatment (independent) variable. Because randomization gives the researcher great power over initial group equivalence, we can be most confident that any difference in posttest score outcomes of the dependent variable is due only to the treatment effects.

Experimentation involves four stages: (1) setting the stage, (2) constructing the independent variable, (3) measuring the dependent variable, and (4) planning the postexperimental follow-up. First, experimenters spend considerable time and thought designing and rehearsing credible props, plausible scenarios, and scripts of experimenter introductions and exits. This process is so demanding that once a researcher produces a credible experimental staging, other researchers may continue using it for decades with only slight variations. Second, the experimenter must also operationalize the independent variable so that it taps realistic variation. Simply designing an independent (treatment) variable with appropriate variation is not enough: The experimenter must design the experiment so that the treatment group randomly receives the treatment while the control group does not. Another problem is designing the experiment so that the subjects do not realize the effects the treatment is suppose to have on their behavior. One of the best ways of doing this is to design experiments in which the subjects are "blind" to what treatment they have received. Another problem is designing instructions that standardize the participant's perception of the experiment. Third, the experimenter must design a realistic dependent variable for pretest and posttest measurements. As a general rule, we have more confidence in pretests and posttests that use behavioral measures than subjective pen-and-pencil measures. Fourth, at the end of the experiment, the experimenter needs to consider "cooling out" the subjects with postexperimental follow-up. Part of this task can be accomplished by sharing a short summary of findings with subjects. Another part of highly appropriate postexperimental procedures is to draw out any deception that the experimenter used, and to ask subjects for their thoughts on how to make the experiment more credible, pleasant, etc.

Methodologists classify true experiments into the classic experiment (pretest-posttest control group), posttest-only control group, Solomon-four group, and factorial designs. All of these designs use randomization into treatment and control groups to minimize such internal validity factors as history and maturation. Each design has its special uses: The posttest-only design simply leaves off the pretests in the classic design because of concern of testing and reactive effects of testing. The Solomon four-group design combines the classical and posttest-only groups primarily to show how much effects of testing and reactive effects of testing actually exist; but the four groups in this design also increase confidence in treatment effects, although it is an extremely expensive design. The factorial design introduces two or more treatment effects for the purpose of testing how strong each is, and whether or not the combined effects are additive or interactive.

The concept of variable interaction is highly important because many independent variables in the world around us have strange but important combined effects. Just as ingesting two prescription drugs separated by a week may be beneficial to your health whereas taking them simultaneously can kill you, many variables in the social world are also strangely interactive. Analysts call the separate effects of two independent variables "main effects," and the combined effects "interactive effects." Only the factorial design can directly disentangle main and interactive effects.

The main problem of experimentation is generalization to diverse populations and times. Four problems of generalizability (external validity) are: experimenter, participant, treatment, and measurement characteristics. Because experimenters may unconsciously influence the outcomes of experiments, methodologists recommend means of making the experimenter "blind" to each condition he or she observes. Similarly, participants who self-select themselves into or out of experiments damage generalizability. Again, the most assured means of controlling for participant characteristics is to design experiments in which participants are "blind" to the condition they are in. Treatment characteristics involves making experiments that have high mundane realism—that is, that appear to realistically mirror everyday situations and activities. Measurement problems are the final problem of generalizability. Because measurements and measurers may be reactive, methodologists advise making a third aspect of the experiment "blind"—the observers. However, none of the above recommendations can completely eliminate the problems of external validity; they simply minimize them.

To increase external validity, many experimenters counsel the use of quasi-experimental designs. In order of increasing experimental control, these are the interrupted time-series, the multiple time-series, the nonequivalent control group, the separate sample pretest-posttest, and the separate-sample pretest-posttest control group designs. The first three of these do not use randomization. The two time-series designs are weakest in controlling for rival explanations of results caused by history effects. The nonequivalent control group design is like the classical design except that it lacks the crucial element of randomization. This makes it particularly susceptible to criticism concerning internal validity. However, it does allow for knowing which group received the experimental treatment and which did not. This does aid confidence in results although the lack of randomization implies that those results could be due to nonequivalent samples.

The separate-sample pretest-posttest design gets around the internal validity problem of testing and reactive effects by giving the control group the pretest and the treatment group the posttest. Because this is one of only two quasi-experimental designs that employs randomization, it provides strong support for ruling out all internal validity problems. By adding two more randomized control groups in which one receives the pretest but no posttest and the other receives the posttest but no pretest, the researcher has a paradoxical situation in which a quasi-experimental design is available that is stronger in ruling out internal and external validity problems than any true experimental design.

The most used but weakest designs in social science are nonexperimental ones. The weakest of all designs is also the most used: the one-time or cross-sectional survey. The reasons for this are: First, because we have only a posttest score we cannot be sure if the independent variable actually came before the dependent variable in our analysis; second, we have no comparison group to use as a baseline for posttest changes. A somewhat better one-shot type of study is the one-time correlational study. However, this type of analysis requires specialized knowledge of advanced statistics and laborious employment of those statistics to approach the confidence in causal explanation the researcher gets from the more efficient experimental designs.

A slightly better procedure than the one-shot study is the one-group pretest-posttest design. Although this design is an improvement because the before-after nature of the pretest and posttest allow direct inference of causal effects, it also has no true control group for comparison. Such comparisons, if they showed a similar change from pretest to posttest scores, are crucial for determining true causality. Finally, the static-group comparison design is the same as the experimental posttest-only control group design except that it lacks randomization. Therefore, it has the same problems of all nonrandomized designs: The researcher does not know how participants were selected into or out of the comparison groups. Such plausible self-selection increases rival alternative explanations of results, and it makes attribution of observed effects to the treatment variable suspect.

Most quasi-experimental and some nonexperimental designs replace randomization with matching. However, you should know by now that matching is a much less elegant and a less sure means of ruling out plausible alternative causal explanations than randomization. Although randomization produces equivalent groups for all variables, matching can only produce equivalence over a few variables.

CHAPTER

7

Scaling Subjective Phenomena

Measurement stands, in fact, as the initial juncture between theory and . . . experience.[1]

Key Terms

Acquiescence bias

Campbell-bipolar scale

Category-rank scale

Extremity bias

Forced-choice scale

Guttman scale

Indice

Indirect measure

Latitude of acceptance

Latitude of noncommitment

Latitude of rejection

Likert-summated rating scale

Scale

Semantic differential scale

Sentence-syntax bias

Social desirability bias

Sociogram

Sociometric measures

Systematic response bias

Thurstone scale

[1]Margenau H. (1959) Philosophical problems concerning the meaning of measurements in physics. In *Measurement: Definitions and Theories*, (C. W. Churchman & P. Ratoosh, Eds.) New York: John Wiley, p. 163.

Study Guide Questions

1. What are the main purposes of creating scales from indices?

2. Explain the reasons for the basic rules for constructing subjective indices.

3. What are the main types of systematic response biases, and how do social scientists attempt to counteract their influence?

4. Why did Likert-summated rating scales replace Thurstone scaling in social research?

5. Compare and contrast the major assumptions, advantages, and disadvantages of Thurstone, Likert, Guttman, forced-choice, Campbell-bipolar, semantic differential, and the method of ordered alternatives scales.

6. What are the advantages and disadvantages of using indirect versus direct measures of subjective phenomena?

7. Explain the basic techniques used by social scientists to study perceptions of group ties?

Chapter 4 introduced the straightforward relationship between the number of items the researcher uses to measure some variable and that variable's reliability. Not only does using more than one item increase reliability, but larger numbers of items—up to a point—normally increase the validity of any measure. In other words, it is normally better to have more rather than fewer indicators of a variable. Researchers term each element or indicator of the research variable an *indice* or *index*. When they have some explicit means of combining these indices into a whole, they speak of a *scale*. An index is, therefore, a single operationalization of a variable, while a *scale* consists of *more than two* indices that have been combined into a single measurement through some procedural rule or rules.

Income is one possible indicator of social class. Other possible indicators might include education and occupation levels. Social researchers often combine such measures of social class into scales they call socioeconomic status (SES) by combining measures of occupation, education, and income. Suppose we wish to measure SES, and use occupation, education, and income with a crude ordinal measure of each (1 = high, 2 = medium, and 3 = low). A union leader might rank high on income but low on education and medium in occupation. An arithmetic mean of these three indicators for the union leader would yield a score of 2, which seems quite a bit more reasonable or valid than a score of 1 (Income), or a score of 3 (Education) as a measure of SES, because we would not expect his SES to be as low as that of an unskilled worker nor as high as that of a justice of the Supreme Court.

Measurement and scaling theory forms one of the most advanced areas of social research and has a long history of important inventions, many of which we all take for granted: voting and elections; censuses to aid taxation and levying of military forces; monetary systems to replace barter; the definition and labeling of social rank; the appraisal of personal quality or performance through contests, examinations, and grading systems; and the degree of excellence for meritorious performance or gravity of offense for criminal offense (Duncan 1984:39–112). Each of these social inventions has a history that goes back thousands of years and was a product of the best minds of the ancient Greek, Roman, and Chinese civilizations. Modern measurement and scaling theory is built on the foundations of these earlier inventions. However, it would be misleading to assume that any intelligent person can replicate a social scientist's observations. This might have been true early in the history of science, but these days, only the trained observer can replicate many of these very complex observations.

Every science uses physical measures of some kind: geometry capitalizes on the plane and solid angles; physics on mass and time; and chemistry on luminosity and electrical charge. Unlike the social sciences, most of the physical sciences have well established, powerful systems of measurement. However, many social measures and scales depend on such primitive scaling properties as nominal (respondent's sex, race, ethnicity) and ordinal (political radicalism, perceived happiness, occupational satisfaction) qualities discussed in Chapter 3.

This chapter discusses many relatively new scaling and measurement inventions that can improve the reliability and validity of our operationalizations. It also focuses on operationalizations of what people *say* they do, think, or feel. Bear in mind that that is often quite different from what they *actually* do, think, or feel, limiting the value of these methods. Usually, for reasons of reliability and validity again, the researcher combines several indices in some manner to represent a particular variable. The rest of this chapter will explicate procedural rules social scientists currently use in the study of various subjective phenomena. Various assumptions, positive features, and drawbacks of each procedure will be noted.

Characterizing the Variable's Domain

To design a measurement or scale, we first need to clearly delineate the domain of our variable. Chapter 3 provides a number of suggestions and rules for abstracting the various components of one's research variables. Exemplary research most typically involves a tedious but necessarily lengthy search of the existing literature. Two such classic searches are outlined below: one for a measure of Machiavellianism; the other for a measure of strength of social ties.

During the 1950s, Christie (Christie & Geis 1970) pioneered interest in those persons who are especially adept at the manipulation of others—so-called Machiavellians. Christie carefully searched the literature from Machiavelli's classic work *The Prince* to Eric Hoffer's *The True Believers* for potential indices. Out of these two decades of searching, he developed the following hypothetical role model of a Machiavellian: Such a person must have a relative lack of emotional involvement in interpersonal situations, a lack of concern with conventional morality, a lack of gross mental illness, and low ideological commitment. Each of these characteristics presupposes two assumptions: First, Machiavellians view humans as basically weak, fallible, and gullible. Second, if humankind is weak, rational individuals should take advantage of the situation to maximize their own gains. Alternatively, if one cannot trust others because of their weaknesses, one should take steps to protect oneself from others' follies.

Christie next gathered statements that might be theoretically consonant with the Machiavellian view. During the first year of the project, he gathered 71 indices. He spent the next few years at the slow but normal process of administering the scale items to various groups, correlating their responses with expected outcomes, and then reconceptualizing the construct. The outcome of this rigorous process was the development of two scales, each of which defined a quite satisfactory cluster of initially interrelated items. Notice that he did not form his scale overnight. Scale methodologists want to know what their items are measuring—which may be quite different from what they originally thought they measured. Therefore, most of their efforts are spent in trying to locate the dimension(s) their scales actually tap.

Systematizing Self-Reported Subjective Phenomena

Any scientific theory must have observable consequences. It also must be possible to make predictions from that theory that can be verified by observations. One area of observation involves self-reported observations in the nature of attitudinal and survey-type data However, these types of data are of a private nature, in that they can be verified only by individuals reporting the behavior. Unfortunately, even though many people are able to communicate their experiences to themselves and others, many others are unable to conceptualize certain of their own experiences for themselves, much less adequately communicate them to others. Most efforts by methodologists interested in such subjective phenomena are directed toward formulating criteria for opening self-reported data to valid comparisons across individuals.

Basic Rules for Constructing Subjective Indices

Christie's aforementioned Machiavellian scale provides a classic example of subjective scale construction. It is important that the researcher making up any such well-constructed scale carefully select and edit indices according to principles that help us evaluate the objectivity of the scale indices. Although I shall mention a few specific reasons and cases for violating these rules in later sections of this chapter, most of these rules are inviolate. When disreputable and ignorant researchers break these rules, we challenge their findings.

First, avoid indices that refer to the past rather than to the present. Memory decay is a major problem in the reporting of subjective phenomena. The further back into the subjective past one attempts to delve, the more unreliable and invalid the data. It is much better to focus only on the present—except in the special case of historical research. Rather than ask "How often did you go to church during the last year?", it would be better to ask "How often did you go to church during the last month?"

Second, avoid indices that are factual or capable of being interpreted as factual. Individuals do not like to appear to be stupid or ignorant. Social researchers, as a normal rule, are not interested in facts, but rather in opinions, attitudes, meanings, and other subjective states. Unlike IQ tests or general knowledge tests, subjective scales ask for personal reactions toward some object, rather than an answer that is externally verifiable as correct ("The majority of lead poisoning cases occur in multiple dwelling units.") Instead, we want indices that help us construct statements that are congruent with a major assumption of research on subjective phenomena; that there will be theoretically important differences in the belief systems of those persons with favorable as opposed to nonfavorable attitudes toward any particular scale item ("Do you feel that lead poisoning is a serious problem in our inner cities or that it is not such a serious problem?").

Third, avoid indices that may be interpreted in more than one way. Although language is always ambiguous, some words or expressions are more vague than others. In everyday life we use such vague questions as "Where are you from?" and "What do you do?" Does the first question refer to place of birth, where a person grew up, or from where one has just come? Does the second question refer to occupation, to the actual type of work on the job, or to what a person does at a particular time of day? We often get away with such questions because we have time to clarify our meanings. But quite often people pass over the ambiguities because they think they understand one another when in actuality they do not. Social researchers strive for great precision in question wording because they recognize that making valid comparisons across individuals suffers if each has a different psychological object in mind.

Fourth, avoid indices that are likely to be endorsed by almost everyone or by almost no one. A question about belief in God is a classic example of a question that in the United States is trivial because some 99% of those surveyed will say they hold such a belief. Similarly, who could say they are not against the spread of AIDS, extramarital affairs, infanticide, or child molestation? The problem with both types of extreme questions is that they are so powerful that a large number of individuals will feel socially compelled to go along with the majority in spite of their actual beliefs or discrepant behaviors. Avoiding the use of such universals as *all, always, none,* and *never,* and such words as *only, just,* and *merely* aids this fourth rule.

Fifth, avoid direct questioning unless the social atmosphere is free from felt or actual pressures toward conformity. Christie and Geis (1970) note that Machiavellianism denotes unfavorable social behavior to many individuals. If you asked individuals to express their opinions of Machiavellian behavior, they might respond simply in terms of *publicly* approved attitudes because of fear of social disapproval. Thus, they attempted to design items that more indirectly measured Machiavellianism. Christie laboriously took pains to find out if people could pick out the Machiavellian items in his scales. Furthermore, simple direct questions are useless in situations where individuals are not aware of their own attitudes. Many people have relatively unformed feelings toward the word "Machiavellian"—they do not know what it means and, therefore, to ask of them their attitude ("Are you Machiavellian?") toward such an object would be absurdly meaningless.

Sixth, select indices that cover the entire range of the affective scale of interest. This is one of the most inexcusably broken rules. Even social scientists who should know better often bias their indices toward their own beliefs. The purpose of legitimate social research is to find out what others really think, not to impose one's own beliefs on others. Results of social investigation indicate that researchers may unwittingly break this rule more often than they realize. For example, rather than state both sides of a two-sided issues, question writers often get lazy and state the second position with an "or not" ending. Respondents treat the following two questions quite differently: Are you in favor of rent controls or not? Are you in favor of or opposed to rent controls? The second question much more fairly presents each side of the issue. Similarly, to make preset attitude scale answers that only include "strongly approve," "approve," and "disapprove" subtly biases the respondent to believe the researcher wishes an answer of approval. Balanced answers of some such form as "Strongly approve," "moderately approve," "slightly approve," "slightly disapprove," "moderately disapprove," and "strongly disapprove" give a more reasonable list of choices.

Seventh, keep the language simple, clear, and direct. This means that: (1) indices should only rarely exceed twenty words in length; (2) each indice should contain only one complete thought; (3) whenever possible, indices should be in the form of simple sentences rather than in the form of compound or complex sentences; (4) indices should avoid words that may not be understood by those who will answer the completed scale; and (5) indices should avoid double negatives. More complex expression of thought can be saved for research reporting. The purpose of making indices of subjective phenomena is not to confuse research participants or to obfuscate the psychological objects under study.

Finally, much of human feeling may be both ambiguous and ambivalent. One may have extremely positive and negative feelings toward an object. Direct questions cannot adequately tap ambivalence. Many people who "hate" violence are often strongly and even unconsciously attracted to violent movies. Attitude measurement techniques cannot now adequately evaluate such opposed feelings.

Systematic Response Biases

Scientific subjective scale construction has matured. Researchers have come to recognize that—no matter how well constructed the scale—there will still be extraneous determinants of the participant's responses that undermine the scale's validity. Even if unconsciously held, systematic biases are part of human nature. This section discusses the major known subjective response biases as well as measures scaling experts employ to minimize their effects.

Humans have *social desirability* tendencies—they will try to give answers that make themselves appear well-adjusted, unprejudiced, rational, open-minded, and democratic. Respondents are often motivated to present overly favorable pictures of themselves. To present such an overly favorable self-concept, the respondent must know what responses the researcher regards as favorable.

The researcher has several alternative ways of controlling social desirability. First, the researcher may attempt to disguise questions that respondents may think of as socially desirable or undesirable; however, this is unsatisfactory for an unknown number of sophisticated respondents. Second, the researcher may give assurances to respondents that their responses will be kept confidential; but this is completely dependent on trust. Christie and Geis give a third, more ingenious, means (1970:26): They asked participants whom they randomly assigned to two groups to read a document on how to fake a test and then to either "fake low" or "fake high." Their rationale was based on the belief that if neither instruction significantly changes the index scores, then one has evidence that social desirability is a relatively implausible explanation. Fourth, some researchers sprinkle their scales with items keyed to measure social desirability. Then the overall scale score is corrected for these known social desirability responses. An interesting variation on this method is to present several items in combination that are equated for social desirability, and to require that the participant choose the one coming closest to his or her own viewpoint.

Acquiescence biases refer to individuals who accept all or most statements ("yeasayers") or reject all or most statements ("naysayers"). Often, this problem can be vastly reduced through phrasing statements unambiguously. Another means of reducing acquiescence is through random *reversal* of half of the item content. Christie and Geis (1970) randomly reversed half of their Machiavellian scale items. For example, they reversed Machiavelli's belief that "Most men are cowards" to read "Most men are brave." Agreement with either item gives opposite attitudinal meaning. If a respondent had marked "strongly agree" ("+3") toward the statement "Most men are brave," later the researchers recoded it as "−3". This is because agreement (or disagreement) with reversed items implies agreement (or disagreement) with the reverse of that scale. In other words, a Machiavellian should agree that "All men are cowards," while a non-Machiavellian should agree that "All men are brave." The converse should also be true; a person disagreeing that "All men are brave" would be a Machiavellian, while a person disagreeing that "All men are cowards" would be non-Machiavellian. However, sometimes sensible reversal of items is not possible, as many would-be revisers have found. For instance, consider the following item from the classic Adorno Authoritarian scale: "After we finish off the Germans and the Japs, we ought to concentrate on other enemies of the human race such as rats, snakes, and germs." Because this item is offensive to many individuals, especially nonauthoritarian individuals, researchers have tried but failed to come up with a sensible reversal.

A final means of controlling for acquiescence tendencies is the most powerful of all: computer-assisted technology. For example, Computer-Assisted Telephone Interviewing (CATI) software, now coming into large-scale use, allows researchers to randomly present numerous indices to their respondents. This method will not cut down on true individual habits of naysaying or yeasaying. However, because every indice has the same chance of order of appearance, the researcher can rule out acquiescence biases due to any particular nonrandom ordering.

Extremity biases include tendencies to check (or avoid) the extremes of answer categories, for instance, the tendency to check (or to avoid checking) "1's" and "7's" on a seven-point scale. Another form of this bias is represented by the respondent who avoids extreme responses by checking "4" (on a scale from "1" to "7") or "don't know." Because of this tendency for some respondents to select neutral scale points, many researchers prefer to "force" the individual to make positive or negative responses by not including such "neutral" categories. This procedure may encourage *cooperative biases,* because the respondent may not actually have an attitude toward an object. Except when the researcher expects less strongly expressed or held attitudes, the exclusion of a neutral response is quite appropriate. Researchers have found that extreme-response sets generally influence scale validity to a small degree, and Nunnally (1967) demonstrated the extent to which this response set can be measured statistically. However, Kuroda, Hayashi, and Suzuki (1986) summarize evidence collected from English, Japanese, and Arabic native-speakers that convincingly demonstrate radically different cross-cultural responses to middle-position responses such as "it depends on . . . " Because each language represents a different way of viewing the world, their work indicates that researchers should be wary of comparing middle-position responses across different language groups.

Sentence-syntax biases also provide a source of response bias. These are systematic sources of bias rooted in linguistic context. Micklin and Durbin (1969) list three types: sentence complexity, voice, and direction. *Sentence complexity* indicates whether an item is stated as a simple or a complex thought. *Voice* denotes whether an item is stated in the active or passive voice. *Direction* expresses whether an item is negative or affirmative. Because we wish to present our respondents with clearly understood stimuli, it seems best to use simple sentences, active voice, and affirmative direction as much as possible. Numerous psychological studies have demonstrated that respondents have much more difficulty understanding statements written in the negative direction, passive voice, or complex form.

There are four primary means of minimizing extraneous response biases. First, the researcher may modify the conditions of administration. The researcher may free conditions of administration of some response bias by establishing rapport with participants prior to scale administration. This includes attempts to convince participants of the importance of participation, of the confidentiality of responses, and of the desire to obtain honest opinions. Sec-

---

Table 7-1   *A Typical Attitude Scale Preface Format*

Listed below are a number of statements. Each represents a commonly held opinion. There are no right or wring answers. You will probably disagree with some items and agree with others. We are interested in the extent to which you agree or disagree with such matters of opinion.

Read each statement carefully. Then indicate the extent to which you agree or disagree by circling the number in front of each statement. The numbers and their meanings are indicated below.

If you agree strongly, circle +3
If you agree somewhat, circle +2
If you agree slightly, circle +1

If you disagree slightly, circle −1
If you disagree somewhat, circle −2
If you disagree strongly, circle −3

First impressions are usually best in such matters. Read each statement, decide if you agree or disagree and the strength of your opinion, and then circle the appropriate number in front of the statement. *Give your opinion on every statetment.*

---

ond, the researcher can modify the measuring instrument. Each of the rules of the previous chapter section may aid this process. Another aid is a clearly written explanatory preface to the instrument such as found in Table 7–1.

Some researchers prefer the use of various indirect measures of attitudes to circumvent participant awareness so that the participant's biases will not influence the assessments. These are discussed in greater depth in a later section on indirect measurements. The use of several instruments is even better because any type of instrument is apt to elicit peculiar confounding factors; a variety of procedures may overcome each others' disadvantages.

Third, the researcher can sometimes detect and discard participants whose responses are largely affected by irrelevant factors. Sometimes researchers build in scale items, with extremely low probabilities of acceptance. If the respondent answers a large proportion of such items, the researcher assumes the respondent is either careless or nonserious and, therefore, discards the responses. However, this procedure risks the alternative possibility of throwing out truly deviant persons.

Finally, the researcher can correct the scores of all subjects in proportion to the amount of their known contamination. Assume, for example that you wish to measure acquiescence response sets. Suppose your scale has ten directly worded items and ten reversed items. If agreements and disagreements balance out, there is no acquiescence response bias; if they do not balance out, you might correct the total scale score for the bias.

Types of Subjective Measuring Instruments

Chapter 3 introduced a number of types of scales: nominal, ordinal, cardinal, ratio, and probability. Each of the measurement techniques in this section assumes one of these types of scale properties. Measurement, in its broadest sense, concerns the assignment of numerals to objects according to some specified rule. However, numerals are just symbols; we still must determine whether or not the scale properties are applicable through a determination of the properties of the variable's measured attributes. The permissible rules for the assignment of numerals to objects depend on the properties of the object, *not* on the properties of the type of scale we utilize. Therefore, the assignment of such numbers as "1" to males and "2" to females is an arbitrary rule because we could have assigned the numbers in another manner.

Category-ranks scales

Often a researcher will present a number of items to a group of participants with instructions for the participants to rank-order the items according to some single criteria. In a study that has become a citation classic, Holmes and Rahe (1967) asked respondents to rank-order events that had caused the most social readjustment in their lives. They then ranked the events over all respondents by assigning the highest-ranked event (death of spouse) an *arbitrary* mean value of 100. They ascribed lesser-ranked events mean values based upon how much readjustment would be required *by comparison to* death of a spouse. Therefore, at one extreme, they established that the second-ranked event, divorce, on average caused a social adjustment 73% of that of the death of a spouse; a marital separation triggered a relative readjustment 65% as large as death of a spouse; and either a jail term or death of a close family member generated a 63% relative social readjustment. Events worth relatively half the social readjustment of death of a spouse included personal injury or illness, marriage, marital reconciliation, retirement, pregnancy, and sex difficulties. At the lowest extreme, a change in number of family get-togethers, vacation, Christmas, and minor violations of the law all occasioned less than a 15% change in social readjustment by comparison to death of a spouse.

Several difficulties present themselves to users of ranking methods. First, with more than 20 items to rank, participants find ranking extremely difficult. With more than 20 items, therefore, most researchers use the following modifications. First, they set up a few rank categories. For example, various studies of graduate-school quality and faculty that the American Council of Education and individual researchers (Gourman 1985) have accomplished normally set up seven ranks: (1) Distinguished, (2) Strong, (3) Good, (4) Adequate, (5) Marginal, (6) Not Sufficient for Doctoral Training, and (7) Insufficient Information. Second, every respondent then rates every item (departments or graduate school programs in this case) according to these categories. Third, researchers compute a mean or median rank for each item. Finally, researchers then reassign a whole rank number because the differences in mean or median ranks do not indicate interval properties but are only ordinal.

Thurstone scales

The rank-order method is an extremely easy method to employ. Many of the methods in this chapter start with—but go beyond—its assumptions. One of the basic assumptions is that attitudes toward various objects can be expressed along a continuum from least to most favorable. Thurstone and Chave (1929) invented three methods that start with this basic assumption. They theorized that the best technique for measuring attitudinal favorability-unfavorability was to measure social consensus concerning a set of beliefs. To achieve this end, the researcher first collected a huge pool of statements that cover the entire range of valued beliefs. Second, independent judges evaluated the favorableness or unfavorableness of each *pair* of items in the scale. This was an inordinately time-consuming task because for n items there are $(n[n-1])/2$ possible pairs. For example, only 15 items would require 105 separate judgments. Third, the researcher chose ten items that represented the full range of subjective feelings. Finally, the researcher asked the actual respondents to choose the statements that best or least expressed their own feelings. After other researchers compared the results of less laborious methods of scaling with Thurstone and Chave's, they abandoned it because they discovered that a far less tedious method design by Likert produced similar or better results.

Likert-summated rating scale

This method is by far the most popular method of scaling subjective phenomena. Like Thurstone scaling, the researcher constructs attitudinal statements that are favorable or unfavorable toward the object or issue under investigation. Unlike Thurstone scaling, it is unnecessary to have *extremely* favorable or unfavorable items because respondents will indicate their *degree* of agreement or disagreement with each item. Generally, the scale design permits only five responses: (1) strongly agree, (2) agree, (3) uncertain, (4) disagree, and (5) strongly disagree, although sometimes researchers modify this rule to four, six, or seven response categories. The investigator used "a priori" judgment at this stage in deciding whether a statement is a direct or reverse measure of the attitude object.

Because the investigator uses only a priori judgments during the preliminary scale construction stage, researchers wish next to do an item analysis for reliability and validity purposes. *Item analysis* is a process involving several steps. First, the researcher pretests all preliminarily selected items on some group of respondents and then sums up all indices into a total score. Second, the researcher orders the respondent's total scale scores toward the attitudinal object. Third, the researcher then selects only those respondents whose scale scores fall in the top (most favorable) or bottom (least favorable) 25th percentile. Fourth, the investigator uses *indices* that fall in the top and bottom quartile to compare the top and bottom quartile of respondents. If an indice is "good," it will discriminate between the two groups; if not, the investigator discards it from the pool of pretest items. Because the investigator originally selected indices only on a priori grounds, this test of indices discrimination is an important means of testing how accurately those priori assumptions were.

Those items that do discriminate will make up the final attitude scale. Final scale scoring is a simple summation of individual indices scores. Low scores on the final scale indicate unfavorable attitudes and high scores indicate favorable attitudes. The Likert method, therefore, has ordinal scale properties.

Guttman scalogram analysis

This scale technique is based on two assumptions: (1) A set of items can be ordered along a continuum of difficulty or magnitude, and (2) such a set of items measures a unidimensional variable. Assume we know a woman can consistently jump a five-foot hurdle. We can predict that she can consistently jump a four-, three-, or one-foot hurdle even though we cannot predict, without more information, whether she can jump hurdles of more than five feet consistently.

We ought to be able to order some subjective phenomena along such a continuum of difficulty. Let us assume that we have a number of attitude statements spanning the continuum of pro- to antihomosexuality: I would not mind having a homosexual for: (1) a chance encounter, (2) an acquaintance, (3) a friend, (4) a roommate, and (5) a date. We should expect someone who was strongly antihomosexual to respond "no" to each of those five indices; some one who was moderately antihomosexual to respond "yes" only to the first statement; another who was only slightly prejudiced to respond "yes" to only the first two indices; still another person who was slightly favorable toward homosexuals to respond "yes" to the first three items; a person who was pro-homosexuality to respond with "yes" to all but the last item on dating; and a strong homosexual rights-oriented person to respond "yes" to all five indices.

Experience suggests that the investigator needs at least 100 individual responses to analyze such a set of attitude statements. After collecting responses, the investigator changes the order of both persons and statements by trial and error until he or she reaches a minimum number of inconsistent response patterns. In the above homosexual example, one inconsistent pattern would be "yes-yes-no-yes-no" because it makes little sense to say "no" to friendship with a homosexual but "yes" to rooming or dating because the latter two require much more intimacy. Response patterns should show such inconsistent patterns in no more than 10% of the cases. Practitioners eliminate statements that show more inconsistency on the grounds that they do not belong to that particular continuum.

Reliability of a Guttman scale involves the use of a special coefficient of reproducibility. To compute it, the researcher needs to know (1) the total num-

Thurstone Equal Appealing Interval*
Check all the statements with which you agree.
(1.5)	_____	We can't call ourselves civilized as long as we have capital punishment.
(10.4)	_____	Any person, man or woman, young or old, who commits murder should pay with his own life.
(5.5)	_____	It doesn't make any difference to me whether we have capital punishment or not.
(2.4)	_____	Capital punishment cannot be regarded as a sane method of dealing with crime.
(7.2)	_____	Capital punishment may be wrong, but it is the best preventative to crime.

Note. Scale values for each item are given in parentheses. A person's attitude score is the median scale value of the statements checked.
*Adapted from Shaw and Wright (1967).

Likert Scale
Circle the response that best represents your opinion.
SA—Strongly Agree A—Agree U—Undecided D—Disagree SD—Strongly Disagree

(4)	(3)	(2)	(1)	(0)	
SA	A	U	D	SD	Capital punishment is just and necessary.
(0)	(1)	(2)	(3)	(4)	
SA	A	U	D	SD	I do not believe in capital punishment under any circumstances.
(0)	(1)	(2)	(3)	(4)	
SA	A	U	D	SD	We cannot call ourselves civilized as long as we have capital punishment.
(4)	(3)	(2)	(1)	(0)	
SA	A	U	D	SD	Capital punishment should be used more often than it is.

Note. For each statement, an item score from 4 to 0 is assigned depending on the response circled. A person's attitude score is the sum of the item scores. Note that items unfavorable to capital punishment are reverse scored, so that disagreeing with these items is like agreeing with a favorable item.

Gutman Scale
Indicate whether you agree or disagree with each statement by circling the appropriate alternative.
Agree	Disagree	Capital punishment should be used only for the most extreme crimes (e.g. multiple murders).
Agree	Disagree	Capital punishment is justified for premeditated murder.
Agree	Disagree	Capital punishment is just and necessary.
Agree	Disagree	Every criminal should be executed.

Note. A person's attitude score is the number of statements with which he or she agrees.

Semantic Differential
Capital punishment is:

Good_____ : _____ : _____ : _____ : _____ : _____ : _____Bad
Fair_____ : _____ : _____ : _____ : _____ : _____ : _____Unfair

Note. For each scale, a score is assigned from -3 to +3 depending on the category checked. (The numbers typically do not appear on the scale, but the blank closest to the negative adjective—e.g., bad—is assigned a value of -3, the next blank is assigned a -2, and so forth.) A person's attitude score is the sum of the scale scores.

Self-Rating Scale
How favorable or unfavorable do you feel toward capital punishment?

       1   2   3   4   5   6   7   8   9   10 11
      Very   Very
      Favorable   Unfavorable

Note: A person's attitude score is the number circled on this scale.

Figure 7–1. Five types of scales for measuring attitudes toward capital punishment.
Source: Petty, Ostrom, & Brock (1981:35)

ber of responses generated by the total sample of respondents, and (2) the number of times participants' choices fell outside of the predicted pattern of responses. The formula is:

$$\text{Coefficient of Reproducibility} = 1 - \frac{\text{total errors}}{\text{total responses}}$$

For example, if in the homosexual example we had only 3 cases out of 100 that deviated from the five patterns described, the coefficient of reproducibility would be $1 - (3/100)$ or 0.97. We would conclude that the reproducibility coefficient shows acceptable reliability.

Guttman scaling is limited to the use of dichotomous and trichotomous variables. One of its advantages is its ability to take *nominal* or qualitative data and order their relationships in ordinal variable form. Koslowsky, Pratt, and Wintrob (1976) demonstrated that physician attitudes toward circumstances of abortions well satisfies Guttman scale criteria. If you will plug the figures from the note at the bottom of Table 7–2 into the reproducibility formula, you will note that the coefficient is 0.95.

If the Guttman scale is composed of dichotomous responses, the scale must use at least ten items in the final version. Second, scale errors must be random because nonrandom errors are a sign of more than one dimension. In fact, most psychological and social psychological theories assume to the contrary that persons normally do not respond unidimensionally; in such cases Guttman scaling is not recommended. In Likert and Thurstone scaling, the researcher does not assume that the acceptance of a favorable item is inconsistent with the acceptance also of a less favorable item because the cumulative

Table 7-2 *Percentage of Acceptance and Rejection and Number of Errors for Each Circumstance in Guttman Scale*

Circumstance	Response (%)		Error	
	Reject	*Accept*	*Reject*	*Accept*
1. Career in education would be disrupted.	60	40	0	3
2. Too young to have the child.	57	43	0	3
3. Financially unable to support the child.	55	45	2	1
4. Too old to have the child	55	45	2	1
5. Does not want the child.	54	46	2	1
6. Being unmarried would be a problem.	48	52	2	2
7. Pregnancy or childbirth is a threat to mental health.	32	68	0	1
8. Pregnancy or childbirth is a threat to physical health.	28	72	1	2
9. Pregnancy is a result of rape or incest.	28	72	3	1
10. Risk of congenital abnormality.	25	75	2	1
11. Pregnancy or childbirth is a threat to life.	23	77	2	0

Note: For response category, $n = 715$; for error category, $n = 32$.

Source: Koslowsky, Pratt, & Wintrob (1976:302)

assumption is often quite unrealistic. For example, pro-civil rights participants will often accept extremely favorable civil rights statements while rejecting milder ones such as "There should be more discussions between white and black leaders." Guttman scaling makes no sense in this type of situation.

Forced-choice scale

An interesting and somewhat new technique requires the respondent to choose which of several equally repulsive attitudinal statements is most true of him- or herself. Christie and Geis (1970:19) note that many respondents understandably object to this procedure, as typified by one who wrote in the scale margin: "This is like asking me whether I would rape my mother or take an ax to my father." Therefore, they modified the forced-choice method by presenting groups of three forced-choice items with instructions to the respondent to choose the one most characteristic and the one least characteristic of the participant. One item was *keyed* to the particular scale of interest. A second item unrelated to the scale was *matched* to the first item in rated social desirability. The third item, the *buffer*, was high in social desirability compared to the other two items.

This procedure has several virtues. First, because there is always at least one highly desirable item—unlike the original procedure of two repulsive items—to choose, participants have little difficulty choosing. Second, the technique makes it difficult for most participants to determine the "social desirability" answer between the *keyed buffer* scale and *matched* social desirability items. One of Christie and Geis' Machiavellian triads in Mach V is

12. **A.** A person shouldn't be punished for breaking a law that he [or she] thinks is unreasonable. (high desirability reverse)

B. Too many criminals are not punished for their crimes. (matched social desirability item)

C. There is no excuse for lying to someone else. (reversed keyed Machiavellian item)

Various methodological administrations of the Mach V scale (Christie & Geis 1970:25) indicate that when even advanced methods students are given the principle underlying the scoring method and are told that the test is designed to measure Machiavellianism, they cannot identify the keyed items. Thus, unlike other types of scales discussed, the forced-choice scale appears to reduce social desirability biases significantly.

The scoring of a forced-choice scale is, however, somewhat more complicated than the previously mentioned scales. One scores according to the response pattern for each item before summing across items. In the Mach V triad shown above, 1 point (low Mach) is given for a "most like me ($+$)" response to 12.C *and* a "most unlike me ($-$)" response to 12.B; 3 points for either A$+$, C$-$ or the B$+$, A$-$ combination; and 7 points (high Mach) for the B$+$,C$-$ combination. This procedure is based on the following rationale (Christie & Geis 1970:30):

Box 7-1 *A Citation Classic on Measurement and Scaling*

Graham B. Spanier (1976) Measuring dyadic adjustment: New scales for assessing the quality of marriage and similar dyads. Journal of Marriage and the Family, 38, 15–28. [*The Social Science Citation Index* (SSCI) indicates that this paper has been cited in over 275 publications.]

This study was one of my first projects after finishing my doctorate. I had been impressed with the fact that marital adjustment was the most frequently studied variable in the field of family sociology, yet surprised that there were few measures of this concept. Moreover, the measures that existed were dated and had never undergone any sophisticated assessment of their psychometric properties. [Because] I had been very interested in the study of the quality of marriage since doing my thesis, I decided I would combine my interest in the subject with my growing background in measurement to develop a new scale.

In the decade since its publication, the Dyadic Adjustment Scale has become the most widely used measure in the field. It has been used in hundreds of doctoral dissertations, as well as in the published articles cited. The scale has some weaknesses that I have acknowledged from the beginning, and the original paper called for further development. Yet no new measure has emerged that has taken the place of the scale. It seemed to meet a critical need at the right time and continues to be widely used.

I never did market the scale commercially; it is generally used without any required permission or fee (commercially available computer and paper versions will soon exist, however). I now wish I had marketed it from the beginning, not for financial gain, but because it probably would have relieved me of the daily burden of responding to correspondence about the scale: granting permission, giving out scoring information, commenting on issues of reliability and validity, and indicating that the scale may be used without permission and may be duplicated without charge. I have answered more than 1,000 letters and an equal number of phone calls in 10 years.

I named the scale "dyadic" adjustment and developed item wording without specific reference to marriage because I wanted to develop a measure that could be used in any committed couple relationship, including unmarried cohabitation. As I anticipated, however, more than 90 percent of the scale's use has been with married couples. I also developed four subscales (dyadic satisfaction, dyadic cohesion, dyadic consensus, and affectional expression) and revalidated the scale and subscales in a subsequent study.

Much of the criticism that followed the article's publication, interestingly enough, is not of the scale itself so much, as of the issue of whether the quality of marriage can be measured. I continue to believe that it can, although I am sure there can be improvements in how it is done. I expect that the scale will continue to be used widely for a few more years and that its use will then diminish as new measures emerge that improve on the psychometric properties and utility of the Dyadic Adjustment Scale.

Source: Current Content, December 22–29, 1986, p. 24.

. . . to have the possible range and theoretical neutral point equivalent to Mach IV, and (b) to take full advantage of the fact that it is probably more Machiavellian to say the Mach item is most like and the matched item least like oneself—a two-step difference—than to say the Mach item is most like and omit the matched item or omit the Mach item and say the matched item is least like oneself—a one-step difference.

It is also important that matched items of this sort be randomized as to order so that participants may not pick up any particular built-in order by which to respond. With the increasing sophistication of respondents taking attitude scales, this type of item will probably come into more usefulness to make it more difficult to cheat on attitude scales.

Campbell bipolar formats

This method was invented by Donald Campbell (1968) and is a cross between Likert and forced-choice formats: The researcher gives the respondent sets of two items that are at opposite ends of a continuum (hence, bipolar). The items, however, are scored in Likert style, as shown in Table 7–3. Therefore, if "A" is

---

Table 7-3 *A Bipolar Format Illustration*

Instructions: This is a survey of your attitudes and opinions. Each item consists of two alternatives, A and B, between which you are asked to choose by circling one of these indicators:

A = I prefer Statement A entriely to Statement B as an expression of my opinion.

a = I prefer Statement A somewhat over Statement B.

? = I cannot choose between A and B.

b = I prefer Statement B somewhat over Statement A.

B = I prefer Statement B entirely to Statement A as an expression of my opinion.

Please show your attitude leanings on each item, even though you do not feel strongly on the topic or do not feel well informed. Please choose between alternatives, even though both may seem acceptable to you, or both unacceptable.

Items in the Assessment of Self (*indicates high self-assessment)

A a ? b B   1.   A. My progress toward the goals of success I set for myself has been disappointing.
               *B. I feel that I have made significant progress toward the goals of success I set for myself.

A a ? b B   2. *A. The conception I now have of myself is more complimentary than the conception I have had in the past.
               B. I now have a less complimentary conception of myself than I have had in the past.

A a ? b B   3.   A. In determining how others feel about me, I am not confident in my ability to do so.
               *B. I am confident of my ability to ascertain how others feel about me.

asterisked, "A" is scored as a "5," "a" as "4," "?" as "3," "b" as "2," and "B" as "1"; this procedure is reversed for items where "B" is asterisked. (Asterisks are not actually used on administered forms.)

We see the advantages of this method mainly in controls for acquiescence response sets and in a clear definition of the attitude continuum for respondents. Campbell's unpublished works indicate that there is not much manifest difference in Likert and bipolar attitudinal assessments. He feels that attention should be placed on making better scales at the outset rather than on scale format (Campbell 1968:6). Nevertheless, it would appear that social desirability response sets more easily influence the bipolar scale format by contrast to the forced-choice triad.

Semantic differential scale

Charles Osgood invented the semantic differential (see Osgood, Suci, & Tannebaum 1957). It is one of the most adaptable scaling methods in our toolbox. In every scaling method I have so far discussed, the investigator must create a completely new scale to measure each attitude object. By contrast, the semantic differential, with minor variations, is adaptable to *any* attitudinal object.

The expression "semantic differential" comes from the ability of this technique to distinguish between the *connotations*, or meanings, of words. An impressive variety of studies in a wide sampling of cultures has suggested that there are three major connotational dimensions underlying a person's judgments: *Evaluation*: (such as good-bad); *Potency* (powerful-powerless): and *Activity* (fast-slow) known by the acronym EPA. With a relatively short list of nine to twelve such bipolar adjective scales, the researcher may measure the affect experienced by a participant toward any object. The fact that the EPA dimensions can be found throughout every culture in which this instrument has been used suggests that the traditional assumption that attitudes have a single dimension is much too simple. We should be measuring attitudinal affect multidimensionally through techniques such as the semantic differential (SD).

The SD measures respondent's reactions to stimulus words, concepts, or phrases in terms of bipolar adjective ratings. An example is shown in the accompanying table. Generally speaking, instructions label "0's" as neutral, "1's" as "slightly," "2's" as "moderately" or "quite," and "3's" as "extremely." Sometimes, researchers add "4's" and label then as "infinitely." In the following example you should read the "x's" placed by a hypothetical respondent as showing that person feels that Communists are "moderately bad," "slightly powerful," and "neutral in activity."

A Communist is:

	3	2	1	0	1	2	3	
good	___;	___;	___;	___;	___;	_X_;	___;	bad
powerful	___;	___;	_X_;	___;	___;	___;	___;	powerless
fast	___;	___;	___;	_X_;	___;	___;	___;	slow

It has been noted that the SD is an extremely general instrument. Heise (1986) has obtained EPA ratings for thousands of word concepts and for social roles. Other researchers have used the SD to study art works, self-concept, and other diverse stimuli. Triandis (1964) developed a variation on the SD concept he calls the behavioral differential (BD), measuring behavior intentions of participants toward particular persons or categories of persons. The following BD example requests respondents to evaluate their behavior toward a black ghetto dweller who is a communist:

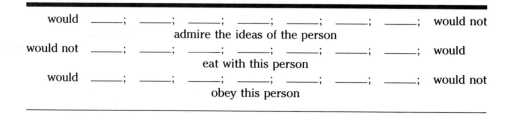

The BD can be changed into a normative differential by asking not what one would do, but rather what one should do, or into a role differential with such stimuli sets as father-son, laborer-foreman, or judge-defendant.

The Semantic Differential has many advantages: It is a generalized method, economical, has instant readiness for use, cross-cultural comparability, standard metrics, and multidimensionality. Further, the Semantic Differential correlates highly with other standard attitude scaling techniques, and is recommended by its good predictive validity.

Heise (1986) has developed a fine piece of Semantic Differential-based software for IBM-PC-like personal computers called INTERACT that he has continued to refine over the past two decades. INTERACT can be used for both research and teaching on how to predict change of semantic ratings from knowledge of the context of particular stimuli. It plugs into 35 equations a special dictionary of semantic ratings on *who* acted, what *action* was performed, the *direct object* of action, individual roles, and social setting to make predictions concerning changes in particular stimuli. The logic is easy to understand from changes in the context of simple sentences. Consider how you feel in each of the following cases: "John smokes," "John smokes marijuana," "John smokes marijuana as part of a legal medical experiment into alleviation of glaucoma," and "John smokes marijuana in church." Each context ought to change your perceptions of John. For example, "John smokes marijauna in church" is usually perceived as much more powerful, much more lively, and much worse in evaluation than "John smokes marijuana as part of a legal medical experiment to alleviate glaucoma."

Although the Semantic Differential has much to recommend its use, it is particularly susceptible to social desirability biases. With especially sensitive topics and respondents special assurance of anonymity of responses is recommended. Second, many groups of respondents, particularly those from lower-class backgrounds, do not feel comfortable with the technique and may refuse to participate in its administration. Third, much research indicates that there is a significant interaction effect between the stimulus and participants that must be corrected using techniques that have long been known to practitioners but not likely to be known to novice users (Osgood, Suci, & Tannebaum 1957).

Fourth, the number of issues or objects evaluated must be quite small (less than ten) when a large number of bipolar scales (more than eight) are used because the tediously large number of responses creates response biases. For example, ten stimuli with nine bipolar ratings each would mean 90 separate responses—an inordinately major request of many respondents. Heise's aforementioned INTERACT computer program comes complete with another, smaller program called ATTITUDE that partially overcomes the tedium of semantic differential scaling. ATTITUDE can randomize the ordering of the bipolar scales helping to cut down on response biases. It also keeps a running record of average scores for any group of individuals using the program to evaluate some set of objects. This cuts down on the tedium of computing semantic scores. Furthermore, this program helps maintain subject confidentiality because it leaves no written record of the subject's response.

The method of ordered alternatives scale

Carolyn Sherif (1980) invented this method in response to criticism that measurement has not kept pace with developments in attitude theory. Specifically, Kelman (1980) faulted earlier theory and methods for the false assumption that an attitude represents a simple point on a scale. Kelman arrived at this conclusion after puzzling through data suggesting that his respondents held contradictory attitudes toward perennial Middle East conflicts. He solved the puzzle by suggesting that the practice of averaging a respondent's judgments to a single point on a continuum is often unacceptable. Instead, Kelman proposed that this average judgment overly simplifies attitudes by representing only the respondent's most typical readiness for action: Such simplifications tell us nothing about particular social contexts or changing situations. Kelman's theory suggests the need to measure the three subjective ranges which depend on particular social circumstances: (1) the *latitude of acceptance,* or the respondent's most acceptable positions; (2) the *latitude of rejection,* or the respondent's most unacceptable positions; and (3) the *latitude of noncommitment* which are positions the respondent neither accepts nor rejects.

Sherif (1980) operationalized Kelman's theory with the method of order alternatives. Sherif's method involves modification of many of the steps we have already encountered in this chapter. The first step involves collecting a set of statements that summarize the entire spectrum of positions concerning some subjective phenomena. The next step, following Thurstone's pioneering lead, is to have judges rank the extremity of each statement. The final inventory uses only those statements for which the judges are in agreement. For example, one of Sherif's doctoral students (Kearney 1975) produced the eleven abortion statements listed in Table 7–4. Notice how they are ordered from extremely conservative (A) to moderate (F) to extremely liberal (K).

Once the investigator has composed the entire scale he or she will print a

---

Table 7-4 *Abortion Statements Used in the Method of Ordered Alternatives*

A. A constitutional Amendment guaranteeing the right to life of the unborn is absolutely necessary; legal abortion should never be available.

B. To protect the rights of the unborn baby, legal abortion should not be available.

C. To protect the rights of unborn children, legal abortion should be available only if childbirth would cause the woman's death.

D. To protect the rights of unborn children, legal abortion should require the consent of the husband (or parents, if the woman is a minor) and be performed only in case of rape or incest, thus severely limiting the number of abortions performed.

E. To protect the rights of unborn children, legal abortion should require the consent of the husband (or parents, if the woman is a minor), and be performed only if children could impair the woman's health, thus somewhat limiting the number of abortions performed.

F. It is difficult to decide whether the rights of the unborn or of the woman are more important in formulating laws regarding abortion.

G. A legal abortion should be available during the first three months of pregnancy, but not after.

H. A legal abortion should be available during the first six months of pregnancy, but not after.

I. A legal abortion should be available during the first six months of pregnancy, but after that time only if the woman's life or health would be endangered by a birth.

J. The law should allow the woman to control her own body by permitting a legal abortion upon request.

K. Abortion on demand and paid by the state should be guaranteed by law to any woman when she asks for it; without this protection, she is a slave to the state through compulsory pregnancy.

Source: Kearney (1975)

---

four-page booklet with the scale printed on each page; but the instructions for each page will differ crucially. On page one, respondents are instructed to circle the *one* statement that comes closest to that individual's position. This instruction produces the traditional modal response found through other scaling techniques. On page two, respondents are instructed to circle other statements that are also acceptable—representing the latitude of acceptance. On page three, respondents are instructed to draw a line through those statements that are personally "most objectionable." On the final page, the respondent is asked to delete any further statements that are objectionable. The results of pages three and four operationalize the latitude of rejection. Statements that are neither crossed out as objectionable nor circled as acceptable make up the latitude of noncommitment.

The method of ordered comparisons often gives interesting visual results. For example, Granberg (1982) demonstrated that members of an antiabortion activist group had significantly wider latitudes of rejection and narrower latitudes of noncommitment than members of pro-choice groups. Figure 7–2 illus-

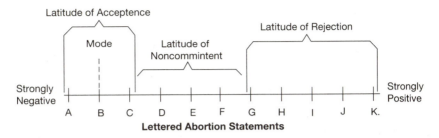

Figure 7-2. A depiction of the modal response and latitudes of acceptance, rejection, and non-commitment for a hypothetical respondent's reactions to the abortion statements used in Table 7–4.

trates hypothetical anti-abortion latitudes of acceptance, noncommitment, and rejection: Note that the modal response is statement B; only statements A, B, and C are acceptable; statements G through K are rejected; and the remaining three statements show no attitudinal commitment.

More importantly than visual representation of each latitude is the fact that the method of ordered alternatives represents human sentiment for many complex phenomena better than traditional methods. For example, Kelman has shown that Arab-Israel attitudes are much more complex than traditional methods indicate; and Granberg's work supports the notion that abortion attitudes are too simply represented by traditional methods. In these, and many other cases, researchers should consider the benefits of using Sherif's invention.

Indirect Measures of Attitudes

In many situations, because the researcher has excellent reason to assume that they are aware of being studied or of what the researcher is studying, participants may attempt to give a good impression, please the experimenter, and so forth. Thus, some procedures provide disguised appraisals. Various researchers have used projective tests (Rorschach, Thematic Apperception Test, Blacky Pictures) to measure such social phenomena as racial prejudice, authoritarianism, and achievement orientations. Less disguised projective techniques have included sentence completion tests with questions like

1. I feel . . .
2. Skin color . . .
3. I hate . . .

However, fundamental data on such indirect tests show their validity and reliability is typically discouragingly low.

Kidder and Campbell (1970) discussed this problem in detail, and concluded that it would be meaningless to compare the results of validity tests of direct versus indirect measures of attitudes for the following reasons. Each type of operation has quite different thresholds. For example, the threshold for recalling stimuli in an indirect measure is lower than that for recognizing stimuli in more traditional direct measures. Therefore, they argued that direct and indirect measures have different thresholds, from lowest to highest being:

1. Autonomic response—eye-blink rates as a sign of nervousness at racist remarks.
2. Verbal report on perceived character of the stimulus—"The average I.Q. of [blacks] is lower than that of whites."
3. Verbal reports on one's own response tendency—"I would not let a *black* move onto my block.
4. Overt locomotor response—refusing to serve black patrons.

Therefore, we expect scales from similar thresholds will correlate higher with each other than scales from different thresholds, according to the logic of discriminant and convergent validity discussed in Chapter 4.

Indirect tests also have some practical disadvantages. First, they may be regarded as an invasion of privacy. Ethically, it is not enough to say science is neutral because its potential use (or misuse) is certainly not value-free. Second, indirect testing often shows deceptive, deprecatory, or exploitive attitudes toward participants. Chronic dishonesty of this type has contributed to a general loss of interpersonal trust in research participant relationships.

Sociometric and Other Interpersonal Perception Measures

The study of social networks tracks back to Georg Simmel but not until the 1930s did social scientists attempt to operationalize social networks. J. L. Moreno first established a core interest in social networks with his editorship of a journal he called *Sociometry*—now changed to *Social Psychology Quarterly* to reflect modern interests. Moreno invented the *sociogram*—a visual representation of social choice, communication, and interaction in groups in which the analyst asks individuals such questions as: With whom would you like most (or least) to work? To whom do you report in your job? With whom would you most like to play?

Based on these types of subjective reports (or even actual observations) the investigator represents individuals by simple points or numbers and network relations between individuals with directed lines as represented by an eight-person group in the left-hand side of Figure 7–3. Let us assume that these hypothetical data are for workmate choices among an engineering team. We can see that person "3" chose person "1," person "2" chose both "5" and "4," person "5" reciprocated person's "3's" choice of herself, person "6" is an isolate, and persons "7" and "8" make up a dyadic clique isolated from the rest of the work group. Persons 1, 4, and 6 chose no one. The sociogram clearly visualizes data for such small groups with few network relationships, but as either the number of relationships or members grow, it becomes virtually impossible to use such graphs because of the number of overlapping lines.

It is important to remember that Simmel warned us that the number of

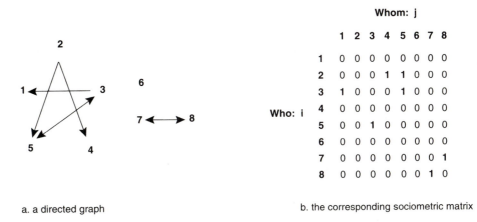

a. a directed graph

Whom: j

Who: i	1	2	3	4	5	6	7	8
1	0	0	0	0	0	0	0	0
2	0	0	0	1	1	0	0	0
3	1	0	0	0	1	0	0	0
4	0	0	0	0	0	0	0	0
5	0	0	1	0	0	0	0	0
6	0	0	0	0	0	0	0	0
7	0	0	0	0	0	0	0	1
8	0	0	0	0	0	0	1	0

b. the corresponding sociometric matrix

Figure 7-3. A who-to-whom sociogram and its corresponding sociometric matrix.

possible group relationships increases as a geometric function of ($[n(n-1])/2$ so that what appears to be an innoculously small increase in group size, in reality can be quite complex; a group of eight has 28 possible relationships while a group of ten has 45 possible ones. Partly for this reason, sociometricians quickly became quite dissatisfied with sociograms and directed graphs. But such informal operationalizations also lead to arbitrarily different representations of the same group structures because the pictorial variations are endless: There are no formal rules for depicting communication structures with directed graphs.

In 1946, Forsyth and Katz introduced matrix algebra as a technique for formally analyzing sociometric data. They proposed using an $N \times N$ matrix with sociometric choices between individuals represented arbitrarily by 1 for the presence of a relationship and 0 for its absence. The right-hand portion of Figure 7–3 illustrates their method of tranforming directed graph data. If you will read across rows or down columns, you can easily verify this translation. For example, row 1 shows that person "1" chose no one, while column 1 signifies that that person was chosen by person "3."

At first glance, this transformation may not seem very significant, but it does have some strong points. First, notice how some 1's cluster; the bottom right-hand corner shows the two-person clique, while the upper middle has a larger cluster of 1's representing the larger clique. Furthermore, by comparing rows and columns we can see interesting phenomena: the two 1's in column 5 show person "5" was chosen most, while the two 1's in rows 2 and 3 symbolize persons "2" and "3" as the persons who chose the most other workmates.

Forsyth and Katz had better reasons, however, for using matrices; they realized that such matrices could be analyzed using matrix algebra. If the Figure 7–3 matrix is squared, the upper-left to lower-right diagonal measures *reciprocated* choices (two persons who chose each other) are the only 1's left:

		Person							
		1	2	3	4	5	6	7	8
	1	0	0	0	0	0	0	0	0
	2	0	0	0	0	0	0	0	0
	3	0	0	1	0	0	0	0	0
Person	4	0	0	0	0	0	0	0	0
	5	0	0	0	0	1	0	0	0
	6	0	0	0	0	0	0	0	0
	7	0	0	0	0	0	0	1	0
	8	0	0	0	0	0	0	0	1

This squaring process gives the analyst a clear idea of who belongs to reciprocated dyads. Similarly, if the original matrix is cubed, the 1's left show members of reciprocated triads. In this particular example, the new cubed matrix

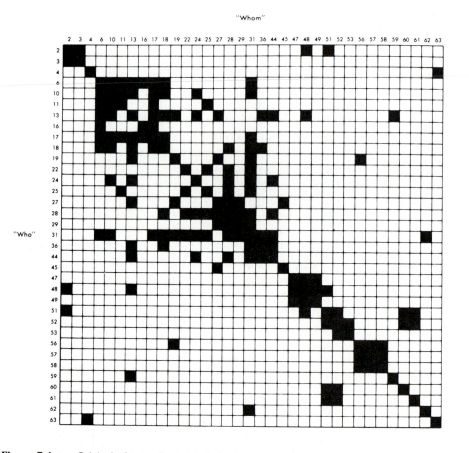

Figure 7-4a. Original who-to-whom matrix for interpersonal communication about family planning in village A. Note: The four isolates have been dropped from this matrix, in order to show more clearly the communication structure.

Source: Adapted from Figure 4.7 of Rogers and Kincaid, 1981, p. 172.

would be left with only "0s" because there are no cases of reciprocated triads. In this fashion, the progression of raising to higher powers highlights larger clique structures.

Other mathematical types of analysis exist for such matrices; for example, measures of social distance. However, these traditional methods simply examined the pattern of 1's along the $i = j$ diagonal without changing the original matrix. More recent approaches have capitalized on the computational strengths of computers systematically to rearrange rows and columns in the search for clusters of *asymmetric* relationships and *group hierarchy* (Rogers & Kincaid 1981). Software exists for measuring the number of links or steps in the shortest path joining any two individuals, the degree to which two people share similar patterns of asymmetric social links, and the clique structures of groups. For example, notice in Figure 7–4b how a computer program has simplified the interpersonal communication structure of a 63-person rural village in Mexico. In the process of six reorderings of the data, this program clearly

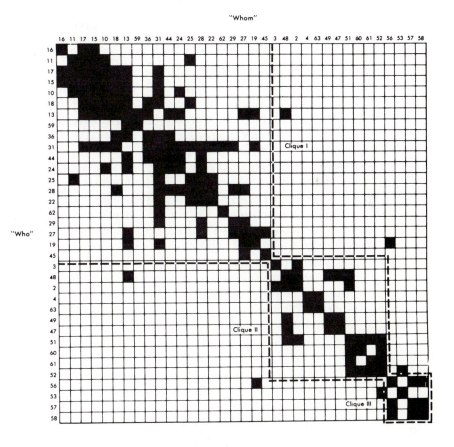

Figure 7-4b. Blockmodeled who-to-whom matrix for interpersonal communication about family planning in village A after six reorderings of data. Note: The four isolates have been dropped from this matrix, in order to show more clearly the clique structure.

Source: Adapted from Figure 4.9 of Rogers and Kincaid, 1981, p. 174.

identifies three village cliques important to the family planning process.

Although sociometric data generally have high reliability, lack of respondent privacy and particularistic or situational applicability can influence their validity. They basically measure only perceptions of attraction and repulsion. Many studies that assess social relationships are interested in the actual interpersonal communications or the accuracy of individual perceptions of such communications.

Summary

The process of operationalization is a never-ending process of improving upon our measurements and inventing new ones. Each operational indicator of the research variable is an indice or index. Researchers often combine three or more indices into a scale. The first step in designing a scale is to follow the rules of earlier chapters on figuring out the domain of the variable. This information is then used to structure the measurements.

One type of observation involves self-reported observation. Because attitudes, opinion, and other subjective phenomena are private by nature, methodologists recommend numerous rules for making them more accessible to analysis. They avoid indices that refer to the past, that are interpretable as factual, that have more than one interpretation, that are likely to receive endorsement by almost everyone or no one, and direct questions. They also recommend selecting indices that cover the entire range of the affective scale of interest; to use clear, simple, and direct language; and with complex affect, to include measures of ambiguity and ambivalence.

Researchers have verified a list of systematic response biases: social desirability, acquiescence, extremity, and sentence syntax. To minimize the effects of such response biases, methodologists recommend standard procedures: modifying conditions of scale administration through establishing respondent rapport, the importance of participation, and confidentiality; using clearly written explanatory prefaces to their scales; detecting and discarding responses largely affected by irrelevant factors; and correcting scale scores in proportion to the amount of their known contamination.

Investigators have invented numerous methods of scaling. The category-rank method simply asks participants to rank order some items according to a single criteria. Thurstone invented a number of more difficult methods that have been simplified and improved upon. In particular, most attitude scales use some form of a Likert scale in which subjects rate items with a common scale of strongly agree to strongly disagree.

A quite different method is Guttman scalogram analysis, which assumes items can be ordered along some unidimensional continuum of difficulty. Although it has the strength of ability to order nominal data, the assumption of unidimensional scaling is often inappropriate. For instance, another scaling method, the semantic differential, has verified three dimensions to any object in any culture: its goodness or evaluation, its powerfulness or potency, and its liveliness or activity level.

More recent methods of scaling attitudes are the forced-choice, Campbell bipolar, and ordered alternatives methods; all of these are variations and improvements on Likert and Thurstone scaling. The method of ordered alternatives, however, gives particularly important information lacking in all the other scaling techniques: the latitudes of acceptance, rejection, and noncommitment toward complex objects. Many other indirect methods such as the infamous Rorschach test exist. However, such methods do not normally have high reliability or validity. They may also introduce problems of invasion of privacy.

A burgeoning area of scaling innovations surrounds the study of social networks. Early methods that used visual diagrams called sociograms have given way to the more rigorous mathematically based techniques of matrix algebra. These methods are important for highlighting reciprocated and unreciprocated social linkages, perceived versus actual social relationships, and strong and weak social ties.

C H A P T E R

8

Surveys:
Use and Misuse

The little men in untold legions
Descend upon the private re-
gions
Behold, my child, the question-
naire,
And be as honest as you dare.

"As briefly as possible, kindly
state
Age and income, height and
weight,
Sex (M or F); sex of spouse
(or spouses-list).

Do you own your house?
How much of your income goes
for rent?
Give racial background, by percent.
Have you had, or are you now
having

Orgasm? Or thereunto a crav-
ing?
Will Christ return? If so, when?
(kindly fill this out in pen)
Do you masturbate? In what
style?
(fill and return the enclosed
vial)
Do you eat, or have you eaten
Feces? Whose?
And were you beaten?
Was your mother? Sister? Dog?
(attach descriptive catalogue.)
Have you mystic inspiration?
Our thanks for your co-opera-
tion."

Distended now with new-got
lore,
Our plump and pleasant men-
of-war

244

Torture whimsey into fact,
And then, to sanctify the act,
Cast in gleaming, ponderous rows,

Ingots of insipid prose.
A classic paper! Soon to be,
Rammed down the throats of such as we.[1]

Key Terms

Card List

Closed-ended questions

Computer-assisted telephone survey (CATI)

Depth interview

Double-barreled question

Frame of reference

Implied alternative

Interview

Leading question

Multiple-choice question

Nondirective probe

Open-ended question

Questionnaire

Quintamentional design

Randomized response technique

Readability formula

Schedule, Survey

Sleeper question

Split-ballot technique

Survey

Two-way question

Study Guide Questions

1. Name some of the most obvious defects of survey design and indicate how they can be overcome.

2. Discuss the three components of ideal communication and how they affect survey research design.

3. When should the researcher consider open-ended versus closed-ended questions? Why?

4. What principles underlie good open-ended question construction? Closed-ended question construction?

5. Explain the use of the quintamentional design.

---

[1]Submitted anonymously in lieu of an anonymous questionnaire in a study of student values and campus religion at the University of Wisconsin conducted by N. J. Demerath III and Kenneth G. Lutterman.

6. When is the randomized response technique useful? How is it operationalized?

7. What are the major novice errors in question design and how may they be overcome?

8. Explain the basic principles of question readability and wording.

9. How can the survey researcher aid question organization and sequencing?

10. How can consumers protect themselves from pseudosurveys?

11. How do pseudosurveys damage legitimate survey research?

12. How can you tell a legitimate from a pseudosurvey?

13. What are the basic differences in using questionnaires and interviews?

14. How do respectable survey organizations select and train interviewers? Why?

15. What types of nondirective probes exist and how can they be used effectively by the interviewer?

16. When is depth interviewing more appropriate than structured interviewing? How do they differ in strategy?

17. What are the main problems of depth interviewing for which interviewers need special training?

18. Why have telephone interviews become important to survey research? What are the advantages and disadvantages of telephone versus face-to-face interviewing?

19. List and explain basic quality control needs for interviewing.

20. What are the major disadvantages of survey methods?

The word "survey" has several meanings, each appropriate to its specialized use in social research: To examine or ascertain some situation, condition, or value; to determine the form, extent, or shape of some thing; and to examine some phenomenon with care. The survey is an extremely old social invention with roots in the ancient practice of voting that can be traced back at least as far as the early sixth century B.C. in ancient Sparta. Farquharson (1969:57–60) unearthed a letter from Pliny the Younger, a Roman orator and statesman who lived from roughly A.D. 62 to A.D. 113, that discussed how the choice among alternatives of acquittal, banishment, or death for persons accused of capital crimes affected the outcomes of voting.

By extension, the nineteenth and twentieth century has continued to produce voluminous scholarly work on the accuracy, reliability, and impartiality of surveys as mechanisms by which nations record and measure citizen reaction to the political and social issues of the day. The early 1900s saw the introduction of "straw votes," or unofficial canvasses of the electorate that recorded popular feelings toward political candidates and issues. The forerunner of modern day canvassing from 1916 to 1932 was the *Literary Digest* which accurately predicted presidential election outcomes. However, it failed spectacularly in 1936 and 1948, mostly because its polls depended on the volunteer responses of mail questionnaires. (Only one-fifth of 10 million ballots distributed were returned in 1936!)

During the Great Depression, the Federal government introduced probability sampling and modern survey methods to study such issues as unemployment and farmers' attitudes toward government programs. Many of those survey programs still continue today, and have been instrumental in producing valuable information on many of the topics introduced in later parts of this chapter. Survey research methods became a staple of academic research just after World War II, when academics who had worked for the U.S. Government on war surveys took up university posts: Paul Lazarsfeld founded the Bureau of Applied Social Research at Columbia; Rensis Likert started the Survey Research Center at the University of Michigan; and Clyde Hart, the National Opinion Research Center at the University of Chicago. These university-affiliated survey centers opened up polling practices to the study of a much wider variety of subjective phenomenon: social issues, attitudes, and trends. In fact, even the normally staid U.S. Bureau of the Census has finally relented to asking subjective questions about happiness, condition of housing, and so on.

The amount of survey research done and reported is staggering. Turner and Martin (1984:30) estimated that the survey industry easily produced gross revenues of $4 billion in 1978. Their sources also indicate that more than 28 million survey interviews by telephone were conducted in 1980. The amount of surveying is obvious to readers of newspapers and magazines; the news media bombards us constantly with survey data that they now often conduct in-house. In fact, the availability of computer-assisted telephone survey (CATI) technology has grossly widened the use of polls because it decreases the cost and time required to conduct polls and analyze data.

This chapter summarizes this huge accumulation of survey methods with an eye toward making you aware of both known merits and defects of survey methods. The problem is that surveys have not only become the most used but also the most abused method. More than 70 million homes will receive questionnaires or interviews this year that start off something like "We're doing a survey . . . and your help will be needed!" Those surveys will ask for the respondents' preferences on consumer products, as well as names, addresses, telephone numbers, occupations, and family incomes. *It is critical that you be able readily to distinguish whether the survey is bogus or legitimate, whether it is likely to lead to benign or Orwellian uses, and whether it is worth your time to fill out.* Although such major pollsters as the *U.S. Census Bureau, National Opinion Research Center, Survey Research Center* of the University of Michigan, *Roper*, and *Gallup* are well-known and respected, it is much more difficult for laypersons to distinguish among the lesser known polling organizations. Some of them may say that cooperation means free samples and discounts from consumer-products companies but not say that your personal information is compiled onto data tapes and sold to marketers plotting to promote their products. In essence, some will say they are doing a survey, but offer your name, address and phone number to anyone who wants it. Others simply use the word "survey" as a guise for getting a foot in your door to sell you something you do not want. Some politicians may use types of questions or designs known to produce misleading information to sell you or others their public policy rather than to use questions to formulate policy; others may mail out "opinion polls" to dress up requests for donations.

Legitimate survey researchers are rightly distressed that such unethical practices misrepresent and misuse their own polling practices, corrupt their professional image, and make people leery of surveys—which ultimately damages public support for legitimate surveys. Legitimate survey researchers are alarmed at the increasing rate of refusals because it leads to bad results. Pseudopolling is designed to show, not to know: It slants questions to elicit sympathetic responses. For example, as part of a thinly disguised fund-raising scheme, one of the nation's capital's economic lobbyists asked: *President Reagan feels too many of your dollars are wasted on subsidizing special interest "programs"—programs which could be provided by private sector businesses more efficiently and cost effectively. DO YOU AGREE?"* This question assumes that (1) the respondent believes "special interest" programs are a waste of money, and (2) that those programs will be covered by the private sector. Such types of "hired gun" pseudosurveys mislead policymakers with what they want to hear rather than saying what is true. Part of the purpose of this chapter is to make you wise to such misuse of surveys.

The seriousness of such unethical practices are appalling. Two organizations calling themselves the American Heart Research Foundation and the American Cancer Research Foundation—both of which have *no relation* to the American Heart Association or the American Cancer Association—mailed more than 12 million questionnaires in 1984 and 1985, in which they asked about stress and diet behavior and solicited donations. The U.S. Attorney's Office filed criminal charges against both organizations in 1986 because the surveys raised $1.5 million—but gave none to charity until after they learned they were under federal investigation. Both foundations pleaded guilty to fraud, yet they were required only to give $100,000 to research, pay $100,000 in fines, and stay out of further "charity" fund raising. Phony polls have proven so effective among fund raisers that such abuses threaten legitimate surveys.

To protect themselves from such unethical practices and to raise the standards for surveying, the National Council on Public Polls developed a code of ethics that requires that members minimally provide public disclosure of eight types of information about how they obtained their poll results. For example, the council requires disclosure of who sponsored the survey; the type of sample, its size, and accompanying sampling error; and complete wording of questions. We have every right to know how, why, and under what conditions particular survey results were obtained. In fact, reputable firms also believe it important that pollsters have an obligation to list other survey organizations that have studied the issues and give a comparison of findings. When presented with a survey, you are encouraged to ask these questions. As students and consumers, it is to your advantage to ask questions and learn to discriminate between legitimate and pseudosurveys.

Types of Surveys

Survey methods include both interviews and questionnaires. The *questionnaire* is a self-administered interview. It requires particularly clear self-explanatory instructions and question design because there is often no interviewer or proctor present to interpret the questionnaire for the participant. An *interview* is a special form of conversation in which one person attempts to extract information, opinions, or beliefs from another. Of course, many occupations involve asking questions to elicit information: nurses for medical histories; police officers in interrogations; journalists in media inquiries; and company personnel officers for job interviews. The purposes of these non-survey related occupations, as in the case of surveys, are to elicit information from one group of people or person and to transmit that information to others. However, the principles that apply to survey questioning should be useful to any type of profession interested in eliciting quality information.

In the extreme case, an interview may be so highly standardized that the interviewer has a *schedule* of questions that he or she must ask in exactly the same wording, question order, and even tone of voice. The reason for this high structuring is based on the desire to present all respondents with the same stimuli so that they are responding to the same research instrument. Even a slight change in question wording or emphasis can cause differences in responses.

The rationale for using highly structured interview schedules or questionnaires is based on the reasoning that participants must have a common vocabulary to elicit similar ranges of responses from similar stimuli (questions). Unfortunately, common vocabularies do not necessarily assure common definitions. The simple question, "Who is the head of this household?" will elicit appropriate responses virtually 100% of the time from white middle-class respondents, while English-speaking Puerto Rican immigrants often assume "head" to mean landlord. Unless the population to which the interview schedule or questionnaire is being administered is relatively culturally homogeneous, a less standardized form of interviewing may be more appropriate. In less standardized, or nondirective, interviews the interviewer plays a more passive and adaptive role, giving only enough direction to the questions so that the respondent will cover a topical area in depth while having more responsibility and freedom of expression.

Questionnaire and Interview Schedule Design

An interview is a conversation with a purpose, specifically the purpose of gathering information. Of course, there are many ways to get information through conversations—some of them better than others. Many of the criticisms leveled against questionnaires and interview schedules hinge upon sloppily designed question formats. As with any type of writing, question design requires much attention to drafting and redrafting. After all, if the question designer carelessly constructs questions, the respondents can not be expected to take the questions seriously: Spelling errors, poor grammar, and complex sentence constructions are among the more obvious detractors that serious students of question construction attempt to purge from their work. Other less obvious detractors are discussed in this chapter. These are also important to learn, if only to understand the difficult decisions that are necessary to formulate quality survey formats. Legitimate survey designers strive for complete and accurate communication of the respondents' ideas. Several general components underlie the ideal communication process: language, conceptual level of difficulty, and frame of reference.

Language typically involves a compromise between formulating the content of an information-getting question and searching for a shared researcher-respondent vocabulary with which to express that question. The survey designer has the responsibility to become aware of the respondents' vocabulary breadth and limitations. Oversimplified or overly difficult questions normally lower respondent motivation to communicate. A physician would probably prefer a question that referred to the actual technical names of the known AIDS viruses—HIV–1 and HIV–2—while the lay public would require a question that simply referred to "AIDS" without such complex distinctions. In all cases, the survey designer strives to keep questions simple, clear, and direct: This means short statements that rarely exceed 20 words; avoiding compound or complex sentence structure; omitting double negatives; and using questions that contain only one thought.

Closely related to the problem of language is the problem of *conceptual level of difficulty*. Even if the respondent shares a certain common vocabulary and grammar with the researcher, they may not share the cognitive organization necessary for the respondent to answer the question. Each of the following questions may appear to ask for simple recall, but are actually conceptually very demanding of human recall processes (Bradburn, Rips, & Shevell 1987: 157):

1. *During the past 12 months, about how many visits did you make to a dentist?*
2. *When you were growing up, how frequently did your father attend religious services?*
3. *During a typical week in your principal job, what percent of working time do you devote to management and administration?*

The time period for the first question is very demanding of memory and almost impossibly so for the second. Administrators who respond to the third question will likely have difficulty with memory retrieval and interpretation. Using an immediate time frame may provide "timely" information—at the cost of minimizing historical value for detecting trends.

Frame of reference refers to the fact that most words may be interpreted from different points of view or perspectives. From some 50 years of research by the U.S. Bureau of the Census' Monthly Labor Survey, we know that when asked the question *"Did you do any work for pay or profit last week?"* that respondents report in terms of what they consider their major activity. Many housewives who do part-time work will answer "no" because they consider such work irrelevant to their major self-definition. The solution to such problems is not always intractable. Census Bureau employees have revised the Monthly Labor Survey by first asking what the person's major activity was. Then those who gave nonworker responses are asked whether in addition to their major activity they did any work for pay. Question designers find it necessary to pretest questions adequately to see if the researcher's and respondent's frames of reference correspond; if they do not correspond, the designers change question wording or order. After the completion of an interview, Belson (1981) had his interviewers ask respondents what they thought the questions meant and how they arrived at their answers. The results document a considerable degree of misunderstanding with even commonly used words unbelievably misunderstood.

Each of us has idiosyncratic frames of references that may confuse the communication process. Although we recognize the need for incorporating specific frames of reference into some question designs, this may not be enough. Sometimes the interviewer will need to supply a nonleading frame of reference for the respondent. This is particularly true of questions that tap retrospective data. For instance,

Interviewer: When was the last time you were hospitalized?
Respondent: Hm. (long pause) Maybe seven or eight years ago.
Interviewer: Well, that would be 1980 or 1981. Reagan's second inauguration was in January 1985. Was your hospitalization before or after his inauguration?

Notice how the interviewer provides a "coat hanger" or frame of reference by which the respondent may measure and place his or her past history.

Language is always ambiguous. The wording of questions has long been considered the number one problem in survey research. Hovde (1936) asked survey designers what the major defects of survey research were and found that 74% named improperly worded questionnaires and 58% named faulty interpretations (frame of reference) as the principle defects. A half century later, standard works on the subject (Turner & Martin 1984) echo that same conclusion. The simple change of "buy" to "fire" in the following question has the effect of yielding a clear majority supporting gun control to a clear majority opposing it (pp. 130–151): *Would you favor or oppose a law that requires a person to obtain a police permit before he or she can buy a gun?*

Researchers use a method called the *split-ballot technique* to test for such potentially biasing effects. This technique involves randomly assigning half the respondents to receive each of several question versions. If a large difference exists between the randomized groups in percentage giving a certain response to the compared versions, the designer has reasonable basis for concluding that the question wording caused the difference. Clearly, this technique is beyond the financial means of many smaller survey organizations because it requires at least twice the number of respondents as normal surveys, but it is an important part of the science of perfecting question design.

Two frame-of-reference issues that have received very little research attention are the abstract-concrete dimension and the hypothetical-actual distinction. It makes quite a bit of difference to ask an abstract question ("*Do you believe in, or are you opposed to, freedom of speech?*") versus more concrete questions ("*Do you think it is acceptable or unacceptable for a person to yell 'Fire!' in a crowded theater?*"). Similarly, many questions are hypothetical ("*Would you be willing to contribute money directly to the Third World?*"). Serious problems arise in interpreting and placing faith in such questions. The frame of references for abstract and hypothetical questions are not of the same order as for concrete and actual issues. The purpose of polling is to communicate, but such questions fail to reveal *why* the public feels as it does.

The Research Issue

Writing questions requires a clear idea of the information the question designer wishes to collect. If the researcher has only a vague conception of the issues, it will be impossible to create questions that are meaningful for the respondents. Defining the issues involves stating them precisely through self-examination, asking oneself, "What am I *assuming* about the issue?" Only after fully recognizing what the issue is that needs researching, can the question designer evaluate any sacrifices in precision called for by the question wording.

In addition, meticulous researchers attempt to judge the meaningfulness of the issue to the respondents who will be answering questions. Often during pretesting researchers are surprised at how unmeaningful their questions are. Gallup polls indicate that less than half of the American adult population say they know what "socialized medicine" or "lobbyist in Washington" means. Ominously, however, when asked such questions as "*Are you generally in favor of, or opposed to, socialized medicine?*" most persons prefer not to appear ignorant by giving some type of answer to this question other than a "don't know."

One of the most difficult tasks is to state exactly what the problem is. A clear understanding of objectives should include the following statements:

1. The population for which the researcher desires information.
2. The kinds of information desired from this population.
3. The required precision of results. (This requires advise on sampling covered in Chapter 5.)

Once the researcher has clarified these objectives, they need translation into specific definitions:

4. Each objective must be operationally defined, so as to depend as little as possible on subjective attitudes.
5. Each objective should be operationally feasible.
6. Only easily understood and comparable definitions of concepts with common understandings should be used.

Open-Ended versus Closed-Ended Question Design

The problem of meaningfulness of the issue to the targeted respondents leads us into the problem of whether one should use open- or closed-ended questions. An *open-ended question* is a question that leaves the respondent free to respond in a relatively unrestricted manner. By contrast, a *closed-ended question* restricts choice of responses by forcing the respondent to answer in terms of given categories or alternatives. Robinson and Meadow (1982:116) speak of this problem as the oldest debate in the profession. The choice between each type of question depends on four considerations: (1) interview objectives, (2) respondent information level, (3) structure of respondent opinions, and (4) respondent motivation to communicate.

When the research objectives call for learning about the respondent's *level* of information, *frame of reference* in answering a question, or opinion structure, open-ended questions are most appropriate. If the objective is simply to *classify* an individual's attitude or behavior on some *clearly* understood dimension, then closed-ended questions are more appropriate. However, sometimes the researcher can use a battery of closed-ended questions that has more than one dimension, as long as the dimensions are not too complex in number or structure in place of one open-ended question which may be more difficult to code. Only after the interview objectives have been clearly defined is it appropriate to examine the next stage, the level of respondent's information.

The *level of respondent's information* calls for open-ended questions if the issues raised may be outside the experience of many respondents because, as we have seen, the respondent might otherwise choose blindly between closed-ended responses so not to appear ignorant. Also, where levels of information among respondents may be extremely variable or unknown, the open-ended question may be especially useful.

The *respondent's thought structuring* also determines choice of open- or closed-ended questions. Closed questions require less effort and ability to recall, order, and perhaps evaluate experience. They generally involve the hazard of offering an easy choice that the respondent might not make if forced to recall, organize, and evaluate personal experience. Open-ended questions demand more motivation on the part of the respondent because the aid of preset structured responses is missing. Closed-ended questions, by contrast, demand little motivation and invite inappropriate responses where the respondent finds it easy to say "don't know."

The respondent's *motivation to communicate* also affects the choice of closed-ended versus open-ended questions. The survey must make the task sufficiently meaningful, rewarding, and enjoyable for the purpose of attaining and maintaining the respondent's attention.

The making of closed questions requires (1) a *limited* number of *known* frames of reference, each of which has (2) a *known* range of possible responses, each of which has (3) *unambiguously* defined choices that approximate well the positions of respondents. But the meaning of what people say to interviewers is seldom self-evident; a solicited opinion may be a reified artifact of the question or interview situation, and the taken-for-granted assumptions underlying the code for classifying responses may beg the question about the meanings of survey data.

Therefore, although closed-ended questions are popular among pollsters because of lower cost, greater efficiency, and minimal ambiguity, they demand greater effort to design than open-ended questions which avoid "researcher-imposed constraint and bias of closed-ended questions" but "require careful and costly coding schemes to make them amenable to analysis" (Robinson & Meadow 1982: 116). Furthermore, closed-ended questions may quickly become obsolete in periods of rapid social change which imparts an advantage in adaptability to open-ended questions for long-term historical comparisons. However, split-ballot techniques (Schuman & Presser 1981) indicate that open-ended questions may not be as superior as previously assumed nor closed-ended questions as biasing in presentation of alternatives.

The interviewer must make the interviewing experience and task "sufficiently meaningful, sufficiently rewarding, and sufficiently enjoyable to attain and maintain the necessary respondent motivation" (Cannell & Kahn 1968:574). It is naive to assume that once a well-constructed schedule has been completed that any person can provide the proper interview atmosphere. Such factors as the participant's and interviewer's personality, attitudes, behavior, skills, and experience may affect the interview product.

Open-Ended Question Design

Experienced designers of open-ended questions suggest several criteria for quality production. First, the question should be relatively directive. It must provide the researcher's frame of reference; if it does not, the respondent may end up answering in any number of dimensions. Consider the following question, "*What are your thoughts concerning abortion laws?*" This question invites responses in any number of frames of reference: opinions, attitudes, past, present, future, laws in particular states, and so on. While this variety of dimensions may well be what the researcher desires to tap, if only one dimension interests the pollster, such as current opinions about present abortion laws in Utah, this question would need more explicit qualification.

Second, it often is a good idea to indicate the number of thoughts expected from each respondent: for example, "*Other than members of your family, what THREE PERSONS have provided the most important influences in your choice of occupation?*" Notice how this question both limits frame of reference to non-family ties and gives an expectation of three answers. Third, an explicit probe after a question may be advisable to job respondent memories: for instance, "*Anything else?*" "*What else?*" or "*Are there any others?*" Fourth, precoded answers for some open-ended questions may be possible and advisable as in "*During the past year, with how many, if any, of your relatives did you have face-to-face contact?*" which we might recode into "0, 1–2, 3–5, 6–10, 11 or more." This type of precoding is particularly applicable to open-ended answers expressible in numbers. Such precoding makes later processing of the data for analysis much more efficient, both in cost and time.

One of the fundamental problems with using open-ended questions is that few people ever use the same words for expressing the same idea. This makes analysis difficult and often relatively unreliable. It is inexcusable to use a closed-ended questionnaire simply to avoid the content analysis problems of open-ended questions. Pretests aid the conversion of open-ended questions to closed-ended questions. The question designer may find that a closed-ended question satisfies respondents' variety of responses, saving considerable labor on later codings of verbatim replies. There are two types of closed-ended questions: two-way and multiple-choice.

Closed-Ended Question Designs

Two-way questions

Experienced question designers (Turner & Martin 1984) recommend a number of criteria for forming two-way questions (where the respondent chooses between two choices). The first criteria is particularly important: *Avoid implied alternatives*, such as the use of "or not." If the "or not" is spelled out in detail, responses will generally be quite different than with the details of the "or not" alternative implied. It may not seem harmful to leave an alternative answer implied by "or not" in a question such as, "*If your party nominated a black man for President, would you vote for him if he were qualified for the job, or not?*" However, experience shows that such implied alternatives usually decrease the alternative response substantially; therefore, an "or not" is usually not sufficient to represent fairly the negative alternative. It would be much better to phrase the question something like "*Suppose your party nominated a black man for President. If he were qualified for the job, would you vote for him or against him?*"

Second, it helps to state both the pro and con sides of an argument just as implied alternatives should be spelled out in fairness to all sides of an issue.

Some people think there should be no commercials of any kind in children's programs because they feel children can be too easily influenced. Other people while perhaps objecting to certain commercials, by and large see no harm in them and think children learn from some of them. How do you feel—that there should be no commercials on any children's programs or that it is all right to have them?

Notice, also, that while the explanation is more than 20 words long, the question itself is close to 20 words in length. Providing information has the advantage of jogging the respondent's memory. However, the designer must take care not to oversimplify the issues in the process. Question designers who persist in using implied alternatives or not explicating all alternatives are either lazy writers or unethically trying to fudge the response distribution.

Third, except in rare instances (*"What is your sex?"*) two-way questions should provide a "Don't know" or "No opinion" answer. It is possible, for example, that many people in the above question on TV commercials have no real opinion. More difficult is the decision of whether to make the "Don't know" or "No opinion" response an explicit part of the question, or simply make it one of the possible coding categories available to the interviewer. Schuman and Presser (1979) used split-ballot techniques to study this issue. Although they found no change in the overall distribution of pro-con opinions they found that the explicit presentation of a "Don't know" (DK) or "No opinion" option to respondents did result in roughly one-fourth more "Don't know" responses than when it was not offered. It is better not to force individuals to express opinions when they do not actually have them.

Fourth, if a two-way question has a true middle position ("stayed the same"), it may be wise to change the two-way question to a three-way one, *"Since the last Presidential inauguration, do you think that presidential-congressional relations have improved, stayed the same, or deteriorated?"*; this would be an improved version of the two-way question, *"Since the last Presidential inauguration, do you think that presidential-congressional relations have improved or deteriorated?"* which does not exhaust the actual alternatives.

Fifth, alternatives should normally be *mutually exclusive* and *exhaustive*. However, where a compromise answer is possible, provision for answers such as "both alternatives" should be made. In the TV commercial questions constructed earlier, some people might view TV commercials as sometimes a good thing, sometimes a bad thing. Unless it is realistic to force the respondent to chose between the alternatives, some form of "both alternatives" answer would be appropriate.

Sixth, it is often advisable to set up separate answer boxes for qualified answers. In the TV commercial question some respondents might be inclined to respond with "TV commercials might be unhealthy in some cases." You should decide whether it is realistic to be forced into a preset alternative or provided with a separate qualified-answer box:

☐ *there should be no commercials on any children's program 1*
☐ *it is all right to have commercials on children's programs 2*
☐ *sometimes it is all right, but other times it is not all right, to have commercials. 3*

Such preset categories should be explicitly provided on the form with checkboxes to the left and codes that will be used for analysis to the right. The reason is simple: categorizing and coding answers by hand is a laborious, demanding task that must be made as easy and inexpensive as it is possible. One of the major reasons many survey organizations have gone over to computer-assisted technology interviewing (CATI) is to reduce such demands and expense. This newer electronic technology still uses electronic equivalents of check boxes, and adds the major advancement of question category coding that is transparent to the respondent and interviewer but which makes the respondent's responses instantly ready for analysis. Therefore, the chance for coding error is dramatically reduced and coding expenses are not necessary.

Seventh, avoid the use of strongly polarized alternatives if you wish the majority of respondents to make choices between them. For instance, *"Should the United States end the current international stalemate by quickly obliterating Iraq with H-bombs, or should we immediately withdraw our troops completely from the Middle East?"* polarizes the choices too bluntly and unrealistically for most respondents.

Avoid such unintended double-choice questions as, *"Is your health better or worse now than it was a year ago?"* which has the double choice of better-worse and now-then. It might be better to remove ambiguity from the above question by rewording it to read, *"Is your health better now or was it better a year ago?"* The idea is to reduce demands on respondents by presenting them with clear, simple choices. Although some types of question-design problems cannot be reasonably written out of a novice designer's question without long apprenticeship and research experience (for example, the subtle semantic differences between the use of "buy" and "fire" in the earlier gun-control question), these rules are much easier to learn and apply.

Multiple-choice questions

As was true of two-way questions, choices need to be mutually exclusive and complementarily balanced so that the number of alternatives on one side does not affect the distribution of replies. Second, all alternatives should be listed. If more than one choice is possible, explicit mention of this should be made. Thus, the decision as to whether the researcher wishes respondents to express one choice or more than one should be clearly given.

Third, if the researcher excludes certain choices in the question, this restriction should be explicitly introduced early in the question and emphasized during the analysis: An example occurs in the question, *"Aside from the expensiveness of abortions, which of these things would you say is the most important reason why some women would not obtain an abortion?"* which clearly delimits "important reasons" in the opening clause. In the analysis of answers to this question, the fact that expense has been *excluded* as a choice must be kept in mind so that readers are not misled by the data.

Fourth, a *card list* should always be given to the respondent if the question has more than three alternatives so that the respondent's answer is not based on just those responses he or she has not forgotten. For instance,

> 21. *Please tell me whether you think it should be possible for a pregnant woman to obtain a legal abortion* (HAND CARD A—see accompanying Figure 8.1—TO RESPONDENT, READ EACH STATEMENT, AND CIRCLE ONE CODE FOR EACH.)

Note also how question 21 highlights differences in the actual question— which is *italicized*—and interviewer instructions —which are CAPITALIZED. The professional question designer employs such standardized visual devices to reduce demands on the interviewer. Also note how each answer on Card A is separated by a line to clearly differentiate each answer for the respondent.

Fifth, "Don't know" and "No opinion" answers should be provided for on the interview schedule. But whether or not they need to appear on the card list is a more complex decision. From the aforementioned research (Schuman & Presser 1979:271), we know that the explicit inclusion of DKs will increase such answers, but should not affect the overall distribution of responses. The researcher who allows for explicit DK choices is making it easier for respondents who actually have opinions to waffle out of expressing opinions, but is also allowing for those who do not really have an informed opinion to more easily take such a position.

Sixth, it is often wise to vary the order of *card list choices* so that the order of stimuli presentation is controlled. This is because there is a response bias for some persons of choosing the first or last choices. Some CATI programs neutralize such biases through random presentation of responses.

Many of these rules for designing questions could be aided by following Dodd's (1947:120) classic standards: "Questions should be so phrased as to analyze the issue fairly to all factions as testable by the percent of agreement on phrasing by a competent panel of persons holding all the diverse opinions on that issue." That is, survey organizations would do well to pretest their questions by having a panel of judges who vary in their own positions on the issue rate various forms of a question as fair or not. Such a pretesting procedure, which is rarely used by modern pollsters would have the virtue of airing disputes over fairness and question bias before survey administration.

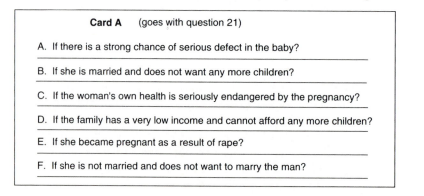

> **Card A**   (goes with question 21)
>
> A. If there is a strong chance of serious defect in the baby?
> _____
> B. If she is married and does not want any more children?
> _____
> C. If the woman's own health is seriously endangered by the pregnancy?
> _____
> D. If the family has a very low income and cannot afford any more children?
> _____
> E. If she became pregnant as a result of rape?
> _____
> F. If she is not married and does not want to marry the man?

Figure 8-1.   Example of a card list.

Other Types of Question Designs

George Gallup (1947) developed an approach to question design called the *quintamentional design* that has much proven merit in tapping opinions and attitudes. Researchers too often use only one question to operationalize specific subjective phenomenon; Gallup's fivefold organization of questions may increase the reliability and validity of subjective phenomena measurement. First, an open-ended knowledge question taps *awareness* of the attitude object. Then, another open-ended question helps ascertain *general attitudes* toward the same object. Third, a closed-ended question then measures *specific attitudes*. Fourth, another open-ended question taps *reasons* for holding this attitude. Finally, the researcher ends with a closed-ended exploration of *intensity* of feeling. The following sequence of questions on abortion follows this design.

1. What, specifically, do "abortion laws" mean to you?
2. What, if anything, should your state legislature do about present abortion laws?
3. Some people have suggested that this state's present abortion laws are adequate. Other people feel that the state's abortion laws are inadequate. Do you approve of abortion law change, or do you feel the abortion laws should remain unchanged?
4. Why do you feel this way?
5. How strongly do you feel about this—very strongly, fairly strongly, or not at all strongly?

A second quintamentional example takes a slightly different tack. (To save text space, responses have been deleted from the first quintamentional set as well as most other questions in this chapter. However, in practice, question designers never leave out such important information.)

1. *Have you heard about fluoridating public water supplies?*
   - ☐ Yes (ASK Q.2)
   - ☐ No (SKIP TO Q.6)
2. *As you understand it, what is the purpose of water fluoridation?* (SPECIFY BELOW)
3. *What is your opinion on fluoridating public water supplies? Do you feel it is very desirable, desirable, undesirable, or very undesirable?* (SHOW ATTITUDE STRENGTH CARD)

   - ☐ Very desirable
   - ☐ Desirable
   - ☐ Undesirable
   - ☐ Very undesirable
4. *Do you think the decision about whether or not to fluoridate the water supply should be made at the federal level, at the state level, at the county level, at the city level, or do you think it should be left to each local community?* (SHOW CARD B)

   - ☐ Federal level
   - ☐ State level

☐ County level
☐ City level
☐ Community level
☐ Some other level (SPECIFY)_____

5. *Who should decide to fluoridate or not to fluoridate—elected officials, a health authority such as the health department, or do you think the public themselves should decide by special vote?*

☐ elected officials
☐ health authorities
☐ the public by special vote

Although there is not always a need for as many as five questions in exploring issues, often times the five components of the quintamentional design—awareness or familiarity with the issue, expression of individual attitudes, reactions to specific proposals, reasons for these opinions, and intensity of opinions—are useful in adequately covering the various dimensions of a research issue.

The quintamentional design points to the need for consideration of multiple-question formats. Too often, novice survey designers try to pack too much into one question. For example, U.S. Bureau of the Census researchers have found that if they ask a single question of women that states *"How many children, if any, have you ever borne?"* they will get many less children than if they ask separate questions about the number of children still living with the mother, the number of children living elsewhere, the number of dead children, the number of stillborns, and so on.

One of the newer survey inventions that is becoming important to the study of very private and sensitive issues, while protecting anonymity, is called the *randomized response technique.* For example, one of the great unknowns in the AIDS epidemic is how quickly the virus will spread in the heterosexual population. To make accurate predictions, answers to sensitive questions are necessary: How many sexual partners do individuals have? How frequently do they acquire new partners? Do they use condoms? How many men and women are bisexual? Stanley Warner of York University in Ontario invented the randomized response technique in 1965 as a method of protecting individual privacy for any type of sensitive behavior or attitude: whether they have evaded paying taxes; whether they have illegally received cable television; whether they have ever misrepresented a vehicle's mileage to close a sale; or whether they have ever used illegal drugs.

The logic of the randomized response technique is as follows: Suppose you want to ask a sample of men whether they had had sex with a prostitute this month. You would ask each man the question, and then ask each to flip a coin. Then you would instruct each respondent to answer "no" if the coin comes up tails and they have not had sex with a prostitute this month. Otherwise, they should answer "yes." Only each individual knows whether his answer reflects the toss of the coin or his true experience. Then you would look at all the responses in your population. You know that half the questionnaire sample who have not had sex with a prostitute are expected to get tails and that half are expected to get heads when they flip the coin. Therefore, half of those who have not had sex with a prostitute will answer "yes" even though they have not done it. So, whatever proportion of your group said "no," the true number who did not have sex with a prostitute is double that. For example, if 5% of the population you surveyed said "no," then you could conclude that the true fraction that did not have sex with a prostitute is 10% and the true fraction that did is 90 percent. It is even possible to use this method with mail questionnaires: Some researchers have enclosed specially designed spinners along with questionnaires with enclosed instructions.

Respondents who have used the randomized response method tell interviewers that they trust the method to maintain their privacy, and that they do not think it employs tricks to invade their privacy. Such data suggest that randomized response techniques may lead to less lying and more truth telling for sensitive questions (Dawes & Smith 1985). In fact, when Tracy and Dawes (1981) used the split-ballot technique to test this method against more traditional, direct methods of questioning for illicit drug use, they discovered that it substantially outperformed more traditional, direct methods; it reduced mean response error as well as what error existed appeared to be random rather than systematic.

However, this method has two potential flaws. First, if a respondent were very anxious to hide any hint of unacceptable behavior, he or she might respond "no" even when the coin toss resulted in heads, simply because the "no" response involves no risk of detection; this method may make it easier for the respondent to admit to unacceptable behavior, but it does not guarantee honesty. Second, the number of cases required to produce estimates having a specified level of reliability would have to be much larger than with conventional methods, because the randomization procedure substantially increases sampling error. Also, in any survey intended to estimate the prevalence of behaviors that affect the risk of many subjects like AIDS, it would be necessary to analyze the resulting data by a *variety of social and demographic characteristics* to certify high- and low-risk groups. For example, we would want to estimate the use of prostitutes by men classified by age and marital status. To make reliable estimates for each cell in such a table, the number of cases in each cell would have to be much larger than the number required in a conventional survey, in which responses can be associated directly with respondents having specified characteristics. This further multiplies the number of cases required. Furthermore, any satisfactory analysis of an AIDS-risk survey would require the *cross-classification* of two or more risk factors, derived from responses to two or more questions. If the responses to these questions were obtained by the randomized response technique, the cell size would have to be unmanageably huge. For example, if one question asked a man whether he had had a sexual relationship with another man, we would surely want a second question asking whether any prophylactic measures had been taken. The resulting 2-by-2 table cross-classifying these two answers quadruples ($2*2 = 4$) the number of cases required.

There are alternatives to the randomized response technique that may equally overcome respondent reluctance to provide truthful answers to sensitive questions: A self-administered questionnaire within a conventional interview, or a flash card to which a respondent may respond with a specified letter—for example, "A" rather than "yes," or a graphic description of the behavior in question. The latter method has long been used for questions concerning contraception. Because these methods do not have the disadvantages of sampling error, but may not be perceived as safely protecting individual privacy, the researcher must weigh the trade-offs of each method.

Sleeper questions are sometimes used to measure how responsibly (validly) a respondent has answered survey questions. The late Robert Winch once had a question asking college students to rank-order the prestige of campus fraternities and sororities with which they were *familiar*. Five of the thirty fraternities and sororities on the list were fictitious. If a respondent ranked any three or more of the five, Winch disregarded the questionnaire during analysis. Some psychologists use the sleeper question, "*Do your eyes hurt when you urinate?*" to test for hypochondria because there is no known condition that causes eyes to hurt during urination. However, only experts should design such questions, and then only under rare conditions: At best, sophisticated respondents may catch a sleeper question for what it is and lose trust in the goals and purpose of the survey; at worst, their use may be considered dishonest and unethical, and may incur the hostility of the respondent because they mislead all respondents to catch the few who mislead the researcher.

Major Novice Errors and Unethical Practices in Question Construction

One of the most common serious errors made by neophyte or unethical question designers is the use of the *leading question* that lures the respondent's answers toward the wishes of the researcher. For instance, "*Aside from murder, under what other circumstances do you feel the death penalty should be used?*" assumes that the respondent believes in the use of the death penalty as justified, particularly in the case of murder. Neither assumption may be correct. Some respondents are likely to be either antagonized by the leading question, or will acquiesce to the question even though they do not believe in the death penalty. A slightly more subtle leading question is, "*How do you feel sex discrimination should be combated?*" which assumes that the respondent feels it should be combated. Such researchers as Kinsey (1948) and Hite (1987) have argued for breaking this rule when the respondent is reluctant to divulge personal information, as in "*When* did you begin masturbating?" However, this technique may backfire. The randomized response technique explained earlier is a superior alternative.

Implied alternative questions (for example, those that end in "*or not*") and questions with *only* a pro *or* con issue stated are even more subtle forms of the leading question. Compare the following questions designs, in response to the stimulus "*If some people in your community suggested that a book stating that blacks are genetically inferior should be taken out of your public library*":

... *would you favor removing this book?*
... *would you favor removing this book, or not?*

. . . would you favor removing this book or leaving it on the library shelves?

You should be able to see that the last design is much less leading than either of the other two.

Legitimate researchers wish to avoid leading questions because they are interested in the *actual* opinions of respondents. Leading questions may give the respondent the idea that the researcher wishes a specific answer because of the built-in biases. Therefore, rather than give an actual opinion, many respondents may "comply," or acquiesce, to the leading question. For this reason, the neophyte question designer must be particularly careful to avoid leading questions. Experienced question designers occasionally break this rule with a specific purpose in mind, but inexperienced researchers would be better off not breaking this rule.

Perhaps the most common error in survey research is the use of *double-barreled* questions that ask persons to respond to more than one stimuli at a time, by asking several questions at the same time. The problem is: To which stimuli will they respond? The only correct solution is to break double-barreled questions into separate questions. An example of a double-barreled question is, "*Would you support imposition of wage and price controls?*" This question is both leading and double-barreled. Double-barreled questions are usually easy to spot: They generally have an "and" or "or" in their wording that gives away the multiple stimuli. The question above ought to be split into two questions, such as "*Do you support, or are you opposed to, wage controls?*" A second example from a recent survey is, "*Do you feel that the increasing incidence of premarital and extramarital sex is basically good or bad?*" Many respondents feel quite differently about premarital and extramarital sex. Therefore, this question should also be split into two separate questions.

Just because respondents are willing to answer such questions is no excuse for using double-barreled questions. Respondents often wish to please the researcher; willingness to respond offers no assurance that frame of reference problems are settled. Even otherwise quite sophisticated researchers unintentionally design double-barreled questions. Thus, the survey designer should always be on guard for this problem.

Special care should be taken in the wording of questions designed to reconstruct the respondent's past actions or history. For example, the question "*How many times, if at all, a month do you attend church?*" could better be phrased "*How many times, if at all, during the past month did you attend church?*" The point is to avoid averaging questions, because event participation (church attendance in this case) may vary so greatly that respondents cannot meaningfully figure an average event frequency in an accurate way. By revising the question to ask for *actual* event frequency over a *short* period of time, the interviewer may get more meaningful data. Also, care should be taken as to the *time* of year reconstructed history questions are asked because of possible cyclical variations. Church attendance figures would be higher than normal during the Christmas and Easter seasons, lower during the summer months.

The researcher also must consider how difficult it is for the respondent to answer accurately due to length of recall period. Consider these questions:

1. *During the last year, how many times did you visit a doctor for any reason?*
2. *During the last four weeks, how much money did you spend on restaurant meals?*

Sudman and Bradburn (1982) relate memory decay to (1) the importance of the event, and (2) improper placement of events in time. The less important the event to the person, the more likely it will be underreported over lengthy time periods. By contrast, placement of events in time usually results in overreporting because respondents "telescope" time by including events outside the given reference period. A good rule of thumb is to keep recall periods no longer than one month, but the best recall period of all is simply "yesterday."

Question Wording and Readability

Attempt to keep sentence structure simple and to make questions less than 20 words in length. Use the simplest wording possible that conveys the meaning intended. Words should always be keyed to respondents with the lowest educational level. Sakiey and Fry (1984) have listed the 3,000 most frequently used English words. For most purposes, these words will express any thought you wish to convey in questions. Of course, you would want to use more technical jargon for some surveys—for instance, surveys of physicians about health practices.

Another good practice is to apply a readability formula. If you do not have access to computer software that can perform this type of function, this can be a tedious task, but one well worth the effort. One of the simpler formulae is the FOG Index which is computed as follows:

1. Take a 100–word sample from your survey report. Compute the mean number of words per sentence. (If the final sentence from your sample runs over 100 words, use the total number of words at the end of that sentence to compute the average number of words per sentence.)
2. Count the number of words in the 100–word sample with more than two syllables. Do not count proper nouns or three-syllable word forms ending in -ed or -es.
3. Add the average number of words per sentence to the number of words containing more than two syllables, and multiply the sum by 0.4.

For example, the FOG Index instructions above contain exactly 100 words, its average sentence length contains 20 words, and there are six words containing more than two syllables. The sum of these is 26. Multiplying 26 by 0.4 produces a FOG Index of the 10.4, or the tenth grade. Because the FOG Index gives only a quick approximation, it does not have great accuracy. A much more complex—but reliable and valid—readability formula is the DRP (Touchstone Applied Science Associates 1985) which is accurate about 85% of the time: The DRP score for the above instructions lowers the readability closer to the end of the eighth grade—which is close to the average reading level of the American population. The most prestigious polling agencies—Gallup, Harris, and NORC—use questions close to a twelfth-grade level.

Although the meaning of a particular word may seem obvious to you, it is often wise to consult a dictionary (and a dictionary of slang) for possible alternative meanings that might confuse the issue. While looking up definitions, look for possible alternative pronunciations which might better communicate the word. Often, good schedules have pronunciation of hard-to-pronounce words in parentheses following the word as an interview aid.

Such abstract concept words as "alienation," "anomie," "cohesion," and so forth should be avoided. If you want to explore such complex issues, more indirect attitude scaling methods are more appropriate.

If words you wish to emphasize are underlined or capitalized, misplaced emphasis can be reduced: *"What are your thoughts concerning LEGALIZED marijuana use?"*

Often, respondents will jump the gun in anticipating a question. One way to reduce this problem is to state the conditions before the alternatives. Consider the following two question formats:

1. *In the case of women who have contracted AIDS, are you in favor of legalized abortion?*
2. *Are you in favor of legalized abortion in the case of women who have contracted AIDS?*

The first question, by stating the conditions first, is likely to receive a more accurate response rate because it forces the respondent to listen more carefully to the full question. The elimination of unnecessary punctuation helps the respondent realize the question is not complete because slight pauses by the interviewer are conducive to premature answers.

"How much?" questions are often too indefinite. *"How long, on the average, is your daily travel to work?"* can be answered in terms of miles or time. Spell out the system with which you wish the respondent to answer.

There are also a number of ways in which a question may be loaded in favor of (or against) a particular issue. These should be avoided. Catch words, stereotypes, and prestige names alter response rates. *"Are you willing to have reasonable price increases with the hope that they will bring back prosperity?"* increased the affirmative response by 11% when the word "reasonable" was added. When a question was restated to include Eisenhower's name (*"General Eisenhower says the Army and Navy should be combined. . ."*). 49% approved compared to 29% when his name was not included (Payne 1951:126). On issues where respondents have weak opinions, they are more likely to cling to key words and phrases. In other words, their responses to marginal issues are distorted by more powerful question words such as "General Eisenhower," "Red China," or "Communist Europe."

Citation of the status quo also provides powerful influences. Any phrase that calls attention to existing conditions—*"As you know . . .,"* *"According to the law . . .,"* *"As it is now . . ."*—gives a predisposition to higher approval for the question, compared to the same question without one of these types of phrases.

Personalized questions normally receive slightly different responses than similar nonpersonalized questions because some people treat "you" singularly (personally) and others plurally (their family, work associates).

1. *"Do you consider it desirable or undesirable to balance the Federal budget?"*
2. *"Is it desirable or undesirable to balance the Federal budget?"*

There are many other danger words, expressions, and question formats that, like "you," change response rates. Before the institutionalization of such methods as the split-ballot method for studying question design, this part of design was basically an art form without clear rules. However, the 1980s saw a significant change toward a science of question design with reference work by Sudman and Bradburn (1982), Robinson and Meadow (1982), and Turner and Martin (1984). Persons wishing to practice survey research ought to consult such references.

One of the most important points almost always overlooked by question designers is how the question will sound five or ten years from now. If one wants to collect data over a period of time, question wording should remain constant. Even with a slight modification, the wording change has to be considered as a possible source of change in response rates. Therefore, the most useful questions are relatively timeless. Tom Smith (1980b) compiled a list of 295 such survey questions for the major survey organizations in the United States. He found that each item had been used an impressive 7.2 times. From this data, he was able to distinguish whether trends exist for particular demographics (background facts such as age, sex, and occupation), attitudes, person evaluations (self-rankings of psychological states), and actual behaviors.

Question Organization and Sequencing

The more complex, or less understood, the issue being measured, the more often a *battery* of questions should be used in preference to a single question. From previous chapters you know that reliability increases with an increase in indicators. Quintamentional question designs are also often useful in this regard because they lead the respondent through a meaningful exploration of the issue.

As with paragraphing in normal prose writing, it is a good idea to facilitate smooth transitions from question topic to topic within the survey, with material written into the schedule or questionnaire. Nothing is more disconcerting for a respondent than jumping from topic to topic. At best, all that the researcher does when making abrupt transitions is to create so much stress that the respondent does not give much thought to any particular question; at worst, many respondents will refuse to finish a poorly designed questionnaire, as is classically illustrated in this chapter's opening quotation. Examples of good transition statements include, *"Now in 1980, you may remember that . . .,"* *"Just thinking about your family now . . .,"* *"Now another kind of question . . .,"* or *"Now, I should like to ask you some questions about . . ."*

Transitions to specific questions from specific answers should also be clearly marked for the interviewer because often particular questions are not applicable given previous responses. Instructions for a hypothetical question 12 might have instructions to "If YES, go to question 13", and "If NO, skip to question 17." Because such directions are extremely demanding of interviewers, it is easy to understand why modern CATI interviewing software that automatically forces the correct question to appear before the interviewer is preferred; correctly programmed CATI interview schedules do not allow interviewers to make mistakes in question sequencing, nor to enter incorrect question responses; instead, they allow the interviewer to concentrate on the primary objective of interviewing rather than trying to decide what question to ask next.

Easy introductory questions (age, sex, number of children) are generally preferred at the beginning of the survey as a "warming up" exercise to engage respondents without taxing or threatening them. These are followed by the main, more complicated, and emotional questions. Riskier questions (such as income) often come late in the survey, so that if the respondent refuses to continue, less information is lost. Finally, a few easy questions are normally given at the end of the survey to provide some tension release, or "cooling off," for the respondent. If this is not done, the researcher risks the possibility of losing later interviews or creating an unpleasant interviewer-respondent situation in leave taking.

Any researcher who plans to have other persons do the interviewing generally provides a detailed interviewer's instruction guide. Instruction guides are an important means of increasing the reliability and validity of one's data because they explicate problems that the interviewer can be expected to encounter, and give standardized means of operationalizing the handling of those problems. Box 8–1 presents an example of parts of any model interviewer's instruction guide.

Box 8-1   *An Example of Portions of an Interviewer's Instructional Guide*

General Instructions

1. The interview quota is 5 per day, preferably more, but 5 is OK. Emphasize quality over quantity to assure 5 interviews a day (the days of arrival and departure count as 1 day together). All respondents have been "warned" by mail, so there is no obligation to call them before you visit them—and telephone-calling may be unwise as it is easier to refuse over the phone.

2. Be sure to write on your white card whether the respondent was

completely	partly	absent, ill, on	unwilling	impossible
interviewed	interviewed	vacation, etc.		to locate

3. Be sure to put on the schedule, upper right-hand corner on the first page, the special number assigned to the respondent. This is our only means of identification; the schedules will be treated confidentially as promised. Put the number in *immediately after* each interview, so as not to make the respondent "feel like a number." Never put the respondent's name on the schedule anywhere.

General Instructions For the Interview:

1. As a general rule, be maximally open-minded, curious, and receptive, without committing yourself to any position. When asked what you mean and think, tell respondents you are here to learn, not to pass judgment.

2. *Introduce yourself something like this:* How do you do, my name is _____, I am one of a team of interviewers under the direction of Professor Smith—I think you got a letter from him some days ago. The interview he mentioned does not last long, and it is completely confidential.

3. Frequently asked questions that need answers memorized are:

Why are you doing this survey? Well, this is a social science study, and we are interested in learning what people think about current social topics.

Why me? We picked some 500 people at random, and you happened to be one of them. You would do us a great favor—

I don't know anything! Very few people know anything for certain in this situation, but we would very much like to hear your opinions.

What will you do with my answers? Well, we will combine the answers from all our interviews to look for general patterns and trends.

4. Know the interview schedule by heart so you can have eye contact with the respondent. Keep the schedule so the respondent does not see what you are writing, but not so that it looks like you are trying to hide it. Check the correct category in a discreet manner. Remember to write down something verbatim, even thought it is covered by the precoding, just once in a while, otherwise the respondent feels you are not interested. However, it is a bad idea to write down too much because that could stop the normal flow of conversation.

5. As a rule, let the respondent lead; do not argue, but cut him or her short if the "story" becomes unnecessarily involved.

6. If the respondent wants to see the schedule, tell him or her to wait until the interview is over. When the interview is over, you may give the respondent a schedule to look at (but not their own), but you must say you need it back "because they are scarce."

7. If more than one person is at home when you call, just introduce yourself by saying, "Well, we drew a random sample, and it happened to be *Mr. (Mrs.)* Smith in this family_____". If this does not work, try, "According to my instructions, I should try to interview the person we have selected." If all else fails, conduct two interviews at the same time using two different interview schedules and say, "If you do not object, I find that what you are saying is so important that I would like to put that down, too."

8. When the interview is completed, and you have left the dwelling and can no longer be seen, look the schedule over, add comments that are still fresh in your memory, making sure that your coding has been correct, etc.

Survey Malpractice

Laypersons may be excused for not knowing these types of rules of good question-writing practice out of ignorance, but professionals who violate them unethically misrepresent social science. The American Sociological Association Council at its August 1986 meeting officially repudiated such violations in the specific case of Paul Cameron, a PhD in psychology who had already been barred from the American Psychological Association for unethical survey practices and who subsequently passed himself off as a sociologist. Cameron is a self-proclaimed "new rights" activist who has long spoken out against gay, lesbian, and women's rights in general. He has published data from surveys he designed and administered that have outraged professional sociologists and psychologists, partly because of highly questionable sampling techniques, and in part because of unethical question design. For example, among the 121 questions from his survey schedule are (with possible "answers" in brackets):

> *When was the last time you read a "dirty" magazine? (within the week/ within the month)*
> *How would you feel about: (a) sharing communal bath or toilet facilities with a homosexual or homosexuals? (very positively/I'd enjoy it greatly/ positive/I'd like it/neutral)*
> *With how many homosexual virgins have you had homosexual relations?*

What makes such absurdly unethical practices so alarming is the fact that normally credible journalistic and legal sources—without proper knowledge of survey practices—have gullibly reported his "findings" as credible. For example, Cameron has appeared as an "expert witness" in a Texas sodomy trial and had a "guest column" printed in *USA Today* and *The Wall Street Journal*.

The American Sociological Association (ASA) Council (1989:2) reports that "It does not take great analytical abilities to suspect from even a cursory review of Cameron's writings that his claims have almost nothing to do with social science, and that social science is used only to cover over another agenda." Although this case is an extreme one, it has become fashionable among some interest groups to invoke "survey methods" to grind social, economic, or political axes. I keep growing folders of such abuses of survey methods for classroom examples of questionable survey design and practice. We should all be concerned with such purposeful abuses of survey methods because ultimately they lead to the discrediting of useful information by gullible, undiscerning sectors of our society.

Questionnaire Techniques

Just as the interviewer and schedule design affect the respondent's motivation to supply information, a questionnaire also affects respondents. The attractiveness of a questionnaire (quality of paper, choice of fonts, neatness, etc.) can make all the difference in the recipient's motivation to fill it out and return it. Questionnaire designers need to take much more care in construction than interview schedule designers because no trained investigator will be present to explain question phraseology or instructions to the respondent. The question-naire respondent will be more likely to misinterpret questions, omit essential items, and make mistakes in filling out the questionnaire than a trained inter-viewer. Thus, the questionnaire must be simpler, less demanding, and more self-explanatory in form than the interview schedule.

The questionnaire also lacks the "personality" of an interview. Most peo-ple would prefer to talk about a subject than write out a detailed answer. Therefore, a questionnaire must sell itself to gain and keep the interest of its recipient. Such simple strategies as using personalized, colorful stamps rather than postage-metered envelopes and enclosing self-addressed stamped enve-lopes may grossly aid return rates. An accompanying letter of introduction that is carefully worded to stress the importance of the questionnaire also greatly helps. For example, the U.S. Bureau of the Census uses such paragraphs as:

> We appreciate your cooperation in connection with our regular survey program. We need this information to help in forecasting the kinds of changes that are likely to occur in the future and to help develop programs to meet changing conditions. Please complete this form, and mail it within the next three days in the enclosed envelope, which requires no postage. We hold all information in confidence and publish only statistical totals.

Experienced questionnaire designers know that they must sell their product to a relatively disinterested audience: Note the appeal about the legitimate and highly important purposes. If one can not sell the importance of the informa-tion needed, response rates will be atrociously low. Goyder (1982) found that *salience of topic* was the most important factor influencing questionnaire re-turn rates—presumably we should expect such highly visible topics as AIDS and cancer to have higher response rates than equally important, but less sa-lient, topics like lead-paint poisoning in slum housing, the transportation of hazardous materials through urban areas, and dangerous toys. Even the Bureau of the Census finds it difficult to obtain response rates of over 70%. Typically, academic researchers without the advantage of prestigious letterheads find it difficult getting even 15% of their sampled respondents to return their ques-tionnaires. When it comes to questionnaire and interview schedule completion rates, one survey interviewer's foot in the door is worth more than two ques-tionnaires thrown in the trash.

Structured Interviewing Techniques

Before any interviewing, interviewers must be selected and *trained*. Even if the researcher him- or herself does the interviewing and has done extensive inter-viewing in the past, he or she will find it necessary to pretest the schedule, preferably on respondents who will demand the most skill in interviewing. Not only does this pretest help in redesigning questions which turn out to communicate inappropriate frames of reference, but it also helps the researcher explicate standardized ways for handling problems that may occur.

There is growing evidence for characteristics that produce good and bad interviewing. Interviewers differentially define their roles—how much they ought to build rapport, probe, record answers, and so on—and those differences do account for part of the differences in results across interviewers. Turner and Martin (1984) summarize research into interviewer feedback indicating that interviewers need more training in proper use of feedback than they typically receive. They found that "Interviewers gave positive feedback indiscriminately for both good and poor respondent behavior; indeed, some of the worst respondent behavior (such as refusing to answer a question) were most likely to elicit positive comments by interviewers (p. 282)." In fact, because respondents often do not have a clear conception of what is expected of them, it becomes important to train interviewers how to improve the responses of respondents through appropriate positive and negative feedback. For example, we know that when respondents receive positive feedback for appropriate behavior that they provide more complete information. Interviewers must have, or develop through training, a considerable degree of social sensitivity or "intraceptiveness": a tactful sensing of the reactions of respondents and appropriate interviewer responses in the interview situation. Button's (1987) imaginative analysis of interviewer-respondent interaction indicates how both participants come to understand that the respondent has not answered a question. Sometimes, interviewer cues or the interviewer's reply to the respondent's answer may not provide the respondent with enough information to know whether or not the answer was entirely appropriate.

From Turner and Martin's (1984) summary, we can conclude that the interviewer must learn (1) to clarify for the respondent what is expected to perform his or her role properly, (2) provide cues as to how to be most effective in answering particular questions accurately, and (3) motivate the respondent to work diligently to recall and organize information and to report even potentially embarrassing material. General instructions to the respondent that clearly define the goals of the interview would include:

> "In order for your answers to be most helpful to us, it is important that you try to be as accurate as you can."

In the case of a questionnaire it is necessary to provide specific cues or suggestions to clarify performance on a particular task, such as:

> "For these next questions we'd like you to be as exact as you can about dates. *Please give me the date of . . .*"

Feedback statements, both positive and negative, help depending on the probable answer to a particular question, as shown in Figure 8–2.

To obtain commitment to engage wholeheartedly in providing the information, it is best to have the interviewer explain the importance of complete information, and then ask the respondent to sign a commitment agreement.

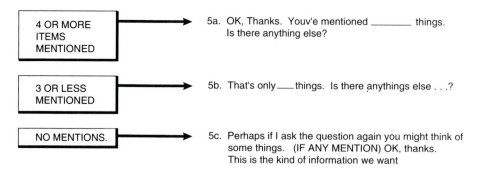

4 OR MORE ITEMS MENTIONED	5a. OK, Thanks. Youv'e mentioned _____ things. Is there anything else?
3 OR LESS MENTIONED	5b. That's only ____ things. Is there anythings else . . .?
NO MENTIONS.	5c. Perhaps if I ask the question again you might think of some things. (IF ANY MENTION) OK, thanks. This is the kind of information we want

Figure 8–2.   Example of a feedback statement.

> "I understand that the information from this interview must be very accurate to be useful. This means that I must do my best to give accurate and complete answers."

In exchange the interviewer then signs an agreement guaranteeing anonymity to the respondent.

Reputable survey organizations spend considerable time and money in teaching—and periodically retraining—interviewers in the types of respondent responses they can expect to encounter, and the types of standardized responses they will find most successful in dealing with them. Interviewer trainees are often intensively given both respondent and interviewer role-playing exercises, videotape feedback, and actual in-the-field training under the supervision of an experienced interviewer.

Most interviews require some type of introductory remarks to give the respondent some minimal level of understanding as to why he or she has been selected, who the interviewer is, and the general nature of the research topic. For example,

> Good day. I'm from the Public Opinion Survey Unit of the University of Missouri (*show official identification*). We're doing a survey at this time on how people feel about police-community relationships. This study is being done throughout the state, and the results will be used by local and state governments. The addresses at which we interview are chosen entirely by chance, and the interview only takes 45 minutes. All information is entirely confidential, of course.

Notice how this introduction gives early assurance of a number of important issues that differentiate the interviewer as legitimate: his or her identity, the legitimacy and purpose of the research, the process for choosing respondents, and general expectations of the respondent. Some type of identification (official letter or identification card) is usually helpful in further establishing legitimate identity, as well as a phone number at the agency where the respondent may call for further proof. Often an advance letter is helpful. With the increasing number of charlatans (sales personnel, fake fund raisers, and bill collectors) who also ask questions, these measures are vital in establishing early rapport with respondents. In addition, the interviewer, consistent with earlier ethical statements in Appendix A, should give enough information to the respondent that he or she can give informed consent. However, there is no need to give complete details, which in many instances would not only be misunderstood but might in some instances, bias the study results, as in a study of homosexual behavior.

Occasionally, the respondent puts up resistance. Typical resistance may take one of several basic forms. First, "Why was *I* chosen?" A good response might be, "We pick some addresses simply by chance, and then talk to somebody at those address to get an accurate picture of how people feel." Second, "How confidential will what I say be?" One good response to this question would be, "When we get through, we put the interviews together and come out with a general picture of the country as a whole" or "We don't identify anybody; we want to get an idea of the general mood of the country." Third, "I'm sorry but I'm busy doing . . ." is a typical excuse. Good answers to this might run as follows: "It'll only take about ____ minutes. Perhaps I could come in and talk with you while you went on doing . . . I wouldn't hold you up any." Fourth, sometimes the respondent will say, "I don't actually know much about ____ anyway. You ought to interview somebody who knows more." Here, the interviewer might respond, "Well, you see, we're eager to get the opinions and ideas of many people. I guess there aren't any of us who know too much about the many complicated things in the world these days. Why don't we try a few questions and see how it goes?" Notice, here, how the interviewer has emphasized that expert knowledge is not necessary, merely opinions and feelings. Fifth, potential respondents often will ask, "What sorts of things will you ask me?" In these cases, typically, it is acceptable to say something corresponding to, "This is part of a study to find out what people are thinking about ____ and what their attitudes are toward ____." Notice that even though this is vaguely stated, it normally satisfies respondents so that a detailed rundown of the interview schedule should be unnecessary. Box 8–1 also gives some typical answers to respondent questions.

Most survey organizations instruct their interviewers, once they have started the interview, not to stray beyond the question wording and order as printed on the schedule. In fact, Turner and Martin (1984) noted that this is one of the most serious contributions to survey errors and is, ironically, committed most often by experienced interviewers who should know better but think they are better judges than the original survey designers. However, occasionally nondirective probing is needed.

There are eight types of nondirective interview probes. First, "I see," "good," "um-hum," and "I understand" may be used as *brief expressions of understanding and interest*. However, research indicates that "um-hum" and "Good" should be used cautiously, if at all, because they may be misinterpreted as encouragement to respond in a biased manner. The second type are *brief, expectant pauses*. The length of the pause is critical: 2–3 second pauses have known positive effects, but those in excess of 10–15 seconds create discomfort. The third type is *neutral requests for additional information* like "*How do you mean?*, "*I'd like to know more of your thinking on that,*" "*Is there anything else?*," and "*Can you tell me more about that?*" Fourth, the interviewer may use *echo or near repetition of the respondent's words*:

Respondent: I've taken these treatments for almost six months, and I'm not getting any better.
Interviewer: You're not getting any better?

Research indicates that sensitive use of the echo and neutral requests forms convey important signals to the respondent that the interviewer is paying close attention or feels sympathy, and it implies encouragement to continue with similar responses. The fifth type of nondirective probe is such *summarizing or reflecting respondent expressions* as "You feel that . . ." or "You mean that . . ." This type is dangerous to use because it may lead to the bias of respondent acquiescence. When the interviewer uses *accurate* summaries within a framework of *acceptance* of the respondent's feelings, this may stimulate further conversation. However, if the interviewer inaccurately summarizes or shows nonpermissiveness, the respondent may well become defensive; or if the summary suggests agreement with the respondent, it may encourage acquiescence bias. Therefore, the summary technique demands attentive listening, ingenuity, and permissive attitudes on the part of the interviewer. Schuman and Presser (1981) demonstrate through the split-ballot method that acquiescence biases are not restricted to those of less education as researchers previously thought.

Sixth are *requests for specific kinds of additional information*: "Why do you think that is so?," "How did that become clear to you?," and "When was that?" A seventh type is *requests for clarification* such as "I'm not clear about that. Please explain what you meant." Eighth, *repetition of a primary question* probing may be used:

Interviewer: What kind of work do you do?
Respondent: Work at the paper mill.
Interviewer: I see. What kind of work do you do there?

These last three kinds of probes are good examples of how the interviewer can lead the respondent toward more appropriate definitions of good respondent behavior. As with echo or summarizing probes, they convey close attention to the respondent's answers, and encourage the respondent to continue in specific ways.

Probably nine out of ten interviews will not tax the interviewer's skills. Most respondents will articulate responses and cooperate without much need for the interviewer to reinforce the "good respondent" role. However, every interviewer finds interview situations that call for particular reinforcement tactics. At one extreme, are situations in which the respondent does *not* give complete, understandable, or unambiguous responses. The brief showing of understanding ("I see," "um-hmm," "I understand") often is sufficient to encourage amplification or continuation of a response. However, the interviewer must be careful not to suggest favorable or unfavorable reactions to the respondent's responses, because such reactions may cause serious reactive effects.

At the other extreme, are situations in which the respondent may be too verbose, giving all sorts of irrelevant information while eating up valuable interviewing time. Here the interviewer must be careful to show interest while tactfully interrupting and leading the subject back into the interview. For instance, "That's an interesting point, Pastor Inqlevist, but . . ." or "I see. Now where were we? Oh yes . . ." Generally speaking, such tactful negative reinforcement will quickly lead the respondent to structure responses more in line with the interviewer's intentions. Sometimes the interviewer may find it necessary to be more forceful by such phrases as, "Mr. Keillor, that's a very interesting story, but I have other interviews to finish today, and I would appreciate it if we could stick more to the questions." Or, "That's nice. Perhaps we could talk about that more after the interview is finished."

Short, staccato sounds like "ah" or the beginnings of words that are not completed during the middle of the respondent's phrase or sentence may help shorten an inappropriately wrong response. If this is ignored, increased gurgling may show the respondent that the interviewer has something to say. Interruptions at the *end* of the respondent's phrase or sentence are less generally effective in shortening responses.

Also, respondents sometimes openly test interviewers for "right" answers. The more effective responses to such situations are the more neutral and vague appeals that show interest in the respondent such as "There is no right answer. We're interested in your opinions." Or, "Your own ideas are what are most important in this survey."

Interviewer "presence" or nonverbal cues may also influence the respondent's answers. It is wise to train interviewers with videotape replays so they can view how their posture, eye contact, and vocal tone affect the interview process. If the interviewer does not show good eye contact and posture through out the interview, the respondent is likely to attribute lack of interest in, boredom with, or unimportance of the interview.

Although the various techniques outlined above are helpful in the interview process, they do not exhaust probing and directive needs of the interviewer. For example, the respondent may give inaccurate or inconsistent responses, irrelevant responses, nonresponses, or only partial responses. Therefore, the interviewer sometimes finds it necessary to provide more adequate frames of reference, interrupt inappropriate responses, or note inconsistencies.

If the interviewer wishes to clarify inconsistencies between responses he or she usually need only have a permissive attitude, summarize the alleged inconsistencies, and request clarification. For example,

> **Interviewer:**   Earlier you said that your husband worked for a research and development firm, but now you say he is a teacher. Please clarify this for me.

The interviewer might also have phrased the clarification request, "Could we go back over that for a moment?" Usually, repeating something the respondent said earlier in the interview will increase the respondent's motivation to respond because it shows that the interviewer feels what the respondent is saying is important, and he is listening attentively. However, the notion of inconsistencies must not appear to be a confrontation. Confrontation will normally jeopardize respondent participation because of its threatening nature. Whenever a question appears to threaten a respondent, it may be wise to break off the subject, change to another topic, and return to the topic after respondent confidence has been regained.

The *pace* or *tempo* of the interview can also be highly influential in motivating respondent communication. Novice interviewers often have difficulty in recognizing that their tempos are too fast or slow for particular respondents. If the interviewer tries to speed up the interview with respondents whose cultural or subcultural way of life is much slower than his or her own, he or she may well create confusion, impressions of harassment, or feelings of irritation or insecurity. By contrast, in interviews with busy corporation executives such respondents might be aggravated if the interviewer does not maintain a pace congenial with their busy schedules.

Finally, more flagrant probing errors by neophyte interviewers include such interviewer behaviors as the overuse of "Could you . . .?" or "Can you . . .?" type of phrasings that *ask* for a "no" answer. Better phrasing would be of the form, "Please tell me. . . ." Particularly at the beginning of an interview it is useful to use this form over the former because the interviewer, by getting the respondent into appropriate role behavior early in the interview, will increase chances that the respondent will continue in that manner later in the interview. A second flagrant error is the phrasing of questions in the leading form "I suppose you would agree or feel that . . ." or "I guess that's all you want to tell me, hmm?" Such pseudoclairvoyant language on the part of an interviewer is likely to elicit either acquiescent responses or hostility. A third common error is the use of the weak word "just" which signifies lack of significance.

One final serious problem is to allow one household member to report for any other. Comparisons of proxy reporting with self-reporting indicates that proxy respondents may consistently and seriously underreport for other members of the same household for some types of information.

Strategies of Depth Interviewing

Earlier in this chapter it was noted that structured interviewing is most appropriate in classifying clearly understood attitudinal or behavioral dimensions. However, there are many situations in which the researcher poorly understands the respondent's frame of reference, information levels, and opinion structures. In these cases, the researcher might resort to more unstructured, or depth, interviewing strategies. Probing and summarizing techniques discussed earlier are relatively unstructured techniques that even the proponents of the structured interview at times acknowledge. Depth interviewing builds upon the use of such techniques. However, because of the relative ambiguity of unstructured interview situations, it takes much more skill and practice to conduct depth interviews successfully.

Banaka (1971:21–30) discusses the need for trainees in depth interview tactics to reflect on (1) *inclusion*—how much they feel part of or excluded from the interview, (2) *control*—their perception of how much they are in control or out of control of the interview, and (3) *affection*—how they feel toward the respondent. Of course, these are problems in structured interviewing as well, but because the depth interviewer has no "prepared script" (interview schedule) on which to fall back, he or she has to develop special interpersonal skills that permit the interviewer rather than the respondent to structure the interview.

Inclusion problems must be tackled before control and affection problems because of the need to establish rapport with the respondent. For the interviewer, this often means coming to grips with the question, "Do I have the right to ask respondents about their private lives or personal opinions?" Unless interviewers can deal with this problem, they tend to give off nonverbal and verbal cues that reveal uneasiness. Any such signs of uneasiness on their part may easily dampen respondents' willingness to continue. Therefore, interviewers must have a wide familiarity with their own emotional self.

In an unpublished pilot study of the social-psychological affects of rape that was conducted during the 1970s, a woman interviewer was required to ask quite obviously personal questions of the rape victims. She had the necessary self-insight and emotional maturity to carry these interviews out without guilt or anxiety over entering into very private areas of the respondent's life. Experience shows that interviewers can ask almost anything of respondents and obtain truthful answers, if they can deal with their own moral-ethical qualms about delving into the respondent's life. By contrast, any displays of moral or ethical qualms on the part of the interviewer generally induce anxiety in the respondent.

The second issue is the problem of control. There is the danger that the respondent may take over control of the interview. The first means of dealing with control has been discussed under the topic of inclusion. If interviewers cannot handle their own emotions, they will easily be led by their respondents. Beyond this, a good tactic is to start with a *written general plan* of action. In the plan, researchers outline a description of their research problem, including a summary of data they feel will be needed to draw conclusions from the study. For instance, in the previously mentioned rape study, we decided on the following general plan:

I. Personal characteristics at the time of rape (age, income, education, religion, occupation, marital and parental statuses, number of brothers and sisters, and own birth order).

II. Personal knowledge of someone who has been raped or attempted rape.
   A. Their relationship to you at that time.
   B. The effect of this experience on them.
   C. The effect of this experience on you.
   D. Similarity-differences of own experiences to theirs.

III. Conception of rape before own experience; differences from actual rape.

IV. Description of actual rape (or attempted rape).
   A. Where and when did it happen?
   B. Distinguishing features of the rapist—age, height, weight, ethnicity, estimated social class.
   C. Personal contact with rapist beforehand.
   D. Description of his behavior. Reaction to his behavior. His reaction to your reaction.

V. Who was told of the rape? Relatives, friends, authorities (police, psychologist, minister). Why did you chose these particular people and not others?
   A. Who told them? What was their reaction to the account? Your reaction to their reaction.
   B. If people told, describe their procedures in handling the case. Your reaction to these procedures.
   C. If police are not told, why not?

VI. What happened to rapist? Was he caught, prosecuted, sentenced, incarcerated?
   A. How you felt about rapist at time of rape?
   B. Afterwards?

VII. Noticeable effect(s) rape has had on life—changes in attitudes toward rape, men in general or particular, other women, sex, police, self.

VIII. What would you do if caught now in same or similar situation? Advice for other women facing same type of situation?

IX Kind of sex education prior to rape.

X. Kinds of sex experience prior to rape.

XI. Motivations for participation in this study.

Unlike structured interviewing, to hold to a general interview plan when doing depth interviewing is often unwise. If my woman interviewer had stuck rigidly to the plan, she would have lost the interview on a number of instances. Rather, the plan is most useful as a *checklist* of points the interviewer needs to cover, but not necessarily in the order of the list no matter how logically laid out.

Inexperienced interviewers often lose control because they may

1. Infer things not stated by the respondent
2. Fixate on the respondent's words by repeating exactly what the respondent said
3. Ask questions that imply the researcher already knows the answer
4. Interrupt or anticipate the respondent's answers
5. Ask several questions before the respondent has a chance to respond to the first one.

By contrast, the respondent may diminish the interviewer's control by (Banaka 1971:17)

1. Being vague; answering "don't know"
2. Asking [the interviewer] a question about her- or himself
3. Resorting to long, rambling monologues
4. Interrupting [the interviewer] before he or she finishes a question
5. Asking [the interviewer] to clarify his or her questions
6. Talking in a very low voice so [the interviewer] can just barely hear.

The skillful depth interviewer learns to be on the lookout for signs that sufficient trust has not been established to control the interview situation.

Good depth interviews can be analyzed in terms of the amount of factual and feeling questions asked. Banaka (1971:101) recommends that about 15% to 25% of the questions should ask for factual material; fewer factual questions make the interview suffer from lack of adequate foundation, and more than 25% indicates the interviewer may be too anxious to avoid asking for personal feelings. Likewise, the interviewer should be asking approximately 15% to 25% opinion and 15% to 25% feeling questions. Less skillful interviewers shy away from asking enough opinion and feeling questions. Furthermore, skillful interviewers ask a lot of probing questions—up to 50% of the questions (Banaka 1971:102)—to get closer to the specifics of the targeted topic.

Good depth interviewers usually use some nondirective feedback to the respondent on what they seem to be stating or feeling as a means of (1) showing the respondents that they have been listening, and (2) encouraging the respondents to expose themselves more. Good interviewers totally avoid the use of giving advice, disagreeing, agreeing, and *inferring* things not explicitly stated by a respondent. (While agreements—for example, "I think that's so"— are bad tactics because they verbally condition the respondent to alter responses, it is acceptable and desirable for the interviewer to show that he or she is listening through occasional encouragements such as "uh-huh" or "I see.") Of course, occasionally depth interviewers, no matter how skilled, may be faced with such complete lack of cooperation that they may have to explicitly raise the need to explore the relational tensions that block the interview.

Such tensions bring up the *issue of emotions, which often create a great problem in depth interviewing.* Because the interviewer will ask highly charged, personal, and emotional questions, the interviewer needs special training in control over strong personal feelings. American culture supports hiding the direct expression of feelings rather than directly dealing with them. Some of the means of avoiding such feelings are (Banaka 1971:17)

1. Objectifying the feeling by expressing an opinion about the other person or object involved
2. Denying feelings
3. Avoiding the use of the pronoun "I"; using "we" or "you" so that [the interviewer] can't tell who belongs to the feeling or opinion
4. Crying or acting embarrassed
5. Asking to be excused for a minute.

To the extent that interviewers avoid the problem of affection, they lose control of the interview. Often these avoidance cues are used to "test" interviewers.

Once respondents discover that interviewers are (1) not made uncomfortable by self-disclosure *and* (2) wish them to explore rather than avoid such feelings, respondents will normally let down these defenses. Several of our rape respondents in response to extremely personal questions went through what they thought were "expected" crying spells. When, to their shock, they found the interviewer was neither sidetracked nor embarrassed by this affective behavior, they stopped these avoidance tactics and started openly discussing their feelings. (Crying is not necessarily an avoidance tactic, but may be used as one.) Had the interviewer been less comfortable with the direct expression of emotion she would likely have lost control of the interviews.

Structured interviews do not normally allow for or encourage variation in question sequence because such variation may lead to unintended response bias. However, the highly charged emotional atmosphere of typical depth interviewing situations requires flexibility in question sequencing. Depth interviewing is closer to field research than to most survey interviewing in degree of unstructuredness; it requires much more training in interpersonal skills than structured interviewing. The serious student of depth interviewing may profit by the role-playing exercises outlined by Banaka (1971).

Survey Method Variations

Traditional survey methods employ interviewers who interview respondents in the field. Such interviewing techniques have become exorbitant in costs; it is not unusual for them to cost more than $300 per interview. For purposes of managing costs, many survey organizations have searched for less expensive means of gaining quality interview data. The telephone interview significantly reduces survey costs, but it also has important noneconomic benefits. Social problems associated with some urban areas where people are nervous about opening doors to strangers, and interviewers who are nervous about entering such areas, create poor response rates that telephone interviewing may help lower. Other important benefits of telephone surveys exist: (1) Coders can quickly inform interviewers of interviewing techniques that create coding problems, (2) staff can meet with interviewers readily and on short notice—which helps raise initially low response rates, and (3) a pool of potential multilingual interviewers can handle non-English interviews from a central location.

Telephone interviews also create new problems. Although about 99% of all U.S. households now have at least one phone, only about 90% of all adults can be reached by phone, due to incidence of transience, institutionalization, and so on. The variability between areas also presents serious problems—at the low end, only 82% of Mississippi households report having a phone (Lavrakas 1987:15). Even within states one finds high variability—although most persons in the St. Louis metropolitan area have a phone, some areas of the nearby Ozarks find rates of phones in as low as 30% of households. Furthermore, for the purpose of privacy, increasing numbers of households now have unlisted phone numbers; for example, as many as 50% of Chicago residential phone numbers are unlisted. To overcome this problem, telephone surveyors have turned to random-digit dialing sampling methods. Such methods offer an attractive, low-cost survey technique. Persons called on an unlisted phone are about as likely to participate in a survey as those called on a listed phone. However, slightly more than 10% of households report having two or more separate telephone lines or numbers—giving them double or more the possibility of being called by this method (Lavrakas 1987:16).

However, telephone interviewing creates currently unsolved problems; it creates a new kind of nonresponse, the broken-off interview that occurs in about 4% of the calls. Telephone interviews also produce less information; interviewers cannot describe housing or talk with neighbors, nor can they describe nonrespondents' characteristics. Another problem with telephone interviews has to do with converting "scale" questions so they can be used over the phone. Comparisons of telephone with face-to-face interviews indicate that it is impossible to give telephone respondents a personal interview scale such as shown in Figure 8–3.

Instead, such question designers need to redesign such scales into "yes–no" questions that have logical branches: "*Is it safe or unsafe?*" IF RESPONDENT SAYS "SAFE": "*Is it very safe or somewhat unsafe?*" Such questioning techniques may make telephone interviews somewhat longer than personal interviews to gain the same information. Controlled experiments on data-gathering techniques also indicate significantly higher response rates by personal visit than by telephone. Therefore, the survey researcher may find some types of issues (more personal or sensitive ones) better handled by personal visit, although the technique is new enough that conclusive comparisons of telephone and person-to-person interviewing do not yet exist (Lavrakas 1987:8).

An even newer variation of survey techniques is Computer-Assisted Telephone Interviewing (CATI), which promises significant improvements in some important areas. First, it eliminates out-of-range answers. If the choices are "1 = yes" and "2 = no," and the interviewer mistakenly keys in a "3," the software will not permit the interviewer to move on to the next question until an acceptable choice is entered. This type of feature eliminates the formerly

Personal interview safety scale

Very safe	10
Safe	{ 9 8
Kind of safe	{ 7 6
A little risky	{ 5 4
Risky	{ 3 2
Very risky	1

Figure 8–3. Example of a personal interview scale.

costly postinterview stage of "cleaning" the data of keypunch errors. Second, open-ended questions can be easily sorted and searched by computer routines rather than laborious human techniques. Third, the question designer can build in logical operations ("IF 'YES' GO TO Q.13") that are transparent both to the interviewer and the respondent, but that insure that the interviewer asks the questions in the intended order. Fourth, known response biases of many attitude scaling techniques can be eliminated through built-in random presentation of items that is transparent to both the interviewer and the respondent. Fifth, questions like economic utility questions—which ask about complex trade-offs between different options that are normally difficult for the respondent to choose between, can be programmed into the software. Sixth, CATI can automatically record numerous built-in quality control checks—random-digit dialing; automatic dialing and quota control; automatic call-back and redialing of busy numbers; automatic control of call by time zone; interviewer productivity reports—that interviewers often forget or improperly record. Best of all, rather than wait months for special staff to clean and verify accuracy of data before it is publicly released, the interview data may be used immediately. Some survey organizations have even set up CATI systems that respondents can use through cable television. Although this method eliminates some visual problems of telephone interviewing, it raises questions concerning self-selection biases: Cable television is not widespread among the general population, and not all cable television subscribers may watch cable programs at any particular time.

Quality Control in Surveys

When things go wrong, interviewers are often blamed. Who are the interviewers? How are they supervised? How are they trained? What kind of quality control exists for their work? Turner and Martin (1984:261) have documented the contribution of interviewers to survey finding variability.

One way to reduce interviewer bias is through training programs. In a training program, supervisors teach interviewers why they will ask specific questions, how to ask the questions, what to do in specific circumstances, how to react to potential refusals, and other essential information. Reputable survey organizations put considerable time and effort into training through week-long training sessions, manuals, and special training guides. Such training normally will also be carried out on the job. Box 8–2 presents a checklist of the types of quality control matters that an interviewer trainer is likely to use to correct undesirable interviewer habits. Another quality control check is to have the supervisor sample each interviewer's work load. Reputable survey organizations wish to verify their interviewers' work to minimize interviews that are faked or sloppily done, to discover errors that call for correction or retraining on special problems, and to identify nonrespondent problems and characteristics.

Box 8-2 *A Sample Checklist of Interview Quality Control Questions*

a. Did the respondent take control away from the interviewer through

(1) asking personal questions?

(2) resorting to long, rambling monologues?

(3) asking the interviewer to clarify questions?

(4) hostility or aggressiveness?

b. Did the interviewer make sufficient use of

(1) eye contact?

(2) pauses?

(3) probes?

c. Did the interviewer

(1) talk too fast?

(2) mumble?

(3) appear to be submissive?

(4) let the respondent take control by asking questions?

(5) give opinions?

(6) criticize questions?

(7) fake data?

(8) not pursue a more precise answer?

(9) force the respondent into certain answers?

(10) have enough knowledge?

(11) give his or her own interpretation of questions?

(12) apologize for the interview?

(13) answer for the respondent?

(14) skip part of the interview?

(15) use such words as "just" or "only"?

(16) give the impression of knowing what he or she was doing?

(17) appear to have sufficient knowledge of the interview schedule?

Editing, coding, and nonresponse adjustments can also have substantial impact on the quality of data. Occupation, industry, place of work, and income are items that frequently require expert coding. One method of coding verification employs a verifier to recode a set of questionnaires with no knowledge of the codes originally assigned by a coder. A second is to have a verifier review the codes originally assigned. Independent verification is more costly than the dependent type, but has been found to give higher quality control. Through these techniques, the researcher may clarify difficult coding choices and questions and to weed out poor coders.

Editing insures completeness of information and resolution of inconsistencies. Because missing data present severe problems for meaningful analysis, survey researchers have long been interested in how to handle missing data in a meaningful way (Kalton 1983). Usually researchers delete missing cases from their analysis, and analyze the remaining data. Often it is possible, although expensive, to estimate the bias introduced by missing data. A lack of attention to these problems usually signals a lack of survey quality.

A final quality control check is to insure that the interviewers faithfully execute the sampling plan. Persons selected may be out of town, at work, busy doing something else, or simply not interested in participating. The evidence indicates that people who are unavailable for interviews at the first interview attempt are normally different from those who are available. They are more likely to be working, to live in a smaller household, and to have abnormally high or low incomes. The Bureau of the Census reports that over three times as many black men as one would expect by chance are lost to nonresponse (Turner & Martin 1984:270). Other groups which have high nonresponse rates are males, Catholics and Jews, white-collar workers, married people, college graduates, and suburban residents. These differences are far from trivial; they clearly show the need for more rigorous follow-up attempts to execute the sampling plan and to estimate the bias introduced by units unsuccessfully included in the sampling plan.

When survey organizations report poll error margins—normally of plus or minus 3%—they are speaking only of the most obvious error which is sampling error. Logically, if we read of differences of more than 3% in two different surveys on the same issue, we ought to be suspicious of the influence of nonsampling errors. Robinson and Meadow (1982) give numerous errors of these types; for example, they note that "In the same 1974–75 survey, *three apparently similar questions* showed that 11%, 25%, and 36% of the public, respectively, agreed that Israel should return the Palestinian land occupied since the 1967 war." Apparently, respondents must have interpreted these three questions quite differently.

Converse and Traugott (1986) note that less obvious forms of quality variation in the complex process of survey measurement add to error problems. One of the most important sources they note is nonresponse, which has more than doubled to an average 30% during the last decade. Converse and Traugott also point out that telephone nonresponse rates are actually higher than those in personal interviews. To show how nonresponse may seriously undermine confidence, they note that during the 1984 presidential campaign, Democratic partisans were more accessible at early calls than Republican ones: an initial "lead" for the Republicans of 3 percentage points after first-round interviewing increased to 13 percentage points after three call backs (p. 1,096).

Converse and Traugott also noted differences in amount of interviewer training and staff turnover rates. Some survey organizations give substantially more and qualitatively different training to their interviewers; some encourage their interviewers to discourage "don't know" responses, while others believe that such encouragement may lead to artificial results. One of the first cost "savings" that less respectable survey organizations use is less training: a 1987 "want ad" from the *St. Louis Post-Dispatch* reads:

> Temple University's Institute for Survey Research conducting NATIONAL SURVEY OF FAMILIES. Must go door-to-door to conduct detailed interviews, have car and flexible A.M., P.M., and WEEKEND hours. Flat rate of $40.00 per interview. Experience not necessary. Attendance at a PAID 3–day regional training conference required.

The idea that anybody can do quality interviewing with minimal training is offensive to survey quality control.

The final area of potential measurement variability is the survey schedule itself. We have already noted that question wording is crucial to interpretation and frame of reference. Type of question—open-ended versus closed, multiple-choice versus dichotomous, explicit versus implicit "don't knows," and so on—may lead to variations across surveys. But even more subtle is the context of particular questions. Converse and Traugott (1986:1097) give a classic example in which an incumbent candidate drew "warmer responses if assessed after a series of questions that highlight dimensions of performance where he had been successful than after items that evoked, however inadvertently, more negative outcomes." These two experts suggest the need to consider more careful wording and question placement in the interpretation of survey findings.

Disadvantages of Survey Methods

Strategies of good interviewing have been outlined in previous sections. Nevertheless, surveys have a number of scientific disadvantages. First, they are open to viewpoint biases. Comparisons of respondents' answers with voting records indicates up to 25% inaccuracy in some forms of the question "*Did you vote in the election last week?*" because some people say "yes," because they believe they ought to have voted when they actually did not. Response rates to such questions become more accurate when the respondent is given a "prefatory excuse": "*Some people may be unable to vote due to illness, vacation, or business trips. Did you vote in the election last week, or were you unable to vote?*" Nevertheless, respondents may still feel obligated to respond with "acceptable" answers: Because respondents feel they ought to have a driver's license or library card, approximately 10% more than actually have them will say they do.

A second problem with survey methods is memory decay. Memory decay is greater with (1) more elapsed time since the event, (2) lesser occurrence of the event, (3) relative unimportance of the event, (4) stronger connection of the question to a person's negative self-esteem, and (5) less accessibility to relevant data. Therefore, many data are often inaccessible to the researcher because respondents often cannot recall events or misrecall various events. The implications of the use of interviews in reconstructing past events should be evident. The more reason we have to assume respondent memory decay, the less reason we should have to depend on the interview as a research technique.

Third, interviewer and questionnaire proctor biases introduce distorting influences. Even though good interviewer training emphasizes that interviewers should always ask structured questions in exactly the same way regardless of the situation, training never erases all the effects of extra-interviewer bias. The Bureau of the Census rigorously trains neophyte interviewers, yet they still find that interviews by neophytes show slightly lower estimates of unemployment rates than those by more experienced interviewers. Maturation effects like boredom, fatigue, hunger, or experience may affect presentation of interview stimuli. Further, even if one could control for such interviewer variations by making them robotlike, nonrational considerations such as their physical attractiveness—sex, age, and social statuses would still introduce bias into interviewing and questionnaire proctoring. Blacks will often answer a questionnaire differently if the proctor is black rather than white, even if responses are completely anonymous. That is, respondents will often respond not only to questions as stimuli but also to interviewer/proctor characteristics. For example, race of interviewer made a startling difference to the question *"Could you tell me who two or three of your favorite actors or entertainers are?"* When the interviewer was a black, 46% and 39% of respondents in two surveys mentioned only black entertainers, but when the interviewer was white, those figures dropped to 15% and 19% (Turner & Martin 1984:137).

Fourth, surveys depend heavily on the respondent's motivation and ability. Although motivation to respond is dependent on question design, interviewer characteristics and interviewer techniques are more important than question design. More specifically (see Figure 8–4), factors like the respondent's dislike for interview content work against complete and accurate information reports, while such interview elements as the research agency's prestige provide motivation to provide complete and accurate information.

Respondents may not be able to answer apparently simple questions, even if they have the motivation to respond. Many respondents are unable to tell interviewers the age of their spouse or children. The Bureau of the Census finds that most wives have little idea of the kind of work their husbands' occupations involve.

Fifth, the most telling weakness of survey research is that it is inappropriate for the study of many social phenomena. That is, the data collected are generally from individuals, and only indirectly (if that) apply to such inter-

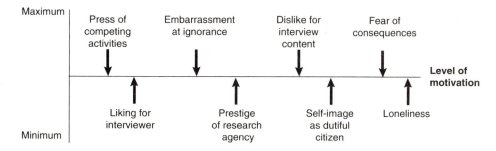

Figure 8-4.   Factors affecting the respondent's motivation to provide complete and accurate information to the interviewer.

Source: Cannell & Kahn from Interviewing (1968). In *Handbook of Social Psychology* (Lindzey and Aronson). New York: McGraw-Hill, p. 652. Reprinted by permission of McGraw-Hill Book Co., Inc.

individual phenomena as interaction, social organization, and dynamic social process. The scientific model is one of direct observation. Unfortunately, the survey method is only a poor approximation of direct observation. Chapter 10 (Field Research) comes much closer to approximating our ideal model of direct observation. The reader of survey research should keep these weaknesses in mind in using or interpreting survey results.

Strengths of Survey Methods

Given the above weaknesses it may seem surprising that social science methodology has become virtually synonymous with survey research. The following reasons may be given in support of survey methods, although not necessarily in support of their widespread use in the social and behavioral sciences.

First, survey methods are often the sole way of retrieving information about a respondent's past history—childhood experiences, recreational activities, or occupational history. This is particularly true with behavior that occurs very irregularly, privately, or rarely. Second, surveys provide one of the few techniques available for the study of attitudes, values, beliefs, and motives. Indeed, many experimental researchers supplement their experimental designs with questionnaires or interviews to learn whether or not an intended treatment variable actually had any effects. Third, survey methods are extremely adaptable to different situations, populations, and settings. Except in the cases of extremely young children and persons with extreme physical or mental incapacities, survey methods have wide applicability.

Perhaps the fourth most typical rational for survey analysis, however, include the following two strengths: data structuredness and collection efficiency. Highly structured surveys have high amounts of data standardization, which makes them particularly amenable to statistical analysis. Fifth, they are extremely efficient in providing large amounts of data at relatively low cost in a short period of time.

Unfortunately, these last two reasons may be the wrong reasons for using survey methods. The fact that large amounts of quantifiable data are collectable in a short period of time and with relatively low cost does not insure that the data will have direct bearing on the researcher's theory. Indeed, survey data often treat society as a simple aggregate of individuals. Therefore, efficiency in data collection may often provide us with information that is of no relevance. Highly structured garbage is still garbage—standardization is only a virtue if it continues to provide accurate and valid responses. Many types of social studies could not have provided meaningful data if they had only employed survey methods. Social routines and patterns are mostly beyond the scope of human consciousness, and require ethnographic methods discussed in Chapter 10 or direct observations discussed in Chapter 9. For instance, classic work on police brutality by Reiss (1968:8) found only 60% of the observations of police brutality by trained observers were consistent three months later with interview self-reports of victimization.

Summary

Survey methods have become the most used method throughout the social sciences. Two generic forms of surveys exist: questionnaires and interview schedules. Because the questionnaire is self-administered, it requires much more effort to produce a clearer, more self-explanatory, quality product than the interview schedule. Ideally, the interview schedule is administered by a rigorously trained interviewer, which relieves the respondent of much of the burden of understanding what information the survey is designed to elicit. Interviews may be subdivided into those which are relatively structured, with preset questions, responses, and question order—and the unstructured, which give only enough direction to the interviewer that he or she knows what topics ought to be covered.

The most difficult part of any type of survey is the formulation of a language that is shared by both the interviewer and the respondent. The burden of shared language falls on the question designer who must consider numerous issues: the demands of the level of vocabulary, grammar, conceptual difficulty, frame of reference, and so on. To test for the potential biasing effects of these types of problems, survey researchers increasingly rely on the split-ballot technique which randomly splits a population of respondents into two groups. The researcher compares different versions of a question for each group. The survey designer can reasonably attribute any differences in responses elicited by the questions to question wording. Most of what we have learned about good survey design has come from this type of technique.

Writing good questions requires that the researcher have a clear conception of the research issue. It also requires that the researcher design questions that are meaningful to the respondent. When the respondent clearly understands and has a high level of information about the issue, and the various dimensions underlying the issue have a known range of limited and unambiguous responses, then a closed-ended question may be most appropriate. Otherwise, open-ended questions may prove more fruitful. Closed-ended questions cost less to administer and analyze than open-ended questions, but they require more effort to design properly and may not prove as useful for long-term use.

Closed-ended questions may be subdivided into two-way questions and multiple-choice questions. In either case, it is important that the question present the entire issue. Similarly, multiple-choice questions that have more pro than con (or vice versa) choices introduce bias, in favor of the more spelled-out position.

Many times, complex issues are better presented by first giving statements that summarize the various positions, and then asking the respondent which side is closest to their own position. But such explicit presentation of the issues may sensitize the respondents to express opinions they do not really hold. The researcher must decide before question design is completed whether or not this is what he or she wishes to do. The researcher must also make decisions about other important issues: whether to use "no opinion" responses, whether choices are mutually exclusive and exhaustive, how to realistically qualify some choices, and so on. Some questions forms are always best avoided: long questions; complex sentences; and double-choice (double-barreled) questions.

Structured schedules require special visual aids: Card lists which present multiple-choice options that the interviewer can hand to the respondent; clearly defined instructions that show the interviewer the exact question order, when to probe, and so on. Because interviewing is a demanding task for both interviewers and respondents, such visual aids are important to reducing those demands.

Too often, researchers design questions that attempt to cover too much material. A better practice is to use a number of separate questions in a multiple-question format. One specific multiple-question format is the quintamentional design; this technique explores specific subjective phenomena in more detail. This design taps attitude awareness, general attitudes, specific attitudes, reasons for holding specific attitudes, and intensity of feelings.

The randomized response technique is a relatively recent survey invention for studying sensitive issues while protecting privacy. In this method, the respondent flips a coin (or similarly manipulates some other randomizing device) just after the interviewer has asked a sensitive two-way question. Because only the respondent knows the outcome of the coin toss, only the respondent will know whether his or her succeeding answer is a response to the coin toss or the question. Another type of survey invention is the sleeper question. It may lead to catching those few respondents who do not take seriously the goals of the survey, but it may lead to loss of trust in the research process because it uses essentially dishonest means of catching dishonest or noncaring respondents.

Novice question designers often make common mistakes that need to be avoided. One common mistake often made by novice question designers is the use of leading questions; these are questions that lure the respondent's answer toward the wishes of the researcher or that employ implicit, but invalid, assumptions. Another mistake is the implied alternative question, which does not give the respondent all sides of an issue. The implied alternative question misleads respondents to think that the interviewer wants a particular answer, rather than actual opinions, because of the built-in biases. An even more common problem is the double-barreled question in which the question designer presents more than one stimuli to the respondent. The problem with this is that the analyst will not know to which stimuli the respondent is actually answering. Such questions need to be broken down into separate questions.

The art of questioning demands much of respondent memory. Questions that ask respondents to recall events that occurred more than a month ago are particularly demanding. These types of questions need special attention to time-span frames of reference. The longer the recall period, the less likely the question designer will tap valid answers. Other features of questions may be overly demanding of respondents: complex or compound sentence structure, infrequently used or frequently misunderstood words, improperly used punctuation, and lengthy expressions. Experts encourage novice designers to consider testing their question formats with standard readability indexes. More subtle response differences occur as a result of using question phrasing that personalizes questions with the use of "you," assume the status quo, or make reference to words that are highly charged because of current stereotypes, prestige, or catch phrases.

Survey designers often do not take into consideration how the question will sound a decade from now. Comparative analysis requires that we use language that will stand the test of time. The reason is that even slight changes in question wording can cause changes in responses rather than measuring actual historical changes.

Questions, once worded properly, must be organized and structured just as sentences in any effective writing need organization into paragraphs with smooth interparagraph transitions. One very effective method of question organization is the quintamentional design. Designers also need to provide transitional instructions that express clearly what questions follow what answers. The heavy demands placed upon interviewers to record accurately—and on respondents to answer validly—makes it imperative that the researcher provide a detailed interviewer's instruction guide and large amounts of question pretesting, off-the-job training, and on-the-job retraining.

Not to provide the above-stated materials is equivalent to malpractice. Because of the popularity of the survey method, we should take special interest in Lakeman's (1970:9) warning that "to tamper with [quality survey methods]— or to tolerate the continuance of their known defects . . . is on a par with using false weights and measures." Because pseudointerviewing has become widespread, legitimate survey practitioners have closed ranks on such unethical practices to protect the validity of their research.

Quality survey organizations teach their interviewers how to get their foot in the respondent's door, build rapport, motivate valid responses, effectively probe for clearer responses, and use proper feedback cues. Some of the means they use to accomplish these goals are standard introductions that establish legitimacy of the research and survey unit and promises of absolute confidentiality of responses, and rigorous training in more subtle tactics like how to stick to the question order, tone of voice, interview pace and tempo, and good eye contact.

The most difficult type of interviewing is depth interviewing. It requires much greater training in social and emotional skills. Depth interviews require special attention to three problems: making the respondents feel part of the interview, keeping control over the interview, and dealing with feelings toward the respondent. Normally, depth interviewing does not involve an interview schedule; instead, it employs a checklist of topics that need coverage. Because the interviewer will ask highly charged, personal, and emotional questions, the interviewer needs special training in control over personal anxiety.

Survey organizations continually search for means of reducing expenses because traditional survey methods are costly. Increasingly they have turned to telephone interviews and Computer-Assisted Techniques of Interviewing (CATI) to reduce costs. Telephone interviewing and CATI significantly reduce problems of costs and human errors in coding and sampling. However, these new technologies create some additional problems: such new types of refusals as the telephone hang-up, greater reliance on such less visually demanding question formats as the two-way question, which may be less appropriate than a more complexly designed question administered in person.

In spite of attempts by legitimate survey organizations to introduce quality control into their methods, critics have become increasingly concerned with the effect of non-sampling errors on survey result interpretations. Some of the more alarming problems are growing nonresponse rates, staff turnover rates, and the differences that question wording and order make on interpretation and frame of reference, memory decay, interviewer biases, and motivating respondents. Further, the survey method is not necessarily the most appropriate form of social research because it does not satisfy the scientific requirement of direct observation. In spite of these problems, survey research continues to dominate social research. The reason is simple: It provides data amenable to analysis relatively cheaply and quickly. Nevertheless, inexpensive, readily available data are not necessarily quality data. Other, more direct, methods of observation are often much more appropriate.

9

Systematizing Observations

. . . while nearly everyone who goes to a zoo sees the animals there, and many even watch some of those animals, very few can be said to observe their behavior.[1]

Key Terms

Central tendency bias

Coding relativism

Concurrent data analysis

Consensual validation

Extralinguistic observation

Linguistic observation

Nonsequential analysis

Nonverbal observation

Observer self-interview schedule

Proxemics

Sequential analysis

Spatial observation

Systematic observation

[1]McCall, G. J. (1984) Systematic field observation. *Annual Review of Sociology, 10,* 263–282.

Study Guide Questions

1. What are the differences between seeing, watching, and observing, and why are these differences important to systematic observation?

2. What are the advantages of using systematic observations versus self-reported data?

3. Explain the importance of each of the five types of generic features of systematic observation.

4. What fundamental problems exist for using popular linguistic measures in social interaction studies?

5. How do nonverbal and verbal behaviors differ? Why are these differences important?

6. Explain the major differences in each of the four extralinguistic dimensions.

7. What types of social cues are given by each of the four major types of body movement dimensions?

8. What does observer self-interview schedules share in common with traditional interview techniques as well as field research?

9. What are some of the advantages and disadvantages of using portable recording devices over simple note taking?

10. What methods are commonly used to check the reliability of observational data?

11. What are common sources of unreliability and invalidity in observational research?

12. What methods are recommended for training observers to make more reliable and valid observations?

13. What special problems exist in the analysis of observational data?

14. Why have researchers started to use more multidimensional approaches in observation? How are these multidimensional approaches like maps? And what are their limitations?

Weick (1985:568) defines systematic observations as "sustained, explicit, methodological observing and paraphrasing of social situations"; each of these four components is a *necessary* condition. First, "sustained" implies commitment to a protracted period of observations rather than the haphazard, punctuated observations laypersons typically make in everyday life. Second, "explicit" suggests observations that satisfy normal scientific criteria of observations that are open to operational replication by other trained observers. Systematic observations are relatively precise about what to observe, ignore, and record. Third, "methodological" denotes intensive, systematic inquiry. This means that the observation plan explicates what should be noticed and what should be ignored. Fourth, "paraphrasing" involves the process of placing observations within a particular social context so that others can understand their meaning. It implies that the observer will consciously manipulate the observational process for the purposes of highlighting who acts, what actions occur, and the relational context of those actions. McCall (1984) neatly summarizes what systematic observation is all about in the opening statement (p. 264): "while nearly everyone who goes to a zoo *sees* the animals there, and many even *watch* some of those animals, very few can be said to *observe* their behavior." The differences between seeing, watching, and observing are critical to understanding systematic observations. *Seeing* involves simple perception with the eyes. *Watching* involves attentiveness that goes beyond elementary visual recognition. *Observation* implies systematically watching for details for the purpose of arriving at explicit judgments.

Not all behavioral research satisfies these criteria. For example, field research (Chapter 10) rarely uses explicit, systematic means of observing: Normally, fieldworkers do not try to systematically control the observational process by imposing specific units of analysis on some social phenomena. Fieldworkers prefer more flexible methods of data collection without explicit preconception of its structure; observational structure that is emergent or implicit. At the other extreme are laboratory experiments and computer simulation studies, which demand highly systematic, preset observational data, and use very explicit preconceptions of how the data ought to be collected. The formality, habituation, regularity, or stability of naturalistic behaviors and social events affects the researcher's ability to collect systematic observation: If the researcher concludes—rightly or wrongly—that an event is not amenable to systematic observation, then such beliefs preclude systematic observational methods.

Work on the measurement of social ties provides a classic example of the systemization of behavioral observation. In 1974, Granovetter (1974) breathed new life into social network studies of job searching by suggesting that the type of personal intermediary used to find a job was associated with income, job satisfaction, and the intensity of the job search itself. Granovetter's methods were quite crude: He used a simple ordinal dichotomy between "weak" and "strong" social ties that was based solely on whether the social tie was a strong tie (friend or relative) or a weak tie (acquaintance). He then measured the hypothesis that jobs found through "weak" social ties provide more jobs and those with higher incomes than those found through "strong" social ties. Because other social network analysts quickly recognized that the weak and strong tie distinction is only an instance of a broader phenomenon—the exploitation of personally held "social resources"—they worked toward empirically improving upon Granovetter's original operationalization. To this end, Bridges and Villemez (1986) proposed an alternative operationalization based upon a simple classification tree for weak and strong ties shown in Figure 9–1.

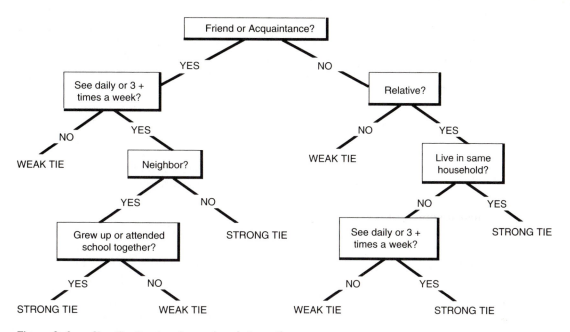

Figure 9–1. Classification tree for weak and strong ties.

Source: Bridges & Villemez (1986)

Bridges and Villemez considerably clarified weak and strong ties through their classification scheme; for them to consider a personal contact as a strong tie, the individual would have to be a relative, friend, or acquaintance who the respondent saw at least three times a week or a relative who lived in the same household. There is one exception: Neighbors are frequently considered weak ties, unless they grew up together with the respondent or they attended school together. All other individuals are weak ties: People who they met on a chance basis or individuals who were former employers. Although the measurement is not perfect, it certainly is a great improvement on the original measure.

Why Use Systematic Observations?

Most of the measurements discussed in Chapters 7 and 8 assume that participants have self-awareness and a willingness to communicate. However, even if persons can and do communicate their true subjective states to the researcher, this in no way assures correspondence of their subjective feelings and actual behavior: Individuals may perceive their group as cohesive, but that does not insure that it is cohesive. In the past, social science has been criticized for being too dependent on verbal self-descriptions. Increasingly, therefore, researchers design behavioral indices and scales as measures of social phenomena.

For example, a classic study of mother-child interaction demonstrates large discrepancies between direct observations and mothers' self-reports (Yarrow, Campbell, & Burton 1964). Mothers reported that they spent about four hours daily interacting with their children aged six or under. Trained observers with stopwatches produced contrasting estimates of approximately one-half hour, of which a good portion of the interaction was of a negative sort ("Go out and play in the sandbox, Johnny"; "Keep yourself busy fingerpainting while Mommy does the dishes.") Systematic observations often fail to replicate "common-sense" experiences.

Self-reported data are simply inadequate for recording the complexities of many kinds of interactions. No parent could possibly remember how many times he or she smiled at an infant during a feeding, nor what stimuli evoked his or her smiles. This points to another, more basic problem: The fact that even intelligent humans may not be able to observe in the same manner as trained observers. Brazelton (1988) has spent a lifetime systematizing films of mother-child interaction in terms of what and how stimuli evoke responses. He has found quite subtle interaction periods in which a mother subconsciously *follows* the baby's *lead* by decreasing her behaviors in response to the baby's own decrease. *Who* is *actually* socializing whom versus *who thinks* she is socializing whom?

Much of the difference between the ways in which the scientist and layperson observe hinges on observational technique. The scientists trained in systematic observational techniques may well use quite different assumptions, rules of logic, and means of communication (both to themselves and to others). Scientific communities also intensively train their graduate students over relatively long periods of time. This training includes techniques of systematically observing various phenomena of professional interest. For instance, ecologists are trained to make quick, yet accurate, estimations of the size of animal herds. Ethologists (biologists who study the social behavior of animals) often come to know *individual* members of beehives, bird flocks, and baboon colonies at sight. As the social sciences have matured, they too have come to recognize the need for reorganizing and systematizing their direct observations of individuals and groups. In large part the recognition of this need has hinged on the scientific dictum of *consensual validation*: Trained observers must produce similar data.

Already listed are important reasons for systematizing observations: The more systematic the measurements, the more clarity that the data can shed on a particular theory. Also, the fact that the *form* of observation schemes reconceptualizing a given phenomenon may lead to reformulated and serendipitous theory. As an analogy, consider different forms of observational schemes as different strengths of microscopes that allow only particular phenomena to stand out in clear relief. Another reason for considering structured observational techniques is that many individuals are in no position to introspect. Children may not be able to respond verbally or in writing; adults may not be detached enough about their own or other's behaviors to recall various events. Or people may be too inarticulate; the English language has but a meager vocabulary for conceptualizing social events.

Generic Features of Systematic Observation

There are a number of features that differentiate what particular systematic observational technique measures: form, duration, frequency, antecedent-consequent behavioral or social structural patterns, and relationships between behaviors, attitudes, and social structures. Of these, *form* is generally the most abstract from common everyday observations. Some observational forms have common-sense meanings. (Bales' [1970] distinctions between questions, attempted answers, and positive and negative reactions). However, many observational techniques are not intuitively obvious valid measurement instruments; eye-blink rates as measures of social anxiety, conversational interruptions as measures of social status, or frequency of word counts as a method of attributing likelihood that someone like Shakespeare rather than another poet wrote a specific poem.

Duration of an observational form refers simply to the length of time the form lasts. Duration can be a particularly important, albeit simple, measure of social and behavioral patterns. For example, deceptive answers are normally longer in length and are preceded by greater hesitations than nondeceptive answers, and the average time taken to begin speaking turns out to accurately predict individual participation rates in groups. For this reason, researchers are turning more and more toward using well-calibrated instruments (computerized clocks, stopwatches, slow-motion filming devices) to more accurately measure the duration of various social and behavioral phenomena.

Frequency of observed social or behavioral units refers to the number of times any event recurs in a given period. The researcher may calibrate frequency either by *absolute* number of recurrences or *relative* (percentage, mean average) number of occurrences. However, normally, relative frequency is preferred because it gives more easily compared data. For instance, if you know that two cities had the same absolute number of homicides last year, you would still want to standardize per some standard (10,000 population) figure to control for size of city: A city of 1 million with 50 homicides last year would have 15 times the homicides of a city of 15 million with 53 homicides in the same time frame.

Ultimately, we are interested in standardized comparisons: If I told you that professors of social science store a greater amount of printed information in their offices than do humanist professors, that would not mean much because the word "greater" is ambiguous. The relative difference, measured in linear feet of office bookshelf space, gives some stark differences: In one study, social scientists averaged 26.5 linear feet of journals versus 3.4 linear feet for humanists—almost eight times as much space (Case 1986)! Social scientists also averaged 35% more office bookshelf space given over to books than did humanist professors. These measures of frequency give interesting comparative figures on the more data-intensive models that social scientists are likely to follow. Similarly, Dreeben and Gamoran (1986) demonstrated stark contrasts between the educational content of black and nonblack high schools with a number of standardized measures: word coverage in nonblack schools averaged 491.7 new words per year versus 260.4 in the black schools; students in the nonblack schools averaged 59.6 minutes of primary instruction daily versus 36.6 in the black schools.

Antecedent and *consequent* patterns direct attention toward the types of behaviors (or social structures) that precede or follow other behaviors (or social structures) in time. In the Dreeben and Gamoran study, the consequent outcome of the above instructional antecedents showed quite clearly in nonblack students learning 80% more words and scoring 79% higher on reading achievement tests than black students. Such antecedent-consequent processes are also important at more macroscopic levels. For example, researchers in the growth of social movements have long wondered why such social movements as the Moonies or Mormons have had tremendous recruitment growth rates while others that appear to have similar messages never make it out of the storefront. Much of the mystery is cleared up by systematic investigation of network features (Snow, Zurcher, & Ekland-Olson 1980) that indicates the importance of such variables as linkages to other networks, rules that limit participation outside the movement, and the strength of social ties within versus outside the movement.

Relationships between behaviors, attitudes, and social structures are final important features for systematic observation. Too often, social researchers presume that they have measured behavior by measuring attitudes and other subjective phenomena. However, behavior and attitudes are not always highly associated. A person may say she hates her smoking habit and wants to quit; another that he dislikes his body image and wants to lose weight. Nevertheless, whether or not either person will change their behavior by giving up cigarettes or sweets is not so evident by those subjective feelings. Observational measures may provide very useful information that subjective measures do not give. Similarly, behaviors and attitudes are individual level phenomenon. Social scientists are often interested in the larger social context of behaviors and attitudes. Observational methods are particularly useful for describing larger social contexts—size of groups, group norms, peer pressures, and so on.

Observational Techniques

Social investigators make four somewhat overlapping distinctions in classes of observational techniques: linguistic, extralinguistic, nonverbal (body movement), and spatial. Because of the overlap between these distinctions, they are somewhat arbitrary.

Linguistic Measures

Social researchers have paid more attention to the development and use of systematic verbal observation than to other types of behavioral observations.

This is somewhat unfortunate because research on the importance of verbal versus nonverbal communication (Birdwhistell 1970) indicates that verbalizations make up only about one-half of human communication. Further, studies of *what* is communicated by either means often show interesting redundancies and inconsistencies, and may be less important than *how* some things are communicated.

For close to half a century now, the most generally known and used linguistic system has been Bales' (1970) Interaction Process Analysis (IPA) categories. It has been widely used because of its general adaptiveness to a large variety of situations. Among other phenomena, IPA has been used to study differences between normal and psychotherapeutic groups, leadership and follower roles, group performance characteristics, and developmental trends in small group discussions. However, the Bales system has not yet contributed much to sociological or behavioral theory. This may be in part due to the fact that it pays little attention to other important aspects of communication: intensity and duration of interaction and such nonverbal phenomena as interludes and transitions in conversations. Part of the reason is also the low reliability and validity of Bales' categories: Lustig (1987) found that the reliability coefficients for the three dimensions that Bales claims underlie his technique are extremely weak. The reliability coefficients for the scales underlying Bales' hypothesized dimensions ranged from 0.0 to 0.62.

There are numerous other systems for systematically uncovering more specific aspects of interaction. Simon and Boyer (1974) have edited an anthology of observational instruments with data on quality, which is worthwhile checking before attempting to formulate a new system. Their anthology includes instruments for the gamut of interaction situations that could be observed. However, any currently available scheme for systematizing social interaction has certain disadvantages. First, the word "interaction" in such schemes is misleading in the sense that the observer does *not* examine interdependent *inter*actions—but rather codes what one person says or does in the presence of other persons. That is, the individuals may only be independently behaving in each other's presence. The observer bases the codes in large part on inferences. Furthermore, such systems ignore much of the *complexity* of interaction because they are traditionally concerned only with *sequentially* occurring interaction, while ignoring *simultaneously* occurring interaction. Observers need to pay more attention to multiple interactional indicators, extralinguistic features, and to simultaneous interaction analysis.

Language-based observational techniques have consistently shown specific coding biases of central tendency, coding relativism, and contamination from associated cues. Bales (1970) was the first to note *central tendency biases*. He noted that observers tend to choose less emotional coding categories. Therefore, he suggested arbitrarily that when the observer can make a choice between a more affective and less affective code, that the coder chose the less affective one). *Coding relativism* means simply that one is coding more recent behaviors relative to past behaviors. While this may not produce much bias within a particular observational setting, it is possible that bias may be much greater *between* quite "foreign" settings (child versus adult, "deviant" versus "normal") because coders are more likely to judge behaviors by the current settings. This implies that contamination from more immediate cues may influence coding.

Extralinguistic Measures

For many decades, communications researchers have known that nonverbal communication is often not redundant of simultaneous verbal communication, and that humans typically spend very small amounts of interactional time vocalizing. Nonverbal behavior can repeat, contradict, or substitute for verbal messages; it may accent certain words, maintain the communication flow, reflect changes in relationships, or indicate a person's feelings toward his or her verbal behavior. Extralinguistic behaviors include vocal, temporal, interactional continuity, and verbal-stylistic dimensions.

The *vocal dimension* include pitch, loudness, and timbre among its characteristics. An instrument known as a voice spectrometer records such variation in verbal behavior with excellent accuracy. Soskin and Kauffman (1961) have shown that judges can, with reasonable accuracy, infer emotional states of speakers from voice spectrometer reading alone.

The *temporal dimension* refers to such things as rates of speaking, duration of utterances, and rhythm. One of the earliest sociologists to concern himself with time patterns, Chapple (1949) developed an interaction chronograph to assess temporal aspects of interaction. More recent inventions are less inferential, in that they do not require an observer's presence to record soundsilence and intensity fluctuation sequences of research participants.

Continuity of speech is a third extralinguistic dimension that includes patterns of hesitation, interruptions, and errors. Social and behavioral researchers have long been interested in sentence changes, repetitions, stutters, omissions, incomplete sentences, tongue slips, and incoherent sounds. The most used speech transcription convention in use presently is Jefferson's (1984) notational conventions. His orthography attempts to preserve actual conversation without rendering the transcript unreadable. The following conventions are among those Jefferson recommends:

(word)   parentheses surrounding a word indicate uncertainty about the transcription.

(0.8)   parentheses around a number on a line or between lines indicates silence, in tenths of a second.

⌈   interlocking open brackets indicate the onset of simultaneous talk between the linked utterances.

⌉   interlocking close brackets indicate the ending of simultaneous talk between the linked utterances.

=   equal signs come in pairs, at the end of one line or utterance, and at the start of a subsequent one; the talk linked by equal

	signs (whether by different speakers or same speaker) is continuous, and is not interrupted by any silence or other break.
?...	punctuation marks indicate intonation contours: they do *not* indicate grammatical status (e.g., question).
<u>out</u>	underlining indicates emphasis: the more of a word is underlined, the greater the emphasis.
::	colons mark the prolongation of the preceding sound; the more colons, the greater the prolongation.
<	the "less than" sign marks a slightly early start of the bit of talk which followed it.
run-	the hyphen indicates the self-interruption of the preceding sound.
(h)	the letter "h" in parentheses indicates aspiration in the course of a word, commonly laughter.

Conventions of notating discourse with such systems have proven much more informative than simply focusing upon the standard forms of speech categories pioneered by Bales (1970). This is most likely because a verbal focus misses well over 70% of what goes on in actual discourse. The purpose of these newer notational systems is to focus on theoretically important areas first offered by Goffman (1974) under the conception of "frame analysis." That is, these notations focus on the *context* of what goes on in conversations, rather than the actual conversations themselves. Therefore, they ask quite different questions about shifting between frames, juggling frames, the resolution of conflicting frames, turn-taking, sequencing of speech discourse, and other routines. However, as with any measure of extralinguistic behavior, their use requires a well-trained observer or sensitive apparatus because extralinguistic behavior varies in subtle ways.

The *verbal-stylistic dimension* has been of considerable interest to social scientists. It involves peculiarities of vocabulary, pronunciation, dialect, and characteristic expressions. Because there are a great many stylistic conventions, the researcher interested in this dimension would be wise to consult the already existing literature on a particular subject matter than attempt to search for a general instrument. For example, if you are interested in styles of suicide notes, Osgood's (1960) classic work on suicide notes recommends itself. When compared to normal letters, Osgood uncovered distinctive features of suicide notes; suicide notes have less diversity of vocabulary, greater repetition, less discriminative use of words, higher redundancy, more distress words, a larger number of all or none words, and more qualifications of verbs ("I might have loved you" as opposed to "I loved you").

Likewise, Lakoff (1975) stimulated much work on the communication of gender differences, when she noted important differences in American men's and women's language: Women used more "empty" adjectives like *divine, cute,* and *sweet;* more interrogative forms (*Is it?*) where men use declaratives (*It is*);

more polite forms such as *please* and *thank you*; and more forms that convey uncertainty like *well* and *you know*. Lakoff's claim that such verbal-stylistic differences create an image of powerlessness for women has been tested in court testimony simulations (O'Barr & Atkins 1978); they found that judges viewed both male and female witnesses who used these relatively impotent speech forms (questions, interrogatives, polite speech, and phrases of uncertainty) as less credible than witnesses who used more powerful speech styles.

Body Movement Measures

Researchers have long known that the body "leaks" information. Freud stated (1905/1959) that "no mortal can keep a secret. If the lips are silent, he chatters with his fingertips." The problem is knowing which channels to observe. Some researchers have observed facial movements, others have focused on posture, eye flashes, and so on. However, Ekman's (1985) summary of research on telling lies is particularly informative. He suggests that some people have less control over their body movements than others, and that different people do leak information in different ways. Therefore, there is no one way of knowing beforehand what body movements to measure. Individual differences in attention to different channels also exist: Untrained female observers pay more attention to actions and verbal style, and untrained male observers attend more to verbal content and appearance (Smith 1983).

Nevertheless, as a general rule, researchers assume that there is a *words-face-body order to leakage*: It is easier to control our verbal behaviors than our facial movements; and our body movements are least under our control. For example, Ekman (1985) demonstrates that the liar who controls his head through nodding and smiling may give away his true feelings through such body displays as clenching and unclenching his fists. Because many of these body movements are too quick for the human eye to catch, many investigators use slow-motion equipment and study the film clippage frame-by-frame.

Specialists distinguish between four different dimensions to body movement: (1) immediacy, (2) relaxation, (3) body appendage movement, and (4) facial expressions. Each of these dimensions provides quite different social clues. Hall (1963) provides a number of *immediacy* (he calls them "proxemic") *dimension* notations systems, as shown in Figure 9–2. He has defined proxemics (1963:1,003) as the study of "man's need to lay claim to an organize territory, as well, as to maintain a pattern of discrete distances from one's fellows." The observer has the option of using either a pictographic symbol, mnemonic symbol, or number code in each case. An illustration of typical proxemic notation is:

1. Two men standing (postural code 55)
2. Facing each other directly (orientation code 0)
3. Close enough that hands can reach almost any part of the trunk (kinesthetic code 101)
4. Touch does not play any part (touch code 6)

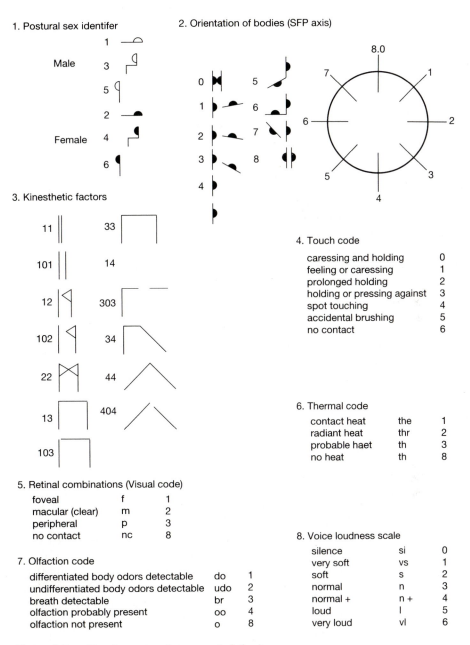

1. Postural sex identifer

Male
1
3
5
2

Female
4
6

2. Orientation of bodies (SFP axis)

0
1
2
3
4
5
6
7
8

8.0
7
1
6
2
5
3
4

3. Kinesthetic factors

11
101
12
102
22
13
103
33
14
303
34
44
404

4. Touch code

caressing and holding	0
feeling or caressing	1
prolonged holding	2
holding or pressing against	3
spot touching	4
accidental brushing	5
no contact	6

6. Thermal code

contact heat	the	1
radiant heat	thr	2
probable haet	th	3
no heat	th	8

5. Retinal combinations (Visual code)

foveal	f	1
macular (clear)	m	2
peripheral	p	3
no contact	nc	8

7. Olfaction code

differentiated body odors detectable	do	1
undifferentiated body odors detectable	udo	2
breath detectable	br	3
olfaction probably present	oo	4
olfaction not present	o	8

8. Voice loudness scale

silence	si	0
very soft	vs	1
soft	s	2
normal	n	3
normal +	n +	4
loud	l	5
very loud	vl	6

Figure 9-2. Notation system for proxemic behavior.

Source: Hall (1963). Reproduced by permission of American Anthropological Association from the *American Anthropologist 65*.

5. Man speaking, looking at, but not in the eye; partner only viewing speaker peripherally (visual code 23)
6. Close enough that radiant heat would have been detected (thermal code 2)
7. Body odor but breath not detectable (olfaction code 2)
8. Voice very soft (loudness code 1)

These proxemic behaviors show great variation across cultures. For example, Japanese come across so very softly in voice loudness that when they learn to speak English they are inclined to carry across their Japanese habit, and often have to be trained to speak in a more "Western" tone of voice to be heard. Touching codes also show wide variation: Business in South America is conducted with a continuous caressing, patting, prodding, and poking that both Japanese and Americans doing business there find extremely uncomfortable. Americans try to stand in face-to-face interaction so that they do not actually have to detect the other person's body odors, while Arabs consciously stand so as to pick up such information as a sign of particular emotions displayed.

In spite of these and other clear differences between cultures, some of Hall's codes would be better replaced with more objective instruments. For example, voice loudness in his system is subjectively defined but can be clearly improved with voice spectrometers. The retinal combination codes also do not pick up on important interactive information. They are defined more by potential for eye contact than actual contact. For example, a coder might code confrontation between American and Japanese negotiators with macular (clear) vision, where an expert could predict that the Japanese negotiator might well drop his eyes when confronted by the American's "look-'em-in-the-eye" stare. Hall's system does not consider coding such important cultural differences.

The *relaxation dimension* normally involves such indicators as degree of arm-position asymmetry, leg-position asymmetry, sideways lean, and hand or neck relaxation. As any good photographer of humans knows, most people unconsciously freeze into highly symmetrical positions that look uncomfortable or unnatural when they know they are being photographed. However, many of the facial expression measures to be considered shortly also are good indicators of relaxation and discomfort.

The *body appendage movement dimension* includes measures of trunk swivel, rocking movements, head nodding or shaking, gesticulation, self-manipulation, object manipulation, and leg and foot movement measures. Once again, these measures embrace impressive variations across cultures and are quite reliable for many investigative uses. For example, Americans use far more expressive hand movements than do Japanese. These ritualistic differences are unconsciously divisive in Americans-Japanese negotiation sessions when neither side has been trained to understand such cultural differences.

Within cultures, these measures may aid communication. Manipulating objects may be a sign of extreme nervousness, as in the shy radio show announcer who continually twirls a pencil in his hand while talking on the air. Men who are nervous may unconsciously pull at their beards or continually run their hand along their shaven chin; women may pull at their ear. People who want to be viewed as together will often sit or stand in some mimicking style, but if they want to be set apart from another person, they will take up a contrasting pose. Therefore, research indicates postural congruence between individuals who like each other and postural incongruence in dislike and status-differentiation situations.

The *facial expressions dimension* is also a particularly rich source of communicative information. Investigators have spent considerable time studying differences in reliability and validity of different parts of the human face. The evidence they have collected shows much complexity: The upper half of the face provides reliable cues for discriminating negative emotions, whereas the lower half provides more cues for discriminating positive emotions. Ekman (1985) suggests that head and facial cues communicate information about *types* of affect experienced while body position may give information about *level of intensity* of affect. However, social context restricts the breadth of such generalizations. For example, eye contact and exchanged glances are normatively bound by the sex composition of the group with quite different norms for male-male, female-female, and male-female group compositions.

Trained investigators can often readily note levels of comfort and discomfort from information leaked through the forehead, brows, or eyelids. Degree of vertically depressed forehead skin creases and speed of eyebrow flutter or eyelid blinking are all good indicators of discomfort levels for most individuals. However, the reliable and valid use of many of these indicators require specialized equipment and training. Many facial, hand, and body movements are micromomentary expressions that are literally quicker than the human eye. If researchers slow motion-picture frames to one-sixth their normal speed, they detect up to two-and-one-half times more expressions than at normal speeds. Ekman (1985) notes that when a falsehood is uttered, a one-sixtieth of a second facial expression of rapid eye movement normally takes place. By way of contrast, the blinking of an eye takes about one-fifth of a second. Such micromomentary movements show much promise for studies of honesty and lying. Numerous researchers have found that the shape and rate of eye blinking is not random, but that blinks are punctuation marks, the timing of which is tied to what is going on in the individual's head. Blink researchers have related specific types of blinking to anxiety, fatigue, boredom, storing information, making decisions, performing difficult tasks, and shifting of visual attention. When information acquisition is important, humans actively inhibit blinking; when routinely checking speed while driving, drivers blink as they shift their eyes to the speedometer and routinely blink again as they register the information; but if a police car is behind them, they do not blink as they turn their eyes to the speedometer.

Nonverbal measures of communication of any type may communicate important information but that information is highly restricted to emotional content. It says little or nothing about other important factors such as what the person is thinking or intends to do. Likewise, most nonverbal expressions are ambiguous because they only make sense within particular contexts: A direct gaze may dispose someone to approach and offer assistance, or to flee the gazer; the "look-'em-in-the-eye" American style of bargaining behavior can be offensive in other cultures. Finally, the sheer number of nonverbal cues available in the normal course of interaction is so huge that the researcher must selectively attend to only a minute proportion of them.

Spatial Measures

How humans use and perceive space is extremely important because it is not random. The study of the nonrandom regulation of human space is one of the more interesting methodological developments. For instance, population densities have been associated with social class, mental hospital admissions, fertility rates, and juvenile delinquency rates.

The mapping of human-space usage can enlighten us. Figure 9–3 is based on the work of Peter Gluck, an architect who studied various subjective experiences of the inhabitants of Shinjuku—the central district of Tokyo and one of the most densely inhabited areas in the world. His mapping visualizes the volcanic–like pedestrian flows from the Shinjuku subway station into the surrounding area. Darker shades show areas of greater human flow; lighter and greyer shades represent more inactive or dormant areas. Human traffic flows along various arteries and is easily visualized.

The mapping technique can highlight important human experiences. One could illustrate "front" (public, formal areas) and "backs" (private, informal areas), perceptions of individual or group "turf" (familiar places), and daily rhythms of territorial activity through graphs of lighted versus darkened areas of any area by time periods of several hours. For other creative examples of social mapping, the journal *Ekistics* specializes in macrostudies of human territorial use. For more microexamples, the journals *Environmental Psychology* and *Nonverbal Behavior* are recommended.

Social scientists have long had an interest in studying territorial and spatial patterns. White and nonwhite residential segregation is not randomly distributed in the United States. Numerous studies of residential segregation indicate that it is greater in northeastern industrial cities than in southern cities, and that it has changed little over the past half century. Another example is provided by aerial photographic studies of traffic on Los Angeles freeways that shows the average vehicle gets on at one exit ramp and off at the next, contrary to the popular opinion that L.A. drivers spend most of their time traveling long distances on their freeways. Often, when we make such systematic observations, we find many surprising facts.

Observational Recording Devices

The observational schemes I have discussed, with a few exceptions, have formats that are adaptable to simple note taking. However, researchers prefer instruments that are more permanent and have better reliability and validity

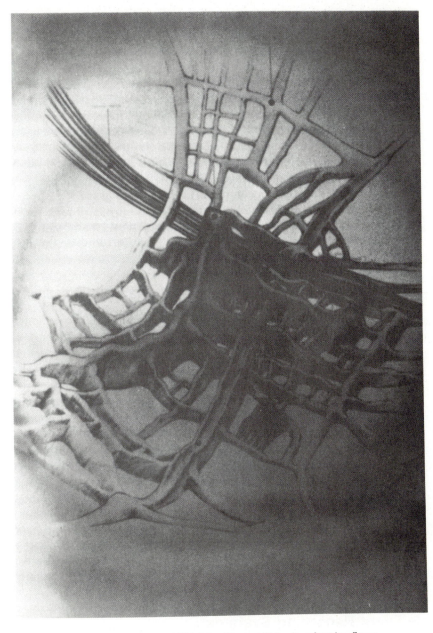

Figure 9-3. Experiental map of Shinjuku (Central Tokyo) pedestrian flows.

Photo credit: H. W. Smith.

than the relatively subjective observations of researchers, no matter how well trained. Some mechanical recording devices grant greater flexibility, reliability, and validity than handmade observations.

Observer Self-Interview Schedules

Reiss (1971) invented a structured observer self-interview format that the observer filled out during, or immediately following each observational transaction. A representative part of his classic police brutality study form follows:

32. Was a personal and/or property search attempted or conducted by the police? (1) yes (go to 32a) (2) no (go to 33).

32a. What kind of search was attempted or conducted? (1) personal ("frisk") (go to 32b) (2) property (e.g., auto or house) (go to 32c) (3) both personal and property (continue with 32b *and* 32c)

32b. If "personal":
1. Would observers say this "frisk" was necessary for the protection of the officer(s) (1) yes (2) no (9) don't know
2. Did the police ask the possible offender's permission before this "frisk" was conducted? (1) yes (2) no (9) don't know

One of the more interesting features of this observational technique is that it may introduce quality in recording as high or higher than that found in research on subjective phenomena, because the instrument does not differ materially from interview schedules and questionnaires. This form was filled out by *trained* observers; and most of the data were of a highly structured, objective nature. It mostly focused on detailed questions about who did what, when, and where: types of weapons or evidence, if the search was conducted prior to an arrest, how police gained entrance, and so on. It included very few subjective questions (32.b.1 is one of the rare exceptions) that might decrease interobserver reliability. However, observers who use it, suffer from what fieldworkers (Chapter 10) term problems of "going native"—the danger of becoming overly socialized into the participant's way of life. For this reason, observers need much training and testing before and after entry into the observational setting.

Portable Event Recording Systems

The increasing interest in observational research has led many researchers to search for means that allow the researcher the ability to record, score, and store behavioral data. Many relatively inexpensive laptop computers—the size of a small briefcase—have software that easily adapts them to such usage. For example, I own an MS-DOS™ compatible laptop computer that runs up to 15 hours on rechargeable batteries. Scientists in fields as varied as sociology, psychology, and animal ethology have used such systems successfully to study such varied topics as child abuse, full-term and premature infants' responses to their mothers and strangers, or animals in the wild. The observer may record behaviors directly in natural settings, indirectly from such original recording media as videotapes, or even through remote entries from the participants themselves.

Software is available that allows for complex behavioral, activity, and location codes. *Behavior Research Methods and Instrumentation* and *Microcomputers in the Social Sciences* are specialized journals that carry valuable reviews of such new technologies. Such technologies are only a means to an end. Researchers must still be carefully trained in the use of any recording device. Digital dexterity as well as an investment of time are two training requirements.

Sound Tape Recordings

These provide a principal source of permanent recording making. However, sound recordings are not adequate for the recording of even fairly simple events. For instance, a three-person discussion, having been recorded with good microphones strategically placed, may prove to have many undecipherable points of verbal interaction, due to simultaneously occurring verbal exchanges between two or three members. Further, it is not as easy as one might think to distinguish speakers by voice (including even the *sex* of the speaker). Nevertheless, a sound recording may be very helpful in recalling of past events. Many researchers find that even a year or more after making a sound recording of some phenomena, they have personally observed that tape replay helps them visually recall much of the original detail.

Camcorders and Motion Picture Films

The mass production of affordable portable camcorders has introduced a record collection method with advantages similar to that of motion picture film. The researcher may record events from different angles to provide independent reliability checks. Both film and tape have permanency. Both, too, have no limits on the size or complexity of the subject matter. Each permits time sampling. Only film can presently be shown in slow motion; however, tapes, unlike film, are immediately usable after taping.

However, both tapes and film have similar disadvantages. The angle choice is highly subjective and may distort the event's nature. More crucially, lenses, especially telephoto lenses, foreshorten perspective. This means that if an investigator filmed a group of persons who were standing quite far apart, on film they would appear to be packed closely together. Lighting also affects both film and tape quality. Finally, films and tapes are subjective documents of what an observer thinks of as important. This last disadvantage may be turned to the researcher's advantage by having naive filmmakers make films. Such documents indicate how individuals feel about themselves and their world.

Some documentary filmmakers (notably Robert Wiseman) claim that there is little if any subject reactivity to openly placed cameras. Wiseman's technique is to go around "shooting" empty cameras for several weeks before he starts filming, to acclimate his participants to the camera's presence. The same technique is recommended for still photography.

Some researchers recommend the use of black and white film or tape in most settings to cut down on irrelevant, distracting stimuli that might affect the observer. Even so, either tape or film is sufficiently complex that it may need magnification, repeat viewing, and slowed motion. At one extreme, it is not unusual to spend an average of six hours simply transcribing an hour of taped small group discussions. At the other extreme, analysis of collective behavior may take as many as 200 hours to produce, code, and analyze a single minute of film record.

Still Photography

Reiss observes (1971:14) that

> The reader may test some of the problems that arise in the use of still and motion-picture photography by examining the highly interesting, if not always definitive, set of pictures assembled by the President's Commission on Campus Unrest to depict violence at Kent State University. . . . The absence of any study design, the sheer unpredictability of events, and the dangers inherent in the situation once violence erupted, limited data collection and analyses. Yet, the Commission was able to assemble 58 photographs depicting the main sequence of events and cast of characters in the situation, by utilizing the work of at least 15 different photographers who were in one observational role or another. Despite obvious difficulties in the use of photographs, investigators were able to document more reliably the roles and events than was possible from separate observer accounts.

Edward Hall used to send his graduate students out into the field with instructions to take at least 150 black and white snapshots of such specific situations as persons waiting at a "Don't Walk" light or individuals entering revolving doors. The analysis of such data is particularly painstaking. One arranges the photos by such different potentially useful criteria as sex or age of participants, size of group, and so on, while looking for distinguishing characteristics of each categorization. If identifying patterns weren't difficult enough, inferring what they mean is never obvious.

Goffman's *Gender Advertisements* (1976) is a brilliant example of how much one can reveal through examining photographs. Goffman's technique resembles Hall's: He focused on particular areas of the body (knees, hands, eyes) and particular forms (finger biting, sucking, head-eye contact). Then he switched sexes for the last several ads as a technique for examining and documenting the symbolic forms of social life.

The Quality of Systematic Observations

As with any data, we measure quality by reliability and validity. These problems are nicely demonstrated in work on catching liars (Ekman 1985). Concern over lying and deceit has become a multimillion-dollar industry in which the Federal government and private industry make over half a million employees take liar detector tests a year. Ekman (1985) examined the paltry research done on the reliability and validity of polygraph tests. *He found that the validity of the polygraph is poor enough that it should never be used alone.*

The problem is that the polygraph measures only the existence of emotional agitation and not the reasons for such emotional turmoil—which may include many things other than concern over being caught lying. In one of the more carefully constructed studies he cited, 8% of the polygraph tests were false positives: Individuals who were actually truthful but judged liars. That would imply that as many as 25,000 individuals each year are wrongly accused with the consequences of losing jobs, being denied loans for mortgages, etc.

Therefore, he researched alternative means of catching liars. He recommended numerous behavioral cues that would add much to the validity of methods of catching liars if used in combination: false (asymmetric) smiles, slips of the tongue, raised voice pitch, and a micromomentary expression on the face among others. For example, Ekman (1985) found that in over 70% of the cases, a liar raises his voice out of fear of being caught. He emphasized that catching liars is so difficult to measure that he proposed a 38-item checklist of systematic data checks in the appendix to his book.

Reliability and Validity

The most common method of checking the reliability of observational data is to correlate observations made by several observers of the same phenomenon. Unfortunately, correlations cannot always detect the differences necessary to show unreliability. First, it is possible for scorers to have similar *total* scores but disagree on many *individual* scores; second, it is possible for scorers to score consistently in different directions—for one scorer to score lower than another.

The structure of the coding scheme may also grossly affect reliability. Fewer categories, greater precision in defining categories, and less inferential categories all contribute to higher reliability. Also, the more intangible, indirect, or abstract the stimuli the more difficulty observers find it is to code reliably.

Observers may also be a source of unreliability and invalidity. Ironically, the nonparticipant observer role is reactive. Subjects who know they are under nonparticipant observation may react with heightened paranoia, hostility, or uncertainty. Concealment of the nonparticipant role may solve these problems, but create new problems of ethics. However, the visible evidence that one is working (recording) may aid the legitimation of the role of nonparticipant observers. The simple demonstration to participants of what one is recording may allay their suspicions. Another strategy of increasing data quality is to chose situations in which individuals are sufficiently engrossed by a demanding situation that their attention is at least temporarily taken off the observer's presence.

Satiation or boredom can also contribute to observer unreliability. Rather than ask observers to code constantly, it is often best to specify short time-interval observation samples. For example, the rhythm of responding to a three-second beeper increases reliability of data. However, this procedure ignores the importance of observing sequences of behavior. For such types of data, the observer might code streams of behavior for short (ten-second or less) intervals, and then break for a standard period.

The second important quality of good data is validity. Because we conceptualize validity as the best approximation to the truth, it is ultimately more worrisome than reliability. The various means of checking on validity discussed in Chapter 4 are all helpful with any type of data. But the complexity of behavioral data demands attention to at least three more aids: first, to adequate means of sampling of behavior; second, to the precision of observational operationalizations; and third, to subtle changes in the environment and persons observed.

Validity is particularly problematic in observational research because a truism of behavior is that almost everything is associated with everything else, and that behaviors that occur close together in time will be more similar than those occurring far apart. A person cannot be both active and inactive at the same time. But some behaviors such as sleep are characterized by other behaviors such as inactivity. These facts raise unique problems of how to code observations validly.

Observer Training

Specialists in observation research recommend some means of simulating the use of their observation schemes in formal training sessions, so that observers are familiar with the situations they will encounter and with the instrument they will use. For example, practice in estimating crowd size is accomplished with films of mass gatherings of humans or animal herds. The trainees may watch and record observations before learning the researcher's system to teach complexity of cues and the need for precise classification norms. Many trainers suggest using consensus sessions in which the researcher meets regularly with observers to discuss problems and methods of coding. The more inferential the system of observation, the more training is needed (Smith 1982).

Special Problems in the Analysis of Observational Data

Observational form, frequency, and duration do not typically present special problems of analysis. Antecedent-consequent, dynamic, or simultaneously occurring events present most of the problems. This section focuses on unique problems of three types of analysis: nonsequential, sequential, and concurrent data analysis.

Nonsequential Analysis

This type of analysis is closest to methods familiar to nonobservational analysts. Therefore, the techniques are relatively simple and straightforward. First, the researcher can total absolute or relative (percentage) frequencies of observational forms. Second, duration of behaviors is also analyzed quite easily. The researcher may find the total duration of some event or measure its relative duration with a mean or percentage of total time. Third, one can calculate measures derived from these others such as average-duration-per occurrence (duration/frequency) and rate of occurrence (frequency/total session time).

The quantitative scores one has collected by the above methods can then be scrutinized by principles of how to go about doing science, several of which were discussed in Chapter 3. One of those principles is to search for regularities. Another is to look for exceptions to those regularities.

Sequential Analysis

Just as one can form data profiles of a nonsequential nature, one can form data profiles of a sequential nature of streams of antecedent-consequent behaviors. The simplest case is dyadic with data collected at two time periods. Consider the problem Vietze, Abernathy, Ashe, and Fawlstich (1978) had in observing effects of mother's vocalization on infant-vocal onset. They separated observations by the ages of children (2, 6, and 12 months old), cases where neither the mother nor the child was vocal, and those where only the mother was vocal. Then they looked at these cases to see how often each was followed by both mother and child vocalizing, and only infants vocalizing. The probabilities that a child will be vocal following the mother's initiation of vocalization increased from 0.02 during the second month of the study to 0.05 by the twenfth month. The baseline (first, neither was vocal and then the infant was vocal) increased correspondingly from 0.01 and 0.04 over the same ten-month period. The difference of 0.01 between these baseline and the other set of conditional probabilities shows the influence of one behavior on another.

Parke (1978) provides another relatively simple example of sequential analysis of antecedent-consequent behavior. He examined the changes in probability of a particular parental behavior in the ten-second interval following an infant's behavior by asking what happens to the parent's behavior in the ten seconds after an infant emits some behavior. Powerful infant signals include such behaviors as coughing, spitting up, or sneezing.

The problem for Parke as well as for Vietze et al. was to come up with an appropriate baseline for comparison because they could not randomize behavior. In either case, the best baseline would be a nonsocial or noninteractive behavior. The baseline for infant vocalizations in Vietze et al. used periods when neither baby or mother was vocal. Likewise, because Parke's question concerned the influence of infant vocalizations on parent's behavior, he chose the contrary case of "stop feeding," when the baby did not behave in an alarming way by coughing, spitting, or sneezing.

The baseline probability in Parke's study—to stop feeding when the baby does not emit one of these powerful signals—was 0.05. This was much lower than the conditional probability of 0.33 of a parent to stop feeding when the infant coughed, spit up, or sneezed. The difference between baseline and conditional probabilities of 0.28 gives us the influence of one behavior on another.

Increasingly, investigators are interested in data collected over long periods of time. Because of the difficulty of drawing random samples of behaviors, most investigators choose to at least include some baseline data for comparative purposes. Greene, Bailey, and Barber (1981) analyzed methods for reducing disruptive behaviors on school buses. Their baseline for number of noise outbursts above a threshold of 93 decibels over a 15-day period ranged from 200 to 1,200 seconds a day. After they introduced high-appeal music and participation in raffles as incentives to reduce noise levels, they measured a significant reduction in noise outbursts with a 50 to 100 seconds of noise per day average range over another 65-day period.

The most rudimentary form of sequential analysis is simply to count instances in which particular behaviors occur within a given time as in the above Green et al. study of school bus disruptions. Patterson and Moore (1979) noted the number of fluctuations in a child's aversive responses for one-minute intervals. The roller-coasterlike fluctuations in aversive responses they observed did not make much sense. This is a typical problem with simple time-series counts of behavior. When Patterson and Moore then analyzed mother-child sequences, they found repetitive interactive patterns that explained the radical shift in complaint behavior on the part of the child.

Concurrent Data Analysis

One of the most difficult problems with observational data is that there are usually many things going on at the same time. Goffman (1974) is one of the more skillful describers of the simultaneous occurrence of many behaviors during social interaction. Unfortunately, there are no restrictions on how many behaviors can occur at once or for how long different combinations can last. Usually the researcher interested in concurrent or simultaneously occurring observations finds it necessary to use permanent records (film strips, videotapes), and to view those sources numerous times to analyze the increased complexity of such situations.

The Logic of Multidimensional Approaches

To this point, mostly single and unidimensional measurements have been discussed. Increasingly, researchers are exploiting the computational power of computers to explore more complex multiple measures and dimensional structures. There are two reasons for this. First, you have already seen in Chapters 4 and 7 that scientists prefer more than one measure of subjective phenomena to increase reliability and validity. For the same reasons, they also prefer multiple measures of behavioral phenomena. For example, if one were interested in measuring who takes out the trash in families, it would be better to observe numerous instances rather than only one. Second, dimensions of personality and social structure may be "mapped out" just as a cartographer maps out terrain in terms of such dimensions as height, length, and width. The mapping analogy is highly appropriate because we can "read" a good social or psychological map much like a good topographical map: The logic is that if two or more phenomena frequently co-occur (happen simultaneously) that the psychological or social distance between them is small. By contrast, we assume that those phenomena that rarely or never co-occur have little or nothing in common; therefore, rarely co-occuring phenomena should be more distant psychologically or socially. To illustrate the use of multidimensional mapping of behavioral phenomena, you should pay attention to the examples shown in Figures 9–4 and 9–5.

Heise and Lewis (1988:70) demonstrate subcultural differences among deviants with the data in Figure 9–5. This figure shows distinctive clusters of good-bad evaluations of marijuana and cocaine use depending on the type of drug activity—nonuse, marijuana-only use, marijuana plus cocaine use, and marijuana plus LSD use. Both male and female nonusers cluster in the lower left-hand corner of Figure 9–4. That is, all non-drug users see both marijuana use and cocaine use as immoral, evil, or wicked. Among men and women who are non-drug users, women are slightly more likely than men to rate drug use as extremely bad (roughly -2 on both scales). Furthermore, women nonusers are much more alike in their negative attitude than men nonusers, as shown in the much smaller variation.

Men and women who have used marijuana do not have such clear-cut objections to either type of drug use. In fact, a small portion of the men and women who have used marijuana rate it from neutral (0) to slightly good ($+1$). Also among this group of deviants, the badness rating for cocaine use is not as objectionable as among nonusers—the average badness rating for cocaine use is close to -1.5 among those who have only used marijuana, but close to -2.2 for those who have never used any drugs. However, unlike nonusers, among those who have used marijuana, a small percentage of men and

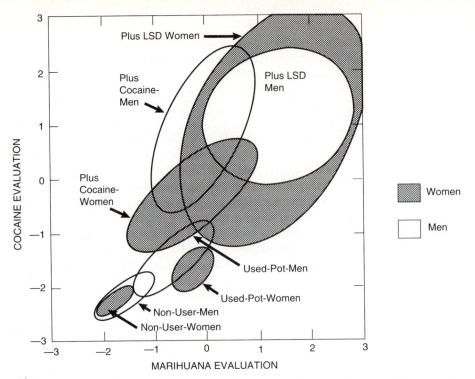

Figure 9–4. Evaluation of drug use, by type of drug used and sex. (95% confidence limits for means. Ns top down: 8, 9, 11, 16, 22, 43, 30, 27)

Source: Data supplied by Prof. David Heise, as reported in Heise & Lewis (1988:70)

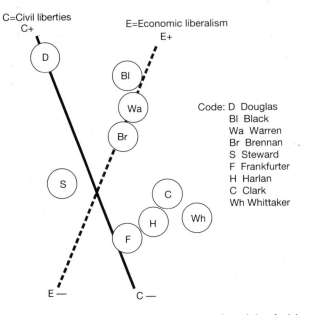

Figure 9-5. Map of supreme court justices from joint decisions.

Source: Schubert (1962)

women rate marijuana use as a positive experience, although the majority of both sexes are more likely to rate cocaine use as a very bad idea.

Individuals who have used marijuana and cocaine show quite different rating patterns from those already discussed. Notice that the size of the area enveloped by women users of marijuana plus cocaine is much larger than for marijuana-only or nonusers. This demonstrates more variation in attitude among cocaine users than marijuana users and nonusers. However, the majority of women cocaine users rated both marijuana and cocaine use negatively. By contrast, compared to women cocaine users, men users of cocaine show more positive attitudes toward cocaine use than toward marihuana use. Furthermore, male cocaine users rated cocaine much more positively than female cocaine users; the women's highest rating was close to 0.7 while the highest men's rating was close to 2.5.

The highest evaluations for marijuana and cocaine use are found among users of LSD. In fact, almost all of the male responses in this deviant subculture cluster in the positive quadrant of Figure 9–4. Among women in the LSD subculture, marijuana is almost always rated positively, but roughly one-third of these men rated cocaine negatively. Over all, as you compare nonusers, marijuana-only users, marijuana plus cocaine users, and marijuana plus LSD users, you can see from this map that the further into the drug culture, the more respectably both men and women rate the two deviant behaviors of using marijuana and cocaine. In fact, the map illustrates what sociologists who study deviant behavior have known for a long time: The further into a deviant subculture individuals get, the more likely they are to treat those deviant behaviors as normal and respectable. Nevertheless, more deviant drug users also show more variation in attitude than less deviant users.

As another example, Schubert (1962:107) analyzed the 1960 U.S. Supreme Court term "on the premise that a justice reacts in his voting behavior to the stimuli presented by cases before the Court, in accordance with his attitudes toward the issues raised for decision." He computed attitudinal distance between pairs of judges by counting "1" whenever judges agreed and "0" in cases of disagreement. Then he standardized by dividing by the number of cases on which each judge made a decision. Multidimensional methods similar to those in the 1984 citations study clarified two primary dimensions that accounted for most of the Court decisions shown in Figure 9–5: first, civil liberties attitudes (the solid black line); second, economic attitudes on conflicts of interest between private individuals and government (the broken line). Notice that then-Justice Douglas was the highest on the civil liberties dimension, Justice Steward was a swing voter who usually sided with anti-civil liberties, and Justice Frankfurter was the most likely to vote against civil liberties in 1960. Furthermore, note that Justices Harlan, Clark, and Whittaker form a cluster with Justice Frankfurher. These four justices' voting behaviors were remarkably similar, and their voting records are almost diametrically opposed to Douglas' on civil liberties issues.

Crosscutting the civil liberties dimension is the somewhat independent dimension of economic liberalism. (If the intersection of the two lines representing each dimension were exactly 90 degrees, the dimensions would be completely independent of one another. Similarly, the closer the two lines, the more they share in common.) Justices Black, Warren, and Brennan form a clear cluster around the economic liberalism end of this dimension. However, note that they are spatially closer to Justice Douglas and civil liberties than to Frankfurter and anti-civil liberties; in otherwords, they tend to vote with Douglas more often than with Frankfurter. Also, the four justices in the lower right-hand area voted more often according to philosophies of anti-civil liberties than economic conservatism, although they all are closer to the conservative than the liberal end of economic philosophy.

Justices Steward and Douglas were independents of quite different colors. Justice Stewart's behavior places him quite clearly in an independent, swing-vote role. He is slightly closer to the conservative than liberal position on both dimensions, yet he is not predictably in either cluster. Justice Douglas's voting record, by contrast, was primarily influenced by civil liberties issues, and secondarily by economic liberalism. He was also closest in philosophy to Justice Black as shown by the short distance between them, but was clearly not in the Black, Warren, and Brennan clique.

Although more than three decades have passed, the same types of dimensions still seem to be important to Supreme Court decisions. Although the court balance has changed toward more conservative voting, the same issues continue to divide the justices. For example, on the continuing controversy over abortions, justices continue to argue in terms of civil liberties of the unborn, women, husbands, and so on.

There are a multitude of multidimensional methods that the researcher interested in scaling can use. Statisticians are continually developing software for making these complex computational methods more accessible to the researcher. Without explicitly taking theory and the statistical assumptions underlying these methods into account beforehand, the researcher runs the risk of producing unintelligible maps. What makes both Figures 9–4 and 9–5 so informative is the fact that their authors used theory to develop and interpret them: In Heise's case, Figure 9–4 developed out of deviant subculture theory; in Schubert's case, Figure 9–5 helps interpret the much discussed influence of civil liberties and economics in high court decisions.

Summary

Besides the systematic measurement of subjective phenomena, researchers are interested in systematic observation and measurement of behavior because self-reports and actual behavior do not always correspond. The techniques for measuring behavior and social structure fall into five types: form, duration, frequency, antecedent-consequent patterns, and relationships between behaviors, attitudes, and social structures.

The types of phenomena that social investigators study can be divided into four broad categories. First, they have developed measures of linguistic content. However, what is communicated is often less interesting than how it is communicated. Therefore, extralinguistic factors often aid in deciphering language: pitch of voice, rhythm of speech, patterns of hesitations, and interruptions are a few of the important indices that researchers have at their disposal. We know that the body "leaks" important information because the body and face appear to be under less individual control than words. Proxemic observations that focus on how individuals organize their territories are also important indices. Such indices prove important in understanding cultural differences. To these microterritorial measures, researchers add more macro indices of spatial patternlike measures of residential segregation.

Most of the aforementioned observational indices and scales are easily administered through simple note taking. However, because mechanical recording devices can grant great flexibility, reliability, and validity, investigators often turn to new mechanical technologies of laptop computers, tape recordings, camcorders, motion picture film, and still photography. All of these methods aid permanency of documentation but they each have specific limitations. For example, any type of video recording is limited by camera angle and type of lens used. Therefore, researchers often use numerous indices or different techniques of scaling to improve the reliability and validity of their measures. Methodologists also have learned how to improve reliability and validity of specific indices or scales through observer training, and using less demanding and less inferential observational schemes.

Observational data have some special problems of analysis not typically found in the study of subjective phenomena. Particularly antecedent-consequent or sequential behavior and simultaneously occurring events call for separate types of analysis. Most of these methods of analysis depend on finding or creating adequate baseline comparison groups because it is rare for social scientists to be able to sample behavior randomly. The reduction in complexity of behavioral data is normally more time consuming than for subjective data. Because observational data are complex, the researcher uses special statistical methods to aid the simplification process.

Although all of the measurement techniques discussed hold much promise for discriminating and highlighting important social information, they can be too subtle to record unless the observer has been properly trained. Untrained individuals normally fail to see things as they are. R. D. Laing (1970:121) proposed a peculiar paradox that neatly summarizes the dilemma:

> The range of what we think and do
> is limited by what we fail to notice.
> And because we fail to notice
> that we fail to notice
> there is little we can do
> to change
> until we notice
> how failing to notice
> shapes our thoughts and deeds

C H A P T E R

10

Strategies of Field Research

If a choice were possible, I would naturally prefer simple, rapid, and infallible methods. If I could find such methods, I would avoid the time-consuming, difficult, and suspect variants of "participant observation" with which I have become associated.[1]

Key Terms

Analytic memo	Ethnography
Backstage role	Field diary
Casing	Field research
Complete observer	Frontstage role
Complete participant	Going native
Constant comparative method	Grounded theory
Contingent acceptance field entry	Hypothesis generation
Cooling out	Introspective skepticism
Cynicism	Methodological note
Derecruitment	Narrative account
Ethnocentrism	Observational note

[1]Dalton M. (1964) Preconceptions and methods. In *Men Who Manage, Sociologists at Work*, (Phillip Hammond, Ed.), Garden City, N.Y.: Doubleday/Anchor, p. 60.

Observer-as-participant

Participant-as-observer

Participant observation

Provisionalizing

Qualitative typology

Retrospective observation

Routine mapping

Skepticism

Sociological calendar

Theoretical note

Study Guide Questions

1. What are the six key ways in which field research differs from most other social research methods? What advantages and disadvantages do these key differences have?

2. What are the three key differences between field research and investigative reporting?

3. Explain three general tactics used to aid self-recruitment and entry into a field setting.

4. Describe six major problems and processes of negotiation involved in collecting field data.

5. How does the field researcher's role affect the risks of going native versus becoming ethnocentric?

6. Describe the relationship between major field-research roles and types of, and access to, information.

7. When is multiple entry a particularly useful technique in field research?

8. Describe some of the problems faced by fieldworkers in handling multiple roles: backstage versus frontstage roles; skepticism, cynicism, and naiveté; and active versus passive observation.

9. Decribe the cycle of observing and recording which is distinctive to ethnography.

10. What techniques are useful in mapping routines?

11. Why is the narrative account so important to ethnography? How are good narrative accounts constructed and maintained?

12. Describe the different information portrayed in observational notes, theoretical notes, and methodological notes, as opposed to narrative accounts.

13. How does the type of role threaten to contaminate the validity of field research?

14. What nine types of data-quality controls does McCall suggest need particular attention? Why?

15. What are the known sources of human filtering about which field researchers must be wary? Why?

16. How do reliability and validity checks differ in field research from other types of research?

17. In what ways is hypothesis generation distinctive of field research?

18. What roles do qualitative typologies play in field research?

19. Why does field research usually handle both descriptive and causal hypotheses poorly?

20. What are the functions of interpretations of incidences and pinpointing operations to hypothesis generation in fieldwork?

21. How does fieldwork compare to other methods in the ways it handles rival hypotheses?

22. What training techniques aid fieldwork reliability and validity?

23. What types of special ethical dilemmas face the fieldworker?

24. Describe some of the special logistical problems in fieldwork.

25. How do social, spatial, and temporal maps aid fieldwork organization?

Science is committed to making direct observations, and some methods contribute to such accumulations of data better than others. Field research refers to a number of techniques aimed at producing direct observations of what people say and do. Of course, numerous professions report direct observations of human behavior, but only field research focuses on *habits* and *routines*. Early sociological masters such as Durkheim and Weber viewed habits as chief determinants of human action, and among the principal supports for the moral fabric of modern societies. Camic (1986) illustrates the central role of habits in Durkheim's sociological analysis, by reference to such diverse human actions as suicides, religion, and the division of labor; he continues (p. 1062) with a discussion of Weber's belief that "habitual action does not occur at random . . . for there is a strong affinity between the way of life within different social groups and the propensity of group members toward various sorts of habitual . . . conduct."

One of the key techniques of field research that separates it from other methods is participant observation. Total participation allows the researcher to experience a social setting from the participant's point of view; it provides insights into routinized and habitual action often hidden even from the participant; and it can create an understanding of groups and experiences about which outsiders may know little or nothing. *This ability to gain insights into the routinized, subjective features of social behavior is the key objective of field studies.* Because we take our habits and routines for granted, they are paradoxically not easily accessible to our conscious minds. The field researcher attempts to understand this "taken-for granted" world. Field research is oriented toward allowing us to see people in the context of their lives, to study the meanings of and consequences of their social reality.

An exemplar of this unique observational contribution of field research is Eliot Liebow's classic study of the black men in a Washington, D.C. ghetto. In one scenario, Liebow (1976:29–34) discusses the subjective view of middle-class whites that blacks are irresponsible men who would turn down an honest day's work. Liebow details a routine scene in which a truck driver attempts to enlist laborers from the men standing around a street corner; the driver recruits only two or three men out of the twenty to fifty he contacts. The truck driver speculates that "these men wouldn't take a job if it were handed to them on a platter" (p. 30). But Liebow's field observations of the black men reveals a very different representation of the man-job relationship. First of all, Liebow observed a large percentage of these apparently "jobless" corner men actually having jobs. There is one who works nights, another who is a trashman—with today being his day off, another who works at a liquor store which has not yet opened for business, and others who have jobs but are temporarily laid off due to the weather. Some of the employed men are off today for personal reasons: One has a funeral to attend this morning, while another has to appear as a witness at a trial. Liebow concludes the "it is not enough to explain (these street-corner men) away as being lazy or irresponsible or both, because an able-bodied man with responsibilities who refuses work is, by the truck driver's definition, lazy and irresponsible" (p. 34). In fact, out of all the men on the corner, Liebow's field notes accounted for all but a handful.

Distinguishing Features of Field Research

Field research techniques in general, and that part of field research known as participant observation in particular, are eclectic. Field research, according to McCall and Simmons (1969:1):

> involves some amount of genuinely social interaction in the field with the subjects of the study, some direct observation of relevant events, some formal and a great deal of informal interviewing, some systematic counting, some collection of documents and artifacts, and open-endedness in the direction the study takes.

To understand the distinctive blend or combination of methods and techniques that make up field research, it may be helpful to contrast it to newspaper reporting which bears superficial resemblance to it. First, although some field researchers, like newspaper reporters, claim they are free of the need to formulate arguments or test hypotheses, gifted field research generates theory. Unlike reportage, which may be done for its own sake, the ultimate objective of field research is committed to the same standards of science that apply in such other settings as the laboratory, library, or computer room. In essence, field research operates through a special "filter" of observational technique and grounding in theory lacking in reportage. Second, reportage is limited by a hit-and-run urgency to report "newsworthy" events for an agency interested in making money from the sale of "stories." By contrast, the quotidian events of interest to fieldwork require long, intensive, poorly renumerated stays in the field. A reporter might rush a report on a particular disaster because of its shock value, "timeliness," and public salability, but a field researcher interested in disaster research is more likely to focus on such enduring components of everyday social life as long-term community and organizational response to the same disaster. Without intensive long-term dedication, an observer is unlikely to come to understand that the field researcher is concerned with normal, everyday life events not usually considered "newsworthy" by the press. The reporter, after all, is in search of a "story," while the fieldworker looks for "data."

Third, reporters usually research what people say and do without concern for what they do not say or do. Some of the most important insights that come out of field research deal with what doesn't happen in particular settings. New reports of the Unification Church "Moonies" movement report flashy, but suspects data on "brainwashing" conversions. But a long-term study of Moonies by Barker (1984) uses data on what does not happen to show the ineffectiveness of Moonies conversion workshops: Although 85% of 1,017 attendees stayed to the end of one two-day workshop, a paltry 4% of those persons converted at the workshop were still members two years later.

It may also further aid understanding of what field research is through differentiating field research from other methods. First, social situations that have a relatively high degree of known organization may be more profitably served through more structured methods, while less structured social situations or those where the structure or organization is not known to the researcher beforehand may be more usefully studied through participant observation—particularly in the early stages of research. All data collection is subject to certain sorts of bias and sometimes the researcher can systematize and deal with those biases. An important difference between unstructured fieldwork and such more structured techniques of social science as surveys and structured observations is typically our *awareness* of bias. Structured observational biases tend to be more explicit, while participant observational biases, though perhaps just as systematic, are normally more hidden from view. More important, they are different types of biases. The source of participant observation biases springs naturally from the interactional nature of the observer's role, while structured observational biases arise from biases built into the coding system.

Second, while the *implicit* nature of participant observation biases is often viewed as a basic weakness of the method's reliability and validity, field methods often incorporate a number of internal checks on reliability and validity. Stated somewhat differently, other techniques normally have reliability and validity built into the observational instrument *prior* to their use; participant observation normally builds in reliability and validity checks *prior to, during*, and *after* observation.

Third, participant observation data, while usually much more open-ended in nature than data based on other methodologies, generally can be systematically coded after the fact. An extended example of these reliability and validity checks and coding procedures is given in a later section of this chapter. The open-endedness of field research may be considered one of field research's strong suits in the study of social situations where little is known beforehand about organization, structure, and other key factors.

Fourth, another key advantage of field research is its ability to shed light on *processes* or *dynamics* of social situations. Field-research data can be gathered over long periods of time for many variables. Other methods rarely approach this adaptability to the study of social dynamics. Structured observations may be gathered over long time periods but usually for only one or a few variables. Surveys, on the other hand, can be used to collect data on a large number of variables, but are generally impractical for reuse on the same populations more than a few times.

Fifth, the field researcher constantly alternates between theory and methods. Nothing in field research is fully prescribed or finally executed in advance of data collection; every component of the research is continually carried on through the fieldwork. No other method allows for this flexibility. Of course, this flexibility has its drawbacks. The unstructuredness of field methods makes it more conducive to the *generation* of hypotheses than to rigorous *testing* of hypotheses.

This relative nonstandardization, unstructuredness, and process-oriented nature of fieldwork is its most distinctive feature. Although other types of research emphasize the need for theoretically directed research, the aim of field research is "to make a virtue of nonstandardization by frequently redirecting the inquiry on the basis of data coming in from the field to ever more fruitful areas of investigation" (Dean, Eichhorn, Dean 1967:275). Although good field-methods usage is as grounded in theory as any method (Glazer & Strauss 1967), it is more flexible and adaptable to the exploration or reformulation of emerging theoretical concerns.

A sixth distinctive quality of fieldwork is field relations; the more the researcher finds it necessary to participate in the field setting, the more the research role will depend on the ability to establish successful trust relationships with participants. Both the difficulty in establishing appropriate trust relationships and the flexibility of field methods contribute to a need for guarding against these becoming major sources of study *bias*. The fieldworker finds it easier to form informant contacts with some persons rather than with others; this raises the question: How will these relations bias data collection toward certain points of view as opposed to other potential, but untapped, field relations? In the same vein, how might the emerging hypotheses attract the fieldworker toward an unrepresentative picture of the field setting? These are the types of questions that the fieldworker must constantly ask throughout the observational period.

Even though fieldwork has a number of such potentially crippling disadvantages and differences, it also has a number of advantages over more structured methods. Dean, Eichhorn, and Dean (1967:276–279) have summarized a number of such advantages.

1. The researcher can reformulate the problem as he goes along. Thus, the fieldworker is less committed to perspectives which may have been misconceptualized at the onset of the project.
2. Because of closer contact with the field situation, the researcher is better able to avoid misleading questions.
3. The impressions of a fieldworker are often more reliable for classifying respondents than a rigid index drawing upon one or two questions in a questionnaire.
4. The fieldworker usually is in direct contact with the data in the field.
5. He may ease himself into the field at an appropriate pace.
6. Categories may be constantly modified for more suitable analysis of the problem at hand.
7. If he starts out on the wrong track, the fieldworker has less reason to jinx his study because of relatively little commitment to standardized collection methods.
8. Difficult-to-quantify variables are probably less distorted by unstructured observation and interviewing.
9. The field researcher has a big advantage . . . in delicate situations where covert research is essential.
10. Surveys are generally more expensive than field observations and interviewing. (On the other hand, Becker [1970:52–53] points out that participant observation is typically much more time consuming—with fieldwork often consuming 12 to 18 hours a day for over a year's time.)

Therefore, participant observation may produce data that are extremely "rich" in detail and specificity. Unfortunately, like a good sauce, it can be "too much of a good thing, more than anyone needs or can put to good use" (Becker 1970:52). Fieldwork often produces data reminiscent of Kurosawa's classic movie, *Rashomon*, is which five plausible but quite confusingly different stories of a murder are told. In later sections, we shall see how this richness can be utilized to logically unfold the truth.

Field research can be characterized by the subjection of the fieldworker to intense—but flexible—periods of social interaction in the search for the descriptions and meanings of social routines and habits. To understand better the dynamics of this social interaction, a conceptualization of six interrelated social processes, which are found in all social relationships, can be employed— recruitment, socialization, interaction, innovation, social controlling, and logistical allocating. These help to determine how the fieldworker goes about doing research (McCall, McCall, Denzin, Suttles, & Kurth 1970).

Fieldworker Recruitment

All organizations, from the smallest two-person group to the largest bureaucracy, have interests in obtaining and avoiding new members. Typically, the major problem for a field researcher involves entry into the field setting, getting a foot in the door of the group he or she wishes to study. It is difficult to give hard and fast rules for this process because numerous organizational characteristics—size of group, degree of organizational hierarchy, formal or informal restrictions on communication, the degree to which reciprocal relations are commonly perceived by all parties, etc.—determine the process of self-recruitment by the fieldworker. Some general tactics may aid this process of self-recruitment: (1) agreeing to meet the rules of the group, (2) actively "selling" oneself to influential sponsors, or (3) offering inducements to the group or its members. More specific tactics can not be given until the field researcher "cases" the proposed research site. *Casing* may involve an informal visit to the proposed research site prior to entry for the purpose of gathering information on project feasibility, needed resources, and means of entry (not unlike a burglar's casing). In some settings, it is easy to gain entry because the group desires new members or wants publicity or legitimacy for their point of view; where secrecy is a factor, it can be very difficult.

The tactics used for entry to informal groups well illustrates these rules. Liebow's (1967) classic study of street-corner blacks was made possible through his adoption of the clothing, mannerisms, and speech patterns of the men he was observing. Humphreys (1970) found that the easiest way to study homosexual tearooms was through accepting the role of "watchqueen" or voyeur-lookout. Adler's (1985) ethnography of a West Coast drug-dealing and smuggling community was made possible only by a mixture of serendipitous events. Because drug dealing is an illegal activity insulated from the straight world by numerous types of subterfuge, Adler might not have gained entry had she not moved into an apartment next to a drug dealer whom she and her husband ended up befriending. However, the ensuing fieldwork was possible only because she followed the above-mentioned rules so that her ever-expanding circle of informants could get to know her and form judgments about her trustworthiness. Fieldworkers who do studies of such types of informal groups normally need to develop a consistent "storyline" to protect their means of access from being terminated.

By contrast, entry into formal organizations often requires more structured approaches. Moskos' (1976) study of U.N. peace-keeping forces was made possible by his status as an accredited correspondent from the Canadian Defense Ministry. In formal organizations, it often becomes necessary to assure the host that you will not be a threat to the organization, and to convey a sense of serious purpose and sincerity concerning your project. Usually it is wise to consent that there will be no journalism, no exposure of hosts, no names, and no publications of results unless agreed upon by both the researcher and the host. Empathy for the host, and respect for the host's point of view is necessary to establish trust and to neutralize any sense of threat. Normally, a general explanation such as "the purpose of the research is to understand the host's organization for scientific reasons of explanation" will suffice.

More formal organizations may minimally require a brief written letter of introduction that identifies the researcher and any sponsors or relevant organizational affiliations, and outlines the proposed research project objectives and methods. Schatzman and Strauss (1973:25–26) present a sample letter of introduction meant to aid entry; this document

> should assure all hosts of confidentiality and very explicitly separate the researcher from any given source of power within or outside the group. . . . It clearly shows the researcher's respect for integrity of the members and their work. . . . [It] should indicate approximately how long, with their permission, the study will go on and how much or how little work will be demanded of them . . . [the researcher] will wisely indicate in the statement that in due time he will have some interesting and useful "observations" to offer. (1973:24–25)

Recruitment is an ongoing process that goes beyond simple entry. Just because one has a foot in the door does not mean the host cannot slam the door shut at a later time. The field researcher is a guest; violations of the organization's code of rules, role reversals, or stepping out of the role of fieldworker may threaten the life of the project and may be unethical. The researcher who violates promises of confidentiality, respect for members' integrity, or takes on a covert observational role is no longer acting as an honored guest.

The field researcher must constantly work at maintaining and renegotiating his or her role of guest from field entry through exit. The role of guest is relatively weak and ambiguous; therefore, the fieldworker's negotiation needs to be imaginative in the quest for interests shared with the host around which to bargain. Often the researcher may promise a "gift" of sharing information with the host after project completion. Sometimes the host offers project-related suggestions that, if accepted by the guest researcher, enhance mutual trust and respect.

Site entry is not an all-or-nothing option. As trust is built up between any host and guest, greater freedom of access to places and information is a normal outcome. The more secret the thoughts or sacred rites, the more difficult the entry. Dalby's (1985) study of Japanese geisha organization nicely illustrates this continuum of access. She had to earn the right to access to increasingly secretive and sacred aspects of geisha life. As she acted and thought more like a geisha, she was able to negotiate successfully with her sponsor for the privilege of entry to more arcane areas of geishahood.

Negotiation for entry refers to a wide-ranging and subtle process of maneuvering oneself into positions from which the necessary data can be collected. Wintrob (1969:67) illustrates the psychological stress underlying this maneuvering from a graduate student's account:

> "I kept thinking: Am I going to be rejected? Am I really getting the data I need? I know I had to set up my tent but I'd put it off. I'd put off getting started in tell-

ing people about wanting to give a questionnaire. I was neatly ensconced in
. . . .'s compound. Everybody there knew what I was doing. I found it hard to
move over to the other camp (a few miles away). I rationalized that a fieldworker shouldn't jump around too much."

The issue of derecruitment is also important. At some point the researcher must wrestle with leaving the particular site because the study is
coming to an end. This derecruitment process often causes much ethical and
moral discomfort for the researcher because of obligations and responsibilities
built up during the course of study. Particularly when the fieldworker has taken
on the more intimate role of participant observer, host group members may
feel they are being abandoned. Strong feelings such as those experienced by
persons undergoing divorce are not atypical for both the guest researcher and
the host. The human bond created in participant observation can become so
strong that all parties find it difficult to completely sever the relationship.
Dalby (1985) says that a decade after completing her geisha fieldwork, she still
keeps up long-distance telephone calls and visits with her former sponsor. Indeed, when her geisha "sister" died in an unexpected accident, she felt morally
compelled to attend the Japanese funeral. This derecruitment process even
affects the researcher's outside relationships. Barker's (1984) own family became upset after she had completed her study of Moonies because she was
able to talk like them; they misperceived her ability to communicate understanding of the Moonie point of view after she had left the field, as recruitment
to the Moonie way of life. These types of strong reactions to the bonds created
in participant observation require that the fieldworker pay explicit attention to
working through plans for leaving the field with all concerned parties.

Fieldworker Socialization

This process requires the learning of beliefs, habits, skills, goals, values, and
norms of a group. Any organization has a vested interest in making members
part of its unique culture. Socialization is a two-way process. The organization
under study will wish to discipline and coordinate the fieldworker's behavior to
protect the continuity of its culture. The field researcher who wishes to understand the organization must cooperate to the extent of learning what is unique
about the group. Without this two-way process, the researcher's initial ethnocentrism will likely impede full understanding of the group's special characteristics. Woods (1981:22) illustrates these processes in discussing his research
on secondary-school pupils:

> One of my outstanding memories from the enormous mass of experience at the
> school is that of pupils talking to me about boredom. They managed to convey,
> largely in a very few words, years of crushing ennui that had been engrained
> into their bones. Great wealth of expression was got into "boring," "boredom,"
> "it's so bo-or-ing here." The word, I realize now, is onomatopoeic. I could never

view lessons in company with that group again, without experiencing that bore- dom myself. They would occasionally glance my way in the back corner of the room with the same pained expression on their faces, and I knew exactly what they meant. This then, provided a platform for my understanding of the school life of one group of pupils.

At the same time, the researcher who is resocialized into the host's group risks the danger of "going native"—that is, uncritically taking the role of the host group. Therefore, the fieldworker finds it necessary to resist the host group's attempts to change beliefs, skills, or values that would damage the observational process. The more extensive the group's efforts to strip or sup- plant the researcher's beliefs or skills, the more important it is that the re- searcher "leave the field" from time to time to regain perspective and keep a low profile within the organization.

As an active participant in his or her own socialization, the field re- searcher must continually work to keep his or her own behavior to "in role" and to appear as nonthreatening as possible. Most researchers who use this method recommend waiting until one has left the field setting before taking notes. The researcher attempts to remain relatively passive during actual time in the field, and not challenge the behavior or verbalizations of the hosts. If the fieldworker acts too obtrusively, the events observed may differ significantly from those that occur when the researcher is absent. The field researcher is in the field primarily to collect data. If the fieldworker participates too actively in the host group, that can interfere with the ability to observe and record the group behavior of interest. Of course, some settings are conducive to nonreac- tive note taking—the "store employee" who sits at a desk or counter, the li- brary patron who had come to study.

On the other hand, the fieldworker who does not participate enough finds that group members may be reluctant to interact in his or her presence or to share information. Treading the fine line between too much and too little par- ticipation is not easy, and causes many new field researchers some degree of discomfort. A good rule of thumb is to participate when it is essential for group acceptance, but not to participate when it would cause competition for status or withdrawal by the host or group members.

These two dangers to data quality of ethnocentrism and going native are inversely related. At the start and finish of fieldwork, there is minimal danger of going native and great danger of ethnocentrism. In the middle of fieldwork, the situation reverses itself with the greatest danger from going native and the least danger from ethnocentrism. Figure 10–1 graphically depicts this normal course of fieldwork development. The researcher who is aware of this inverse relationship should weigh each in accessing the quality of his or her data.

There are a variety of roles that the researcher can assume and each can be useful for gaining some types of information, getting in and out of certain places, and talking to certain people. But each role also has its disadvantages: Places that can't be visited, people to whom one can't talk, and information that can't be gained. Dean, Eichhorn, and Dean (1967:284) have listed the fol-

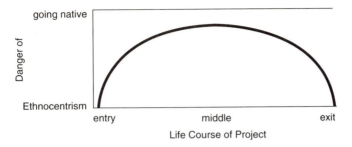

Figure 10-1. Hypothesized relation of going native and ethno-centrism to data quality over project life course.

lowing kinds of informants as useful sources of information; of course, the field researcher is a special kind of informant who takes on some of these roles as well:

1. Informants who are especially sensitive to the area of concern.

The *outsider*, who sees things from the vantage point of another culture, social class, or community.

The *rookie*, who is surprised by what goes on and notes the taken-for-granted things that the acclimated miss. And, as yet, he or she may have no stake in the system to protect.

The *nouveau statused*, who is in transition from one position to another where the tensions of new experience are vivid.

The naturally *reflective and objective person* in the field. He or she can sometimes be pointed out by others of his or her kind.

2. The *more-willing-to-reveal informants*. Because of their background or status, some informants are just more willing to talk than others.

The *naive informant*, who knows not whereof he or she speaks. He or she may be either naive as to what the fieldworker represents or naive about his or her own group.

The *frustrated person*, who may be a rebel or malcontent, especially the one who is consciously aware of blocked drives and impulses.

The *"outs,"* who have lost power but are "in-the-know." Some of the "ins" may be eager to reveal negative facts about their colleagues.

The *habitué* or *"old hand,"* or *"fixture,"* who no longer has a stake in the venture, or is so secure that he or she is not jeopardized by exposing what others say or do.

The *needy person*, who fastens onto the interviewer because he or she craves attention and support. As long as the interviewer satisfies this need, he or she will talk.

The *subordinate*, who must adapt to superiors. He or she generally develops insights to cushion the impact of authority and may be hostile and willing to "blow up."

However, not only does each of these types of informants give useful and unique types of information; they each also present unique dangers. Too much association with one type may cut the researcher from other types of information. Hence, the researcher must always be aware of the dangers of reliance on each as a source of data. Dexter's (1970:22) field research on the United States Congress notes the importance of cross-checking informants:

> [In my research] I sometimes appear to rely chiefly upon interviews, but in fact I was living in Washington at the time, spent much of my "free" time in a congressional office, saw a good deal of several congressional assistants and secretaries socially, worked on other matters with several persons actively engaged in relationships with Congress (lobbying and liaison), had participated in a number of congressional campaigns, had read extensively about congressional history and behavior, and had some relevant acquaintance with local politics in several congressional . . . districts. All these factors made my analysis of interviews somewhat credible. And, as I look back, interviews sometimes acquired meaning from the observations which I often made while waiting in congressional offices—observations of other visitors, secretarial staffs, and so forth. And, finally, most important of all, it happened that interviews with constituents, lobbyists, congressmen of different views and factions, could be and were checked and rechecked, against each other. Yet in the book we say little about all this; and in fact it is only now . . . that I realize how much these other factors affected what I "heard."

There are four ideal-typical field roles: complete participant, participant-as-observer, observer-as-participant, and complete observer. Each of them, as with informant and host roles, has its unique biases and uses in fieldwork. Figure 10–2 summarizes salient components of each role.

The *complete participant* conceals his or her observer role from those observed, and remains a covert observer "in disguise." Two major problems are inherent in this role. One is that the researcher may become handicapped by being too self-conscious about performing in an assumed role. Hammersley and Atkinson (1983:94) note that "passing" as a member over a protracted period may place great strain on the fieldworker's role-playing abilities and

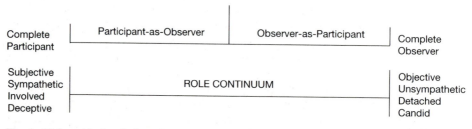

Figure 10-2. Ideal typical continuum of fieldworker roles.

psyche, and the field researcher's cover risks being blown. Adler (1985) explained that throughout her study of West Coast drug wheeling and dealing, she avoided the total participant role and sought a conversion of her covert role to an overt one by developing trust; her reasoning was not only because of the psychic strains and ethical dilemmas covertness encourages, but also because covertness prevented her "from asking some necessary, probing questions" (p. 18). Furthermore, covertness inhibits the researcher from taking anything but already established roles. In more open research, the researcher may switch established roles or innovate a role more conducive to data collection. Also, how can the fieldworker who is not frank and honest with his hosts expect his hosts to be frank and honest in return?

Another problem with the *complete participant* role is that the fieldworker may play the role so convincingly that he or she may actually "go native" because of total immersion in the culture. Because the role expectations for a true native will often conflict with those for an observer, it is likely that the social routines of the host group may severely limit data collection. Beyond these practical limitations, the complete participant role is often ethically suspect. Thus, for both ethical and practical reasons a more explicitly defined observer role is more appropriate in most situations.

The opposite extreme is the *complete observer* role which is illustrated by systematic and detached eavesdropping and reconnaissance. Hammersley and Atkinson (1983:96) point out that this is rarely a dominant fieldworker role; usually it is used only to "case" a setting prior to committing oneself to the site. The reason it is so little used in later stages of field research is because the complete observer has virtually no human contact at all. Consequently, it is difficult to generate and test theory rigorously, to question participants about their beliefs and actions, or to observe freely. In other words, the complete observer role has the sterility inherent in observing behavior through a one-way mirror, without the benefit of the host feedback that makes less extreme forms of fieldworker roles so adaptable and modifiable.

Stein's (1990) study of a pornographic bookstore provides a good example of the structural limitations of the complete observer role. Because management made him promise that he would only observe in the capacity of a "store clerk," his ability to collect data became severely limited in terms of what and when he could observe, and he was not allowed to freely ask questions of people who frequented the store nor to openly seek informants who might clarify the *meaning* underlying the routines he observed in the bookstore. Furthermore, the silence inherent in the adult bookstore he observed created an additional structural barrier. Therefore, this type of role makes it difficult to overcome the fieldworker's ethnocentric biases, and to collect the more sensitive types of data that are necessary in the study of any poorly understood phenomenon.

The two extremes of complete observer or participant are rare in most field research because of their limitations, but the two less extreme roles although more likely employed are also limiting. The *participant-as-observer* spends more time participating than observing, and those observed are generally aware of his or her role. But the building of rapport presents the danger of informants overidentifying with the fieldworker and his or her role. To avoid this, participant observers recommend the need for breaks during participation to reflect back and analyze field behavior. Probably most serendipitous data are noticed in the beginning stages of fieldwork, before the observer has grown accustomed to the research setting. The strategy of "leaving the field" at periodic intervals also contributes to fresher perspectives. Upon reentrance into the field setting, the researcher will have regained some of his or her ethnocentrism that, however short-lived, may give much leverage in terms of observing things that otherwise might have been unnoticed or taken for granted. For example, as a result of being part of the group for a long time, it becomes harder to see small changes, in the same way as a visiting relative finds children more changed than parents or friends who are with them daily.

When contact with subjects is relatively brief, formal, and openly classified as observations, we speak of the *observer-as-participant*. Here the major sources of bias are likely to be misperceptions caused by the brief and formal nature of the fieldworker's contact. The danger is that the fieldworker will see "motion" rather than "action" because the observer-as-participant role, like the complete observer role makes it difficult to interpret meaning. In part this limitation is due to the fact that the observer-as-participant engages in telling him- or herself what he or she is seeing as opposed to understanding action from the point of view of the participants. However, the limitation is also a function the fact that the observer-as-participant role is not as conducive to the establishment of trust relationships as a strictly participatory role.

Hammersley and Atkinson (1983) have pointed out that field relations often call for somewhat more complex operations than the above typology suggests. The fieldworker rarely takes on just one of the four typical roles. In the least complex of settings, he or she may use the complete observer role to case the site, and then move increasingly into a participant role. In more complex sites where cliques, factions, or multiple authority structures exist the task of access becomes even more complex; in these cases the fieldworker needs to plan for multiple entries to the site. If the researcher does not provide for gaining simultaneous access to different cliques or factions, he or she risks (1) being identified with particular groups, and (2) the appearance of slighting or bypassing particular leadership factions. For example, in an auto assembly plant, a researcher who contacts only management or union at the start risks alienating the other faction; the "other side" is likely to identify such a fieldworker as part of "them."

Multiple entry is particularly useful in studying complex overlapping and hierarchical authority structures. Kahn and Mann (1952:7) suggest that "since the researcher requires spontaneity and cooperation rather than docility and obedience, it is not enough for (the fieldworker) to use the ready-made authority structure." Rather, they (1952:8) propose that the researcher "ask the head of the organization only that he himself agree to the project and that he agree to have the question put before the next level in the organization" and go on down the hierarchy. This procedure, so-called "*contingent acceptance*" by various levels of the organization, has risks of rejection by particular echelons, but it provides better cooperation and information if followed through successfully.

Janes (1961) has emphasized that the fieldworker role undergoes five separate phases: newcomer, provisional acceptance, categorical acceptance, personal acceptance, and imminent migrant. Rapport builds up throughout the first four phases. As a newcomer, the fieldworker is labeled as a stranger through such references as "that sociologist who is doing a study." As the fieldworker gains acceptance, the labels may change to "friend" or even "one of us."

The last phase, imminent migrant, is an often ignored yet extremely crucial period for field studies. As the researcher starts "cooling out" of the field in preparation for ending the study, field relations take on a particularly new character: Rarely will new information be informally volunteered by subjects, and anxiety increases among the study population over the researcher's impressions and findings. The researcher often finds it useful during this stage to spend most of the time interpreting and reviewing the study findings with the study group.

Of course, the researcher's role definitions will not be completely self-defined—they will also by partly defined by those within the group studied and partly by the social situation. To control for reactivity of the observer and to guard against "going native," many researchers have cautioned that the fieldworker not become "too active" in the group being studied. However, the observer's choice in this matter may be limited by social setting and circumstances.

Fieldworker Interaction

Interaction may be defined as "WHO comes together for WHAT activities WHEN and WHERE." (McCall, McCall, Denzin, Suttles, & Kurth 1970). The desire to collect high-quality data circumscribes the type of interaction necessary in the field researcher's role. Two types of interaction are important for this analysis: first, the type of interaction appropriate for the fieldworker and, second, the most appropriate ways to observe and record interactional occurrences on the part of the host group.

Field Roles

The fieldworker interacts in a role of participant-observer that gives rise to intrinsic tensions, because he or she is at the same time both an insider and outsider. Although the fieldworker starts out as an outsider, as he or she becomes absorbed into the group and its culture, the act of leaving the group setting becomes difficult. The role of insider also makes it difficult to view objectively and to examine critically the group's definitions of reality. Early in the recruitment process, the researcher uses such tactics as courting, charming, or cajoling to be allowed into the hosts' world. Later, to understand this subjective world, the researcher allows the hosts to seduce him or her. From this may evolve a dangerous process of "going native": The researcher may forget his or her place on the outside.

In interaction with our hosts, we play at being one of them; this may lead to being mistaken for one of them. Hosts often offer insider roles (resident sociologist, visiting friend, honorary member, affectionate mascot) to legitimize the fieldworker roles: To be an insider means that one is guided by the experiential world of the participants of a particular social setting. An outsider to that system is not guided by the rules and prescriptions of this experiential world; as such, he or she is a potentially threatening figure, and may find it too easy to adopt an insider's perspective to reduce the tension. This may result in uncritically accepting the host's perspectives.

The fieldworker must fulfill simultaneous, recurring, and often conflicting roles. At the same time that he or she is establishing rapport with a particular organizational faction, the fieldworker may be attempting to deal with rumors that threaten already established relations with other factions, directly participating in ongoing events, rummaging through organizational archives for important historical documents, and keeping track of and sorting through large masses of observations. The multitude of activities required in field research makes it difficult to lay down specific procedural rules for fieldwork interaction. However, fieldworkers are in general agreement concerning good fieldwork roles: The researcher, while in the field, must become quite conscious of the roles he or she is playing and must be detached from the field setting. The researcher must be able psychologically to stand off to the side as he or she gathers data and views the situation with *introspective skepticism* ("Is that really what is happening?"), *cynicism* ("Can I believe that?"), and *naiveté* ("What is going on here?").

The complexity and difficulty of the fieldworker role is made more obvious when we consider the fact that as the observer utilizes the above backstage "objective self" for analytic perspective, he or she must also present frontstage behavior that creates an acceptable rapport with the study group. This frontstage behavior implies that one avoids actually asking the host: "Is that really what is happening?" or "Can I believe that?" Rather, one asks questions that help the hosts express true opinions and concerns. The trick is to avoid questions that might intimidate the hosts or lead them to tell the researcher only what they think the fieldworker wants to hear. One of the most important—but most difficult—components of the fieldworker's role is *not to take anything for granted*. Howard Becker, one of our foremost participant observers, counsels his fieldwork trainees to play dumb by using phrases like "I don't understand what you're saying," "What do you mean?", or other ways of pressing the hosts for clarification.

The fieldworker must walk a tightrope between *active participation* in the group, which may help to gain acceptance within the group but tends to interfere with introspection and *passive observation*, which cuts down on the possibilities of "going native." Nevertheless, although it can help his or her analytic perspective, it can also lead to ethnocentrism and loss of rapport. It is usually more practical to separate recording of the observations from the actual observation themselves. Note taking during observation is usually extremely reactive; notes that are taken down in the field often are kept to a minimum and, where possible, unobtrusively made.

Observing and Recording

Fieldwork is a manner of observing and recording the rush of ongoing events in a particular setting. But it involves more than observing and recording motion. *The objective is to discover patterns and routines in commonplace sequences of social interaction.* The fieldworker sets out to observe directly the things people actually say and actually do as they occur in some specific setting. Because he or she is normally a participant in the group being observed, those observations include observing him- or herself. Inferring such mental phenomena as motives, intentions, or attitudes are more often than not more distracting than helpful to the fieldworker. Similarly, tests, questionnaires, and other devices that seek indirectly to indicate or measure what people might say or might do are usually more distracting than helpful to the fieldworker. The reason is simple: Fieldworkers want to know precisely what goes on in some particular place at some particular time; other methods give information on what people *think* goes on, or think *should* go on, is not necessarily what does go on.

Fieldworkers are convinced that their method will ultimately lead to uncovering highly regularized patterns of interchange between two or more individuals that they call routines. Routines are largely hidden from conscious awareness and, therefore, if they are to be examined, they must first be revealed. To uncover such routines, the fieldworker uses an established set of procedures that may be termed provisionalizing, monitoring, analyzing, routine mapping, and resolving (see Figure 10–3).

Provisionalizing refers to the earliest stages of field research, when the investigator knows little about the group or organization. First days in the field are normally spent in simple selection of problems, concepts, indices, and their definitions. Schwartz and Jacobs's (1979:10) position is that

> It might also be well for the discipline to begin at the beginning as so many have repeatedly recommended—that is, first observe, describe, and categorize

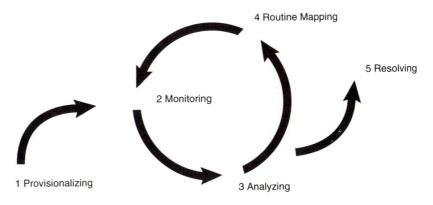

Figure 10–3. Discovering routines through fieldwork.

social events. . . . Such studies should be encouraged and require no apology to those who contend field studies offer "only descriptions." Without descriptive data to build upon, theories of social behavior are likely to continue to prove to be "only theories."

Although some field researchers claim that their observations, descriptions, and categorizations are not guided by theory, in reality that is an impossible claim: Because they make choices of what to observe much less what not to observe, theory is always implicit in field research. It is better, therefore, to be explicit about the problem one wishes to study from the very start. After all, the malleability of field research always allows for restating that problem as the investigation unfolds. Freilich's study of Mohawk Indians well illustrates the use of theory in provisionalizing:

> New Yorkers sometimes read in their newspapers about a unique phenomenon in their midst: the Mohawk Indians who work on the steel structures of various buildings in and around their city. Articles, at times accompanied by pictures of smiling Indians, discuss these "brave" and "sure-footed" Mohawks. The question of why so many Mohawks work in structural steel is one that is often researched by students enrolled in colleges located in and around New York. In 1956, this problem was, in fact, my first professional research assignment. I used A.F.C. Wallace's paper, "Some Psychological Determinants of Cultural Change in an Iroquoian Community," as the foil in my proposal for research support. Wallace's paper suggested that Mohawks lack a fear of heights, and that this lack of fear explains their involvement with the steel industry. I argued that a negative trait (lack of fear) cannot have specific positive consequences (lead a tribe into steel work). I argued further that there is no functional value in a lack of fear of heights for steelwork, and that in actuality the opposite is true: a normal fear of high places leads to caution that saves lives. A more plausible argument seemed to be that Mohawks frequently act *as if* they have no fear of heights. In presenting a subsidiary problem, "Why these acts of daredevilry?", I put forth my theoretical belief that sociocultural factors explain social and cultural phenomena better than do psychological factors. I had a vague notion that Mohawks in steelwork represented some kind of cultural continuity. Thus, the questions I posed were (1) why is it good, culturally, for a Mohawk male to be a structural steelworker? and (2) How does such a cultural "goodness" relate to Mohawk cultural history? (Freilich 1970:185–186)

The provisional stage of formulating a hypothesis in field research differs from other social research methods. The field researcher assumes a *learning* role (Agar 1986:12) in which the observer encounters a social world he or she does not understand at the start, but of which—through firsthand experience—he or she will try and make sense. As Glazer and Strauss (1967) outline *grounded theory*, the researcher constantly compares emerging hypotheses and field data. This comparison forces the researcher to reexamine data in the light of emerging theory, and thus leads to analysis which of necessity goes beyond description.

The utility of making the research problem explicit becomes most apparent after comparing different ethnographic accounts of the "same" thing. Lewis' (1951) restudy of an isolated rural Mexican village by Redfield (1930) provides the classic example. While Redfield found virtually no indication of interpersonal conflict within Tepoztlan, Lewis found the village to be conflict ridden. There is good reason to believe that the village had not significantly changed in the two decades between studies. Rather, the differences were largely due to different focuses of concern of each researcher. Redfield seemed more concerned with describing *ideal* cultural life, while Lewis appeared more concerned with *actual* village interaction and organization. Freedman (1983), in a restudy of Margaret Mead's famous Samoan field site, provides more recent evidence for the need to make professional fieldwork concerns more explicit: His work indicates Mead's work may have been more concerned with ideals rather than actual sexual behavior of Samoans.

The second through fourth stages of ethnography give it its distinctive flavor: Figure 10–3 depicts this as a circular process of *monitoring, analyzing, and routine mapping*. Once one has provisionally decided what to observe and not to observe, one starts watching actions as they occur in their normal course of development: Who did what, who said what to whom, the context of what happened, and notations of potential field researcher biases. The first stages of this recording process usually will entail simple self-debriefing recall processes, in which one records those things one recalls having happened over some specified short period of time. (However, some roles that the observer takes do not allow such brief encounters; for example, Stein's aforementioned [1989] research on adult bookstores.)

Because field research involves observing complex phenomena that will easily exhaust the novice observer, most experienced field researchers recommend periods of no more than 15 minutes of intense monitoring at a stretch. Even the most well-trained observer finds it demanding and fatiguing to observe and record for more than two hours at a stretch. Longer stretches unduly tax human recall processes that are already burdened by the richness of interaction surrounding the observer. Although 15 minutes may seem like a very short period to the novice, experience indicates that each hour of field observations translates into roughly six to eight hours of self debriefing immediately after leaving the field. Therefore, to observe for a quarter of an hour is to plan on investing several more hours in reconstructing the details that one has observed.

Because note taking during observation is usually extremely reactive, fieldworkers rarely take down more than a minimum of notes while in the field. Instead, where possible, notes are made unobtrusively. Therefore, the field researcher needs occasions for literally and figuratively "leaving the field" for periodic reviews of what has happened and where the research is going. Part of the need for leaving the field will also include a critical self-examination of habits of attention and inattention that inadvertently filter the fieldworker's observations.

Effective field observation can be destroyed by not paying attention to known sources of human filtering habits of ignoring social use of physical space, nonverbal behaviors, listener behaviors, actions of peripheral persons, and actions in peripheral physical settings. First, physical space constrains social behavior and is modified by it. As some naive architects have belatedly discovered, many modern architectural spaces intended to humanize our large cities have actually encouraged sales of illicit drugs and crime. Second, non-verbal behaviors may be as important as, or more important than, the talk they accompany; people often give off nonverbal behaviors that contradict what they say. Third, listener behavior is as important as speaker behavior in any interaction. You might test this statement by not responding to someone who greets you. Fourth, persons who are peripheral to the "main arena" may be important to what is going on. Consider the case of an observer of a baseball game who pays attention only to the pitcher and batter, without considering "peripheral" actions of where outfielders positioned themselves or baseline umpire's actions and positions. Fifth, actions in peripheral settings may be important to the routines on "center stage." Just as the baseball manager must not only consider today's immediate game, but also such "peripheral physical settings," other organizations and groups do not act in isolation of their peripheral environment. A good fieldworker takes time out occasionally to consider how to compensate for these types of habits of inattention.

Analyzing goes on both in and out of the field. In the field, the worker reflects on what is going on by incessantly asking him- or herself various forms of the question "What happens when. . . ?": For example, when (some action) occurs, what other actions regularly precede or follow that action? The field researcher must never forget that routines are so embedded in social life that they are difficult to tease out. Good writers of fiction often provide useful sources of insight into social routines. For example, Howard Mohr in his *How to Talk Minnesotan* (1987) cleverly uncovers many of the social routines most Americans are unaware of using. In his chapter on "The Minnesota Long Good-bye," he notes that American departures take place in stages. In the first stage, he says that we never speak directly to those we are leaving. Instead, we speak directly to our spouses (or ourselves) such that those we are leaving will over-hear us. In this process we use routine phrases such as "We better head out," "It's getting late," "It's past my bedtime," and "Let's hit the road." For example, picture this insightful example of a routine "Minnesotan" dialogue in which a couple about to leave their hosts after a day's visit say (Mohr 1987:216):

— "Well, Doris, I suppose we oughta hit the road."
— "You bet, honey. It's about that time."
— "You two just got here. Stay awhile. Did we do something wrong?" You will be offered another cup of coffee and a light lunch. Go ahead and eat, let your food settle, then with a halfhearted lunge from your seat and a yawn, speak directly to your host:
— "It's past our bedtime. We really gotta go."

and so on through numerous other social routines we unconsciously, but ha-bitually, use to extricate ourselves "politely" from social situations. Although Mohr intends to be humorous, his book works largely because of attention to real social routines which he has observed and in which he has participated. For instance, Mura (1987) used Mohr's insights to analyze similarities between Japanese and American social routines of gift giving and face saving.

When the researcher leaves the field this process of analysis continues with a focus on what to observe (or not to observe) during proceeding entries into the setting. An important part of this analysis is the mapping of routines. Many field researchers use flow charts to graphically depict the natural course of what they have observed. The purpose of such flow charts are several fold. First, the mapping of routines makes explicit the generic question, "What happens when. . . ?" Second, the process of mapping provides the fieldworker with a means of taking stock of whether or not he or she really understands the flow of events. Third, a flow chart provides a logical means of checking for all possible courses of action that need to be watched in future site monitorings. Because not all of those logical courses of action will be observed at the site, important questions can be more easily visualized such as "Why does such and such happen after such and such an event, but not some other event take place instead?"

Such mappings of routines might be as crude, but helpful, as Broadbent's (1989) ordering of political actors in Japan shown in Figure 10–4. Even though

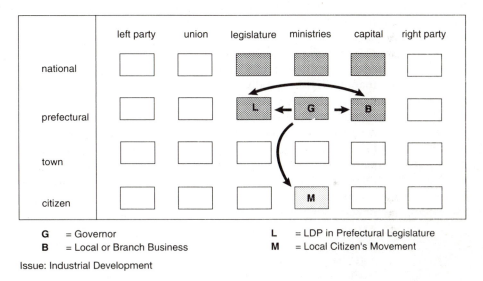

| | G | = Governor | | L | = LDP in Prefectural Legislature |
| | B | = Local or Branch Business | | M | = Local Citizen's Movement |

Issue: Industrial Development

Issue–Context:
1. National fervor for rapid economic growth.
2. Prefectural government pride in successful development.

Ideology or Value Motivation of Actor:

=Pro-Development Stance.

=Pro-Environmental Protection Stance.

Sanction Used in Influence Relation:

1. Economic: Business Elite influences LDP (Liberal Democratic Party) through campaign financing.
2. Political: Business Elite influences Governor through electrol power.
3. Political: Governor has institutional power over the legislature, where he initiates most of the bills.
4. Political: Governor has institutional ability to reject citizen demands.

Figure 10–4.   Elite Alliance on Industrial Development.

Source: Broadbent (1989:187)

Broadbent's categorizations are crude, they highlight important group relationships. Note that only six of the potential 48 alliance channels of influence were utilized by the actors in this particular alliance of elites over industrial development. His map provides means of identifying lines of possible and actual communication, power and influence, what actors think ought to be versus what actually is, and so on. Furthermore, his basic diagram provides a means for cross-cultural comparisons in future field research.

By contrast, some routine mappings may be so complex and pregnant with meaning that their use is neither immediately evident nor transparent without considerable exploration. For an exemplar of such a diagram, I refer the reader to McPhail and Wohstein's (1986:455) flow chart of processes underlying collective behavior. Nearly a decade and a half of participant observation work, in various forms, of collective behavior led to their formulating a complex flow chart involving such variables as individual perceptions, error signals, self-instructions for behavior in collectivities, muscle contractions, etc.; it was developed because collective behavior is an exceedingly complex phenomenon involving such numerous dimensions as direction, velocity, spacing, and tempo of collective locomotion, and vocalization and gesticulation in concert by various individuals.

The goal of this cyclical course of monitoring, analyzing, and routine mapping is the production of a *narrative account* of what went on in the sequence in which various actions occurred. Field researchers follow a fundamental principle in constructing their narrative accounts: *If it isn't in their notes, it didn't happen*. A good narrative account is meant to assist memory in recording events for analysis because memory is always selective and distorted. The construction of a high-quality narrative account involves following important guidelines. First, even before the fieldworker starts to observe and record the events that transpire, he or she visits the site and sketches a ground plan of the scene and its physical setting. This ground plan includes such important information as features of the physical setting, including identification of fixed and movable objects, identification of zones of activity and nonactivity, and the locations of individuals identified by clear descriptive devices (grey hair streaked red down the middle, blue jump suit, etc.). Later on, the details of this rough ground plan can be filled in. Many software companies now offer relatively inexpensive mapping and graphics programs that modern field researchers are starting to utilize.

Excellent quality fieldwork involves paying special attention to the construction of the narrative account. During the monitoring of the research site, it is neither possible nor practical to take down more than a shorthand, skeletal account of what happened for two reasons. First, while one is writing, one may hear what is said, but one cannot also be watching and writing simultaneously. Second, the public act of note taking is usually highly *reactive*. Nevertheless, note taking is necessary to correct for faulty memory. Therefore, experienced fieldworkers have learned to compromise in numerous ways. Sometimes, they develop notation skills that permit them to jot down notes without looking down, so their eyes never leave the scene. Other times they use portable computers—which may be reactive devices in many settings—to allow them the same convenience of typing while watching, or tape recorders, cameras, or video recorders. Still other times, they may take short absences from the primary site to make quick and unobtrusive notes.

Because the fieldworker cannot both write and watch simultaneously, as soon as possible after leaving the field, he or she needs to write out the narrative account for that period. Although some field researchers immediately debrief themselves after leaving the site by using tape recorders, such records should still be typed out into a first draft narrative account before going to bed the same day. This narrative account usually takes a special form. The page will be divided into two parts: The left-hand third of the page will form a column for theoretical and methodological notes, and is not used for the narrative account per se. The right-hand two-thirds of each page will be used for writing the actual narrative.

For example, note how the *novice* field researcher below has constructed her New Year's Eve celebration in Japan in the following example. (These notes are raw, unedited notes. In succeeding paragraphs, these notes provide good examples for second-draft editing.) The left-hand third of the above notes are left blank for later more theoretical notes added during the analysis stage. The right-hand portion displays the first-draft narrative account. Some of the most glaring points that need editing are underlined:

December 31, 1988

10:30 p.m.   We arrived early at the temple. There were already many Japanese there. I was starting to feel cold. From past experiences, four years ago, we knew that it was necessary to arrive early, if one was going to find adequate places to observe the midnight rituals.

10:45 p.m.   By now, there were already over 100 people in the main compound—an area of about 50 meters by 100 meters. Some were in warm Western-style clothes, but others wore the traditional Japanese kimono. There seemed to be an especially large number of young Japanese women in kimono with clashing colors. Many used only a small fur cape as protection against the cold and wind.

11:05 p.m.   Two Buddhist monks emerged from the monk's quarters dressed in beautiful monk's robes. Both had completely shaven heads, and were about 30 years old. They set up two roped-off walkways—one leading into the area housing a large bell, and they roped off the immediate 20 meters diameter around the bell.

11:20 p.m.   Despite the fact that the crowd now numbers over 500, everyone files in—orderly without any pushing or shoving. The area is filling rapidly.

11:30 p.m.   The crowd must number well over 1,000 throughout the whole temple complex, and continues to grow. Despite the late hour, there are many children and most are playing with little apparent adult supervision.

11:45 p.m.   My husband estimated the crowd at over 2,000 persons. Despite the fact that it is now becoming hard to move around freely, everyone is well behaved. There is no evidence of any drunks or <u>unruly</u> behavior.

11:53 p.m.   Five monks emerged from the same quarters as before. The oldest monks came out, first carrying <u>various religious icons</u>. The monks' initial silence <u>made the bystanders restless</u>. They then carried out a <u>short Buddhist service</u>, and then removed the icons back to their quarters.

12:00 p.m.   At exactly midnight, the most senior member of the Buddhist monks came out and rang the bell once. Those of us in the second circle closest to the bell are being slowly moved forward by the surging crowd who <u>wish to get a closer look at the ceremony</u>.

12:05 a.m.   The last of the monks have each now rung the bell once. Now those in the inner circle are being given the chance to ring the bell once. The bell "striker" is always guided by one of the younger monks. In the case of children and the infirm, he actually adds momentum to help strike the bell with enough force.

12:10 a.m.   I can no longer see the bell. I am being propelled forward by the crowd against my will. I <u>feel</u> the need to escape; the crowd is pressing in, and is so dense that there is no way but to go with the crowd. The bell is still ringing. We are going down the stairs away from the bell. I <u>feel</u> as if one person misses a step, we will all fall and be crushed. It is a <u>terrifying feeling</u> even though the crowd seems calm.

The first step in editing these notes is to distinguish between the most *inferential* (what people "mean") data and the least inferential (what people say or do) data. The fieldworker wants to describe, not evaluate, when recording notes. The good fieldworker would not evaluate the young women in kimono as wearing "clashing colors." Instead, it would be better to describe some of the traditional kimono patterns that "clash" according to Western standards but do not from the Japanese standpoint—for example, red and pink plaid kimono with dark green and purple sashes are not uncommon in Japan. "Small" fur cape is very ambiguous. It would be better to say how small—roughly 3-inch wide fur collars. "Many" needs specifying—100 women? 40%? "Unruly" behavior is vague. Perhaps it would be better to clarify that sentence to read. "There is no evidence of any drunks, persons hitting others, yelling, screaming, pushing, or shoving in spite of the fact that everyone is standing with no room to move in any direction."

The final comments about the observer's feelings at 12:10 P.M. are inappropriate. The same is true of the first comment that the observer "*was starting to feel cold.*" Such comments do not belong in the running description of events. Instead, the fieldworker records them as "researcher's feelings" in a *separate account* called methodological notes or deletes them.

Rather than generalize observations and events such as "various religious icons," the observer should provide specific descriptions ("small wooden trays with Japanese *omochi* [rice cakes] stacked three high; 18–inch–high statues of Buddha" and so on). Verbal interaction is often modified by nonverbal interaction that highlights or modifies the meaning of the words: compare the information provided by "they then carried out a Buddhist service," with the more descriptive, "The oldest monk bowed before the altar, hit a small, hand-sized gong. Then the remaining, four younger monks rose to a standing position from lotus position, clapping their hands once in unison. The oldest monk then turned to face the crowd and fellow monks. In unison, the monks chanted 'Nam myoho renge kyo' for approximately four minutes." Richness of detail is important to fieldwork, as well as distinctive of it, because—unlike most other methods—it is difficult to replicate field research. Hence, the richness of information in quality field research allows other researchers to derive their own conclusions if they do not agree with the analysis.

During the period between the first draft and the finished product, the field researcher revises the draft according to certain rules. First, the narrative account is editorially combed for words, phrases, sentences, and paragraphs that do anything other than describe the actual events; those events will be deleted or moved to the left-hand column. Experienced fieldworkers remove (underscored material in the following examples) three principal types of items from the narrative column: statements of attribution, motives, or psychological states ("the surging crowd who *wish to get a closer look at the ceremony*"); valuational statements ("dressed in *beautiful* monk's robes"); and statements of cause and effect ("The monks initial silence *made the bystanders restless*"). The left-hand column may contain notes used to explore future monitoring periods: "Is there an association between periods of leader inactivity or silence and bystander restlessness?"

Among the major telltale signs of unclear narrative are pronouns, vague referents, and passive voice. "*We* arrived *early* at *the temple*," "*many* children," and "The area is filling *rapidly*" all need clarification. The first example would be better as "My husband and I arrived at Kiyomizu Temple at 10:30 P.M." The objective is always to produce a sufficient record of who did what, how, when, and where. The field researcher is not interested in the question "Why?" during the writing of this narrative account. Although the field researcher cannot record everything, he or she can produce a quality narrative through focusing on some manageable portion of the site with appropriate attention to observational filters, and by working on and reworking the accompanying narrative account with the above rules before retiring for the day.

The field researcher finds it necessary to organize and sift through this collected mass of rich information before memory decay becomes a serious impediment. Two suggestions beyond the previously mentioned self-debriefing exercises should be kept in mind. First, reread and "free associate" from raw data to reconstruct the field events, and thereby uncover observations not noted earlier. Second, note changes in field relations for similar reasons:

Changes in roles, as is true of changes in any inferential perspective, create dangers of falsely attributing changes in oneself to changes in the group being studied. Thus, the researcher often starts out by keeping a field diary that is distinguishable from an ordinary personal diary in the above-noted important ways.

Retrospective observation also entails more abstract processes. This involves the painstakingly reiterative process of running through the considerable number of field notes collected to redirect and reconceptualize the observation. Sometimes new lines of pursuit are noted during observation. However, *experienced fieldworkers believe that more frequently hypotheses emerge, are redesigned, and are generated through data filing and processing.* To give easy access to data based on such indexing and to avoid the time-consuming process of thumbing through a chronologically ordered field diary to search for particularly indexed materials some workable system is needed. McCall and Simmons (1969:76) suggest making folders for each variable, category, and hypothesis. Then type field notes on mimeograph stencils and run off several copies. (One copy is placed in a cumulative file in chronological order, acting as a regular field diary.) Other copies are filed in appropriate variable, category, or hypothesis folders. Each folder should be reviewed periodically and interpreted. This filing system makes data on each subject readily accessible; one does not have to go through the entire diary. The folders help with the analysis of incoming data and may suggest new categories that need indexing.

Schatzman and Strauss (1973:99–105) recommend that the field researcher keep separately labeled notes according to whether they are observational (ON), theoretical (TN), or methodological (MN). An *observational note* is a statement of who said or did what, when, where, and how. *Theoretical notes* are the researcher's self-observational notes, or concern the methodological process. In addition, Schatzman and Strauss recommend the use of *analytic memos* that elaborate on or tie together theoretical notes.

This process of recording the cycle of monitoring, analyzing, and routine mapping is a sizeable and time-consuming chore. For this reason, qualitative researchers are increasingly turning (Becker 1985) to personal computer-based, file-management software for the purpose of finding facts and mastering massive amounts of data generated by field research. Quality file-management software make data entry, manipulation, and sorting, storage, and so on much more manageable than conventional pencil-and-paper methods. Good methods of field-note management provide sufficient means for (1) storage and retrieval of the observed times, places, and circumstances, and for (2) control over the analysis process in terms of facilitating the need for more observations for negative, conflicting, or supporting evidence.

This discussion of fieldworker activities has emphasized the participant-observation role. However, other field data often are used in conjunction with field notes to gain a greater understanding of the setting; interviews, historical records of the organization, newspaper morgues, correspondence, official documents, and diaries are often sources of additional information. Because these methods are covered in other parts of this text, they will not be covered in duplicate here. (See Chapter 8 on interviewing for suggestions on open-ended and more formal interviewing skills, and Chapter 11 for dealing with already available data sources for suggestions on historical records or archival data.)

As the fieldworker's findings increase, the study will turn further away from discovery of hypothesis and more toward testing hypothesis. This process is one of resolving, because certain questions must be answered to achieve closure: How do field researchers know when they have collected enough data? When are their samples of data large enough? How do they know when they have understood the culture they are studying? Agar (1986) also speaks of this final stage of fieldwork as one of *resolution*. In a nutshell, his argument is that fieldworkers are finished once they are satisfied that they have schematically *understood* the phenomenon they are watching. Schatzman and Strauss (1973) argue that it is when the categories are "saturated"—when new information does not change the categories of a typology—that there is enough information. A large part of this process of understanding takes the skeptical posture of saying to one's self "what I think is going on probably isn't, but what is going on in that case?"

Fieldwork emphasizes the holistic nature of the phenomenon under observation. This process of resolving the patterns that connect the fieldworker's rich sources of data present a danger of "overemphasizing integration of the data at the expense of conflict and disharmony" (Agar 1986:30). The resolution stage consists of a repetitive process of developing higher order schema that show the relations among several lower order patterns of data. Agar suggests that the fieldworker ask three questions at this stage: What inferences do I need to make to understand why two (or more) behavior patterns follow in a particular order? What inferences help in understanding the routines I've observed? Of the inferences I've made for one particular routine, which are helpful in understanding other routines?

Box 10–1 provides an excellent example of the end product of the laborious field-note-taking process: the published account. Note in this boxed insert how one could work backwards from the published account to the actual field notes. At times Kotarba explicitly quotes from his field notes; at other times he condenses and synthesizes them into a lively whole. In any case, the routines and meanings of the bar-world in Kotarba's observations come through very clearly in this excerpt. By contrast, the first-draft Japanese New Year's Eve notes above lack Kotarba's richness of detail and, *most importantly, his sense of routine life.* The Japanese New Year's Eve notes give no idea of the *routinized, subjective nature* of a typical Japanese New Year's Eve. Kotarba's published account (1984) by contrast, reeks of routinized, subjective features of bar behavior.

Fieldwork Innovation

Any change in the social setting's division of labor, norms, or goals that might result from the fieldworker's presence may threaten the validity of the study.

Box 10-1 *An Exemplary Published Ethnography*[2]

In order to get a feeling for the drinking/driving experience of the tavern regulars, the reader must first understand the setting where the behavior originates. The taverns included in this study are located in an all-white, lower-middle-class neighborhood. They lie within a one-square-mile area that consists primarily of single family residential units. The taverns are all located on major traffic arteries, in buildings that have "store front" appearances. Three of the taverns have adjacent apartments, or "flats," in which the owners and their families reside. This live-in feature of the taverns is common to this type of community . . . and serves an important business function. The taverns are all family businesses in which the father, mother, and older children all take part in tending bar, socializing with the customers, and tending the business. In this respect, they have a minimum of private family life. Only on specific occasions, such as Sunday afternoons or vacations, will a non-family member be hired to tend bar, and these employees are always regular and trusted customers who take on the part-time work more as a favor to the tavern owner and an indication of status among their peers, than as a source of extra income. . . One owner indicated the lasting nature of tavern proprietorship in his family line as follows:

Hell, my father used to run a tavern up in Bridgeport, even before prohibition. He was smart enough to get me started here, when the neighborhood was still vacant lots . . . Some day, the Good Lord willing, the kid (referring to his ten-month-old grandchild) will be serving drinks to your kids!

****

An essential theme of tavern interaction is the fact that, for the majority of the clientele, drinking and driving are virtually inseparable activities. Both of these activities are indulged in regularly and occupy large amounts of the habitués' time. One of the taverns, for example, serves a "hard core" group of 17 regular customers. Seven of these men will stop in every morning for a "bracer" (i.e., a shot of whiskey) before they drive to work. Three customers, because they work relatively close to the tavern, will normally go there for a "liquid lunch," again traveling by car. All 17 men will either stop in the tavern right after work for several drinks, or will do so right after dinner. Moreover, all these men will spend anywhere from 10 to 25 hours in the tavern in an average weekend. Those regular customers who frequent the tavern less often will stop in for the proverbial "quick one" before driving off to more pressing social engagements, such as relatives' parties, weddings, or dates. . . .

The constant mixing of drinking and driving is a result of the taken-for-granted importance of these two activities in the customers' everyday lifes. Stopping in for a few drinks is an activity that can occur almost any time of any day when the men have at least a few minutes to spare. Having a drink is a prerequisite for almost any activity, from going to work or the racetrack to attending the First Holy Communion of one's child or the funeral of one's union steward. Inevitably, these other activities involve transportation by car. The heavy

[2]An excerpt from Josephy A. Kotarba. (1984) One more for the road: The subversion of labeling within the tavern subculture. pp 152–160. In Jack D. Douglas (Ed.), *The Sociology of Deviance.* Boston: Allyn and Bacon, Inc.

reliance placed upon the automobile is, of course, not unique to these men. Nevertheless, the tavern customers generally look down upon walking or taking public transportation in getting from one place to another, for these are perceived to be means of transportation utilized by children, old ladies, and poor people.

. . . a typical tavern habitué in these settings is a regular at several taverns for several reasons. He will ordinarily visit one tavern to place his gambling bets, another to have a drink with the men from work, another to plan a softball team, and still another where members of his own ethnic group gather. . . . Quite often, all of this visitation is accomplished in one evening or afternoon. Whereas the amount of driving is increased from simple tavern-to-home, (as is common-sensically thought) to tavern-to-tavern-to-tavern-to-tavern-to-home, the amount of alcohol consumed along the way increases in somewhat geometric fashion. At each stop along the way, the customer feels distinct normative pressure to drink as if it were his first stop. He is obliged to have drinks in order to renew old acquaintances and to fulfill his obligations as a new member for the evening, even though he may only stay in the tavern for a few minutes to take care of some other business. If he plans on making several stops in one evening, the time allowed for each stop may be consciously shortened, but the amount of alcohol consumed at each stop may not.

****

During the course of this study, I encountered only three cases of DWI convictions, but the effects of this labeling process were widely known among all the tavern regulars. In all three cases, the wives of the drinkers/drivers forced them to sharply curtail the amount of time spent in the taverns. One wife stated her reaction to her husband's conviction as follows:

> If I told him once, I told him a thousand times to quit burning himself out at the bars. He wouldn't listen to me, though. He said I had nothing to gripe about . . . Everybody had shame in our family before . . . He thinks it's a big joke. Wait, someday he's gonna lose his job over his drinking, then he'll learn. Six months without driving is one thing, but no paycheck? Then, it's goodbye, buster . . .

The threat to the habitué's substantial self is also present at the mention of the other label he could acquire as a result of a DWI conviction. That label is "alcoholic." Within the general interaction of the tavern, alcoholism is never discussed openly, for it hits too close to home. It's a taboo word. . . . The shame associated with the label of alcoholic would force a drinker *out* of his deviant subculture, for he would be known by his peers as a "weak" person.

The larger the group under study, the less probability that the researcher will have any such undesirable effects. The types of roles discussed earlier in this chapter have different innovating effects. The covert observer's low "spy" profile may mean that his or her role as a *researcher* will not cause any innovations per se. But the covert observer who comes in as a complete participant may have innovating effects—particularly in small groups. At the other extreme, the fieldworker who takes on the complete observer role has potential innovating problems through high profile as an observer, but not as a participant.

It should be pointed out that most people in natural situations find it difficult to act unnaturally for any length of time. Documentary films such as those done by Wiseman clearly show that the innovating presence of participant observers and their equipment (tape recorders, movie cameras, portable personal computers) may be quite minimal over a long period of fieldwork, particularly in large groups or formal organizations. The best strategy would appear to introduce obtrusively the equipment or role but not to actively employ it for a few days. For example, Wiseman "shoots" an empty 16 mm camera for a few days. Because his subjects believe his camera has film when in fact it does not, he is able to have them adjust to the innovation without large film expenses. However, any change in the fieldworker's role over time—which is a very likely outcome—may have short-term innovating effects to which the fieldworker must be constantly alert; the fieldworker must be able to adequately differentiate between natural internal changes in the host group, and changes introduced by the field researcher's presence.

Data-Quality Controls

Because of the potential vulnerability to invalidation and unreliability that the innovating roles of fieldworkers may induce, McCall (1969a:132–135) has listed some appropriate quality-control checks:

Observational Data

Fieldworker

1. *Reactive Effects*—Where available, comparison of informant interview accounts of similar events where the fieldworker was and was not present; if the above is not possible, then he or she should ask informants if the observer's presence seems to affect the events observed.
2. *Ethnocentrism*—Comparison of fieldworker interpretations with relevant respondent and informant interviews for incomplete or inaccurate interpretations.
3. *Going Native*—Comparison of field notes on comparable observational setting at different points in the research for changes in viewpoint. Reflection on researcher's sympathies and antipathies toward the subjects as sources of bias.

Interview Data

4. *Knowledgeability*—Reflection should be given to whether the interviewee gave direct, firsthand data; confidence in his or her objectivity, introspectiveness, interpersonal sensitivity.

5. *Reportorial Ability*—Knowledgeability and ability to report one's knowledge may be independent of one another; therefore, the researcher must consider the reliability of the interviewee's memory, the interviewee's ability to express him- or herself well in detail and on issues that may seem obvious to him- or herself.
6. *Reactive Effects of Interview Situation*—Did the interviewee seem to be straining to give the researcher the kinds of information he or she thinks the researcher wants, or did he or she appear to withhold information?
7. *Ulterior Motives*—Was the interviewee trying to rationalize, muckrake, slant results, expose something, and so on, casting doubt on the account's accuracy?
8. *Bars to Spontantaneity*—Did the interviewee seem overanxious about possibilities of being overheard?
9. *Ideosyncratic Factors*—Did factors immediately prior to interviewing—the subjects' immediately past mood, fatigue, or drinking—affect the testimony uncharacteristically? Was there notable discontinuity with previously expressed reports?

Each of these checks illustrates how model fieldworkers adhere to the norm of scientific skepticism in evaluating their data. For instance, a field researcher who has noted potential reactive effects of her presence four times during observation of a single observational event, and absence of reactivity in nine other notes of the same event, would note that the data quality was acceptable for that event (9/13 or .69 cases of nonreactivity). The purpose of such data-quality checks is twofold: The first is to serve as a quality-control check for particular factors that may contaminate the data with the intent of reducing their influence on future data. The other is to note in the write-up of the research to what extent the contaminating factors have been avoided.

One of the unique features of fieldwork is that reliability and validity checks are usually built into field research as it proceeds or after it is completed, rather than before research is initiated as in most other methods. Again, unlike other methods, fieldwork checks on data quality require an unusual attention to self-awareness: However, there is no one blinder than one who either will not or cannot see oneself. Thus, ironically, McCall's technique helps but is affected by the same biasing effects it is designed to counter.

McCall's nine quality-control checks also explain why the researcher must maintain *backstage* attitudes of skepticism, cynicism, and introspection. This is not to say that the fieldworker has to be cynical about human nature. Rather, these attitudes are necessary components of the scientific process. One can be no less cynical toward oneself than one is toward one's subjects if one is to be able to properly evaluate the data. In other words, by taking on the role of cynical introspectionist, one tries to give the data the most rigorous data-quality evaluation possible, given the qualitative nature of field data. Such evaluation must include cynical and skeptical role playing toward all instruments of data collection, including oneself.

Becker (1970) takes a somewhat different approach to measuring data-quality control. Although he does not employ strict formulae as does McCall, he suggests ground rules for interpreting data quality. First, there should be more statements that are volunteered by the host group members than are directed by the participant observer. Second, there should be a similar or greater number of statements made to others than to the fieldworker alone. If the number of statements made to the observer alone is over 50, then the observer ought to question the proposition. Third, actual host group and individual activities should make up 20 to 25% of the total data collected.

Hypothesis Generation

Part of the fieldworker's innovating role will be to generate hypotheses. Simple submersion in an observational setting is an insufficient, albeit necessary, component of field methods. But hypotheses cannot be formulated in a vacuum without knowledge of the field site. Furthermore, the fieldworker can rarely anticipate developments in the field that inevitably guide his or her investigation. Many fieldworkers claim that hypotheses formed without regard to these considerations turn out to be trivial or banal. What field researchers do best is enter a field site with grounding in the theory of their discipline, and with as much knowledge of their chosen site as they can glean from secondary materials. The field then takes over, and the outcome depends on the interaction of fieldworker and field setting. Theorizing, thus, is usually only done after the generation of much data.

However, the advantage of this after-the-fact theorizing is the generation of *serendipitous* data. Serendipity refers to the making of fortuitous discoveries through the combination of sagacity and accident, of things a person is not in search of. The surprising, anomalous, and unexpected observation has long proved of interest to sociologists. Barton and Lazarsfeld (1955:322) indicate two different uses of serendipitous data. The first is that they create such problems as trying to explain what they are and what they do. The second is that some variables may be found in the qualitative observations that cannot be measured directly.

Observations that raise problems go against our theoretical and common-sense expectations. Therefore, they provide challenges to scientific inquiry. Because the fieldworker is a stranger or newcomer to the field site, he or she is in a good position to pick out problematic facts that are taken for granted by those accustomed to the locale. Hence, probably, most serendipitous data are noticed in the beginning stages of fieldwork, before the observer has grown accustomed to the research setting. The strategy of leaving the field at periodic intervals also contributes to fresher perspectives. Upon reentrance into the field setting, the researcher will have regained some ethnocentrism that, however short-lived, may give much leverage in terms of observing things that otherwise might have been unnoticed or taken for granted. Informants who hold particular types of marginal or deviant roles may also be helpful in generating unexpected data.

Some observations, while not surprising in and of themselves, may have usefulness as indirect measures of qualitative social and behavioral variables.

Barker (1984:285), not surprisingly, found that 85% of 1,017 persons who attended a Moonie workshop in London stayed to the end of the two-day session. But her longer term assessment of "brainwashing" conversions by the Moonies painted a much more interesting picture: only 30% came back for a second session; only 10% became members for at least a week; and only 4% were still members two years later. Even more serendipitously, when she compared Moonie joiners to nonjoiners, she found that a higher proportion of joiners than nonjoiners had advanced educations, high self-esteem, and high-school grades, contrary to the popular press reports that Moonies have more mental health problems than average. Such serendipity was possible only because of Barker's refusal to settle for unsystematic observation. Her fieldwork has had a large impact because she systematically counted comparable observations, rather than proceeding by hunch and suspicion alone.

Qualitative Typologies and Analytic Induction

One of the best means by which field researchers take large amounts of raw data and summarize them is through qualitative typologies, which are nominal classifications. Because of the qualitative nature of most field data, it is not always possible to have the rigor of ordinal-, cardinal-, or ratio-scaled measures, but such nominally scaled categories as Barker's (1984:230) differentiation between Moonie joiners, nonjoiners, leavers, and general-population comparison groups may prove enlightening for understanding differences in such things as perceptions of control over their own life, others, or the world around them.

At one end of a continuum of making typologies are simple, crude lists of types used for comparison. Snow and Anderson (1987) elaborate how homeless street people construct and negotiate their personal identities through three generic types of identity talk, which they categorized as distancing, embracing, and fictive storytelling. First, they may use *distancing*: They may attempt to disassociate themselves from others ("I'm not like the other guys who hang out at the 'Sally' [Salvation Army]). (p. 1349)." Second, they may use *embracing* in which they verbally or expressively confirm acceptance of a role such as "I've tramped my way across the country" or "I'm a bag lady." Third, some homeless people engage in *fictive storytelling* in which they resort to fanciful claims and fabrications: Snow and Anderson (p. 1359) provide an example of a 40-year-old homeless male "who spent much of his time hanging around a transient bar, boasting about having been offered a job as a Harley-Davidson mechanic for $18.50 per hour, while constantly begging for cigarettes and spare change for beer. Each of these qualitative types proved important in quantitatively discriminating such things as the amount of time on the streets. For example, homeless people who fantasized about future-oriented fictions were four times less likely to have been on the streets during the past six months as those who embellished their fictive storytelling with past or present events.

Agar's observations of how junkies chose places for their drug transactions offers another highly systematic and logical analysis based on only four

---

Table 10–1   *Summary of Questions to Ask in Place Selection with Effect on Value of Individual Place*

Question	Answer	Effect of Value
1. How much heat is there on X?	More	Lower
	Less	Higher
2. How much can you expect people to hassle you for dope at X?	More	Lower
	Less	Higher
3. How hip a spot is X?	More	Lower
	Less	Higher
4. How far away is X?	Farther	Lower
	Closer	Higher

*Where X is any place.

Source: Agar (1980:153)

attributes (see Table 10–1). In essence, these four questions illustrate the logical sorting process of "cost" of the place of "getting off" on drugs. A place that "has the heat on" (for example, the police were just there, a new superintendent of buildings prowls the halls, the place has been busted two or three times) has low value and the junkies will rarely frequent it unless very sick. A place that is "hip" ("It's groovy," "You can always hang out after you get high") has high value and is frequented often. Logically, the more factors that have high value, the more likely an addict will visit the place, and vice versa.

Oftentimes, one finds it useful to take two or more such qualitative typologies and cross-classify them to obtain a set of logical typological combinations. A classic example is Becker's (1963) typology for the study of deviance:

	Obedient Behavior	Rule-Breaking
Behavior Individual perceived as deviant	*Falsely accused deviant*	*Pure deviant*
Individual not perceived as deviant	*Conforming*	*Secret Deviant*

Glazer (1965) suggests using what he terms the *constant comparative method* for generating typological categories. In his method (p. 440), one starts out by "coding each incident in the data in as many categories of analysis as possible." After a few codings, the fieldworker may find a conflict in how or why to code some instance that will call for logically reconciling recordings. This process aids the change from comparisons of incidents to incidents to comparisons of incidents with properties of some theoretical framework. In essence, this is how Agar (1980) proceeded from classifying drug addict statements of how they selected a place. Agar looked for similarities and dissimilarities among such statements as "The lock is broke."; "It's not cool."; "Too many people coming in and out."; "We might be seen."; and "There's too many people." He eventually categorized such statements into one of the four place selection questions in Table 10–1. What makes fieldwork methods different from other methods is partly the *simultaneous* nature of such operations: While the researcher is gathering data, he or she conducts important parts of the analysis.

Hypothesis Evaluation

Fieldworkers often distinguish between two types of hypotheses; *descriptive* and *causal*. A descriptive proposition infers only simple association between two or more variables such as in the hypothesis; "Lesser amounts of physical size or strength are associated with lesser use of physical aggression." A causal hypothesis adds the inference of determination of one variable from the other to that simple association, as in "lesser amounts of physical size cause lesser amounts of physical aggression."

There is always the danger in fieldwork of treating both types of hypothesis poorly. The reason is that many hypotheses quite normally emerge during *later* stages of field research or *after data collection has ended.* In such cases, the researcher may not have enough data to test a particular hypothesis adequately. Also, explanations may be tautological: They may emerge from the data and be suggested by the data. To guard against these possibilities, field researchers often can assess descriptive hypotheses through two different techniques: interpretation of incidence and pinpointing operations (McCall 1969b:237) In the *interpretations of incidence* approach, the researcher sifts through the data, sorting according to similarity of account content; he or she then attempts to make theoretical sense out of these sortings. *Pinpointing operations* refers to the formulation of uniform and specific combinations of theoretical indicators that are applied to all cases relevant to evidence for or against a proposition.

Causal hypotheses require even stricter evaluation because, in addition to the association factor already mentioned for descriptive hypotheses, the fieldworker must assess (1) proper time sequencing of the variables, and (2) rival causal explanations. While field research rarely discredits most of the rival causal hypotheses, the more rival explanations discounted, the greater the credibility of the fieldwork data conclusion. The time sequencing of the variables implies that the independent variables must have either preceded, or occurred simultaneously with, the dependent variables. Therefore, as long as the dependent variable can be shown not to have preceded the independent variable, causal explanation is rendered plausible. Notice, however, as with other types of nonexperimental research, that the field researcher can never prove that just because two variables are associated and time-ordered, and other rival explanations are discounted, that therefore one variable causally determines the other—he or she can only add substantial weight to the argument of causality.

Fieldwork Social Controlling

Social controlling is an ever-continuing process: The fieldworker who takes on the role of participant observer does well to remember that someone is observing his or her activities. We think of rewards for conformity, or punishments for deviancy, as ways of reinforcing a group's culture, but there are more subtle ways of social controlling that may affect the field researcher. Role definition is one of the more important yet subtle ways of controlling a fieldworker. As a fieldworker, the researcher may be limited to having access to some places, times, or people but not to others. It is partly for this reason that fieldworkers try to cultivate informants. Informants are people who can do things for the researcher or who have access to places from which the researcher is barred.

Social controlling through the fieldworker's role as defined by the hosts is a particular problem in organizations with a complex or highly hierarchically defined division of labor. If the fieldworker is authorized by management to study assembly-line workers, the workers may define the fieldworker, at worst, a "spy" and, at best, as "one of them rather than one of us." Therefore, the fieldworker must always be aware of how his or her role is or might be defined by various members of the host group, the potential social controlling effects of those role definitions on the goal of obtaining data, and potential ways to circumvent these constraints to data collection without threatening the project's continued existence.

Implicit in fieldwork, social controlling is the awareness that there is reciprocity in any role relationship or transaction. Unlike the role of the researcher in other methods, the participant observer is an integral part of the situation he or she is observing; Schwartz and Schwartz (1956:348) state that "Together the observer and the observed constitute a context which would be different if either participant were different or were eliminated." Therefore, unique field-work-related problems of data collection and ethics are created by the intimate reciprocal influence of observer and observed.

Field Training, Reliability, and Validity

While reliability and validity are matters that can be handled to some extent while in the field, concern with reliability and validity should be built into training sessions before fieldwork begins. Unfortunately, little thought has been given to field training techniques in the past. Training techniques used in survey research and structured observations may be profitably used in fieldworker training. On the other hand, Bennett (1960) points out that fieldwork is more than a set of techniques for the collection of data. Bennett, accordingly, has developed a course designed to train fieldworkers. The first part of his course has standard formal instruction in such specific fieldwork techniques as rapport, informant interviewing, and the like. The second part of the course is designed to make students aware of individual perspectives as a significant element in observation and interpretation. Ethnographic documentary films unfamiliar to the students are shown to the classes for the students to practice observational note taking. Finally, students actually put these techniques to use in some social setting. During the second and third phases of the course, students and professor analyze each other's notes.

Bennett (1960) noted three general observational patterns in fieldwork: (1) The *empirical ethnographer* records events in chronological order, details descriptions, and makes few interpretations. (2) The *holistic ethnographer* notes gestalts, emphasizes the emotional-esthetic whole, and adds some interpretation, and (3) The *social anthropologist*, with an interest in social structure and system, summarizes details and emphasizes interpersonal relations. Additionally, some students showed highly idiosyncratic variations in observation and interpretation: Some were more likely to note odors, tastes, sensual textures, or emotional states of characters. Some avoided the use of adjectival descriptions while others used them with care. Still others interjected their personal experiences and cultural comparisons ("This society resembles my own . . ."), while others framed their notes with such abstractions as "feudal, authoritarian system," "rigid sex mores," and "the woman's role is subordinate to the man's."

If fieldworkers are to make significant progress in higher reliability and validity, thought will have to be given (1) to making fieldworkers more aware of these types of biases in their own work, and (2) techniques for training fieldworkers into or out of these perceptual patterns as dictated by the nature of particular field-research needs. Noted earlier in this chapter is that the model fieldworker starts out by noting the "what, when, where, and how much" of any field setting. This is comparable to Bennett's "empirical ethnographer" pattern. Toward the middle portions of the field project, more time is spent on the "how" of the setting. The researcher becomes more interested in interpretive reconstruction of data near the end of the project. Finally, the "analytic memo" scheme of note taking proposed by Schatzman and Strauss (1973) comes into play during later stages of model field research, and is comparable to Bennett's "social anthropologist" pattern.

Apprentice fieldworkers can be trained to be sensitive to their individual observational biases (Smith 1982). It is not enough simply to ask fieldworker trainees to observe and record factual information. Enormous differences in perceptual biases, states of consciousness, and observational paradigms exist between people that influence what they observe. But it is possible to sensitize trainees to such important descriptive categories as absolute number of observations recorded, proportion of descriptive versus inferential observations, the duration of events, and antecedent-consequent descriptive details.

Field-method reliability and validity depend in large part on what is being observed when. By comparing social survey data to his key informants' reports, Poggie (1972) found his informants gave the most valid information in response to directly observable public phenomena, concrete referents, and noncontroversial responses requiring little evaluation of inference (e.g., "What percentage of the houses here are made of adobe?"). The least valid responses were those to questions concerning information about non-directly observable matters (e.g., "What percentage of the people sleep in beds?").

In the past, field studies have given little attention to means of evaluating and increasing reliability and validity. Because of the unique contributions to knowledge that are possible when field studies are carried out in a manner consistent with standards of scientific rigor, *this chapter section has emphasized that quality fieldwork may be collected with good validity and reliability.* We know now in large part due to the persistent experimentation of such fieldworkers as Schatzman and Strauss, McCall, and Bennett, that fieldworkers can be trained in ways that meet high standards of reliability and validity (Smith 1982).

Ethics

Because of the normally intimate roles that fieldworkers engage in, compared to other types of researcher roles, the ethics of fieldwork becomes somewhat problematic. On the one hand, most fieldworkers normally explain who they are, and what they want to the groups they study. This act of accountability for their actions may be handled by such a simple statement as "I'm here to write a book about your group." Agar (1980:55–56) observes that such a statement implies two things to most people: First, that the researcher will observe different aspects of the group's life; second, the fieldworker will eventually publish something about the group.

It is this second implication that is most bothersome because identification of who was studied is usually much easier to deduce in field research than in other, more anonymous, types of social research. John Lofland's (1966) chronicle of a small, deviant religious sect provides an excellent example. Although he attempted to disguise names and places for ethical reasons, another social scientist "blew" his cover (Lynch 1977) through deductive disclosure. Similarly, Vidich and Bensman's (1968) two-and-one-half year study of "Springdale" created a furor in the community he had studied, and in the university he had been associated with at the time he did the study because of the difficulty of disguising identities. Because the number of village officials was small, it was impossible to disguise completely references to each individual. Furthermore, community dynamics were impossible to discuss without identifying individuals.

The problem of fieldwork ethics creates special problems of accountability: At whose insistence should the field researcher cut out, distort data, or lie? Although the fieldworker wishes to protect the privacy of the host group, many host groups wish to control the final written product. The result can be disastrous: Agar (1980:186) writes of a group that cut his final written report "in half, changed technical terms, and altered the analysis," even though he had carefully protected anonymity. He vowed never again to make an agreement allowing a host group to control the final product of his fieldwork.

Another important issue that crops up in fieldwork ethics is: On whose side is the fieldworker? Ethnographic work has occasionally been used against the very people who hosted the fieldworker. Agar (1980:186–187) reports an offer from a federal law-enforcement agency to provide research money in exchange for monthly reports; he refused because it made him uncomfortable that the agency's goal was the elimination of his informants. Although other ethnographers argued with Agar that as long as they controlled the research process, they saw no reason to turn money down from any source, he raises an important dilemma of the "unknown number of informational strings attached" to this enforcement agency's offer. Although Agar offers no absolute guidelines for resolving these types of complex, ethical dilemmas, he correctly observes that the field researcher must evaluate the potential political effects of his or her participation in any project.

Punch (1986:83) sums up the ethical problems in fieldwork, when he states that

> Often fieldwork means getting to like the researched, and hoping they will get to like you. On that basis, it is reprehensible if we train students to purloin documents, betray confidences, and abjure the strong obligations surrounding friendship in our society. A healthy academic community concerns itself with responsibility to the researched, accountability to colleagues, and integrity in terms of responsible conduct between senior and junior staff (to avoid feudal exploitation).

One of my colleagues, Michael Stein, relates that in his graduate student days, the late Harry Crockett, Jr. had a summary ethical rule that all fieldworkers might well heed: *People should not be in any worse shape after you leave the field than when you entered it.*

Fieldwork Logistics

Fieldworkers have numerous demands placed on their time and energy. Likewise, host groups under study may feel threatened by the additional demands placed upon them by field researchers. Field entry, therefore, raises logistical problems of how research roles and other resources (time, energy, money) will be distributed.

The fieldworker has multiple identities that may lead to a necessary segregation of roles and audiences. He or she may find there are problems of scheduling his or her roles, so that both the researcher and the host group minimize inconsistent demands of competing roles or unrealistic pressures of too many role demands. In highly stratified organizations, in particular, the fieldworker is often placed in highly unrealistic multiple identities. Managers may expect the field researcher to report any irregular activities of the rank and file, while the rank and file may see the fieldworker as a threat to their privacy or even as a means of improving job conditions.

Even in small groups the fieldworker finds it impossible to study everything. In Liebow's study of black street-corner men, he got to know about 20 of the men on a relatively personal level over an intensive year-and-a-half study. Decisions on how to collect information best inevitably end up weighted against the realistic needs for budgeting one's roles. The constant public nature of the fieldworker's role may create special stresses that lead to exhaustion. Even if the fieldworker leaves the field for short time periods, psychological preoccupation with the study may prevent relaxation.

Organizing Field Operations

In the earliest stages of gaining formal entry to the research setting, we saw that it is important for the investigator to case the site. Once entry has been achieved it becomes necessary to *extend* this casing to gain a picture of the parameters and complexity of the universe to be observed and its components. This is the only means by which the researcher can attempt to be systematic in organizing field operations. Schatzman and Strauss (1973:36) suggest that the researcher organize operations through three maps: social, spatial, and temporal.

The "social map" notes frequencies (the *how much*) and types (the *what*) of persons, roles, channels of communication, status hierarchies, and so on. The "spatial map" locates the *where* of persons, events, power, organizational segments, and channels by which persons and resources pass from one location to another. The "temporal map" deals with the *when* of people and events. Dalby (1985) provides a good example of a sociotemporal map shown in Figure 10–5.

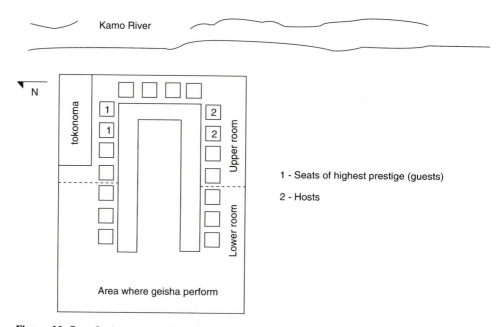

Figure 10–5. Sociotemporal map of geisha activity area. (Floor plan of a typical banquet room in Pontocho. The space enclosed by the three sides of the tables serves as a no-man's-land where geisha can move about freely.)

Source: Dalby (1985:287). Reprinted with permission of the University of California Press.

These mapping routines have several important functions. First, they help the researcher know what the *boundaries* and *substance* of data gathering will be. Second, from these mappings, the field researcher may form strategies of sampling since he or she cannot possibly look at everything. Third, the maps help to *organize times* and *locations* in the field. Fourth, the maps help to anticipate potential problems (demanding time schedules, problems of hierarchical communication) and unanticipated research foci. Fifth, the maps help him or her judge the magnitude of the research task. Sixth, the mapping tour acts as a means of introduction to the people he or she will later study more intensively. In the New Year's Eve notes used earlier, a well-made map would have aided our confidence in estimates of crowd size, aided the observer in organizing information, and helped the reader better understand the various descriptions.

The final step in organizing research is to start observations with the *higher* echelons and *quickly move on* to lower echelons. Schatzman and Strauss (1973:47–48) explain that this move has two rationales. First, the researcher wishes to establish *independence* from the leadership. Therefore, he or she "must not appear to be reporting findings." Second, the "view from the top" is typically a rather special one, where the researcher will be able to get a good working start on organizational overview, operations, functions, present and future rationale, and history from which to branch out in observing at lower echelon subsites.

Because humans measure their activities and developments through time, a good practice is the construction of a *sociological calendar* as a device for condensing and analyzing data about social processes. In constructing a sociological calendar, the fieldworker attempts to work out the *latent* units of time in a social organization by contrast to manifest units such as days, weeks, and months. Light (1975) reanalyzed classic work on the socialization process of medical students through the natural pacing of social events (Table 10–2). His calendar suggests that the medical-school year shows clear changes in student perspectives from broad, idealistic concerns with the sick, through pragmatic "getting through" concerns, to a more tempered idealism. Each of these phases is associated with particular social demands on the student's time and energy. Therefore, the sociological calendar helps the fieldworker think more rigorously about his or her data, and brings out structural relationships between data that might not have been noticed otherwise.

Summary

Certain problems and procedures recur in all fieldwork that have been touched upon: types of general and specific knowledge about a host group obtained before entering the field; sources from which information about an organization of community may be obtained; preparation for entry into the field; initial field research activities; the structuring of the field researcher's role; the se-

Figure 10–6. *Calendar 1 Changing perspectives on Idealism, based on "Boys in White"*

Structure	Premed.	High pressure, highly structured lectures, reading, exams		A variety of clinical experiences		Anticipating graduation
Time (Semesters)	Point of entry	1st	2nd-4th	5th	6th-7th	8th
Perspectives (Mid-1950s)	General idealism	From idealism to getting through	Getting through (GT)	From GT to maximizing experience	Maximizing experience (ME)	From ME to tempered idealism
			Suspended idealism			

Source: Light (1975: 1155)

quence and timing of field activities; the selection of sponsors and informants; incentives the field research offers informants; ethical problems involved in field research; means of insuring high data quality; and human relations and emotional costs of doing fieldwork.

The eclectic nature of field research is its hallmark: It involves at least three broad types of field strategies: (1) participant observation, (2) informant interviewing, and (3) enumerations and samples. Participant observation includes watching and being a part of the events under study, and maintaining stable relationships in a host group. Using a restricted definition of "informant," informant interviewing is interviewing a knowledgeable person only about other people (not him- or herself) or only about events that are not currently happening. Enumerations and samples include surveys and observations involving little participation that can be repeated and easily counted. Although interviewing, sampling, and observations are discussed in other chapters, a distinctive feature of interviewing, sampling, and observation is that they are unstructured and ongoing processes in field research, but conceptualized before research begins in other types of research. These unstructured and processual qualities give field research an edge over other methods for uncovering routines and habits and for research in as yet little explored areas of social life.

Participant observation, however, is not as useful at unearthing institutionalized norms and statuses; informant interviewing is a generally useful means of collecting such data. Informants, when properly interviewed, may explain rules and status relationships, accounts of what roles exist and who occupies them, what constitutes such things as adultery or illegitimacy, how political power is supposed to be passed from one person to another, and so on. However, informant interviewing depends on the firm establishment of trust and the type of role the informant occupies.

Field research is weakest in enumerating and sampling events and in showing causality. The distributions and frequencies of members, number of times members have or do things, etc. are best handled by more structured observational techniques and survey methods introduced in other chapters of this text, and which have clearer standards of reliability and validity. Similarly, the massive number of potential causal explanations of any particular event are poorly handled by field research because it has no means of adequately and logically reducing alternative explanations. Field research is good at generating hypotheses that may be more rigorously tested by other methods.

McCall's six fundamental organizational process—recruitment, socialization, interaction, innovation, social control, and logistics—highlight the process of doing fieldwork. Their order is arbitrary because all six processes occur simultaneously and because they influence each other. But the advantage to their use is the highlighting of the *unique processual nature* of fieldwork which is oriented toward the complex task of unearthing social habits and routines normally hidden from consciousness.

Recruitment concerns techniques for gaining and maintaining access to a particular group or organization. Most researchers case potential research sites prior to entry to weigh project feasibility and costs. Formal organizations require more elaborate assessment of methods of entry and access: letters of introduction, promises of acting in the role of guest at all times, elaborate maneuvering to gain access to different levels of an organization, and so on. Recruitment is an ongoing process throughout the history of a field project, and involves careful attention to derecruitment as the project nears completion.

It is important to give careful consideration to the choice of roles before attempting entry into the field: The field researcher can overparticipate in host group activities, leading to problems of "going native" or underparticipate, leading to problems of ethnocentrism. The participant role may lead to unintended and unwanted changes in the group, but lack of participation may result in lack of trust and a general reluctance to share information with the field researcher. Therefore, the fieldworker usually finds it necessary to use a variety of roles and informant relationships to gain access to different parts of a field site.

Fieldworker interaction is oriented toward roles that help the researcher in gaining access to information on WHO comes together for WHAT activities WHEN and WHERE. It also involves a complex of attitudes of skepticism, cynicism, and naiveté that help the fieldworker not take anything for granted, and more objectively assess information.

Quality field research involves special attention to the manner of note taking employed. A cyclical pattern of provisionalizing over what to watch or not to watch, monitoring, analyzing, routine mapping, and resolving the patterns of data they have decided to watch gives much distinctive flavor to how field research operates. The complexity of social life makes this process particularly exhausting: Fieldworkers recommend short periods of 15 minutes to no more than several hours at a time in actual monitoring. Furthermore, each hour of monitoring translates into six hours or more of debriefing, note revisions, and preliminary analysis. Much of this note writing and revision calls for special attention to human problems with memory-recall and observational-filtering habits that may block out the production of quality narrative accounts essential to the reconstruction of what occurred. The rule is: *If it is not in your notes, it did not happen.*

An important, but often overlooked part of field observation and analysis is the making of physical maps and flow charts of routines and habits. The richness of field data needs such means of data reduction and management. Other means of qualitative aids to analysis include the construction of indexes through systematic filing and sorting systems that aid management and data storage and retrieval. Later stages of field research emphasize more holistic analysis of behavior patterns that have been observed and recorded, and resolution of conflicting data and meaning.

The presence of the fieldworker may introduce unwanted innovations into the group studied. Part of the solution is to wait a few days after introducing a new role or new technology (movie camera, personal computer) before resuming note taking, to allow the host group to resume a more habitual course of behavior. Even so, because of the particular vulnerability of field research to unreliable and invalid observation, particular skeptical attention to checking the quality of data is needed: attention to such problems are ethno-centrism, going native, informant knowledgeability, etc.

An advantage of this process is the serendipitous generation of theory. The fieldworker's role of stranger or newcomer may aid him or her in discovering things too close to the host group because the host group is accustomed to their life patterns and do not question habitual actions. But another part of theorizing in field research comes from ordering the mass of data they have gathered through typologies and analytic induction methods. Because the field researcher lacks control over the variables he or she is observing, the investigator can rarely test causal hypotheses rigorously. However, the fieldworker can sensitize future research to possible and plausible relationships between variables.

Field researchers must always realize that they are also being observed by their host groups. Observation implies social control and reciprocity. One of the unique qualities of fieldwork is reciprocal influence of observer and observed. This quality affects the ethics, reliability, and validity of field research. Therefore, field researcher training needs special attention to these aspects of field study.

Finally, field research is so demanding an activity that logistical problems of distribution of research roles and resources is a constant problem. Field research normally requires attention to multiple role-identity scheduling, what information to collect, when to collect it, how to organize field operation, boundaries of field operations, and so on. But the attention paid is worth it when it produces structural relationships between data that have not previously been noticed.

CHAPTER

The Historic Imagination and Method

Historians generalize all the time . . . and sociologists are forever dealing with particularities. . . . Historians are likely to feel that a given outcome is explained if they can relate a credible story about a sequence of events that led up to it or the motive that impelled it, while sociologists are likely to feel that an outcome is explained if they can trace its connection to other institutions and forces in the surrounding environment.[1]

Key Terms

Accretion measure	Croce's problem
Archival record	Erosion measure
Boolean truth table	External criticism
Case-study approach	Life-history method
Cliometrics	Method of agreement
Comparative-historic method	Method of disagreement

[1]Erikson, K. T. (1970) Sociology and the historical perspective. *The American Sociologist, 5,* 331–338.

Oral history

Physical trace

Primary data source

Secondary data source

World systems theory

Study Guide Questions

1. What are key differences in the way sociologists and historians use historical data?

2. Why are many sociologists unhappy with the term "historical sociology"?

3. What are the differences in History-as-Ideas versus History-as-Facts? Why is History-as-Ideas more important?

4. Why is it a good idea to start by standing on the shoulders of the giants of historic studies, rather than starting out on one's own?

5. Explain the four fundamental types of comparative-historic method. What are the advantages and disadvantages of each method?

6. What is world systems theory; and what are its strengths and weaknesses as a sociological method?

7. What types of physical trace measures exist and what kinds of historic information do they provide?

8. What are the differences in public versus private archival records from the point of view of the historic information they provide? How can they distort historic studies?

9. How does the historic researcher judge authenticity, meaning, and credibility of historic sources?

10. Primary and secondary sources have different biases. Explain these differences and how they effect historic research.

11. What are the advantages and disadvantages of using documents-as-direct-indicators and documents-as-correlates methods?

12. How do historic scholars use psychological principles of memory to assign different weights of plausibility to evidence?

13. What types of special sampling problems confront the historic researcher?

14. How does the oral-history method differ from more traditional historic methods?

15. Why do oral-history methods appear to be exciting and glamorous to the outsider but are actually quite the contrary?

16. **Why is the presumption that the historic researcher must be either quantitative or qualitative a narrow-minded presumption?**

17. **How is the historic researcher caught in a dialectic between past and present? Writer and reader? How can the researcher attempt to break out of these dialectics?**

It is no accident that the word history originally enveloped either the chronology of actual or that of mythological events; the muse Clio in Greek mythology was, after all, the goddess of both history and epic poetry. For the Greeks and their admirers, the Romans, actual and mythical events were one and the same. It is somewhat ironical, therefore, that the history of history has been one of an increasingly relentless attempt to separate out fact from fiction. The process of separating out fact from fiction is one of challenging detective work, requiring both special skills and attitudes.

Many nonhistorians think of history as an onerous task of memorizing names, dates, and places; learning about dead people and obsolete ideas that have little relevance for their lives today. Other people have difficulty perceiving the relation of history to sociology. They think of sociology as the study of the "here and now" of society and of history as the "then and there" of society. However, the great master builders of sociology—Durkheim, Weber, and Marx—were all adept at the use of history in the aid of sociological interpretation. Indeed, if these masters were living in the United States today, they would surely be members of the Historical Comparative section of the American Sociological Association. After all, sociology sprang from their attempts to understand "the roots and unprecedented effects of capitalist commercialization and industrialization in Europe" (Skocpol 1984a:1).

Ever since the late nineteenth century, most historians have written in an ironic mode. History, more than any other discipline, can claim to rest on the theory of unintended consequences. Nevertheless, such theory undertheorizes because it is vague. To say that an outcome was unintended does not specify why or how that unintended outcome occurred, rather than some other outcome. Historic accounts also tend toward vagueness in specification of large-scale processes, and toward insufficient rigor in methodology that might inform the causal process underlying social change.

Conceptualization is not sufficient to build theories. To build theories, the scholar must study internal variation and dynamics, which calls for comparative cases and the search for patterns. The historic scholar assumes that change comes in patterns. As Barzun and Graff state (1970:168) ". . . where Cause is, there is Regularity." Ideas of what form those patterns take can come from the scholar's own hunches, but for the novice, a more practical procedure is to start with suggestions made in the relevant literature. Burke's (1980) monograph on the convergence of history and sociology nicely illustrates numerous social structural concepts: social role, kinship and family, stratification, bureaucracy, etc.

The next step is to translate those hunches and theories into hypotheses with falsifiable implications. In Tilly's work on collective action, for example, he proposes that structural differentiation dissolves traditional social bonds. If that is true, we would expect to observe a rise in indicators of collective violence during the periods of accelerated urbanization or industrialization.

Next, the scholar needs to gather the data necessary for testing such inferences. The fit between the data and specific implications of the theory indicates whether the hypothesis needs rejection or modification. When the scholar finds numerous hypotheses that point in a similar direction, the scholar realizes the potential for a general model. The historic scholar must give shape to events through interpretation of constellations of facts.

This process of shaping, comparing, and verifying, calls for somewhat different methods than those which researchers trained in traditional quantitative methods are inclined to use. The historic scholar usually does not find safety in the large samples known to quantitative researchers. Instead, the richness and complexity of a small number of cases, as in field research, is a hallmark of historic studies. As Tilly (1984:77) states, there is no safety in numbers—"large numbers give an illusory sense of security . . . The lesson reads: Stick with careful comparisons of small numbers until you have a very clear idea what you need from large numbers and how to make the comparisons valid." It makes no sense to generalize until the scholar gets the facts right.

The 1970s and 1980s have witnessed a resurgence of interest in the remarriage of sociology and history. Increasing numbers of sociologists have swelled the Historical Comparative section. Over the same two decades, a disproportionate number of awards have been presented to sociologists who make the historic method the central method of their work. These social scientists hold the belief, well expressed by Abrams (1982:2) that

> Sociological explanation is necessarily historical. Historical sociology is thus not some special kind of sociology; rather, it is the essence of the discipline. All varieties of sociology stress the so-called "two-sidedness" of the social world, presenting it as a world of which we are both the creators and the creatures, both makers and prisoners; a world which our actions construct and a world that powerfully constrains us. The distinctive quality of the social world for the sociologist is, accordingly, its *facticity*—the way in which society is experienced by individuals as a factlike system, external, given, coercive, even while individuals are busy making and remaking it through their own imagination, communication and action.

Stinchcombe (1968:108) succinctly adds that "explanations of the start of traditions may or may not be sociological. But the reasons that traditions get maintained are sociological."

Many social scientists who employ historic methods are not happy with the invention of the term "historical sociology" because the term implies the existence of a separate field of study—parallel, say, to the sociology of education. Social scientists who employ historic methods recognize that their methodology is *a set of eclectic techniques and styles of argument*, rather than a theoretically coherent field of study. For instance, Skocpol (1984b:363) notes, at one extreme, such sociologists as Kai Erikson who apply a general model to explain historic instances through a single case study. Erikson (1966) is well-known for his use of the Durkheimian model of communal definition and regulation of deviant behavior through reanalysis of historic data on the Puritan community in seventeenth-century New England. At the other extreme, is Barrington Moore's (1966) classic work on the social origins of dictatorship and democracy which used comparison of the French, Russian, and Chinese revolutions. Moore's work, although published in the same year as Erikson's, analyzed three cases with the goal of understanding causal regularities across time.

Still a third pattern of historic research is more modest in scope: It uses concepts to interpret history. Whereas the other two approaches search for hypotheses or models of broad scope, this third approach focuses more narrowly on the historic contexts in which particular individuals or groups find themselves. Skocpol gives Paul Starr's (1982) acclaimed work on the social transformation of American medicine as an exemplar of this approach. Starr's approach is closer to traditional historic research in that he uses historic context to locate the rise in status, authority, and professionalization of physicians in America. His work eschews interest in global models or broad generalization. Starr's approach is still different, however, from the historian who seeks to persuade through dense texture of detail. Instead, Starr employs the strategy of persuading in terms of social context and social patterns.

Conceptualizing Historic Analysis

Every thinking human who searches for sources is a practicing historian. Mommsen (1874) states this maxim as: "There is no other way to understand the events that take place before your eyes. Every business man who handles a complicated transaction, every lawyer who studies a case, is a searcher for sources and a practicing historian" (translated into the English by Barzun and Graff [1970:v]). However, because some individuals more intelligently practice history than others, we wish to learn from those who practice it best. History involves painstaking research in the name of getting the facts right; but it also involves using facts in the service of generalization to guard against knowing too much and using too little knowledge. Ultimately, then, we are less interested in History-as-Facts than in History-as-Ideas.

Historians have long considered Max Weber's contribution to the study of China an indisputable tour de force because it is a History-as-Ideas par excellence. Indeed, van der Sprenkel (1963) marvels at the paradox that Weber accomplished so much in Chinese historic scholarship, considering that he considers Weber's approach fundamentally flawed; that Weber was not a Sinologist (one who is expert on Chinese matters); and that he had a severely limited range of sources. Van der Sprenkel points out that Sinologists revere Weber's Chinese scholarship despite the fact that his translations were

(1963:348) "often in versions that were faulty and sometimes grossly misleading; and despite the fact that his writings on China abound in errors of detail, while some of his generalizations are as dogmatically wrongheaded as they are sweeping."

No one was more painfully aware of van der Sprenkel's charges than Weber himself who only reluctantly allowed this part of his work to be printed. Van der Sprenkel's (1963) exposition of why Max Weber's Chinese scholarship persists as a classic despite its flaws is central to understanding good historic sociology. Yes: Some of Weber's evidence is insecurely founded and some of his judgments are wrong. But he was a genius at conceptualizing. His work stands as a giant among the pygmies not because it was correct but because he raised all the important issues; he asked all the important questions. Weber generated innumerable ideas that have served, and will continue to serve, to initiate productive new lines of inquiry. No other means can grant a greater gift to scholarship.

Weber's work demonstrates the usefulness of proceeding from clearly defined questions or hypotheses. Historic research is so broadly based that there are an unlimited number of different questions to which historic sources can provide answers. Therefore, those who would do historic research need to continually ask themselves: What problem am I addressing? What knowledge do I seek? Of course, a comparative sociology must also begin with a universal quest concerning such questions as the problems of power and authority, or the tensions between tradition and modernity or between coercion and freedom.

Historic researchers end up asking the Big Questions. These questions (Tilly 1984:35) include: "Why do poor regions stay relatively poor, why did capitalism radiate from western Europe, under what conditions do ordinary people rebel, what causes persistent inequality among races and sexes, what conditions promote tyranny, when and why do wars occur. . ." Although the Big Questions are demanding, they lead to great payoffs. Nevertheless, "the *historicist* search for truth asserts that for all who seek truth the right understanding can be made compelling only for a time—even with the best available methods" (Bendix [1984:9]).

Those who use historic methods are sensitive to the continual need to reinterpret "the facts" within the current social context. Historic scholars know that the intellectual frames of earlier scholars need continual reassessment. For example, for most of us, modernity is an answer to past inconvenience and poverty. But for the historic scholar, modernity begs the question: Why do nations that have undergone modernization have so many characteristics that vary together (i.e., in the same direction), if only imperfectly? The Marxian tradition sought solutions to this question through noting changes in their common basic forms of production (infrastructure). During the 1960s, many scholars attempted to seek answers to the same questions through studying "modern" attitudes and motivations (superstructure). We must ask: Are infrastructure and superstructure connected? How? Which impels which? Now some researchers are focusing on "the revolution in communications," suggesting that modernity is tied to the linkage between (both) information *production* and *attitude* transformation. Each generation, indeed, must rewrite history in accord with its own evolving social context.

The world has become more modernized and is modernizing. But that doesn't solve the problem for the historic minded investigator. As Tilly (1984:15) points out, such processes raise more questions than they answer. Questions like:

1. What fundamental large-scale processes must we distinguish in order to understand how the world has changed and is changing?
2. How do those processes relate to each other?
3. What social structures experience those processes?
4. How can systematic, large-scale comparisons help us understand the structures and processes involved?
5. In approaching these questions, how much should we rely on the intellectual frames we have inherited from the nineteenth century?

Some individuals would skip the study of the master-historic scholar's Big Questions as an exercise in noncreativity. Clearly, however, these master questions enlarge upon—rather than obstruct—profitable avenues of research for the most individualistic and creative of scholars.

Tilly graphically illustrates the above questions in Figure 11-1. This diagram visualizes classic nineteenth-century arguments concerning the relationship between societal integration and differentiation. First, the ordinate (vertical axis) suggests that as integration increases, order increases. Second, the abscissa (horizontal axis) specifies that as differentiation increases, disorder increases. Third, the A-B relationship indicates that decreases in integration lead to disorder. Fourth, the C-D relationship implies that differentiation which outstrips integration will lead to disorder. Fifth, E-F conveys the idea that increases in both integration and differentiation may still produce disorder, unless there is greater integration than differentiation.

Although all five ideas seem reasonable, Tilly's work (1984:51–53) suggests two competing explanations based on his years of historic work. The first is that social integration—rather than lack of social integration—is a necessary condition for such types of *collective* action as collective violence and

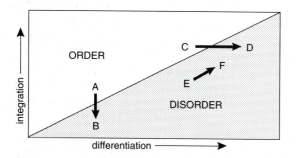

Figure 11-1. The historic relationship between societal integration and differentiation.

Source: Tilly (1984:50–51)

protests. The second is that collective action may result from the rational pursuit of shared interests rather than from disorder or irrationality. In effect, Tilly challenges us with reformulated *Big Ideas* to be skeptical of older interpretations of historic data. Such is the pattern of good historic research: It challenges us to sharpen our questions and search for data critical to chosing between alternative hypotheses.

The process of conceptualizing historic analysis may not even involve the collection of new data. Although Tilly's brand of intellectual inquiry challenges us to collect new data, some important types of historic analysis use reconceptualized models to shed light on already existing historic data. Erikson's (1966) study of deviancy in the Puritan colonial history is such a venture. Erikson borrowed from the *Big Questions* Durkheim posed concerning deviancy, to add understanding of deviancy in general rather than to shed new light on the Puritan period. Erikson's question is not a "scissors-and-paste" type that focuses narrowly on one historic period; his is a scientific history that asks questions, and then searches for ways to answer them.

As with any scientific question, the historic researcher must pose the question so that it is operational—that is, so that it is resolvable through the use of empirical means. Further, the historic question (Fischer 1970:38) "should be open-ended, but not wide open. It should dictate the kinds of facts which will serve to solve a problem, without dictating the solution itself." Those who would not heed Fisher's advice are likely to experience Alice-in-Wonderland's confusion (Carroll 1960:72):

> "Cheshire-Puss," she began, rather timidly. . . . "Would you tell me please, which way I ought to go from here?"
> "That depends a good deal on where you want to get to," said the Cat.
> "I don't much care where—" said Alice.
> "Then it doesn't matter which way you go," said the Cat.

My advice for the novice user of historic methods is similar to that for any method: Use the shoulders of the giants of the field to see further. In other words, go back to the classic thinkers who posed the Big Questions, rather than try to pose your own Big Questions. They'll lead down interesting enough pathways until you gain enough experience to follow your own path. The great thinkers cared enough where their questions led that they beat a well-worn pathway for other explorers to follow them and continue their search. Not incidentally, such a strategy would lead to continuity and cumulation of significant *knowledge*, rather than an amassing and accretion of mere, interesting *information*.

Comparative-Historic Approaches

The historic scholar is not interested in a mere collection of haphazard facts. Facts, concepts, and hypotheses must be coordinated, results compared, likenesses recognized, anomalies explained or rejected, and essential components discerned. In particular, the scholar typically uses one of two approaches that Mill (1950) labeled the "method of agreement" and the "method of disagreement." In the *method of agreement*, the scholar tries to establish that several cases sharing crucial similarities he or she wishes to explain also have in common the hypothesized causal factors. That is, the researcher choses cases with the same outcome, and identifies the similarities among those cases, despite other differences. The problem with this method is that those same cases may also vary in ways that allow for alternative hypotheses. In the *method of differences*, the scholar compares cases where the presumed independent and dependent variables are both present with cases where they are absent. That is, the researcher matches cases with different outcomes on every possible antecedent dimension, except the one thought to be causal. The different outcome is thus induced from the structure of the match. The logic is to compare overall similarities between positive and negative cases with the presumed only case in which there is one crucial difference. This method is more powerful than the method of agreement because it focuses upon true variation in the phenomenon to be explained. Better yet, the analyst might try to combine the two methods by comparing several positive cases along with a contrasting set of negative cases.

Ragin (1987) gives an even more sophisticated variation of the combination of these methods using the truth-table logic of Boolean algebra. Boolean algebra deals with logical concepts and true-false statements. The "or" in A or B implies an addition operation in which one plus one does not add up to two or zero, as you might think from the binary base, but adds instead to one. That is, positive plus positive is still positive. Another way to look at the function of a "not" is that it is an inversion: the inverse of zero equals one, and vice versa. Also, the "and" in A and B implies a multiplication operation: Think of anything times zero has to be zero, or that it takes two positives to produce a positive. From these basics follow a wealth of interesting theorems, which Ragin explores in his monograph.

For example, Ragin tests Rokkan's thesis that the outcomes of the Reformation, the Democratic Revolution, the Industrial Revolution, and the timing of state formation were the important historic factors shaping cleavage structures in Western European polities. He did this by creating truth tables with "1" for presence and "0" for absence of five variables for each of 16 Western European countries: (1) establishment of a state church allied with the Roman Catholic church; (2) a significant Roman Catholic population, and Roman Catholic participation in mass education; (3) state protection of landed interests; (4) whether a state formed early or late; and (5) whether there was a major split in the working-class movement following the Russian Revolution. Basically, this clever combination of the methods of agreement and differences through the use of Boolean algebra suggests (Ragin 1987:130) that the "the Russian Revolution divided working-class movements (1) in countries with national churches that had experienced nation building more recently (Norway, Finland, Iceland, Germany), and (2) in countries without national churches (that is, Catholic countries) that had denied the Roman Catholic church a major role in mass education (Spain, France, Italy)."

Another technique known as the comparative-historic method consists of four fundamentally different ways of seeing (Tilly 1984:81): individualizing, universalizing, encompassing, and variation finding. Scholars who *individualize* use the case-study approach. In the *case-study approach*, the scholar treats each case as incomparable and peculiar. For the social scientist, this practice is usually not very interesting; social scientists are trained to look for regularities, not peculiarities. Although the establishment of what is distinctive about a particular historic period is a worthy enterprise, if a modern social scientist uses the case-study method, it is probably due to lack of funds or data for larger-scale multiple comparisons. The case-study method (see the section on nonexperimental designs in Chapter 6) is the logically weakest method of knowing. The study of individual careers, communities, nations, and so on has become essentially passé: Recurrent patterns are the main product of the enterprise of historic scholarship.

The *universalizing method* emphasizes the search for common properties among all instances of a phenomenon. Tilly's work (1978) on collective action is an exemplar. Tilly has spent a lifetime collecting evidence that demonstrates the importance of organization in promoting collective action, regardless of the country or type of collective action. For Tilly, such master trends as industrialization and urbanization change the nature of collective action in highly regularized ways. His belief in universals propels him to collect massive sets of continuous data on contentious events. In the final analysis, he posits that collective actions are a direct outgrowth of power structures, opportunity/threat structures, mass mobilization, organization, interests, and repression.

The *encompassing approach* (Tilly (1984:83) "places different instances at various locations within the same system, on the way to explaining their characteristics as a function of their varying relationship to the system as a whole." Wallerstein's (1974) world-system approach is a classic example. He proposes one single world economic empire dominated by one strong center and many weak periphery states. Core states amass wealth and promote global accumulation through a system in which core countries promise weak, peripheral ones eventual wealth, as long as they stick by the rules of liberal capitalism and allow themselves to be exploited. This all-encompassing system is generated and sustained, in Wallerstein's theory, by rivalry and competition between core powers, inadequate demand, wage pressures, and the search for cheap raw materials. The central problem with Wallerstein's approach is inherent to any encompassing approach: *It is impossible to falsify because there is only one case.*

The final approach is the *variation-finding approach* which uses multiple cases in the search for all shared instances of degrees of patterned variation. The problem is that it is difficult to attain in historic research. The qualitative nature of most historic data, the few cases of large-scale processes and social structures, the general problems with attaining data of comparable accuracy and worth for numerous cases, and the lack of experimental rigor all impede the goal. Usually, the result is data on a meager number of variables for a large number of cases. Ragin (1987:53–68) compares several classic cases of the variable-oriented approach and concludes that it gravitates toward abstract, even vacuous, generalizations, and that it poorly handles complex causal arguments. This approach therefore may be better suited to nonhistoric methods.

Concept Formation and Measurement

Scholars evaluate concepts in terms of their advantages and disadvantages. How the historic-minded researcher formulates and measures concepts matters greatly because some definitions are more advantageous than others. Most of my generation learned history as a history of epochs, dynasties, and reigns. The presumptions of such a conception of history is that certain events are keys to interpreting social transformations; but such presumptions may prove at worst incorrect or at best inaccurate. Although it is true that some historians may think of themselves as "medievalists," "Tang dynasty experts," or whatever, many historic problems do not neatly fit into either a historic period or generational framework. The history of modern science would seem silly categorized under such concepts as Hitler's Third Reich, twentieth-century America, or the period of Eisenhower's administration. The history of science is much more international and temporal in scope than such narrowly defined periods.

Similarly, conceptualization into eras presumes the importance of Great Persons or Great Events to the interpretation of social change or stability. Although particular individuals or events may unduly influence history, such conceptualization downgrades the potential of alternative concepts. It is a value judgment to focus on the doctors, lawyers, and Indian chiefs of a society rather than the midwives, peasants, and peddlers. It is a value judgment to consider wars and revolutions more important than routine, everyday life. Increasingly, historic researchers have turned away from the traditional conceptions of history toward more mundane topics such as Puritan family-life patterns, medieval tilling practices, or everyday slave life.

How we conceptualize phenomena aids analysis, but also constrains it. Traditional historic analysis depends on such temporal and social units of analysis as reigns, dynasties, and empires, implying clear-cut demarcations of social change. Students of modernization may chose "national" units, although such a choice implies the independence of each nation state and a smooth evolutionary transition from less to more modern. *World-systems theory* (Hopkins 1982a; Chirot & Hall 1982) challenges those presumptions by conceptualizing an integral world capitalist system that has been expanding since the sixteenth century. World-systems theorists presume that the present economic well-being of advanced ("core") nations allows them the ability to exploit economically weaker periphery states. Hopkins (1982b:152) gives a succinct overview of this conceptualization in which he says, we say, "Here's a core-country and here's a periphery-country; now, how are they related? Why, through 'trade'." And with that, a set of activities and interactions we call "trade" ceases to be just one of many ways in which the interrelations linking the partial-production-operations formative of "cores" and those formative of "peripheries" are actualized, in given times and places. And instead "trade" (almost invariably as "market-trade") becomes *the* form of *the* relationship between *the* core and *the* periphery. We now have two kinds of "things" (world-regions), "cores" and "peripheries," related by (usually) international trade—hence, exchange rates—a world market, terms of trade, and the like. With that the figure-ground inversion is complete, and the basic conception ceases to frame analysis or to guide interpretation.

The world-systems concept itself has disadvantages. Although the world-systems concept has much intuitive appeal for explaining the persistence of the rich-poor nation gap, it fails to describe or explain "why the reaction to capitalist penetration was so different from place to place and continues to vary in important ways today" (Chirot & Hall 1982: 99). It does not explain why such precapitalist "world economies" as existed for over two thousand years in India before the British colonization or in North Africa before the Ottoman conquest did not develop along lines similar to that of Europe. In Chirot and Hall's terms (p. 99), the world-systems concept lumps ". . . all precapitalist societies into two simple types (which is) perilously close to the ahistoric eurocentrism that characterized modernization theory."

Throughout these examples of conceptualization runs a common axiom: One scholar's abstraction is another scholar's problem. Categories are useful to the extent that they allow the scholar a means of classifying more concrete events. However, classification is an abstract process that cannot satisfy all scholars. World-systems proponents treat "core" and "periphery" nations as viable abstraction, but have difficulty with such similar abstracting methods as Skocpol's (1984a) notion of revolutions. Hopkins (1982b:147), for instance, complains that revolutionary transformations of social relations seem very abstract to him yet he has no comparable difficulty with conceptualizing core-periphery trade relationships!

Clearly, we do need abstractions. The problem is matching of the abstract with the concrete. Competent historic scholars, as with other methodologists, formulate their concepts based on the theory derived from their questions. They then tie those concepts to associated ideas that lead them toward the selection of specific concrete indicators or indexes. To make their case stand up, the scholar finds it crucial to move back and forth between the concrete and the abstract.

There is no magical formula for showing how best to do this—particularly when dealing with such large-scale processes or organizations as the historic researcher is used to investigating. The boundaries between nations seem tangible enough to some peoples but not others: The boundary between the United States and Canada appears to have sharp definition that is well guarded at major entry points, but North American Indians do not consider themselves members of either nation, and many carry special Indian-tribe issued passports as proof. Similarly, the boundaries between North African nations are real enough to cause war between those who would think otherwise, yet to nomads of border regions they are fictions that are dangerous to the nomad's livelihood.

In spite of the inherent fuzziness of many concepts, all social description involves three fundamental tasks (Tilly 1984:29). First, the researcher must construct analytic classifications of social structures; revolutions, war, core-nations, or whatever. Second, the researcher has to fashion empirically distin-guishable cases for each category. Third, the investigator must demonstrate observable sequences of social events or individual behavior that fit those clas-sifications. Of course, the wise investigator does all of this with much trepida-tion because (Tilly 1984: 42) "history . . . resists the forcing of complex events into simple, abstract categories."

Whether or not a concept survives will depend on whether its advantages outweigh its disadvantages. Strict Marxian analysts define capitalism in terms of the relations of production, but world-systems theorists emphasize the con-ditions of trade and exchange in capitalist nations. Each conception commits each side to observing different phenomena. The world-systems theorist be-comes committed to search for an integrated, holistic world economy; the Marxian to looking at technology, size of firm, concentration of capital, worker autonomy, and other measures of the forms of production.

Types of Evidence

The researcher must turn concepts and abstractions into evidence at some point. The historic scholar—because the investigator did not live at the time he or she is researching—must depend on evidence the scholar did not directly pro-duce. This evidence often is some form of a document, but there is a variety of other primary and secondary sources of data open to relatively unobtrusive and systematic observation that may be creatively utilized. On the one hand, there are primary data sources known generically as physical traces and signs; on the other hand are secondary sources that can be noted as archival records.

Physical Trace Measures

Physical traces and signs fall into two classes: *erosion measures*, or signs of selective wearing of some material, and *accretion measures*, or signs of mate-rial deposit. Because these types of measures have been largely borrowed from archeology, some scholars refer to them as part of the subfield of historic archeology. Erosion measurements most often involve measurement of the se-lectivity of wear and tear on various objects by some population. As examples, researchers have considered the "souvenir habit" theft patterns in large urban hotels as one index of hotel residents' feelings of estrangement; and use-patterns have been studied through wear on library book page corners and wear on museum tiles.

Accretion measures, by contrast to erosion measures, gauge social deposits or accumulations: frequency of dirt smudges, finger markings, and page underlinings indicate differential usage of books; the frequency and kind of calendars or paintings hung in businesses or residences, and whether they are hung in public or private areas, indicate much about norms and values; and the types and amounts of trash left by various populations are both indicators of affluence and values.

The entire field of archaeology is a science of inference from garbage and other residues. Broken pots, bones, and other fragmentary rubble accumulated over hundreds or thousands of years at a single site may give insight into the daily life of ancient peoples and differences between social classes. Similarly, changes in type and placement of graffiti over time indicates much about territoriality, areas of conflict, and scatologic (obscene) interests of differing epochs. (Some nonhistoric-minded researchers have even used these types of data in studies of current societies.)

Webb, Campbell, Schwartz, and Sechrest (1966:46) point out that "physical-evidence data are best suited for measures of incidence, frequency, attendance, and the like." Physical trace measures rarely provide critical tests of theory. Normally, the historic scholar uses a series of them to build up a more complete picture than other forms of evidence alone could provide. The main virtue of erosion and accretion data is their relative inconspicuousness or unobtrusiveness, compared to archival records which are materials that authors consciously presume might be used by future investigators. Therefore, physical traces are materials with which the producers are less likely to have tampered because they do not purport to record information about things that happened.

Archival Record Analysis

Historic scholars have used archival records of various sorts more often in their research than physical trace measures. Archival records are testimonial documents because they purport to record information about things that happened unlike pieces of pottery, poems, and codes of law. We may distinguish between two generic types of archival records: public and private. *Public* archival records are normally prepared for examination by some audience and *private* archival records are generally not prepared for an audience.

Public archival records

There are four types of public records: actuarial records, political and judicial records, other governmental documents, and mass-media productions.

Actuarial records include formal records kept on birth, marriage, death, and disease. Birth and marriage records may be matched to estimate the incidence of premarital sex relations across time. Incidence and spread of sexually transmitted diseases may give an indication of nonmarital sexual activity. Many organizations other than governments produce actuarial records. Many professional organizations keep member directories with potential usefulness such as that found in *American Men of Science* and *Who's Who in America*.

Political and judicial records have also been much used by historic scholars. Critical role-call votes, aggregate voting records in relation to prointegrationist characteristics, and court decisions are among the vast storage of political and judicial records that have been and can be further utilized by investigators of social change. Governmental records in some countries are remarkably complete and accurate going back centuries. For example, the Swedish and Japanese have kept extremely well-documented actuarial, political, and judicial records for hundreds of years.

Other sources of public records are more unorthodox yet informative. Water treatment plant records on amount of water supplied and types of treatment may inform changes in basic living patterns and the spread of diseases. Historically minded criminologists have learned much about changes in the definitions of crime by looking at police logs, studying the history of strike and strike-breaking activities, and studying old prison records. Presumably, private security guard agency records and store shoplifting records could be put to similar creative use.

The mass media also presents an enormous public archive to which scholars often turn. Changing styles of obituaries, letters-to-the-editor columns, and cartoons in newspapers indicate much about changes in everyday concerns of particular peoples. Television networks have huge repositories of old films, news, and videotapes that scholars have rummaged for various types of evidence of social change.

Dibble (1963) terms public archival records "social bookkeeping" documents because they are the products of groups and organizations and not of individuals. Dibble pointed out (p. 206) that we have an unwarranted bias in believing that all documents are produced by individuals as in the classic examples of ". . . the secluded monk, the diarist alone in his room at the end of the day, and the solitary traveler. . ." But such public archival records as transcripts of parliamentary debate, calendars of saints, bank books, tax returns, court records, crime statistics, censuses, and lists of college graduates are kept for, of, and by specific groups of people. Dibble rightly contends that only a very small fraction of any group of documents of interest to the historic scholar were produced in individualized circumstances.

Because public archival documents are produced by social systems, it behooves their analyst to consider the social system that produced them. Different social systems use quite different rules for freedom to alter a document. "Stricken from the record" rules can work for or against accuracy. Members of the U. S. Congress are free to amend their remarks in the Congressional Record before it goes to press, which works against accuracy. At the other extreme, a professor who requests that the editor of her book add items missing from her bibliography may either add to accuracy or to embellishment, depending on her request.

Furthermore, the social system that produced the record required communication to carry through the mandate. At one extreme are court reporters in the United States who are physically present during the stenography of court proceedings, and who have no power to change or alter the stenographic output. At the other are bureaucracies where a memo written by a low-level civil servant may pass through any number of higher-level offices, be freely altered without documentation, and finally signed by a bureaucratic functionary who does not even read the document.

The consideration of public documents must involve a working knowledge of the mechanics of the particular social system that created or underwrote any particular document. Did the system allow the freedom to embellish; the freedom to build in independent checks; secrecy; materials to be stricken and, if so, for what purposes; alternative means of recording events? What individuals might be served by the public archival document? Who might a document threaten or injure? Who carried it out? Who, if anyone, checked on the creators of the public document? What were the motivations underlying the creation of the document? How attentive were the record keepers to the wishes of those who legislated its creation? These questions are only a few of those important to a critical understanding of the existence of any public record.

Social bookkeeping documents, then, have special problems of distortion, as does any set of documents. Rather than discard a document that is suspect, the historic scholar may turn those problems to advantage. The process of distortion and alteration is an indicator, after all, of how the social system works: how malleable it is, whom it protects, or how efficiently it carries out its mandate. Marx's claim that every state is a *class* state cautions us to consider how social systems shape public archival data. For example, the definitions, conceptualizations, and *interests* of ruling groups produce unemployment rates.

Private archival analysis

While a central problem associated with public records is the normally large mass of such data that exist, the central concern with analysis of private records is their episodic nature and, thus, limited usage for analysis of lengthy time periods. We may distinguish between three classes of private archives: sales records, institutional records, and personal documents. Webb et al. (1966:90–91) report the use of air-flight insurance sale data to infer changing patterns of anxiety over air travel. Coleman, Katz, and Menzel's (1957) classic study of the diffusion of drug prescription innovations among physicians depended on pharmacy records. Industrial and institutional records may shed light on absenteeism and job turnover in relationship to age, seniority, and worker's home-factory distance. Union grievance records may inform studies of racial, gender, and ethnic conflict.

Personal documents include autobiographies, diaries, letters, and life histories. *Autobiographies* must be treated with particular caution, as Denzin (1970:227) warns.

the author of the autobiography may not always be fully aware of what has occurred in his life. Furthermore, he may dress up, beautify, or hide what he is aware of. It is the job of the (scholar) to probe and uncover such topics. . . . In the autobiography the (scholar) must keep the record of experiences separate from the interpretation given them.

The *diary* is less susceptible to fallacious reinterpretation of past behavior by its author. The diary is a set of personal outpourings written discontinuously. Scholars have used diaries for a variety of social scientific purposes, including the study of suicide and acculturation among immigrants to a country. *Memoirs* are more impersonal than intimate journals and normally are written in a relatively short period of time as are autobiographies. While the memoir's impersonality reduces its psychologic importance, its data may be of great interest as a history of organizational development. *Logs* are accounts of meetings, events, visits, trips, and happenings. The log may provide a systematic time-budget record. It may also give an excellent picture of patterns of interaction in social settings. *Letters* were the primary source of information in Thomas and Znaniecki's (1927) classic study of Polish immigration to America. During World War II, the United States government employed social scientists to research letters and diaries captured from German soldiers to assess the impact of propaganda on German troops.

The Evidential Status of Documents

Milligan (1979:177) says that "every historian knows the special excitement that is derived from perusing the documents, the primary sources that are the basic, if incomplete and imperfect, evidence from which (the historic scholar) seeks to recreate the past." However, the sophisticated analyst tempers this excitement with a respect for the need to ask questions that historians subsume under the heading of *external criticism*: Is the document authentic? The tedium of the painstaking care needed in scrutinizing documents tempers the initial excitement of reading primary sources with boredom.

In other types of social research, the researcher is normally painfully aware of the limitations of the data he or she has collected because the researcher was directly involved in their collection. The survey analyst, for example, is usually well aware of the self-inflicted warts and blemishes of question wording. The problems of historic scholars are the mirror image of this: They have a duty to make themselves aware of the warts and blemishes of the producers of documents. This is their duty, in spite of their natural reluctance to question the veracity of a document's contents, let alone its authenticity. But the whims of human nature sometimes call for the historic researcher to reach conclusions at odds with the testimony presented in particular documents. One of the first duties of the historic researcher is not to be duped; we all know that individuals may forge or falsify wills and other legal documents, attribute literary works to authors who did not write them, and naively take jokes and satires at face value. A good example of doctoring history is the attempt by the National Aeronautical and Space Administration to "improve" Neil Armstrong's famous statement "That's one small step for man, one giant leap for mankind" when he stepped on the moon's surface. In spite of the fact that the quote is clearly audible on tape recordings and Armstrong has confirmed that he did not use the word "a," NASA has changed the official version to read "one small step for *a* man" which significantly changes the meaning of what he said.

As with other disciplines, history has had its share of forgeries. The faked papers of Hitler come to mind as ones of which the general public is largely aware. The publishers of the West German magazine *Stern* embarrassed themselves in the early 1980s when they paid a huge sum of money for exclusive rights to publish a "newly discovered" diary of Hitler, only to find out that they had become part of a major hoax. Milligan (1979:179) asserts that the cunning needed to uncover such hoaxes can be quickly gained through practice. For example, Milligan states that "as the number of documents of the same nature grows, so does the probability that each of them is authentic" because it is more difficult to believe that a forger has made a whole file of bad documents rather than just one. (The forger of the Hitler diaries was clever enough to forge a huge output of documents.)

Furthermore, the investigator searches for corroborative evidence that lends authenticity to the document—such things as diction, style, versification, personal language, manner or expression, and writing habits of the ascribed author that is consistent with other already verified documents. For example, the scholar studies types of paper and styles of handwriting typical of a particular individual or period, or searches for characteristic errors. Furthermore, the historic scholar will want independent verification of the document; for instance, if the document includes a date or place, the scholar must verify that the author was actually in that place at that particular time.

Platt (1981:34) produced a worthwhile list of checks for inauthenticity in documents:

1. the document as it stands does not appear to make sense, or has obvious errors in it
2. different versions of the same document are current
3. it contains internal inconsistencies of literary style, content, typeface or handwriting
4. the document is known to have been transmitted via many copyists
5. it is known to have been transmitted via someone with an intellectual or material interest in the version given passing as the correct one
6. the version available is derived from a secondary source suspected on other grounds as being unreliable
7. it contains anachronisms
8. it fits too neatly into a standard formula or literary form.

Once satisfied with the document's authenticity, there comes the second part of the investigator's external critique in which the researcher asks: What is the real meaning or intent of the document? We cannot always take authors literally; they may employ a host of such subtle meanings as jest, sarcasm, or allegory. As Milligan (1979:182) asks: "Was the person given to ambiguity or obliquity, to jokes, irony, or fables to make a point?" Therefore, the investigator attempts to disentangle real from apparent meaning.

The third part of the external critique is determination of the document's credibility. Even if a document is authentically attributable to a specific person, that document may not be credible. The investigator will want to know how reliable a witness the author was. Did the author actually observe the phenomena or base the document on hearsay evidence? Obviously, actual observation is more credible than hearsay evidence. Similarly, documents written soon after an observation are more credible than those written later. Because no individual enjoys total recall, Milligan (1979:182) warns the historic document critic to regard every recollection as suspect; he also alerts the researcher to consider for whom the document was intended: It may have been discredibly written "to please hearers and readers, advance one's own interest" or more credibly written as "a private remark . . . the fewer the intended audience, the more credible."

Additionally, the researcher asks: Did the witness have the social or physical ability to observe accurately? Numerous factors might destroy the credibility of a physically able-bodied witness: During warfare, it may have been impossible for the most observant of combatants to hear or to differentiate particular noises or lights; during working hours, the supervisor may have been stationed so she could not actually see a machine break down. The investigator may also have good reason to suspect that self-interests of the witness worked against credible accounts.

Research into the appalling internment of Japanese-Americans on the West Coast during World War II indicates that the predicament in which the authorities placed the internees could not have led to credible responses among the internees to the following two crucial questions of the War Relocation Authority Application for Leave Clearance (Thomas & Nishimoto (1946:56–58):

Question 27: Are you willing to serve in the armed forces of the United States on combat duty, wherever ordered?

Question 28: Will you swear unqualified allegiance to the United States of America and faithfully defend the United States from any or all attack by foreign or domestic forces, and forswear any form of allegiance or obedience to the Japanese emperor, or any other foreign government, power or organization?

To the American patriot, these questions may seem harmlessly fair, but the Japanese immigrants—who already had been denied American citizenship for over forty years—feared that if they renounced their allegiance to the Emperor, they would be without a country; and if they left the relocation centers, they would find themselves without resources in a world they had every reason to believe would regard them with hostility. After all, the war authorities had forced them to leave all but the clothes they could carry with them. So the Japanese immigrants pleaded with their American-born (and American citizenship-vested) sons and daughters to answer these questions in the negative. The result was that nearly half of the second-generation males and their immigrant parents answered negatively. Still today, the aftershock of these "unpatriotic" no-no and yes-no sets of responses is so great that sophisticated researchers know better than to trust respondents to say how they answered these questions, or to ask them if they know any Japanese-Americans who returned to Japan after the war. The social stigma of the no-win situation into which these people, through no fault of their own, had been placed during the war still hangs over many of them and colors what they feel is safe to say in public.

Milligan (p. 182) lists three steps in historic testimony at which credibility may be lost: observation, recollection, and recording. Because human recording is fallible at any of these three steps, the researcher does not wish to accept the testimony of single witnesses. The historic investigator will search for corroboration from other documents or other witnesses. Similar to the problems of narrators in field research (see Chapter 10), the historian must recognize that different witnesses have special vantage points that color their credibility. No one is capable of observing, recollecting, or recording everything. The seasoned historic researcher has learned to place each witness within the *context* of his or her account; each witness has special self-interests, social stresses, or physical ailments which the researcher must learn to recognized and take into account.

Platt (1981:41) cites Naroll's ranking of types of secondary sources by the degree of proximity to the original in the following order: datum report, participant report, observer's report, derivative report, scholar's report (citing primary sources), and reader's report (not citing specific passages from primary sources.) The further from the original primary source, the less trust and confidence the cautious investigator places in a particular document. But even primary sources have their own problems, which increase to the extent that there are greater time lapses between an event and a report, the more professional stake the author has in the report, and the less agreement between authors with opposing viewpoints. Also, authors may publish to seek practical advantage, they may be compelled to violate the truth, their vanity may color their remarks, they may wish to please their public, or they may be led by illusion or prejudice to misreport events. Also, they may plagiarize or popularize the works of others.

Users of historic documents may still be interested in using documents with questionable veracity. After all, if the scholar is interested in forgery, lying, or the social pressures to conform, it is important to verify independently the veracity of the testimony. Therefore, the clever researcher may turn forged or questionable documents to advantage, by focusing on the specific adaptations individuals make to their social situations.

Similarly, what particular authors do not record may be as important as what they do record. The investigator must be on the lookout for selective silences as well as selective confessions. As Ekman (1985) has shown, when given a choice, deceivers would prefer to conceal than to falsify information. By focusing on particular events, the author may attempt to mislead the reader through an incorrect inference dodge. Less cynically, etiquette, social convention, or custom may keep an author from accurate reporting.

Because any document is open to a variety of biases, historic scholars feel a compunction to marshall numerous sources of primary and secondary evidence as a means of correcting for the particular biases of any one documentary source. The competent scholar realizes the need to become an expert on numerous concerns that are seemingly peripheral to any particular document. The scholar will want to know the particular institutional constraints that bracket the document, the organizational routines that produced the document, the time-lapse between observation and writing, and whether the document was confidential or public. These days, studies of the Puritan settlers rarely focuses on Puritan-era documents themselves. Rather, scholars want to know the context of the documents: What did the colonists eat and wear, the tools they used, how their bartering system worked, the number of offspring they produced, and so on. The social atmosphere and dynamics of early American life pervades the documents that were left behind.

Dibble (1963:213) states that some researchers use the *documents-as-direct-indicators method* of historic research in which "all or part of the document itself, as opposed to external events, which are recorded by or correlated with the document, is the datum under investigation." For the purpose of answering limited *factual* questions such a procedure poses no problem. During the late 1970s, Caldwell (1983) stumbled onto the "confessions" of 51 first-generation American Puritans from the First Church of Cambridge, Massachusetts, which pastor Thomas Shepard had recorded in his notebook between 1637 and 1641. As a fact, either those documents had the ring of truth or not: Either Shepard had recorded true confessions of his parishioners or not.

But Caldwell did not stop with the documents-as-direct-indicators approach because to do so would be to reify the document; she did not wish to confuse the documents-as-indicators with use of facts-or-events-as-indicators. Because it is much more interesting to classify a number of relatively less general items under some general heading, Caldwell started to compare these newly discovered confessions with ones in the Royal Library of London. She noticed that these early British conversion testimonies did not *sound* American.

Caldwell's comparison indicated a difference both in tone and structure: The American voice sounded more anxious, and expectant. She inferred this was due to the voyage across the ocean—a sort of biblical Red Sea deliverance experience in which the Americans found that the promised land does not lie just on the other side of the sea. She inferred that the Puritan immigrants found themselves alone in the wilderness, with the Bible as their only refuge. While the English Puritans used biblical examples and similes in their confessions, the Americans spoke as though they were living inside the Bible. The Massachusetts Puritans' difficult experiences come through in their confessions with a sense of unfinished business and struggle. Their speeches were tougher, more muscular. To stick to a purely document-as-indicators approach would have proven barren compared to Caldwell's.

A more important form of the marshalling of evidence is the *documents-as-correlates method* (Dibble 1963) in which the scholar attempts to test the fit of a document with other known documents and knowledge of the evidence in question. A classic example is the clever detective work that Prof. John Morrison, a classical scholar and a retired president of Wolfson College at the University of Cambridge, did on designing and building the first Greek trireme (a ship equipped with 170 Athenian oarsmen) in 1,500 years. Morrison's quest began with two thorny problems (Green 1988:75): In a boat roughly 118 feet long and 18 feet wide, where could all 170 oarsmen possibly have sat, and how did the Greeks keep so many oars in perfect harmony?

Morrison's detective work was all the more astounding when one considers the limitations of his sources: There were no plans and no preserved ship timbers; only four visual representations of triremes remain from classical times. Much of the reconstruction of the trireme rests on a pottery fragment the size of a minnow's length, another from a fifth-century B.C. limestone relief from the Athenian acropolis, and two even cruder bas reliefs. But these four fragmentary representations tally with each other, and it is possible from the size of the oarsmen in each representation to guess the approximate size and shape of a trireme. Furthermore, the triremes were sheltered from the blazing Mediterranean sun in ship sheds. From archaeologic excavations of the only trireme shed yet discovered, Morrison corroborated his guess concerning the length and width of these ships.

A brief description in Plato's *Republic* and accounts from the Greek historians Herodotus and Thucydides give the number of officers, deckhands, petty officers, and oarsmen. Xenophon adds another clue from his account of a 140-mile voyage under oars from Byzantium to Heraclea along the Black Sea's southern coast that took a "long day." Assuming a 16-hour day, Morrison deduced that a trireme's cruising was at least seven or eight knots. The Greek government underwrote Morrison's cleverly deduced project and in the summer of 1987, he tested the first trireme in 1,500 years using British amateur rowers. With a modicum of work, Morrison's rowers learned how the Greek must have synchronized all 170 rowers and confirmed that a trireme is capable of speeds of over 8 knots. Morrison's work panned out because of the clear correlation of fragments of data—a process known to all competent historic scholars.

As these examples indicate, historic scholars do not establish facts from documents simply by examining testimony to events which is recorded by witnesses who have seen or heard about these events. They find it necessary to use a wide variety of testimonial and documentary sources, and then fit these pieces together into a meaningful whole. They must judge the weight of each piece of data to reach an overall conclusion. Some of this judgment comes from the use of syllogism of the type:

The distance from Byzantium to Heraclea is about 140 miles.
Xenophone says it took a "long day."

In the summer, a "long day" would be, at most, 16 hours.

Therefore, a trireme must be capable of roughly 8 knots at cruising speed.

The next step—confirmed with Morrison's trireme—was to test how fast a trireme can actually go. Typically, historic researchers do not have the luxury afforded Morrison to test their syllogisms with tangible data. Instead, historic scholars know that the syllogisms they make are not all equally solid; therefore, they combine the differently weighted conclusions of each syllogism to reach an overall conclusion.

Historic scholars wish always to seek such independent sources of evidence because they recognize that no witness or document provides the perfect evidence. This means that the historic scholar uses rules for evaluating any type of evidence. Two such laws are those of probability and of memory.

Laws of probability suggest that some authors are or are not plausible candidates of particular testimonials or documents. Because individuals use sentence styles, words, phrases, and so on that are peculiar to themselves, some scholars test for word or phrase frequency. Statisticians settled the several-hundred-year-old debate over who wrote *The Federalist Papers*, by comparing the known works of James Madison and Alexander Hamilton (Kolata 1986:335) by means of a statistical analysis of the vocabularies of each man, compared to the statistical profile of these papers. The evidence clearly supported Madison, and not Hamilton, as their author.

Scholars also depend on laws of memory. They assign more weight to testimonials and documents recorded shortly after an event occurred; that describe specific details rather than give general conditions; that are addressed to audiences who share the witness' beliefs rather than to those who do not share the testifier's ideology; that appear disinterested rather than politically charged; that are spoken in one's own language rather than a less natural one; that are unprompted testimony; and that were recorded before many versions of the event spread. The reasons for these preferences follow. First, recordings shortly after the occurrence of an event are likely to be fresher in the witness' mind. Second, specific details are more easily verified with independent pieces of information. Third, addresses to like-minded ideologues are less likely to be colored by attempts to hide or distort information than those made to unsympathetic groups. Fourth, disinterested witnesses are less likely than interested ones to give unbiased accounts; the "stranger," as Simmel noted long ago, has a privileged position from which to view events. Fifth, accounts in a primary language are probably more natural or less constrained in expression. Sixth, unprompted testimony is likely to be more spontaneous and freely given. Seventh, after the recording of many versions of an event, the possibilities of coloring of memory with rumor becomes much greater.

Particularly when chosing between conflicting accounts of an event, the historic scholar attempts to assign weights according to the above principles. The scholar is not only obligated to reference the source of each fact; he or she must also estimate the value of each source. From the prospective of the consumer of historic research, there is a tension between the appeal of authority of the scholar versus the authority of the display of data. The authority of the historic scholar is no better than the method of historic research.

The Availability of Documents and Sampling Problems

Webb, Campbell, Schwartz, and Sechrest (1966:54) point to what they termed "Croce's Problem"—that is, "either one is uncertain of the data when only a limited body exists, or uncertain of the sample when so much exists that selection is necessary." The second part of Croce's Problem is solvable through modern probability sampling methods discussed in Chapter 5. The first problem presents the major obstacle because the missing data might well alter the evidence. Physical evidence data often survive and are deposited selectively. Government officials routinely edit or secretly classify information of great import to a balanced picture of their work. Tombstones made of concrete or marble survive longer than wooden ones, producing oversampling of the remains of wealthier individuals. Bookkeeping methods may subtly change, generating pseudochange of unemployment definitions. Documents may become lost or destroyed. Thus, the historic scholar must become adept at gleaning knowledge in selective survival and depositing of the evidence. Small subsamples of documents lead to the problem of overinterpretation, in which the scholar carries generalization from one or a few known documents too far.

The scholar blessed with an abundance of documents has a quite different problem: Where to start sampling? Some historians suggest that the scholar should start with documents that have no apparent theoretical interest. The reason is to prevent preconceived hypotheses from biasing one's selection. But this solution leaves us with little guidance, particularly when no catalogue exists from which to sample.

I believe Tilly (1984:28–29) gives much better advice; he suggests starting by considering "basic social units: category, network, and catnet. *Categories* distinguish populations of two or more people by some characteristic they share: all Japanese-Americans, all farmers with tractors, or all politicians. A *network* denotes a population connected by the same social tie. The ties may be direct as with mother-father, supervisor-supervisee, or two lovers; they may also be indirect as in a group of Japanese and Americans connected by a translator." It may be more abstract yet (Tilly 1984:29) as in "web of debts among people who have borrowed money from one another."

Tilly coined the term *catnet* from the combination of category and network to represent those cases in which both common characteristics and network links exist. Examples would include extended families, churches, armies, and political parties but *not* more amorphous social phenomena such as civilizations, cultures, or societies. The point of these distinctions is they give the scholar some types of social frameworks from which to start sampling. Furthermore, the scholar will want to sample from adequate time frames. Because the historic researcher typically is interested in social change, it makes sense to represent a variety of time periods adequately.

Finally comes the problem of when to stop sampling. The best advice is to stop when the scholar has thoroughly sampled all potential types of sources without bringing anything new to light. The theory of sampling is well developed with known populations. By knowing how the scholar collected the observations, or by knowing the number of observations, we can often say quite precisely what kinds of observations are consistent with the theory of sampling and the theory of large numbers. However, the historic scholar may not have good information on the population of documents available. Therefore, the scholar is often reduced to inferences about quality control. If the researcher has sampled a wide variety of documents, times, places, categories, networks, or catnets without uncovering startling new evidence, he or she gains confidence that further searches would be unproductive.

Although a large number of cases may aid confidence in a causal relationship, paradoxically, only a single deviant case casts doubt on causal hypotheses. Although much historic scholarship is based on single-case analysis, scientific analysis eventually moves toward a variable-oriented strategy, in which competing theories play a part in determining how much and what to sample.

Producing History: The Oral History

Oral history is actually a misnomer for the process of oral data collection methods. Most oral historians trace the roots of the oral history back to the 1940s, when Louis Starr and Allan Nevins started organizing less traditional means of historic-data collection at Columbia University. It actually is traceable further back to the "life-history method" of two sociologists, Thomas and Znaniecki (1927). Thomas and Znaniecki taught their graduate students at the University of Chicago, as early as the 1920s, to combine data gleaned from autobiographies, letters, and diaries where available, and to supplement these sources with unstructured interviews and structured questionnaires for a more systematic coverage of gaps in the life history. Their guidelines for the life history included data on the subject and his or her family, including (Denzin 1970:235)

> . . . experiences confronted in childhood, preadolescence, adolescence, and
> adult life; the nature and meaning of the inner (subjective) life, including such
> topics as emotional stabilities, sense of the self, power devices, recreational and
> avocational activities, basic satisfactions, and work as value. This proposal
> completely covers the life cycle. It has the advantage of being so complete that
> it could be used with a group, or members of an organization. It also contains
> recommendations concerning data on demographic and sociopersonal aspects.

More traditionally oriented scholars often disdain the oral-history tradition; Barzun and Graff (1970:146) state that "(W)hat a person did or thought thirty years ago is past and dead, even if that person is technically alive. The living relic is his own ancestor (who) . . . tidies up embarrassing disorders of his dead past, reverently conceals his own skeleton in a hidden closet." Some such traditionalists decry that oral histories lead to "a few veins of gold and a vast mass of trash" (Tuchman 1984:76). However, this charge is not particular to oral histories; all research involves the tedium of sifting for the few gold nuggets of information. Those who would confuse the tape recorder with the vacuum cleaner are ill-suited for understanding the potential of the oral history or any data-gathering device.

Scholars who use the oral-history method realize that it is no panacea: Memory is elusive, and many factors color the articulation of memory. To a large extent, oral history is not simply the reconstruction of the past but is a new construction of reality. However, to disregard oral histories on these grounds alone is not justified because the scholar should regard all historic documents as constructions of reality rather than actuality. The point is not to confuse history making with history gathering. After all, scholars know that other documents are routinely doctored, altered, falsified, or destroyed. The doctoring may be ever so subtle: Some important individuals prefer to telephone others rather than write letters because they believe it is a "safer" means of keeping secrets. Ironically, if it wasn't for former President Nixon's desire to tape-record all incoming calls to the White House, we would have little knowledge of the Watergate Scandal. And, of course, he tried in vain to erase those tapes.

Before the 1960s, scholars employed the oral history primarily in the interviewing of elites. In the years before the invention of the tape recorder some historians lamented that important people like Grover Cleveland had died without a good estate of historic documents. (His widow tried to destroy all records of his past affairs.) These scholars envisioned biographies of important personages aided by oral interviews. Since the 1960s, scholars have used the oral history chiefly as a means of empowering the nonliterate and historically disenfranchised: Appalachian mountain peoples, poverty-stricken blacks, unwed mothers, nonunionized Mexican farm laborers, or Asian "boat peoples." The oral history, then, has come to represent groups of people who have paltry written records. Oral historians pride themselves on doing "grass roots history," or the history of the nonelite, or the history of ordinary people leading ordinary lives. The result has been an interdisciplinary approach useful not only to the historian but also to the sociologists, the folklorist, the gerontologist, and the anthropologist.

The result has led to a virtual explosion of articles and books on oral history, and a shift in focus toward a more democratic history; a history viewed with evidence from the underside. Furthermore, Nevins (cited in Starr 1984:5) recognized, as early as 1950, that the confidential letters, memos, and other types of written records of old were being replaced by the telephone, the airlines, and other means of contacting other persons. Further, the published oral history has aided the documentation of modern events that might otherwise be lost to future generations. Finally, taped or videotaped oral histories can give the user access to nuances of voice that otherwise would have to be inferred from a transcript.

Oral-data collection methods are based on the frailties of recall, the distortions of personal ego, self-delusion, shyness, and unresolved contradictions. They thus lack the immediacy of memory that scholars prefer in their data. But even more immediately collected data are open to question. Therefore, oral collection methods are like other methods, in their need for tests of internal consistency and external corroboration. For example, in a series of oral histories, individuals consistently denied that they received any aid from local church groups when they first arrived in St. Louis. However, there is considerable evidence from the records of the St. Louis chapter of the International Institute that certain churches actively provided aid, if only in the form of lending their building to the newcomers for religious services and social events. Where such inconsistencies emerge, oral historians suggest that the interviewer actively encourage the narrator to resolve the contradictions. However, there is a fine line between pursuing contradictions to their conclusion, and putting words in the mouth of the narrator.

On the other hand, long-term memory is not always as fallible as some scholars posit. Some cultures have remarkable oral-history traditions that appear to be highly accurate to ethnographers. Some American Indian groups carefully groom "keepers of the talking stick"—official oral historians who must prove to the entire village council that they can repeat verbatim the entire history of the tribe without variance from tradition. They spend years in training to improve their memory capacities so that they do not vary their stories. Such oral-history traditions are strongest in nonliterate cultures. Alex Haley traced his genealogic roots back several hundred years by tapping into the memories of relatives who passed down their oral history systematically through the generations. Of course, in any case it behooves the researcher to search for independent verification as he or she must even with written accounts.

Sometimes such independent verification of oral histories comes from physical objects or cultural artifacts: the existence of buildings, farming tools, handcrafted artifacts, or other signs. Other times, independent written records may corroborate the oral traditions. Still other times, the scholar searches for underlying values, attitudes, beliefs, and feelings expressed in exaggerated facts, in the belief that what people believe happened is often as important as what actually happened.

Collecting Oral Histories

Most people associate the oral history with the exciting taping of an interview with an interesting narrator. To listen to the oral history of a former black slave, a Jewish holocaust survivor, or a Japanese-American war internee is a moving experience—one that the listener is not likely to forget for a long time.

In reality, however, to produce the oral history is not a very glamorous process; the oral history is a demanding art that is filled with drudgery if it is done correctly. The researcher must have specialized skills not only in nondirective and structured interviewing, but also in equipment operation and historic research. All of the special demands of the depth interview (see Chapter 8) are present in the oral history: the need for extraordinary sensitivity, alertness, and empathy.

A good oral-history interview, like a virtuoso performance, is good because it appears effortless to the listener. However, I would suggest that the more effortless the interview appears, the more effort went into its production. A good part of this preparation is research into whom to interview. In my own current project, I spent close to nine months talking to various members of the St. Louis Japanese-American group, gathering lists of potential respondents, and then assigning priority to older and key members.

During this same period, my research assistant rummaged old newspaper files, public documents, manuscript collections, and other historic materials in a search for the types of open-ended questions that ought to be the project's priority. We borrowed questions from several related sources because of the similarities and differences experienced during World War II. We also grappled with the problem of who would be the best choice for interviewing particular narrators. After all, some interviewers have better rapport with particular narrators and their subjects. This process also involves becoming knowledgeable in the special vocabularies of the narrators.

However, the researcher has to be careful not to spend too much time in research. Many desirable narrators are old and in frail health. If the researcher spends too much time in preparations, some key narrators may become too frail for interviews, may move away, or actually die. It becomes imperative, therefore, to plan the research phase efficiently so that the interviewer knows whom to interview and what to ask without wasting time that might end in lost data.

At some stage, the project is ready for actual interviews; but before an actual interview can be conducted, the interviewer must make sure all of the needed equipment is present and functional. Many interviewers spend up to an hour in preparation for the interview before it starts. They carry standard checklists of all equipment to make sure they do not forget tape recorders, extension cords, many hours of tape (unwrapped and ready to use), oral-history forms, release forms, note pads, and several pens and pencils. Because of the possibility of equipment failure, they will have back-up machines. They pretest all machinery before the interview to make sure they are working properly before the interview starts.

The professional oral history is much like a professional theatrical performance in this regard. Everything must go off without a hitch, so that unforeseen glitches do not disturb the interview process. The oral-history interviewer carefully selects the place of interview to be a one of few interruptions and distractions: the noise of clocks, refrigerators, fans, open windows, running water, rustling paper, rambunctious pets, and telephone interruptions can make tapes undecipherable. The interviewer will have set up the interview so that he or she interviews only one person. The presence of multiple narrators is extremely bad practice for a number of reasons. First, people talk simultaneously and it becomes impossible to transcribe. Second, the presence of other's influences what people say. Second, the interviewer wants narrators to think for themselves and not to parrot what others have said. The interviewer sets up the interview so that spouses or other individuals know that they will have their own turn at a later date.

The actual interview requires multiple demands on the interviewer. The interviewer must be attentive to what the narrator is saying, noting down things that need further probing and clarification. This requires sympathy, friendliness, tact, and the courage to be inquisitive. At the same time, the interviewer must remain alert to the possibilities of equipment failure, tapes that may be shortly in need of changing, and so on. The interviewer must be sensitive to the candor of the narrator and should keep notes on any possible lack of candor. The oral-history schedule is generally more of an outline of basic points that are central to the overall project. The interviewer and narrator need to be sensitive to the point that these records will be used by people who do not know them, and so, details that the narrator assumes the interviewer already knows have to be drawn out in incredible detail: narrator's name, age, birthplace, likes, dislikes, etc.

The interviewer must ask questions that this future audience will want answered. This means that the oral history depends heavily on *probes*: Who? What? Where? When? How? Why? It depends also on numerous *cues*. The interviewer must juggle the innumerable facts, clues, and references that the narrator makes to add specifying dates, places, and actors. *Props* are essential to jarring long-term memory: We ask the narrator to bring old family albums, photographs, slides, newspaper clippings, and so on. Additionally, we keep running lists of the names of old-timers to refresh our narrators' memories. Props need social location: Because the tape-transcription user may not have access to these props, they need very careful description on the tape. This process of description involves clear physical descriptions. One of our respondents brought a fish-scaler made in the relocation camp in which he had been interned during World War II; the interviewer described the type of wood, the exact size in inches, color, etc. Then she had the narrator describe how the fish-scaler was used. She probed for context, and the narrator responded that it had been quite normal for the camp authorities to bring supplies into the camp from which the internees made household furnishing more to their tastes similar than those which had been taken from them before they were relocated.

One of the hardest tasks in oral-history interviewing is being patient. A common problem is that of silence when the narrator is trying to recall events that happened in the distant past. Many interviewers learn to count to ten slowly to give the narrator adequate time to recall particular events. If the interviewer rushes or interrupts the narrator, he or she may become even more flustered at recall. Rather than openly challenging discrepancies in narration, a better practice is to probe tactfully to pin down dates and events in relation to other dates and events. Being a good listener is a demanding task.

Another task is to keep the questions open-ended: closed-ended questions with simple yes or no replies are of little help. The interviewer must be ever inquisitive and flexible in pursuing leads. If the interviewer thinks of a question while the narrator is speaking, he or she ought to write it down for future reference. Oral histories are fatiguing for both the interviewer and the narrator. The interviewer must remain alert to the need to cut off the narrator and to set up an appointment for a later continuation.

A difficult question concerns requests for off-the-record information. The interviewer will ask the narrator to sign an unconditional release of the tape and its transcription. Some narrators may wish to sign a conditional release— for example, one in which the tape will not be released until after their death. Others may wish that the interviewer delete some information that is particularly sensitive or kept otherwise off-the-record. For ethical reasons, the oral historians must always remember that people are more important than the study and therefore should honor such requests. Starr (1984:7) points out that an oral history which has a release form has much the standing of a legal deposition. It is also an essential component of the informed consent process. The oral historian must be careful, therefore, to protect the narrator from victimization or harm in the quest for historic fact. On the other hand, the oral history can have the benefits of increasing self-esteem, uniting social groups, and aiding the search for collective identity.

At the end of the interview session, the interviewer should immediately break the copy seals on the tape so that it can not be inadvertently erased. Then the interviewer should make a back-up copy of the tape. Both tapes need labels that include the date, narrator's name, interviewer's name, and tape number if it is part of a series. The tape transcriber should use only the back-up tape to protect the data on the original. The interviewer must also make sure that all notes and word spelling lists accompany the backup for transcription.

An important and often overlooked detail is to appropriately thank the narrator. Special efforts should be made to express appreciation for the time and effort of the narrator. The narration process is often a very emotionally charged and draining experience for the narrator.

Processing and Disseminating Oral Histories

The collection of oral histories is the exciting, romantic part; the processing portion is the drudgery. Because the history is permanently recorded on tape, many individuals feel that the process need go no further than depositing the tape. However, it is a rare scholar who will actually listen to hours of tape. A well-written transcription is much more efficiently read. Therefore, if it is to be of much value, the project director needs to find means of adequately transcribing the tapes. The magnitude of the drudgery involved in good transcription is shown by the fact that an hour of tape may take ten hours of tedious labor to transcribe and index properly. The ideal transcription is more than a verbatim rendering of the narration. The transcriber must attempt to convey the conversational quality of the narration and the essential individuality of expression and dialect. It is tempting to clean up grammar and syntax to protect the ego of the narrator, but such efforts work against the clear portrayals of the narrator's background. Consider differences in the two transcribed versions where the first version is closer to the natural language flow of one of my respondents:

NATURAL VERSION

Respondent: That's camp life's story and ah . . . here ah . . . in the St. Louis . . . Where is it? (Referring to a photograph) This is a 1943 or 44, no, no, no, no, no, after I evacuated, 19 . . . 50 or '51, we, all Japanese, get together had a New Year's party. One of Chinese restaurants. All those peoples gone. I have checked that. All, everybody gone.

OVEREDITED VERSION:

Respondent: That is the story of camp life in the St. Louis. Where is it? This (picture) was taken in 1943 or 44 . . . No, it was after I was evacuated. In 1950 or '51, all of us Japanese got together and had a New Year's party at one of the Chinese restaurants. All of those people are gone. I have checked all of that. Everybody's gone.

The flavor of nonnative speech is lacking in the edited version. Therefore, it is not enough to hire someone who can simply type. The transcriber must become familiar with means of conveying particular qualities of speech. This also involves full description of the narrator's mannerisms and gestures. The interested reader is referred to the detailed instruction in Baum (1977) or Davis, Back, and MacLean (1977) for specific information on the art of quality transcription.

At the end of the laborious process of transcription comes the editing process. Normally, all of our project members pass tapes we have transcribed in a round robin of editing. The editing process is much quicker than the transcription process. Sometimes, one person hears things differently than another person. The editing process gives a partially independent check on the transcription veracity, its punctuation, and ability to convey the narrator's meaning. In many cases, the transcriber did not adequately understand what he or she heard and ends up mistranscribing the narration. The editing process allows the project staff to correct these errors. Finally, the narrator is offered the chance to review, correct, and approve the edited draft transcription. It is wise to provide the narrator with specific guidelines for this task; clearly labeled inquiries where the transcriber or interviewer did not understand the tape recording or think that specific narration is vague and wish some type of follow-up details for clarity. The entire object of editing is to correct for clarity and accuracy, rather than style.

The last step involves a detailed table of contents and index, just as a professional book would have. Many researchers never complete this important step, but it is crucial to the dissemination process. Because most word processors now include search and sort functions, this task is not nearly as odious as it used to be. The value of a well-indexed transcription is hard to overstate. Calls for such transcriptions are a thousand to one over the actual tape because tapes are awkward to use efficiently (Starr 1984:7). The entire process is an expensive one: It is estimated that an average six-hour oral history in my project costs upwards of $1,500 in 1988 dollars.

Historic scholars should demand external proof of the authenticity of oral histories as they would with any document. This means checking the taped voice with electronic voice-analysis devices, matching the tape with transcription for suggestions that it was tampered with, falsified, or edited; if it was, why, by whom, to what extent, and under what circumstances. Furthermore, the scholar needs satisfaction that the narration was not staged or manipulated. As with any document, the oral history always needs corroboration from other documents.

Analytic Strategies

Attempting to separate out analysis from description in historic research, as in field research, is nearly impossible. As does the field researcher, the historic scholar must learn to move back and forth between each level with ease and to employ a wide variety of means to achieve the ends of the historic scholarship. More and more, the historic scholar finds that the social sciences and humanities are united by the elusiveness of meaning and the challenges of scientific verifications. Historic scholars find it increasingly necessary to poach intellectually: to borrow and absorb new methods and materials from other disciplines; to tolerate multiple, and conflicting, definitions and methods of analysis. But the fact is that the world of our experience does not come to us in the pieces scholars have traditionally carved out. Scholars need to get away from the ethnocentrism of looking at phenomena in isolation, thereby divorcing themselves from either cultural or temporal commentary.

Although all scholars find it necessary to specialize, the pattern of specialization therefore is becoming more one of splitting, merging, and rearranging the borders of knowledge. (Much of this rearrangement of knowledge is part of the "hidden" university—study groups, symposia, conferences, and institutes outside of departments.) This is all quite new and upsetting to the old-guard disciplinary purists who concentrated on how their disciplines were distinctive. In traditionalist English departments, the old pattern was to defend disciplinary autonomy by focusing on literary works in isolation. Now, however, some historians and sociologists alike study literary work, and contend that the older methods divorced those works from the cultural and social structure in which those works were born. This newer generation challenges the idea that culture is static, unchanging, or homogeneous and that no method of description can ever be more than a representation that changes with the angle of the observer.

Meaning is elusive and never completely verifiable; it is not isolated from culture, but imbedded in it. The historic scholar who uses letters must know not only the language in which the letter is written, but the social conventions underlying it. Japanese and French letters use writing conventions that emphasize obliqueness in the service of politeness, whereas American letter-writing conventions emphasize a straightforward, get-down-to-business-like approach. No letter writer is beyond such constraints of society.

The historic scholar must learn to know many such social conventions—those of the legal system when reading a contract, those of social norms when looking at an advertisement. The same is true of what is "meant" by a pun, satire, or joke. The literary Japanese pun emphasizes the huge number of homonyms that exist in that language; a Japanese author may write out a sound combination in the Japanese syllabary, rather than employ a Chinese character, because a specific set of syllables may represent numerous characters—each with its own distinctive meaning. The intent is to "soften" the meaning, so that the literate reader is amused by the multiple images. Puns in English—and other alphabet-based languages—have no such linguistic equivalents.

Cliometrics: Quantitative versus Qualitative Approaches

Cliometrics grew out of the marriage of economics and history. Like most marriages, this one has built-in tensions threatening its continued existence as well as factors which aid its cohesion. Much of the tension comes from the unnecessary pitting of qualitative Clio (the Greek goddess of history) against quantitative econometricians. After all, science is ultimately the business of quantification and measurement. Historians who cite "typical" documents or "representative" cases make quantitative statements; they are implicitly measuring when they speak of "significant events," "widespread communication," "growing trends," "intense debates," or "high probabilities."

The tensions are produced out of the narrow-minded presumption that one must either be quantitative or qualitative. Certainly there is no safety in numeric or qualitative facts: The scholar must control the historic material rather than the material control the scholar. Numbers must be made meaningful. Quantification may broaden and deepen the scholar's understanding of historic materials, or it may lead to an empirical dust bowl, depending on how conscious the scholar is of methodology. Unfortunately, as the French historian Moheau recognized over 200 years ago, there are more individuals who know how to calculate than how to reason.

The value of quantification in historic research is not much different from other disciplines; it is limited by access to countable data that clearly operationalize some phenomenon of interest to the scholar. The complexity and paucity of historic materials may exacerbate this problem. It can be difficult to get accurate information because the sources can prove inconsistent, unreliable, or lacking. When large amounts of high quality data do exist, quantitative analysis ". . . establishes how many examples there are to support each side of the argument, and thus reveals not only the main features of the evidence but also, more important, the exceptions to them, the nuances, the degree to which the emerging generalizations need to be quantified" (Aydelotte 1969:5).

Therefore, at its best, the quantification process can aid the historic scholar hone the process of the systematic verification of hypotheses and legitimate generalization of results. At its worst, it can result in disconnected, individualized bits of quantitative information. Quantification for the sake of quantification and quantification that disguises the inadequacies of evidence are a sham. The value of qualitative methods in historic research is in the supplying of meaning, of getting behind the facts and figures to the lived reality—which may reside more properly outside of the realm of quantitative history, and in bringing life to the coldness of the barren count.

Tilly (1981:34) further clarifies the quantification versus qualification debate, by stressing that historic arguments abound with many more-or-less statements, for which "available quantitative models and statistical techniques are inadequate." Numeric wizardry does not automatically amplify understanding. Indeed, the focus on quantification detracts from other important analytic devices (Tilly 1981:34): "deliberate conceptualization, explicit modeling, painstaking measurement, and self-conscious comparison."

The introduction of highly efficient, inexpensive computers has both exacerbated and benefited the quantification issue in scholarship. Any scholar trained in quantitative methods prior to the large-scale introduction of computers can attest to their benefits. Large scale computational procedures that were time-consuming, costly, and human error-prone when accomplished by hand have come to be commonplace, error-free, and inexpensive. Computers give extraordinary impetus to the capacity to store and manipulate huge data banks and to do analysis efficiently and easily. At the same time, computers can simply compound the process of trivialization through piling more facts on the heap, of mistaking statistical results for reality, and of dehumanizing history.

Cobb's (1971:1528) critique of quantitative historians in his essay "Historians in White Coats" well illustrates the above potential for exacerbations:

> [The end product of] the computerization of 516 urban riots, turbulences, disturbances, . . . lynchings, stabbings, . . . [and] provocative songs . . . will no doubt reveal some highly interesting patterns: that, for instance, market riots occur on market days, on or near the market, that marriage riots will take place after weddings, that funeral riots take place either outside the church or near the cemetery. . . . Perhaps we knew already, but now we *really* know; we have a Model. Riots has been tamed, dehumanized, and scientificated.

However, Cobb's critique borders on a premature divorce of Clio from her quantitative husband. Although many historic problems do not reduce to quantitative analysis, many problems are more informed by quantitative analysis (Tilly 1981:62); (1) more complex models; (2) problems with greater numbers of variables; (3) greater the variation to be explained; and (4) and more easily quantifiable data. Additionally, historic scholars too often undertheorize, produce vague specifications of large-scale social structures, and use insufficiently rigorous methods. The marriage of quantitative and qualitative methods should be one of satisfaction of complementary needs. Two examples follow to illustrate this point.

During the late 1970s, Efron and Thisted (1976) decided, just for fun, to analyze Shakespeare's vocabulary statistically. Their fun was not mindless, however: Should a new literary work be found, they wished to determine whether Shakespeare could have written it. To their delight, two scholars a decade later discovered copies of a new poem in both the Bodelain Library in Oxford, England and in the Yale University collection. Part of the poem includes the following stanza:

> Shall I die? Shall I Fly
> Lover's baits and deceits,
> sorrow breeding?
> Shall I tend? Shall I send?
> Shall I sue, and not rue
> my proceeding?
> In all duty her beauty
> Binds me her servant for ever,
> If she scorn, I mourn,
> I retire to despair, joying never.

Some Shakespearean scholars regarded the new poem with much skepticism. However, because a West German scholar had already put all of Shakespeare's known works into computer-readable form and had counted all of the published words he used with a computer, Thisted and Efron realized they had a golden opportunity for quantitative analysis of qualitative data. Shakespeare's known works included 884,647 total words and a vocabulary of 31,534 different words. Of those words in Shakespeare's vocabulary, 14,376 appeared just once, 4,343 appeared just twice, 2,292 appeared just three times, 1,463 appeared four times, 1,043 appeared five times, 837 appeared six times, 638 appeared seven times and so on.

Although the quantitative questions open to Efron and Thisted were limited, they are quite interesting and answerable: How many words did Shakespeare know but *not* use? If a newly discovered poem written by Shakespeare appeared, how many words would be in it that he had never used previously? How many words in it would be among those he had previously used only once before? How many would he have used only twice before? From such questions, for example, they predicted that if Shakespeare's known works were doubled in length, the new half would contain 11,430 ± 178 new words he had not previously used.

The newly discovered poem contains 430 words. Efron and Thisted predicted that it should contain 6.97 ± 2.64 new words. In fact, the new poem contained 9 words Shakespeare had never previously used. Another of their predictions was that this new poem ought to contain 4.21 ± 2.05 words Shakespeare had used only once previously; the actual number was seven. As further test of their questions, they compared the poems of John Donne, Christopher Marlowe, and Ben Johnson to the new poem. None of these poems gave even a close approximation to Shakespeare's style. For example, in a poem by John Donne, there were 17 words that Shakespeare had never used. In typical statistical conservatism, Efron and Thisted concluded that there is no convincing evidence for rejecting the hypothesis that Shakespeare wrote this new poem.

Interestingly, numerous literary experts who have read the poem felt that the quality of the poem did not sound anything like Shakespeare. Nevertheless, Efron and Thisted's work gives a solid probabilistic basis to the historic scholar's analysis of who could or could not have written this poem.

Although Efron and Thisted's approach is limited in marriage of quantitative and qualitative techniques, not all historic scholarship need be; Long (1987) shows an easier coupling of the two through his use of obituaries to study changes in identities and organizations. Long investigated the terms individuals use to interpret, depict, and legitimize the self-images and biographies of the deceased through the use of content analysis of 630 randomly selected newspaper obituaries over a century. For example, some 30.8% of the American Civil War era obituaries mentioned such personality characteristics of the deceased as: "[Oakley's] . . . intellectual powers were great . . .;" and "[Slote] . . . was a man of medium build . . .;" "[Comstock] . . . was a good workman, and very much of a gentleman. . . ."

This earlier period was also characterized by references to friends and acquaintances; pleasures, hobbies, and distractions; habits and routines; and travels. However, within the hundred and twenty years of Long's analysis, such depictions reduced to near zero. By the late 1930's, obituaries had become more formal: Occupational tags or titles replaced the particulars of work histories; and family mentions increased dramatically over the study period. Long (1987:993) concluded that "obituaries are the products of obituary producers, of the practices, sounds, and routines of the reporters who write them." As with Efron and Thistle's study, because of the lack of rigorous control over alternative hypotheses in historic studies, the nature of the study compelled Long to admit (p. 994) that "it seems probably that the changes are, at the least, partial, indirect effects of changes in their production and in the organization and operation of the newspaper industry."

Application of Concepts

Concepts are always socially constructed. In the case of historic scholarship, the researcher constructs concepts out of the tension between past and present because writing about the past inevitably reflects experience in the present. A second tension in which the historic conceptualizer is imprisoned is that between the writer and audience. As Barzun and Graff (1970:137) write, ". . . the reader is always more sensitive to a (person's) *expressed meaning* than the writer. . . . It is not hard to see why: the writer has his intended meaning at the forefront of his mind, and it too often comes between him and the actual words he writes down."

Attention to these two tensions is of great concern to the historic scholar because each introduces subjectivism into historic scholarship. The first-rate scholar attempts to battle and overcome each potential bias, although these are not easy tasks. *The writing of historic scholarship demands a rethinking of the past—recapturing bygone events and thoughts.*

To overcome the dialectic between the past and present, the researcher must ask questions that probe the minds and social structure of the period under scrutiny: How did the people think and act? What were their motives? How did they behave? How might they have differed from ourselves? What was their social context, and how might that context have influenced them?

Sewell's (1985) study of nineteenth-century social structure and mobility is an example of relatively unproblematic concept construction. His long-term interest in social inequality, combined with fortuitously good data from French marriage registrars of the nineteenth century, allowed him to construct three status measures of men's occupations based on (1) the percent literate in each occupation, (2) the percent of witnesses to the marriage who were business-men, professionals, or rentiers, and (3) the percent of men in each occupation whose wives were not employed. Of course, no operationalization is ever perfect: Sewell's data allowed him only to infer literacy by an individual's ability to sign his or her name; and the ability to procure a bourgeois witness to one's marriage does not necessarily depend on one's own social standing. Neverthe-less, these data allowed Sewell to infer that migrants to Marseille—contrary to the common assumption that migration was an uprooting, disruptive pro-cess—had some literacy skills that helped them in the labor market in their new residence. Also, whatever disruption migration might have exacerbated was probably lessened by the tendency to undertake migration with family members.

Contrast Sewell's relatively clean conceptualization with the task before Otis (1985) in studying prostitution in medieval society. Because our present conceptions of prostitution have roots in sixteenth-century prohibition, it is difficult to cross the past-present dialectic time warp and understand twelfth- and thirteenth-century tolerance of prostitution. Rather than expel prostitutes to beyond the city wall, French Languedoc authorities authorized red light dis-tricts or "Hot Streets," and municipalities created public brothels and granted both royal and seigneurial privileges. This was also a period in which the insti-tutional repression of women reached new lows. Otis failed to examine the legalization of prostitution in relation to other social background factors which severely reduces the value of her work. She never spells out its relation to plagues, economic depression, war, or turmoil of the period. The reader ends up neither with an understanding of the relationship of prostitution to social structure nor of the attitudes of the day.

Part of the problem with the operationalization of concepts in historic— or other—studies is the danger that the operation will "freeze" the fluidity of social life and change. As Bendix states (1963:70)

> Definitions of structures like feudalism, bureaucracy, etc., usually take the form of enumerating several, distinguishing characteristics . . . They say nothing about the strength or generality with which a given characteristic must be pres-ent, nor do they say anything about the structures in which one or another ele-ment of the definition is missing. The result has been uncertainty. Abstractions are needed to define the characteristics of a structure and thus they remove the definition from the evidence. On the other hand, when we approach the evi-dence "definition at hand," we often find its analytic utility diminished, because the characteristics to which it refers are in fact neither unequivocal nor general.

Essential components of any valuable theory include an exact definition of which aspects of social structure have what relevant consequences, and exactly which consequences feed back to what selective impacts on structures. Interestingly, most individuals seem "naturally" inclined to regard psychologic factors as more salient that social structural ones. Therefore, it is easier to identify strong or weak leaders, than to consider (structural) conditions as conducive to effective or ineffective leadership. Among historians, this tendency is reflected in The Great Man Theory of History. Similarly, sociologists interested in understanding crime in society had, for a long time, studied criminals, rather than crimogenic milieux or criminal opportunity structures. Rather than consider institutional or opportunity structures and their effects on ambition, most individuals think of ambitious or lazy people. We seem to focus more readily on heretics and beliefs in heresy, rather than on the social process through which heretics are made; on the heresy hunt in which the individual is labeled a heretic, rather than on the anxiety-relieving ritual produced by the heretic-labeling institution and the social arrangements that originate and support the individuals in the heretic belief system.

The individual is not a basic social unit; the meaningful interaction of two or more individuals provides the simplest social unit. As complex as "meaningful interaction" is to operationalize, less salient social units exist that are easily as complex to identify and study: power, capitalism, modernization, and westernization. However, the scholar engaged in historic studies has just as much of an obligation to formulate clear conceptualizations, as is demanded in any other type of research. The basic problem is not whether it is possible to operationalize concepts, but whether it is worthwhile doing so. The acid test of worthiness is whether the concept proves important for understanding the working of some theory.

The normal process of doing any type of study results in an interplay of concept formation and data analysis. The researcher formulates concepts grounded in past studies; these serve as initial guides to what data to collect. After data collection, he or she reformulates and refines the concepts because of deficiencies that the data make apparent. Future research further refines those concepts as new evidence accumulates that uncovers new flaws. It is the scientific attitude of skepticism that ultimately protects concepts from becoming reified—that is, frozen into our brain synapses as if they were reality. Only the mind that seeks to discriminate between what is true and false, that is curious enough to seek clarification always, can overcome the danger of reification. As Barzun and Graff (1970:128) conclude: "There is no substitute for well-placed skepticism."

Summary

All of the early great sociologists used historic methods in their search to study large-scale and master social changes. Historic and sociological methods are complementary rather than separate fields. First, the start of traditions may have historic roots, but the maintenance of traditions is of sociological concern. Second, social structure may contribute to historic regularities and changes. Third, sociological concepts may aid in the interpretation of historic events: It aids in generalization (History-as-Ideas) rather than particularization (History-as-Facts).

The master scholars of history have focused on asking important questions. The Big Questions have great payoff, but they need continual reassessment within particular social and temporal contexts. Rather than collect new data, some of the most interesting historic scholarship reconceptualizes and reevaluates older theories and data. Metaphorically, the novice scholar of history does well to start by standing on the shoulders of the giants of the field. With the historic giants as firm grounding, the novice may see further.

Researchers who use the comparative-historic method fall into four generic camps: individualizers, universalizers, encompassers, and variation-finders. The individualizers trust the case-study approach in examining a case for its distinctive qualities. This approach is the least appealing to social scientists interested in generalizations. The universalists study all instances of a phenomenon in search of common properties. The classic social theorists generally fall into this camp. The last two methods emphasize variation. Scholars who use the encompassing approach search for variation within one total system. The variation-finding approach uses multiple cases in the search for degrees of variation.

The formation and measurement of concepts is an important part of historic scholarship. All concepts have advantages and disadvantages. Some, such as dynasties, lend themselves more to Great Persons interpretations; others, such as medieval tilling practices, serve more mundane views of historic processes. Therefore, conceptualization is a necessary part of historic research, yet it also constrains it. Conceptualizations aid in abstracting reality. Therefore, the historic scholar finds it necessary to move back and forth between the abstract and the concrete. Although the scholar does not want to force complex events into simple categories, the scholar must construct analytic taxonomies, fashion empirical cases for each category, and demonstrate observable instances of cases that fit those taxonomies. The ultimate survivability of a concept depends on whether its advantages outweigh its disadvantages.

The scholar needs evidence to support concepts. Evidence comes from primary or secondary sources. Primary sources include archaeologic physical traces caused by the erosion or the depositing of materials. Because of their relative unobtrusiveness, physical traces provide useful records of incidence or frequency. A second major source of evidence is that of public and private archival records. Because public archival records are normally prepared for particular audiences, they are a product of groups rather than individuals. Therefore, the scholar who uses them must consider how they were produced, altered, embellished, distorted, or altered.

Private records are usually more episodic and meager than public records. As with public records, the scholar must scrutinize them for authenticity, alteration, reinterpretation, and distortion. Historic scholars make it their business to question documents. The authentication process involves rules of external critique: Larger numbers of documents, nonanachronistic features, correct handwriting styles, and papers are among the checklists of items that increase the probability of authenticity. By contrast, if the document has internal inconsistencies, was transmitted through numerous copyists, is derived from secondary rather than primary sources, and so on, suspicions of inauthenticity increase. External critique also involves a search for the meaning underlying particular documents and the credibility of documents.

To counteract the particular biases of any one document, historic scholars prefer large numbers of documents as correctives. Documents may be used as direct indicators for answering only a limited number of factual problems. It is more interesting and useful for the scholar to correlate documentary evidence: To search for consistent patterns into which documents fall.

Modern probability theory adds sampling from large depositories of documents when good catalogues of documents exist. However, much of the problem with sampling documents occurs when catalogues do not exist or when there are large gaps in the records. Historic research must account for selective survival and depositing of evidence. The scholar may also sample evidence based on basic social units and time periods rather than on the basis of documents themselves. Because scholars may not always have the luxury of using probability methods, they need rules of when to stop sampling. A rule of thumb is: Stop sampling when no new evidence comes to light.

A relatively new historic data collection method is the oral history. The oral history is a particularly eclectic means of recording and preserving the long-term memories of respondents. Because of the potential for distortion of events that occurred long ago, the oral history may represent a construction of reality rather than reality itself. However, for the nonliterate and historically disenfranchised, the oral history may provide a means of doing history of the common people. The oral history demands much more of the interviewer than traditional interviewing.

Historic scholarship is eclectic: Because facts are grounded in specific times and places, scholars need to become experts in such areas as language, social conventions, and legal systems. The scholar need work back and forth between facts, documents, inferences, and events that are external to the documents and facts, but give them context and meaning.

An unproductive debate in history has raged over quantitative versus qualitative research. The debate was first introduced by econometricians interested in quantification of history. Because all historic research involves at least implicit quantification and probabilistic logic, the debate is false. Numbers are necessary to scholarship but they are not sufficient: They always need interpretation.

Two tensions complicate objective historic accounting: the tension between the past and present, and that between the reader and writer. The challenge for the historic scholar, therefore, is first to reflect history as it was rather than as an artifact of the present, and second to decrease the gap in expressed meaning between the scholar and audience. The first tension challenges the scholar to consider how people thought and acted, and how their social context structured their acts and thoughts. Because the act of conceptualizing the past holds the danger of artificially representing and freezing it, the scholar is challenged as to how to represent social change.

Good theory-building is a means of getting beyond the static nature of concepts. Theory-building is a search for internal variation and dynamics. Because the scholar assumes change is represented by patterns, he or she searches for regularities. Regularities that become evident lead the scholar to posit hypotheses that are falsifiable. The scholar then searches for data with which to test those hypotheses and their inferences. Historic scholars disdain haphazard collections of facts; each of these components—facts, concepts, and hypotheses—need integration and generalization. The classic methods of providing this integration are the "method of agreement" in which several cases that share crucial similarities imply common causal factors, and the "method of differences" in which several positive and negative cases lead to a crude implication of causation of the variation. The Boolean truth table may aid the process of refining these two basic methods.

C H A P T E R

12

Simulation and Modeling

A game—nearly any game, not merely those termed "simulation games" constitute a kind of caricature of social life. It is a magnification of some aspect of social interaction, excluding all else, tearing this aspect of social interaction from its social context and giving it a special context of its own. . . . [games are] an introduction to the idea of playing under sets of rules, that is, the idea of different roles. . . .[1]

Key Terms

Algorithm

Artificial intelligence

Backward reasoning

Best-first searching

Bidirectional reasoning

Brute-force searching

Chunking

Expert system shell

Forward reasoning

Fuzzy logic

[1]Coleman, J. S. (1966) In defense of games. *American Behavioral Scientist, 10*, 3–4.

Heuristic knowledge	Prisoner's dilemma
Inference engine	Rule-based knowledge
Knowledge base	Simulation
Mixed-motive game	Symbolic logic
Model	Turing test
Nonzero sum game	Zero sum game

Study Guide Questions

1. What are the advantages and disadvantages of simulations?

2. How do simulations differ from experiments?

3. Simulations may be descriptive or analytic, holistic or partial, macro- or microanalytic, static or dynamic. Describe these properties.

4. What are the fundamental differences between human gaming, human-computer simulations, computer simulations, and artificial intelligence?

5. How are size of group, perfect vs. nonperfect information structure, and zero sum versus nonzero sum structure important to classification of human games?

6. How does artificial intelligence differ from true intelligence?

7. What three kinds of knowledge exist? How do these types of knowledge complicate attempts to form artificially intelligent computer programs?

8. Chess has provided a good model for artificial intelligence simulations. What are the different reasoning methods that have been tried, and what are their deficiencies?

9. When using expert advisory systems, in what five ways do social science goals differ from knowledge engineering goals?

10. What strategies aid in validating simulations and games?

Although not every instructor will choose to include this chapter in a one-semester undergraduate methods course, it is an area of growing importance in social science. For this reason, students should at least be exposed to the contributions and logic of simulations. The fast-paced growth of simulation by social scientists during the 1980s will undoubtedly continue in the 1990s, and add important information not possible through the methods already discussed.

Abelson (1968:275) has defined *simulation* as "the exercise of a flexible imitation of processes and outcomes for the purpose of clarifying or explaining the underlying mechanisms involved." A simulation, therefore, is a symbolic abstraction, simplification, or substitution for some system. In other words, a simulation is a theoretical model of the elements, relationships, and processes that may reasonably symbolize some system. It is *not* an attempt to get a perfect replication of that system. Indeed, the beauty of simulations is often that their simplicity reduces the complexity of some system to its very essence.

The perfect model is not one that precisely represents reality. Such a simulation would have the same drawbacks as a map as large and detailed as the city it represents, a map depicting every park, every street, every building, every tree, every pothole, every inhabitant. Were such a map possible, its specificity would defeat its purpose: to generalize and abstract. Mapmakers highlight such features as their clients choose. Whatever their purpose, maps and simulations must simplify as much as they mimic the world. Simplification can pay off: By abstracting only the essence of the system—*by boiling it down to the barest skeleton—simulationists often recognize familiar patterns and behaviors*.

Simulations can be used to teach students about the operations of complex social systems. Gamson designed SIMSOC (shorthand for simulated society) to teach students about the essential workings of societies. He included personal goals of power, wealth, and popularity to mimic the individualistic level. Food and energy supply, standard of living, social cohesion, and public commitment, and other components of modern nation-states found representation in public programs, societal consumption levels, intergroup conflict representations, measures of alienation, and subsistence, and so on.

Simulations also may be used to test and develop theories. INTERACT, (Heise & Lewis 1988), a simulation to be explained in greater detail later in this chapter, has proven highly productive for testing balance theories of attitude change, criminal victimization, and deviance, along with many of the assumptions underlying the symbolic interactionist viewpoint in social psychology. Simulations help the theorist make a theory more explicit. Many advocates of simulations see them as ways of testing whether one really understands some phenomenon as well as one thinks one does. In the process, the rigors needed to produce a good simulation help weed out fuzzy ideas and unspoken assumptions. Heise's INTERACT (Heise & Lewis 1988:1) started out in 1973 as a simple attempt to see whether Heise could mathematically predict what would happen if one person insulted another person. Heise (p. 2) has since spent over 15 years improving the simulation of a very simple theory that "people try to have experiences that confirm their basic sentiments." The result has been a much more thorough explication of a large body of social psychological theory than would have been possible using other methods.

Simulation Versus Experimentation

Experimentation, as has been demonstrated in Chapter 6, has virtues of control and replication. As was explained, when one moves out into the field, one normally loses some control over one's research variables, particularly in more macrosocial settings. One of the major advantages of simulation is that the researcher can artificially manipulate variables in such macrosocial settings in ways that one could simply not do in ordinary life, either for practical or ethical reasons.

Furthermore, it was also demonstrated that experiments can normally extrapolate to, at best, a few variables. By contrast, simulations (particularly computer simulations) may often handle a multitude of variables including both intrapersonal and interpersonal processes at the same time. Sometimes experimentation may be used in conjunction with simulation and gaming. Indeed, some simulations utilize experiments within their context.

Both experiments and simulations are criticized for their artificiality or lack of validity. Again, as in Chapter 6, it is emphasized that methods per se give neither validity nor invalidity to scientific knowledge. Simulations, as well as experiments, have been designed that closely approximate social processes. Simulations, unlike experiments, are best justified in the study of systems. *System* is a very general term that refers to any set of interrelated and interdependent entities: cognitions, sentiments, families, courts, bureaucracies, and nations.

Simulations can compress the study of large stretches of time into seconds. Therefore, simulations are also well suited for the study of long-term processes. By contrast, few experiments allow for the study of processual change over more than two points in time. The simulationist has a great advantage over the experimentalist in ability to study long-term effects of a great many variables.

Dimensions and Properties of Simulations

There are at least four questions that the simulationist can consider while developing a simulation. First, will the simulation use a descriptive or analytic model? Some simulations are interested in simply describing relationships and variations in systems—SIMSOC is such a simulation. Similarly, Greenhalgh and Bongaart's (1987) simulation of five alternative fertility policies is a descriptive simulation. These researchers projected China's population size, old-age economic support, family economy, and the status of women in the years 2000 and 2025 based on five models: stop at one child, stop at two children, stop at two children with a delay in child bearing until the woman had reached age 25 to 29 with spacing of children between four and six years apart, a stop at two children option with no requirement on delay of first child but a delay of second child until the mother was age 30, and a mixed policy of stop at one child in the cities, and stop at two and space them in rural areas. Ironically, although the Chinese government hopes to abandon its strict one-child family policy by the year 2000, these simulations showed superior methods of reducing fertility without the disruptive effects of the current, highly restrictive policy on population aging, physical safety of females, and cultural acceptability of fertility policy. Other simulationists are more interested in analytic cause and effect statements. The WORLD CRISIS simulation disk (Wilcox 1984) that accompanies this text is such a simulation; it attempts to explore the probable causal effects of changes in such variables as population increase, available natural resources, and pollution.

Second, will the simulation employ a holistic or partial model? Some simulationists may be interested in examining the total phenomenon, while others may hold parts of the phenomenon constant while examining its impact on some subsystem. As a general rule, at the start of any simulation, the user is better off trying to understand only a very small portion of the model, while holding other variables constant. As understanding increases for smaller portions of the model, then the researcher may proceed to working with larger, more holistic models. In INTERACT, Heise recommends working first with two-person scenarios because three-person scenarios are much more complicated. Similarly, I prefer students to introduce only one small change at a time when using INTERACT because otherwise they will not be sure which among different changes they make actually produced the observed change. This is one of the ironies of simulations: Although, *unlike experiments*, they allow for a multitude of controlled changes, the researcher is better off proceeding conservatively in the introduction of complex changes.

Third, the simulationist must decide whether to focus on macro- or microanalytic models. Some problems deal with aggregate levels and flows as fundamental units. The WORLD CRISIS simulation gives macro-level changes in population, energy, food supplies, and pollution for the entire world (see Figure 12–1 for one such projection), although most population experts now think analysis should focus on somewhat smaller national differences because of the wide variations across nations—from negative population growth in a few Western nations to enormous population growth in some African nations. Other simulations, such as INTERACT, are concerned with more basic, elemental units: attitudes, emotions, and interactional outcomes.

Fourth, the decision to focus on static or dynamic models is important. Most simulations deal with change and trend development, but some explore equilibrium or static models. The purpose of WORLD CRISIS is to find an equilibrium point, in spite of the fact that the student is lead through a series of changes in population to arrive at that equilibrium. By contrast, INTERACT, although it is predicated on the static notion that individuals will try to confirm their basic feelings, is most interesting for its predictions of change in affect.

In the next several sections, several types of simulations shall be discussed—human gaming, human-computer simulations, computer simulations, and artificial intelligence. The order of my discussion follows from their his-

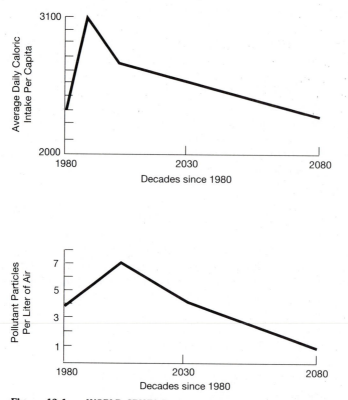

Figure 12-1. WORLD CRISES Projections through the year 2000.

toric order of appearance as tools for understanding social phenomena. The appearance of each has added much to the rigor of modeling social structures and processes, but that rigor sometimes comes at a price of breadth of usefulness of each method.

Human Gaming

Games generally are classified as two-person (dyadic), three-person (triadic), or *n*-person (more than three participants). Each of these sizes has special features not found in the other sizes (Davis 1983). For example, sociologists have long recognized that a two-person group makes for poor organization because by taking any one of its two members away, it becomes impossible to continue the group. By contrast, a triad can lose a member and still maintain its collective identity as a group. Triads also have special features of coalition formation not found in dyads. *N*-person groups also have unique features. There are many solutions to group power and coalition formation for two- and three-person groups for which no known solution exists in groups larger than three-person groups. The reasons for this are the expanded structural dimensions that must be considered (see chapter 11 in Smith [1987] for a discussion of social network properties). For example, the simple addition of a new member increases the potential dyadic ties by a function of $n (n-1)/2$: A four-member group has six possible dyadic coalitions but a five-member group has ten, and a six-member group has fifteen. As more members are added, researchers find it necessary to consider such properties as the actual number of linkages between members, the degree of hierarchy, linkages to persons and groups outside the group in question, strength of ties, reciprocity of ties, and so on.

The importance of this increasing complexity of larger sized groups is simple: The fewer the players, the simpler the game in general. The more complex the game, the more forces a player is faced with that neither the player nor the simulationist can control. The result is increasing difficulty in defining and understanding the game's decisional processes.

The structure of information is also highly important in games. Theoretically, games of perfect information are strictly determined, but very rarely can perfect information be assured. For example, only in parlor games can one usually find perfect information, as in chess. However, even such games as bridge and poker are games of nonperfect information. Similarly, most decisions in everyday situations involve much less than perfect information. To illustrate how much difference lack of information can make, consider the classic prisoner's dilemma game in which the police have arrested two suspects to a crime. The police, after placing each suspect in a different cell, informs them of their choices to remain silent or to confess and of the following consequences of their choices. First, if one suspect turns state's evidence and the other suspect does not, the squealer is set free and the other receives a 20–year sentence. Second, if both confess, each receives a five-year sentence. Third, if both remain silent, they each receive a one-year sentence for a lesser charge of carrying a concealed weapon. Figure 12–2 illustrates each choice of the classic prisoner's dilemma.

The outcome of this simple game would appear to hinge on lack of trust (where there is less than perfect information) about what one's partner will do. But the results of thousands of prisoner's dilemma games shows that even if players are told the normal outcome—which is for both to confess—they will still consider only their own self-interests (to be set free), and ignore information that their partner holds power over their outcomes. Even game theorists lose prisoner's dilemma matches! Therefore, the objection can be raised that determinism of games of perfect information depend on players acting rationally. However, such games as the prisoner's dilemma demonstrate convincingly that players do not always play according to their "best" interests. For this reason, games often raise enticing questions of the circumstances under which individuals do not behave rationally. The matter of imperfect information seriously complicates game outcomes because there is no predetermined

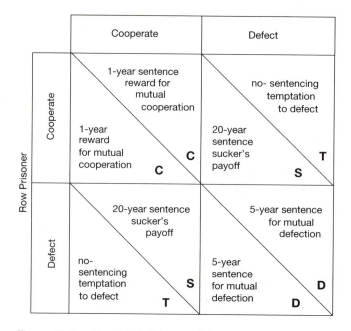

Figure 12-2. The Classic Prisoner's Dilemma.

rational play with which to predict outcomes. The choice of either strategy to simulate will depend on the purposes of the game, although imperfect information is more probable in social life.

Another important component of games is the generic reward-cost structure: zero sum, nonzero sum, or mixed motive. *Zero sum* structures depend on the assumption of fixed rewards or payoffs; if rewards are constant, then if one person receives increased rewards, the other person's rewards must decrease. Whether rewards are actually fixed does not matter—simulationists often run games where the participants only think rewards are fixed, with results similar to actually fixed rewards. Many social situations are zero sum by nature: war, time spent in social relations, and so on. Therefore, in zero sum games, the players have no common interests, making them purely competitive by nature. *Nonzero sum* structures, by contrast, are based on an assumption of non-fixed rewards and costs; both parties might win or both might lose. Negotiation strategies are typically predicated on attempts to show both parties how they will both win or both lose. *Mixed-motive* games more often approximate reality than either purely zero sum or nonzero sum games. Outcomes are usually a complex mixture of competitive zero sum and noncompetitive nonzero sum strategies.

The Prisoner's Dilemma game by definition is a mixed-motive game; the upper-left hand and lower-right hand cells are nonzero sum, and the remaining two cells are zero sum. Figure 12–3 illustrates clear-cut examples of each type of game: zero sum, mixed-motive, and nonzero sum. Note that in every cell of Figure 12–3A, that if one player wins points, the other must lose points—

making it a zero sum game; in Figure 12–3C, either both players win or both lose in each cell combination—making this a nonzero sum game, and the Figure 12–3B game is a mixture, in which the upper-left and lower-right hand cells are nonzero sum and the upper-right and lower-left hand cells are zero sum. (By the way, none of these are prisoner's dilemma games; by definition [see Figure 12–2], (1) the temptation to defect (T) must be of greater value than the reward for mutual cooperation (C), which must be of greater value than the punishment for mutual defection (D), which must be of greater value still than the sucker's payoff (S); and (2) the combination of the temptation (T) and sucker's payoff (S) divided by two must be smaller than (preferable to) the reward for mutual cooperation (C). In Figure 12–2, remember that the numbers are all negative because they represent jail terms. Therefore, Figure 12–2 does satisfy these two requirements.)

Such games as SIMSOC are closer approximations to many everyday social settings than two-person experiments, which depend on zero sum or nonzero sum strategies, or three-person games which are a simple function of the relative power of each player. N-person interactions typically have mixed-motive strategies that lead to relatively complex solutions. For example, SIMSOC simulates individual motives of power, which most people perceive is zero sum; popularity which may be nonzero sum; and wealth, which may be zero sum if one perceives a fixed-pie distribution, or nonzero sum if one considers increasing everybody's wealth through an expanding pie. Experiments that use only two- or three-person groups pay the price of low applicability: They pertain to only a relatively narrow set of conditions.

On the other hand, games have such a wide range of criteria by which they may be played that it becomes difficult to know how to predict and interpret their outcomes. There are a number of criteria that can affect the interpretation of game outcomes to greater or lesser degrees; for instance, the duration of play; player preparation time; amount of player involvement; participants' age range, homogeneity, prior knowledge, and sophistication; the number of players; the level of abstraction of game rules; flexibility of play scenarios;

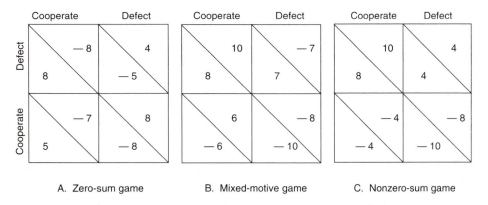

Figure 12–3. Examples of zero sum, nonzero sum, and mixed-motive games.

observability; validity and acceptability of the game message; and responsiveness of the game to player actions; and so on.

This list of possible variations that the designer can build into games illustrates the problems of their use, when we consider the problems of internal and external validity presented in Chapter 4. The more complex (and presumably more lifelike) the game, the less control over threats to internal validity that the designer has. The following steps in designing games to operationalize social structures and processes illustrate how complex a game can get.

1. Define the overall simulation objectives, attempting to give operational definitions of key components and processes.
2. Determine *scope* of the game in terms of time, place, and issues.
3. Identify key actor's roles, social groups, or organizations making critical decisions.
4. Determine actors' objectives in specific contexts (power, wealth).
5. Determine actors' resources (physical, social, economic, informational, political).
6. Determine the interaction sequence cycle or structure among actors.
7. Determine the decision rules or criteria on the basis of which actors decide what resources and information to transmit and what actions to take.
8. Identify potential constraints on actions of actors such as trust, legitimacy, coalition formation, and reward-cost structures.
9. Formulate clear scoring rules or win criteria. This should include the time of winning, number and types of criteria (money earned, zerosum), and, if there are more than one criteria for winning, the degree to which those criteria are interrelated. If more than one winner is possible, Inbar and Stoll (1972:275) suggest that the arrangements by which the winners are produced should be spelled out according to one of the following methods:
   a. hierarchical structure (players rank-ordered on winning criteria)
   b. group reference structure—that is, within each of the various competing or noncompeting groups in a game, a winner might be selected.
   c. task structure—the difficulty of the task herein determines the number of winners and losers the game will yield.
10. Determine the methods of allocation of resources.
11. Choose the forms of game presentation, manipulation, and sequences of operation. Some practical considerations should include duration and availability space, materials, and facilities.

Gamson attempts, in SIMSOC, to capture all the relevant features of some aspect of social life in a single game. Imagine you are a member of SIMSOC. Sixty of your classmates also represent citizens of SIMSOC. All members of SIMSOC live in one of four partitioned regions, widely separated from each other. The rules regulate travel between each region through public and private transportation tickets. You have a job as broadcasting chief of MASMED (mass media) by which you earn pay in SIMBUCKS for your responsibilities in running the National Broadcasting System. Your classmates have such positions as sales vice-president of BASIN (basic industry), regional representative for INNOVIN (innovative industry), fund-raising chairperson of POP (party of the people), SOP (society party) membership chairperson, chief organizer for EMPIN (employee interests), and appeals judge for JUDCO (judicial council).

During the last class period, you fired one of your reporters who, unable to find another job, died because, as an unemployed individual, she could not obtain the subsistence necessary to pay her room and board. The regional police force has arrested your best friend, the chief organizer of EMPIN. You are upset because you haven't enough SIMBUCKS to buy a travel pass to his region of SIMSOC to counsel him.

You have just published the latest SIMSOC TIMES edition, showing that while the standard of living is rising, social cohesion is at an all-time low, and the nation's food and energy supply is decreasing. A news item has been delivered stating that an earthquake has just hit one of the nations' four regions, and all communications with that region are disrupted indefinitely. You decide to run an editorial blasting SOP's political philosophy of decentralization as the basic cause of SIMSOC's ills. As the editorial is going to press, your class instructor halts the game to assess your society's and your own personal progress during the previous hour. As you can see from this brief example, SIMSOC represents major components and problems of any modern society.

The irony of this ability of games and simulations to introduce complexity into research is that the complexity can obscure the most important features of social structures and processes. It is wise to remember that parsimony is always a virtue in science. Sometime researchers are surprised that reducing social structures to their essence leads to processes similar to those found in seemingly more complex system. Although it is true that just because a stripped-down simulation of social structure leading to similar processes as found in everyday life does not prove that the simulation mirrors essential reality, it may do so. Some of the most interesting features of science come from the discovery that the world is not always as complex as it appears on the surface.

A good example of the simplicity of apparently complex events is demonstrated in a simulation of the stock market (Smith, Suchanek, & Williams 1988). After the great October 1987 stock-market crash, these researchers wondered whether it was necessary to search for the mechanics of trading in the complex of suggestions given by so-called Wall Street experts. Smith and his colleagues designed a clever game simulation of a few fundamental aspects of stock-market workings. Briefly, they used roughly 12 volunteer economic students connected by a computer network to duplicate trading on the stock-market floor. They gave each volunteer a number of "shares" of stock, along with some working capital. They simulated a trading day with four-minute sessions, in which traders entered between two and three dozen bids, and made offers resulting in from five to twelve trades. All traders started with the same information, and each session ended with a payout. Not known to the traders was that the simulationists determined the amount of payoff randomly as 0, 6, 28, or 60 cents. Because the average daily payoff was 24 cents, a share's dividend value on the first trading day in a 15-day experiment was $3.60 (24 × 15).

Smith and his colleagues found that in a typical four-minute day, nine of the twelve traders entered into trading. One might open a bid to sell a share for

$1.50, which would be quickly accepted because it was $1.90 below market value. Then someone else might offer $1.30 to someone who would snap the share up at this value. Such bargain basement prices triggered a flurry of rising bids, and a boom quickly developed. By the middle of the fourth day, the price topped $5.50 even though the stock's value had now dropped to $3. At such high prices, offers to sell began to outnumber offers to buy. By day eleven, prices were below the stock's dividend of $1. At the end of the 15–day period some astute traders were able to post gains of $50, while others ended up with $5. Ironically, had the traders traded at or near the dividend value, all traders would have ended up with profits of $16.

Smith and his colleagues then varied the simulation to test some hypotheses currently in circulation among Wall Street watchers. First, they used Tucson business persons with real trading experiences, but this group created the biggest boom-bust of all! Next, they tried using persons experienced in their previous simulations as traders; These sessions created somewhat smaller boom-bust cycles, apparently due to learning experiences. Then they tried market regulations that would restrict trading, but found this actually fueled the bubbles. Price curbs were even worse: They created the longest lasting boom because everybody knew the stock couldn't fall below 15 cents. Smith et al. argue that market crashes are caused by nothing more than the traders themselves speculating on prices, rather than paying attention to the stock's basic values. These simulations created cyclic effects remarkably similar to those observed in normal stock market affairs. They also suggest that boom and bust cycles would not be helped (and might well be hindered) by most of the suggestions that Wall Street and government analysts have made. Note that this simulation does not offer proof of boom and bust cycles. Smith et al. use the results of their simulation as a form of rhetoric to argue their ideas.

Orback (1979) has commented on the motivational aspects of learning that simulation games cause. He points out that researchers using simulation games have been somewhat baffled by the fact that participants normally find these techniques more interesting than traditional techniques—including experiments to which they show superficial resemblance. Orback's conclusions are that participants' responses to simulation games can be largely accounted for by the facts that they (1) allow persons greater freedom of thought, expression, and action; (2) have greater amounts of novelty involved; and (3) are not restricted by the judgmental or sanctioning inhibitions found in more traditional techniques. Most simulation games are closer to quasi-experiments—particularly multiple time-series designs—in this respect than to true experiments. True experiments generally use simple before-after designs, rather than time-series, and highly restrict the introduction of treatments for purposes of control over internal validity. Although simulations often do employ randomization, such employment is not normally used to introduce or deny treatment to the subjects. In the Smith et al. (1988) simulations, note that all traders received the same treatment, whether randomized or not. What simulations lose in internal validity, therefore, they attempt to gain back in external validity, or generalizability.

Because simulationists take this loss of internal validity seriously, they sometimes invent stricter simulations that use computers. These computer-based simulations allow for much greater control over plausible alternative explanations of events, but they can come at the price of loss of generalizability.

Human-Computer Simulations

In human-computer simulations, so-called computer games, or gaming simulations, individuals play the role of decision makers, but the computer is also a participant, responsive to the players' activities, and thus the simulation combines elements of both games and computer simulations. To be responsive to players, the simulationist must provide the computer with a script, analogous to an actor's script in a dramatic play. This script must comprise two different kinds of messages: first, every action the player makes must have an appropriate response programmed; second, the program must apprise players of actions they must take to respond appropriately to the computer's screen displays. For example, in a classic computer game called HAMMURABI, the following computer-person "dialogue" could take place:

Computer: Hammurabi says: Welcome, New Village Manager. Your population is 1,000 people. You own 70 acres. You have 200 bushels of grain in store. Land is trading at 20 bushes per acre. How many acres of land do you wish to buy?
Player: 1.
Computer: You now have 71 acres and 180 bushels. How many acres do you wish to plant?
Player: No.
Computer: Error in format. That does not make sense.
Player: 300.
Computer: But you only have 71 acres.
Player: 30.
Computer: The population is now 1,071. How many bushels do you wish to use as food?
Player: 80.
Computer: There were 80 accidental deaths, 30 deaths from disease, and 120 deaths from starvation. The population is now 841. You have been replaced by a military junta.

Notice how the script structures the player's alternatives. If the player communicates outside of the program-given alternatives, the simulationist has instructed the computer to print out something like "Error in format. That does not make sense." We can guess a good part of the flow chart that underlies this program. Clearly, for example, when the computer screen asks a question that requires a numeric answer ("How many acres. . .") if the player responds with a nonnumeric answer, the program responds with "Error in format. . . ."; if the player responds with an out-of-range answer, such as 300 acres when the computer memory shows only 71, similarly it has a built-in mechanism to remind the player that anything larger than 71 is impossible. Also, the player may deduce that political instability depends at least in part on successful economic policies from the concluding computer script.

Other portions of such computer programs are not intuitively obvious to the reader, but are important to understanding how closely such a simulation mirrors reality: The welcoming statement and the ending statement in the above program use a random-number generator to mimic accidental events beyond the individual's control. As any farmer can tell you, no matter how technologically advanced the farming methods, accidents of weather and other natural forces may nullify the blood, sweat, and tears of farming effort. HAMMURABI includes random-number generation to mimic the probabilities of such events as earthquakes, floods, or being born into a family with a certain number of acres of arable land.

Computer games of the type illustrated by HAMMURABI are more for teaching than research purposes because of their structured scripts. However, another type of human-machine simulation is productive in the area of research. This is a two-step gaming simulation. During the first step, the simulation takes place with probable characteristics such as described by Coleman (1964: 1058–1059):

1. First, a delineation of the principle roles in the system, and the structure of the system.
2. A general model of purposive behavior of persons in roles, following the expanded notion of economic man set down in recent theoretical statements.
3. Detailed (through largely qualitative) observation of behavior of persons in each of the roles in the system, to determine the principal costs and returns involved in each possible action by a person in the role.
4 A synthesis of the above information into a simulated social system.

In the second step, the information gleaned from the human simulation is fed into a computer simulation as its database. The value of this is apparent, in reconsidering that computer simulation builds steps of selecting appropriate *processes* and *sequencing* of units. There may be many alternative processes and sequencings that seem plausible until one has simulated, after which one may narrow down the choices to flow chart and program. Conceivably, one may alternate human and computer simulations like this for some period of time before one hits upon the best modular fit.

Computer Simulations

Unlike human simulations, where human actors make the decisions, computer-simulation decision making depends on extremely precise definitions. If the simulationist wished to emulate racial equality and inequality processes, computer operationalization would require precision in defining "racial equality" to mean something such as equal proportions of all racial groups in each occupation and at each level of education and income.

Second, computer simulation requires that large amounts of data on the system to be analyzed be stored in the computer's memory. These data must be quantitative (ordinal, cardinal, or ratio) in nature. Generally speaking, these data must be reasonably accurate if the old computer wisdom "garbage in, garbage out" is not to prevail. Abelson (1968:283–308) gives a number of steps in the process of building computer simulations, as summarized below.

1. The problem should be too complex to be handled by traditional methods, but not so global as to defy analysis.
2. The model must have identifiable *units* (individuals, groups, roles) with precisely defined *properties* (variables and constants). There must be some system *inputs* that put system *properties* into motion through specified *processes* and specified *phasing* or sequencing of processes through time, from which *consequences* may be drawn.
3. Organize the sequences of specified processes logically through flow charts.
4. Investigate to determine a suitable computer because all computers do not have the same memory-storage capacities for data and programs.
5. Choose a programming language that is efficient and can accommodate the various processes and sequences in the flow-charting.
6. Write the computer program.
7. "Hand simulation" of the program—run slowly through a simulation step-by-step to uncover unanticipated shortcomings in the program.
8. "Debug" the program. That is, check the program for flaws that must be corrected.
9. Revise the model to improve it theoretically in terms of input specifications or programming options.
10. Utilize data to (a) explore a large set of reasonable assumptions during simulation runs to see which assumptions, if any, are critical to what degree; and (b) gather data relevant to those propositions about which there is considerable quantitative ambiguity.

Heise's work (1988) on INTERACT well illustrates these ten steps. He chose his first problem because *he felt he knew the answer already, and therefore, he could readily verify whether the simulation produced an expected answer*. The question was: What happens when one person insults another person? However, even with the more primitive equations he worked with in those days, it took Heise days using a hand calculator to work through this simple problem. Even then he couldn't be sure he had correctly analyzed the situation. The number of independent variables and equations has become large enough now that a computer is absolutely essential to the analysis. INTERACT, from its inception had clearly identifiable individual and role units with precisely defined properties—ratings of their *goodness, powerfulness*, and *liveliness*. By inputting these ratings for *subjects, behaviors*, and *objects* into Heise's equations, the researcher can quickly identify consequences. The functioning of these equation depends on a logical flow of who does what to whom in what situation. A judge who hands down a sentence to a criminal in a court room is completely in character, and we expect no change in our fundamental feelings toward such a judge. A judge who murders his wife in a sleazy hotel is quite extraordinary, and anyone can conclude that our feelings of such a judge's goodness ratings ought to plummet.

To understand the types of analysis possible with INTERACT, you must understand a little about the semantic differential technique (SD) discussed in Chapter 7. The SD measures three dimensions for any object—goodness (from very bad -4 to very good $+4$), powerfulness (from very impotent -4 to very potent $+4$), and activity (from very inactive -4 to very lively $+4$). Normally, researchers have used the SD to measure particular objects without taking into account the social context of those objects. INTERACT simulates what happens to our feelings toward particular objects based upon the interaction between actors, actor's behaviors, the objects of those behaviors, and the social contexts of those behaviors.

Consider a typical SD set of ratings for a physician $(1.8, 2.1, -.03)$, which implies that physicians are typically perceived as quite good (1.8), very powerful (2.1), and slightly inactive (-0.03). What if a physician were to do something quite out of character with those ratings such as doublecross $(-2.35, -0.35, 1.5)$ a colleague? Certainly we would hold such a doublecrossing physician in lower esteem. In most situations we would predict that a physician who doublecrossed another physician would drop dramatically in our perceptions of goodness. INTERACT goes on to predict that such a physician would also lose power, and be seen as more active than typical because of the somewhat negative (-2.35), impotent (-0.35), and somewhat lively (1.5) effect of doublecrossing a person of the physician's own status. The basic premise of INTERACT is that our actions (and who we act toward, and the social context) at least temporarily change our conceptions of the actor, behavior, object, and context. In fact, INTERACT makes quite specific quantitative predictions about how social situations affect our emotions.

INTERACT quite often produces quite reasonable and interesting conclusions, even if given problems far out of the range of normal experiences. Consider a scenario in which the mother (the object) is manipulated by (behavior) a baby (the actor). Although experts on infant development (Brazelton 1988) clearly show that babies socialize their mothers through their behavior as often as mothers socialize their babies, most adults do *not* perceive this reciprocity. In fact, when INTERACT is told the baby's repertoire of actions are "managing" and "training" types, the program protests that *no such act is fitting* for a baby toward its mother, this is because INTERACT's dictionary of semantic ratings suggests that adults do not normally perceive that babies coerce, deter, shackle, or socialize adults. When I keyed in "the baby manipulates the mother," INTERACT quite reasonably indicated that the mother should "feel afraid, insecure, embarrassed, petrified, terrified, cowardly, or ashamed." This is consistent with reports from mothers of colicky babies; such babies cry incessantly and uncontrollably. Their mothers report feelings of helplessness, frustration, insecurity, embarrassment, and fear—all indicators of lack of control. The program *again predicted that no word describes how the baby feels*; this prediction makes sense, in that adults often wonder what a baby really does feel, and because we find it hard to imagine that a baby might control us. In the case of a baby who manipulates a mother, Heise's program predicts that

SUMMARY

The setting is: unnamed

	E	P	A
Baby sees himself as			
baby	2.0	−2.6	2.5
transient	2.0	−2.6	2.5

In general, Baby can take roles which are: male casual.

Baby sees Mother as

	E	P	A
mother	2.5	1.5	-0.1
transient	2.5	1.5	-0.1

Baby sees their relationship as: physical primary managing training.
Baby has perceived no event.

Mother sees herself as

	E	P	A
mother	2.3	1.9	0.0
transient	2.3	1.9	0.0

In general, Mother can take roles which are: female casual.

Mother sees Baby as

	E	P	A
baby	2.9	−2.0	2.0
transient	2.9	−2.0	2.0

Mother sees their relationship as: verbal primary. Mother perceived no event.

From Baby's perspective:
No act is fitting for [1.1 −1.0 1.9] Baby to Mother. _____
Mother should [1.8 1.1 0.3] please Baby (or compliment, interest, encourage, talk to, welcome, uplift him)._____

From Mother's perspective:
Baby should [1.7 − 0.3 1.4] play with Mother (or sleep with, laugh with, desire, notice her)._____
Mother might [1.8 1.6 1.4] interest Baby (or cheer, assist, apologize to, support, inform, welcome him). _____

From Baby's viewpoint, Baby does manipulate Mother, so [21.7]
No word describes how [−1.8 2.3 0.5] Baby feels._____
Mother should feel [−1.2 −2.1 − 0.3] afraid, insecure, embarrassed, petrified, terrified, cowardly, ashamed. _____

From Mother's viewpoint, Baby does manipulate Mother, so [20.0] Baby should feel [−1.6 1.6 0.7]
contemptuous. _____
Mother feels [−1.0 −1.8 − 0.2] insecure, afraid, cowardly, terrified, scared, self-pitying, petrified.
_____

Annotations (right margin):
— Original Attitude
  E = Evaluation column
  P = Power column
  A = Activity column
— **EPA Status quo scores start here**
— **Suggested status quo EPA ratings and status quo behaviors**
— **Total change in EPA caused by "Baby does manipulate Mother"**
— **Separate EPA change in attitude scores and predicted change in emotions**

Figure 12–4.   Summary output for INTERACT simulation of "The baby manipulated the mother."

the mother should feel like the baby is contemptuous of her inability to control the baby rather than be controlled. This seems reasonable because mothers of colicky babies often feel total loss of control if the situation lasts for weeks without change.

The numbers in Figure 12–4 also aid the interpretation of the simulation. Note that most of the numbers are given in triplicates. These triplicates first give semantic differential (see discussion in Chapter 7) scores of goodness, powerfulness, and liveliness ratings for the original, contextless attitudes. The "transient" attitude line in each case is the same as the line above it because no interaction has yet taken place. The summary in Figure 12–4 indicates that

Americans impute that male babies perceive themselves as very good (2.0), very impotent (−2.6), and very active (2.5) creatures, on average. Americans also impute that babies perceive that mothers are even nicer (compare 2.0 with 2.5), somewhat potent (1.5), and neutral in activity level (−0.1) in general. The way in which Americans perceive the average mother in her role of mother is fairly close to the imputed perceptions of the average baby toward her mother—compare 2.5 with 2.3 in goodness; 1.5 with 1.9 in potency; and −0.1 with 0.0 in activity. However, Americans perceive male babies are considerably nicer than their mothers (2.9 compared to 2.0), a little less impotent (−2.0 compared to −2.6), and less active (2.0 compared to 2.5). (These differences in perceptions are due to gender differences in our culture; not to real mother-baby differences.)

Because I constrained the baby's perception of its relationship to its mother as being managed and trained, INTERACT protests that no act is fitting (see under EPA status quo scores start here). It would take an act that was slightly good (1.1), slightly impotent (−1.0), and quite active (1.9) for the baby to act in such a relationship, and INTERACT has no such word programmed into its dictionary so there is a blank following "Baby to Mother." By contrast INTERACT next suggests behaviors that are "in role" for a mother to her baby from the baby's perspective, such as "compliments," "interests," etc. Then the program gives very appropriate status quo (in-role) behaviors from the mother's perspective. For example, it is appropriate for the baby to play with or notice his or her mother. The program also suggests that the mother might try to interest her baby, or cheer, assist, apologize to, support, inform, or welcome the baby because those actions have EPA scores that satisfy the mother-child role relationship (require EPA of 1.7, −0.3, and 1.4).

INTERACT, in response to the request to check on the outcome of a "baby who manipulates its mother," projects radical changes in the emotional outcomes of such an outrageous act—a *total change* in feelings of goodness, powerfulness, and liveliness of 21.7 points for the baby and 20.0 for the mother. The act is beyond normal words for our newly perceived "super-baby," and its mother feels overwhelmed by the "coup d'état" of the normal mother-child relationship. This is shown from both baby's and mother's perspective. Notice that the only emotion that satisfied INTERACT's equations for the baby's feelings is "contemptuousness" of the mother's weakness of control. The mother, by contrast, from both the baby's and her own perspective has very specific changes in emotional reaction: She may be afraid, insecure, scared, self-pitying, and so forth.

If a program such as INTERACT does not make such an intuitively obvious prediction, the simulationist must explore why it does not, by either revising the model that gave a false conclusion, or by revising theory to accept the new finding. The predictions given by INTERACT often surprise individuals who are naive about criminal victimization theory. Although it seems unjust that humans lower their esteem for a victim by blaming them for being in the wrong place at the wrong time, such theory is well substantiated. For example, most individuals judge the rape victim who was walking her dog in Central Park at 11 P.M. when she was attacked as "asking for it." On the other hand, in other situations the program may be wrong. As with any simulation, INTERACT is no better than the information it has at hand with which to make predictions. Rather than assume that INTERACT or any other simulation is correct, the user must check the results against reality.

The point is that the simulationist should check the results of any simulation against intuition and other information about what constitutes reasonable outcomes. When such a check reveals disagreement, then the simulationist should consider the following possibilities: the formal development of the model is mistaken; the starting assumptions are incorrect or oversimplified; the simulationist's intuition about the field is inadequately developed; or the simulationist has discovered a penetrating new principle.

Robert Axelrod's (1984) work on the evolution of cooperation provides another classic illustration of the advantages of computer simulations in social research. He started off with a very simple question: "When should a person cooperate, and when should a person be selfish, in an ongoing interaction with another person?" (p. vii) Axelrod set up a round-robin Prisoner's Dilemma tournament in 1979, in which he asked leading game theorists to submit computer programs that mimicked whatever strategy the simulationists thought would win the tournament. Only two rules restricted the simulationists: First, the program could use only a binary response of cooperate or defect; and second, it had to store the results of the preceding responses of the other computer program in memory for use on succeeding trials. Fourteen academic simulationists sent Axelrod programs to which Axelrod added a fifteenth program, RANDOM, which simulated a control group through a simple random-number generator that cooperated when it generated "0" and defected on the appearance of a "1."

As in any round-robin tournament, Axelrod pitted each program strategy against every other one in a variation of the prisoner's dilemma, in which both players received 3 points for mutual cooperation; both received 1 point for mutual defection; and if one cooperated and the other player defected, the cooperator's "sucker's payoff" was a no-point accumulation and the temptation for a lone defection was 5 points. He decided the winner by the total number of points each strategy accumulated over the course of roughly 150 trials in five separate tournaments to control for chance factors. Anatol Rapoport—a highly respected Canadian psychologist—submitted a program, TIT FOR TAT that won the tournament. His four-line program was the shortest, and encompassed just two rules: Cooperate on the first move; then mimic the other player's move in succeeding trials.

It helps to compare the various strategies to understand why TIT FOR TAT did so well. For example, a mathematician submitted a program named after himself: JOSS. JOSS also began by cooperating on the first move, and normally it mimicked the other player's moves in succeeding trials. However, JOSS used a random-number generator to pull a "surprise defection" 10% of the time, following the other player's cooperation. Immediately following this surprise defection, however, JOSS returned to cooperation. Against TIT FOR TAT, the two players ended up in an even worse position for the rest of the match: the mutual defection cell.

Axelrod stressed that it was not the combination of strategies that was at fault. JOSS beat TIT FOR TAT with an average of 230 to 225 points for the five games, but TIT FOR TAT averaged a first-place winning 504 points overall against all other players versus a twelfth place 304 points for JOSS. (RANDOM came in dead last in this tournament with just over half of TIT FOR TAT's overall points.)

Axelrod next opened up a second tournament to anybody who wished to enter, through a series of advertisements in computer hobby magazines. He sent a detailed analysis of the results of the first tournament to all the applicants. He received programs back from 62 individuals from six different nations and eight different academic disciplines. This new set of programs, due to the results of the first tournament, was considerably more sophisticated. Whereas the longest program in the first tournament had run 77 lines of instruction, the longest in this tournament was 155. Interestingly, neither length of program nor programming language—FORTRAN or BASIC—made any real difference in explanation of the results.

Although Axelrod had allowed entrants to resubmit any of the programs from the previous tournament only Rapoport resubmitted TIT FOR TAT. Once again, TIT FOR TAT won the round-robin play, and RANDOM came in dead last again. As an example of an unsuccessful program, we might consider a "super-nice" strategy, TIT FOR TWO TATS, which only came in twenty-fourth out of the 62 (not counting RANDOM) entrants. Other program strategies simply took advantage of this super-nice strategy of "turning both cheeks" when the other person defected. The poor results of this program show that there are limits to being forgiving.

The reader can see the advantage of computer simulations over true experiments quite easily by now compared even to doing simple two-person gaming with simple rules such as TIT FOR TAT has. It would be nearly impossible to get humans to stick to one particular strategy under laboratory conditions, and even if that were possible, it would be exceedingly costly to pair 63 individual conditions (including the last-place RANDOM), each with at least 15 individuals for statistical purposes. The 3,969 combinations (63×63) of strategies would be beyond the province of time and money in the most well endowed of laboratories. Furthermore, even in Axelrod's study, the number of simulation combinations was so large that for the purposes of understanding why TIT FOR TAT succeeded, he found it necessary to compare differences in program strategies based on their rank order. By comparing the top 15 finishers with the bottom 15, he noticed some interesting patterns: a "not-nice" strategy (defect after the other player cooperates) appeared in only one of the top 15, a "nice" strategy (cooperate after the other play cooperates) appeared in only one of the bottom 15; winning strategies were typically uncomplicated and transparent; and successful programs were "forgiving," in that they went back to cooperation as soon as the other player did.

It is doubtful that Axelrod could have completed this award-winning work—it won the American Association for the Advancement of Science's 1981 annual Newcomb Cleveland Prize in social psychology—using human experiments. It is ironic, also, that Axelrod uses anthropomorphic terms to describe the results of this computer simulation tournament; he uses such words as "trust," "nice," "retaliation," and "cooperation" as if these strategies simulated human intelligence. It is also ironic that no entrant tried techniques inspired by artificial intelligence programs used to play chess (Axelrod 1984:39). Had someone used a "look ahead" rule in the second tournament, as someone had in the smaller first 15-rule tournament, Axelrod demonstrated after the fact that it would have won with 520 points to TIT FOR TAT's 504 points. In the next section just such newer techniques and goals are considered.

ARTIFICIAL INTELLIGENCE

How would you feel if you overheard a conversation with the following types of sentences, "The computer knows that . . .", "The computer feels that . . .," "That computer is intelligent," or "The computer is knowledgeable"? These sentences challenge our definitions of intelligence and knowledge. The field of artificial intelligence combines highly immodest ambition with a suggestion of deceit. Its proponents have created nonnumeric computer programs that can emulate expert knowledge within very narrow fields. These programs work well in sorting facts, but are presently out of their depths when called to generate new knowledge to solve a problem. On the other hand, artificial intelligence experts have also written programs, which simply trick humans into thinking a computer is intelligent. Consider the following dialogue between a patient and her "understanding therapist":

> I'm depressed much of the time.
> *I'm sorry to hear that. In what way are you depressed?*
> People are always bugging me.
> *Can you think of a specific example?*
> Well, my husband made me come here.
> *Your husband made you—that's interesting.*
> It's true. He's as domineering as my mother.
> *Tell me more about your family.*
> My mother and I are always fighting over the phone.
> *Who else in your family do you have regular contact with?*
> My father.
> *Let's talk about your father.*
> You are like my father in some ways.
> *Tell me about the resemblance.*

Although this dialogue seems realistic, a computer program called ELIZA created the *italized* portion. Joseph Weisenbaum (1976) of the Massachusetts Institute of Technology created ELIZA in 1965 to sharpen the growing debate over what is real versus artificial intelligence. Because ELIZA has tricked many individuals into think they were interacting with a psychiatrist, it has come to have something of a cult following among computer aficionados. In actuality, ELIZA is a clever program that simply scans the input messages to locate keywords that are part of its existing knowledge base; for example, "father" is easily matched with "family" and "like" with "resemblance."

This debate over what is true knowledge goes back to the 1940s, when a British mathematician, Alan Turing, proposed a test that, in his honor, has come to be known as the Turing test (Hofstadter 1979). The *Turing test* consists of an interrogator communicating via teleprinters with a human and a computer: It would be the interrogator's job to determine which is which via conversation over the communication links. Turing predicted that it would become commonplace among the well-educated public to speak of machines thinking by the year 2000. Indeed, artificial intelligence (known by its acronym AI among its proponents) has grown into a full-time pursuit with just this goal in mind.

Although ELIZA fools many people, the Turing test presumes that an intelligent machine would have to pay attention to the actual *meaning* of the sentences—not just to the presence of certain words—if it were to fool people. Clearly, ELIZA fails this test. However, such programs have helped shape our recognition of the communication problem because experts now realize how closely interwoven are communication and knowledge. The approach that early work in artificial intelligence took was "to translate input sentences into a internal formal language that, theoretically, would allow the system to perform inferences, without needing to handle all the subtleties of ordinary conversation" (Roberts 1981: 166). Work during the 1980s changed toward more promising approaches.

AI researchers no longer like to differentiate between the computer program and the knowledge embodied in that program. As newer computer languages like LISP (short for Listing Processor) and PROLOG (short for Programming in Logic) have been developed and have become available at more reasonable prices on personal computers, AI researchers have found it increasingly possible to develop knowledge systems that learn and grow through self-modification. Buchanan and Shortliffe (1985) developed MYCIN to provide diagnosis and therapy selection for blood infections and meningitis. It has outperformed human diagnosticians in the identification and treatment of diseases in both classes. Similarly, geologists (Marble, Calkins, & Peuquet 1984) have reported the use of AI in PROSPECTOR to locate important mineral deposits heretofore not uncovered through traditional geologic methods. Social scientists are not as far advanced in developing such programs, but are having successes that will be described in later sections. In the meantime, AI researchers have produced a remarkable base of knowledge about the nature of knowledge and workings of the human brain that are useful to all simulationists.

Types of Knowledge

We need to distinguish between intelligent behavior and behavior that only appears to be intelligent before we discuss knowledge. ELIZA is a good example of a computer program that appears to be intelligent but is not, but even humans may appear to be intelligent but not be so. Daniel Dennett (1984:264) designed the "Chinese Game" after John Searle's thought experiment, in which people might behave as if they were perfectly fluent in a foreign language while, in reality, not being able to understand a word of it. In Dennett's work computers operate as simple sets of rules which may be applied to one set of symbols in order to produce another set. This is seen in numerous instances of the "funny English" used by Japanese who appear to know our language. Japanese coin phrases like "From now" (When meaning to say "from now on"), patterned after the Japanese "Ima kara," which make no sense to an American unless you understand the rules of Japanese grammar. Similarly, the Japanese might coin a new word like Calpis©—the trademark for a popular milk-based soft drink—without any comprehension of the nausea they have created in an American's mind. (Of course, Americans also use "funny Japanese" in the mirror-image of this process by applying English rules to Japanese.)

Clearly, then, there are different aspects of knowledge. First, there is *factual knowledge* which may consist of textbook facts. Although such knowledge is relatively easy to build into a computer program, it is also the most trivial aspect of knowledge. Human brains are not simple repositories of facts or information, and knowledge is not simply a mass of data such as the individual words: "from," "now," and "on." Psychologists have long known that human intelligence operates by *chunking* things into units: People remember a phrase or units of meaning rather than abstract strings of letters or words.

Humans don't randomly solve problems. They invent rules of thumb to organize facts: Chess masters don't reason any better or faster than anybody else—their mastery comes from more than having learned thousands of board positions and strategies; it also comes from having learned how to put that knowledge to use when needed. Expertise consists of hundreds of rules of thumb that have been laboriously distilled from such experience. AI experts therefore claim that human knowledge is organized into *schema*—sets of pigeonholes or boxes for related facts and rules of thumb; and *frames*—elaborate structures for making sense of data.

Second, therefore, humans use heuristic knowledge. *Heuristic knowledge* consists of the complex and normally fuzzy set of problem-solving strategies we use. We often use a few vague rules of thumb to make the multitude of choices confronting us more manageable. Heuristic knowledge also includes our intuitions, associations, judgments, rules, pet theories, and general inference-making procedures. Whereas our factual knowledge consists of such bits of information as what clothes are in our wardrobes, how we decide what to wear normally is based on heuristic knowledge. A working woman might have 15 outfits and 10 pairs of shoes. She probably uses a few simple heuristics for deciding which shoes to wear with outfits: matching colors are okay, black and brown do not go together, pink is not suitable for work hours, and so on.

Heuristic knowledge most often consists of rules based on context or situation. Consider the knowledge required to understand the differences in the use of "seized," "club," and "drove off" in the following sentences:

David seized the steering mechanism, and drove off.
David seized the burglar's hands, and handcuffed them.
David seized the club and drove off.

A human with knowledge of golf could understand that the "club" in the third sentence implied golf, that the ball flew down the fairway, and that the first sentence involved some sort of vehicle. A human could also easily understand the three different uses of "seize." Presumably, the second sentence refers to David in the role of an authority of the law. Even more subtle is the context required to understand the meaning of "Mary had a little lamb." "Had" in this sentence, depending on context, could imply owned, ate, had sex with, gave birth to, etc. Much of the effort of artificial intelligence experts is spent in programming much simpler heuristics into programs.

A third type of knowledge is emotional. *Emotional knowledge* consists of human needs and affect that assume an intelligence that can experience, share, empathize, and grasp "the problem." Although ELIZA fools many people into thinking it has emotional knowledge, it has no ability to understand human problems. John Updike, in his novel *Roger's Version*, cleverly illustrates the difference between artificial and human intelligence, when he has a young computer programmer state that "Hofstadter can talk all he wants about Strange Loops, but until he builds one that can make a computer reprogram itself or get so bored inside its box it commits suicide, it's in the same category as life assembling itself in the primordial soup." Similarly, one of my students after working for two semesters with INTERACT, correctly noted an irony in its program: It can correctly predict changes in emotions that humans experience in different social contexts with a high degree of accuracy; however, it can neither understand those emotions nor does it get bored with endless repetition.

One of the great challenges before AI is the establishment of machines that behave purposively and use feedback to approximate closer human knowledge. Such a machine would also need to have intentionality—humans can empathize with the characters of a story and understand "hunger, fright, anger" symbolized by these words. It takes more than just using one set of words or language to code or define another. Artificial intelligence is concerned with mechanizing processes we do not fully understand, although we may routinely perform them without apparent effort or difficulty.

Rule-Based Systems

Allen Newell and Herbert Simon of Carnegie-Mellon University created the first true AI program, LOGIC THEORIST back in the late 1950s. LOGIC THEORIST demonstrated that a computer could perform a genuine intellectual task: It could prove a theorem in symbolic logic, and it could use the process of deduction. The starting point in symbolic logic resembles a high-school geometry proof: It begins with a set of premises, and the goal is another statement known as the theorem. The logician combines and modifies premises through a half-dozen rules of inference, until the manipulation applied in the right order produces the theorem.

Consider such a statement as *A leader decides what shall be done, or assigns subordinates to particular tasks.* In symbolic notation, let the symbol *P* stand for the phrase *A leader decides what shall be done*; let *Q* stand for *The leader assigns subordinates to particular tasks*; and let the symbol *v* stand for *or*. Then this statement can be written in symbolic logic as

P v Q

Additionally, symbolic logic represents IF-THEN statements with an arrow: →. Consider the following two facts from knowledge of triads and coalition formation for any three persons *A, B,* and *C*: (1) *The coalition of BC dominates the more powerful individual, person A* and (2) *If BC dominates person A, then the coalition is revolutionary*. We can represent the deduction about the coalition in this way:

R (statement 1) is true
R (statement 1) → *S* (statement 2) is true
Therefore, *S* is also true

Simply translating verbal statements into such types of symbolic statements is not so important as the fact that once translated, the logician may manipulate rules of inference, in much the same way as one manipulates an algebraic equation by adding or subtracting from each side.

Symbolic logic-based programs using such languages as LISP and PROLOG translate symbolic logic into what logicians term *predicate calculus* with a rigorous syntactic structure. A sentence in predicate calculus is called a "*well-formed formula*" (*wff*) and is made up of simpler "atomic formulae" which, in turn, consists of "predicate symbols," "variable symbols," " function symbols," and "constant symbols." Constant symbols are like nouns and predicate symbols are like verbs. Thus, "Rick likes Judy" would translate into the following predicate calculus as

LIKE(RICK,JUDY).

More generally, we could employ such sentences as LIKE (X,Y) to substitute any liking pair. Similarly,

—LIKE(X,Y)

is a general statement for X does not like Y. How do you think Rick will feel if he finds out that

—LIKE(JUDY,RICK)?

Using LOGIC THEORIST, Newell and Simon were eventually able to complete proofs of Newton's classic *Principia Mathematica* theorems. In fact, Alan Turing (1936) had already predicted that a simple-minded symbolic logic machine would be capable of computing any logical reasoning process, no matter how complicated through the use of algorithms. An *algorithm* is a procedure that must be followed to solve a problem, a set of instructions to be implemented in a given order. For the mean average, a three-step algorithm is necessary: (1) count the number of figures to be averaged; (2) add up all the individual figures; and (3) divide step 1 by step 2.

Newell and Simon's work led them to work on more general human intellectual tasks. This work culminated in their book *Human Problem Solving* (1972). In this important work, Newell and Simon introduced the prototype for later AI programs: **General Problem Solver (GPS). GPS** was the first computer program to attempt separation between general problem-solving heuristics that applied across the board, such as the rules of symbolic logic, and specific rules of thumb that applied only to the task at hand—what AI researchers call domain-specific knowledge. No longer did programmers have to tell in minute detail what to do, step by step, but they could instead focus on what to know.

Although Newell and Simon's work revolutionized work in AI, the focus on what to know has proven incredibly tedious and time-consuming in and of itself. As an example, consider game playing which has been one of the most successful branches of AI. Backgammon and checkers programs now exist which consistently beat the top-ranked players. The top Chess program, DEEP THOUGHT, produced at Carnegie-Mellon University, was seeded at the grandmaster level of over 2,500 points (compared to the top human level of 2,800 points) in 1990 for the first time in history.

In theory, game playing poses problems which can be solved only by some set of logical rules. the concept of a game (or a task or problem of any kind) presupposes a given set of rules or logical constraints, a variety of alternative states, and the transformation of any state. Some parts of this problem are easily solved. You can see this in the standard "look-up" tables by which computer chess games operate—they can play the first few moves with standard responses if the human opponent uses a standard move. Using these standard look-up tables, a computer may be programmed to look ahead a certain number of moves.

But the heuristics get complicated quickly with nonstandard moves because of the number of possible permutations of moves. One means of solving this problem is to have humans collaborate by programming the machine to ask for advice. The human then gives advice, and the machine modifies its heuristics if the advice differs from its own conclusions. However, for a human, rules are made to be broken. The chess master knows when to concentrate on a certain area of the board, and to ignore others which are not relevant to the developing strategy. The chess master then can be ready for an unexpected opening outside the province of any yet known look-up table.

Theoretically, much of human problem solving is like a game, in that it, too, is always in a certain state. The problem for the problem solver is to discover the quickest way from the starting state to a solution or goal state. To do this, the machine has to keep a list of known states. This means that only problems that are well-defined and fairly limited in known states are currently under the province of AI research. To understand why, let us consider a few of the strategies by which AI programs may work: brute-force, best-first reasoning, forward and backward reasoning, and bidirectional searches.

Brute-force searches are the simplest, but they are also totally undiscriminating. The program must generate each branch of a logic tree and explore each in turn. An expert knows that all knowledge is not equal, but this type of rule ignores that wisdom. The first computer-based chess games usually employed the brute-force method in spite of the fact that there are at least 10^{120} possible moves in the game—well beyond the limits of any foreseeable computer's memory. Nevertheless, a chess program that can look ahead eight moves in a few seconds clearly has an advantage over a non-Master-level player. But the brute-force search is not intelligent; it reminds us of the legendary monkey who works at the typewriters of the British Museum, and eventually completes production of the works of Shakespeare through random typing methods! Such a feat defies reasonable imagination.

The true expert uses some form of a *best-first search rule*. Experts do not think faster than nonexperts: rather, they know gestalts; they search for patterns. Normally, the expert does not need to search everything, but can jump around through the search space, generating a series of possible solutions in rapid succession, and quickly discarding those that lead nowhere. Just as the chess master need not consider all of the possible moves in turn, studies by cognitive scientists into expert human problem solving shows that experts do not think faster than nonexperts. The expert knows a wealth of material, but more importantly, the expert imposes particular schema onto new problems to more quickly look for similarities and differences with problems the expert already knows how to solve. Much of the progress in expert-consulting systems comes from learning and applying the rules by which experts decide their best-first searches.

Forward reasoning is a third method of arriving at intelligent solutions. If a problem has only one starting state but many alternative solutions, forward reasoning is a highly appropriate method of problem solving. Chess gives a classic analogy: It has only one starting state for both players, but an incredible number of means by which one may win. Without "looking forward" at least four moves, a player will quickly be eliminated by a good player. Similarly, for writing a text such as this one, there are an infinite number of alternative solutions for arriving at a satisfactory product. The first draft must consider the steps needed to achieve some desired goal. This is another reason why our mythical monkey in the British Museum will almost assuredly not type out even one sentence of Shakespeare's work at random: It has no meaningful rules with which to order the characters on its keyboard. Expert systems may be structured to use forward reasoning. The program may apply the rules to facts already known, and deduce whatever additional facts it can.

This third means of intelligent action employs *backward reasoning*, where the individual works backward from the finished product or goal to the original state. For proving a theorem already known, it makes sense to work backwards from the goal state to the starting state. Engineers often employ this type of reasoning when they reverse engineer; that is, when they take a competitor's finished product and break it down to understand how the competitor made it. Expert consulting systems may be structured to simulate backward reasoning through starting with one or more hypotheses and testing them one at a time.

But what seems like a promising sequence of state changes may lead, not to a solution, but an impasse or deadlock. For this reason, many complex problems require both forward and backward reasoning. *Bidirectional reasoning* uses both forward and backward rules of knowing. The goal of bidirectional reasoning is to compare logic paths to discover which one is the shortest, or to find out whether the forward and backward paths diverge or are the same. If one path is shorter, then that path is preferred. If the paths are the same in both directions, then the researcher gains confidence that the results indicate the preferred rule. However, if the paths diverge, the results suggest at best alternative solutions and at worst uncertainty over the best path.

The predicate calculus spoken of earlier operationalizes uncertainty through the concept of fuzzy logic. *Fuzzy logic* is reasoning based on uncertainty and vagueness. Humans use maddening amounts of fuzzy logic; we used such vague comparisons as old-young, good-bad, and beautiful-ugly; we say "maybe I'll come," and "probably it'll rain." The simulationist employing predicate calculus tries to tighten up human vagueness with probability statements. For example, if you played by TIT FOR TAT rules with another person who appeared to play by the same rules "occasionally," the simulationist might try to find out how often "occasionally" was. In the case of JOSS, mentioned earlier, we know that "sometimes" is 10% of the time after a cooperative move. In predicate calculus, this would translate into:

COOPERATE (TIT FOR TAT) > DEFECT (JOSS, 10%)

which denotes the conclusion that TIT FOR TAT's cooperative moves will be followed 10% of the time by Joss's defection, although we cannot know for sure when it will defect. This is a mirror of life when we say "It is pretty certain that. . ." or "It is unlikely that. . ."

Expertise requires accumulation of a lifetime of such chunks of information, with all its maddening, apparently illogical exceptions. Indeed, some of the most interesting components of social life defy logic. There are numerous social exceptions to the mathematical law of transitivity that if A > B, and B > C, then A > C. In sports, team A consistently beats team B, which invariably beats team C, yet team C may beat team A consistently. Similarly, human liking relationships between three individuals tend toward transitivity, and the exceptions to that rule also appear to follow a few simple rules. The strain toward transitivity in friendships may depend upon such factors as salience and amount of inequality. Some individuals are simply insensitive to intransitivity in their relationships; and the more inequality that exists, the more salient that intransitivity may become. The designer of expert systems must take these types of exceptions into account

Expert Systems and Intelligence Amplifiers

The most successful by-product of AI research is, unquestionably, the pre-packaged expertise of expert systems. Some specialized knowledge domains such as tax laws and governmental regulations are well codified and routinized. Such domains seem especially suitable for the development of what has been termed expert systems, consultation systems, or knowledge-based system. Schuerman (1987:14) states that "an area is a candidate for the development of expert systems, if it requires reasoning about the facts of a given situation, followed by exercise of judgment in an area requiring professional skill and knowledge. . . .However, areas characterized by a great deal of novelty or creativity are unlikely to yield to an expert system approach."

MYCIN—a physician's consultant for blood and meningitis infections—provides a classic example of a successful expert system program. Below is a sample output from the middle of a consultation between MYCIN and a physician:

> **MYCIN:** Is the meningitis a hospital-acquired infection?
> **DOCTOR:** NO
> **M:** IS Pt103's (NOTE to reader: Denotes patient 103) clinical history consistent with EPIGLOTTITIS?
> **D:** NO
> **M:** Is Pt103's clinical history consistent with OTITIS MEDIA?
> **D:** NO
> **M:** Has the patient ever been to an area that is endemic for coccidiomycoses?
> **D:** UNKNOWN

MYCIN, like any intelligence-amplifying software, consists of a *knowledge base* that consists of a structured collection of facts and rules with which to communicate knowledge or expertise. For MYCIN, this knowledge base is equivalent to the knowledge about infection that physicians carry around in their heads. In MYCIN's cases, there are just less than 500 rules such as:

IF   (i)   the infection is meningitis, and
        (ii)   organisms were not seen in the stain of the culture, and
        (iii) the type of infection may be bacterial, and
        (iv) the patient has been seriously burned,
THEN there is suggestive evidence that *Pseudonomas aeruginosa* might be one of the organisms causing the infection.

MYCIN is programmed to ask specific questions, using this existing general knowledge base to build up a data base about the patient which holds the equivalent of the patient's clinical history that a physician would normally write down on paper forms attached to a clipboard. The physician may add or delete knowledge from this knowledge base, just as the physician would with traditional paper-and-pen form.

Separate from this knowledge base is an *inference engine*, which is a routine that performs the actual logical operations (inference building) that reaches conclusions. Expert system designers have found it necessary to separate the inference engine from the knowledge base, so that they can easily add or modify rules without drastically changing the behavior of the whole system. The inference engine controls the program—it controls what the program does next.

An expert system may also have an *explanation system*. MYCIN provides a credible consultation system; that is, the physician may question and evaluate its advice. For example, a physician may query why MYCIN wants to know, if patient Pt103 is a burn patient. So the physician types in "WHY." MYCIN responds: Rule 478. Furthermore, MYCIN will list as explanation a list of the rules that it applied, which support the conclusion and which do not, and will list a table of probabilities that the rule supports the conclusion. For example, MYCIN might list five rules with probabilities ranging from 0.1 to 0.4 that bacterial infection exists, and one rule that suggests that bacterial infection does not exist with a probability of 0.1. The physician can then weight the evidence as clearly favoring bacterial infection.

MYCIN *doesn't know why a rule is valid, so it has no way of knowing when to break the rules. This is always a problem with expert systems: They treat the world as a self-contained set of rules that does not encompass all of knowledge.* Knowledge engineers start by making a list of things the program ought to know, and by putting some rules into the program. Then, they try the program out on some test cases, they see how it goes wrong, fix the rules, and start over, testing the program with new cases. The knowledge engineer needs to sit down with experts who relate exceptions to rules to which the knowledge engineer attempts to recast the IF-THEN rules. It took over 20 person-years to build up the rules in MYCIN by this procedure. Although Artificial Intelligence systems can reason by analogy, at this writing there is no such system that can learn from its own mistakes.

The designers of MYCIN were so successful at diagnosing and prescribing treatment that they took the inference engine from MYCIN, and developed an expert system *shell* to which they could add other medical knowledge. Most commercial expert systems shells are based on MYCIN's original design: Shells are bare bones of knowledge domains to which the purchaser can add. But humans also have a methodology—a means of reasoning about facts which allows us to infer other facts and take appropriate actions. The shells are no better than the means by which they allow such reasoning processes to be incorporated into their structure.

PLACECON is an experimental consulting system for the placement of child welfare cases modeled after MYCIN. An example of one of its production rules is (Schuerman 1987:15)

IF	Placement is needed, and
	Relatives are available, and
	Relatives are able to care for the child, and
	Relatives are willing
THEN	Place the child with relatives.

Schuerman's program, as with MYCIN, queries the user to build up a set of facts about particular cases; for example, it would have "yes" and "no" answers to "need for placement" and the availability of relatives that could be changed over time as the child's situation changed or new cases were entered. It also has an inference engine that uses both *forward chaining* and *backward chaining*—the inference engine's operationalizations of forward and backward reasoning discussed earlier—to represent hypotheses about the merits and demerits of returning the child to the home, placing the child with relatives, or placing the child elsewhere. As with any quality expert system, the user can query PLACECON to justify the reasoning process it used in placement.

Although PLACECON is still in the experimental stage, a few successful expert systems do exist in the social science for specialized purposes. Brent (1987) created EX-SAMPLE as a means of routinizing the decision-making process involved in sampling. As Chapter 5 notes, probability sampling involves a number of well-known rules concerning such things as the amount of funds available, time necessary, response rates, and so on. Such a well-defined, but technically complex, body of expert knowledge is well suited for expert systems.

The complexity introduced by expert systems has led some researchers to search for more parsimonious uses of expert systems. Garson (1987), for example, set about comparing a 51-rule expert system for explaining satisfaction levels in 198 legislative bodies. Although a 51-rule system came close to explaining all cases, Garson found that a six-rule system explained 52% of the cases, while most of the remaining rules only covered one or two cases each. For example, the mean majority party legislative satisfaction level was high, if the number of days was less than 93.5 and the percentage of chamber bills passed was more than 68% (Garson 1987:19). Garson's point is well taken: Although a physician using MYCIN would care greatly about the rules that explained the minority of cases, a designer of any expert system set of rules ought to be most concerned with those that are most important. Always remember: All knowledge is not created equal.

Expert systems do not always impress experts. Experts do not care so much about help with routine tasks so much as with tasks they themselves find difficult: The expert system ultimately ought to be knowledge-enhancing. Therefore, Heise (1986) has programmed a special type of inference-building and testing machine he calls ETHNO (short for ethnography) for systematizing the analysis of social interaction, with the goal of explicating the necessary and sufficient conditions underlying the structure or dynamics of any set of events.

ETHNO is structured to ask questions designed to reveal the logical order in a set of, or series of, social events. Among the major problems of sequential analysis of social behavior are setting priorities for social events, analyzing their logical consistency, understanding the constraints a particular set of events places on the generation of new interactional sequences, and generating new interactional sequences that flow from the structure of given social settings. ETHNO can aid the understanding of all of these.

ETHNO, unlike many other expert systems, comes with no built-in factual base about the event to be analyzed because fieldwork is predicated on lack of such knowledge. It starts out by asking what appear to the expert user to be dumb questions. ETHNO queries the user to give a brief account of what events occurred, and the logical relationships between those events. As it builds a logical data base of user-answers, it stops repeating its early "dumb" questions. In fact, many of its later queries become a challenge to the best of experts. It operates by using the rules of symbolic logic to systematically ask the user to validate or refute whether any particular event is essential for another event to occur.

As an example, I have used the classic game between TIT FOR TAT and JOSS discussed earlier in this chapter (Axelrod 1984:37). In that description, both players cooperated (CC) on the first five moves, before JOSS's random-number generator pulled its first surprise defection or CD (TIT FOR TAT cooperates, JOSS defects). This set up a series of 19 plays, in which the two players alternated cooperating and defecting—CD,DC, CD . . . . The reason for the alternation is that neither side has a memory span larger than the very *last* move of the opponent. Therefore, on the twentieth move TIT FOR TAT remembers only that JOSS defected on the nineteenth, and JOSS remembers only that TIT FOR TAT cooperated on the nineteenth. As a result, each "mimics" the last move each remembers, causing them to alternate between CD and DC. After roughly 10 more plays, JOSS pulled its second surprise defection, and the remaining 176 moves became a boring exercise of both players defecting.

Figure 12–5 below shows why—once JOSS made its first surprise defection—this outcome was inevitable. The game is essentially reduced to the relationships between four moves. An ETHNO diagram should be read by first looking at the top most three-symbol icon (T&J in this case), and then working backwards from the bottom (Coo in Figure 12–5). The initial reciprocated cooperation between the two players over the first five moves is shown by the Coo–T&J path. That is, one starts off by keying in "Coo" for "cooperate" because TIT FOR TAT is always programmed to start off by cooperating. ETHNO then asks if T&J requires this action. Because it is necessary, the researcher replies "Yes." This action leads to the screen appearance of the right-hand ninety-degree line between T&J and Coo, which represents the necessary "tie" between each. Then, when the researcher keys in another "cooperate" to represent JOSS's rule to cooperate with a cooperator, the program asks, "Does Coo require this action?" and "Does T&J require this action?" As it requires both, the researcher types in "Yes" and the program assigns "Clo" to this new rule of the game, and places the "Clo" notation along the line between T&J and Coo.

Once ETHNO establishes that cooperation is essential to cooperation by both players and to the game, it does not bore the researcher with asking that question again throughout the remaining cooperation-cooperation moves. However, after JOSS's first surprise defection, ETHNO is designed to query

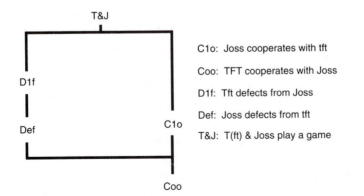

Figure 12–5.   An ETHNO simulation of a typical TIT-FOR-TAT game with JOSS.

once again. Because this defection is not essential (it is random), and is outside the cooperation-cooperation rule that ETHNO knows, the screen display splits this first defection (Def) off from the cooperative move, and places Def on the left-most line. Notice that it does *not* draw a special line with both Def and Coo or Def and Clo.

In a sense, ETHNO suggests in Figure 12–5 that this first defection is critical because it no longer queries (is surprised by) any cooperate-defect sequences. However, at move 24, JOSS pulls its surprise defection for the second time. This time TIT FOR TAT does defect, setting up an infinity of DD moves. When TIT FOR TAT defects in response to JOSS's second defection, ETHNO asks if a defection is a requirement for a defection. Because both players are programmed to defect in response to a defection, the correct answer is "yes." This response sets up the Def D1f relationship shown on the left side of Figure 12–5. Like TIT FOR TAT, ETHNO needs *one* lesson to learn that JOSS is a sneaky player to be watched carefully in the future. Basically, Figure 12–5 suggests that two persons playing by TIT FOR TAT's and JOSS's rules have only two ways to play—use cooperation (alternate between Coo and Clo) or use defection (alternate between Def and D1f). That is, the two players can live in a spirit of mutual trust or mutual distrust. The first defection sends a message to TIT FOR TAT to be on the lookout for a second sucker's payoff, in which case TIT FOR TAT will not be burnt twice!

Because most event structures may involve chains or sequences of events that are very long, the implications of relationships between events may easily tax and warp the human sensory system. Chapter 10 (Field Research) and 11 (Historical Research) have already discussed some of the problems with the human sensory system in collecting data relevant to some of ETHNO's rules. For example, historians do not trust facts in and of themselves. A fact must always be checked and weighed against other evidence. ETHNO includes important checks on the status of facts: whether prior events are essential for the current one, whether one event implies another, and so on. Because ETHNO is based on psychologic evidence that "no" answers are less trustworthy than "yes" answers, and that humans poorly consider events widely separated in a chain of events, the program will tediously ask questions of the user to explicate the actual relationships between events. Similarly, because not all information is of uniform use, Heise's (1988, p. 140) program operates by heuristics like "events with fewer prerequisites should have lower priority; higher priority events will occur more often and with shorter intervening periods." ETHNO transcends these heuristic ideas; it computes priorities precisely, although we still have more to learn about which computations are appropriate.

Toward Truly Intelligent Computer Systems

To date, most efforts of AI researchers have involved writing ad hoc programs that focus only on one minute aspect of any particular phenomenon. A general program's reasoning will always be characterized by false starts and dead ends. It has no way to simply recognize the solution the way an expert will say "AHA!

That's a (fill-in blank) type of problem." For this reason, most AI research has turned increasingly toward a focus on the specific domains of knowledge encapsulated by expert systems.

Although some of these programs outperform even the human experts, when they encounter an unusual problem that its rules do not cover, they come to an abrupt halt. They have no way to know what to do. A human expert in such a situation would simply go back to first principles and start over from there, using whatever general reasoning methods necessary. The challenge for AI has been to program how the computer is supposed to find that sequence, rather than to tell it what to do. Allen Newell (in press) and his colleagues have made progress toward this goal of creating a computer program that can learn from experience called SOAR.

To understand how SOAR works, it is useful to think of the rule-based system as a society of little demons. These "IF x, THEN DO y" rules spend most of their time in quiet contemplation of something called "working memory," which is a kind of internal blackboard that records data about the current situation. However, when one of them sees something it likes—that is, when the conditions on the IF side of the rule match the current situation in working memory—it jumps up and shrieks out the command listed on its THEN side: "DO *this*." The program obeys, taking whatever actions are demanded, and makes the appropriate changes in working memory. And then everyone settles down again to wait for another demon to jump up.

As long as all goes well, the computer simply follows the orders of each shrieking demon in turn, moving from step to step until it reaches a solution to the problem at hand. However, there are two worst-case scenarios that crop up when: (1) none of the rules apply, and (2) when several demons are activated simultaneously and start struggling for power. What Sewell's team had done is teach the demons some manners, by operating much like an exceedingly polite business conference. Instead of letting the activated demons fight over who gets to give orders, SOAR lets all of them have their say. Only when everyone's opinions are on the table does the program decide what to do. In this way, SOAR automatically uses the most powerful knowledge it has available.

The second difference in SOAR from earlier expert systems is that it treats impasses, or conflicts between the rules, not as crises but as opportunities. Just as a commuter might deal with a traffic jam by turning off on the first available side street and finding a new route home, SOAR automatically deals with each impasse by setting up a new problem—"solve this impasse"—and going to work on it.

The third difference is known among psychologists as *chunking*. Whenever SOAR resolves an impasse, it remembers how. More precisely, SOAR encodes the results of its problem-solving as a new IF-THEN rule—a "chunk"—and then stores it away in memory, where it operates like any other rule. In this way, it does not have to keep reinventing the wheel. Its memory is cumulative. In fact, the next time it encounters the impasse, it "sees" it. For example, in one test, SOAR had originally taken 1,731 steps to solve a problem; on the next attempt, it solved the same problem in only seven steps. These features of SOAR show promise for refining other expert advisory systems.

Expert Advisory Systems and Social Science

Social scientists who use expert advisory systems typically diverge from knowledge engineers in their goals. Shangraw (1987) notes a number of ways in which each differ. First, knowledge engineers usually presume that one expert's theory is as good as another's in building their systems, in spite of the fact that good evidence exists showing that expert judgments vary significantly; two different experts may use quite different rules that lead to different solutions. The solution is to use their systems as guides for postulating theory that "must be verified with other methods or by a larger sample of the expert population" (Shangraw, p. 167). Second, knowledge engineers typically are untrained in good methodologic strategies of observing and questioning their informants that could be made more objective by using social science techniques described in other chapters of this text. Third, Shangraw (p. 168) observes that "the knowledge engineer is confident in his ability to identify expertise; the social scientist is more concerned with setting standards for eliciting expertise." Because all expert advice is not of the same quality, knowledge engineers could learn much from social scientists who compare actual performances of experts and nonexperts in forecasting. Fourth, the intelligent advisory system software that a knowledge engineer uses constrains knowledge to a particular preestablished format. Not all knowledge fits neatly into present rule-based systems. The self-contained, molded representation of knowledge in such a system makes it difficult to follow standard social scientific procedures of refining and reworking theory that is disproven or unworkable. Fifth, knowledge engineers are worried about practical questions of how to get a program implemented and running, rather than whether the system is ultimately a valid representation of expert knowledge. Shangraw argues, therefore, that knowledge engineers and social scientists need to work closer together in testing the validity of intelligent advisory systems.

Validating Simulations and Games

The basic principle for establishing the reliability of a simulation is that *successive runs should give similar results*. In the case of computer-based simulations, this principle is rarely a problem, but in human games it may be. Thus reliability in human games requires physical equipment that is practical and easily moved, and clear, simple, and complete sets of rules that do not "overtax the player's span of attention" (Inbar & Stoll 1972:280).

Reliability, while important, never insures validity of any method. Validity is aided by asking numerous questions about face validity. Does the simulation appear reasonable? Did any unexpected events occur? Did expected events pan out? How do the results compare with theoretically or empirically expected outcomes in the natural world? Did unexpected processes, sequences, or structures emerge that violate the assumptions of the model? Do components of the simulation parallel those in the system the simulation is attempting to represent?

Most of the simulations chosen have been discussed in this chapter because their creators have attempted to answer these types of questions satisfactorily. Where these simulationists know of sources of invalidity in their programs, they communicate those sources, and attempt to correct them. Heise's INTERACT provides a classic example. He and other social scientists (Smith-Lovin & Heise 1988) have gone to great efforts to test the generalizability of his model and to correct its weaknesses.

Unfortunately, none of the techniques mentioned can completely validate a simulation. A simulation may give correct results for the wrong reasons. Simulations are no better than other methods. It is always wise to consider testing simulations against the results of other methods (see Chapter 14 on multiple-method approaches), and to change various components of the simulation, to measure how robust results of a simulation really are. To the extent that a simulation produces results reminiscent of real world events, the simulationist gains confidence in the veracity of the simulation. The irony is that the more complex—and, therefore, lifelike—the designer makes the simulation, the more obscure the processes and results of the simulation become. Axelrod's round-robin tournament gives results that make sense in the everyday world, but he found complex interactions between strategies—a cooperative strategy like TIT FOR TAT—might win most of the time, but lose occasionally to a strategy like JOSS that was on the whole an inferior player—reminiscent of the complexity of everyday intransitive experiences, without explaining those experiences. Similarly, increasing the number of participants in INTERACT from two to three grossly complicates the results. The general lesson is: Although simulations may aid us in more validly representing the complexities of social life, valid representation does not inevitably lead to understanding.

Even so-called knowledge-enhancing software is presently no better than the humans that programmed it or the customer who uses it. Simulationists reluctantly work with a "closed world" assumption—that nothing outside the program is relevant. Expert systems are presently shallow: They have no general principles, just hundreds of rules of thumb. They are unable to infer missing knowledge. They do not learn: Their "expertise" has to be put in by hand. The expert knowledge system is just one rigid mapping of the world, but humans are not always so rigid. Knowledge inside our heads is both highly structured and wonderfully reshapable. Simulations do not provide the magic method for doing away with theory-building and testing.

Another set of validity issues in artificial intelligence clusters around the banner of *nonstandard logic*. AI languages represent standard logic dealing with simple truth and falsity, but human reasoning includes statements like "She *believes* this," or "He *knows* that." Also AI represents human uncertainty with probability, but much of human uncertainty is not random but vague. In spite of the vagueness of much of human reasoning, human experts seem able to look at a problem and use recognition based on pattern matching from their huge store of memory and experience rather than from reasoning. Perhaps more important than if-then rules, humans use semantic networks to group concepts and objects: We might use the word "animate" to include "tree" and "root." Finally, Humans may look at a problem and see the whole: "AHA!" By contrast, knowledge engineers seem bent on simply building bigger bases of facts and rules.

Summary

Simulation and gaming as a research techniques evolved out of such historic games as chess, which were designed originally to mimic medieval warfare. A simulation is not meant to be an exact replica of reality; instead, it is meant to highlight the essence of some particular phenomenon. The construction of simulations requires understanding the rules that constrain life. Just as our genetic code must consist of relatively few rules that govern our sex, the color of our eyes, and our height, a good social simulation makes explicit the essential rules that control social relationships, institutions, or whatever. One of the main values of simulations is an explanation of such rules or heuristics. Simulations are often used for teaching theories about the construction of heuristics, and for doing research into testing and developing theories.

Although the purpose of simulations is to clarify and explain underlying social processes, the designer must already know a great deal of precise information about the process and conditions the designer wishes to simulate before starting.

Simulations differ from experiments in important ways. Experiments are quite useful in manipulating and controlling a few variables, but simulations offer the possibility for control over and manipulation of a multitude of variables. This ability of simulations to manipulate many variables makes it particularly well suited for the study of large-scale processes. Because simulations can compress the study of large stretches of time into seconds, simulations are also well suited for the study of long-term processes.

The nature of the phenomenon the designer wishes to simulate constrains the nature of the simulation. First, although simulations are particularly suited for the study of social process, some phenomenon or research questions are relatively descriptive, while others call for more analytic designs. Second, designer may employ a holistic or partial simulation of some phenomenon. Although holistic simulations may mirror reality, their complexity may lead the designers to study smaller portions of their operations to reduce the complexity to more manageable means. Third, some social problems deal with macroscopic models of the entire world, while others may focus on more microscopic models of attitudes, emotions, etc. Fourth, some models focus on static systems, while others explore more dynamic systems.

The earliest simulations in social science modeled themselves after existing games. Gaming simulations must take into account the size of the group because social theorists have long known that groups of different sizes have special structural characteristics. Structure of information is another important feature in games. Most everyday situations involve less-than-perfect information. Both differences in amount of information and uncertainty of quality of information are among the important features of everyday life for which some game designers try to create simulations. Other important gaming simulations have focused on differences created by zero-sum strategies in which there are both winners and losers, nonzero-sum strategies in which there may be more than one winner or loser, and mixed-motive strategies, which combine features of both zero-sum and non-zero sum strategies.

Mixed-motive strategies are most common in everyday life, but they lead to relatively complex outcomes that are challenging to understand. The general rule is: The more complex and lifelike the game, the less control the designer has over threats to internal validity. Paradoxically, although the designer may wish to study a distilled model of reality to highlight important processes, the more distilled the model, the more likely the model loses generality or external validity.

The operationalization of games requires close attention to specification of objectives, components, and processes; time, place, and issues; key actor's roles, objectives, and resources; interaction sequences and structures; decision rules; the constraint of trust, legitimacy, and other important social structures; the formulation of clear scoring rules; and methods for the allocation of resources. Rather than introduce large amounts of complexity into the simulation, designers often wish to keep the simulation as parsimonious as possible as a test of the need for complexity in arriving at normal processual outcomes. What appears to be necessary complexity often turns out to be frills.

Participants in simulations typically like them better than experiments because they allow greater freedom due to the greater amounts of novelty involved and fewer restrictions in individual judgments. Simulations come closer to such quasi-experimental designs known as time-series studies, in part because of this relaxation of control. The relaxation of control implies a loss of internal validity, which the designer tries to trade off against increases in generalizability or external validity.

Early social science simulation designers started toying with the interaction of humans and computers during the 1960s. As rudimentary as these human-computer simulations were, they provided the prototype for later work, in that they focused on providing the computer with a script. The challenge was to make a script that had an appropriate response for every action the human player might make, and to program the computer to advise the player of appropriate and inappropriate courses of actions and their outcomes. The general purpose of these exercises in programming were to explicate principle roles and social structures.

By the 1970s, a number of social scientists had graduated to more complex computer-based simulations. This graduation was made possible, in part, by the reduction in price of computers and the vastly greater memories of the newer generation of computers. But, more significantly, it was aided by greater understanding of the needs of simulations: more precise operationalizations than normal research requires, clearer understanding of the units, properties, and sequencing of social processes than theory had previously allowed. Designers found it increasingly possible to quickly change the assumptions underlying their simulation, run a simulation, check the simulation against known theory, and redesign the simulation once again. The interplay between simulation and theory became grossly more efficient.

The latest step in simulation has brought social scientists closer to the relatively new field of artificial intelligence. Artificial intelligence arose out of the attempts of cognitive experts to try and understand what made for real intelligence. The challenge of answering this question has proven more difficult than earlier researchers and theorists imagined it would take, but the outcome has not been a failure. Instead, the work into intelligence has produced a better understanding of the different types of intelligence as well as interesting and useful by-products under the guise of intelligent or expert-consulting systems.

The major thrust of artificial intelligence advancement has come from programming machines to use symbolic logic to simulate deductive processes. This is quite an advance over pre-artificial intelligence programs that could only work with high-order data in ordinal, interval, or ratio form. Symbolic logic can use nominal data and test for their truth or falsity, relationships to other data through if-then statements, and so on. It requires the price of rigorous syntactic structure found in predicate calculus. But the trade-off is the ability to emulate any logical reasoning process. All current artificial intelligence programs are based on such logic processors.

Nevertheless, the heuristics that humans use have proven to be difficult to simulate. Cognitive scientists often use human experts as informants for their intelligent advisory systems. The program will ask for advice which it then uses to modify its heuristics when that advice differs from its own conclusions. Although this has improved the advice such advisory systems give, unlike humans who often know when to break the rules, these programs are still unable to make such decisions. Teaching machines when to break the rules may prove one of the most difficult of the last frontiers of intelligence emulation.

The earliest artificial intelligence machines tried brute-force searches of memory for rules and strategies. Because not all knowledge is equally important, that strategy is not very intelligent. More recent studies of how experts solve problems has led to programming computers to use a best-first search rule in which they search for patterns, discount certain strategies, and focus upon only part of their memory. Also, because humans' intelligence involves "looking ahead" or intentionality, programs now use forward searching strategies, backward searching strategies, and combinations of both called bidirectional strategies.

However, humans often use fuzzy logic; we use vague conceptualizations like old and young or uncertain statements like "I think that. . ." or "Occasionally I . . ." Undaunted, artificial intelligence designers have used probability to mimic fuzzy logic. The outcome of all these efforts has been a growing number of prepackaged expert systems that hold a wealth of specialized knowledge domains for well codified and routinized parts of social life. Furthermore, they have used these original systems to create shells for the creation of future knowledge-based systems. These shells use an inference engine that performs the symbolic logic and a knowledge-base to which the human user may add knowledge in interaction with the system. The more sophisticated systems include an explanation system with which the user may consult to obtain explanations—the rules the program used in its deductions—for particular advice. The outcome of all this effort, therefore, has been the creation of machines for inference-building and testing that can enhance any knowledge concerning humans.

The goals of social scientists and those who create intelligence advisory systems—called knowledge engineers because they "mine" the knowledge from the expert's heads—may diverge. Most knowledge engineers presume that any expert may be used to create a working expert system. Social scientists, concerned with validity and generalizability, have challenged knowledge engineers to use better sampling methods in an effort to come up with more representative expert populations; to use higher quality observational and questioning methods; to be concerned with setting standards for what expertise is; to consider less standardized representations of theory that do not fit neatly into rule-based systems; and to consider the validity of their system.

Validity becomes the greatest challenge to using any intelligent advisory system. As simulations are becoming more complex, their validity becomes more challenging to assess. Because no one method insures validity, simulation designers must go back and forth using their simulations to test theory, but also using theory to design more valid simulations.

CHAPTER

13

Evaluation Research

When people become so intelligent that they know how to choose as their representatives, persons of decided ability, who know something of human nature, who recognize that there are social forces, and that their duty is to devise ways and means for scientifically controlling those forces on exactly the same principles that an experimenter or an inventor controls the forces of physical nature, then we may look for scientific legislation.[1]

Key Terms

Accountability

Boomerang effect

Cost-benefit analysis

Cost-effectiveness analysis

Direct cost

Effort variable

Facility-equipment cost

Indirect cost

Performance variable

Personnel cost

Project goal

Program input

Project objective

Program output

Quick-analysis

Situational variable

Social audit

[1]Ward, L. (1906) *Applied Sociology*, New York: Greenwood Press, p. 338.

Study Guide Questions

1. What are the ideal functions of evaluation research; how does evaluation often diverge from those ideals?

2. Where does the demand for evaluation research come from?

3. How do basic and evaluation research differ? How are they similar?

4. How do interest groups affect evaluation research?

5. How does evaluation research differ in basic research design and measurement from basic research? Why?

6. Why is the distinction between performance and effort variables important in evaluation research? Efficiency and process?

7. Why do administrative and political considerations come into conflict with ideal evaluation research design?

8. Explain the uses of and basic differences between quick-analysis, social audits, cost-benefit analysis, and cost effectiveness.

9. How do evaluators typically measure costs and benefits? Why do some evaluators recommend cost-effective measures as an alternative?

10. What strategies aid and detract from the utilization of evaluation research findings?

Brooks lists four *ideal* functions of evaluation research.

1. The *accounting function*—to provide information to some agency on the benefits of some program relative to projected costs
2. The *feedback function*—to use evaluation results for the program being evaluated to draw upon
3. The *dissemination function*—to provide a basis of knowledge for other programs to draw upon
4. The *theory-building function*—"to clarify, validate, disprove, modify, or otherwise affect the body of theory from which the hypotheses underlying the program were derived." (Brooks 1965:34)

More practically, however, the evaluator discovers the purposes of evaluation to include the following covert or overt rationales (Weiss 1972:11–17): postponement of decisions, ducking of administrative responsibility, public relations and prestige, or as a grant requirement imposed by outside authorities. To this list is added that many project administrators may wish to use scientific advice to (1) justify decisions already made or pet theories, (2) disprove the wisdom of rival theories, or (3) weaken the power of another administrator by subjecting his or her project to scrutiny. Most of these rationales involve resistance to change. Glaser, Abelson, and Garrison (1983:81–84) suggest that such resistance to change comes from at least six specific sources: fear of loss of status, prestige or power; threatened job security; threatened work philosophy and practice; fear of loss of self-esteem; fear of the unknown; and forced change.

Of course, some evaluation programs have much more honest and scientific grounds for existence. But the evaluator must be alert to other possible project rationales and roadblocks. The existence of such nonscientific rationales and roadblocks affects the project evaluation process. Indeed, these rationales and roadblocks indicate potential conflicts of interest between the evaluator and project staff with which the evaluator must deal if the evaluation effort is not to be compromised.

The Demand for Evaluation Research

The 1960s and 1970s were a period of robust federal interest in applying social-science methodology to the evaluation and solution of large-scale social problems. Putt and Springer (1989:20–21) point out that the optimism for social scientific applications to public problems reached its zenith in 1965, when President Lyndon Johnson ordered the Program Planning and Budgeting (PPB) system. The PPB system required the categorization of budget expenditures into "programs" with specifiable objectives. Although the PPB system was officially discontinued in 1971, the idea underlying it continues to be resurrected with such neologisms (coined words) as "zero-based budgeting."

Federal fiscal policy has not shown the same level of financial support for social science solutions to social problems during the 1980s as in the previous two decades, but there appears to be an enormous demand for the use of social-science methods under the rubric of "evaluation research." Evaluation research is now commonly understood to mean the assessment of the effectiveness of social programs that were designed as tentative solutions to existing social problems. The very complexity of modern societies requires a broad range of information to make decisions.

This is quite different from most other types of applied research that attempt to search for solutions to social problems. The evaluation researcher is not like a consulting engineer searching for means to reach a given end. Rather, the evaluation researcher is more like a quality-control inspector who tries to determine whether things are working as they were designed to work. Evaluation research seeks not to find solutions (as in applied research) but *to assess programs designed as tentative solutions to social problems*. The social sciences have had few individuals in the past whose roles corresponded to this evaluation role. Increasingly, however, organizations demand individuals trained to perform such evaluation functions. Weiss' (1972: viii) comment still applies

There are enormous demands today for skilled evaluators in all the new federal programs in education, vocational education, rehabilitation, crime and delinquency, mental health, antipoverty, health, community planning, model cities, family planning, addiction services, and so on. There is a need, too, for greater understanding of evaluation purposes and process by practitioners and administrators in these fields who are expected (and often legally required) to cooperate with evaluation efforts and to put to use the findings that emerge.

In assessing our department's M.A. program in evaluation research, we found an average of 1.6 jobs per graduate student. These jobs, many of which did not exist several years ago, had such titles as Evaluation Specialist (State Planning Agency), Internal Evaluator (Neighborhood Health Center), Planning Associate and Specialist (United Way), Research Analyst (Metropolitan Police Department), and Community-Staff Coordinator (University Department of Community Medicine). If anything, Weiss' comments on demands for evaluation experts are even more apropos today at the state and city level.

Donald Campbell (1972) has envisioned a society of the future that has an explicit evolutionary evaluative mechanism built in; his future society uses social-scientific methods for changing itself through evaluation of innovations and solutions to problems. It then attempts further innovations and scientific evaluations as a feedback mechanism for resolving problems that arise. While Campbell's society is only visionary at the moment, the United States and several Northern European countries are taking steps in that direction. Indeed, both socialist and nonsocialist polities, and both developed and developing countries, have attempted to rationalize decision making over the last several decades through employment of evaluation research that identifies national priorities, aids choice in assessing the pros and cons of those priorities, searches for effective means of attaining those priorities with least cost, and continually monitors the evidence for and against programs designed to execute those priorities.

Some examples of evaluation research studies reported in *Evaluation Quarterly* show the diversity of this demand. Some reports were for public-policy assessments: work release effects on criminal recidivism; and an assessment of gun-control laws on armed robbery, assaults, and homicide rates. Another group evaluated the effects of different programs: psychologic effects of day care and pathway design effects on reducing bicycle accidents. A third group was concerned with outcomes: Long-term impact of water-conservation measures; compensatory treatment for disadvantaged college-student assessment; and the impact of increased enforcement of sanitation laws.

Basic versus Evaluation Research

Strickly speaking, there are no formal methodologic differences between basic research and evaluation research. The methods, techniques, and research designs discussed in other chapters of this text may be used in either research realm. However, evaluation research differs from basic research in several ways. First, evaluative research utilizes deliberately planned intervention of some independent variable(s). Second, the programs it assesses assume some objective or goal is desirable. Third, it attempts to determine the extent to which some program has reached the desired goal or objective. Suchman (1969:15) states that evaluation research "asks about the *kind* of change that program views as desirable, the *means* by which this change is to be brought about, and the signs according to which such change can be recognized."

The critical difference between evaluative and basic research is one of objectives rather than methodology. Both depend on the canons of scientific logic, but evaluative studies apply these canons to programs with social, political, economic, and administrative objectives, while basic research is more likely concerned with theoretical objectives. Rather than test a *theoretical* hypothesis of the form "a change in X will produce a change in Y," the evaluation researcher needs an *evaluative* hypothesis of the form "by a planned change in X, the probability of Y (judged desirable) *increases*." As an example, it is of little use to an educational decision maker to learn that high social status and high educational achievement are related (a theoretical hypothesis), *because the decision maker cannot change status*. What the administrator needs is evidence showing how to raise the learning levels of children from lower-status minorities.

Great variations exist in project objectives. Although evaluation research is typically restricted to program impact, the administrator may not care so much about hypotheses as just plain facts: How much drug abuse exists and who uses illegal drugs? Who uses the mass transit system? In other administrative environments, the decision maker may face a choice between two or more programs and ask: Does Plan A or B most effectively solve the nuclear-waste problem? Or, an administrator may be interested in causation: Do block-watching programs reduce crime?

Although the critical difference between evaluative and basic research hinges upon project objectives, the organizational context of the project creates other important differences. First, in addition to learning traditional research management skills, the evaluation researcher must learn new skills— the evaluation researcher must learn how to adapt to organizational and policy decision-making environments. As Putt and Springer state (1989:xii) "understanding *what* decision makers need to know, and *why*, is a fundamental part" of the evaluation process. To understand what decision makers want to know, the evaluator may spend much time with policy-makers that would normally be spent collecting data in actual research settings.

Second, the basic researcher is accustomed to the freedom of formulating research questions. The evaluation researcher, by contrast, must become familiar with answering a client's questions as to whether a program is accomplishing what the client wishes to accomplish. Sometimes this feature gives the evaluator very little freedom because the client has a good idea what questions to ask or how to answer them. More often, the client has little idea, and so the researcher has a lot of freedom in designing the evaluation.

Third, the evaluation researcher wishes to measure whether the project attains program goals. Basic researchers concern themselves with "what is." The evaluator compares "what is" (alternative programs) with "what ought to be" (the program objectives).

Fourth, unlike basic research where the investigator normally has control over research procedures, the evaluation researcher works in a setting where priority goes to programs, as opposed to the evaluation. This feature has several important consequences. On the one hand, program priority means that the evaluation researcher's world, unlike the basic researcher's world, is constrained by real time. The evaluation researcher finds it necessary to deal within the time structure of the program. Also, program priority over evaluation produces conflicts of interest and conflicts over control of resources because the interests of the program staff and the researcher are inherently competitive. The program staff are typically service-oriented, and see data-collection procedures as disruptive, potentially worthless (because they already believe in the worth of their program), and possibly threatening (because the evaluation may produce negative results).

Fifth, other researcher-program staff conflicts are inherent in their different frames of reference. Each party has a different paradigmatic stance. The researcher's obligations lie in objectivity in evaluation, public dissemination, and cumulation of project intervention results. Project staff usually feel that project data should be limited to in-house usage—particularly where negative results appear. The reason is that negative results threatened the continuance of their programs, and therefore, of their jobs. As Putt and Springer (1989:33) state, this type of research "cannot be separated from the conflict of values and interests which lies at the core of the political process."

This brings us to a sixth difference. We have seen that scientific hypotheses strive for parsimony of explanation. Scientists wish to generate a small number of predictions (laws and theories) that organize a great deal of diverse information. But the world of action typically finds redundancy of *results* useful for policy decisions.

Given that there are definite differences between evaluation and basic research, there are still many similarities. Both types of investigation are subject to the same problems of reliability, validity, and operationalization, and each uses the same store of research methods, techniques, and principles discussed in other chapters. The evaluation researcher, then, must be competent in the use of the methodologic principles and the tools presented in other chapters. While differences between evaluation and basic research are emphasized throughout later sections of this chapter, one must never lose sight of the need for a grounding in basic methodology.

Knowledge for What and for Whom

It has been pointed out earlier that the sharpest distinction between evaluation research and basic research lies in the evaluation researcher's concern with program objectives and goals. These objectives and goals are normatively based in ways that the goals of basic science are not. Each type of research asks different types of questions. As discussed in Chapter 3, nothing is more important than the way the researcher defines the problem. Questions limit and orient all investigation. The basic researcher asks questions concerning *what is, what will be, or what can be.* By contrast, the evaluation researcher is interested in the program client's problems concerning the *gap* between what is and what "ought to be" or "should be." The basic researcher might ask: What are (or can be or will be) the effects of a negative income tax on the stratification system? The evaluation researcher's *client* might ask how the stratification system (as is) can be changed to some ideal state (eliminated or reduced). The client would then ask the evaluation researcher to assess the effectiveness of the client's proposed solution. Basic and evaluation researchers, then, define their problems differently. In the language of Chapter 1, each operates by quite divergent paradigms.

From a social frame of reference, the evaluation researcher's problems arise from the client's belief in the need for social change. Only direct action or a change in some state of affairs can solve the client's problem. On the other hand, increased knowledge solves the basic researcher's problem. Ideally, increased knowledge yields a testable explanation that allows the basic researcher the ability to predict and control. Therefore, basic science is more conservative by nature than evaluation research.

Nevertheless, evaluation research is not ideologically radical. Groups interested in radical or rapid social change are unlikely consumers of evaluation research. Furthermore, evaluation research is often used for conservative purposes; some outside agency usually defines the problem or project goals. The agency calls in the evaluator as an expert or as someone with specialized competence in understanding, predicting, and controlling the project. The evaluator says, "Define the goal, and I will see what means can attain it, and what it will cost you." Therefore, the contracting agency may predetermine (through its goals) costs and benefits of the status quo.

Because evaluation research concerns social problems as opposed to theoretical problems, ideological issues are important to evaluation research. An important question that often arises is: Who cares about the problem? Various interest groups may define the problem differently. The Caucasian-defined "black problem" becomes the "white problem" for many black groups. Therefore, the crucial problems for evaluation research are political by nature. Representatives of various groups with vested interests in the program may have conflicting interests. Coleman (1972:15) noted that

> those interests likely to be *threatened* by a potential policy change are more likely to be activated than those interests likely to be *benefited*—simply because persons and corporate bodies experience a loss arising from change in the status quo as greater than an objectively equivalent gain arising from change in the status quo.

This tension between those threatened and those benefited acts as a strongly conservative force. The result, as Suchman summarizes, (1969:28) is likely to end in the threatened party's attempt to abuse the evaluation through

(1) eyewash—limitation of attention to favorable program aspects; (2) white-wash—avoidance of any objective appraisals; (3) submarine—evaluation designed to eliminate a program; (4) posture—adoption of the objective and scientific pose without any substance; (5) postponement—delay of action while awaiting needless evaluation; and (6) substitution—disguising failure in an essential program activity by shifting attention to a less relevant but more defensible program aspect.

Some parties, therefore, may try to nullify the prestige of expert evaluators, so that the study ends up with preset conclusions that protect the threatened parties' statuses, rather than by finding out what actually works. Because evaluators are much less independent than the typical social scientist, the evaluator's loyalty to good evaluation implies the need to balance scientific criteria with pragmatic criteria that are critical to useful evaluation results. Also, the solutions to all social problems involve compromise, bargaining, coercion, or negotiation. Political conflicts and cross-pressures often lead to the political reality that it is better to do nothing at all than to implement a program that will certainly alienate some interest group. The result of all these conflicting pressures most commonly is close-to-zero effects rather than effective programs (Rossi & Wright 1984).

This relative lack of independence of evaluators is reflected in the magnitude of tasks faced by most evaluations. Social scientists are rarely equipped to handle the breadth of skills required. Sociologists and anthropologists are most likely able to provide ethnographic or field observation skills. Political scientists are more comfortable with dealing in political and policy-making environments. Economists feel most at ease in discussing costs and benefits of programs. Most large-scale program evaluations require the efforts of numerous specialists who are unaccustomed to working in such interdisciplinary settings. Furthermore, evaluators are normally unaccustomed to the need to reconcile many conflicting desires: to stay in business, political convictions, commitments to sponsors, to benefit the larger society, and promises to informants. The outcome is that evaluators have political influence even when they do not aspire to it.

Experienced evaluators advise a five-step process for dealing with political influence. First, identify interest groups with a likely vested interest in the evaluation outcomes. Second, determine these interest groups' concerns. Third, establish the types of information relevant to these concerns. Fourth, ascertain the optimum means to get this information. Fifth, decide how to report the results. The first three of these five steps are particularly germane to the present discussion of for whom and for what purposes one seeks knowledge. To ignore conflicting interest groups' concerns creates the danger of selecting criteria for evaluation that favor one interest group over others. Furthermore, selection of biased criteria creates the danger that measures of importance to accepting (or rejecting) conflicting interest groups' assessments of the program will be ignored.

Paradigmatic differences between program administrators and researchers also complicate the questions of "knowledge for what?" and "for whom?" First, program administrators look for solutions to immediate problems, while the evaluator is more interested in measuring long-term effects, and certain stakeholder groups may be interested in long-term outcomes. Second, administrators are disposed to conceal inefficiency and resist disruptive change, while evaluators are more oriented to the measurement of social change. Third, administrators (and many interest groups) are usually threatened by negative results because such results threaten the agency's public image and program continuation. Administrators advocate most reforms as though they are certain to be successful, in spite of a wealth of evaluation studies that show otherwise (see Rossi & Wright 1984). The evaluator, lacking this ideological commitment and armed with a history of past negative findings, therefore often threatens programs.

Specifying Evaluation Goals and Side Effects

There are a multitude of interest groups that may have vested interests in the evaluation process. The question then arises: *Whose* purposes shall be assessed? Shall the evaluator orient to the needs of scholars, evaluation practitioners, the project director, the project staff, the program's clients, the agency requesting the evaluation, or the funding agency? Each of these groups may assess the evaluation from different—probably conflicting—perspectives. Some interest groups may wish to drop or add program goals. Others may wish to reallocate project resources among competing projects. Still others may be interested in simple rejection (or acceptance) of the program's approach. Some groups may not even see a problem worthy of evaluation. Some parties may wish a project which allows them the possibility of choosing the best prospect from among several proposed lines of actions, while others may desire only to fine-tune an existing program. One administrator may simply wish to force subordinates to comply with instructions, another bureaucrat may desire to create support for a pet proposal, and yet another may try to use the project to cast suspicion on a political opponent's policy. Putt and Springer (1989:33) note that evaluation cannot erase such value differences or make them irrelevant—it can only clarify ideals and provide empirical evidence; the information produced by the evaluation process "is not 'neutral' and 'apolitical' but is itself based on assumptions and preferences."

Therefore, the evaluator must find out who cares about the "problem," and why they care about it. This means the evaluator will have to explore the *values* of the groups with vested interests in (and opposed to) the project. Suchman (1969:158–159) shrewdly observes how values affect the objectives of the evaluator and program staff.

> In general, the evaluator will seek to measure achievement, while the program personnel will be more likely to emphasize effort or technique. The evaluator will be more concerned with higher levels or ultimate objectives, while the practitioner will be more involved with lower level or immediate objectives. To the evaluator, the criteria of success will deal more directly with improvements in the status of the recipients of services, while for the staff, the tendency will be to seek criteria which reflect the smoothness and efficiency of the services themselves rather than their effect upon the people to whom the services are provided.

The types of questions the evaluator must ask of these interest groups at this stage are

1. What is the present state of the system? How does it work?
2. What is the desired state of the system? That is, what norm is desirable for what groups? How would that system work in its desired state?
3. How can the present system be moved toward this desired state? What would this cost with respect to other norms in the society; that is, what would be the side effects of such change?

Furthermore, because the need for the evaluation is socially problematic—that is, not all interest groups see a "problem"—it is necessary to ask,

4. Why have certain groups defined the situation as a social problem, while others have not?

These types of questions are means of defining and clarifying the interest groups' values in relation to the program objective. Indeed, as Coleman (1972:7) points out, because "the research problem enters from outside any academic discipline, it must be carefully translated from the real world of policy or the conceptual world of a client without loss of meaning." It may be that half the battle in evaluation research is over after the evaluator has helped the client define and clarify the problem. Most organizations and decision makers have only fuzzy ideas about their problems, and even vaguer notions about how to solve those problems. To assist decision makers and organizations in recognizing and defining the issues, and in clarifying their personal and organizational needs and solutions, are skills to be admired. Clarification of program objectives and solutions requires that the evaluator show the full context of social and organizational implications of the project, rather than just the narrower personal or vested interest implications.

Perhaps an analogy to theory-testing in basic research will further clarify the need for clear definitions of program objectives. The model basic researcher throughout preceding chapters undertook research only after formulating testable hypotheses. Likewise, the evaluator wishes to treat the evaluation project as the independent variable, and the *desired* state of change as the dependent variable. As with basic research that is not tied to theory, it is not surprising that programs that fail to define their objectives prove unsuccessful at assessing those programs. Williams (1971:xiv) grimly observes that social-science research has seldom been relevant to federal program evaluation, simply because of *lack* of communication over the needs and goals of federal policy programs. For this reason, Putt and Springer (1989:102) emphasize the need for the evaluator to work at creating quality ties to key participants. Political interaction is a fundamental part of the evaluator's role.

Program managers are rarely explicit about their objectives, and programs usually have multiple objectives. Evaluators need, therefore, to guide the defining of objectives in measurable terms. Closer collaboration between evaluators and project staff in the identification of project goals and criteria has beneficial outcomes: It leads to more adequately defined, realistic, and comprehensive objectives. Suchman (1969:29–410) suggests the following list for explicating program objectives:

1. *What* is the nature of the objectives?
2. *Who* is the target of the program?
3. *When* is the desired change to take place?
4. Are the objectives *unitary* or *multiple*?
5. What is the desired *magnitude* of effects?
6. *How* is the objective to be attained?

To this list we should add

7. What are the *unintentional* effects or side effects of the program objectives?

Let us now follow through with a hypothetical agency, and examine a set of questions the evaluator might ask. Our agency is the United World Population Society. They are concerned with the "population explosion crisis," and wish our evaluator to provide them with answers about the outcome of the current program to "control population growth." Our evaluator will first want to know *what* they are trying to change—birth-control attitudes, knowledge, behavior, or some combination of these? Then the evaluator will want to know *who* is the target of the program—men, women, adults, members of some social class? *When* do they expect the change to take place—immediately, in the short-, mid-, long-range future? And how long is "long-range"—a year, five years, ten years? Are the program objectives unitary or multiple? Are they interested only in attitudes or attitudes and behavior? If the goals are multiple, what is their relative importance to the program? Are any of these goals incompatible? What is the desired *magnitude* of effect of the program—zero population growth, a 5% decrease in births, or what? *How* are these objectives to be obtained: through literature distribution, formal classes, or tax incentives? What are the side effects of a change in birthrates on gross national productivity, environmental pollution, changes in proportions of youngsters to old people, etc?

Another question concerns how the program objectives are to be attained? What are the program "inputs?" Inputs are the program activities that are designed to bring about the attainment of project goals. Inputs refer to organizational charts, personnel staffing, and interorganizational relationships that show administrative patterns; they also denote statistics on services provided including standards and quotas.

Evaluators often refer to project goals as "outputs" or "outcomes." Sieber (1981) has made a convincing case that evaluators need look beyond outcomes of social interventions as they are more narrowly defined. More traditionally defined surveys (Rossi & Wright 1984) of the outcomes of social programs lead to the conclusion of "no effect" or "little effect." Sieber's broader examination discloses numerous examples of nontraditional outcomes that indicate *boomerang* effects: a raise in Old Age Security Insurance benefits that makes poor, elderly persons ineligible for Medicaid; the Drug Enforcement Administration's promotion of the spraying of a toxic herbicide on marijuana fields in Mexico for the immediate goal of destroying marijuana fields at the expense of public health—when samples of confiscated marijuana show up in the United States; and higher unemployment rates and criminal recidivism among the pre-trial accused, who received more rather than less employment counseling!

Such boomerang effects have lead Sieber (1981:xiii) to propose that more attention needs to be paid to program inputs. Some reverse effects may be caused by "inadvertent slippage" in program inputs. Because vaguities, inconsistencies and incompatibilities are inherent in most programs, certain interest groups may "reinterpret features of the design, change goal priorities, or synthesize previously sovereign ideas and practices." The evaluation industry itself is partly to blame: It has become a multimillion-dollar industry in which some practitioners are willing to ignore negative outcomes.

It would be wrong, however, to conclude that boomerang effects are due primarily to programs as they were originally conceived. Sieber (1981) explores numerous causes of boomerang effects of which only a few are listed. First, any social intervention is likely to lull some groups into believing action has been taken which permits the situation to deteriorate. Second, other groups may rebel against a particular social intervention in a burst of ungovernable grievance. Third, resource scarcity may lead administrators to abandon costly procedures necessary to the accomplishment of the project objectives. Fourth, bureaucracies are notorious for displacing goals: Gratification comes from adherence to the letter of the law, rather than the objective underlying the law. Clients who acquiesce to the rules and routines of agencies often unwittingly allow the agency to make them into individuals with a "trained incapacity" to function outside the agency. Fifth, hostile parties may undermine or subvert well-intentioned programs. Sixth, larger federal budgets call for larger and ever-increasing bureaucracies. Power, prestige, and political ambition of administrative leaders add to the size.

Evaluation is basically an appraisal of value. The formulation of project objectives depends in large measure on *whose* values the evaluator considers and who the intended user of the results is thought to be. Because values are part and parcel of politics, the evaluator needs continually to assess the expression of values through an examination of program inputs and outputs. The next section addresses problems of operationalization of inputs and outcomes—how to make the evaluation researchable in valid and reliable ways. This is necessary because the failure of many programs is due to poor conceptualization.

Design and Measurement

The methods of evaluation research follow the same scientific principles as in basic research. Any differences between the two methods of research, therefore, are due basically to differences in objectives and the conditions under which each type of research normally is conducted. Because evaluation projects typically measure large-scale, complex, and nonrepetitive politically motivated events, it would be a mistake to become enthralled with research technique. *"Right" evaluative decisions cannot replace power and authority*.

Experimental Control

One of the basic differences in conditions between evaluation and basic research is experimental control. The evaluation researcher rarely has the control over research variables that is possible in basic research. In basic research, investigators typically speak of independent and dependent variables. But in evaluation research, evaluators speak of *project outcomes* or *outputs*. Outputs are not strictly equivalent to dependent variables because some of them may not be *intended* outcomes. Also, there are *project variables* or *inputs* that are the study's equivalent to independent variables—those variables which, under the evaluator's control, were intended to bring about some social change. Then, there are *situational variables*.

Situational variables are any variables that are not subject to project control, but are plausible candidates as independent variables. The evaluation must control for the confounding or distorting effects of situational variables, if the results are to have any meaning. Because the number of extraneous (situational) variables over which the researcher has control decreases as one moves from basic into evaluation research, the evaluator has to learn how to control for the influence of them on study outcomes, if this research is not to be subject to the criticism that the results are meaningless. Therefore, the evaluator needs to give hard thought to selecting the strongest possible research design employable in the evaluation (see Chapter 6).

Basic researchers normally employ designs that emphasize high internal validity, but are weak in external validity. Because elegant designs that increase internal validity usually reduce the relevance or generalizability of evaluations, evaluators need to focus more on external than internal validity. Cronbach (1980:8) reaches a similar conclusion when he states that "adding a control costs something in dollars, in attention, and perhaps in quality of data: a control that fortifies the study in one respect is likely to weaken it in another," and in a later paragraph where Cronbach states that "a strictly representative sample may provide less information than a sample that overrepresents exceptional cases and deliberately varies realizations." Because evaluation research consumers expect relevance and responsiveness to their needs, the evaluator often needs to forego the bells and whistles of control, in favor of data with more generic applicability to public policy. Also, the nature of most programs is beyond the scope of believable controls. As Rossi and Wright (1984:345) note

> An estimated 5%–10% of the persons eligible for Old Age and Survivors Insurance (Social Security) benefits have not applied for them. These nonapplicants cannot realistically serve as controls for estimating the effects of social security benefits, however, because of self-selection factors. . . . (and) it is ethically unthinkable to use randomization in the evaluation of some programs.

Time, Space, and Roles

A second major difference between basic and evaluation research deals with the time frame of each. Evaluation research has built-in time scheduling that places unusually heavy demands on the researcher for timely research. Time pressures also affect the choice of research design and strategy. It is necessary to fit the evaluator's time schedule to the project's rather than the reverse, as is usually possible in basic research. The evaluator does not work alone; he or she must consider the constraints of the organizational staff. Decision makers are action oriented; they prefer partial data now to full data later. They are doers who live in the present; persons who have little interest in the future. After all, if they do not act now, they may not have a chance to act later.

Third, evaluation research is not only more time bound than basic research, it also is more spacebound. Pressures typically exist to test immediate needs of a specific program. Little encouragement is given to generalizing from the results as in basic research. Therefore, the evaluator may find little encouragement to transcend the immediate evaluation to make sure project results that work in one situation will work in others.

A fourth major difference between evaluation and basic research concerns the researcher's role. The evaluation researcher's role is highly marginal: The evaluator is in the position of "being a doctor without patients or a professor without a class" (Rodman & Kolodny 1972:135). The evaluator's marginality creates the danger of political exploitation. The evaluator must stick by the canons of scientific verification and must *not* even *appear* to be partisan toward or manipulated by any group with vested interests in (or opposition to) the evaluation process. To give such impressions can only serve to compromise the evaluation process. "Scientific research . . . does not rely on personal intuition or individual authority to determine what is 'real.' Rather, it depends on empirical evidence." (Putt & Springer, 1989:29)

Establishment of trust and credibility with decision makers and other participants is a difficult but necessary process that the evaluator makes easier by staying "in role." Good evaluator role modeling includes: developing explicit communication networks with all interest groups, clarifying project goals, interpreting ideological implications, making value-laden assumptions clear, coordinating communication between interest groups, and minimizing intrusiveness in the organization's day-to-day operations.

Operationalization of Variables

A final difference between evaluation and basic research concerns the ways in which each operationalizes variables. While operationalization in basic research is concerned with independent and dependent variables, evaluation research operationalization typically takes place using one or more of the following indicators: (1) effort or activity; (2) performance or accomplishment; (3) adequacy of performance or impact; (4) efficiency of input versus output; and (5) process, or the conditions of effectiveness.

Strictly speaking, *effort* or activity variables are input variables because they measure what the program is doing or how it is doing it rather than program outcomes. Types of input variables that may need to be measured are characteristics of the program participants (race, sex, and relevant preprogram attitudes), length of program service, program staffing, and so on. Effort variables should not be used as measures of output even though program personnel like to be evaluated in terms of effort. As Suchman (1969:61) aptly states, "evaluation at this level has been compared to the measurement of the number of times a bird flaps its wings without any attempt to determine how far the bird has flown."

Performance measures programs in terms of policy objectives. There are countless examples of evaluations that have shown performance failure, even though the program itself had excellent effort indicators. Therefore, the researcher needs to evaluate how the program outcomes measure up to the program's objectives. If the program is intended to reduce the social stigmatization of Aid for Families with Dependent Children, does it actually do this? If it is designed to reduce the juvenile delinquency recidivism rate, does it reach this objective?

Adequacy of performance depends on the degree to which the total magnitude of the problem is reduced. Therefore, rather than test for *total* program effectiveness or simple effectiveness versus no effectiveness, the evaluator may be asked to research the *relative* effectiveness of program policy. Consider the relative worth of several federal experiments run during the 1970s. Four income maintenance experiments in Seattle and Denver cost approximately $110 million: $31 million in payments to individuals and $79 million for data collection and research. Although that may seem like an enormous outlay of tax monies, it was actually a very good buy for the money: Not only did these income maintenance experiments save more than would have been spent on traditional welfare programs, they would have paid for themselves through serendipitous findings that had nothing to do with the research objectives originally used to justify them. Aaron (1981:97) reports:

> A direct outgrowth of the requirement of the income maintenance experiments for continuous information on income and earnings was the system of monthly retrospective reporting . . . its application reduces case loads and cut program costs by roughly 4 percent. Monthly reporting also reduces the frequency of underpaying benefits. . . . If savings of 4 percent could be achieved nationwide, the savings would approach $300 million a year. And these savings would not include other benefits from monthly reporting such as accurate addresses that permit a reduction in the number of medicaid cards incorrectly sent to ineligible persons.

Efficiency is a measure of program performance (output) in terms of effort (input). It asks whether the program outcomes can be justified in terms of project costs. In a later subsection, several means of assessing project efficiency will be introduced.

Process measures *why* a program is successful or unsuccessful. Traditionally, evaluation research has researched only whether a program works or not. Process analysis goes into analysis with more depth by asking: What are the conditions that made the program successful or unsuccessful? Answers to this in-depth probing are then used to modify the program, with the hope that the program will now be more successful. However, growing concern over the number of projects with close-to-zero effects has led to a broadened scope of evaluation studies that includes (Rossi & Wright 1984:348)

> (1) basic research on the relevant social processes involved in social programs; (2) needs assessment studies that gather data on the incidence, prevalence, and distribution in social and physical space of the social problem involved; (3) implementation research to explore alternative ways of delivering programs to ascertain which are most cost effective and/or achieve the greatest impacts; (4) program monitoring research to explore the issue of how well social programs, once enacted, are actually implemented; and (5) impact assessment, the traditional concern of evaluation research.

Control over Research Design

Administrative and political considerations have a way of coming into conflict with ideal research design. Program personnel will rarely let the evaluator have the freedom necessary to carry through the ideal evaluation. It is a rare program staff that will easily agree to randomized control groups or treatment variations. The use of control groups may mean denial of service; most policy makers and practitioners strongly oppose denial of service for whatever reasons and for however long. Therefore, the evaluator usually has no choice but to select some nonequivalent comparison groups for quasi-control. Evaluators often end up using participants in different projects as comparison group surrogates for one another, so that they can compare the relative effectiveness of two or more program strategies because it is difficult to justify denying treatment to individuals.

Boruch, McSweeny, and Soderstrom (1978) nevertheless have cross-referenced over 300 randomized evaluation studies in such areas as health care and juvenile delinquency to show the feasibility of such field tests in spite of managerial, political, and other constraints that often exist. Powers and Alderman (1979) suggest creative ways to apply true experimental designs in field settings. They point out, first, that where schools offer programs several times in an academic year, the researcher can delay treatment to a randomly created control group that can obtain the treatment at a later date. Second, where there are multiple sections of a program, one can randomly assign sections to experimental and control groups. Third, scarce resources may preclude access to the program for all individuals. In this case, one can choose randomly from those participants desiring the program. As an alternative ethical and practical procedure, one might randomize participants who express no preference between control and experimental conditions. Evaluators, then, often have more power over randomization than one might suspect.

A further problem of control concerns the sensitizing or reactive effects of evaluation measures (see Chapter 4). Rather than measure actual program effects, the evaluation researcher may be measuring placebo effects of people who know they are being evaluated and how they are being evaluated. In one of the largest social experiments ever run, the New Jersey Income Maintenance Experiments (Watts & Rees 1977), the treatment was so complex that the evaluators found that the more disadvantaged the participants, the less they understood and used the income maintenance benefits due them. This differential understanding created problems of experimental control over treatment allocations—a problem not uncommon to large social experiments.

While it is not a complete solution to the sensitizing problem, the evaluator should use behavioral rather than attitudinal measures to evaluate project outcomes. A common dilemma is that recipients' perceptions of benefits occurring tend to be positive despite signs to the contrary. Recipients may report reduced anxiety or increased self-esteem, but lower levels of such behavioral variables as reduced unemployment or recidivism rates may not occur. The attitudinal measures are more suspect than the behavioral measures because of known reactive effects of perceptual distortion.

In sum, sound evaluations require attention to at least four methodologic concerns. First, the evaluator needs to clearly operationalize a set of treatment variables that can be implemented in the field setting. Second, the research design should be broadly defined so that it has high generalizability. Third, the measurement of project inputs and outcomes require an adequate data retrieval system. Fourth, treatments must be diverse enough to allow meaningful comparisons.

Special Types of Research Designs

An essential first condition for evaluating a program's impact is the ability to isolate what would have happened in the absence of the program. That is, we wish to distinguish between effects of the program and the effects of other forces. Because the major types of research designs are thoroughly discussed in Chapter 6, only a few designs are added here that are more specifically related to particular types of evaluation research: quick-analysis, social audits, cost-benefit analysis, and cost-effectiveness analysis.

Quick-Analysis

Evaluation and policy researchers normally operate under heavy time pressures in large part because policy and decision makers must act on the basis of whatever information is available; their general rule of thumb is that it is better to act on the basis of incomplete information than to wait for more information. Patton and Sawicki (1986:43) state the trade-off in the following way: "It is better to analyze roughly appropriate existing data exhaustively, than to conduct a superficial analysis of hastily collected new data." Quick-analysis has at least two functions in evaluation research. First, it may be a type of needs assessment. Second, it reflects the pragmatic time and budgetary constraints of policy and decision making.

Putt and Springer (1989) devote a whole chapter to quick-analysis techniques based on the principle of "more thought and less data." The term "quick-analysis" is not synonymous with "intuition," or with careless or superficial analysis. In fact, it discourages lack of focus based on the maxim: "If you don't know how you will use the information, don't bother to . . . answer the question" (Hawkins & Nederhood 1986:39). Quick-analysis encourages keying in on the fundamental aspects of the evaluation or policy problem. It entails the active and rapid employment of a gross outline of what is known about some problem or policy to figure out the logical implications of general courses of action.

As an example, consider the problems facing politicians concerning the threat of an AIDS epidemic: Should they or should they not act quickly on pending AIDS legislation? Assuming current U.S. Center for Disease Control estimates are correct, Bloom and Carliner (1988) estimate that the cumulative costs of medical treatment alone in the United States will not exceed $22 billion, but that lost output to the morbidity and mortality of American AIDS patients will range from $1.4 to $1.7 trillion. The economic impact on San Francisco, New York, and some other large American cities in this scenario will be a rise in taxes and health-insurance premiums to finance a portion of the costs.

Politicians cannot afford to wait on basic researchers to solve the problem: Basic researchers often spend a lifetime studying some particularly worthy problem in detail. An evaluation researcher, knowing that time is of the essence might make a quick analysis of the general decisions—and their consequences—facing the politician, as shown in Figure13–1. In this case, let us assume that an individual legislator needs focus in trying to decide whether to support legislation or not. The worst case scenario would be for politicians to do nothing, and for the epidemic to materialize according to the worst predictions. The politician who does not respond to this scenario seriously by working toward effective AIDS legislation risks appearing weak, ineffectual, or irresponsible if such an epidemic performs according to Center for Disease Control projections. The best case scenario would be for politicians to do nothing, and for the epidemic not to materialize—for at least two reasons. First, legislative processes are long and grueling without promise that the output will pay off as hoped. Second, if the epidemic were not to materialize, politicians would have shown that they can stand up under pressure and make the right decision not to be cowered into panic.

The consequences of passing legislation fall somewhere in between these two extremes. If politicians produce effective legislation and the epidemic does spread as fast as predicted, this becomes the second best outcome. Effective legislation makes the politicians look good in the public eye, as well as responsive and responsible to real threats. However, if the predicted spread of AIDS does not materialize, the politicians end up in the third best scenario because

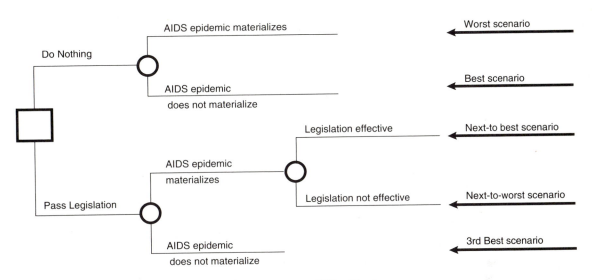

Figure 13-1. A decision sapling for political response to an AIDS epidemic.

the legislative effort was unnecessarily wasteful of time and money. Here, they have at least shown that they were prepared for responding to a crises that happily did not occur. Finally, the next-to worst case scenario is one is which politicians pass ineffective legislation.

Ineffective legislation is probably better than no legislation because politicians can at least claim to have tried to respond quickly. But ineffective legislation may exacerbate the crisis. For example, in Missouri, individuals have introduced various bills that would require the reporting of the identity of anyone who tests positive for antibodies to HIV to the Department of Health, and Department of Health plans to use this information to conduct contact tracing of all past sexual and needle-sharing partners of such persons. The bills would prohibit or put into question the legality of existing anonymous testing programs for HIV. All the bills would require mandatory testing of various groups, depending on the bill, such groups would include prisoners, those who plead guilty to certain crimes, certain mental health patients, marriage license applicants, persons getting treatment at methadone clinics, and hospital patients.

However, it is doubtful that any of this legislation will prove effective for the following reasons. First, the reporting of identity with follow-up contact tracing, will make any confidentiality provisions in the bills meaningless. As soon as contact tracing begins, a person's social contacts will quickly learn the person's test results, with devastating consequences for the person. Second, requiring doctors to report the identities of patients who test positive is a breach of physician-patient privilege. This breach will cause individuals to avoid seeking information from the medical profession concerning their own risk for HIV infection, and will drive those at risk underground. Third, a substantial percentage of individuals will be falsely labeled as positive for HIV. The tests are not foolproof, and in low-risk populations, up to 90% of persons who test positive for the HIV antibodies may in fact not have HIV infection. Fourth, the proposed reporting and contact tracing program is extremely expensive, involving an attempt to trace sexual or drug contacts for seven to ten years. Such money might better be spent on public education concerning the facts of HIV transmission. Fifth, many of the proposed groups presently have such a low risk of infection—marriage license applicants, hospital patients—that such legislation requires too wide a net, leading to unnecessarily high costs.

Because probabilities that the AIDS epidemic will stay on its predicted course, and that particular legislation will be effective would greatly clarify the politicians alternatives, the second step of quick-analysis is to estimate the probabilities for each outcome based on available evidence. One set of subjective probabilities for the alternatives is given in Figure 13–2. Present figures show that AIDS is spreading remarkably close to 1985 Center for Disease Control estimates. Politicians aware of this fact are likely to assign probabilities close to 100% for the continued spread of AIDS. Therefore, the politicians will be propelled to act rather than risk the high certainty of a worst-case scenario. Their problem becomes one of producing effective legislation.

Most experts, for the reasons given above, feel that current legislation will prove highly ineffective and costly. Therefore, a subjective probability has been assigned of .10 to currently proposed legislation—not a very happy conclusion because it leads to the next-to-worst case scenario. Because of the high probability of AIDS spreading throughout the general American population, it becomes imperative for evaluation researchers with expertise in social epidemiology to increase quickly the chances that politicians will produce more effective legislation. Because resources are finite, the longer one waits to produce

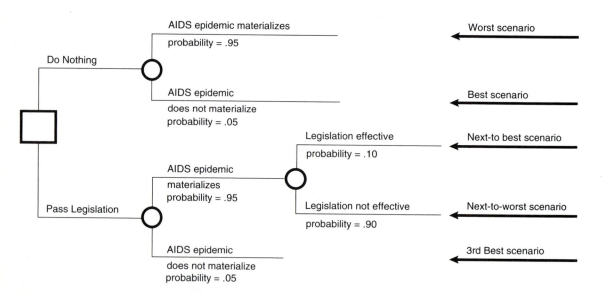

Figure 13-2.   A decision sapling for political response to an AIDS epidemic with subjective probabilities.

effective legislation, the more resources we can expect AIDS to sap over time. Herein lies ones of the strengths of quick-analysis: It helps the evaluator focus on the efficient use of resources.

Social Audits

In the social audit, the researcher traces policy-initiated resource inputs "from the point at which the agency disburses them to the point at which the ultimate intended recipient of those resources receives them" (Coleman 1972:18). The evaluator then relates this social audit to program outcomes. The social audit allows for distinguishing between two sources of program ineffectiveness: (1) The resource inputs may have been ineffective, or (2) they may never have reached their intended recipients. Unlike most traditional research designs that examine primarily project outcomes, this design focuses on possible losses or diversions of resource inputs. This technique does not explain the effectiveness of particular resources, but it does show what resources are available at particular points, and it graphically depicts where and how resources get lost. The social audit is an effective supplement to more traditional research designs because it uncovers process and relative efficiency of programs.

Public agencies typically monitor activities to identify staff accomplishments and audit programs and activities to insure lawful expenditures of public monies. As Putt and Springer (1989:3) state, "Monitoring and auditing require a tremendous amount of information—records of client contacts, records of eligibility for services, records of services provided, and precise accounting records." Putt and Springer continue by noting that (p. 12) "monitoring the activities of individual counselors, for example, may provide information for keeping them accountable to program intentions, or for improving the efficiency of their work." However, because public record keeping is notoriously uneven in most public agencies due to staff inexperience, conflicting and heavy workload demands, and concerns for individual privacy, the evaluator should not use them uncritically. Independent social audits are preferable to official ones.

LaFree's (1980) study of the disposition of forcible sex-offense cases reported to the police beautifully demonstrates the value of the social audit shown in Figure 13–3. Out of 881 cases of rape, armed raped, sodomy, armed sodomy, assault and battery with intent to rape, and assault and battery with intent to gratify reported to the police in a large, midwestern city between January 1970 and December 1975, LaFree noted that a full 62.8% resulted in no arrest. Of the 37.2% in which the police made an arrest, felony charges were filed against 46.6%—or only 17.4% of the original cases reported to the police. Of filed felonies, 81.77% were prosecuted, bringing the percentage of cases brought to trial of the original down to 14.2%.

The audit of case disposition becomes somewhat more complex at this point because some of the accused pled guilty and some did not. Of prosecuted cases, 59.7% (N = 74) of the accused pled guilty, but the court handed down a guilty verdict in only 40% of those. Of those accused who did not plead

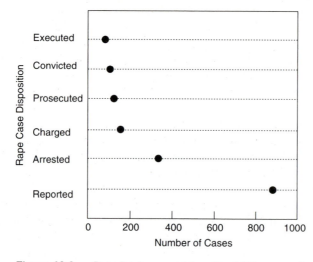

Figure 13-3. Dot plot for a social audit of 881 cases of rape in LaFree's (1980) study.

guilty, the courts sentenced 60%. In total, therefore, 11.8% of the original forcible sex offenses ended up with guilty verdicts. Among these 104 convicted felons, the court executed sentences for 79.8%. About half of those (50.6) ended up incarcerated in a penitentiary, and the others with some other form of incarceration.

For someone who is knowledgeable about the criminal selection process, the results of this social audit are certainly not surprising. However, LaFree used the results of this audit to examine which cases do or do not end up in the final 9.4% that received incarceration. Although other criminologists have noted the disproportionate numbers of blacks in prison, LaFree's analysis demonstrated that racial composition of the victim-offender dyad most strongly affects official reactions of criminal justice personnel in the disposition of the case. In five of the nine processing decisions listed above, when controlling for evidence and legal severity, black men accused of sexually assaulting white women received more serious sanctions. LaFree (1980:852) concluded that the justice system imposes "more serious sanctions on men from less powerful social groups who are accused of assaulting women from more powerful social groups."

As another example of a social audit, universities have become increasingly concerned about policies for retaining students because of the impending demographic squeeze as fewer high-school graduates become available for recruitment. At a commuter-based, public urban university, only slightly more than one-fourth of the students traditionally graduate with a degree. (Large public universities with residential halls average 50% retention rates, and the most elite private universities average 80% retention.) At one institution, concerned administrators (Grobman 1983) did a social audit to trace the entrance and exit points of students who were enrolled during the fall 1975 semester through January of 1982. Almost equally half of 3,260 newly admitted students in the fall 1975 semester came straight to the university from high school (53.1%) or had transferred from other colleges (46.9%).

The administration audited each of these two groups of students separately—presumably on the theory that transfers from other colleges were different from straight-out-of-high-school enrollees. In terms of the percentage receiving a degree by January 1982, both groups were identical—26% of both groups had earned a UM–St. Louis degree. The social audit, however, did demonstrate some interesting exiting differences between each group. Almost half (47%) of the other college enrollees had transferred to still another university during the seven-year-period, compared to one-third of those admitted directly from high school. Another important difference was in students of unknown status—those who had not yet graduated and were not currently enrolled, but who had not requested that a transcript of work be sent to another institution. More than one-third (35%) of those admitted directly from high school fell into this category, while less than one-fourth (23%) of transfer students did. The remaining 4% of transfers and 6% of high-school enrollees were still currently enrolled.

The administration argued, based on these data and surveys of student needs, that policy must emphasize the creation of a wider variety of majors because the largest enrollee attrition is due to students who transfer elsewhere to seek a major that does not currently exist on campus. Without denying the merits of this proposal, it may be suggested that this social audit could be improved in several ways. First, divide up the transfer students into two groups—junior college and other—and trace the flow of each to judge whether their patterns of attrition are more like that of other transfers of high-school enrollees. Second, using the LaFree study above as a model, this student attrition study could profit from attention to suspected correlates of attrition—hours worked at a part-time job, family income, educational status of parents, and so on. Third, a good evaluation of alternative policies would include measurements of the costs and benefits (see the next section) of additional college programs, residential housing, and increased scholarship aid.

As a final example of social audits, consider the tracing of resource inputs from the point of disbursement in such voluntary organizations as the American Red Cross to the point at which the intended recipients experience those inputs. One might analyze, first, which inputs (or portions of inputs) never reach the intended recipient. Of voluntary contributions, how much actually reaches the intended recipients in some form (sand bags, food, clothing, medical supplies)? Of that portion that does not reach the intended recipients, where does this loss of input go—for instance, public relations for more fund raising or organizational salaries?

More subtly yet, consider identical dollar amounts of disbursements by the American Red Cross to two different communities. If the disbursements to one of the communities depreciates more rapidly (through loss or abuse), then the flood victims in that community receive less resource inputs than in the other community. President Lyndon Johnson's Great Society promise to "measure the performance of our programs to insure a dollar's worth of service for each dollar spent," during the 1960s, has great irony: Few programs give more than 20 cents on the dollar. One value of the social audit is to yield data on inefficiencies in disbursements so that policy makers may design more effective means of disbursal.

Cost-Benefit Analysis

It was noted earlier that the evaluator is often interested in measuring program efficiency. In other words, rather than asking whether a program is effective, it is often more profitable to ask whether it is effective by comparison to other alternative programs. Cost-benefit analysis makes decisions among alternative programs, by calculating the probable costs and benefits of alternative programs, and then ordering these programs by favorability of cost/benefit ratios; it is premised on the efficient and effective application of scarce resources. It would be more rational to allocate priority to a mental health program with 60% recovery rates, as opposed to another program with 65% recovery rates, if the first program costs only half as much per patient.

Thompson (1980:1) traced the history of cost-benefit analysis to Sir William Petty who

> found in London in 1667 that public health expenditures to combat the plague would achieve what we now would term a benefit-cost ratio of 84 to 1. In the United States, benefit-cost analysis (synonymous with "cost-benefit analysis") achieved statuatorial authority with the passage of the River and Harbor Act of 1902 and the Flood Control Act of 1936. These pieces of legislation mandated that individual projects were to be justified by comparing their benefits ("to whomsoever they may accrue") with the costs.

The early history of cost-benefit analysis naively focused on main program effects, valuing those effects monetarily, tabulating costs and benefits, and comparing costs and benefits through subtraction or division. For example, many evaluators divide the benefits of a program by its costs to achieve a standard of comparison across projects. If the ratio produces a value less than 1.0, the evaluator concludes that the program has more costs than benefits. As the ratio becomes greater than 1.0, the evaluator concludes greater benefits than costs.

However, evaluators have come to understand that social programs have secondary and tertiary effects that are subtle and complex: valuing human life and productivity, depreciation, lifetime effects of policy changes, and so on that require collaboration across such diverse fields of expertise as economics and political science. Evaluators also recognize that what is a "cost" or "benefit" reflects values; they spend much time, therefore, assessing the perceived costs and benefits of different interest groups. Given that federal agencies alone commit more than a billion dollars each year to program evaluations, policy-oriented demonstrations, promotion-oriented demonstrations, and research, the importance of cost-benefit analysis is readily apparent regardless of the complexity and subjectivity of cost-benefit analysis.

Cost-benefit analysis has several inherent problems. First, it is rarely easy to calculate costs and benefits in standard terms—"work satisfaction," "marital happiness," or "labor productivity of a philosopher" are all difficult concepts to measure. Second, because a change in one part of the social system will affect other parts of the same system, it is necessary to make decisions about which effects are the important ones. A program for reducing mental illness may in turn create the need to retrain mental health personnel for other occupations. This points to a problem of how costs and benefits should be aggregated or scaled.

Cost-benefit analysis depends on reliable, valid, and widely available data that may not be readily obtainable. When only suspect data are available, evaluators arrive at extremely divergent cost-benefit conclusions. Errors can creep into either of the two crucial tasks necessary to cost-benefit analysis (Putt & Springer, 1989, p. 496): "(a) identifying the full range of resources required by a program, and (b) attaching dollar values to those resources."

Consider, for example, the gross differences in costs per AIDS patients from nine different studies which have ranged from $23,000 to $168,000 per case (Bloom & Carliner 1988). Those costs cover only the personal medical care costs in 1986 dollars. It is important to foresee many other costs not covered under personal medical care: the direct costs of prevention, diagnosis, and treatment of the illness, and the indirect costs associated with the lost value of market and nonmarket output due to increased morbidity or mortality resulting from illness. Direct costs of AIDS should include

> personal medical care costs as well as nonpersonal costs for educational campaigns, biomedical research, and blood screening. Indirect costs are the foregone earnings of AIDS patients and the value of any household services they would have provided. Nonpecuniary (more intangible monetary) costs include the value that AIDS patients, their families and friends, and other members of society place on the suffering and death of AIDS patients and on the need to behave differently to avoid contracting or transmitting AIDS.

The costs of countering the AIDS epidemic like any program, then, are not at all obvious. It is not sufficient simply to count government or insurance company outlays of funds; that would be only a small portion of the costs of AIDS: such indirect costs as deterioration in quality of life; hidden costs of "nonprofit organization" that receive partial support from governmental, private, and charitable sources such as Planned Parenthood organizations that do AIDS testing; and such opportunity costs as missed job promotions.

Opportunity costs are an important factor that investigators sometimes forget. Cook and Campbell (1979:218) relate the famous British experiment in 1967 to test the economics of breathalyser tests on making the roads safer. The data at the time showed a precipitous decline in intoxicated driving following the abrupt introduction of breathalyser tests. However, the police found the evidence necessary to gain a conviction burdensome and, therefore, started limiting their use of the test. As soon as British drivers realized that the odds of being caught and convicted were minimal, they returned to their previous habits. More importantly, police realized that the time consumed by the breathalyser tests produced *lost opportunities* for patrolling for more serious crimes.

An adequate accounting of costs is no simple task, but Putt and Springer (1989:504–511) suggest the following are minimal criteria:

1. *Personal Cost.* In addition to salaries, the evaluator must recognize a wealth of less visible costs: employer contributions to dental, medical, and disability insurance, retirement plans and social security.
2. *Direct and indirect costs.* Clerical assistance, telephone answering services, and custodial services are all indirect, or overhead, cost. The time a lawyer spends helping a client win a lawsuit case is a direct cost. The difference is that direct costs are those needed to provide specific mandated services while indirect costs are those needed to support the program outside of any specific services.
3. *Facility and equipment costs.* These are such indirect costs as word processors, fax machines, office supplies, vehicles, fuel, and office footage needed to run a program.
4. *Other costs.* Any special personnel, facility, and equipment costs not typical of routine programs. These may include "depreciation" guidelines for equipment or technological obsolescence.

In the typical assessment of costs, evaluators do assess these categories for government units and agencies that implement government policies. For example, to implement a particular social service, administrators typically add up the costs of operating the entire supplemental services needed ($18,000 yearly salary and benefits, a secretary at a $10,500 yearly salary, $9,000 for office space, and $6,000 for supplies), and divide by the number of clients per year. Then, if the average client stay in the program is for nine months, the administrator divides the yearly cost per client by 0.75 and so on.

Less often, evaluators consider the private costs of policies and programs. For example, if AIDS spreads as rapidly as epidemiologists believe it will, by the 1990s there will be a number of contributed and imposed private burdens: AIDS-cases filled hospital beds that compete with non-AIDS related cases; diversions of health staffs and supplies from other critical areas; outlays in welfare for children of AIDS-infected parents; health and disability insurance diversions from other areas; and market value of foregone labor. These are costs that need critical assessment, but which change depending on the values and preferences of evaluators and decision makers. For example, market value of foregone labor is typically based on current market pay—which devalues women's work to about 60% of a man's for the same type of work, although many individuals would object to valuing the loss of a women's work as less than a man's in the same work.

Evaluators often measure *benefits* by estimating the reductions in social costs. If it costs $20,000 a year to keep a convict in prison for an average stay of five years, while some new parole-training program costs $4,000 a year per parolee with an average length of eighteen-months of rehabilitation, then the program's economic benefits are a savings of $94,000. Of course, recidivistic criminals' costs should be figured into this analysis. If 30% of the parolees in the training program are reinstitutionalized, the researcher must add the costs of their new confinement, court costs, and victim costs. The benefits of full employment should also be added in, as such other gains of the program.

Many social costs and benefits are purely speculative. How could one financially express the anguishes of rape, the emotional costs of assault, or murder? Nevertheless, some social costs and benefits can be rationally expressed. The costs of heavy drug usage could be viewed from the point of view of society's loss of the drug user's work power, the loss of the potential tax dollar, and the losses resulting from accidents on the job.

Similarly, the cost of life can be measured through the willingness-to-pay life value (WTPLV). Thompson (1980:197) defines the WTPLV for any person who suddenly developed a life-threatening condition and had no insurance against it. Such a person has only his or her own life value (OLV) "consisting of his savings plus his discounted future earnings minus his discounted future consumption."

The most objectively supportable costs and benefits are more appropriate than more speculative ones, if the researcher is interested in making a strong argument for the validity of the data. Therefore, while this practice may understate cases, individuals with vested interests are more likely to accept understated than overstated costs and benefits. It is a myth to suggest that such program effects as threat to human life, fear of crime, or environmental pollution cannot be reasonably quantified.

A word on institutional records is in order, given that social audits, cost-benefit analyses, and other more traditional forms of evaluation depend on accurate records of inputs and outputs. Institutional records (see Chapter 11) are notorious for being incomplete, unstandardized, and disordered. Therefore, the evaluator cannot depend on the quality of records kept by program personnel. While more expensive, it is probably worthwhile developing precoded observational forms to aid standardization.

Cost-Effectiveness Analysis

A closely related technique to cost-benefit analysis is cost-effectiveness analysis. Because it is often difficult to construct cost-benefit calculations, some evaluators advocate measuring the costs of alternative treatments or programs because cost information is usually easier to uncover than benefit information. A comparison of the steps involved in each approach shows more similarity than dissimilarity. Thompson (1980:247) notes that "cost-effectiveness is most appealing when exactly one dimension of program effects is hard to value monetarily." Without such a dimension, they are essentially equivalent; with more than one such dimension, cost-effectiveness becomes less attractive because of difficulties in proving commensurability of dimensions.

The Experimental Housing Allowance Program of the 1970s illustrates the use of cost-effectiveness methodology. In the housing allowance program, the federal government set up three primary experiments. First, the program created a demand experiment which offered housing allowance subsidies in two cities to a randomly selected group with another group serving as a true control. The evaluators observed the effects of this program on the households. Second, in a parallel supply experiment, the researchers observed that the effects of housing allowance subsidies on landlords, developers, homeowners, mortgaged lenders, real-estate brokers, and others was to improve housing conditions in two other housing markets. In a third experiment, evaluators observed eight administrative agencies in six other cities to understand how they managed this type of housing allowance program.

Kain (1981:365) analyzed the effects of these experiments and concluded that

> particular program requirements also affect the fraction of allowance payments spent on increased housing expenditures. Somewhat surprisingly, the program evaluated in the supply experiment appears to have induced the smallest increases in housing expenditures of any of the allowance plans considered. . . . Not only did the housing requirements fail to increase recipients' housing consumption by much, but they also seem to have adversely affected participation, especially among households of greatest need.
>
> . . . program analyses confirm the finding of earlier studies that housing allowances and similar programs that exploit the existing housing stock have subsidy costs per assisted household about half as large as conventional public housing, section 8 new construction, and similar production-oriented programs.

Putt and Springer (1989: p. 521) note that cost-effectiveness comparisons are most appropriate "*when policy alternatives are not expected to differ in effectiveness. (emphasis added)*" Under such conditions, the least expensive alternative is preferable.

Analysis, Recommendation, and Dissemination

The real test of evaluation research is its impact on the implementation of policy. The ultimate product should not be a contribution to existing basic scientific knowledge, but rather, a social policy that the evaluation results modify. All too often, however, individuals who commission evaluations complain that the messages from the evaluations are not useful while evaluators complain their message is not used. Putt and Springer (1989: p. 31) state that

> the relevance of information for decision making depends on numerous factors—the nature of the policy concern, the constellation of interests surrounding the problem, the degree of power to make policy decisions, and the type of organization in which the decision will be made . . .

Notice how this role differs from the more traditional basic researcher's role, where it is more likely that little interest is shown in the utilization of research findings. Of course, some researchers feel data interpretation is the responsibility of the agency whose policy is being evaluated. This is a naive viewpoint, because agencies have historically shown a poor track record in policy analysis, recommendation, and dissemination. There are a number of reasons for this. First, one of the major reasons for agency failure to utilize results is ideological. Agencies feel committed to particular ways of doing things despite evidence that the program is ineffective. This is true of the general public too. As Suchman (1969) aptly puts it, "the public must be given what it needs, or it will learn to like what it gets." That is, the public is likely to become so accustomed to policy that it resists changing ineffective programs. The outcome is that "evaluators who see themselves as fearless seekers after truth come to feel that they have been assigned walk-on parts in the political pageant" (Cronbach 1980:47). Second, revisions in programs threaten more than ideology; they threaten relationships between funders, clients, and organizations (Weiss 1972: 114). Revisions also threaten organizational economics. It may not be economically feasible to change an organization's practices.

It should come as no surprise, then, that organizations resist change unless there is strong reason to do otherwise. Coleman (1972:13) stresses that unless the evaluator transmits the research back to the organization through *open publication*, the "results will ordinarily not be acted upon nor will they be openly disclosed to others, unless it benefits [the organization's] interest." He points to the Equality of Educational Opportunity study, which criticized existing education policies that HEW kept inaccessible, until the mass media picked up on its value. Therefore, the evaluator may find it necessary to insist on public dissemination of project results even *before* committing him- or herself to the evaluation task. The crucial ethical problem in evaluation research is the freedom to communicate during and after the study, subject to legitimate concerns for privacy, national security, and faithfulness to contractual commitments. As Cronbach warns (1980:4): "An open society becomes a closed society when only the officials know what is going on. In so far as information is a source of power, evaluations carried out to inform a policymaker have a disenfranchising effect."

Another reason for the evaluator to take the responsibility of reporting findings for dissemination to a larger public is that project decision makers are usually not capable of analyzing data in terms of the sophisticated tools (test factor analysis, regression analysis, and other tools discussed in advanced research and statistics courses) that social scientists have at their disposal. Therefore, it is the evaluator's responsibility to brief the policy decision makers on the utility of project results. Putt and Springer (1989:604) go even further. They stress the need for the evaluator to give oral presentations; such presentations are useful in clarifying and exploring research information. Because much of the most significant communication of findings is informal, and not all of it is deliberate; some of the most significant effects are indirect, affecting audiences far removed from the program under investigation. Oral presentations to such audiences may aid in personalizing support for the program.

Other roadblocks to high utilizations have to do with methodologic weakness and design irrelevance. On the one hand, policymakers are more likely to rely on their own experience rather than trust results of poorly done studies. On the other hand, even if the study is well executed, its design may not bear on the "critical issues." Therefore, investigators need to design evaluation studies from a knowledge of the effects that the design will have on analysis and recommendations.

On Increasing Utilization of Results

As stated, the importance of evaluation research will depend on its effectiveness in implementing policy. There are three factors that determine the relevance of evaluation research: (1) pertinence, (2) soundness, and (3) timeliness of information (Williams 1971:55). Good research design and measurement cover the first two points. The factor of timely information needs some exposition. The evaluator must always be mindful that—from the policymaker's perspective—partial information now is better than complete information later. Most studies have constant deadlines and demands. If the evaluator fails to supply current information at those deadlines, his or her value to the policy-decision process decreases accordingly. Policy issues can shift too rapidly to make application of findings and recommendations useful. So timely information is important, but not sufficient.

It is a political mistake, furthermore, for the evaluator to judge programs in all-or-none or success-failure terms. Ideological resistance can be strong enough to override strong "failure" analysis. As Cronbach (1980: 11) states "the evaluation must aim to be comprehensive, correct and complete, and credible to partisans on all sides." Evaluation is not likely to provide unequivocal answers. No report will extinguish controversy over the merits of a social program. Therefore, the researcher should focus on the *relative* effectiveness of alternative programs and policies where possible.

This may mean that evaluators need to encourage policy makers to build program *variations* into their policies. Program variations and information redundancy is highly useful to policy makers. Multiple-method approaches explained in Chapter 14 may aid in this process, because all studies have deficiencies that limit their policy applicability. Acknowledging the limitations of the design and analysis used in the evaluation can aid policymakers in arriving at more responsible decisions.

Finally, good, clear writing of project results is important. Technical jargon will put off interested parties. If the evaluator cannot write up a nontechnical report he or she should engage someone with social science journalistic abilities to write up the report for maximum dissemination. As McCloskey (1985:189) states "bad writing . . . does not get read . . . the writer who wants to keep his audience always bears in mind that at any moment it can get up and leave."

The Future of Evaluation Research

We live in an age marked by grand-scale social changes. Virtually all advanced nations have evolved into some form of welfare state. Part of this social change shows in the increasing pressures for governments and industries worldwide to be accountable. *Accountability* is a major battle cry in today's public and private sectors: "Sunshine laws (requiring open public meetings)" and "freedom of information" acts are signs of the times. However, accountability has long and respected roots in the Platonic image of the good society as one which is socially responsible and rational. One problem is that this ideal conflicts with the ideal of pluralist accommodation and compromise in modern societies. Another problem (Cronbach 1980:4) is that "a demand for accountability is a sign of pathology in the political system. . . . Accountability emphasizes looking back . . . to assign praise or blame; evaluation is better used to understand events and processes for the sake of guiding future activities."

Currently, because of this political climate, the act of *doing* evaluation research studies, not their results, provides impact to our complex political mosaic and important policy decisions. It was possible to justify heavy federal participation in "Sesame Street," guaranteed annual wage experiments, and experimental school programs *because* these programs would be subject to evaluation.

Until the late 1960s, most evaluation research conducted in the areas of health, social, rehabilitative, and welfare services was done either by university-affiliated researchers or private research agencies—usually hired through contract. Since then, public and private service agencies have been hiring their own staff researchers and have been conducting more in-house evaluation research. As a consequence, more well-trained social and behavioral scientists have gravitated toward research jobs in public and private agencies.

Growing interest and faith in evaluation have been unparalleled in history. Requests for technical assistance to establish evaluation systems within local facilities have climbed steeply. The consequence has been the phenomenal growth of masters and doctoral degree programs in evaluation research, literature dissemination (600% increase in subscribers to *Evaluation* magazine over two years), and summer institute participation and requests. Although this growth was arrested at the federal level during the era of the Reagan administration, it increased at the state level during the same period (Rossi & Wright 1984). With the establishment of their own professional identity, evaluation researchers have progressed toward creating higher standards of credibility to protect themselves from fly-by-night quackery and client, consumer, and governmental cross-pressures. Much of the excitement to be derived from this growing field lies in working on these developing problems and prospects.

Summary

Evaluation research is a growth area for individuals with social-scientific research skills. Governmental agencies increasingly either want, or are required, to assess the effectiveness of social programs. Governments wish to rationalize the identification of national priorities, choose between priorities, search for methods of attaining those priorities with minimal cost, and monitor programs used to execute those priorities.

The specific methods explained throughout this text are used in evaluation research, but such research differs from more traditional basic research in terms of objectives. Basic researchers examine hypotheses of a theoretical nature: As x increased, y increases (decreases). the evaluation researcher examines the effects of planned changes in some economic, political, administrative or social objectives. Many theoretical hypotheses concern variables over which researchers have no control, but evaluative hypotheses involve only variables over which the evaluator has control.

Because evaluation takes place within organizational settings, evaluators must learn to cope with politics. The evaluator has less freedom of choice of problems than more traditional researchers because of the political climate: Policymakers often define those problems, and impose strict time constraints on answers. Furthermore, program staff often feel threatened by research because they feel it may disrupt their routines or because they fear negative results. Because of such conflicts, program staff may pressure evaluators to limit project findings to in-house use. Policy-and decision makers may also pressure evaluators to produce much redundant information; this is quite different from basic research where parsimony is preferred.

Objectives also separate evaluation from basic research. Basic researchers more often focus upon the question of what is, while evaluator's clients are interested in what might be. The program administrator must deal with a social problem that either he or she, or some other interested party, has mandated. Because different parties may have conflicting interests, evaluators then have unique responsibilities for protecting their evaluations from some parties' attempts to nullify their efforts: To do this they must become adept at compromise, bargaining, coercion, and negotiation. The skills needed to do effective evaluation, therefore, go well beyond the scope of traditional scientific disciplines: Economist, political scientists, sociologists, anthropologists, and other specialists may find it necessary to work as a team.

This multitude of interest groups raises an important question: Whose purposes shall the evaluator assess? It is naive to think the evaluation can negate conflicts of interest. Pragmatically, the research can only clarify objectives of each group and provide empirical support for or against particular objectives. The evaluator accomplishes this task through asking a series of such focused questions as what is the state of the present system, what would the desired change in that system be, and how can that system be moved toward this ideal? Most important in this questioning process is to ask: Why have certain groups defined the situation as a social problem while others have not, and why have such groups chosen particular means of achieving that desired end and not other means? One of the primary reasons why programs fail is lack of well-defined goals and objectives. The evaluator who aids explication of program goals accomplishes much.

Evaluators do not speak of independent and dependent variables. Rather, they refer to inputs and outputs or outcomes. Inputs are measures of effort expended in a program. Outputs are the effects of the program. It is not sufficient to measure only inputs or outputs: Program staff like to focus on inputs because they wish the evaluation to recognize their efforts. However, effort does not necessarily lead to desired outcomes. By contrast, if the output shows little or no effect, without considering the actual program inputs, the evaluator cannot demonstrate that the program actually functioned as it was suppose to do. Indeed, some programs that ostensibly have so-called "boomerang effects," when properly evaluated demonstrate improper program functioning. Evaluators speak of intended and unintended outputs because some programs actually do boomerang.

Situational variables are a third important factor in evaluation; these are variables that are not subject to project control, but which might be plausible candidates as independent variables. Because situational variables may confound study results, evaluators are concerned that they be able to employ the strongest possible research design. Whereas basic research traditionally is strong in use of designs with high internal validity, the political nature of evaluation research calls for designs that emphasize high external validity, or generalizability. Ironically, the inherent political nature of evaluation research is likely to compromise this ideal: Believable controls are unlikely because of political cross-pressures. Time pressures also compromise research design and strategy: Decision makers prefer some data now to all of the data later. These pressures force evaluators to consider more creative means of producing quality data fast.

Control over research design in evaluation research normally presents political problems because program staff rarely understand the need for true experimental conditions. The benefit of randomization is based on long-term goals, but program staff are more likely to focus on the short-term detriment of denial of service. The result is pressures to stick to nonequivalent comparison group designs. However, creative and persistent evaluators sometimes do convince program authorities of the value of true experimental controls. Large-scale social experiments that use randomization may suffer from reactive effects of measurement, offsetting gains of randomizations. Part of the solution to this problem is to employ behavioral rather than attitudinal measures of project outcomes.

Evaluation researchers have added several new research tools not normally found in traditional research: quick-analysis, social audits, cost-benefit analysis, and cost-effectiveness analysis. Quick-analysis evolved in response to the time pressures of politics. In quick-analysis, the evaluator analyzes whatever partially appropriate data which already exist rather than produce a whole new data set that would take much time. The evaluator must often think quickly about fundamental aspects underlying the policy problem and how the problem may be roughly but logically answered. One technique of quick-analysis is the decision tree; another is the use of subjective probability analysis. Decision trees aid the researcher in tracing out the best to worst case scenarios. Subjective probabilities give a rational means of deciding how likely any particular scenario might occur.

The social audit provides a means of tracing resource inputs throughout the life course of a program to find out whether inputs actually reached intended recipients and, if so, whether they were effective. Sometimes inputs get lost or diverted; this technique aids the analysis of such possibilities. Social audits also assist policymakers who monitor the efficiency of monetary disbursements and services.

Cost-benefit analysis provides another means of measuring program efficiency. Because resources are typically scarce, cost-benefit analysis is premised on the efficient and effective application of those resources. Early use of cost-benefit analysis focused on main program effects and monetary costs and benefits. However, evaluators have come to understand that social programs often have complex and subtle costs and benefits and that what is a "cost" or a "benefit" is a valuation. Perceived costs and benefits may not match up across competing interest groups. In addition to more easily researched direct costs of programs such as staff salaries, evaluators search for such indirect costs as deterioration in quality of life, opportunity costs, and the value of foregone labor. Other costs and benefits are more speculative: for example, the emotional loss from homicide or rape. Evaluators attempt to focus on the most objectively supportable costs and benefits. Although this adds an element of conservatism to their work, it makes their results more politically viable.

Cost-effectiveness analysis is closely related to cost-benefit analysis; it compares the cost and benefits of alternative programs. Cost-effectiveness analysis is most appealing when exactly one dimension of a program is hard to value monetarily or when policy or program alternatives are not expected to differ materially in effectiveness. In either case, cost-effectiveness analysis may shed light on the least expensive alternatives.

The bottom line of evaluation research is its impact on policy implementation. Although traditional researchers may not care whether or not their research is used, evaluators strive to influence policy. Unfortunately, ideology and interorganizational relationships often impede the use of evaluations. Evaluators find it necessary, therefore, to contract for public dissemination of project results before they start work. They also find it necessary to maintain good working relationships with the staff throughout the project. The continued briefing of key decision makers and audiences affected by the results may smooth over some of those ideologic problems.

Of all the factors that are important to the use of evaluations in implementing policy, perhaps timeliness of information is the most critical. The evaluator must keep in mind that partial information now is better than full information later. Policymakers work under strict deadlines and policy issues can change rapidly: Both of these facts pressure evaluators for timely analysis. The credibility of evaluation, however, depends on evaluators focusing on relative program effectiveness, rather than equivocal success or failure. To do otherwise is to invite perceptions that the evaluator is partisan.

The disparity between social science and policy is the fundamental reason why evaluation is so difficult to complete. The objectives are totally different. In social science, the goal is to formulate theory that is innovative and original. Scientific theory must be plausible and convincible; it must also be internally consistent. Theory proceeds through argumentation; it thrives on criticism and argumentation.

Policy, by contrast, is a series of guidelines for action. It must be geared to the fulfillment of widely accepted or powerfully supported goals. It must hold promise for tangibly meeting those goals. It must be economically feasible and cost effective. It must appeal to a large section of the relevant public and show potential for gaining strong support. Without these criteria, policy has little chance of implementation.

CHAPTER

14

Triangulation: The Necessity for Multimethod Approaches

We must use all available weapons of attack, face our problems realistically and not retreat to the land of fashionable sterility, learn to sweat over our data with an admixture of judgment and intuitive rumination, and accept the usefulness of particular data even when the level of analysis available for them is markedly below that available for other data in the empirical area.[1]

Key Terms

Aggregative analysis	Ecological correlation
Cohort analysis	Ethnocentrism
Contextual comparisons	Fallacy of the wrong level of analysis
Cross-sectional study	
Cultural analysis	Galton's problem
Ecological analysis	Institutional analysis

---

[1]Margenau, H. (1959) Philosophical problems concerning the meaning of measurements in physics, (C. W. Churchman & P. Ratoosh, eds.) *Measurement: Definitions and Theories*, New York: John Wiley, p. 163.

Interactive analysis

Longitudinal study

Organizational analysis

Panel study

Replication

Reputational method

Social network

Societal analysis

Time series data

Trend study

Triangulation

Study Guide Questions

1. Explain the basic rationales for using multiple methods.

2. Explain the seven procedures for improving theory triangulation.

3. Why do studies that do not take time into account produce misrepresentative conclusions?

4. What are the principle advantages and disadvantages of panel, cross-sectional, and trend studies?

5. Explain the primary strategies of cross-national research.

6. What fundamental problems plague cross-cultural comparisons? In spite of these problems, what are the benefits of cross-cultural research?

7. How does the use of multiple investigators aid validity and reliability of research? Multiple sources of participants?

8. What are the principle differences between and uses of within- and between-methods triangulation?

9. What differences in information come from the seven dimensions of analysis?

10. Describe the fallacy of the wrong level of analysis and discuss how social scientists can guard against it.

Just as a wood chisel and jackhammer each have different functions and uses, each method, tool, or technique has unique strengths and weaknesses. Closed-ended questions are most appropriate when the researcher clearly understands a variable's domain or dimensions, but inappropriate when the question is highly reactive or obtrusive. Hidden cameras may be nonreactive, but raise ethically sensitive issues and may distort data because of camera angle or coverage. One of the earliest sociologists to give recognition to the strengths and weaknesses of different methods was Zelditch (1962). He argued that surveys were the most adequate and efficient means of gathering frequency distributions, participant observation the prototype for incidents and histories, and interviewing informants the most efficient means of learning about institutionalized norms and statuses. He explained not only why these three types of information and methods provided the best matches, but why each of these methods were inefficient and inadequate for collecting other types of information.

Traditionally most social and behavioral researchers have not given much serious thought to the quality of their research endeavors. Chun, Barnowe, Wykowski, Cobb, and French (1972) showed that researchers select such psychological measures as attitude scales according to the convenience of their immediate availability rather than by the rational criteria of reliability or validity. In addition they noted that 63% of these measures had only been used once and 19% only twice while only 3% had been used more than ten times. Brown and Gilmartin (1969:288) revealed that 64% of all research reported in the two most prestigious social science journals in 1965–1966 were based on verbal reports collected through questionnaires or interviews. They also noted that 75% of mid-1960s social-science research had its setting in the United States, and 85% referred to only one point in time. Furthermore, 54% of the studies they surveyed used the individual person as the primary unit of analysis. Bahr, Caplow, and Chadwick (1983) classified 300 deliberate replications in social science research during the period 1973–1981 according to variation in time, place, method, and subjects. They found that 48% of these replications only varied subjects or subjects and methods. They were particularly dismayed that these replicators paid no attention to varying time, place, and methods; time, methods, and subjects; and place, methods, and subjects.

These surveys of research methods paint a dismal picture. Theories of social life cannot progress if they focus solely on individuals. Advancement in the social sciences depends on data that are not culturebound or timebound, that are replicable and replicated, involve macroscopic problems, are concerned with the correspondence between what is done and what is said, and pay more than lip service to reliability, validity, and replication.

Since the publication of the Chun et al. (1972) and Brown and Gilmartin (1969) studies there has been an explosion of calls for more use of multiple methods. Through on-line searches of psychological and sociological data bases I located over 250 research titles in the psychological literature and over 70 research paper titles in the sociological literature published between 1980 and 1987 that refer to multiple methods or triangulation of theory or methods. Clearly, social scientists are moving beyond the methodological parochialism of the past. Fewer researchers push particular methods as superior to all others; social investigators more clearly recognize the constraints imposed by particular methods and theories.

Boring (1953) was among the first behavioral scientists to warn of such "method-boundedness." He warned (p. 172) that

> as long as a new construct has only the single operational definition that it received at birth, it is just a construct. When it gets two alternative operational

definitions, it is beginning to be validated. When the defining operations, because of proven correlations, are many, then it becomes reified.

Others have since continued to reemphasize the need for such multiple operationalizations as a corrective for irrelevant components of any measurement procedure. Campbell and Fiske continued this line of reasoning in a citation classic (1959) when they asserted (p. 82) that

> When a hypothesis can survive the confrontation of a series of complementary methods of testing, it contains a degree of validity unattainable by one tested within the more constricted framework of a single method. . . . Findings from this latter approach must always be subject to the suspicion that they are methodbound: Will the comparison totter when exposed to an equally prudent but different testing method?

Research methods are never atheoretical or neutral in representing the world "out there." They act as filters through which the researcher selectively experiences the research environment. By using one's knowledge of how each method may selectively bias or distort the scientist's picture of "reality," the researcher may select combinations of methods that more accurately represent what is "out there."

Let us consider, first, a navigator's plight in locating the ship's position. If the navigator picks up signals from only one known navigational aid, the navigator may know which course the ship is following, but still cannot ascertain the distance from that signal. However, if the navigator can locate *two* known navigational aids, and knows their distance from each other, then elementary high-school geometry solves the ship's exact location.

Second, consider the military strategist's concern with knocking out a *known* enemy position. The strategist knows that the likelihood of achieving this aim is greater if the enemy is caught in a crossfire from several different positions. What these two examples have in common is the use of several locational markers aimed at pinpointing a single objective.

Now let us consider this triangulatory logic in terms of use of scales. We may view scales as primitive triangulatory devices. We have seen that they are more reliable and valid than single indicators of any phenomenon. In terms of our navigational and military analogies, scales use a number of locational markers to pinpoint a particular objective. Therefore, why all the fuss about using a number of locational markers? Because we cannot *directly* observe most of our variables. When researchers attempt to measure such abstractions as quarks or social groups, they are really like blind people led into an arena and asked to identify an elephant by touching only its leg. Certainly, we might make better guesses if we could pool the information of a whole group of blind people, each of whom has touched a different part of the elephant.

Previously I said that scales are only primitive triangulatory devices. The reason for this is that most scales, while composed of more than one locational marker, use locational markers *with the same biases*. If you ask people about their feelings toward UFOs (Unidentified Flying Objects), some of them may believe they exist. However, some of those same people may also believe that you might think them strange if they said they existed or that they thought

UFOs were "good." Such persons are likely to give you a false response because they give only the socially acceptable response. Another means of getting at feelings toward UFOs might be to observe behavior. Some 13 out of every 10,000 Japanese voters chose the UFO Party in the 1989 Upper House elections. This might measure extremely strong positive feelings toward UFOs (and the contributions their passengers might make to cleaning up the social problems on Mother Earth) for some of those people, but of course some UFO Party votes may have been simply protest votes against the other political parties. As you can see, each type of measure has advantages and disadvantages.

Likewise, scientists wish to use *complementary* methods because each method has advantages and disadvantages that limit its ability to measure such abstractions as "social class" and "cohesion." Therefore, just as we prefer scales to single measures, we prefer the use of several methodological approaches to a single approach.

Triangulation extends beyond multiple method approaches. The following sections introduce triangulation through testing competing theories, analysis across different times, problems and prospects of cross-cultural and cross-national triangulation, investigator triangulation, participant triangulation, and methodological triangulation. Time and financial limitations normally preclude individual investigators from employing all of these devices. Nevertheless, researchers who build as many of these devices into their research as their financial and temporal budgets allow help build a more theoretically rigorous science.

Theoretical Triangulation

Adherence to particular theoretical biases can lead to investigative ethnocentrism. The researcher with a social change or dynamics orientation often unwittingly ignores evidence about social stability. Further, particular theoretical biases support certain methods more than others, and vice versa: Survey researchers who study the stability of attitudes and opinions are most likely to use such methods as interviews; those interested in change are more drawn toward field research or experimentation. If there is a moral here, it is that investigators need to actively design research to adequately test competing theories.

Blumstein and Cohen's (1987) research into characterizing criminal careers clearly demonstrates this need. They observed that most knowledge about crime and criminals derives from one-shot data collections, in which the analyst links crime rates in a community with such community attributes as racial composition, age distributions, and percent of broken homes. Their own approach was to focus on the criminal-careers of individual offenders, and to observe offender crime participation rates over time.

Blumstein and Cohen's theory led them to observe offender participation rates, initiation rates, termination rates, and the associated length of criminal careers. Their innovative theoretical approach reveals important new insights: Annual offending frequency was reasonably constant for those offenders who stayed criminally active; termination of criminal behavior rates were relatively low for active offenders in their 30s; and offending frequencies were relatively insensitive to such attributes as age, sex, and race for active offenders. From the point of view of theoretical triangulation, these are important observations because they are opposite to those derived from one-shot analyses on understanding and controlling crime.

Another exemplar is Fiorentine's (1987) work on the persistence of the gap between men and women applicants to college premedical programs. In this study, he focused on quantitative comparison of two theoretical approaches: the structural barriers approach and the normative approach. The *structural barriers* approach hypothesizes that sex differences in occupational aspirations and commitment are consequences of blocked opportunities; that is, this approach theorizes that colleges and medical schools discriminate against women applicants. The *normative barriers* approach takes a different tack. It presumes that young women are likely to view the pursuit of success in a high-status career as a transgression of norms. In other words, the normative approach presumes that young women anticipate social rejection if they are successful in a career so they limit their ambitions to more "appropriate" female-typical occupations.

Fiorentine (1987) tested each theory. He used numerous quantitative measures, such as cumulative grade-point averages, and required science course grades of applicants to test for discrimination between the sexes; he also used qualitative evidence from unstructured interviews with applicants. He concluded that neither theory was completely adequate, and (p. 1133) that "the persistence rate of female and male premedical students [is] not so much the result of normative *barriers* to female career commitment and success [as] the result of normatively appropriate *alternatives* to these demands that are currently afforded women." A man's achievements are still tied to his own occupational success, but a woman continues to have *two* routes to adult status: She can tie herself to her husband's status or to her own socioeconomic achievements. Because women have socially acceptable alternatives to achievement for the purpose of attaining adult status, many of them choose marriage rather than pursue careers of their own.

Although studies like Fiorentine's or Blumstein and Cohen's appear to be becoming more typical of social science research, theoretical ethnocentrism still exists in the majority of published research. Progress toward unifying theories of human life and behavior depend on taking theories at odds with each other more seriously in the design of research. Westie (1957:150, 153) recommended seven procedures for improving theory triangulation.

1. List all existing and plausible propositions in a given subject area.
2. For each of these propositions, construct a list of plausible interpretations.
3. Conduct actual research to determine which of the presupposed empirical relationships actually exist.

4. Discard those presupposed relationships and interpretations that fail to survive empirical tests.
5. Reinstigate empirical investigation to select the best interpretations from any contradictory propositions.
6. Use the list of those propositions that pass the empirical test to reassess the theories from which they were derived.
7. Reformulate the theory based on the empirical tests conducted.

The advantages of Westie's procedure are fourfold: (1) This procedure minimizes the chance of constructing *internally* consistent logical theories that ignore plausible contradictory propositions outside the theoretical system; (2) the procedure builds in means of testing a whole range of plausible theoretical interpretations; (3) the procedure extends confirmation or doubt to a larger number of theoretical propositions than the usual, more particularistic method of testing a particular set of propositions; and (4) because these procedures make alternative explanations explicit from the start, they are more likely to survive as alternative explanations after investigation, thus encouraging research programs as opposed to isolated research projects.

Time

Maines (1987:306) states the need for time-based studies bluntly: "*Studies . . . that do not take into account fundamental differences in temporality will always produce misrepresentative conclusions* (italics in original)." We all recognize social change through words that have come into current use: for example, modernization, individual maturation, and bureaucratization. Researchers use several types of research designs to study such temporal processes: cross-sectional data, cohorts and panels to study social trends and do longitudinal analyses.

Cross-Sectional Studies

Sometimes, an investigator makes an attempt to study change and process through *cross-sectional* data—data collected at *one* point in time with the intention of making statements concerning *time-related* process. Child development researchers often compare children of different ages at one point in time. These researchers may *wrongly* conclude that any differences they find are due to aging. Cross-sectional studies are open to more rival alternative explanations than data collected on the same group of people over many points in time. For example, cross-sectional data indicate a general trend toward closed mindedness with age. With only cross-sectional data, one could explain this observation as due to aging processes *or* to such other differences as the lower educational attainment of older persons. One could better test the aging explanation through following a *cohort* (a specific age group) through the life cycle.

One must be careful in choosing time-series versus cross-sectional methods because each, like every method, has its own weaknesses and strengths.

Cohort Analysis

Hastings and Berry (1979) compiled an interdisciplinary set of classic papers on cohort analysis and the problems of separating age, period, and cohort effects that the analyst interested in cohorts ought to read. A *birth cohort* is a set of people who are born within the same time interval: the years of the Great Depression, World War II, the Vietnamese Conflict, the Reagan Administration years, or the decade of the 1910s provide several examples of birth cohort intervals. Quite separate from particular years in which people are born is biological *age*. For example, intuitively we assume that persons age 18 are different than persons age 65, *independent* of the birth cohorts into which they were born. Finally, a *period* is a specific time interval *independent* of ages of the persons included in that time interval. The Vietnamese Conflict is a period; The persons born during the Vietnamese Conflict make up a specific birth cohort.

Until the 1980s, researchers had no satisfactory method for separating the effects of age, period, and cohort in studies of social change. Furthermore, the standard cohort tables they used in their research were difficult to read even by well trained cohort analysts. Table 14–1 gives an example of a standard cohort table for homicide frequencies per 100,000 persons in the United States. If you read across every line, you can see a general trend, regardless of age group, indicating that homicides increased in frequency over each time period. Furthermore, if you read down each row, you can verify that ages 25–29 are the most likely age for becoming a homicide victim. More difficult to judge is (1) how much affect age and period have independently of one another on homicides; and (2) what the separate cohort effects, if any, might be. For example, a

Table 14-1   *Age-Period-Cohort Crosstabulation of Homicide Frequencies per 100,000*

Age Group	1952–1956	1957–1961	Period 1962–1966	1967–1971	1972–1976	Cohort
1. 15–19	6.2	7.5	8.6	15.1	17.1	11
2. 20–24	11.88	13.6	14.2	22.9	25.5	10
3. 25–29	12.4	11.9	13.6	19.3	22.2	9
4. 30–34	10.8	10.6	10.9	15.5	16.9	8
5. 35–39	9.4	8.8	9.1	12.5	13.4	7
6. 40–44	7.7	6.8	7.1	9.6	10.2	6
7. 45–49	6.1	5.7	5.5	7.3	7.4	
Cohort	1	2	3	4	5	

Source: Smith (1979)

group age 15–19 in 1952–1956 would be age 20–24 in 1957–1961, and age 25–29 in 1957–1961. For this reason, the 11 cohort numbers shown in Table 14-1 are for the *upper left to lower right diagonals*. The lower left hand-most 6.1 number and the upper right hand-most 17.1 number are cohort homicide rates for only one point in time. The lowest most diagonal of numbers 7.7 and 5.7 give homicide rates for the same cohort at two points in time; the 9.4, 6.8, and 5.5 in the next lower right-hand diagonal give numbers for the same birth co-hort at three different points in time; and so on. You can readily see how complex these changes are to visualize and understand.

Nakamura (1986) solved both the statistical and visual problems of co-hort analysis with a technique illustrated in Figure 14-1. First, he demonstrated that to use the technique he had in mind, the data for periods and age groups had to have the same time interval. In Figure 14-1, this requirement is satisfied by the fact that both age groups and periods are for five-year time periods. Next, Nakamura wrote a computer program that computes the overall arithmetic mean score for all of the data. Then, his program uses statistics to compute deviations of age, period, and cohort effects from the expected average value. Finally, the program displays these deviations in standardized units so they can be compared directly with one another.

With the above simplified principles in mind, look at Figure 14-1. You can easily see that the period effects increased over time from about − 0.2 to + 0.3 over the five periods from 1952 through 1976. By contrast, age effects are close to the statistical average for 15-19 year olds, then jump to a high of almost 0.4 standard units higher than average for 20-24 years olds before starting to drop off to almost − 0.5 standard units below average for persons age 45-49. Finally, there are no cohort effects at all; all of the 11 cohort periods are close to the mean. In sum, Nakamura's method demonstrates a clear trend toward increasing homicidal violence in America from 1952 to 1976 and also substantiates the belief that young people age 20-24 are particularly at risk.

The only remaining problem with this approach concerns the problem of size of ages, periods, and cohorts. Nakamura has played with different statistical assumptions—for instance, assuming that cohorts have the same or different numbers of individuals represented—and came up with slightly different graphs. For example, when he added the assumption that cohorts 5 and 11 were equal in size the resulting graph showed a small cohort effect. He also points out that other researchers (Knoke & Burke 1980) using a still different set of assumptions came to conclusions opposite his own.

The Knoke and Burke assumptions led to figures showing a decreasing period effect, an increasing age effect, and a huge increasing cohort effect. Knoke and Burke's results seem much less probable than Nakamura's for several reasons: First, the Knoke and Burke results, unlike Nakamura's, led to results *the opposite* of what a careful reading of Table 14-1 suggests. This indicates that one or the other set of results is wrong. Second, it is hard to imagine how cohort effects could be as huge as Knoke and Burke found: They ranged from − 1.4 for cohort 1 to 1.9 for cohort 11.

What kinds of differences in persons only five years apart in birth data could create such huge increasing risks over a period of only 11 cohorts that

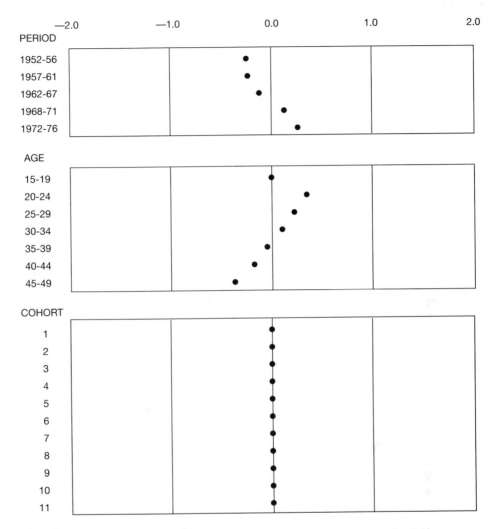

Figure 14-1. Statistically estimated effects of period, age, and cohort on homicide rates per 100,000 in the Untied States.

Source: Adapted from Nakamura (1988:363)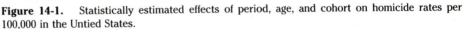

only show up after World War II? Third, homicide data has long indicated results closer to Nakamura's visual aid than to Knoke and Burke's. For example, other studies have indicated that young persons in their twenties have the most danger of being murdered and that the chances of murder decrease after that age. Also, there has been a consistent trend toward more homicides since World War II. Nevertheless, there are two reasons for uncertainty. First, none of those earlier studies tried to separate out age, period, and cohort effects. Second, it is impossible presently to know for sure which set of statistical assumptions is closer to the truth. The wide differences in outcomes of each set of assumptions indicate that cohort analysts should pay close attention to their assumptions before assuming their method of interpretation is correct.

Panel Analysis

Researchers often use *panel analysis* to compare the *same* measurements for the *same* sample at several *different* points in time. A special type of panel analysis already briefly mentioned is cohort analysis. Cohort analysis depends on a sample of relatively narrow-ranged ages. A researcher interested in socialization might take a sample of individuals between the ages of five to ten, and study this *cohort* at several yearly intervals. By contrast, a researcher interested in unemployment might take a sample of all individuals legally old enough to work full-time (14 years of age and older), and study this *panel* over several years. It is important in both cohort and panel analysis to analyze the data in unaggregated (individual) form because aggregated data can mask actual change. If 20% of people change from more to less positive attitudes, while an equal percentage change from less to more, separate data in aggregate form could not reveal such changes.

Panel studies also often involve invalidity problems of subject mortality and reactive testing effects (see Chapter 4). In most studies of Japanese-Americans and other immigrant groups to the United States, the researcher separates them out into first-generation immigrants, second-generation offspring, and so on. A 1988 research project into the 40-odd Japanese-American families who settled in St. Louis after World War II, found only three first-generation immigrants left, and a couple dozen second-generation offspring. The remainder had mostly died, and a few had moved elsewhere.

Kohn and Schooler (1978) were more fortunate in a follow-up study of the effects of occupation on personality. Of 883 randomly selected men, they succeeded in locating 820 (93%) ten years later. Through the cooperation of the post office, telephone company, past employers, and unions, they traced these men even though many had changed residences a great many times. Reactive effects—the question of how the process of measurement may *change* that which the researcher is measuring—also creates problems. Chapter 4 explained the reactive effects of the longitudinal study of American health. We know that repeatedly measuring the healthiness of individuals changes their personal health care habits.

Sometime, to avoid problems of reactive effects and participant mortality, the researcher foregoes panel or cohort analysis and takes different samples at different times. While this cuts down on costs of finding the same individuals twice, it is a much less effective approach to the study of change than is panel or cohort analysis. Its disadvantages are that it (1) may introduce invalidity through equivalent samples (history, maturation, differential selection of participants), and (2) can only be examined in aggregate form because the same participants are not measured at each point in time.

In addition, the panel study is actually a time series of static "snapshots" or cross-sectional analyses. For this reason some researchers use *trend studies* of selected processes, not at a few isolated points as in a panel study, but continually over time. The major disadvantage of this procedure is that practically one can focus only on relatively few processes in comparison to panel analysis.

Figure 14-2 displays the unmistakably related trend relationship between cigarette smoking and lung cancer. The nature of this relationship was obscure for a long time because of the long latent period between the increase in cigarette consumption and the increase in the incidence of lung cancer. In men (top two lines), the habit of smoking began to increase at the beginning of the twentieth century, but the corresponding trend in deaths from lung cancer did not begin until after 1920. In women (bottom two lines) smoking began later, and lung cancers are only now appearing.

Disadvantages of Temporal Studies

There are also many practical drawbacks to temporal studies. Perhaps the most obvious is the fact that they often require long waiting periods. Few scientists have the job security to play this waiting game. Rarely is a university enlightened enough to sit patiently for a decade or more while one of its scientists "just" collects time-series data. Some researchers bypass this problem through retrospective time-series techniques that are more economical and less time-consuming. Studies on careers and social mobility use retrospective

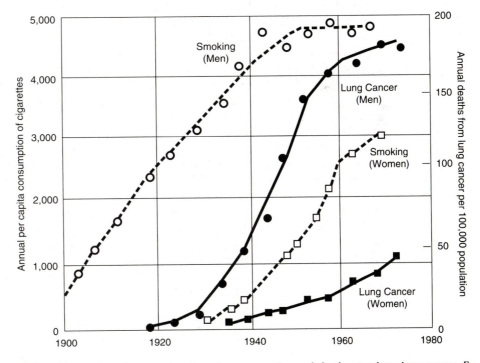

Figure 14-2. Annual per capita cigarette consumption and death rates from lung cancer, England and Wales 1900–1980.

Source: From "The Cancer Problem" by John Cairns, *Scientific American* (November 1979), p. 72. Copyright © 1979 Scientific American, Inc. All rights reserved.

time-series techniques quite often (by asking respondents what job they had five years ago, ten years ago, and so on). However, memory decay presents severe problems for the analyst of such data.

Second, changes in various conditions may affect the quality of one's time-series data. A researcher often words an interview question slightly differently at a later date. However, changes in responses may occur not due to actual social conditions but rather to interview technique or instrumentation change.

Third, changes in one's variables of interest may have to be standardized in terms of other extraneous changes. As an instance of this, consider absolute changes in birth rates. Absolute birth rate changes are meaningless—contemplate an absolute birth rate of 100 new births in a city of 10,000, compared to the same city 20 years later with a population of 40,000 and 400 yearly births. Absolutely the birthrate has risen fourfold; relative to population size, however, it has not increased relatively.

Fourth, the researcher must chose time periods appropriately. Some social processes are relatively short run, such as those found in many attitude-change experiments; but developmental changes may take years to work themselves out. The development of HIV infections takes at least five years. Women's life expectancy rates in the United States took 180 years to double from approximately 40 to 80 years. Most of the changes in homicide and motor vehicle thefts between 1946 and 1984 can be accounted for by 40–year changes in the American age structure, business cycles, criminal opportunity structures, and rate of imprisonment (Cohen & Land 1987). Thus, repeated observations must correspond with the time of actual change to gauge the process accurately.

This comparison of cross-sectional and longitudinal analyses underscores the need for combining approaches where the researcher observes structure, structural changes, and intervening processes. Kass (1977) compared the longitudinal and the cross-sectional perspectives in examining changes in male income from 1950 to 1970. In a longitudinal cohort study, he found that as men age, up to their retirement, their income continues to increase. However, a cross-sectional analysis comparing groups of different ages, at the same point in time, leads to the conclusion that there is a decline in income during the later working years. Even after adjusting for change in the cost of living and productivity levels of workers, these conflicting conclusions do not change to any great degree. This type of paradox should lead the analyst of social data to be wary of the type of analysis of findings.

Location

If the social sciences have neglected the time dimension they have been equally negligent of the location dimension. Brown and Gilmartin's (1969) study of sociology found that the settings of 75% of American sociological research published in the 1960s were in the United States. Throughout the 1970s and 1980s, there was little sign of encouragement: Easily 95% of citations in the three most prestigious journals of sociology in the United States are to works published in English. Yet many scholars write research as if they have discovered basic principles that would hold true anywhere, anytime. As with other methodological decisions, the convenience of available populations is often counterproductive to generalization.

By the use of relatively homogeneous populations, we lose potentially large amounts of variation in social life and its causes. Even a cursory perusal of differences between nations leads one to the conclusion that social variation in the United States is relatively meager. To name only a few: We live in a country with an annual gross national product per capita of over $15,000, while most of Africa suffers from annual per capital GNP of less than $250; our annual inflation rate has been less than 5% during a period when Brazilians experienced annual inflation in the hundreds; and the Japanese experience less than 1.4 murders per 100,000 population a year because of strict gun control, while some Americans experience 6.8 per 100,000 population, or nearly five times the Japanese rate (United Nations 1985).

In his 1987 presidential address to the annual American Sociological Association, Melvin Kohn spoke of the indispensability of cross-national research for (p. 713) "establishing the generality of findings and the validity of interpretations derived from single-nation studies." Fundamentally, Kohn argues for two locational strategies: The researcher may search for statistical regularities or cultural and historical differences. When the researches uncovers cross-national similarities and regularities, the breadth of our knowledge increases. Kohn's (see Kohn & Schooler 1978) own work provides a classic illustration of this first strategy. He has clearly demonstrated that social stratification consistently affects personal values and thoughts. His work (1987) in the United States, Italy, Japan, and Poland has shown that people with higher income, occupational status, and job self determination enjoy greater occupational self-direction which in turn leads those persons to value the self-direction in other parts of their lives and for their children.

The second strategy of cross-national research is the search for cultural and historical differences. Kohn (1987:729) points out that

> In interpreting cross-national *differences*, historical considerations cannot be merely implicit; history must come to the forefront of any interpretation. For example, after demonstrating remarkable parallels in both the causes and consequences of the French, Russian, and Chinese revolutions, Skocpol (1979) had to explain differences, particularly in revolutionary outcomes, in terms of historically unique circumstances.

Of course, historical differences are the basis for cultural differences, so the investigator must also pay attention to cultural explanations of cross-national differences. The historically rooted cultural norms underlying Japanese marriages are quite different from those in the U.S.A. Schooler and Naoi (1988) state that in Japan, the adult couple relationship is seen as much less important than that of mother and child, compared to the United States. In addition,

Japanese women rank the importance of their roles as individuals less than their roles as mothers or wives; this is the reverse of ranking of American women. Such normative differences pervade other such areas of social life as work organization identification; American men do not identify with their work place roles with the same degree of ferver as Japanese men.

LeVine (1966) pioneered a comparative strategy of convergent validation, in which the researcher measures each hypothesized difference between populations with different instruments, designed to capture the same type of choice pattern in different situations. His analysis of dream reports, values, and public opinion poll data across different ethnic groups in Nigeria produced strong convergence of findings. This convergence of findings strengthened his conviction that the differences among the three ethnic groups was not an artifact of his measuring instruments.

Analysis across space, particularly with comparison of divergent cultures, presents some fundamental problems of analysis: (1) causal inferences from statistical associations; (2) societal or subsocietal unit definition; (3) sampling bias; (4) Galton's problem, the problem of interdependence of cases; (5) data-quality control, the problem of trustworthiness of data; (6) categorization, the problem of defining concepts for categories that are suitable in any cultural context; and (7) costs of time, logistics, and money. Each problem is discussed below.

Causal Inferences from Statistical Associations

A standard cross-cultural objective is to show statistical associations between two variables. Bourguignon's (1976) work on trance and spirit possession provides a good example. His survey of over 480 societies showed clear distinctions. He found spirit possession practiced by itself with no reference to trance only in noncomplex, nomadic societies with small populations where the principle occupations were hunting, gathering, or fishing. These societies also had a local decision-making structure at the level of the band or community, and had no class structure. By contrast, those societies that practiced *both* spirit possession and trance were relatively complexly stratified sedentary societies that engaged in animal husbandry or agricultural subsistence. These societies also practiced decision making that went beyond the local community. Bourguignon asserted another possibility: that the *type of society causes* such practices. He based his assertion on much cited work by Barry, Child, and Bacon (1959) that described how subsistence societies discourage qualities of independence and initiative, and hunting and gathering societies encourage autonomy and initiative.

This temptation to assume that association and correlation means causation is often great, even though any introductory statistics text states that correlation is only a necessary, not a sufficient, condition for causation. The problem is even more critical in cross-cultural than in single-culture research because the observed relationship may well be an artifact of one or more of the following problems: definition of unit of analysis, sampling bias, Galton's problem, data quality control, or cross-cultural categorization, each of which will be discussed in turn.

Societal and Subsocietal Unit Definitions

Naroll (1968:248) lists six criteria that researchers used to define societal or subsocietal units of comparison: (1) distribution of some particular variable, (2) territorial contiguity, (3) political organization, (4) language, (5) ecological similarity, and (6) local community structure. Defining such large-scale units of analysis is complex and somewhat arbitrary. For example, language is often inadequate. Some African nations have adopted English or French as the official bureaucratic languages because they consist of many mutually unintelligible dialects and languages; Chinese, itself, is actually a collection of such languages as Cantonese and Mandarin which are as dissimilar as French and Italian. Similarly, although the United States and Canada are politically distinct nations, economically and socially, they are difficult to separate as anyone who studies communication flows, markets, personal acquaintances, or other means of interaction soon discovers.

Vallier (1971) argues that cross-cultural researchers have an *overconcern* with society as the unit of selection and observation. While he concedes that societies are of special theoretical interest because of problems of "integration, legitimacy, continuity, and order" that are not exhibited in other types of collectivities, he asserts that the chief drawback in characterizing societies in terms of such cultural terms as "dominant values," "modal personality," "overriding beliefs," and "typical patterns" is that they close off other explanatory levels. Numerous researchers (see the summary by Kohn 1987) have followed Vallier's suggestion to balance cultural explanations with such structural interpretations as role systems and status hierarchies. As Vallier (1971:210) states, "the 'cultural' fallacy in certain kinds of macro-structural studies is as prevalent, and perhaps as misleading, as the ecological fallacy in studies of behavior." (See the final section of this chapter.)

In addition to the theoretical problems of defining societies, there are practical problems. First, it is extremely difficult to observe a total primitive society, much less a total contemporary, complex society. Therefore, the use of total societies as the unit of analysis puts the researcher under pressure to search for summary data, "typical" patterns, and "distinct essences." These procedures have the unfortunate consequence of representing societies as more homogeneous and harmonious than is actually the case. Both the Japanese and American mass media misrepresent the Japanese as much more homogeneous and harmonious than scholars know they are. For example, few Westerners know of the environmental protests that still go on, such as the one that continues unabatedly over the heavy-handed way in which the Japanese government imposed Narita Airport on the rural outskirts of Tokyo in the 1960s, or the frenetic tension built into the almost unbelievably competitive

educational system, or the Japanese *yakuza* (mafia) and its influence on cocaine use. Cross-cultural researchers have an obligation to explore such societal cleavages, competition and conflict, and social strains.

Second, using the total society as the unit of analysis limits the number of
cases the researcher can study. There are officially slightly more than 130 nations that are United Nations members. Perhaps some 5,000 distinct societies
exist; of these, there is ethnographic data for only about 2,000. The most as-
sessable and complete documentation—Murdock's Ethnographic Sample—
contains data on only about 750 societies.

Sampling Bias

Most cross-cultural data depend on nonrandom sampling of societies. Ideally,
it would be desirable for researchers to use stratified probability sampling,
based on geographical area, because neighboring societies are usually more
alike than nonneighboring societies. Such similarities between neighboring societies create problems for correlational analysis because cultural diffusion *in-
flates* correlations spuriously—what we call Galton's problem.

Galton's Problem

The major weakness of cross-cultural methodology is Galton's problem: Using
cultural units as *independent* tests of correlations between variables when
each cultural unit may not actually represent independent trials. Both the Hopi
and Navajo Indians use a rain dance. Although these neighboring tribes have
different cultural origins, it would be a mistake to assume these dances exist
independently of each other. Cultural diffusion of the rain dance from one culture to the other is a distinct possibility, and independence of cases may be a
false assumption.

Indeed, variables are often highly associated cross-culturally because of
geographical diffusion of traits between neighboring cultures. Some types of
Chinese noodles entered Japan about a thousand years ago and became a staple part of the Japanese diet. In fact, when Western culture opened up trade
routes to the East, a number of major cultural diffusions in eating habits took
place. Marco Polo brought back the Chinese noodle to Italy so that most of us
who eat "Italian" food do not realize that Italian noodles are a post-thirteenth-
century adaptation of Chinese cuisine. The "hot" curried foods we associate
with Korea, Thailand, and Mexico are due not to the indigenous cultures, but to
Dutch traders who introduced cayenne pepper from the Northern Caribbean
Sea into many trading posts before the local cultures adapted it to their own
agriculture. Likewise, Japanese who believe their traditional culture is distinctive, have difficulty explaining the similar musical scales (Pentatonic or five-
tone), musical instruments (the Biwa which is mandolinlike), language similarities, and Sumo wrestling similarities with Mongolia. Although it is conceivable

that such similarities developed independently, it is historically improbable, given what scholars now know about the influence of the Silk Road on Japanese culture. Galton suggested measuring the possible effects of geographic closeness and cultural diffusion in cross-cultural studies, as a means of checking whether such associations hold up independently of either.

Data-Quality Control

In the chapter on fieldwork, means of checking data-quality control was introduced. The same reliability and validity problems occur in cross-cultural research, but are usually more suspect due to the greater possibilities of ethnocentrism, lack of awareness of the complexities of different societies, and translation difficulties. Normally speaking, data quality increases with amount of time spent in the field, more fieldworkers, greater degree of participation in the daily life of the group, higher familiarity with the native language, and greater numbers and diversity of native helpers and informants. Unfortunately, these means of assessment will not always work nor always be possible. Many of the greatest anthropologists have worked alone. Edmund Leach lost his field notes, yet wrote a highly regarded work on a Burmese tribe. And Margaret Mead had no field experience in Japan nor knowledge of Japanese in writing her acclaimed *The Chrysanthemum and The Sword*, but instead used good judgment and acumen in picking from the scanty secondary sources available to her during World War II.

The solution to data quality control in cross-cultural research ought to be a familiar one to you by now: Use multiple measures. The reason is that they allow *independent* means of testing whether each is measuring the same thing. Because some measures may be culturally specific, it may be possible to test whether these items measure the same dimension cross-culturally through measuring the degree to which these culturally specific items cluster with items that are "identical" across cultures.

Cross-Cultural Categorization and Phenomenological Differences

If operationalization of noncomparative research presents problems, then cross-cultural operationalization is even more difficult. In addition to typical operational problems of finding reliable and valid indicators or classifications, one is faced with maximizing equivalence of stimuli cross-culturally. While the concept "mother" may be compared cross-culturally, such terms as "uncle," "aunt," and "cousin" have numerous ambiguous usages cross-culturally. In Japan, "ojiisan" signifies one's grandfather or it can be used as a sign of respect for *any* old man, depending on context. The problem is: How can one faithfully translate or reproduce the *ambiguity* and *complexity* of one culture into another culture's language. The more complex (multidimensional) or ambiguous a stimuli, the more difficult comparisons become.

Even pictographic materials are subject to different cultural responses. Consider the following four Japanese symbols that have pictographic origins in China—although not all Chinese symbols are pictographic—meaning, from left to right, fire, mountain, and river:

火　　山　　川

None of these symbols are intuitively connected with the English-equivalent meanings, although the reader can readily "see" how each might represent each of the three concepts. But even the English-equivalent meanings leave much to be desired for translation purposes. For instance, Japan is a narrow mountainous country with very short, steep rivers that, by U. S. standards, remind one more of dry creek beds most of the year rather than deep flowing rivers. Similarly, 300-foot high hills in Japan are often officially labeled "mountains."

Because it is more difficult to compare across cultures than within cultures, most analysts end up doing *contextual comparisons*. That is, they make relative within-culture comparisons for several cultures and then look for similarities and differences in those patterns. This is the tack that Lin and Wie (1987) took in their study of occupational prestige in China. They measured Chinese rankings of occupations, and found at the top physicians followed by electrical engineers, university teachers, natural scientists, social scientists, and so on through the bottom rankings of miners, loaders, garbage collectors, pedicab drivers, and housemaids. Although these rankings turn out to be remarkably similar to rankings in the United States and other industrialized countries, Lin and Wie did *not* focus on whether China is similar to other nations but on how occupational ratings differ within each nation. For example, they compared Chinese occupational rankings by sexes and ages of their Chinese respondents. Chinese males assigned higher prestige to drivers, mechanics, and waiters than did males in other societies.

Contextual comparisons achieve several positive results. First, they control for many possible differences in the cultural systems (educational level, social class, gender). Second, the ordinally ranked comparisons across societies are easier to justify than to presume absolute comparative measures. Third, the researcher need not look for items that are equivalent phenonologically in all respects. Rather, the investigator may use "functional equivalents"; that is, the researcher may make use of the fact that alternative institutions may perform the same function. Although some occupations may not correspond across nations, the function of manual/nonmanual labor does. It may be better to begin comparative research by searching for such *general* variables, before searching for precisely equivalent measures. Status may be best measured by wealth in one nation, ownership of cattle in another, and multidimensionally by an index of wealth, occupational prestige, and educational attainment in still another. Therefore, *the cross-cultural researcher need not be concerned with total equivalence of measures.* What is important is that the measures be equivalent in terms of the dimensions they tap or functions they serve.

By contrast, items that appear on the surface to be equivalent (political positions, occupational rankings) may not be phenomenologically equivalent cross-culturally. Rather, individuals in different cultures may interpret, or otherwise give subjective meanings, dissimilarly. Acts of prostitution are subjectively viewed negatively in most contemporary Western countries, yet they may be viewed as religious acts of a most positive nature in some other cultures. Americans have a very strong resistance to dependence on any other persons that is deeply rooted in our sense of individualism. Japanese socialization, by contrast, glorifies the dependence of persons on their family and work group. Although the word "individual" has very strong positive connotations for Americans, the translation of "individual" into Japanese (as "kojin") carries a strong negative connotation of being cut off from one's group. Such qualitative methods as field research or historical studies may often aid locating rich or subtle similarities and dissimilarities between cultures that more structured methods fail to pick up.

Costs of Cross-Cultural Research

Kohn (1987:727) says that it "would be hard to exaggerate the amount of time, thought, and analysis that must go into the effort to achieve comparability of methods, concepts, and indices" cross-culturally. It simply may not be worth the effort to overcome the various costs of time, money, and complex logistics. Kohn, speaking from his own experience, noted that governmental authorities in the United States and academic colleagues in Poland both imposed their own unjustifiable standards on what data he could and could not collect, which grossly complicated replicability of studies. Furthermore, Kohn notes that because few researchers are experts in other cultures, that most such research demands collaboration with experts in other cultures. From my own experience in Japan, seemingly irrelevant factors may complicate such collaboration. For example, American academics are often frustrated by Japanese cultural politics, which demand that the senior member of a Japanese research team have final say on projects, although junior members may be much more expert and intelligent choices as collaborators.

Also, translation is far more complicated than most laypersons realize. At the very least, once the researcher has had research materials translated into another language, he or she ought to have them independently translated back into the language of origin by a "blind" translator, to make sure the forms clearly carry the same meanings as originally intended. However, as a first step, the researcher ought to also consider several independent translations to compare the differences in nuances. Although this process is expensive, it recognizes the phenomenological subtlety of language in conveying thought. These types of considerations led Kohn (1987:728) to conclude that cross-national research is not worth the effort, unless the researcher has very good reasons.

Benefits of Cross-Cultural Research

Given the unique pitfalls and problems of the cross-cultural method, what are its advantages? First, it acts as a check on the culture-boundedness versus generality of our findings. Second, it increases the range of variation of many variables. For example, the correlation between per capital income and the effects of primary-school quality on academic achievement for 29 countries is a huge − 0.72 (Heyneman & Loxley 1983). That is, the more GNP per capita, the less school quality explains differences in academic achievement. Such extremely poor countries as Uganda, Botswana, and India have school systems that explain very large amounts of academic performance—ranging from 46% to 90%. At the other extreme, school quality in rich countries like the United States and Sweden explain from 25% to 35% of the student academic achievement. Apparently, students in wealthier countries who wish to succeed have academic achievement opportunities outside the traditional classroom setting not available to students in poorer countries. This type of finding is not apparent from studies of single countries.

Third, Whiting (1968:696) further points out that

> The cross-cultural method, by studying cultural norms, holds individual variation constant. Psychological studies of individuals in a single society do just the opposite, in that cultural norms are held constant and individual variations are studied.

Of course, the logic of Whiting's comments holds for sociological studies in single societies because there, too, the researcher holds cultural norms constant while studying social variations. The virtue of this is that it allows one to focus on social and cultural explanations rather than individual explanations.

Marsh (1961) lists three other advantages to cross-cultural research: Fourth, comparative analysis aids the replication of studies done in similar societies; fifth, the researcher may generalize propositions from one type of society to other types; and sixth, discrepant findings over different societies may lead to the development of a more encompassing theory to account for those discrepancies.

Investigator Triangulation

Researchers increasingly recognize the need for employing more than one observer in their research. When properly handled, the use of multiple observers can lead to more reliable and valid data quality controls. As shown in Chapter 10, participant observers have quite different phenomenological observational patterns—some are more "empirical," others more "holistic," and still others act more as "social anthropological ethnographers." Further, there are wide variations in how some people identify odors, tastes, and emotional states, and there are differences in observational frames of reference. Investigator bias is always a potential problem, regardless of method. If researchers are multiple observers, they can compare their data to check for such potentially biased reporting.

Even though more systematically structured methods have less need for investigator triangulation, the need is always there for reliability and validity quality controls of phenomenological biases. Interinvestigator reliability correlations can tell much about the adequacy of our methods. Strauss, Schatzman, Bucher, Ehrlick, and Sabshin (1964:36) illustrated this in an observational study of mental hospital interaction. They employed a minimum of three fieldworkers throughout their study, in the search for corroborative and negative evidence. Data that two or more observers independently reported the same observation increased the team's confidence in the reliability and veracity of the data. Of course, sometimes no colleague was able to corroborate a colleague's observation. When the unverified observation appeared to be important, the team would initiate further inquiry into similar situations as a means of checking the evidence.

Perhaps the greatest use of investigator triangulation centers around validity, rather than reliability checks. Investigators with differing perspectives or paradigmatic biases check out the extent of divergence in the data each collects. Under such conditions, if the data divergence is minimal, then one may feel more confidence in the data's validity. On the other hand, if their data are significantly different, then one has an idea as to possible sources of biased measurement that the researchers should further investigate.

Research Participant Triangulation

Social scientist's accumulated knowledge suggests that there is a danger of bias whenever researchers do not explicitly verify or test distinctions between certain categories of research participants. In particular, to avoid misinterpretation of research results, the Committee on the Status of Women in Sociology (CSWS) of the American Sociological Association (1988) recommends more sensitive treatment of gender and racial categorization in research.

The CSWS points out that much research implicitly translates the difference between the genders and races as absolute differences, with little theoretical respect for the actual diversity of within-gender or racial experiences or the malleability of differences. For example, some sociologists of the 1950s made claims—that with hindsight now seems outrageous—that the task (male) and socioemotional (female) labels within the family developed out of biological necessity. Specifically, some social scientists asserted that the allocation of socioemotional specialization to women arose out of the biological acts of childbearing and nursing. Rossi (1977) challenged such research with a call for new research based less on the status quo of biological factors, and focused more on explicating the power imbalances between men and women and the supporting ideological structure.

Furthermore, the CSWS notes that much research on families, social classes, and other social groups and aggregates fails to consider the differential effect of change in prevailing policies or practices on male and female members of the aggregate. Yet, in many cases, the interests of men and women diverge, and they are quite differently affected by change. For example, while most social researchers presumed that "no fault" divorce laws would equalize divorced men and women's relationships, they have in fact led to much greater injustice in part because of the ways in which the courts have interpreted "no fault."

Although the CSWS was most interested in righting injustices in research on women, their suggestions are applicable to any group of research participants who lack empowerment. Many of their suggestions follow. First, researchers have an obligation to make their assumptions explicit to avoid the danger of limiting the range of possible findings about gender and race. One means of doing this is to explore gender, race, or age as forms of sociocultural organization. Second, research should always build on empirically verified features of the research participants' social worlds, and not on unfounded assumptions about the participants' nature or life conditions. Third, research should include sufficiently large subsamples to allow meaningful analysis of such subgroups as sex and race. If data are from single sexes or races, therefore, those samples should serve only as a basis of generalizations relating to that sex or race. Fourth, when researchers know relatively little about the social worlds of their participants, they have an obligation to use qualitative approaches to provide more richly detailed information. Fifth, when researchers employ more systematic approaches, they have an obligation to take care that their instruments are equally appropriate for both sexes and other racial groups. Sixth, much care needs to be taken in applying gender neutral, and explicit terms to avoid biased assumptions. One specific means of doing this is for the researcher to explore whether gender differences are indeed greater than sex differences of race, age, social class, or sexual orientation. Another means is to explore interaction effects. Many apparent gender effects turn out to be attributable not to gender, but to the interaction of gender and other variables (Smith 1983).

Methodological Triangulation

Triangulation of methods takes two forms: within methods and between methods. Each will be discussed in turn in this section.

Within Methods

Triangulation within methods usually involves *replication* for purposes of reliability and theory confirmation. That is, within-methods triangulation provides a test-retest check on data quality, and a means of confirming the validity
of earlier findings through checks on the stability of earlier findings. Ironically,
while replication is a basic tenet of scientific advancement, few researchers or
journals show interest in published replications in the social sciences. Indeed,
some social-science journals have traditionally rejected true replications, particularly those showing evidence contrary to originally published materials.
Even more dismaying from this standpoint is the fact that much of published
research produces theory after the completion of the research. Such ex post
facto theory is particularly in need of confirmation by replication because unanticipated results may be due to chance factors. Remember that, by chance
alone, five out of 100 results should be statistically significant at the .05 level.

Form (1987) bluntly posits that the whole of replication is in a state of
disarray. He says (p. vi) that scholars "cannot even reproduce the marginals of
tables found in articles (and) . . . authors are reluctant to reply and provide full
details on how they collapsed categories, omitted some cases, and so on." The
result is that editors of the better journals are now demanding that scholars
provide (p. vi) "full citation of the data source: the official name of the data
source, its institutional origin, the exact title of the series, the exact address
where the data may be provided, and other information."

Fortunately, some researchers are becoming more concerned about the
lack of true replication in social science. Bahr, Caplow, and Chadwick (1983)
have reported on the third follow-up of the classic study of Robert and Helen
Lynn's Middletown studies. Based on their experiences, they strongly urge social scientists to resist the temptation to "improve" such baseline studies by
including topics absent in the original study. For example, they deeply regret-
ted "wanton" changes such as changing "men," in "Some men have much more
money than others" to the more trendy word "people" because it obliterated
possible changes in the pattern of different male and female responses. In the
furtherance of future replications Bahr, Caplow, and Chadwick deposited their
third-stage classic replication in the Center for Middletown Studies at Ball State
University.

Similarly, Alwin (1986) has replicated Lenski's classic work on the "religious factor," and demonstrated that although the Catholic church has com-
manded considerable moral authority on a number of issues linked to family
and household decisions, that obedience to Catholic doctrine is decreasing.
Alwin showed that these patterns are consistent with a growing "privatism"
among American religious institutions.

These types of data sharing and replication are extremely important for
the development of social science. Hauser (1987) called for standard procedures for making data available to readers. The advantages he lists include
(p. vi):

reinforcement of open scientific inquiry; the verification, refutation, or refinement of original results; the promotion of new research through existing data; encouragement of more appropriate use of empirical data in policy formulation and evaluation; improvement of measurement and data collection methods; development of theoretical knowledge and knowledge of analytic techniques; encouragement of multiple perspectives; provision of sources for training in research; and protection against faulty data.

Hauser's call is a timely one. Machine-readable technology, like floppy disks, now makes the sharing of huge amounts of raw data and supporting technical documentation inexpensive and transferable.

Between Methods

Triangulation through the use of different methods, finds its main use in *disconfirming* the tenability of arguments that findings are artifacts of particular methods. Conversely, it may show findings to be simple artifacts of particular methods. Hovland's (1959:13) classic paper on attitude-change studies demonstrates some of the limitations of experiments and survey methods.

> What seems to me apparent is that a genuine understanding of the effects of communications on attitudes requires both the survey and the experimental methodologies. At the same time, there appear to be certain inherent limitations of each method, which must be understood by the researcher if he is not to be blinded by his preoccupation with one of the other types of design. Integration of the two methodologies will require on the part of the experimentalist an awareness of the narrowness of the laboratory in interpreting the larger and more comprehensive effects of communication. It will require on the part of the survey researcher, a greater awareness of the limitations of the correlational method as a basis for establishing relationships.

Table 14-2 displays some strengths and weaknesses of five different data-gathering devices. This table shows how much better it would be to combine methods, to take advantage of the strong points of each type of data, cross-check data collected by each method, and collect information that is available only through particular techniques.

Sieber (1973) gives an exemplary rational for integrating particular methods. He shows how fieldwork may contribute to survey data design, collection, and analysis, and vice versa. He points out (1973:1343) that fieldwork may often valuably precede surveys by providing "information about the receptivity, frames of reference, and span of attention of respondents." On the other hand, surveys may contribute to fieldwork through (1973:1354) "(1) correction of the holistic fallacy [tendency of the field observer to perceive all aspects of a social situation as congruent], (2) demonstration of the generality of a single observation, (3) verification of field interpretations, and (4) the casting of new light on field observations."

One of the more glaring needs is for the use of triangulation in the analysis of verbal data on behavior. Survey data often correlate very poorly with

Table 14-2 *Comparison of Five Methods for Researching Informal Communication in Organization*

Method	*Operational Approach*	*Principal Data Secured*	*Main Strength(s)*	*Main Weakness(es)*
Participant observation	Long-run operational contact	Examples and judgments	Provides insights into on-going communication	Time consuming; often nonquantitative; may influence data
Continuous observation	Observation of one person or job	Information flow through one person or job	Portrays communication role of one job; quantitative	Does not reveal broad patterns of communication; may influence data
Communication sampling	Statistical sample of communication	Variety of communication events	Sample is more economical than 100% observation	Interrupts work
General communication surveys	Questionnaire and/or interview	Unlimited quantitative and qualitative information	Secures more data for less cost	Responses based mainly on memory and judgments
Network surveys	Timely survey of communication episodes	Information on communication flow and networks	Relates networks to communication and organizational variables	Effective only in smaller groups up to 500 persons

Source: Keith Davis (1978). Methods for studying informal communication, *Journal of Communication, 90,* 112–116.

observational data, yet survey results that ask people what they did or do are generally accepted at face value. A long line of research on perceptual biases (see Chapter 4 in Smith 1987 for a review) indicates that research that relies on people's introspective reports about the causes of their behavior may have little value as a guide to the true causal influences.

Community power studies have also afforded an interesting debate in recent years over the possible theoretical biases particular research methods may have (Kerbo & Fave 1979). There are two controversial methodological orientations in this debate. The first is the *reputational* method in which the researcher asks panels of "judges" to identify community leaders. The second, in contrast, is the *decisional* method or, in other words, some combination of methods in which the investigator uses such relatively eclectic methods as case studies collected in an anthropological or journalistic manner. Researchers who use the reputational method exclusively find more centralized decision-making structures than researchers using other methods. That is, the reputational method appears to channel descriptions of community power structure toward "elistist" interpretations, and away from a "pluralistic" state of affairs. As Polsby (1969:118) described pluralistic power structures, they tend to have

> dispersion of power among many rather than a few participants in decision making; competition or conflict among political leaders; specialization of leaders to relatively restricted sets of issue areas; bargaining rather than hierarchical decision making; elections in which suffrage is relatively widespread as a major determinant of participation in key decisions; bases of influence over decisions relatively disperse rather than closely held; and so on.

Studies of theories of crime afford another assessment of the effects of method on theory testing. Hindelang (1978) indicates that black overrepresentation in arrestees for common personal crimes can be attributed to at least two causes: (1) disproportionate involvement in criminal offenses, and (2) criminal justice system selection biases. Studies relying on official data have generally supported the *differential involvement* hypothesis, while studies relying on self-report techniques generally have supported the *differential selection* hypotheses.

While there are several other plausible explanations for method-theory correspondence in community power and crime studies, nevertheless *particular types of methods are usually interpretable only through particular types of theory, and will generally produce only selective theoretical explanations.* Thus, increasingly, social scientists plea for a social-research norm that gives lowest degrees of confirmation to propositions confirmed by only one method, and higher degrees of confirmation when multiple methods are used. This brings us back to Campbell and Fiske's (1959) rationale for convergent and discriminant validation of research operations, because measures should correlate more highly with other measures of the same concept using different methods (convergent validation) than with measures of a different concept using the same method (discriminant validation).

Dimensions of Analysis

Although there are a multitude of levels at which one can collect sociological data (voter precinct, individual, top-level management, census tract), there are quite basic differences among, and uses of, seven prototype levels or dimensions of data collection and analysis: (1) *aggregative (individual)*, (2) *relational*, (3) *organizational*, (4) *ecological*, (5) *institutional*, (6) *cultural*, and (7) *societal units.*

Aggregative variables derive from accumulations of individual characteristics. Most demographic studies (birth- and death-rate statistics) and survey sampling are aggregative by nature. Per capita income is an average income standardized on individuals that researchers often used to characterize the wealth of geographic regions. Indeed, one must be particularly wary of the fallacy of the wrong level of analysis in the use of such aggregative data. Many studies that *appear* to focus on the marital dyad actually sample one member of the dyad, and use that person's data *as if* they represented the entire dyad. However, aggregative analysis fails "to establish social links between those observed" (Denzin 1970:302). By contrast to such aggregative analysis, the other six levels of analysis are more global in that they characterize the collective as a whole, and do not derive from an accumulation of individual characteristics.

Relational analysis concerns interactional network patterns between individuals and groups. Smith (1987:377–412) summarizes this important and burgeoning area of research. Relational analysis includes various measures of group properties: size, density of interpersonal connections, centrality of connections, clique structures, weak and strong ties, tranfers of resources, joint activities, and so forth. Each of these cases uses group characteristics without reference to individual properties. The journal *Network Analysis* specializes in reporting these types of studies.

While researchers may view organizations as made up of individual members, they may also additionally see organizations as having qualities unattributable to those individuals. We infer this from the simple observation that organizations persist with membership change. Thus, we simply cannot infer many organizational properties from cumulations of individual properties. Some examples of *organizational units of analysis* that have consistently proven worthwhile to examine are: bureaucratization, criteria (universalistic versus particularistic), rigidity of rules, and type of organizational control (public versus private, sectarian versus nonsectarian, decentralized versus centralized).

Ecological analysis involves spatial explanations. The field of crime and delinquency has used ecological data quite often for analytic purposes. Studies abound using such variables as proportion of broken homes, average voting rates, mean rental rates, or average income levels for particular areas like census tracts to explain crime rates, delinquency rates, or patterns of social disorganization. Some of the classic studies of cities used ecological analysis as a primary descriptive or explanatory device. Land-use patterns prove to be a function of transportation networks in a large number of ecological studies.

Institutional analysis compares relationships within and across the legal, political, economic, or familial institutions of society. On the one hand, the investigator may compare elements within institutions. Many researchers interested in kinship patterns examine the relationships between such variables as kinship authoritarian structures and kinship division of labor. On the other hand, comparisons across institutions also prove interesting. What similarities and differences, for example, exist in the relationship between authority structure and division of labor in judicial as compared to religious organizations? Institutional analysis has been the mainstay of sociology since its inception. Marx analyzed political, scientific, legal, artistic, and religious institutions in terms of their economic foundations. Similarly, Weber probed historic trends in rationalization and bureaucracy in the arts, education, and government.

Cultural analysis refers to the association of norms, values, practices, traditions, ideologies, technologic objects, and other artifacts of culture. *Societal analysis* typically involves such macroscopic indicators as degree of urbanization, industrialization, education, gross national product, and distributions of political wealth and power. Cultural and societal analysis are the most macro levels of social analysis.

The distinctions between these seven types of analysis are blurred by the fact that properties of one type of characteristic sometimes may be constructed from properties of another type. In network analysis, the researcher may work with such data as individuals, or change the focus to compatible network data on who-choses-whom, the individuals at the intersection of cliques, and so on. Because many different levels of an organization may influence individuals at any particular time, it is often useful to design a study that focuses on more than one level simultaneously, much as one might analyze the human body through plastic overlays of skin, muscular materials, and skeletal and organ fabrics. Therefore, inhabitants, precincts, and cities might all be elements of the same study. As Denzin (1970:302) has aptly noted, those sociological studies that we have commonly come to regard as classic usually have *combined* several levels of analysis.

Fallacy of the Wrong Level of Analysis

The particular *level* of analysis often defines disciplinary problems. However, researchers working at a particular level of analysis occasionally assume uncritically that they can generalize their findings to some other level without additional empirical verification. Some researchers treat small, informal groups as microcosms of the larger society. On the other hand, other researchers believe that society is more than its constituent groups and that societal processes involve complex ties not exhibited by small, informal groups. Clearly, we have here an instance of different paradigms concerning the legitimate *scope* of our empirical generalizations.

Scientists term this problem of scope the fallacy of the *wrong level of analysis*. Researchers who make inferences, *without empirical justification*, to a theoretical unit that is smaller or larger than the unit of observation, have this problem. One must take caution to avoid this fallacy because social researchers often shift between individual- and group-level data. Changing levels of analysis would not be a problem, if researchers would make the effort to *test empirically* changes in theoretical analysis, rather than *assume* that their theory generalized to different levels of analysis.

As a matter of practicality, the researcher's data limit the attempt to deal empirically with this problem. Research based on census data deals with pooled data on individuals to protect individual privacy. Nevertheless, researchers often feel no hesitancy about making generalizations at the individual level from this aggregated data. Generalizing aggregated data to individuals is most susceptible to the fallacy of the wrong level of analysis.

Yule and Kendall (1950) provide the classic example of aggregation effects. They calculated the degree of association between wheat and potato yields for 48 counties in Great Britain. The association was pitiably low (it was only + 0.22 on a scale from 0.0 to 1.0). However, when they *pooled* data on contiguous counties they obtained an impressive association of + 0.77 between wheat and potato yields. As a general rule they discovered that *measures of association increase with increasing aggregation of any kind of data.*

Robinson (1950) termed a common occurrence of this fallacy the *ecological correlation*; he demonstrated that it is *fallacious* to assume that properties correlated or associated at the group level are correlated at the individual level. Therefore, in designing research involving different levels of analysis, it is wise not to assume that associations computed for variables at one level of analysis (census tracts) hold for variables computed at another level (individuals living in those census tracts). This is always an empirical question, and quite often, researchers make this error. The Bureau of Federal Narcotics based its original fallacious claim that marijuana smoking leads to heroin usage on a weak association between marijuana and heroin usage among lower-class blacks. They argued from a relatively small group of users to the total society. A second mistake was their assumption that an association implies causality.

The fallacy of the wrong level continually pops up in disguised or partially disguised form. Some investigators of community power assume that it must be similar to societal power. Again, this is a matter of empirical verification and not an unquestioned assumption. We know that some state governments differ from the national government because they have unicameral (one) legislatures, balanced budget requirements, or differing veto powers; why, therefore, should community, state, and national power necessarily be formed in the same way?

Firebaugh (1978) provides a rule for knowing when aggregate-level data provide unbiased estimates of individual-level relationships: Bias is absent when, and only when, the group mean of the independent variables has no effect on the dependent variable, with the independent variable controlled. Therefore, the researcher can make cross-level inferences from higher to lower levels of analysis when, and only when, effects of the means of the independent variables are absent. By contrast, inferences from individual to group or higher levels are no problem because the researcher can group the data as desired and can always disaggregate the data. Because modern statistical methods can control for the effects of this fallacy (as long as the researcher uses appropriate statistical controls for all of the independent variables in the theory), the problem of ecologically inflated correlations is not a problem.

The essence of this logic is for the researcher to use computer programs that independently set all independent variables to their mean values, and then to observe how these adjustments affect the relationships between each independent variable and the dependent variable. This type of analysis asks the question: If all individuals were the same (had the mean value) on one independent variable, how would this affect the other independent variable-dependent variable relationships? By setting each variable to its mean value, and then observing the independent-dependent variable relationships, the researcher is "controlling" for the effects of each independent variable.

Summary

The word "triangulation" evokes means of measuring and mapping some area through knowledge of several pieces of information. Because each method has unique informational strengths and weaknesses, researchers should use a combination of methods, with the intent of counterbalancing the merits and demerits of each method. Multiple methods aid reliability and validity, through providing a corrective for irrelevant components of any measurement procedure. Because we can not normally observe most of our variables directly, we may pool information from numerous sources to arrive at a better picture of the puzzle.

Triangulation in its broadest sense extends beyond multiple methods to testing multiple theories, data collected at different time and locations, large- and small-scale processes, and differences in investigators and participants. The aim of each of these types of triangulation is to strengthen confirmability and generalizability of results.

Researchers have discovered that particular theories are biased to support certain methods and vice versa. The antidote for such biases is to design research that tests competing theories using a variety of methods. To do otherwise is to engage in theoretical ethnocentrism that may be internally consistent but that ignores external hypotheses inconsistent with the theory. Researchers, therefore, have an obligation to list all existing and plausible hypotheses in their field of study, to consider plausible interpretations of those hypotheses, and to design research which tests all rival hypotheses.

Data collected over many points in time foster concern with social change and process. Five types of temporal study designs exist: cross-sectional, cohort, panel, trend, and longitudinal. Because cross-sectional designs simply compare individuals of different ages at only one point in time, it is an extremely weak form of time analysis. Better yet, the researcher can collect data on a particular narrow-ranged age group, called a cohort, over a period of time. Then, the researcher can apply known techniques for separating age, cohort, and time-period effects.

Panel analysis uses the same measurements for the same sample at several different times. It is particularly subject to participant mortality and reactive testing effects. Although some researchers try to short cut these problems by employing different samples at different times, this procedure raises questions about the validity problems herein defined as history, maturation, and differential selection of participants. Also the researcher can compare data from each time period only in aggregated form. This means data on individual change do not exist in this pseudopanel form. Furthermore, panel analysis is really a series of static snapshots.

One final form of temporal analysis is longitudinal analysis in which the investigator collects a continuous stream of data. Typically, longitudinal analysis employs data on many periods of time but only one (or a few) variables, while panel analysis allows for only a few time periods with many variables. Because of the expensiveness of any such temporal data collection, some researchers do retrospective time-series analysis, in which they ask respondents for information that may be years old. Memory decay is a particular problem with this method.

Collection of similar data across different nations or cultures may also aid generalization of results. Data collected only in particular locales may allow for too little variation to be useful for broadening our knowledge of social life. When we find similarities across different nations or cultures our confidence in results is strengthened; by contrast, cross-national or cultural differences lead us to look for historical or cultural explanations.

Although we prefer such comparative data, analysis across space is beset with particular problems. First, defining societal and cultural units proves extraordinarily difficult in practice. Once defined, such units are subject to the problem of how to reduce information to a manageable summary of distinctive patterns. More often than not, this attempt leads researchers to view societies and cultures as more homogeneous and harmonious than they actually are. Second, few cross-cultural researchers use nonrandom sampling techniques, which leads to particular problems of sampling bias. Third, Galton warned us during the last century that because of cultural borrowing, cultural units may not be independent of one another. Therefore, apparent similarities between cultures may not be independent of geographical closeness and cultural diffusion. Fourth, because of difficulties of cross-cultural comparisons, data quality often suffers. Fifth, operationalization is more difficult in cross-cultural than single-nation studies because of the difficulty of translation equivalence of essentially dissimilar concepts. Sixth, the time and expense of cross-cultural research is often outrageous. In spite of these problems, many researchers continue to maintain that cross-cultural research is essentail to broaden the generalizability of our findings. This is because it provides a check on culture-boundedness of our findings, aids replication, helps generalize findings, and leads to more encompassing theories.

Known variations in how individuals perceive the world around them led many researchers to suggest the use of multiple observers. If several investigators independently observe the same phenomenon, our confidence in the robustness of those observations increases. If only one individual observes a particular phenomenon, then the investigator may initiate an independent corroborative search of similar situations. Such similarities and differences in observations aid us in locating possible sources of biased measurement.

Gender and racial distinctions are categories for which researchers have particular concerns because much research implicates gender and racial differences as due to biology than to power imbalance. Professional social science organizations warn of such ideological bias and encourage closer attention to explicating the social construction of gender and race, verifying assumptions underlying research, including large subsamples of racial and gender groups for analysis, using qualitative approaches to provide rich detail, and exploring interaction of race or gender with other variables.

Methodological triangulation involves within-method replication and across-method checks on data quality. By repeating the same methods with different samples or at different times, we gain evidence of the stability of our findings. By using different methods, we can disconfirm particular theories as artifacts of particular methods when different results occur systematically. The bottom line is that particular types of methods normally produce selective theories.

Seven fundamental social levels of analysis are the aggregative, relational, organizational, ecological, institutional, cultural, and societal. Researchers often uncritically assume that they can generalize their findings to some other level without empirical verification. This is the fallacy of the wrong level of analysis. It can only be solved by testing theories at different levels and, when using aggregated data, using appropriate statistical controls that can disaggregate individual effects.

PART

III

Analysis and Presentation of Data

C H A P T E R

15

Data Management

The method of analysis then defines what the information is and may or may not endow this information with certain properties. A "strong" method of analysis endows the data with properties which permit the information in the data to be used, for example, to construct a unidimensional scale.[1]

Key Terms

Backup

Codebook

Coding

Conditional-cleaning

Database program

Data cleaning

Data entry

Electronic data processing (EDP)

Keypunching

Machine-readable data

Optically scanned data (OpScan)

Precoding

Postcoding

Recoding

Spreadsheet

[1]Coombs, C. (1953) Theory and methods of social measurement (L. Festinger & D. Katz, eds.) *Research Methods in the Behavioral Sciences*, New York: John Wiley, p. 472.

Study Guide Questions

1. What are the advantages of electronic data processing versus hand processing?

2. Under what conditions does it make sense to precode data?

3. What viable solutions exist for coding of multiple answers? Why?

4. When is postcoding a more appropriate type of procedure than precoding?

5. What are the functions and most important features of a codebook; how does the researcher put these functions into practice?

6. What are the standard practices for dealing with missing data? What are their advantages and disadvantages?

7. What practices are standard for recoding data? Why is it still necessary to keep a set of the original unrecoded raw data?

8. Describe good habits of data backup and saving data.

9. Why is it necessary to worry about cleaning data? What methods aid data cleaning?

One of the most formidable tasks in research is condensing and managing data. The objective is to control the data rather than be controlled by them. Neophytes are often surprised with (and at a loss of what to do with) the huge mass of data they have collected. Consider for a moment a set of actual survey data for a random sample of Americans that is available to users of this text with access to an IBM-PC compatible machine. These programs known as *SocialTrend* and *SocialScene* (Savage 1988) include data collected in 1975, 1980, and 1985 on 699 randomly selected Americans for 65 separate survey questions.

One way to look at the massive amount of data in these two programs is to consider the number of discrete pieces of information amassed on the *SocialTrend/SocialScene* diskette: 65 variables times the 699 randomly selected individuals equals 45,435 distinct pieces of information. How can the researcher suitably organize this mass of data for analysis? As a start, the researcher might organize the data by variables, ignoring individuals. Seemingly, this procedure reduces the choices to separate analyses of the 65 variables. However, because scientists are minimally interested in relationships between variables, this actually reduces to 65×64, or a still unmanageable 4,160 possible two-variable relationships.

This is where theory-guided research shows its advantages. The vast majority of those two-variable relationships are meaningless. Many make no sense theoretically. There is little reason theoretically, for example, to examine the relationship between the respondent's age and race because age cannot cause race nor race cause age. (It does make sense to look at a table breaking down age by race to see how closely the sample resembles the actual population; but this type of table is not used for theoretical purposes.) There is also little theoretical reason to examine the relationship between respondent's current religious affiliation and spouse's labor force status for similar reasons. The researchers who conducted this series of three surveys in 1975, 1980, and 1985 never intended that these data be used blindly. They requested particular survey questions with specific hypotheses in mind. Although those researcher's specific hypotheses do not exhaust all sensible hypotheses, the novice researcher should keep in mind that the number of intelligent hypotheses in any similar large data set is probably only a small fraction of the possible combinations of variables.

It makes much more sense to study hypotheses that have some root in theory. Because experts on voting theory predict that social class affects voting it makes sense to cross-tabulate social class by political party affiliation. Similarly, because existing theory supports the expectation that religious attendance should have a negative influence on sexual permissiveness, a cross-tabulation of sexual permissiveness by religious attendance would provide a reasonable check on this hypothesis.

Preparing Data for Electronic Analysis

The advantages of electronic data processing far outweigh analysis by hand. Electronic data processing can (1) grossly reduce the errors in tabulations, (2) take much of the toil and drudgery out of coding, and (3) increase the speed of calculation. As recently as the 1970s, the preparation of data for electronic analysis was a multiple stage process in which Murphy's Law—if it can go wrong, it will—operated. The researcher (or a trained assistant) might have had to spend countless hours looking over each of hundreds of survey forms that interviewers had filled out by hand. The researcher laboriously might then have reduced these data to special numeric codes and transferred these distilled data to special lined paper which used columns for variables and rows for cases. For example, all male respondents might have been coded as "1s" and all females as "0s." Then, another person was likely to use these special forms to keypunch rectangular holes into computer-readable cards with a typewriter-like keyboard.

Essentially, this process allowed the introduction of errors into electronic data preparation at three different stages: data collection, coding, and keypunching. Inventive computer engineers have created means for reducing the need for so many stages. For example, interviewers in the more established survey organizations now use personal computers to key in interview responses in computer-readable form bypassing the tedious coding and keypunching stages. The bottom line: Fewer stages for data preparation produce fewer possibilities for human errors, quicker data preparation, and tremendous cost savings for personnel and supplies.

Coding

Coding involves the assignment of symbols for each category of a variable in a study. For example, in survey research, a "yes" answer might be coded as "1" or "Y", and a "no" answer as "2" or "N". Electronic data processing most often depends on numeric codes. Rather than store words or sentences in computer memory, the researcher is most likely to reduce words and sentences to numeric symbols. Although the researcher could store the words "resident of the South" and "nonresident of the South" or the alphabetic symbols "s" and "n" in machine-readable form, many forms of data analysis depend on the more convenient, but arbitrary, assignment of "1" to residents and "0" to nonresidents.

The first chore of data management, therefore, is numeric coding. The task of coding is less onerous and laborious where standard conventions exist for coding particular variables, the data already occur in numeric form, or the researcher knows which categories to employ prior to data collection precoding. Through experience, researchers have learned to formulate standard conventions for some variables: Sex, income (collapsed into a small number of mutually exclusive but exhaustive ordinal categories), socioeconomic status, "yes-no" type closed-ended questions, and Likert-type attitude scales are among the multitude of standardly employed social variables, for which precode conventions exist or are easily manufactured.

Precoding

Precoding refers to those situations where the researcher decides before starting data collection what symbols to assign for any particular variable. Table 15–1 lists some examples of such conventional precodes. Likert-type attitude items (see Chapter 7), by convention, are scored from 1 to 5. The much used Duncan SEI (socioeconomic index) scores occupations from a theoretical low of 0 to a high of 99. Although the Duncan SEI is useful for many statistical analysis, clearly, it would not be useful in tabular analysis (without gross modification) because of the huge number of cells that would exist. It might be more practical to round off these scores to the nearest whole number—for example, 9.3 to 9—for many purposes. The researcher might consider further refinements in education and religion, but more refinements would call for larger samples. For example, with large samples, Protestants might usefully be subdivided into the various sects and mainstream churches. However, it makes little sense to divide Jews into orthodox, conservative, reformed, and secular Jewish groups under most circumstances, because Jews make up only 2% of

Table 15-1   *Some Examples of Standardly Employed Precodes for Social Variables*

Variable Name	Precode Description
Likert-scale items	1 = strongly agree, 2 = agree, 3 = uncertain, 4 = disagree, 5 = strongly disagree (or for "reversed items" 5 = strongly agree, 4 = agree, 3 = uncertain, 2 = disagree, and 1 = strongly disagree)
Occupational status	Duncan SEI score (i.e., lawyers = 94, physicists = 86, health administrators = 72, librarians = 67, dental hygienist = 54, draftsmen = 44, railroad conductors = 34, postal clerks = 25, electrician apprentices = 17, unpaid family farm workers = 07)
Education	1 = less than high school, 2 = high school, 3 = some college, 4 = college, 5 = master's degree or PhD
Religion	1 = Protestant, 2 = Catholic, 3 = Jewish, 4 = Other, 5 = None

the total American population. Similarly, although it might make some sense to subdivide those with less than a high school education into 8 years or less, and more than 8 years, but less than 12 years, subdividing "master's degree or PhD" does not because less than 1% of the American population has a PhD. Out of a sample of 1,000 individuals, we would expect less than ten with a PhD.

Other types of data may already exist in a manner amenable to precoding: age, income expressed in dollars, and educational attainment expressed in years. Once again, such codes present few problems for the researcher. In each of these cases, it is always better for the researcher to store the data in as close to their original form as possible and to create wholly separate variables for collapsed data, because future researchers may find it useful to use the original variable in the creation of their own codes. For example, in the National Opinion Research Center data used in SocialScene™, the original data have been combined into three categories: individuals with less than 12 years of schooling, those with a high-school diploma, and those with more than 12 years of schooling. Once the researcher has combined the data through recoding, unless the original data set still exists, it is impossible to disaggregate the recoded data into their original form.

Once the researcher has chosen how to code each and every category of a particular variable, he or she must chose how to store that variable in machine-readable form. Before the advent of optically scanned data (op scan forms) such as are often used for computer-graded multiple-choice tests, researchers used the margins of their interview schedules and coding forms to note the column in which a particular code ought to be placed. For example, consider the following two questions from a longer survey:

20. Are you now married?   51/

      yes. 1

      no. 2

21. What is your exact date of birth? _____   52–53/
                                    month

                                   _____   54–55/
                                    day

                                   _____   56–59/
                                   year

The columns to the far right indicate the places in which the coder must put each answer. For example, if the first respondent says she is presently married and was born on November 10, 1947, then, in row 1, the coder marks a "1" in column 51, an "1–1" in columns 52–53 (a "1" in each of these two columns, not an 11 in each), "1–0" in columns 54–55, and "1–9–4–7" in the remaining four columns from 56–59 of the appropriate electronic spreadsheet.

    Occasionally, the researcher discovers that not enough columns have been apportioned. In the process of coding a huge archives of data on women seeking abortions, coders discovered that we had not considered enough codes for the question "Who accompanied the patient on the day of the procedure?" Originally, we had conceived of a one-column variable in which we assigned codes for husband, POSSLQ (Persons of Opposite Sex with Same Living Quarters), steady boyfriend, girlfriend, parent, sibling, other relative, other (nonrelative), and no one. However, we found we needed to consider combinations of those categories; for example, parent and boyfriend, boyfriend and friend, and so on. We ended up with a two-column variable with 19 separate categories of companions. Of course, sometimes, the researcher may decide to collapse categories into a smaller number of columns. In some, but not all, of the analysis of this aforementioned abortion data, all of the 10 through 19 codes were collapsed into the 9-equals-other code because of the small numbers of individuals who had multiple companions.

    Not all variables are as easy to code as the above examples indicate. Many variables are more open-ended and do not have a known range of potential answers. In this same abortion project, the abortion counselors had asked the patients the reasons for the abortion. This proved to be a very difficult question to code. Some women said "because of a new job" or "I'm in the process of divorce" or "for financial reasons." The first two of these reasons were coded under 02 = the time is not right. On the other hand, many women said they were "too young" or "too old," but they were not coded as 02 because we felt there were so many of these latter cases that we wanted a separate code for each. The general rule is that where many cases of particular answers exist, give each answer a separate code. If few cases exist, remember that they will be spread too thinly in later two-variable and multivariable analysis. For example, a study of religious effects in a metropolitan area of 2.5 million such as St. Louis, with only 50,000 Jews, would need a huge random sample to analyze this small category of persons; a random sample of 1,000 individuals would produce only 20 Jewish individuals.

Another set of problems exists in the case of variables that allow for multiple answers. In the abortion study, the method of birth control that the patient had used prior to the abortion and the one she planned to use afterward were coded. Although the patients mentioned 14 distinct methods, some of them included such combinations as diaphragm and foam, foam and condom, or condom and suppositories. Similarly, many questionnaires and interview questions allow for multiple answers by including such instructions as "circle all that apply." In such cases, the researcher may code each answer as a separate binary or dichotomous response. For example, with the birth control question we could have coded "0" if the patient did not use a particular birth control method, and "1" if she had in 14 separate columns representing each type of birth control method. We did not because there were only a few patients who used multiple birth control methods. We found we needed only two columns to code 18 different birth control patterns.

If the patients had used a large number of the possible 182 combinations of birth control, it would have been much less confusing for coders to code a separate column for the 14 separate types of birth control. The disadvantages of this process are twofold. First, it takes up valuable computer memory—14 columns versus 2 columns. Second, "0" can present a problem in computer analysis because it is easily confused as part of missing data. Major statistical analysis systems solve the problem of missing data through placing a period (.) in place of missing data or by assigning some number such as −(minus) 99 for missing data. Most computer programs treat such periods or −99s as missing data—that is, they do not run calculations on them.

Precoded data can save much time and money. For example, closed-ended interview schedules and questionnaires printed on op scan sheets obviate the need for coders. Similarly, precoded data forms can take the place of a special codebook for recording the meaning of each code. Because precoding only works with easily codeable data, researchers often need to postcode data and record the postcodes in special codebooks for future reference.

Postcoding

Postcoding refers to coding of data after they have been collected. As a rule, it is inefficient and wasteful to postcode data, if it can be precoded. There is no good reason to leave open-ended such easily precoded data as sex, race, religion, or state of residence. Rather than write an open-ended question like

What is your race?_____

it would be much better to add precodes as in

51/

What is your race? (circle one)

     white   1.

     black   2.

     other   3.

The first procedure makes unreasonable demands on coders to remember postcodes and the column in which to place the code, requires that coders waste time better spent on other tasks, and increases the chance of clerical error. It would be better to use op scan forms or some other form of electronic input during data collection to overcome these disadvantages of postcoding and nonelectronic precoding.

Nevertheless, postcoding does have its place. Many archival files of interest to social scientists contain masses of uncoded information. Also, true open-ended survey questions cannot reasonably be precoded. Postcoding proceeds in a several step process. First, the researcher must examine all of the data for unique categories. Second, each new category requires that the researcher assign a separately required code. Third, the researcher summarizes frequencies for all categories. Fourth, the researcher decides whether or not all categories are mutually exclusive and totally inclusive; if they are not, the researcher must either recode the data or decide on a means of coding multiple categories. Fifth, the researcher allots the necessary number of columns to the postcoded data.

Furthermore, because some data allow for multiple codes, the researcher may find postcoding useful for reducing the possible number of combinations of codes down to some smaller subset. Recall the earlier example of combinations of birth control used in the abortion study. Originally, the clinic where this study was conducted had postcoded those data, and found that there were only 18 different birth control patterns used (out of a possible 182). This postcoding enabled us to reduce the data to 18 possible codes within only two, instead of three, columns.

Finally, postcoding allows for more flexibility than precoding. The point of such research designs as open-ended questions and field methods, after all, is to allow for more responsiveness in the discovery process. It makes no sense to make true closed-ended data, such as sex of the respondent, flexible. However, it makes much sense to allow those individuals we study the flexibility to express themselves as they see themselves, and then, to let that expression guide postcoded categorization.

The Codebook

The codebook serves at least two vital functions: first, it specifies the meaning of each numeric code; second, it indicates the column in which each variable is located, and where more than one line of data is needed, on which line the data are to be found. It can also serve other useful functions. Because most statistical programs written for the computer save space by limiting a variable name to as little as eight spaces, researchers often used the code book to write in both a short mnemonic variable label as well as a longer, more widely understood label. Researchers who code secondary souces of data also give the sources of their data in the codebook so that other researchers may verify the quality of their sources. For example, Figure 15–1 reproduces part of an electronic spreadsheet of demographic data. These data are not intelligible without further explanation. The purpose of a codebook ought to be to make the data

COUNTRY $	POP INC	GN PPR CAP	INFLATION	LABOR GROW
Algeria	3.200	6.000	6.000	10.000
Egypt	2.600	8.000	6.000	6.000
Libya	3.300	3.000	6.000	10.000
Morocco	2.600	8.000	5.000	7.000
Sudan	2.900	9.000	7.000	7.000
Tunisia	2.700	7.000	5.000	7.000
Benin	3.000	9.000	6.000	6.000
Burkina Fas	2.600	10.000	6.000	4.000
Ghana	3.400	9.000	10.000	8.000
Guinea	2.300	9.000	1.000	4.000
Ivory Coast	3.000	8.000	6.000	8.000
Liberia	3.100	9.000	3.000	6.000
Mali	2.800	10.000	6.000	6.000
Mauritania	2.900	9.000	4.000	5.000
Niger	2.800	10.000	6.000	7.000
Nigeria	3.000	8.000	6.000	7.000

Figure 15–1. Partial reproduction of an electronic spreadsheet for a study of worldwide demography.

in such a spreadsheet intelligible to a wide audience. The top row in Figure 15–1 lists short variable names of less than eight characters length. The first one is what is technicaly called a string variable; the dollar sign tacked on to "country" tells the reader that this is a numerically coded variable. By looking down the first column, the reader may easily verify that no string variable can consist of more than 11 characters. For example, this statistical program cuts short the full name of Burkina Faso. The variable label in the second column, POPINC, is short for the rate of population increase in 1985. For example, by reading across row 1, the reader can verify that Algeria's rate of population increase was 3.2%. The remaining three columns—GNPPRCAP, INFLTION, and LABRGROW—stand for annual gross national product per capita, the rate of inflation, and the relative growth in the labor force. However, these three variables are rank-ordered variables. A good codebook should list how the true cardinal data in each case were recoded. (A full codebook and data on the total 132 nations does exist, and accompanies the instructor's manual for this text.)

The reader may have noticed that the variable columns in Figure 15–1 each contain 12 spaces (actually columns). Although some of these spaces may appear to be wasted, this practice is good from the standpoint of reducing human error. Under the formats of the older technologies, the data on line 1 would have simply been introduced as a stream of data as in

ALGERIA326610. . .

The researcher then tediously had to program the machine to recognize where each variable was located and where the decimal point went. This introduced much room for human error. Some programming innovations improved the situation slightly by introducing commas or spaces between variables as in the forms

ALGERIA,32,6,6,10,. . .

ALGERIA 32 6 6 10 . . .

but the abstractness of these forms still produce room for unnecessary human error. For example, a space between variables might actually be missing data, it is not clear what the variable name is for each number, and the viewer has no idea where the decimal point should be placed. Whenever possible then, the spreadsheet format is highly superior because of the concrete connections between variable labels, decimal placement, columns, and variable value entry.

Box 15–1 illustrates the most important features of a codebook. First, notice that the introduction to the codebook explains important information about the number of cases in the data file, primary sources of the data, and how missing data were coded. This information is followed by separate data on each variable in the format of short variable name, columns in which the data are located, and a detailed description of how each variable was operationalized. A properly prepared codebook ought to give other researchers enough information that they can judge the adequacy of operationalization, understand all codes, and be able to use the codebook to do his or her own analysis of the same data set.

Even if the researcher alone will analyze a data set, he or she should make up a codebook based on the main principle of human fallibility: If you don't write it down, it doesn't exist. This point should not be taken lightly. Years after publishing a study, researchers often tear their hair out in exasperation because they wish to reanalyze old data, but did not adequately document their earlier work.

The Problem of Missing Data

It is inevitable in research to have missing data. Respondents to questionnaires and interviews often give no response or don't know answers, and bureaucracies and organizations keep incomplete records. Researchers normally do their best to keep missing data to a minimum. Question designers find that some question wordings lead to less nonresponse than do other question wordings. Similarly, observers find some behavior-coding systems more difficult to employ, leading to more missing data than other systems.

Various computer programmers have tried numerous systems to deal with the problem of missing data. Comparisons of these different systems has lead to some standardization, as researchers have learned by trial-and-error that not all systems are equally effective. Early programmers often assigned zeros, nines, ninety-nines, nine hundred ninety-nines, etc. to missing data. However, these systems suffer disadvantages that have led modern programmers to abandon these systems for missing values. For one thing, computers

Guide to Using Demograf.sys

by Herm Smith

This file gives access to important data on the 130 largest nations in the world. Use this codebook to understand how each variable was operationalized.

The data used here come from the Population Reference Bureau's *1987 World Population Data Sheet*. The PRB warns that data from their work should not be used as a time series because fluctuations in values often reflect revisions based upon new data or estimates, rather than actual changes. For developed countries, nearly all vital rates refer to 1985, and for less developed countries for some point since 1980. The primary sources of this data are: *United Nations Demographic Yearbook, 1985* and *Vital Statistics Report, Data Available as of 1 January 1987* of the UN Statistical Office; *World Population Prospects, Estimates and Projections as Assessed in 1984* of the UN Population Division; *World Population Profile, 1985* and unpublished estimates and projections of the Center for International Research of the U.S. Bureau of the Census; and estimates and projections of the World Bank.

IN ALL CASES, MISSING DATA ARE REPRESENTED WITH A PERIOD(.).

POP87   COLS 1–12

This is the mid-1987 population estimate. Where possible, the effects of refugee populations and large numbers of foreign workers are taken into account.

CRUDBRTH   COLS 13–26

The annual number of births per 1,000 population. It is called the crude birth rate because these rates are affected by the population's age structure.

CRUDEATH   COLS 27–39

The annual number of deaths per 1,000 population. It is called the crude death rate because these rates are affected by the population's age structure. For example, a country like Japan, with a relatively large number of people over age 65, will often have a higher crude death rate than a less developed country with lower life expectancy.

Box 15-1   *Part of a Codebook for World Demographic Data* do not always handle blanks and zeroes in the same way. Therefore, the coder naively may simply not enter a zero into a particular column in the mistaken belief that the computer will treat a blank as a zero. For another thing, researchers may confuse zeros, nines, ninety-nines, etc. with codes for true non-missing data.

There are two types of non-missing data responses for which researchers typically assign special codes. The first are DK (don't know) responses for which the standard is to code each column of the variable with 8: 8, 88, 888, etc. The second are NA (not applicable) responses for which some researchers assign 0s. For many types of analysis, it is important to know the distributions of DK and NA responses. For example, certain groups of individuals may give higher frequencies of DKs than other groups.

Recoding

For use in many sophisticated statistical analyses, the researcher needs to recode DK and NA responses as missing data. For example, in an analysis of race using the simple codes 1 = white, 2 = black, and 3 = don't know, to do an analysis requiring dummy variables, the researcher might recode the DK responses as missing values. Similarly, sometimes such qualitative variables as the string variable "country$" above might be assigned a meaningful numeric code. For example, numerous studies of the world economy point to extreme differences in poverty between countries in the northern and southern hemisphere. It might be useful to form a new variable NORSOUTH, in which 1 equaled northern and 0 equaled southern countries as defined in such analyses.

It is very important when coding or recoding to keep the original data in their uncoded, and original coded, raw form. There are several reasons for this. First, the researcher might very well wish to do another type of analysis at a later date, and it may not be possible to disaggregate recoded data into their original form again. Second, in the process of coding or recoding, errors may be made. If the original data set is gone, there is no way to make corrections. Third, it is possible to lose all of the original data through electronic power surges, machine failure, or other natural calamities. In the next section the need to keep adequate backup copies of the data set is stressed, so that this possibility is minimized.

Data Entry

Once the researcher has decided on an effective and coherent set of codes, and column and line placements for each set, he or she may start entering the data onto an electronic diskette or magnetic tape via a computer. Because there are fewer errors possible and greater efficiency in the use of such electronically readable formats as op scan sheets or archival work stored on diskettes, where the possibility exists, these formats are preferable to manual data entry. Inexpensive electronic data-transfer systems such as Kermit™ exist for all major computer systems. This public domain software now gives little excuse for manual reentry of data that exist on one computer system to another. However, where data entry must be performed manually, it can be performed using a computer keyboard patterned after standard typewriter or numeric pads.

Whether the researcher enters data manually or electronically, it is crucial that the researcher keep adequate backup copies of the data set. When one considers the huge amount of labor and time that goes into data coding and entry, the few extra minutes it takes to make a backup is the wisest investment. I recommend not only keeping two electronically readable backup copies of the data, but also storing them in physically separate places—perhaps one at home and one at work. The reason for this is that if lightning (or some other act of nature) does destroy one data set, it is less likely to destroy a backup kept miles from the original. Electronically destroyed data is similar to data destroyed by fire, except that it takes a fraction of the time to complete the act.

Furthermore, as the researcher engages in the act of entering data, work should be saved after every 15 minutes or so of entry. Some data entry programs now automatically save work after a certain number of minutes or keystrokes to help prevent unnecessarily large data losses. Although saving work is a crucial component of data entry, it is not the same thing as backing the work up with a separate copy on a separate disk, tape, or other electronic medium because any electronic medium is subject to damage *without warning*. Imagine your feelings if the air-conditioning failed in the computer room you use over a weekend, and several months or years of work were destroyed days or hours before the final report was due. This scenario has happened to many researchers who did not take the necessary precautions.

Data Cleaning

Just as one ought to proof one's written work for errors, one ought also verify one's data entry. Very large samples or lengthy numbers of cases and variables can make this a tedious job. For this reason, computer programmers attempt to create less odious ways of performing this vital aspect of data entry. Remember: No study is better than its data base. The rule is known in some circles as the GIGO rule: garbage in, garbage out. The problem is that human errors are most often nonrandom. The best way to guard against human error is to have an independent clerk re-key the data in, and to resolve any discrepancies between the two clerks.

One of the most error-free means of verifying and cleaning data is that which is used in MicroCase, Inc.'s MicroCase™ program. MicroCase includes an automatic re-key checking option. If the user selects Micro-Case's data-entry option, the program screen queries whether this is original data entry or a re-key. When the user presses the re-key option, the program will compare each entry for each variable on each case with the value already entered. If the two keys fail to match the program beeps, displays the discrepant values, and asks if the clerk wishes to replace the original value with the new one. A similarly accurate method would be to take independently coded data, and transform the two sets through subtraction of the one coder's data from the other coder's. The newly created variable ought to have only 0s for each case. Instances where a code other than 0 exists imply the need to reenter these particular pieces of data.

Another, less complete way, but nevertheless useful means of checking the veracity of a data set is to run simple frequency checks of codes for each variable. For example, the researcher might check the frequency of various codes for sex (1 = male and 0 = female). If the researcher finds any numbers out of range—from 2 through 9—he or she will know those are illegal codes, and can then search for those illegal codes in the electronic spread sheet, and compare them with the original raw data. Many times clerks key in data into the wrong, but adjoining, columns. For example, a clerk may inadvertently skip column 22, throwing all remaining data off for that case by one column. Because cleaning data by checking for illegal codes cannot find all such cases, this is only a weak substitute for full verification of data. It can only lead to discovery of illogical entries and does not catch all typographical errors.

One final means of checking the veracity of data that is useful is *conditional-cleaning*. Sometimes, a code for one variable is dependent on previous variable codes. For example, in the abortion study, only about one in ten of the patients sent in a follow-up form given to all of them. I created one variable, FOLLOWUP, which my coders coded as 1 if yes and 0 if no. All proceeding variables were contingent on the coding for this variable. If a 0 existed in the FOLLOWUP column, then all remaining columns should have consisted of periods (indicating missing data). By contrast, if anything other than periods existed in the remaining columns, then the FOLLOWUP column for that particular case ought to have had a "1" keyed in. Because I was dealing with close to 6500 cases, I used a computer program to check for any such illogical conditional occurrences. In each illogical conditional case, the program printed out the entire case on a separate piece of paper so that I could examine it for correction.

Logical inconsistencies in data are red flags that the researcher should check the veracity of the data. For example, the total suicide rate should equal the average of suicide rates by age groups, properly weighted by age group totals. Similarly, it is most unlikely that a 19-year-old young woman has 12 or more children. When the researcher finds such inconsistencies, he or she has an obligation to recheck the original raw data for possible errors.

Summary

The first task of data analysis is to organize the data for statistical processing. Because most data files in the social sciences are huge, this means managing the data so that they can be processed by computer. Until the 1980s, this was a laborious process. Newer computers and statistical software have grossly simplified and speeded up the preparation of data for analysis.

The first task of data management is coding data into numeric forms. For some forms of data, conventional precoding systems already exist or are easily developed. For open-ended questions, questions with multiple answers, and qualitative data, the process is much more challenging. Another tricky coding problem is the issue of how to code missing data because "0s," are easily confused with missing data, and because the researcher often wishes to separate "not applicable" and "don't know" answers as special types of missing data. Precoding can save valuable time and money. However, sometimes the researcher has no choice but to postcode data, or needs the flexibility of postcoding to express some set of desired categories.

Researchers keep codebooks to specify the meaning of each numeric code, to show where the variable data are located, and to make the records intelligible to themselves and other researchers at later dates. The codebook normally gives a short variable name used in computer analysis, a less cryptic long name for use by the researcher and others, the spreedsheet column and row in which data are located, the range and meaning of variable values, sources of the data and the manner of operationalization. Where the original data have been recoded, the researcher wishes to document how it was recoded.

Researchers normally find it easiest to visualize data as a rectangular spreadsheet with cases down rows and variables across columns. Because data entry is labor-intensive, researchers advise saving the data every 15 minutes or so and keeping adequate backup copies of them in electronic form. Just as with proofing written work, researchers stress the need to clean data. This can mean simply checking for logical inconsistencies, out-of-range responses, and other illogical codes. However, the best way is to recode the data in a form that the recoded data can easily be checked against the original data.

C H A P T E R

16

Fundamentals of Data Analysis

Seek simplicity and distrust it.[1]

Key Terms

Asymmetric relationship	Marginal
Beta weight	Mean
Bivariate analysis	Median
Column percentage	Mode
Correlation	Outlier
Counter-rate	Pearson's correlation
Data transformation	coefficient(r)
Ex post facto interpretation	Percentage table
Exploratory data analysis	Quartile
Histogram	Rate
Line of best fit	Ratio
Logarithmic transformation	Raw frequency distribution

[1]Alfred North Whitehead.

Reciprocal relationship   Spurious association
Row percentage   Standard deviation
Scatterplot   Stem-and-leaf plot
Slope   Univariate analysis
Spearman's rho   Variance

Study Guide Questions

1. Why is it better to use theory and test inferences drawn from the interpretation in analysis, rather than do ex post facto interpretation?

2. Explain the general rules for testing inferences.

3. What is the logic of exploratory data analysis? What are the advantages and dangers of exploratory data analysis?

4. What is the intrinsic worth of univariate analysis?

5. How do raw data distributions, histograms, quartiles, outliers, and such representative values as the mean, median, and mode contribute to our understanding of the shape of data distributions?

6. What different types of information are given by means, medians, modes, rates, counter-rates, ratios, quartiles, variances, and standard deviations?

7. What is the purpose and logic of transforming data?

8. What are the advantages of two-variable analysis over univariate analysis?

9. Describe the three possible types of bivariate relationships and their common forms.

10. What are the four basic criteria for inferring causality?

11. Explain the two fundamental rules of percentage-table reading.

12. How does the researcher demonstrate association or lack of association with percentage tables?

13. What problems face researchers in choice of measures of association with percentage tables?

14. What strategies can the researcher employ for analyzing nonpercentage tables?

15. Explain the logic of scattergrams and correlations for testing for causality? What dangers do these techniques present for such tests?

16. How does regression analysis help guard against the dangers of simple correlational analysis?

17. When is Spearman's rho more appropriate than Pearson's r?

Researchers who do well-constructed studies rarely make data-analysis decisions solely after they have collected their data. Instead, the ideal is to anticipate data analysis in earlier phases of the research. To do otherwise risks the chance of ending up with insufficient or inappropriate data. It is not uncommon for researchers to fail in their ability to analyze the data they have collected, even though they may have ended up with a massive repository of data. Ironically, these massive data stockpiles frequently go unanalyzed, perhaps due to the fatalistic what-do-I-do-with-all-this-data dilemmas they may create.

One solution, offered repeatedly in this text, is to collect only data that have some direct linkage to theory. This helps reduce data to a relatively manageable size, and also focuses collection efforts on data that are most relevant to hypotheses. In their classic analysis of the American occupational structure, Blau and Duncan (1967:18–19) note that

> the general plan of the analysis had, therefore, to be laid out a year or more before the analysis actually began, although there turned out to be "serendipitous" elements in the tabulation specifications we drew up; some tabulations proved to be amenable to analytical procedures not initially comtemplated. . . there are many combinations we might have desired but could not afford, and many others we would later have liked to see but that we simply had not thought of when dummy tables were drawn up. We were conscious of the very real hazard that our initial plans would overlook relations of great interest. However, some months of work were devoted to making rough estimates from various sources to anticipate as closely as possible how tables might look. This time was well spent, for, on the whole, the tabulations have proved satisfactory.

Herein lies the core of successful research: letting one's theory guide the analysis. As Blau and Duncan's statement makes clear, this procedure does not necessarily stifle or suppress the serendipitous. Theoretically directed research often leads to unexpected findings, and it also guards against data-collection overkill. Research that is tied directly to theory helps focus analysis on the most plausible variable(s) of interest while ignoring those of least importance.

Although much of social science and all of historical research is done "after the fact," scientists frown on after-the-fact interpretation of data. The habit of *ex post facto* (after-the-fact) interpretation of data can lead to excessive flexibility; to change one's interpretation at will is no way to *build* theory. No datum stands in isolation from other data. It is better to consider how data are tied and related before collecting them. Although novices may start out by saying "I'm going to use Weber (or some other well-known theorist) to interpret my data," they do not actually have such freedom to choose theory. Theory limits the type of data with which one can choose to test that theory. Therefore, hypothesis testing ranks higher than ex post facto interpretation.

There are times, of course, when researchers have no choice but to interpret data ex post facto. In the process of doing routine scientific investigation, scientists do uncover serendipitous findings which appear to lack a theoretical reason for existing. However, the scientific attitude is to treat such isolated findings with a grain of salt, until they have gained corroboration from independent means.

A wise general rule is *to test inferences drawn from the interpretation*. That is, the scientist reasons: I can only accept an ex post facto interpretation if I find other non-ex post facto evidence that supports my interpretation. The scientist knows that an opinion is not sufficient to convince other scientists. Therefore, the scientist reasons: If my interpretation is correct, it must have *empirically verifiable consequences*. The more empirically verifiable consequences the scientist can muster in support of his or her interpretation, the more confident all scientists become that the interpretation is supported. By contrast, if attempts to empirically verify such consequences work out contrary to expectation, then the scientist must go "back to the drawing board" to reconsider where the original interpretation might have gone awry. Remember that although it takes only one piece of contrary verifiable information to shoot down an interpretation, no number of verifiable sets of consequences ever prove an interpretation.

Rosenberg (1965:86) provides a classic case of the search for explanation of serendipitous findings. Rosenberg found unexpectedly that the average child of divorce had lower self-esteem than children from intact families. He interpreted this to be due to stigmatization of divorce and relative discordant family life. He then reasoned that *if* his interpretation were true, *then* groups in which divorce is strongly condemned (Catholics, Jews) should lead to greater social stigma and, therefore, lower self-esteem than among groups where divorce is not as great a social stigma (main-line Protestants). Because further data analysis supported this interpretation, Rosenberg could feel more comfortable that his interpretation might be on the right track. Although Rosenberg did feel more comfortable with his interpretation, a quarter of a century later he is still on the lookout for contrary, as well as, supporting evidence.

Exploratory Data Analysis

Exploratory data analysis (Tukey 1977) requires deductive methods for looking at data in as many ways as possible, and actually thinking out the implications of emerging patterns. One learns more from the process of analyzing the data than from the results. It is important to try out "what if" scenarios. Very often this process leads to relationships and patterns the analyst had not expected. For novices, the advantage is that if they grasp the full significance of their data, they will be much less likely to make mistakes. Data analysis has come a long way in a very short time. Only about a decade ago, scientists like Tukey needed an IBM mainframe dedicated to the sole task of constructing plots in three dimensions, and spinning them around to see new relationships between points of data. Now anyone can do that on a personal computer.

Before one can perform various statistics one must have some number of objects—individuals, groups, nations, etc.—from which to sample and analyze. For analysis, the data are conventionally arranged in a spreadsheet-like matrix, in which the rows correspond to the objects and the columns correspond to the variables, or the values of measurement. An ideal statistical software system ought to enable the user to visualize and manipulate this matrix, allowing the user to reach conclusions about the structure of the data. The computer should not get in the way of the user, but instead should provide transparent access to the raw data, be able to render powerful graphical manipulations, and perform the classical statistical procedures.

The first step in analyzing data is to get the data into the statistics program. Commonly, as shown in Chapter 15, the data are stored in tabular columns. Most of the statistical programs can import such data files from other electronic spreadsheet or database programs, so that the user does not have to rekey in all of the data, which would be both a waste of time and a new means of introducing errors. Even better programs allow data input directly from laboratory devices.

A good statistics application should let the user freely play with the data, using interactive graphics, tranformation of variables prior to an analysis, and creation of new variables. It may help to think of a statistics program as a set of tools for viewing data from different angles. Just as an individual might rotate a spherical world atlas to get a better idea of geography, the statistical user wishes to manipulate and vary ways of simplifying a mass of data to reveal various aspects of the data: which observations deviate from the average, which ones cluster and how they cluster, how one set of observations differ from another set of observations, what two sets of observations have in common, and so on.

What statistical software cannot yet do is advise the user when he or she has violated particular statistical assumptions, or when to use a particular statistic. The analyst must know enough about statistics to know when to use any particular one and how to interpret the outcome. The following sections of this chapter are meant as a basic introduction to commonly used statistics in the social sciences. Because a solid understanding of statistics would take up a separate text, the reader is encouraged to become more proficient in the use of statistical tools through outside readings and course work.

Univariate Analysis

Univariate analysis refers to the examination of only one variable at a time. While of no intrinsic explanatory worth, the researcher often needs to use univariate analysis for descriptive and exploratory purposes. The researcher may wish to describe the ages of a sample of respondents to demonstrate how similar (or dissimilar) this sample is to some population. This description is possible using several basic techniques.

Distributions and Shapes of Data

As with the human body, social data come in many recognizable shapes and sizes. The problem with social data is that the researcher needs some means for recognizing those shapes. One of the oldest means of producing recognizable distributions of data is the raw frequency distribution. The *raw frequency distribution* simply displays the number of cases for each category of a variable. A quick way to see a number of frequency distributions is to run the SocialScene™ diskette and chose the "frequencies" option for any variable. For example, the raw frequency for male respondent is 319 and 380 for female respondents. Females, who make up 54% of National Opinion Research Center (NORC) respondents, are slightly overrepresented, in part because they are more likely to be at home when the NORC interviewer calls. Similarly, Social-Scene tabulates the *grouped* frequency distribution for age categories of respondents as:

18-30	181
31-44	180
45-65	211
66+	123

Such tabulations are easier to read for variables with large numbers of categories, than are simple raw distributions by actual age: 18, 19, 20, ... However, in the process of grouping categories, the researcher loses some information (the actual numbers of persons 18, 19, . . .) and may make arbitrary groupings, or "cutting points" as some researchers call them. For example, the researcher could just as well have used the cutting points 18–30, 31–40, 41–50, 51–60, and 61+.

The histogram

Some researchers use the *histogram* as a display of the sample density and distribution of a continuous numerical variable. For example, Figure 16–1 displays a histogram of the crude birthrates (number of births per 1,000 population), with a superimposed normal, or bell-shaped curve. The fit of the normal distribution is quite poor: the third, fourth, and eleventh bars are too high; the first, sixth, and seventh bars are too low; and the right-most bar is well outside the normal range.

Although the histogram is quite appropriate for displaying the shape of data, it is not appropriate for counting data values. By looking only at the left-hand side of Figure 16–1, the reader can only get a rough estimate of the number of nations with particular crude birthrates; for example, there appear to be 25 nations with a crude birthrate of about 10 births per 1,000 population.

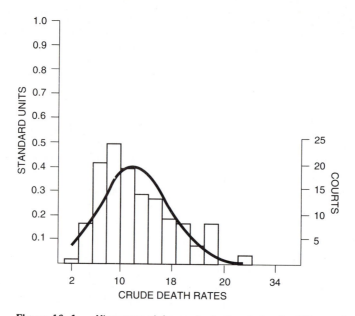

Figure 16–1. Histogram of the crude death rate for the 130 most heavily populated nations of the world, with a comparison overlay of the normal distribution.

Tukey (1977) invented the stem-and-leaf diagram as a more accurate measure of counting, as well as shaping of the data.

The stem-and-leaf plot

The *stem-and-leaf plot* looks like a sideways histogram or tally. The stems are on the left side of the display and indicate the most significant digits in which variation occurs. The leaves are on the right side, and represent the next decimal digit after each stem for each case. Between the stems and leaves, the reader will see a column with an "M" and two "Hs." The M designates the "median," which is the midpoint value for which half the cases lie below and half lie above this value. The Hs represent the quartiles; the values for dividing the total values into fourths. Figure 16–2 demonstrates the value of a stem-and-leaf diagram for actual counting.

The stem-and-leaf plot shown in Figure 16–2a shows the exact number of values for each crude death rate value; there are exactly eight values for the median value of 11.0. (You can verify this for yourself by counting the eight 0s.) Figure 16–2 also demonstrates clearly which two values—crude death rates of 28 and 29 for two nations—that are deviant cases. In the terms of statistics, these two values are *outliers*, because they are outside the normal expected range of values for crude death rates; in this case they are over two and a half times the median value.

The data in Figure 16–2b (look only at the right-hand side) are even more interesting. Although it appears difficult to understand at first glance, once you

MINIMUM IS: 3.000	MINIMUM IS: −620.000
LOWER HINGE IS: 8.000	LOWER HINGE IS: 24.000
MEDIAN IS: 11.000	MEDIAN IS: 28.000
UPPER HINGE IS: 15.000	UPPER HINGE IS: 57.000
MAXIMUM IS: 29.000	MAXIMUM IS: 3465.000

3	0	−62	0	
4	00	−46	2	
5	000000	−30	1	
6	0000000	***OUTSIDE VALUES***		
7	0000000000000	1	8899	
8H	0000000000000	2 H	00000001111222222223333334444444	
9	00000000000	2 M	555555566666777777777788888888899	
10	00000000000	3	00223333333334444	
11M	00000000	3	5588	
12	00000000	4	144	
13	000000	5	13	
14	000000	5 H	789	
15H	0000000	6	1	
16	000000	7	67	
17	000	8	568	
18	00000	9	012	
19	000	10	22	
20	000	***OUTSIDE VALUES***		
21	0	12	4	
22	0000	14	17	
23	0000	17	8	
OUTSIDE VALUES		18	2	
28	0	22	4	
29	0	25	77	
		28	9	
		30	1	
		40	8	
		46	2	
		57	8	
		63	6	
		115	5	
		173	22	
		346	55	

a. Crude Death Rates	b. Population Doubling Time

Figure 16–2.   Stem-and-leaf diagram of the crude death rate (left-hand side), and the estimated time it takes for the population to double in size (right-hand side) for the 130 most heavily populated nations of the world.

understand the logic of the layout you will see how easy it is to work with. First, to understand this data, locate the H, M, H values. Each number on the right represents the last digit of a value. Those on the left represent all the other digits of the number. If you look at the first value "−62 0" you know this number is to be read −620 from reading the top line "MINIMUM VALUE IS: −620). In a similar fashion the second and third values are −462 and −301. The fourth line represents four values: 18, 18, 19, 19. That is, each of the numbers to the right represents the last digit of a value. All other digits are the same for each value on the same line. Now, go to the twelfth line 5H 789. For now, ignore the H. How many values are on this line? What are they? Following the above example, you can count those numbers on the right; there are three. Each one begins with the number on the left so the values are 57, 58, and 59.

Now that you understand the basics, let's look at the figure more closely and examine some of the parts. There are three interesting outliers with negative values. These three nations—Denmark, Hungary, and (former) West Germany—all have declining populations. That is, rather than double, these three figures— −620, −462, and −301—estimate the number of years it would take to half their present populations without fundamental demographic changes in births, deaths, or migration patterns. Now look at the lower outside values. The figures also show nineteen (you should be able to count these to verify my figure) outliers that are doubling at a snail's paces. For example, there are two nations that will take 3,465 years to double at their present rate of growth. Although the doubling time variable has many more deviant cases than does the death rate variable, it has a larger cluster of cases close to its median value. For example, you should be able to verify that there are 81 of the 130 nations with doubling times from 20 years to 34 years (recounting all the numbers to the right of 2H, 2M, and 3).

For purposes of gaining skill at interpreting a stem-and-leaf graph, note also that there are nine nations with the median number of 28 years doubling time by counting all of the 8s following the "2 M," and no cases of countries with doubling time values from 62 through 75 years. From this data, the reader can gain an appreciation of concern over world population growth. Although the industrialized nations are those making up the slowest growth (or contraction in three cases), these nations are mostly outliers. Almost two-thirds of the nations (you should be able to count 85) have doubling times of 34 years or less:

1	8899
2H	00000001111222222223333334444444
2M	555555566666777777777788888888899
3	00223333333334444

We do not count the three negative cases (the outliers) because they belong with the "slow" growing nations in terms of doubling time.

Representative Values

In the last subsection, several ways were demonstrated in which researchers organize a whole set of data to understand its form. Quite often the researcher wants to know what the "representative value" is for such a set of data. Probably the most commonly used statistical summary measure is a statistical "average." "Average" is a vague word in statistics, because it can be used to mean one of many different measures of central tendency. The three most commonly used measures of central tendency are the mode, the median, and the mean. Each of these values has their place in research, but each can also be abused and misused. It is important to understand the function and place of each in summarizing typical values.

Mode

The mode, or modal value, is simply the one that occurs most frequently. *The modal value is particularly useful for summarizing data that have a two (or more) humped-camel form or two normal curves joined together.* In Figure 16–2a, there are two modal values for the crude death rate: there are exactly 13 nations with crude death rates of 7 and 8 per 1,000 population. Because the data in this figure has only one hump, the mode does not describe this data much differently than would the mean or median values.

The problem with using the median or mean values to summarize the representative case with two- (or more) humped data is illustrated in Figure 16–3. In this figure, either the median or mean value will actually produce a measure farther from the representative case than will a modal value. Note that there are two "representative cases," as described by the modal values with the highest number of counts, yet the mean and median values in this figure would give misleading values because these values have few tallies. A small number of industrialized countries hover around the left-hand mode of 1.5 very near the near-zero-population growth mark of 1.8, with a much larger number of nations that have an annual modal growth rate of 2.9% each year. Clearly this right-hand mode of 2.9 is the more representative (and ominous) figure of the four. The median (2.3) and mean (2.0) values fall between these two modes, and represent a much smaller number of nations. In this example, therefore, the right-hand mode becomes the measure of choice for the single most accurate description. (Note that because the right-hand hump has the largest area it represents the most cases.)

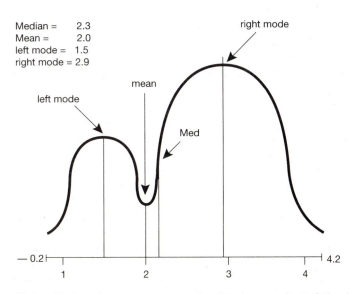

Figure 16–3.   Summary representative data for annual population increase throughout the 130 most heavily populated nations of the world.

Median

Another simple measure of typicality is the median. The median is measured by collecting all the values and ordering them by increasing value. After the numbers are in order, the median value is the middle value with an odd number of cases, or the average of the two middle values with even numbers of cases. Therefore, half of the values in the sample with fall below and above the median value. The median value is highly appropriate in two different situations: first, when the data, unlike in Figure 16–3, are not bimodal; and second, for reasons I shall explain shortly, when the data are highly skewed. That is, they depart significantly from the normal distribution by having one "tail" which is much longer than the other tail. To state it differently, the median is appropriate when the data have a disproportionate number of outliers on only one side of the distribution. The estimated population-doubling time variable shown in Figure 16–2b is a good example of a case where statisticians prefer the median as a measure of typicality. In this case the median is 28. Compare this with the arithmetic mean of 138.8, which would be a misleading figure, because this suggests that a value among the bottom outside values is representative. Clearly, in this case, the median outshines the mean as a representative value.

Arithmetic mean

The arithmetic mean is defined as the sum of all data values, divided by the number of such values. Mathematically, the mean is quite easy to calculate: It is equal to the sum of all the data values, divided by the number of data values. For example, for the population doubling time, the researcher could add up -620, -462, -301 . . . . 3,465, and 3,465, and then divide this summation by the 130 values. Remember that the mean value for world population-doubling time gives a misleading 138.8 years, while the median value of 28 years is closer to reality. The mean is a good measure only when the data are approximately bell shaped. When the data have a few extreme values on one side of the distribution, as is true in Figure 16–2b, those extreme values will unduly attract the mean value. The mean, therefore, is not a good measure of representativeness with highly skewed data, because it is unduly affected by outliers.

There are innumerable variables for which the professional statistician always eschews the mean in favor of the median. Almost any measure of wealth—income, housing value, etc.—is skewed typically toward only a few deviant wealth cases. A favorite example was a naive comment by former-president Ronald Reagan, during his presidency, that there was a wealthy New York school district in which children received free school lunches in spite of the fact that the parents made more than $75,000 a year. He was referring to Pocantico Hill, N.Y., where the mean family income was $88,689. That figure, however, was skewed by the income of one family that calls Pocantico Hills home: the Rockefeller family. The 24 in that school district who received free school lunches came from families which met the guidelines of $15,630 or less family income, and the median income of the school district was $26,004 at that time.

These examples indicate just how unreputable or naive individuals can misuse statistics. Statistics do not twist numbers; people do. To avoid the misuse of statistics, it is imperative that the user learn which summary measure of the data is most appropriate, and to use it carefully. In fact, by comparing the mean, median, and modal values for a distribution, the experienced researcher can often make some good educated guesses about what the form of the data must look like. For example, if the researcher has mean and median values which are close numerically, the data are probably symmetrical. If all the reader knew was that the mean for the crude death rate was 11.9 and the median was 11, then the reader could guess, without looking at Figure 16–2a, that the distribution was skewed toward a few somewhat larger numbers. A mean value that is significantly larger than a median value, as in the case of the world population-doubling time variable shown in Figure 16–2b indicates likelihood of very extreme values "pulling" the mean value away from the most typical scores.

Rate and counter-rate

The rate is another simple, frequently used tool in statistics that is easily understood by the nonprofessional. At the simplest level, a rate standardizes the relative frequency of occurrence of some event, by dividing the number of occurrences of some event by the size of the total group in which that event might take place. The monthly unemployment rate published by the U.S. Bureau of Labor Statistics is a highly visible example. The monthly unemployment rate is simply computed by dividing the total of individuals reported as unemployed by the total of persons eligible for employment in a given area. If there are 100 million individuals eligible for employment, and 6 million of them are reported as unemployed, then the unemployment rate is 6 million/100 million = 6%. The counter-rate to a 6% unemployment rate would be a 94% employment rate.

All percentages are rates, but some rates use a slightly different standard of comparison than the base of 100 implied by a percentage, because some phenomenon occur relatively infrequently. Social scientists compute suicide rates by dividing known suicides by the total population of an area, and then standardize that figure by multiplying that figure times 100,000. The highest state suicide rate in the United States is Nevada's 23 per 100,000 population. If we used only a normal base of 100, the rate would be a less understandable .023 percent.

Demographers use the standard unchanging, arbitrary constant of 100,000 for very rare phenomena such as suicide, robberies, attempted murders, hospital admissions for alcoholism, and homicide. They use the standard of 1,000 for somewhat more frequently occurring events like fertility, births, infant mortalities, and abortions. For example, in 1976, there were an estimated 9.5 abortions per 1000 Canadian women in the childbearing years, compared to the Cuban rate of 61. Quite frequently occurring events use 100 as the constant multiplier as in some cause-specific death rates. For example, demographers divide the total number of deaths from cancer by the total number of deaths, and then multiply the outcome by 100. In Israel 27.8% of all deaths in 1975 were caused by cancer. Similarly, the rate of urbanization is so widespread that the multiplier of choice is 100: It ranges from 2% urban in Burundi to 100% in Singapore.

Ratio measures

The percentage is only one of many types of ratio measures; it uses the total number of cases converted into a base of 100 for direct comparison of populations of different sizes. However, size of a population is only one of numerous factors that can introduce distortion into comparisons of figures. Ratio measures can aid more valid comparisons of different populations. The *sex ratio* is a classic example; it is computed by dividing the number of males by the number of females in a particular population, and multiplying the result by 100. The result expresses the number of males per 100 females. At birth, the normal sex ratio in the United States is about 105, or 105 male per 100 female births. However, because females outlive males, by age 85 this ratio drops to approximately 60 males per 100 females.

Another widely used ratio measure is the dependency ratio. The dependency ratio is measured by dividing the number of dependents (those individuals under age 15 and over age 64) by the number of potentially productive adults in a population (between age 15 and 64), and multiplying the outcome by 100. In 1980, this ranged from 113 dependents per 100 productive adults in Zimbabwe to a ratio of 47 in Japan and Canada.

The logic of ratio measures is based on the fact that different populations are not of the same size. Because we expect a larger population to have more individuals who are males, females, dependents, productive adults, or whatever, than smaller populations, a ratio measure standardizes population size for purposes of comparison.

Summary Measures of Variation

The various averages and ratio measures discussed reduce the raw data to single scores. However, it is often more useful to summarize the distribution of data through some measure of dispersion or variation in values. From the standpoint of the nonprofessional, the range of values is the easiest to understand, but also the least useful. The range of values in Figure 16–2 for the crude death rate spans the numbers from 3 to 29 deaths per 1,000 population. The range of population-doubling time is much greater: It varies from −620 years to 3,465 years. Although the doubling time has a much greater span of numbers than does the crude death rate, the reader already knows that this is because there are many more outliers among the doubling time values. The reader also knows that more values cluster close to the median value of the population doubling time than of the crude birthrate. What we need is an exact measure of such clustering to see its effect on variation.

Quartiles

One easily comprehended measure of variation is the quartile. The quartile simply divides the data into quarters just as the median divides it into halves. Clearly, for the data in Figure 16–2a, the quartile is superior to the range for many purposes. The lower and upper quartiles are shown by the two Hs. (H stands for "hinge," or quartile.) Half of the values for the crude death-rate cluster between 8 and 15 deaths per 1,000 population in Figure 16–2a, while for population doubling time the quartile range is from 24 to 57 years in Figure 16–2b. (To figure out the quartile range in this case, simply divide 130 [nations] by 4, which produces 32.5. Then count the thirty-second and thirty-third cases from both ends of the diagram. You will note that you end up in both cases on the two lines which are designated with an "H." In the case of the lower hinge, you will end up between the last 23 and the first 24. In the upper hinge case, you will end up between the 57 and 58.) With highly skewed data where the median is the preferred measure of central tendency, the quartiles often provide satisfactory measures of variation.

Variance and standard deviation

When the data are approximately normally distributed, the measures of choice are two special types of mean averages known as the variance and standard deviation. The variance is simply the mean of squared deviations of scores from the arithmetic mean. Consider the following data for the number of Roman Catholic Churches in the St. Louis metropolitan area:

Jefferson County	11	$(35- 11) =$	24	$(24)^2 = $ 576
Clinton County	15	$(35- 15) =$	20	$(15)^2 = $ 225
St. Charles County	18	$(35- 18) =$	17	$(17)^2 = $ 289
Franklin County	18	$(35- 18) =$	17	$(17)^2 = $ 289
Madison County	18	$(35- 18) =$	17	$(17)^2 = $ 289
St. Clair County	29	$(35- 29) =$	6	$(6)^2 = $ 36
St. Louis County	69	$(35- 69) = -34$		$(-34)^2 = 1156$
St. Louis City	102	$(35-102) = -67$		$(-67)^2 = 4489$
SUM	280		0*	7349

Note: As a check the sum of differences from the mean should always be zero (or if rounded numbers are used, close to zero).

$$\text{Mean} = \frac{280}{8} = 35$$

The Variance, then is easily computed by taking the sum of the squared differences above in the right most column and dividing by the total number of observations:

$$VAR = \frac{7349}{8} = 918.625$$

and the standard deviation is simply the square root of the variance, or

$$s.d. = \sqrt{918.625} = 30.3$$

This means that roughly 68% of the counties ought to range between 4.7 churches ($35 - 30.3 = 4.7$) and 65.3 churches ($35 + 30.3 = 65.3$), *if the data are normally distributed* (see Figure 16–4).

Statisticians prefer the standard deviation over other measures of variation when dealing with normally distributed data, because it has well-known properties that allow interesting and useful interpretations across variables, and because it is the basis for numerous other statistics, just as the arithmetic mean is related to the standard deviation. As a hint of its usefulness, consider the following properties of the standard deviation. First, the range is approximately equal to six times the standard deviation for many distributions. Second, plus or minus one-standard deviation includes slightly over two-thirds (68.26%) of all values, two standard deviations include over 95%, and three standard deviations over 99%. Third, the researcher can use fractions of standard deviations to locate how far a particular value is from the mean value. Figure 16–4 illustrates the second and third properties visually.

Some researchers cheat by using the standard deviation for non-normally distributed data. However, this is not considered good practice. Most statisti-

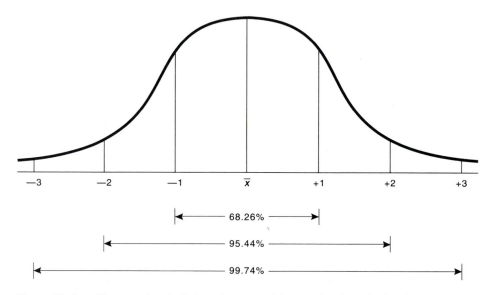

Figure 16–4. The normal, or bell-shaped, curve and its associated standard deviation patterns. (X-bar is the mean.)

cal techniques taught in elementary statistics courses assume the user has normally distributed data. Although some techniques are robust enough for use with data that is not non-normally distributed, unless used with appropriate caution by an experienced statistician, use of such techniques is likely to produce inaccurate information.

Transforming Data

Quite often, the researcher finds that a variable is far from normally distributed. Size of various populations and income are variables that are normally heavily skewed. The researcher might consider mathematically transforming those variables to normalize them. A very common method of statistical graphing is to use logarithms to exaggerate or simplify visual patterns. Commercially produced logarithmic graph paper uses unequally (i.e., exponentially) spaced Y-axis scale points to visualize the mathematical transformation of data. The base of 10 logarithm of 100 is 2.0 because $10^{2.0}$ is 100, log of $10^{3.0}$ equals 1000, log of $10^{4.0}$ equals 10,000, and so on. Because the logs 1, 2, 3, 4 . . . correspond to the numbers 10, 100, 1,000, 10,000 . . . logarithms become a convenient way for transforming highly skewed data, or data that has huge variation.

Once you understand the principles underlying mathematical formulation, you need not actually do the computations by hand because good statistical software exists that can do it faster and more accurately. What you do need to learn is when to transform data, and what kinds of mathematical formulations might be appropriate. As a starting point, it is worthwhile exploring transformations of any data that is highly skewed.

The world population data shown on the left-hand side of Figure 16–5 provides a good example. Notice how there are only a few very large populations. (The last figure in the upper graph represents China's 1.062 billion population, which is the most extreme case). By contrast, 67 nations with less than 200,000 population are shown on the first two lines at the top of the stem-and-leaf diagram. Also, the median indicates that half of all nations have less than 9.3 million in population. However, logging the populations produces a nearly perfect bell-shaped curve in the right-hand stem-and-leaf example. In fact, there is only one outside value at each end, and one could almost draw the bell-shaped curve freehand using this figure as a guide. As most statistical analysis is based on normally distributed data, this is a very important technique. Regression analysis, presented in the next chapter, is a good example.

When researchers want to compare two independent data sets, they often consider transforming data using a mean of zero and replacing original scores with standardized scores. Many sets of transformed data can then be compared. By using standardized scores for homicide rates and suicide rates, a researcher could make more valid comparisons of each. For example, a country with a homicide rate of 3 standard deviations would be comparable to a country with a suicide rate of 3 standard deviations in rarity.

```
     1987 POPULATIONs   (expressed in 1000s)              1987
POPULATIONS   (logged)

MINIMUM IS:      0.200
LOWER HINGE IS:      3.900                    MINIMUM IS:      – 1.609
MEDIAN IS:      9.200                         LOWER HINGE IS:      1.361
UPPER HINGE IS:      23.500                   MEDIAN IS:      2.219
MAXIMUM IS:      1062.000                     UPPER HINGE IS:      3.157
                                              MAXIMUM IS:      6.968

 0 H  000011111111222222222223333333333334444444    – 1      6
 0 M  5555666666667777777778888999         ***OUTSIDE VALUES***
 1    000000001234444                      – 0      9
 1    5566667789                           – 0      22
 2 H  012233334                             0       0122344
 2    59                                    0       6667888999
 3    11                                    1 H     0111112223334444
 3    789                                   1       5556667888888899999
 4    2                                     2 M     00000111122333333334
 4    6                                     2       5666667777788899
 5    011                                   3 H     00111111112344
***OUTSIDE VALUES***                        3       666789999
 5    3567                                  4       000114
 6    112                                   4       66689
 8    1                                     5       14
10    478                                 ***OUTSIDE VALUES***
12    2                                     6       69
14    1
17    4
24    3
80    0
106   2
```

Figure 16-5. Stem-and-leaf plots of the original data for the populations of the 130 most heavily populated nations (expressed in 1,000s) on the left, and logarithmically transformed data on the right.

Two-Variable Analysis

Because scientists are primarily interested in variable analysis, as opposed to pure description, univariate analysis is of limited value. Rather, the first analytic step normally will be to examine two-variable (bivariate) relationships. There are three possible types of bivariate relationships: (1) *noncausal correlation*, where *neither* variable influences the other variable; (2) *asymmetrical*, where *one* variable influences the other variable; and (3) *reciprocal*, where *both* variables influence one another. The problems of assymmetry and reciprocity present the key problems for scientific explanation.

Noncausal Correlation

Noncausal correlation generally is due to one of three possibilities: (1) alternative indicators of the same concept, (2) effects of a common cause, or (3) functional interdependence of the parts of a common "system" or "complex."

Alternative indicators of the same variable are often highly associated due to the fact that they are components of the same phenomenon. The following two items from a scale measuring attitudes toward abortion are highly correlated because they measure nearly the same thing:

G. A legal abortion should be available during the first three months of pregnancy, but not after.

H. A legal abortion should be available during the first six months of pregnancy, but not after. Although these two statements are highly correlated, social scientists would not say that either variable causes the other.

By contrast, *effects of a common cause* means that the same conditions independently promote the development of other variables. The number of newspapers read per 1,000 population is positively correlated with the Gross National Product, not through one variable causing the other, but rather as effects of industrialization. Industrialization causes the Gross National Product to rise. It also requires a highly educated work force who are likely to want to keep abreast of news.

In any organism, all the parts are dependent on one another. This *functional interdependence of the elements* insures a positive correlation between presence or absence of the various component elements. The facts that most known societies have incest taboos and stratification systems may mean only that these units perform interdependent functions for social systems. While functional interdependence implies indispensability of units to the system, some system elements are dispensable and are arbitrarily associated; in other words, they occur together as part of some nonfunctional complex. In the United States, many citizens assume that burning the flag is antipatriotic, even though in many countries, such behavior would not be associated with antipatriotism; the two traits hang together in American society because of "style of life," not because of causality.

From the preceding examples, it should by now be apparent why variable correlation and association do not necessarily imply causation. Indeed, because the preceding examples present interesting scientific problems in and of themselves, causal analysis is not the only phenomenon of interest to the scientist.

Reciprocal and Asymmetrical Relationships

An *asymmetric relationship* refers to one-way causation of the sort that x can cause y but y cannot cause x. Quite often, social scientists make this assumption. It is quite reasonable to presume that neighborhood transiency could affect suicide rates. It is much more difficult to understand how the suicide rate could conceivably affect neighborhood transiency. A *reciprocal relationship* suggests that x causes y and that y causes x. Homan's classic hypotheses that "liking causes friendship" and "friendship causes liking" satisfies the requirements for a reciprocal set of causal relationships. Reciprocal relationships are much more difficult to study than asymmetric ones. The only way one can judge their scientific authenticity is (1) to study the effects of x at time 1 on y at time 2; and (2) to study the effects of y at time 2 on x at time 3. Few social or behavioral studies exist that do this. Kohn and Schooler's (1978) work on the reciprocal effects of substantive complexity of work and intellectual flexibility is a classic in such longitudinal assessment. They found that more substantively complex work increases individual flexibility and that, in return, individual flexibility increases the chances that a person will take on more substantively complex work.

Of course, it is not always possible to specify causal relationships. Homans' classic propositions that liking leads to more interaction that, in turn, leads to more liking is a reciprocal relationship that is appealing, but difficult to test. Methodologists often propose that reciprocal relations are actually *alternating* causal forces, because it is unlikely that two variables can simultaneously cause each other. In Homans' propositions, the methodologist would assume, as Kohn and Schooler did in their study of work and personality, that liking promotes more interaction at a later time that generated more liking at a still later time. Therefore, scientists often view reciprocal relationships as special cases of asymmetrical (unidirectional) relationships.

The Criteria for Inferring Causality

When the scientist's interest does center on assignment of causality, he or she can make the decision on direction of influence through four criteria: (1) statistical association, (2) time sequence, (3) variable permanence, and (4) tests for spurious association. Scientists assume that temporarily prior variables and such fixed or unchangeable variables as race and sex influence such later-occurring and alterable variables as friendship cliques.

Statistical association implies that the researcher can demonstrate that the variables vary using a measure of association or correlation. *Time sequence* refers to the order of occurrence of the variables; the causal, or independent variable, must come earlier in time than the dependent variable. No statistic can tell the causal order. Only the human brain and good theory can specify causal order. *Tests for spuriousness* mean that the association between the independent and dependent variables being tested should *not disappear* when the effects of other variables causally prior to the original variables are removed. *Variable permanence* alludes to the necessity for the variables to exist over an extended period of time. Tests for spurious are covered under three-variable analysis in Chapter 17.

The methods for demonstrating these requirements differ, according to whether the researcher uses tables or measures of association. For this reason, it is necessary to consider statistical tables separately from measures of association.

Percentage Tables

Table 16–1 illustrates the basic principles of tabular analysis, using percentages based on the National Opinion Research Center data in SocialScene[TM].

Table 16-1 *Supreme Court Decision Approval by Religion of Respondent, Expressed in Percentages (Raw Number of Cell and Marginals Cases are Shown in Parentheses)*

Decision Approval	Religion of Respondent				
	Protestant	*Catholic*	*Jewish*	*Other*	*Totals*
Approve	39	43	87	85	44
Disapprove	61	57	13	15	56
	100	100	100	100	100
	(409)	(191)	(15)	(48)	(663)

Source: SocialScene™ random subset of case drawn from the National Opinion Research Center's 1985 General Social Survey data. The questions asked were: "What is your religious preference? Is it Protestant, Catholic, Jewish, some other religion, or no religion?" and "The United States Supreme Court has ruled that no state or local government may *require* the reading of the Lord's Prayer or Bible verses in public schools. What are your views on this—do you approve or disapprove of the court ruling?"

Note: The relationship is significant at the .01 level with a chi-square of 48.767.

The first rule of reading a table is to read and understand all nonnumeric portions: the title, subtitles, variable headings, and other identifying information shown in the table. Without this basic information, the reader cannot understand the meaning of the numbers placed within that table. The heading for Table 16–1 suggests that it is a bivariate table for the dependent variable, "approve or disapprove of the Court decision," and the independent variable, "religion of respondent." The tradition in table layout is to place the dependent variable on the left-hand side, and the independent variable across the top under the table heading.

Causally, religios status ought to precede and influence religious opinions. The variable heading, "Religion of respondent" and "Decision Approval," point to the location of each variable. Under each variable heading, the table lists the variable categories: Protestant, Catholic, Jewish, and Other for the respondent's religion, and approve or disapprove of the court decision. Beneath the table is listed important information researchers used to evaluate the sample and variable operationalizations. First, the data come from a well-known, nearly annual, survey done by a highly respected survey organization. These data re then followed by the exact questions used, so the reader can evaluate the quality of question wording. Finally, outside of the eight percentage cells (39, 43, 87, 85, 61, 57, 13, and 15) the reader should consider the so-called "table marginals," total percentages, and "Ns." Table marginals are the row or column totals that appear at the bottom or right-hand side of a table.

The researcher normally presents tables in a percentage format, rather than as raw data. The reason is that the researcher does not normally want to compare absolute cell frequencies because "*N*'s" or "*marginals*" (the column marginal N's are 409, 191, 15, and 48 in this table) are usually unequal as in Table 16–1. Therefore, the researcher controls for these inequalities through percentaging. Where there is an explicit independent variable, the researcher uses the total number of cases for each of that variables' categories as the standard base for percentaging. The reader can work backwards to see the original raw data used to formulate Table 16–1. For example, using the column marginal of 409 Protestants, the reader can take 39% of 409 to arrive at 159.51 to find the actual number of Protestants who approved of the court decision. Most probably, then the actual number of such cases is the rounded 160. Similarly, by subtracting 160 from 409, the reader arrives at 249 Protestants who disapproved of the court decision.

The five column totals of 100(%) are an important redundant element aiding the researcher to quickly understand which variable is the independent and dependent variable, and therefore which way to read the table. The second important rule of table reading is: *Make comparisons opposite to the computation of percentages*. In Table 16–1, because the percentaging is *down columns*, the reader must compare percentages *across columns*. Therefore, the reader should compare the percentages across the "approve" row with each other, and then compare the percentages across the "disapprove" row. One can readily see an effect of religious preference. Protestants are less likely than Catholics to approve of the Supreme Court decision, and Jews and Others are more than twice as likely to approve of that decision than either Protestants or Catholics.

Patterns of association in tabular data

The purpose of formulating a table is to search for patterns in the data. Because many tables use variables that are neither ordinal- nor cardinal-based, the pattern of covariation between variables in a table is referred to as an *association*. At the simplest level, a percentage table with no association would have exactly the same percentages across the row (or column) that does not add up to 100%. For example, if there were no association between the two variables in Table 16–1, we would expect that each of the cell percentages for the "approve" row would have the marginal frequency of 44%, and each of the "disapprove" row percentages would be 56%.

A quick perusal of Table 16–1 indicates that this is not the case. There are differences between each row percentage pairing, and those differences are ordered from lowest at the left to highest at the right for the approve row, and just the reverse for the disapprove row. Furthermore, SocialScene™ computes a simple measure of statistical independence of two variables called chi-square. Chi-square is a statistical test that indicates whether or not statistical association exists. The pattern in Table 16–1 is significantly different from the no-association null hypothesis prediction; in fact, the chi-square of 48.767 for this table indicates that we could expect significantly different results in only 1 out of 100 samples (= .01 level of significant). Because Table 16–1 does not employ at least ordinal variables, it makes no sense to speak of *direction* of the association. Nevertheless, some of the differences are strong and patterned enough to suggest a strong association between the two variables: Notice the more than twofold difference between Catholic and Jewish approval of school prayer as one reason.

Table 16–2 illustrates a case of close-to-perfect *lack of* association. Because most social scientists would predict that astrological sign has no causal effect on social variables, I have provided a test of the possible effects of respondents' astrological sign on satisfaction with their financial situation. Remember that if astrological sign has no effect on personal satisfaction with financial situations, that we expect all of the cell percentages to be close to the row marginal figures of 29, 45, and 25%. Unlike Table 16–1, in which there are huge differences in cell percentages read across rows, this table indicates no more than a 7-percentage-point spread from the expected cell frequencies. For example, the difference in astrological signs across the "not at all satisfied" row is 12 percentage points (a low of 18% compared with a high of 30%). None of these percentages are more than 7 percentage points from the row total average. Furthermore, the chi-square of 11.335 is not significant statistically, as a more objective indication that there is no association between these two variables. (If you have SocialScene™ and an MS-DOS-compatible machine at your disposal, you could have some fun looking for associations between astrological sign and other NORC variables.)

Table 16–2   *Satisfaction with Financial Situation by Astrological Sign of Respondent, Expressed in Percentages (Raw Number of Cell and Marginals Cases Are Shown in Parentheses)*

	Astrological Sign of Respondent				
Satisfaction with financial situation	*Earth*	*Air*	*Fire*	*Water*	*Totals*
Satisfied	33	30	25	28	29
More or less satisfied	43	52	45	41	41
Not at all satisfied	24	18	29	30	25
	100	100	100	100	100
	(179)	(170)	(173)	(172)	(694)

Source: SocialScene™ random subset of case drawn from the National Opinion Research Center's 1985 General Social Survey data. The questions asked were: "We are interested in how people are getting along financially these days. So far as you and your family are concerned, would you say that you are pretty well satisfied with your present financial situation, more or less satisfied, or not satisfied at all?" and respondent's astrological sign was recoded from birthdate information. Earth signs include those persons with birthdays from March 21 through June 21; air is from June 22 through September 22; fire from September 23 through December 21; and water from December 22 through March 20.

Note: The chi-square of 11.335 is not significant statistically.

Choice of measures of association

Because chi-square simply informs whether or not there is an association between two variables, the researcher needs to know something about true measures of association. However, there are many statistical measures of association. Choosing the best measure of association is very complex, and beyond the scope of this text. However, it is important for even the novice researcher to learn as much as possible about when statisticians prefer one particular measure over another. For this reason, it is useful to examine Table 16–3 which describes some important features of the most widely used measures of association. For the purpose of deciding which measure of association to choose, the user must know information about direction of causality, type of variable, number of variable categories, raw cell frequencies, and so on before using any particular measure of association. The problem is that most measures of association are dependent on specific assumptions that are best not violated. For example, some measures of association are highly sensitive to cells without cases. The result is that different measures of association can lead to wildly varying results.

A few of the major decisions that the user must make are listed in Table

Table 16-3 *Characteristics of Selected Measures of Association*

Measure	Type of Variable	Type of Measure	Magnitude	Strength	Weakness
Lambda	Nominal	Asymmetric	0.0 to +1.0	Modal prediction; PRE	Nature of association
Tau-y	Nominal	Asymmetric	0.0 to +1.0	Modal prediction; PRE	Nature of association
Gamma	Ordinal	Symmetric	−1.0 to +1.0	Appropriate for r x c table; Same as Yule's Q for 2 x 2 table	Ignores ties in rank; Ignores causal relationship
Somers' d_{xy}	Ordinal	Asymmetric	−1.0 to +1.0	Accounts for ties; Accounts for predictor variable	Ignores pattern of frequency in different cells
Tau-b	Ordinal	Symmetric	−1.0 to +1.0	Accounts for nontrivial ties	No clear PRE interpretation
Spearman's rho	Ordinal	Symmetric	−1.0 to +1.0	Equivalent to Pearson's r	Only useful with variranked from 1 to N

16–3. The best-known measures are listed down the left-hand column. Across the top are a few of the major decisions the researcher must make to choose among the measures. The first major decision depends on the type of variable. As a rule, it is best to chose a measure based upon the weakest variable of the two to be analyzed. If the table has a nominal *and* an ordinal variable, then because nominal categories are weaker than ordinal scales, the choice must be between nominal measures. If both variables are ordinal, it makes sense to choose an ordinal measure.

Both the nominal measures—lambda and tau-y—are asymmetric measures that range from 0.0 for no association to 1.0 for perfect association. The designation of asymmetric means that there are two measures of each—one for predicting x from y, and another for predicting y from x. Knowing which to use means theorizing the appropriate causal order. For example, if the researcher had two nominal categories—sex of respondent and presence/absence of sex discrimination—the only lambda or tau-y that would make sense is the one that treated sex as the predictor of sex discrimination. Like most of the measures in Table 16–3, these measures are P.R.E. (Proportional Reduction in Error) ones. PRE measures give improved guessing rules for making predictions about the association of two variables. Those predictions depend on information inherent in the table. Lambda$_{yx}$ predicts the modal values for each category of the dependent variable y, based on knowledge of the modal values of the independent variable x. Lambda$_{xy}$ reverses the roles of each variable, so that one makes predictions about x based on knowledge of y. Tau-y makes guesses about the *distribution* of the dependent variable by assuming a minimum guessing rule that all categories of the independt variable are *randomly assigned* to the distribution found in the dependent variable's margins. Because tau-y and lambda use different guessing rules, each may lead to different values.

The choice of measure is more difficult yet with ordinal data. Some of these measures are symmetric such as gamma, while others are asymmetric. One of the most grave problems with ordinal measures is whether to base the rules on prediction of the same rank order or the opposite rank order. If Jane is ranked higher in social class than Mary, we might use the "same rank order" rule to predict that she will also rank higher in occupational prestige; but in predicting her alienation, we would probably do better to use the "opposite rank order" rule, because alienation and social class are negatively related.

Because most measures of association vary between 0 and 1, or between –1 and 1, they are easily interpreted in terms of lack of association or association. The problem with chosing between measures of association becomes most apparent when they give different values. As you can see from this discussion, the process is not easily reduced to a neat set of cookbook rules. The novice user has little choice but to either take a course in their use, or consult with a statistician over which measure is most appropriate when the values differ.

How the researcher percentages can also grossly affect results. Cole (1979) challenged the long-standing belief that age is negatively associated with scientific productivity and creativity, by demonstrating that earlier methods of percentaging were incorrect. If one examines the percentage of scientists making important discoveries, by dividing total scientists into the number of scientists making important discoveries at ages under 30, 30–39, 40–49, 50–59, and age 60 and over, the percentages of scientists making important discoveries would drop from 40% at age 30 and under to 4% at age 60 and over. The problem with this type of percentage is that it ignores the fact that there are many more younger scientists than older scientists, due to mortality rates and increasing graduate-school enrollments over time. Therefore, when Cole percentaged the number of scientists making important discoveries based on the total number of scientists *of each age group*, he found a slight curvilinear relationship between age and productivity with increases in productivity through the thirties and forties.

Tables Where Percentaging Is Impossible

Percentage tables are possible means of analysis, only when researchers are cross-tabulating complete raw or group frequency counts for two or more variables. Some of the time, however, they wish to cross-tabulate some other type of data, such as averages, variation measures, correlations, or incomplete frequency counts (where the percentages do not total 100%).

The researcher sets up nonpercentaged tables similarly to percentaged tables, in that they must have headings for variables and variable categories and rows and columns with cells. But these cells, unlike percentage tables, do not contain (or are not based on) frequency counts, but rather are based on some summary statistic. For instance, Table 16–4 contains data expressed with medians in each cell. Normally speaking, the reader reads across the categories of comparison—in this case the City and County of St. Louis—after reading the various tabular headings. For example, reading across row one, the median household size in 1980 was 1.94 in the county and 1.50 in the city, or about one-half person (one-seventh) larger in the county than the city; the median age of city resident was a half year older than county residents (31.2 versus 31.7); and county residents had completed a whole year more schooling (11.7 versus 10.7) on average than had city residents.

It is important for the nonpercentage table heading to contain information identifying the statistics in the cell. The fact that the Bureau of the Census statisticians chose medians in each of these cases is a good sign that the data were skewed (as was discussed early in this chapter, under the subheading of representative values). In cases where the statistic summarizes arbitrary scoring systems (nominal or ordinal), it also is necessary to identify the meaning of the scoring system. If one of the table variables was Machiavellianism scored from 1 to 7, then it would be necessary to identify whether I represented high or low Machiavellianism, if the table reader is to understand what cell figures mean. (In Table 16–4 this presents no problem because the tables have a cardinal base.)

Table 16-4 *Median Household Size, Median Age of Population and Median Years of Completed Schooling for the City and County of St. Louis in 1980*

	St. Louis County	St. Louis City
Median household size	1.94	1.50
Median age of persons	31.2	31.7
Median years of completed schooling	11.7	10.7

Source: 1980 U.S. Census data

Correlation and Regression

Many researchers do not analyze their data in tabular form, but instead use correlational analysis, or some type of analysis based on correlations. Correlations presuppose that the researcher is using cardinal data. The logic of these approaches is the same as that employed in tabular analysis, but it requires somewhat more of an understanding of statistics on the user's part.

Unlike looking at percentages, or other summary statistic differences, the researcher using correlational analysis expresses the relationship between two variables through such measures as Pearson's correlation coefficient, *r*. To get a feel for what a correlation coefficient summarizes, consider the graph in Figure 16–6. This graph is called a scatterplot. A *scatterplot* is a two-dimension plot similar to the two-variable tables in that the researcher charts one variable on the vertical axis and the other on the horizontal axis just like in tabular analysis where one variable goes along the rows and the other along the columns. Each of the nine hatch marks in Figure 16–6 represents the intersection of the scores for the two variables for each of the eight counties and one city defined by the U.S. Bureau of the Census as the St. Louis Standard Metropolitan Statistical Area (SMSA). For example, in the lower right-hand corner, observe the "star" plot for St. Louis County. That hatch mark stands at the intersection of 11.7 years median schooling and 20.3 years median housing age.

A scattergram is a visual means of examining the question: If we know an individual (person, county, or other unit) score on one variable, how well can we predict the paired score on another variable? By examining the scattergram, the reader can usually get an intuitively close idea as to how closely related two variables are. If all the hatch marks are truly scattered across the graph, there is no correlation between the two variables. If, as in Figure 16–6, those hatch marks cluster close to a line known as the regression line, or line of best fit, then the two variables do covary; and if all the points fall directly on a straight line, then there is perfect correlation between the two variables. The

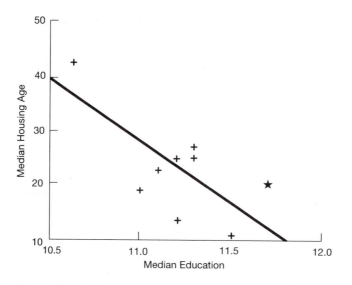

Figure 16-6. Scatterplot between median years of schooling and the median age of housing in 1980 for counties in the St. Louis Metropolitan Area.

Source: 1980 U.S. Census data

closer the dots are to falling on the line of best fit, the higher the correlation between the two variables.

The usual measure of correlation, Pearson's *r*, is mathematically a special type of mean average score between two variables; it varies from −1.0 if the two variables have a perfect negative correlation to 0, indicating no association to +1.0 indicating a perfect positive correlation. The line of best fit also gives visual information concerning the correlation. If the line of best fit, as in Figure 16–6, runs from the upper left to lower right, the correlation is negative. Remembering that median education reflects only persons 25 years of age and older (so that they have mostly finished their formal schooling), the r = −0.69 shows a strong negative correlation between median education and median age of housing in the St. Louis SMSA. In other words, persons with higher education have a propensity to reside in areas with younger housing, and vice versa: the lower the education, the older the median age of the housing. If the relationship were positive, the line of best fit would run from the lower left-hand corner to the upper right-hand corner. This latter type of relationship suggests that as one variable increases, the other also increases.

Each of the conjunctions of variables represented by hatch marks in the scattergram contributes to the total summary correlation just as does each case in computing a mean score. Similarly, just as an outlier may grossly influence the mean, so, too, can hatch marks further from the line of best fit. To illustrate how much difference is possible, if we were to remove the St. Louis County dot in the lower right-hand corner of Figure 16–6, the correlation for the remaining eight cases would jump from −0.69 to −0.80—a very strong negative correlation. (All correlation coefficients in this book are Pearson's r unless otherwise stated.) The line of best fit would also change and become steeper, reflecting the way the line is computed. Outliers, then, have great influence on the correlation coefficient.

Actually there are two lines of best fit. It is possible to compute a line predicting x from y as well as y from x. Of course, if the researcher has a good sense of the causal order, it rarely makes sense to compute both regression lines. As with the correlation coefficient, r, the regression lines serve two important functions: Because the regression lines offer a graphic picture of the relationship between x and y, they (1) summarize that relationship, and (2) can be used to infer one set of variable values from another set of variable values.

The regression line is the line of best prediction for x from y or y from x. That is, if one took all of the actual scores and the predicted scores (those along the regression line) in Figure 16–6, and squared the differences between actual and predicted scores, the sum of these squared deviations around the regression line would be smaller than for any other straight line. Therefore, this regression line gives the best prediction of x from y. There is also a regression line that gives the best prediction of y from x.

Just as means and standard deviations provide summary statistics for univariate distributions, researchers rarely use scattergrams to report their data, but instead, rely on *correlation coefficients* and *regression coefficients*. From high-school mathematics, the reader may recall that any linear equation of the form $y = bx + a$ is composed of several important pieces of information. First, the b, or beta, is the *slope* of the straight line that the linear equation predicts. Therefore, it gives information that as x increases by some amount, y will increase by some other amount. If in Figure 16–6, the regression line were $y = 1.5x$ the researcher would know that as x increases one unit, y increases 1.5 units. Second, the a, or y-intercept, tells where on the y-axis (vertical axis) the line crossed. Therefore, in Figure 16–6, because a is approximately 11.4, it crosses the vertical axis at approximately that point.

The *beta weight* does not measure the same thing as a correlation. A correlation coefficient measures the strength and direction of coincidence of two variables. If the researcher squares the correlation, he or she produces a measure of the amount of variation in one variable, which is explained by its linear covariation with the other variable. For example, a correlation of 0.9 squared suggests that 81% of the variation in y is attributable to variation in x. A *beta weight*, by contrast, measures the predicted linear unit change in values of the dependent variable based on knowledge of the independent variable values. A beta weight of 0 suggests no ability to predict one variable from the other, because the line of best fit is parallel to the x-axis. A beta of 0.9 means that as x (the independent variable) increases by one standard unit, y (the independent variable) is predicted to increase by 0.9 standard units.

Although the difference between a slope of 0.9 and 0.8 might seem trivial to a novice researcher, the difference is as nontrivial (assuming adequate measurement) as a "slight error" in computing the correct trajectory for sending a rocket to Mars. Just as miscomputing the correct trajectory to Mars by one degree would end up sending a rocket hundreds of thousand of miles off course, a change in slope of 0.1 compounds errors of prediction of the dependent variable over larger units of the independent variable. Furthermore, a slope has no limit to its range unlike the correlation coefficient which ranges only from $+1$ to -1.

As an example, consider a regression equation for predicting male college graduates income suggested in Conklin's (1982) Clear5™ software on income inequality. This equation is

$$\text{Income} = \text{year} * 279 - \$538009$$

In 1990, the equation predicts an average salary of $17,201 and in 2020 $25,571. However, simply changing the beta from 279 to 280 would produce $19,191 and $27,590, respectively; the difference in prediction between this "slight" change in 1990 is $1990, and is $2,019 in 2020.

Scattergrams have another important visual use. Sometimes the correlation between two variables is low because the relationship is nonlinear. Quick inspection of a scattergram can give an idea of whether the relationship is curvilinear or linear. For example, Figure 16–7 shows a curvilinear relationship (The hatch marks and the points on the graph do not fall along a straight line.) between the number of Roman Catholic Churches in the St. Louis SMSA and the median family income. Most statistics books recommend using a special statistic called *eta squared* and comparing it to the Pearson's correlation coefficient to get a more objective measure of nonlinear relationships. When *eta* is larger than Pearson's *r*, the researcher infers the relationship is curvilinear. Neverthe-

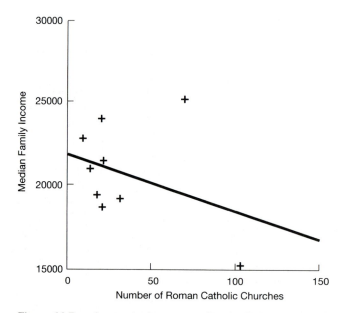

Figure 16-7.   Scatterplot between median family income and the number of Roman Catholic churches in 1980 for counties in the St. Louis Metropolitan Area.

Source: 1980 U.S. Census data.

less, an inspection of a scattergram can at least give a quick-and-dirty inference to this question in many cases.

Another commonly used measure of association between variables is Spearman's *rho*. This measure is used only with rank-order (ordinal) data. For example, the interval data used in Figure 16–7 and the associated rank ordering for each county in the St. Louis SMSA for the 1980 census data are listed below:

SMSA UNIT	Number of Roman Catholic Churches	Rank	Median Family Income	Rank	D	D²
Monroe County (IL)	7	1	22.801	7	−6	36
Jefferson County (MO)	11	2	21,042	5	−9	81
Clinton County (MO)	15	3	19,469	4	−1	1
St. Charles County (MO)	18	4	24,167	8	−4	16
Franklin County (MO)	18	5	18,788	2	3	9
Madison County (IL)	18	6	21,419	6	0	0
St. Clair County (IL)	29	7	19,239	3	4	16
St. Louis County (MO)	69	8	25,266	9	1	1
St. Louis City (MO)	102	9	15,265	1	8	64
						Sum = 188

The data in columns two and three reflect the well-known propensity for American Roman Catholics to live in large metropolitan areas, rather than rural areas. However, note that median family income has a distinctly different rank order. Spearman's *rho* uses the following formula to comput a measure of association:

$$\text{Spearman's } r_s = 1 - \frac{6\Sigma\,D^2}{N(N^2 - 1)}$$

where Σ stands for sum, D^2 refers to the squares of the differences in rank order between columns 5 and 6 above, and N equals the number of cases. For example, the rank order for Monroe County is $1 - 7 = 6$, and the square of 6 is 36. Spearman's *rho*, in this case, then is

$$\text{Spearman's } r_s = 1 - \frac{6(188)}{9(9^2 - 1)} = 1 - \frac{1128}{720} = -.57$$

Compare this with the Pearson's *r* of .06—which indicates no relationship between Roman Catholic church membership and median family income. Spearman's *rho*, on the other hand, suggests a relatively strong negative relationship ($-.57$). Areas with stronger Roman Catholic church membership have lower median family income. (The reason for this has more to do with the fact that Roman Catholics live in urban areas with less income than with their religious affiliation.)

In the next chapter regression analysis and path analysis shall be discussed. These techniques now dominate quantitative methods of analysis in a variety of academic disciplines, and depend on summary statistics such as the correlation coefficient and regression coefficient.

Summary

In the ideal data analysis, the researcher anticipates the types of data analysis he or she will need in earlier phases of the research. A primary means of anticipation is to collect data linked to theory; to let theory guide the analysis. That is, the ideal is to use the data to test empirically verifiable consequences of theory.

Once the data are entered and clean, the researcher examines the data for each variable one at a time to explore the shape of the data. This exploration depends on fundamental statistical tools: measures of central tendency and distribution. Visual means of displaying these measures include the histogram and the stem-and-leaf diagram. These visual displays, and summary statistics like the various averages can help the researcher organize a set of data to find the "typical value." Other simple, frequently used tools include the rate expressed as a percentage and ratio measures. The researcher also summarizes variation away from the typical value with quartiles, standard deviation, the variance, and other measures. In the process of visualizing the shape of the data, the researcher may transform the data with logs, z-scores, or other mathematical means of reshaping the data into a more statistically and theoretically appropriate form.

The next stage of analysis is usually two-variable analysis. The purpose of bivariate analysis is to search for causal relationships. Researchers depend on summary measures of statistical association and correlation and visual diagrams, known as scatterplots for this stage. However, they realize that association is only a necessary and not sufficient step in causal analysis.

For percentage tables, the first rule of analysis is to read all nonnumeric portions: title, subtitles, and other identifying information. The second rule is to compare percentages in the direction opposite to computation of percentage marginal totals. If the percentages add to one hundred down the columns, then the researcher compares differences in percentages across rows. Usually this comparison is standardized by using a statistical measure of association.

A second major technique of analysis is correlational analysis. When the researcher uses cardinal data, the correlation is generally the most appropriate summary statistic of coincidence of two variables. Associated with the correlation coefficient is the line of best fit or regression line. This line gives a measure of predicting the dependent variable from the independent variable, and the correlation coefficient tells how strong the relationship is.

C H A P T E R

17

Further Analytic Techniques

The sciences do not try to explain, they hardly even try to interpret, they mainly make models. By a model is meant a mathematical construct which, with the addition of certain verbal interpretations, describes observed phenomena. The justification of such a mathematical construct is solely and precisely that it is expected to work.[1]

Key Terms

Antecedent variable	Intervening variable
Component variable	Multicollinearity
Conditional variable	Multiple r squared
Distorter variable	Nonrecursive relationship
Dummy variable	Panel study analysis
Extraneous variable	Path analysis

---

[1]Neumann, J. von, (1963) Method in the physical sciences, *Collected Works*, New York: Pergamon Press, p. 16.

Recursive relationship	Statistical elaboration
Regression analysis	Suppressor variable
Robust	Test factor
Spurious relationship	Turnover
Standardized beta weight	Trend study analysis
Statistical control	

Study Guide Questions

1. Explain the basic logic of test factor analysis.

2. What does a beta weight explain that a correlation coefficient can not?

3. Why is regression analysis not as good as true experimental controls but still better than simple correlation?

4. How can one statistically demonstrate spurious relationships? What must account for a relationship that is spurious?

5. Under what conditions would a researcher suspect a component analysis is justified? How would the researcher demonstrate this effect?

6. What statistical evidence is necessary to support an intervening variable relationship? How does this differ from antecedent variable evidence?

7. What conditions lead the researcher to suspect a suppressor variable? A distorter variable?

8. Conditional relationships require what kinds of evidence? Why do researchers say they demonstrate interaction effects?

9. Why is multivariate analysis difficult in traditional tabular analysis?

10. What assumptions must researchers who use techniques of multivariate regression analysis be wary?

11. How do the three basic assumptions of path analysis differ from those of multiple regression?

12. What are the basic techniques necessary to trend analysis? Why are they necessary?

13. How does panel study analysis differ from trend study analysis?

14. What are the major advantages and disadvantages of panel study analysis?

One of the major assumptions in social science is that unicausal explanations (*A* causes *B*) should be distrusted. The social sciences lack the simplicity of explanation found in many other sciences. Generally speaking, it is rare to find correlations higher than ± .40 in the social sciences. Perfect explanation, remember, would require correlations of ± 1.00. Therefore, social scientists suspect that social and behavioral research that deals with such two-variable distributions as zero-order correlations (normal two-variable correlation coefficients) and two-variable cross-tabulations are too simplistic. Parsimony is a scientific ideal, but one should remember that explanations may be too simplistic. Therefore, researchers increasingly find the need to study the relationships between more than two variables at a time.

The objective of this chapter is to introduce students to the logic of multivariate analysis. For those students interested in in-depth knowledge of these techniques, a course in intermediate or advanced statistics is recommended. This chapter focuses on a fundamental understanding of the logic and importance of these methods.

Three-Variable Relationships

The simplest means of statistical control, just seen in the last chapter, is to use relative frequencies expressed as percentages rather than absolute frequencies, or raw cell scores. The researcher can also view the two-variable relationship profitably through "controlling for" some third variable—that is, by holding constant the third "test" factor. Researchers term this third factor a "test" factor because they introduce it to test properties of the original bivariate relationship.

Basic Ideas

The *test factor* is a means of examining the relationship of independent and dependent variables through use of a third variable. The logic is the same for both tabular and correlational analysis, although the researcher calls each by a different name; test-factor analysis and regression analysis, respectively. Regression analysis controls for the effects of third (and even other) variables using cardinal data in the same way that test-factor analysis does for tabular data in nominal or ordinal form. For instance, when methodologists say that a tabular relation disappears after introduction of a test factor, they imply that the cell frequencies in the three-variable table now show *no association*; that is, there is no significant variation in the appropriate cell percentages that the researcher compares.

In a similar manner, regression analysis sets each of the independent variables to their arithmetic mean value as its basis of statistical control, and then computes a statistic known as a standardized beta weight. The beta weight takes the correlation between a set of possible independent variables and a dependent variable, and removes the multiple effects of all the independent variables save one, by setting all their case values to their arithmetic means. In this manner, the researcher sees only the distilled, purified effect of each independent variable. A *standardized beta weight* is a measure of the *net* effect of an independent variable. Regression analysis also measures the *combined effects* of all the independents variables with a measure knows as the *multiple r squared.*

For example, if one were interested in the causes of car thefts, one might run a series of correlations of car thefts per 1,000 population against the hypothetized independent variables. Because some juvenile delinquents steal cars, the researcher might study the effects of high-school dropout rates. Also, because one might expect cars parked in public parking lots to be particularly vulnerable to theft, one might run a correlation between the per capita receipts in parking lots and car thefts. As expected, these correlations are positive and nontrivial using national data in Stark's (1987) Showcase™ program:

parking lot receipts per capita - car thefts per 1,000 = 0.42
percent high school drop outs - car thefts per 1,000 = 0.26

Having shown that a correlation exists is only the first step in causal analysis. Step two involves setting all cases—state data in this example—of dropout rates to the national mean level as a measure of statistical control, and then computing the beta weight for the effects of parking lot receipts per capita. The resulting *beta* is close to the correlation; it is 0.42. Then, the researcher sets all cases of parking lot receipts per capita to the national mean level, and computes the beta weight for the high school dropout rate, which also does not change drastically; this beta drops slightly from the correlation of 0.31 to 0.26. Finally, the researcher computes the multiple r squared measure of total explained variance which is 27%.

In effect, the researcher knows a great deal more than with the correlations. Because the beta weight is standardized, the researcher can directly compare the beta weights. The beta for parking receipts is more than 50% larger than the beta for the dropout rate, so the researcher knows that the net effect of parking lots on car thefts has more effect than high-school dropouts. Then, because this regression analysis can explain car thefts in only 27 out of 100 cases, the researcher also knows that there must be other independent variables that are yet undiscovered.

Although regression analysis controls for whatever variables the researcher analyzes, it is never as strong at asserting causality compared to true experimental controls, because the true experiment controls for all extraneous factors, while regression analysis controls only for those independent variables entered into the analysis. This is one good reason why scientists can never say they have proven anything. In the above explanation of car thefts, I controlled only for one other variable for each beta weight. However, adding the percentage of area urbanized as a third independent variable would actually reduce the effects of parking lot receipts to an insignificant beta weight of 0.05, without substantially reducing the effects of high-school dropouts. Without the control for urbanization, parking lots appeared to be robust; with controls for urbanization, the regression shows the effects of parking lots to be fictitious. The moral of the story is: Regression analysis is no better than the theory the researcher tests.

Cut to the bare bones, the logic of test-factor analysis has three possibilities. First, if after introduction of a third variable into the relationship, the original table percentages (or beta weights) do not change significantly from the original table percentages (or correlations), then the researcher gains confidence that the test factor has no effect on the original bivariate relationship. Second, if the original relationship washes out—that is, shows no association or correlation after introduction of the test factor—then the researcher assumes that the original relationship is spurious, and that the test factor is the genuine independent variable. Third, if the original association or correlation becomes stronger, then the researcher assumes that there may be several causes, rather than one cause of the relationship.

However, test-factor analysis is not a substitute for clear thinking about the causal relationship. The researcher needs to keep in mind the possible causal order of the three or more variables. It makes no sense to introduce test factors haphazardly. To better understand the logic of test-factor analysis, let us return briefly to the bivariate relationship between religion of respondent and approval of the court decision in Table 16–1. In that table, there was a significant relationship between the two variables, with religion making quite a difference in approval. Protestants were the least likely to approve of the court decision concerning use of the Lord's Prayer in public schools, Catholics approved slightly more often than Protestants, and Jews and persons of other religions were most likely to approve the decision. A three-variable table allows for the examination of the independent-dependent variable relationship under each *condition* of the test factor. Note that a three-variable table is actually a set of subtables—that is, there is a separate subtable for each partial relationship, or condition, of the test factor.

Table 17–1 adds a test factor, sex of respondent, to Table 16–1. Because sex has two conditions, the researcher makes two separate subtables; one for each sex. The idea is to examine whether or not the test factor of sex has changed the original independent-dependent variable relationship. *The first rule for reading three-variable tables is to compare cells across test-factor subtables that share the same independent-and dependent-variable values.* For example, in Table 17–1, the researcher would compare the Protestant approval cells across males and females; then the Catholic approval cells for each sex, and so on.

If we compare the male and female subtables, we find essentially the same relationship between approval of the court decision and religious preference. The rank order of approval is still the same, with Protestant at the lowest end and Jews and Others at the highest end. However, we can also see that there is an independent effect of sex of respondents. With the exception of Catholics, males are more approving of the court's decision than females. For example, 42% of Protestant males approve of the court's decision, while 36% of Protestant females feel the same way. Although the column marginals are very

Table 17-1 *Approval of Court Decision by Religion and Sex of Respondent, Expressed in Percentages (Raw Number of Cell and Marginals Cases Are Shown in Parentheses)*

Sex of Respondent	Court Decision	Religion of Respondent				Totals
		Protestant	*Catholic*	*Jewish*	*Other*	
Females	Approve	36	43	78	75	41
	Disapprove	64	57	22	25	59
		100	100	100	100	100
		(231)	(101)	(9)	(20)	(361)
Males	Approve	42	43	100	93	48
	Disapprove	58	57	0	7	52
		100	100	100	100	100
		(178)	(90)	(6)	(28)	(302)

Source: SocialScene™ random subset of case drawn from the National Opinion Research Center's 1985 General Social Survey data. The questions asked were "What is your religious preference? Is it Protestant, Catholic, Jewish, some other religion, or no religion?" and "The United States Supreme Court has ruled that no state or local government may *require* the reading of the Lord's Prayer or Bible verses in public schools. What are your views on this—do you approve or disapprove of the court ruling?" and the interviewer coded sex of respondent by sight.

Note: The chi-squire measure could not be calculated because at least one expected cell frequency was smaller than five cases.

small for Jewish respondents (only 6 Jewish men and 20 Jewish women), we can see that Jewish men (100%) are, like Protestant men, more much approving of the court decision than women (78%).

The researcher's theoretical perspective is important in analyzing three-way tables. Rosenberg (1968:40) emphasizes that the researcher should not introduce test factors into the table unless "(1) there is a theoretical reason or empirically based reason for assuming that it accounts for the relationship; and (2) there is no evidence indicating that it is not related both to the independent and dependent variable." Clearly, we have good reason to believe that sex and religious preference precede religious opinions. We also know that women are more likely to attend church than men, and therefore, might well have different attitudes toward prayer outside of church. We also know that different religious affiliations influence a wealth of variables. Therefore, we have satisfied Rosenberg's criteria for introducing the tabular forms shown in both Tables 16–1 and 17–1.

Test Factors: Control through Elaboration

This section considers seven prototype *test factors*: extraneous, component, intervening, antecedent, suppressor, distorter, and conditional variables. This process is called *elaboration*, because the researcher is interested in obtaining greater information about the two-variable relationship, or stating and developing that relationship in more detail.

Extraneous or spurious relationships

One theoretical reason for introducing a test factor involves the testing of hypothesized extraneous variables. The general rule is: The more particular variables that the researcher can introduce *without substantially* changing the original bivariate relationship, the more confidence that the original relationship is real and meaningful rather than *spurious* or accidental. Unfortunately, it is impossible to control all extraneous factors, which means that there can be no complete proof that some extraneous factor yet uncovered is not actually responsible for the relationship. This is one good reason why multivariate analysis does not have the power of controls found in the true experiment.

The causal form of the extraneous relationship is

rather than the original hypotheses, which has the generic form of

$$X \rightarrow Y$$

In other words, the *XY* relationship here is spurious and symmetrical, rather than causal and asymmetrical. The original relationship disappears when controlled on the test factor, simply because *X* and *Y* are related due to the dependence of both on a common antecedent variable. Figure 17–1 gives some simple examples of extraneous variable relationships. Note that the relationship between number of fire engines at the scene of a fire and the amount of fire damage disappears when size of fire is taken into account (controlled for). Notice also that while the *interpretation* of the original relationship is spurious, this interpretation is due to some extraneous variable. For example, the reason that hospitalization is associated with the death rate is because of an outside variable that actually affects each variable independently. Seriousness of illness causes hospitalization, and it also causes the death rate to go up.

Because of the possibility of spurious relationships, researchers who find statistical support for causal relationships are normally cautious in claiming "proof" of causality. The prudent researcher is always aware that he or she may simply not have found a test factor that actually causes the original rela-

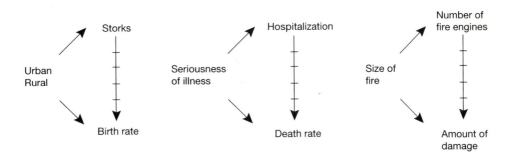

Figure 17–1.   Spurious causal interpretations.

tionship to vanish. *This is particularly true where the association or correlation is not supported by existing theory.* The famous philosopher Friedrick Nietzsche claimed that eating piles of potatoes led to liquor use, based on the statistically positive association in Europe between potato production and production of vodka, whiskey, and wine; and because he described the aftereffects of too much alcohol as leading to a mouth that felt like an old potato! The correlation between potato production and liquor production is simply explained by the fact that potatoes are a main ingredient in liquor production in Europe as well as a nonalcoholic staple. Alcoholism in the United States and other places where liquor is non-potato-based would provide a better test of Nietzsche's outrageous claim.

To call a relationship spurious, the first thing the researcher must show is that the original, hypothesized relationship exists statistically. The relationship in Figure 16–1 between religion of respondent and opinion of public-school prayer is a candidate for testing, because the chi-square here shows significance, while the relationship in Figure 16–2 is not, because the chi-square for testing the relationship between respondent's astrological sign and satisfaction with financial situation is nonsignificant.

The second thing the researcher must do is demonstrate that a test factor significantly changes the original relationship. Table 17–1 gives one such test for the test factor of sex of respondent, using the data introduced in Table 16–1. However, here the original relationship appeared to withstand the test. Although the approval rates for males appears higher than for females, if you compare female approval/disapproval rates with male approval/disapproval rates, you will see that the pattern is very similar; Protestant and Catholic approval rates for males and females are lower than their corresponding disapproval rates. Also, note that the Catholic rates are the same for both males and females. When the original relationship withstands the introduction of a number of such test factors, researchers say that the original relationship is *robust* because the relationship appears to be durable and sturdy. For example, in my earlier example of the causes of car thefts, both parking lots and dropout rates appeared to be robust, because there was little change between the correlations and corresponding beta weights. However, with further controls, it was demonstrated that parking lot receipts was not robust.

When the researcher uses correlational analysis, the same logic applies. For example, in Stark's (1987) Showcase™ computer demonstrations, his data illustrate the spuriousness of a well-known correlation between the number of police per 1,000 population, and the number of property crimes per 100,000 population. The correlation of 0.47 between these two variables nearly vanishes to a beta weight of − 0.01 when controlled for the percentage urbanized. The reason is twofold: Governments in larger urbanized areas hire larger numbers of police; and larger metropolitan areas are the places where property crimes are more likely to occur. Similarly, the bivariate correlation between readership of *Playboy* magazine (and other girlie magazines), and the rape rate of 0.31 nearly disappears—it reduces to a nearly insignificant beta equal of − 0.14—when the researcher controls for areas with large numbers of all-male households. Again, the reason is because mostly men rather than women read

Playboy, and men account for the vast majority of rape. In fact, all-male households are a fairly decent operationalization of where the young, single men live.

In the above-mentioned examples, the naive analyst might believe the test of significance which shows both correlations to be statistically significant. However, substantive significance is a matter of logic and theory. Theory contributed the test factors that ultimately showed the original bivariate relationship to be spurious. The moral is: *Statistical significance is no panacea for good theory*.

Finally, lack of an association or correlation is different from spuriousness. The bivariate correlation between pickup trucks per 1,000, and per capita spending in bowling alleys in the United States (Stark 1987) is a paltry and statistically insignificant 0.08. It is incorrect to call that essentially nonrelationship spurious. Spurious is a word researchers reserve for statistically significant bivariate correlations that can be shown to be false, due to a third variable that explains the entire bivariate relationship, by reducing the original relationship to near-zero and statistical insignificance.

Component variables

Scientists spend a great deal of time specifying which component or element of a global independent variable is responsible for effects on some dependent variable. A biochemist may try to isolate which component of all the chemical compounds in a strain of HIV produces AIDS. Similarly, the social scientist may introduce various components of an independent variable into a bivariate table to specify each component's effect on the relationship. For example, which element in alienation (powerlessness, normlessness) is responsible for voter registration apathy? Which element of status inconsistency (education-occupation inconsistency, income-ethnicity incongruity, visible versus nonvisible lower statuses) produces political liberalism? Which element of social class (respondent's occupation, father's education) is accountable for attitudes held toward work?

Component analysis is a sort of "reverse engineering" approach to statistics, because it allows the researcher a means of breaking down a complex variable into its constituent elements. Social class provides a classic example; social scientists are often interested in researching the components of social class—education, occupation, income, subjective class identification—to discover the strength of each element in contributing to variations in attitudes and behavior. Table 17–2 provides an example of a tabular breakdown of two elements of social class, in the determination of fear of walking alone at night in the respondent's neighborhood. This table only focuses on the proportion who answered in the affirmative to the question about fear of walking alone at night. The abridged portion of the original table is not necessary for this particular analysis because that portion can be derived by subtracting each percentage from 100%. It is a good idea, particularly when first starting out analyzing multivariate tables, to treat them in this less complex, subtable manner for ease of analysis.

None of the subtable analysis comparisons for *subjective* social class in

Table 17–2 *The Percent of Individuals Claiming They Are Afraid to Walk in Their Local Neighborhood at Night by Their Subjective Class Identification and Respondent's Income Level*

	Less than $10,000 Income		$10,000 to $22,499 Income		Income More than $22,499	
	Middle Class	*Working Class*	*Middle Class*	*Working Class*	*Middle Class*	*Working Class*
Proportion agreeing that they are afraid to walk alone at night	40	48	35	34	29	16

Source: SocialScene™ random subset of case drawn from the National Opinion Research Center's 1985 General Social Survey data. The questions asked were "In which of these groups did your earnings from (respondent's occupation), for last year—1984 (1972, or whatever)—fall? That is, before taxes or other deductions. Just tell me the letter. A. Under $1,000 . . ."; "If you were asked to use one of the four names for your social class, which would you say you belong in: the lower class, the working class, the middle class, or the upper class?"; and "Is there any area around here—that is, within a mile—where you would be afraid to walk alone at night?"

Note: The chi-square measure for each subtable differences in respondent's income were significant statistically at the .01 level, but the subjective class differences were not significant.

Table 17–2 (40 and 48; 35 and 34; and 29 and 16) are significantly different statistically. However, the *objective* income levels do appear to be meaningful. In fact, the chi-square for the bivariate differences in income levels is statistically significant at the .01 level. Interestingly, the differences are greater for the working class than the middle class when separated out by income levels. For example, the difference between the working-class respondents with less than $10,000 and those with more than $22,499 incomes is 48 minus 16%, or a 32 percentage point spread while the comparable difference for middle-class respondents is a spread of only 11 (40–29) percentage points. Clearly, respondents with more income report less fear of walking alone at nights, but the difference is greater for those who see themselves as working-class respondents than middle class.

Rosenberg (1968:47) aptly reports that this type of analysis "*suggests that the 'same' variables are not always the same.*" That is, the components of a more general variable may produce different effects on various dependent variables. For explanation of variation in some dependent variables, occupation may be the most powerful explanation, with other variables, education may be the most efficacious; and with still others, income may be the most potent cause. In Kohn and Schooler's (1978) research on work and personality, they found various features of occupation (whether one works with things, people, or ideas) to be the strongest determinant of personal flexibility among these independent variables. National surveys show educational attainment has a stronger effect than income level on attitudes toward abortion. However, among these three measures, income is the most strongly related to increasing trash problems: Trash is largely a product of affluence.

Intervening variables

Intervening variables are test factors that take the form

$$X \rightarrow T \rightarrow Y$$

That is, the researcher proposes that a third variable, T, mediates the original XY relationship. Stark (1987) provides a clear example of an intervening variable that also elucidates the interpretation of spurious relationships. Some individuals have long assumed that poverty leads to such a variety of social pathologies as homicides.

The bivariate correlation between the percentage of households below the official poverty line and the homicide rate is a respectable 0.51; on the surface, this correlation supports the hypotheses that poverty leads to higher homicide rates. However, Stark notes a few other interesting correlations and facts. First, the correlation between overcrowding and homicides is a huge 0.72. (Stark measured overcrowding across the various states, by simply tabulating variations in the percentage of individuals who live in households with more than 1.01 persons per room.) More interesting yet, Stark then used beta weights whereby the researcher controls for the net effects of each of these two possible independent variables. In the process, the net effect of overcrowding remained at a robust level, with a beta weight equal to 0.67, and the poverty variable and the net effect of poverty fell to a seemingly spurious level based on a beta weight of 0.07. Stark warns that the reduction of the 0.51 to 0.07 does *not* mean the effect of poverty on homicide is spurious. Instead, he suggests the plausibility of causal chain of the type:

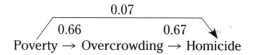

First, Stark reasoned that poverty probably does not directly cause homicides. Instead, poverty leads to people living in overcrowded conditions. He underscores this hypotheses by demonstrating that the correlation between these two variables is 0.66. Second, he reasoned that overcrowding leads to homicides; again, the correlation of 0.67 bolsters this conclusion. The direct path between poverty and homicide is an insignificant beta weight of 0.07, because poverty only indirectly affects homicides through the test factor of overcrowding by Stark's logic.

According to the logic of statistical analysis laid out by Rosenberg, Stark's theory is impeccable. Rosenberg (1968:74) states that "if the test factor is intervening, the relationship between the independent and dependent variable should vanish" when controlled on the test factor. Furthermore, the bivariate correlations between the test factor and the independent and dependent variables must conform to the theoretical expectations as they do in Stark's analysis.

Antecedent Variables

The antecedent variable is a test factor that takes a causal chain form

$$T \rightarrow X \rightarrow Y$$

Testing for antecedent variables requires the support of much more empirical evidence than spurious or conditional causal relationships. Rosenberg (1968:74) lists the following requirements:

1. All three bivariate relationships (*XY, XT, and YT*) must show statistical association.
2. After controlling on the antecedent variable (*T*), the independent-dependent relationship should *not* vanish.
3. After controlling on the independent variable (*X*), the antecedent-dependent relationship *should* disappear.

Therefore, the researcher must generate a number of statistical tests to demonstrate antecedent characteristics: three bivariate tables and two three-variable tables with the independent variable controlled. In fact, to examine the logic of his intervening theory of homicides, Stark actually produced all five statistical tests; the only difference was his labeling of the test factor and independent variable. To understand this point, let us presume that Stark had started out by suggesting that overcrowdedness directly causes homicides, and then assumed that poverty causes overcrowding. The proposed causal structure is

$$\text{Poverty} ----\rightarrow \text{Overcrowding} ----\rightarrow \text{Homicide}$$

or,

$$T -------\rightarrow X -------\rightarrow Y.$$

First, he would have listed all three bivariate correlations:

Poverty-overcrowding	$r = 0.66$	(TX association)
Overcrowding-homicide	$r = 0.72$	(XY association)
Poverty-homicide	$r = 0.51$	(TY association)

These three bivariate correlations satisfy the first of Rosenberg's requirements. Second, Stark would have shown that after *controlling for the antecedent variable* (T or Poverty), that the effect of the independent variable (overcrowding) on the dependent variable (homicide) did *not* vanish but was in fact a robust 0.67. This satisfies Rosenberg's second requirement. Third, he would have shown that the effect of the antecedent variable, poverty, when controlled for overcrowding (X), *nearly vanished* to a paltry beta weight of 0.07. This satisfies Rosenberg's third requirement. As one can see, he would have still used all of the same information in a slightly different order. The test variable decision, therefore, is not so much one of statistics as it is basically theoretical, logical, and empirical. The researcher must determine causal order before knowing what kinds of results to expect from statistical tests.

Suppressor Variables

A suppressor variable is a test factor that acts to overpower the "true" strength of some variable relationship. The actual strength of the *XY* relationship becomes apparent only after controlling for the test factor. In contrast to every other type of test factor discussed, controlling for the suppressor variable *increases* the original relationship rather than reducing it to near zero. A positive bivariate relationship after controlling for an appropriate test factor ought to become even stronger (more positive); a negative bivariate relationship even more negative (stronger).

The reason is that the true relationship is "purer" in separating out the effects of other influences. For example, in Stark's (1987) ecological data set for Seattle he found the following two bivariate correlations:

unmarried males per 1,000 population-rapes per 100,000 $r = 0.71$
unmarried females per 1,000 population-rapes per 100,000 $r = -0.04$

These correlations reflect basic information about rapes. Rapes occur in areas close to where unmarried men rather than unmarried women live. More interestingly, however, are the comparable statistics for unmarried males per 1,000 population controlled for unmarried females, and vice versa. After controlling for each variable, the beta weight for unmarried males is an impressive 0.88 and for unmarried women falls to -0.41. In other words, after purifying each variable, one can see that rapes are very strongly associated with areas inhabited by single males, and not with areas where unmarried females live. Without taking out the suppressing effect of each variable, we would not learn a major set of lessons. First, that single women are not likely to be raped in their own neighborhoods. Second, it is when single women risk venturing into territories inhabited by single males that they risk rape. It is much safer for a single woman to live in and frequent areas inhabited primarily by other single women or married couples. Furthermore, single women living or frequenting neighborhoods that are inhabited by a large percentage of single males are at very high risk of being raped.

Distorter Variables

The distorter variable is a test factor that actually reverses the original *XY* relationship. Because the sign of the original relationship changes from positive to negative (or negative to positive), the logic is that the test factor distorted the true relationship until the test factor was "partialled out." (The term "partial out" is often used in place of "control." The two terms refer to the same process of purifying the original relationship.) Again, Stark's Showcase™ (1987) demonstrates a good example of a distorter variable. In Canada, the simple bivariate correlation between the percentage of Roman Catholics and per capital alcohol consumption is -0.25, contrary to the United States where it is positive.

However, after controlling for the effects of the percentage of persons with a religious affiliation (essentially controlling for Catholics who live in predominantly Catholic areas, versus predominantly Protestant areas), the sign of the comparable beta weight between percentages of Roman Catholics and per capita alcohol consumption changes to $+0.33$. This makes more sense on three counts. First, the beta weight in Canada now matches the correlation and beta weight signs for the United States, which indicates that the effects of the independent variable have the same effects in each country. Second, Roman Catholics, unlike those of many Protestant faiths, have never discouraged alcohol consumption. Third, Roman Catholic liturgy encourages the use of alcohol in communion, whereas numerous Protestant churches substitute grape juice for alcohol. Essentially, the original correlation of -0.25 must reflect the subcultures in which Catholics in Canada live. In provinces such as Quebec, which are primarily Catholic, Catholics find it easier to hold to Roman Catholic values. In provinces such as Ontario, which are primarily Protestant, the Protestant environment must mask Catholic values. This is also an example of the kind of distortion or masking problem you can run into if you see aggregate as opposed to individual data. It demonstrates how test-factor analysis aids the researcher in solving the problem of the ecological fallacy.

In comparing types of test factors, Rosenberg (1968:99–100) notes that the consideration of distorter test factors enables the researcher to avoid the danger of accepting as true a false hypothesis—what is termed a *false negative* in Chapter 4—as well as avert rejecting a true hypothesis known as a *false positive*.

The reader can view a summary of important test-factor similarities and differences in Table 17–3.

Conditional relationships

Davis (1970:22) observes that to say "the relationship between X and Y is due to T" is not the same as "the relationship between X and Y depends on the *level* of T." Therefore, when one introduces a test factor, it is possible to find a partial association that is strong at one level of the test factor, weak at another level of T, or even to find reversed associations for different levels—one positive, another negative. *A conditional relationship demonstrates an interaction effect, because the effects at each level are not uniform.* For example, turning back to Figure 16–2 for a moment, the differences between the working class and the middle class are *not* constant. The difference for individuals making less than $10,000 income is 8%, for between $10,000 and $22,499 is only 1%, and for over $22,499 is 13%. If these differences were similar (which they are not), we would say their level of income did not make a difference.

Income maintenance experiments carried out in Denver and Seattle (Tuma, Hannan, & Groeneveld 1979) afford another example of conditional effects. They found that the effects of income-maintenance support on white women's marital dissolution rates were conditional on the level of income maintenance. Women receiving $5,600 in annual support were much more

Table 17-3   *Properties of Test Factors*

	Extraneous Component Intervening	**Antecedent**	**Suppressor**	**Distorter**
1. Original association between independent and dependent variables is	Positive	Positive	Zero	Positive
2. Relationships in contingent associations are	Zero	Positive	Positive	Negative
3. Compared to the original relationship, the relationships in the contingent associations	Vanish (reduce)	Remain unchanged	Emerge	Reverse
4. Test factor related to independent and dependent variables with	Same signs	Same signs	Opposite signs	Opposite signs
5. Independent, test factor, and dependent all related	Yes	Yes	No	Yes
6. Steps involved in procedure	1	2	1	1

Source: Chart 4–1, from *The Logic of Survey Analysis*, by Morris Rosenberg. Copyright © 1968, Basic Books, Inc., Publishers, New York, p. 101.

likely than women receiving $3,800 and $4,800 in annual income support to become separated from, or divorce, their husband.

The condition where an original *XY* relationship with an apparent lack of association is actually due to partial associations—one negative, the other positive—canceling each other out is particularly interesting because it shows the danger of spurious *non*correlations. Lipsitz (1965) found that roughly the same percentages of working- and middle-class men agreed that "any good leader should be strict with people under him in order to gain their respect." But, when he controlled for education, the discrepancy in education and social class indicated that the upwardly mobile (high class with low education) showed less authoritarianism, while the downwardly mobile (low class with high education) showed more authoritarianism.

Such findings challenge us to try to find a single, as opposed to separate, interpretation for the contradiction in findings. Davis (1970:101) warns that conditional specifications are delicate and complex operations, because it is often hard to tell whether differences in the conditions, or levels, of the test factor are minor statistically or worthy of consideration. Nevertheless, because conditional relationships demonstrate the effects of statistical interaction, they tremendously increase the amount of information concerning a causal relationship.

Beyond Three-Variable Relationships

As the reader can well imagine, traditional tabular analysis quickly becomes unmanageable for test factor analysis. Several of the three-variable tables introduced in the last section ended up with such small marginals that some cells had too few cases for statistical significance testing. Tables with four or more variables would simply create even more empty or near-empty cells, even with large samples. Furthermore, three-variable tabular analysis is difficult enough for the expert, much less introducing still more variables.

Because even statisticians have trouble reading multivariate tables, statisticians have spent decades trying to invent the equivalent of a better mousetrap. The result has been mathematically complex methods known as loglinear analysis. Loglinear analysis is well beyond the scope of an introduction to methods text and hand computations. The reader interested in a relatively lucid nonmathematical introduction to this method could profit from reading Gilbert's (1981) introduction for the novice.

By contrast, when the researcher is working with cardinal-based data, regression analysis is easily extended to beyond three-variable relationships. However, *multiple-regression analysis* is based on several assumptions that must be met before the researcher can properly use it.

First, the independent-dependent variable relationship must be related in a *linear* fashion, as seen in the earlier discussion of linear regression lines. Therefore, it is useful to check the scattergrams for violations of this assumption. More objectively, the researcher can check the Pearson's r coefficient against a less restrictive measure of association known as eta. When the two measures are similar, the researcher knows that the relationship approximates a straight line. When the two measures are dissimilar, the researcher needs to consider transforming the independent variable—for example, using the log or square of one variable—and revising the theory, to account for the fact that the dependent variable is a function of the log (square, etc.) of the independent variable.

Second, normally the researcher using multivariate regression analysis is limited to cardinal-based data. However, it is possible to use categorical data in a regression analysis through creation of a "dummy" variable (*Dummy variables* are nominal variables dichotomized into the presence [scored 1] or absence [scored 0] of a certain characteristic for each individual respondent.) For example, religious affiliation may be recoded as separate dummy variables so that "Protestant" is a recode of Protestants to the value "1" and all other religions to "0"; "Catholics" is a recode of Catholics to the value "1" and all other religious affiliations to "0"; etc. A variable with k categories can be recoded into a maximum of $k-1$ dummy variables.

Third, in its simplest form, we assume that there are no interactive effects in regression analysis. In this case, the effects of all independent variables must *add up* (they must be additive) to form a prediction of the dependent variable. However, this is not always the case.

To better understand these situations consider the following two examples. WHO DOES WHAT TO WHOM makes a differences in our evaluations of individuals. Change (in impressions of an actor's activity level [fast-slow] appears to depend primarily on the simple additive effects of three dependent variables: the generic impressions of the actor's overall activeness beforehand, the generic impressions of activeness of a particular behavior, and the general impressions of activeness of the object (Heise 1979)).

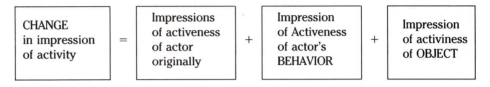

Consider the difference in how active you feel each of the following actors becomes:

The old man kissed the young girl.
The young girl kissed the old man.

The old man in the top sentence is doing a very lively thing to a lively object. We presume this will make him much more lively. The young girl is doing a very lively thing to an unlively object. This should dampen our impression of her liveliness. This demonstrates strictly additive effects.

By contrast, changes in impression of goodness are more complex. They involve three simple additive effects: impressions of the actor's, behavior's, and object's initial goodness. However, they also involve an *interaction effect* between the behavior and object (Heise 1979).

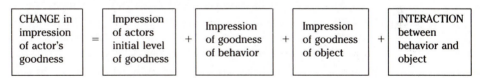

This particular *interaction effect* is predicted by balance theories of attitudes. Consider the following two sentences:

My enemy's enemy is my friend.
My friend's enemy is my enemy.

Now consider how you feel if your enemy burglarizes your friend versus if your friend burglarizes your enemy. Those sentences show that friendship and dislike depend on an interaction between persons and how those persons behave. Although it is possible to enter interaction effects into a multiple regression equation, theory is important because it helps you know what kinds of interaction effects to look for.

Fourth, the correlations between independent variables should not be extremely high. If two independent variables are highly correlated, the high correlation—termed *multicollinearity*—can make the computation of the effects of each independent variable on the dependent variable highly unreliable. Methodologists have a general rule for accepting or rejecting such high correlations: that the correlation should be at least twice as large as the the *standard error* (the standard error being a special type of standard deviation which is defined as the square root of the sum of all the predicted scores from actual dependent variable scores divided by the total sample size) of the correlation before assuming multicollinearity presents no problems. For example, if the correlation was 0.5 the standard error should be no larger than 0.25. Much of the problem with multicollinearity involves unreliability of measures. Multicollinearity problems are in large part assumed to be a function of relative size of the correlation to poor measurement.

Economists have a long tradition of working with highly correlated variables (often above 0.90). Their methods suggest three ways to assess potential problems of multicollinearity. First, look at the standard errors, as suggested above. Low standard errors are a sign that multicollinearity problem are generally low. Second, look at the betas when other variables are added to the equation. If the betas are stable (do not change much), then multicollinearity is probably not a problem. If, on the other hand, betas change, then multicollinearity may present problems. For example, if the beta changes from a plus to a minus sign (or vice versa), multicollinearity may be a problem. This is not a sure sign, however, because a change of sign may also mean that the newly introduced independent variable is an intervening variable. Third, take random subsets of the sample and run the regression equations. If the equations remain essentially the same, then multicollinearity is probably not a problem. When the researcher meets these tests, multiple regression provides a basis for comparing the *relative* contributions of numerous independent variables in predicting the dependent variable.

An extension of multiple regression much used in the social sciences is path analysis. *Path analysis* uses variations on multiple regression to examine theoretical models like the Finke and Stark (1988) model of the religious economy in Figure 1–2 (Chapter 1). The objective is to examine the fit of the model to the data. If the fit is close, the researcher retains the model; if not close, the researcher modifies the model to fit the data better, and then subjects them to further tests on the new data. The most interesting use of path analysis is in the tracing of indirect relationships of the type

$$x \rightarrow y \rightarrow z$$

where x only indirectly influences z through y.

To use path analysis, the researcher must make several assumptions, in addition to those already specified for multiple regression. First, the researcher must have confidence in the causal ordering of the independent and dependent variables; the independent variables must change first and the dependent variable later. Second, the researcher treats the model as a closed system—all relationships in the system should remain unchanged by controlling for any variables omitted. Finally, the influence of one variable on another must be asymmetrical (path analysts use the term *recursive*). In other words, there can be no reciprocal (*nonrecursive*) variable relationships where both variables influence one another causally.

When these assumptions are met, statistical methods for evaluating causal models provide clear decision rules regarding model adequacy. When these assumptions are not met, the researcher risks misusing regression and path analyses. Yet even where the assumptions are met, with large samples, virtually any model may be rejected, even if the degree of causal misspecification is very minor. Therefore, Bentler and Bonett (1980) proposed a psuedo-chi-square test ranging from zero to one, which has been much overlooked by researchers, as a guide in evaluation of various causal models.

When the researcher analyzes simple multicausal relationships, such as the one shown in Chapter 3's Figure 3–2, simple regression analysis suffices.

However, most multicausal relationships are not a simple summation of the effects of numerous independent variables. Researchers more typically grapple with complex multicausal relationships, such as those shown in Chapter 1 (see page 27) and Chapter 3 (see page 86), where the researcher must test for the logic of numerous possible chain reactions. For example, Finke and Stark's (1988) theory of the religious economy (see page 27) posits four direct effects (religious diversity, Sunday schools, percentage Roman Catholic, and population growth) on religious adherence. The remaining three effects are indirect (Religious Diversity, % Roman Catholic, and Population Growth) and operate through the effects of Sunday Schools.

By contrast, although Figure 3–1 (see page 86) has only five variables in the causal paths it visualizes, it includes no simple direct effects of social disintegration and resource deprivation on homicide rates. Instead, social disintegration and resource deprivation are highly correlated; social disintegration has two indirect causal connections to the homicide rate; and resource deprivation has three indirect causal paths.

Dynamic Study Analysis

The methods of analysis presented to this point illustrate means of interpreting cross-sectional data. However, in addition to static cross-sectional analyses, the researcher is often interested in analyzing trends or panels over time.

Trend Study Analysis

In the trend study, the researcher examines a small number of variables over a large number of points in time. The main problem in such studies is to control for all variables extraneous to the variables of interest, because the researcher wishes to study the "pure" effects of the variables of interest, not the confounding effects of extraneous variables. One means of controlling for extraneous variables is to *standardize*. Demographers often standardize marriage rates for any particular year by multiplying the rate in each age category by the number of persons in that category in the standard year and then totaling over all age categories. This method gives a weighted (standardized) marriage rate based on population distributions, which change from year to year. This weighting is important for comparing marriage (and other) rates over time, because relatively younger populations normally have lower marriage rates, and vice versa. In this manner, social scientists study changes over time *as if* the variables of interest were equal to standardized variables at each time period. Notice how the change in marriage rate is less pronounced when standardized on population distribution than when compared as a crude percentage rate.

Year	Crude percentage Married	Percentage married standardized on 1950 Age Distribution
1890	52.1	61.2
1930	58.4	62.1
1950	68.0	68.0

Much of the original trend toward higher marriage rates is seen as largely spurious; that is, attributable to a shifting age distribution.

In addition to standardization, identification of which parts, or properties, of a system are contributing to the trend is important to many trend studies. Similar to component variable analysis, trend studies often map particular wholistic trends and then break these down into their main components for comparative purposes. The unemployment rate provides a classic example. Although labor experts are interested in the gross monthly unemployment rate, usually they also wish to know specific unemployment rates for whites, blacks, hispanics, teenagers, and so on because of the wide variation in unemployment among such groups. The black, hispanic, and teenage rates of unemployment are much larger than the white adult unemployment rate which usually rises much more slowly and falls more quickly.

A good example of the identification of key components in trend analysis comes from the NORC data in SocialTrend™. The original tabulation (not shown) indicates that approval of abortion when there is a chance of birth defects fell from 86% in 1975 to 83% in 1980 to 79% in 1985. This difference is significant at the .05 level. However, Table 17–4 indicates, while it is true that that there is a general trend toward conservatism in attitudes toward this abortion question, that the main drop in approval occurs among older individuals. In fact, only the percentage differences for persons 66 years of age and older are significant at the 0.05 level.

Panel Study Analysis

Panel studies, in contrast to trend studies, usually involve a larger number of variables from a single sample followed over a smaller number of times. In trend analysis, the concern is with what researchers term *net shifts* in totals over time periods. However, it is possible that a trend analysis will show no net shifts, even though individuals may have shifted. For example, in the Social-Trend™ data set, many of the dependent variables show no net effects—Respondents age 31 through 44 provide an example in Table 17–4. The difference

Table 17-4   *Changes in Approval of Abortion If There Is a Chance of Birth Defects in 1975, 1980, and 1985, Controlling for Age of Respondent*

Approval of abortion if there is a chance of birth defect by age	Year		
	1975	*1980*	*1985*
18–30 years of age	89	83	84
31–44 years of age	85	86	85
45–65 years of age	84	85	78
66 years of age or older	86	72	68

Source: SocialScene™ random subset of case drawn from the National Opinion Research Center's 1975, 1980, and 1985 General Social Surveys. The questions asked were: "Please tell me whether or not *you* think it should be possible for a pregnant woman to obtain a *legal* abortion if there is a strong chance of serious defect in the baby?" Age was recoded from date of birth.

Note: The chi-square measures for each subtable of respondent's income were not significant statistically, except for respondents age 66 and older for whom the differences are significant at the level of 0.05.

of 1% between each five-year period may mask individual changes; it is possible that some individuals who approved in 1980 did not in 1985, and a nearly equal number who did not approve at the earlier time period did five years later. However, it is impossible to know, using this table or the data from which it is generated, how many individuals changed attitudes between time periods.

Compare that with panel analysis, where the characteristic we are interested in is termed *turnover*, or shifts over time. Table 17–5 uses retrospective data on the religion in which NORC respondents were raised along with their religious affiliations, at the time of interview to illustrate panel analysis. The method of reading turnover tables in a little different than traditional percentage tables. The first rule is to compare the cells in the diagonal from upper left to lower right, in which there is no turnover to compare the percent of stayers. Protestants appear to have the least turnover with 91% who were "stayers," 85% of Catholics were stayers, 71% of Jewish respondents were stayers, and 40% of those with other religious affiliations were stayers. The second rule is to look down the columns to find out where the "movers" (those who were no longer in the religion of birth) had moved. For example, those who had been raised in nontraditional religions were most likely to have moved. The largest category of movers among those raised in other religions were the 46% of respondents with an "other" religion who moved to Protestant religions; the least number was the 3% of respondents who converted to Judaism.

Actually, Newport (1979) used another, larger, set of NORC data to study not only the mover-stayer patterns shown in Table 17–5, but the mover-stayer patterns among the various Protestant denominations. Protestants, while they appear to be stayers in Table 17–5, actually move more often than Catholics; but they move to other Protestant religions. In fact, Newport demonstrated, using turnover tables, that Protestant movers move "up" to churches of higher socioeconomic status. For example, Methodists who move move to Unitarian-Universalist Churches more so than to Southern Baptist ones. By using a series of further subdivided tables, Newport determined that this trend toward denominations of higher socioeconomic status is associated with Protestants "shopping around" for religions more compatible with their present socioeconomic status. It is those in the more liberal (and higher status) churches, like Unitarian-Universalists, who move up and out of religion.

The major advantage of a panel study is that it provides information on *what* changed, how much, and in what direction. However, panel analysis does have limitations. First, it has "ceiling effects," or limitations, in comparing change over time; for instance, individuals at the top of a scale (high socioeconomic class) have little chance to improve relative to someone at the lower end of the scale. Second, unreliability in the measurement instrument may create pseudochanges rather than real change. In particular, this means the panel researcher should be on the lookout for statistical regression effects (see Chapter 3).

Lazarsfeld (1972:358) argues, in stating a position sympathetic to this view, that theory and research should go hand in hand, that "turnover measures should be related to substantive ideas about the nature of change." He himself followed this rule in the same paper by studying an "oscillation model" in which he assumed that respondents in his study had a basic position, from which they stray occasionally, but to which they are continuously "pulled back again." He then linked this model to observed data over time.

Table 17-5 *A Turnover Table for Religious Affiliation in 1985 by the Religion in which Respondents Were Raised* (Expressed in Percentages)

Religious Affiliation in 1985	Religion in Which Raised			
	Protestant	**Catholic**	**Jewish**	**Other**
Protestant	91	10	12	46
Catholic	3	85	0	11
Jewish	0	0	71	3
Other	5	5	18	40

Source: SocialScene™ random subset of case drawn from the National Opinion Research Center's 1975, 1980, and 1985 General Social Surveys. The questions asked were: "What is your religious preference? Is it Protestant, Catholic, Jewish, some other religion, or no religion?" and "In what religion were you raised—Protestant, Catholic, Jewish, None, or Other?"

Note: The chi-square measures for each subtable of respondent's income could not be computed, because some expected cell frequencies were smaller than 5 cases.

Summary

The next stage in analysis uses the logic of statistical control to test correlations and tabular associations for spuriousness. The researcher accomplishes this task through the introduction of third, test, factors. The idea is that if the original bivariate relationship stays essentially the same after the introduction of the test factor, then it is a robust relationship. However, if the original relationship vanishes, then the researcher may suspect the true relationship is spurious. The relationship may also become stronger or change signs from positive to negative, or vice versa. The new relationship, after controlling for the original relationship, is a "purified" one, in which the effects of the test factor have been eliminated. There are a number of logically possible types of test factors, each of which describes an ideal typical relationship of the test factor to the independent and dependent variables.

As the researcher comes to understand these more complex three-variable relationships, he or she then tries to model still more complex relationships using the same logic. The primary technique used to model more complex causal relationships is called multiple-regression analysis. This technique breaks down the effects of the analysis into the net effects of each independent variable and the total effect of all independent variables. However, regression analysis, and its offspring, path analysis, depend on assumptions that the researcher must be cautious to follow; linear relationships between independent and dependent variables; logical time sequences of variables; and so on.

Each of the above methods is a cross-sectional method of analysis. In addition to these methods, the researcher may study trends over time, by examining a small number of variables over a large number of points in time. Or the relationship may use panel analysis to study the same sample for a large number of points over a smaller sample of times.

In closing, there is a close interplay of theory and research in data analysis. The data suggest, stimulate, and generate theory, but also restrain, control, and discipline theory. The logic and strategies of elaboration and other multivariate analysis cannot lead the researcher far off track in interpretation of data, because such techniques control the assaying of the evidence and, at the same time, are unpredictable enough that they are open to new and serendipitous theory.

APPENDIX

A

Ethical Commitments in Social Research

Knowledge of man is not neutral in its import; it grants power over man as well.[1]

Key Terms

Accountability

Debriefing

Deception

Deductive disclosure

Ethical absolutism

Ethical relativism

Ethics

Fraud

Individual autonomy

Individual risks

Link-file system

Morals

Nuremberg Code

Privacy

Secrecy

Social benefit

[1]Friedrichs, R. *A Sociology of Sociology*, 1970, New York: Free Press, p. 164.

Study Guide Questions

1. Describe the dilemmas that exist between ethics and morals on the one hand, and science on the other.

2. What are the primary social obligations described in major social science codes of ethics?

3. What ethical considerations propelled social scientists to start considering social benefits versus individual cost analysis?

4. Why does Kelman believe harm-benefit analysis is a risky and uncertain business?

5. What are the minimal conditions necessary for informed consent? What are the obstacles to informed consent?

6. What issues of informed consent divide researchers from their research participants?

7. Why is deception usually perceived as a tangible form of invasion of privacy? Do social scientists believe deception is ever acceptable—why or why not?

8. What are the ethical absolutist and relativist positions? What justification is there for either position as the superior one?

9. What are some of the problems associated with the ability to destroy privacy?

10. What social conditions are most susceptible to invasions of privacy? Why?

11. How does a link-file system work to protect privacy?

12. Why is no privacy protection system foolproof from deductive disclosure?

13. Why must social scientists be protected from required disclosure?

14. How do the roles of scientist and citizen conflict for individual scientists?

15. Why is a free marketplace of ideas essential to protection from fraud?

16. How does secrecy chill scientific progress?

17. Should the public be protected against "dangerous" or "threatening" ideas?

In its narrowest sense, ethics refers to the moral principles by which single individuals are guided. But we are most interested in its broader meaning: The rules of conduct recognized in certain associations or departments of human life, because one person's actions often affect others. This idea has a long history in the social sciences: Durkheim (1958) said that professional ethics was the *collective conscience* of the professional group. Collegial obligations of ethics codes serve principally to affirm professional membership and solidarity. Therefore, violators disaffirm the group itself and, minimally, take lower rank within it.

Ethics concerns morals. Following Durkheim, morals have a corporate rather than individual basis. After all, individuals receive their professional status by virtue of group membership. Groups require sharp boundaries to avoid responsibility for the failures of outsiders. Charlatans and quacks provide the rallying point for professional cohesion. If the corporate body does not take moral control of individuals, group members forfeits control over their own status.

Strictly speaking, ethics and morals prescribe an *ought* world, while science describes an *is* world. The world described by science is not always a pleasant one: We may wish the social world was different from the way it actually is. Thus, science and ethics often exist in a delicate state of tension, because what we wish were true and what is true may not necessarily be the same. Some of the ethical dilemmas that occur in the social sciences do so as a result of this naturally built-in tension, rather than to individual character or manners per se.

But there is another side to the problem of ethics in research; if science were just about the description of reality, there would be no dilemma. The dilemma, however, rests in a paraphrase of the quotation at the beginning of this appendix: Knowledge of humankind grants power over humankind. Scientific knowledge is not ultimately divorceable from its use by humankind, because scientists are not interested in simply describing present reality, but wish ultimately to predict future events. Science as a descriptive enterprise implies science as prediction. Prediction may lead to greater control, and control of other humans is not, or should not be, only a scientific decision. Control of other humans also involves moral or ethical decisions: In a world of finite resources, who is allowed the privileges of new vaccines, economic-incentive programs, leadership-training skills, more effective crime prevention, or high-technology job training?

Some social scientists would object that the social and behavioral sciences have thus far been limited to data *about* humans—that they have little concern with the *manipulations* of humans. However, recent events support the contention that social investigations are increasingly concerned with manipulation of humans. Even in research where manipulation of humans is not evident, such talk only disguised ethical problems. As noted by Ernest Nagel (1961: 452)" . . . every branch of inquiry aiming at reliable general laws concerning empirical subject matter must employ a procedure that, if it is not strictly controlled experimentation, has the essential logical functions of experimental inquiry." In other words, just because a researcher has never depended on research through experimentation does not mean that he or she can be absolved of producing knowledge that is without the *logic* of experimentation. Sociologists who depend heavily on survey research (and most still do) increasingly use techniques in their analysis that *approximate* experimental controls. Hence, experimental control is a relative matter.

A general maxim of science is: The more control the scientist has over participants in a study, the more valid are the findings. Paradoxically, the more experimental control there is over participants, the greater the ethical problems created. Social scientists are not free from values; all scientific research has an implicit or explicit commitment toward change. Unless one is willing to take the social scientist as some sort of priestly overlord of the social order, the researcher is forced, whether he/she likes it or not, into value stances.

The code of ethics of the American Sociological Association asserts thirteen social obligations of any sociologist. These obligations can be subsumed under three broad areas of ethical dilemmas that present themselves: (1) the social benefits of research versus risks to individuals; (2) scientist versus citizen roles; and (3) application-of-knowledge. Greater accountability and social utility of the social sciences best proceeds by considering each issue before, during, and after conducting research.

Box A-1 *Code of Ethics of The American Sociological Association*

Preamble

Sociologists recognize that the discovery, creation, transmission, and accumulation of knowledge and the practice of sociology are social processes, involving ethical considerations and behavior at every stage. Careful attention to the ethical dimensions of sociological practice, teaching, and scholarship contributes to the broader project of finding ways to maximize the beneficial effects that sociology may bring to humankind and to minimize the harm that might be a consequence of sociological work. The strength of the Code, its binding force, rests ultimately on the continuing active discussion, reflection, and use by members of the profession.

Sociologists subscribe to the general tenets of science and scholarship. Sociologists are especially sensitive to the potential for harm to individuals, groups, organizations, communities, and societies that may arise out of the incompetent or unscrupulous use of sociological work and knowledge.

Sociology shares with other disciplines the commitment to the free and open access to knowledge and service, and to the public disclosure of findings. Sociologists are committed to the pursuit of accurate and precise knowledge and to self-regulation through peer review and appraisal, without personal and methodological prejudice and without ideological malice. Because sociology necessarily entails study of individuals, groups, organizations, and societies, these principles of access and disclosure may occasionally conflict with more general ethical concerns for the rights of clients and respondents to privacy, and for the treatment of clients and respondents with due regard for their integrity, dignity, and autonomy. This potential conflict provides one of the reasons for a Code of Ethics.

The styles of sociological work are diverse and changing. So, also, are the contexts within which sociologists find employment. These diversities of procedure and context have led to ambiguities concerning appropriate professional behavior. The clarification of ethical behavior in diverse contexts provides a second reason for this Code.

Finally, this Code also attempts to meet the expressed needs of sociologists who have asked for guidance in how best to proceed in a variety of situations involving relations with respondents, students, colleagues, employers, clients, and authorities.

This Code establishes feasible requirements for ethical behavior. These requirements cover many—but not all—of the potential sources of ethical conflict that may arise in research, teaching, and practice. Most represent *prima facie* obligations that may admit of exceptions, but which should generally stand as principles for guiding conduct. The Code states the Association's consensus about ethical behavior, upon which the Committee on Professional Ethics will base its judgments when it must decide whether individual members of the Association have acted unethically in specific instances. More than this, however, the Code is meant to sensitize all sociologists to the ethical issues that may arise in their work, and to encourage sociologists to educate themselves and their colleagues to behave ethically.

To fulfill these purposes, we, the members of the American Sociological Association, affirm and support the following Code of Ethics. Members accept responsibility for cooperating with the duly constituted committees of the American Sociological Association by responding to inquiries promptly and completely. Persons who bring complaints in good faith under this Code should not be penalized by members of the Association for exercising this right.

I. The Practice of Sociology

A. *Objectivity and Integrity*

Sociologists should strive to maintain objectivity and integrity in the conduct of sociological research and practice.

1. Sociologists should adhere to the highest possible technical standards in their research, teaching, and practice.

2. Since individual sociologists vary in their research modes, skills, and experience, sociologists should always set forth *ex ante* the limits of their knowledge, and the disciplinary and personal limitations that condition the validity of findings, which affect whether or not a research project can be successfully completed.

3. In practice or other situations in which sociologists are requested to render a professional judgment, they should accurately and fairly represent their areas and degrees of expertise.

4. In presenting their work, sociologists are obligated to report their findings fully, and should represent the findings fully and without omission of significant data. To the best of their ability, sociologists should also disclose details of their theories, methods, and research designs that might bear upon interpretations of research findings.

5. Sociologists must report fully all sources of financial support in their publications and must note any special relations to any sponsor.

6. Sociologists should not make any guarantees to respondents, individuals, groups or organizations—unless there is full intention and ability to honor such commitments. All such guarantees, once made, must be honored.

7. Consistent with the spirit of full disclosure of methods and analysis, sociologists, after they have completed their own analyses, should cooperate in efforts to make raw data and pertinent documentation collected and prepared at public expense available to other social scientists, at reasonable costs, except in cases where confidentiality, the client's rights to proprietary information and privacy, or the claims of a fieldworker to the privacy of personal notes necessarily would be violated. The timeliness of this cooperation is especially critical.

8. Sociologists should provide adequate information and citations concerning scales and other measures used in their research.

9. Sociologists must not accept grants, contracts, or research assignments that appear likely to require violation of the principles enunciated in this Code, and should dissociate themselves from research when they discover a violation and are unable to achieve its correction.

10. When financial support for a project has been accepted, sociologists must make every reasonable effort to complete the proposed work on schedule, including reports to the funding source.

11. When several sociologists, including students, are involved in joint projects, there should be mutually accepted explicit agreements at the outset with respect to division of work, compensation, access to data, rights of authorship, and other rights and responsibilities. Such agreements may need to be modified as the project evolves, and such modifications must be agreed upon jointly.

12. Sociologists should take particular care to state all significant qualifications on the findings and interpretations of their research.

13. Sociologists have the obligation to disseminate research findings, except those likely to cause harm to clients, collaborators, and participants, or those which are proprietary under a formal or informal agreement.

14. In their roles as practitioners, researchers, teachers, and administrators, sociologists have an important social responsibility because their recommendations, decisions, and actions may alter the lives of others. They should be aware of the situations and pressures that might lead to the misuse of their influence and authority. In these various roles, sociologists should also recognize that professional problems and conflicts may interfere with professional effectiveness. Sociologists should take steps to insure that these conflicts do not produce deleterious results for clients, research participants, colleagues, students, and employees.

B. *Disclosure and Respect for the Rights of Research Populations*

Disparities in wealth, power, and social status between the sociologists and respondents and clients may reflect and create problems of equity in research collaboration. Conflict of interest for the sociologist may occur in research and practice. Also, to follow the precepts of the scientific method—such as those requiring full disclosure—may entail adverse consequences or personal risks for individuals and groups. Finally, irresponsible actions by a single researcher or research team can eliminate or reduce future access to a category of respondents by the entire profession and its allied fields.

1. Sociologists should not misuse their positions as professional social scientists for fraudulent purposes or as a pretext for gathering intelligence for any organization or government. Sociologists should not mislead respondents involved in a research project as to the purpose for which that research is being conducted.

2. Subjects of research are entitled to rights of biographical anonymity.

3. Information about subjects obtained from records that are opened to public scrutiny cannot be protected by guarantees of privacy or confidentiality.

4. The process of conducting sociological research must not expose respondents to substantial risk of personal harm. Informed consent must be obtained when the risks of research are greater than the risks of everyday life. Where modest risk or harm is anticipated, informed consent must be obtained.

5. Sociologists should take culturally appropriate steps to secure informed consent and to avoid invasions of privacy. Special actions may be necessary where the individuals studied are illiterate, have very low social status, or are unfamiliar with social research.

6. To the extent possible in a given study, sociologists should anticipate potential threats to confidentiality. Such means as the removal of identifiers, the use of randomized responses, and other statistical solutions to problems of privacy should be used where appropriate.

7. Confidential information provided by research participants must be treated as such by sociologists, even when this information enjoys no legal protection or privilege and legal force is applied. The obligation to respect confidentiality also applies to members of research organizations (interviewers, coders, clerical staff, etc.) who have access to the information. It is the responsibility of administrators and chief investigators to instruct staff members on this point, and to make every effort to insure that access to confidential information is restricted.

8. While generally adhering to the norm of acknowledging the contributions of all collaborators, sociologists should be sensitive to harm that may arise from disclosure and respect a collaborator's wish or need for anonymity. Full disclosure may be made later if circumstances permit.

9. Study design and information-gathering techniques should conform to regulations protecting the rights of human subjects, irrespective of source of funding, as outlined by the American Association of University Professors (AAUP) in "Regulations Governing Research on Human Subjects: Academic Freedom and the Institutional Review Board," *Academe*, December 1981: 358–370.

10. Sociologists should comply with appropriate federal and institutional requirements pertaining to the conduct of research. These requirements might include, but are not necessarily limited to, failure to obtain proper

review and approval for research that involves human subjects, and failure to follow recommendations made by responsible committees concerning research subjects, materials, and procedures.

II. Publication and Review Process

A. Questions of Authorship and Acknowledgment

1. Sociologists must acknowledge all persons who contribute to their research and to their copyrighted publications. Claims and ordering of authorship and acknowledgments must accurately reflect the contributions of all main participants in the research and writing process, including students, except in those cases where such ordering or acknowledgment is determined by an official protocol.

2. Data and material taken verbatim from another person's published or unpublished written work must be explicitly identified and referenced to its author. Citations to ideas developed in the written work of others, even if not quoted verbatim, should not be knowingly omitted.

B. Authors, Editors and Referees Have Interdependent Professional Responsibilities in the Publication Process

1. Editors should continually review the fair application of standards without personal or ideological malice.

2. Journal editors must provide prompt decisions to authors of submitted manuscripts. They must monitor the work of associate editors and other referees so that delays are few and reviews are conscientious.

3. An editor's commitment to publish an essay must be binding on the journal. Once accepted for publication, a manuscript should be published expeditiously.

4. Editors receiving reviews of manuscripts from persons who have previously reviewed those manuscripts for another journal should ordinarily seek additional reviews.

5. Submission of a manuscript to a professional journal clearly grants that journal first claim to publish. Except where journal policies explicitly allow multiple submissions, a paper submitted to one English language journal may not be submitted to another journal published in English until after an official decision has been received for the first journal. Of course, the article can be withdrawn from all consideration to publish at any time.

C. Participation in Review Process

Sociologists are frequently asked to provide evaluations of manuscripts, research proposals, or other work of professional colleagues. In such work, sociologists should hold themselves to high standards of performance in several specific ways:

1. Sociologists should decline requests for reviews of work of others where strong conflicts of interest are involved, such as may occur when a person is asked to review work by teachers, friends, or colleagues for whom he or she feels an overriding sense of personal obligation, competition, or enmity, or when such requests cannot be fulfilled on time.

2. Materials sent for review should be read in their entirety and considered carefully and confidentially. Evaluations should be justified with explicit reasons.

3. Sociologists who are asked to review manuscripts and books they have previously reviewed should make this fact known to the editor requesting review.

III. Teaching and Supervision

The routine conduct of faculty responsibilities is treated at length in the faculty codes and AAUP rules accepted as governing procedures by the various institutions of higher learning. Sociologists in teaching roles should be familiar with the content of the codes in force at their institutions and should perform their responsibilities within such guidelines. Sociologists who supervise teaching assistants should take steps to insure that they adhere to these principles.

A. *Sociologists are obligated to protect the rights of students to fair treatment*

1. Sociology departments should ensure that instructors are qualified to teach the courses to which they are assigned. Instructors so assigned should conscientiously perform their teaching responsibilities.

2. Sociologists should provide students with a fair and honest statement of the scope and perspective of their courses, clear expectations for student performance, and fair, timely, and easily accessible evaluations of their work.

3. Departments of Sociology must provide graduate students with explicit policies and criteria about conditions for admission into the graduate program, financial assistance, employment, funding, evaluation, and possible dismissal.

4. Sociology departments should help students in their efforts to locate professional employment in academic and practice settings.

5. Sociology departments should work to insure the equal and fair treatment of all students, by adhering both in spirit and content to established affirmative action guidelines, laws, and policies.

6. Sociologists must refrain from disclosure of personal information concerning students, where such information is not directly relevant to issues of professional competence.

7. Sociologists should make all decisions concerning textbooks, course content, course requirements, and grading solely on the basis of professional criteria without regard for financial or other incentives.

B. *Sociologists must refrain from exploiting students*

1. Sociologists must not coerce or deceive students into serving as research subjects.

2. Sociologists must not represent the work of students as their own.

3. Sociologists have an explicit responsibility to acknowledge the contributions of students, and to act on their behalf in setting forth agreements regarding authorship and other recognition.

> *C. Sociologists must not coerce personal or sexual favors or economic or professional advantages from any person, including respondents, clients, patients, students, research assistants, clerical staff, or colleagues.*
>
> *D. Sociologists must not permit personal animosities or intellectual differences vis-à-vis colleagues to foreclose student access to those colleagues.*

Source: Code of Ethics of the American Sociological Association, Washington, D.C. (Effective August 14, 1989)

Social-Benefits Versus Individual-Risks Dilemma

While social scientists are far from complete consensus on a universal set of ethical rules for research involving human participants, they are in general agreement that researchers must be prepared to think in terms of the costs and benefits of the research: *Are the scientific objectives of the study proportionate to the risks to the study participants* (World Medical Association 1964; U.S. Department of Health, Education and Welfare 1971)? The necessity for cost-benefit thinking is clearest in a worst case scenario, such as a study of the effects of syphilis by the U.S. Public Health Service in 1932. Several hundred Tuskegee, Alabama, black men known to have syphilis were medically examined at regular intervals by Public Health officials. From the moment the study began, government officials apparently withheld treatment of the disease for the purpose of determining what effects syphilis has on the body. Worse yet, when the study finally came to public attention some four decades later, some of the study survivors charged that they had never even been informed that they suffered from the ravages of syphilis. Most ethics experts have concluded that the costs of untreated syphilis were unacceptable when compared to the Tuskegee study's professed objectives. Indeed, the National Medical Association went so far as to charge the study officials with genocide of poor and uneducated blacks, many of whom died slowly and painfully, or who were severely incapacitated as a result of their syphilis. Although the Tuskegee study is far from typical of sociobehavioral research, it raised the need for procedural safeguards in regulating social and behavioral research.

After the outrage against such unethical studies died down, more reasoned voices have prevailed with questions intended to prevent future problems: Whose interests should count for what in the calculations in such risk-benefit assessments? Risk-benefit assessment is not a value-neutral exercise. Researchers' ideas of risks and benefits quite often differ radically from those of the larger community. Consequently, most universities and research centers invite philosophers, priests, rabbis, social workers, lawyers, and others to sit on standing committees known as institutional review boards (IRBs) that review the individual risks and social benefits of all research proposals.

Harm-benefit analysis is itself a risky and uncertain business. General public service obligations implicit in the social benefits of research are extremely important as claims but extremely vague in practice. Kelman (1982) believes that such analysis will always be of limited aid, because the harm and benefits accruing in the long run to the larger society cannot be accurately measured. Proposals to IRBs often contain such statements as "there is no evidence that enduring damage has actually resulted in this type of experiment," and "the experimental manipulations may affect such significant life resources as income, housing, or conditions of parole." Such phrases as "is no evidence" and "may affect" are neither tangible nor particularly enlightening. Kelman has aided researchers by developing a relatively exhaustive taxonomy of potential harms that should be considered by researchers before they commence their research: (1) direct injury, stress, and indignity; (2) privacy and confidentiality in terms of public exposure, reduced control over private space; (3) impaired capacity to make decisions because of deception and lack of informed consent, deprivation of respect, and erosion of trust; and (4) social control in terms of governmental regulation.

The main issue is: Who is concerned with the participant's welfare and the larger societal fabric? Whose side are we on? In the Tuskegee syphilis study, the potential scientific benefits were not just clearly outweighed by the risks to participants; all participants' health statuses and lives were endangered by the study design, and a clear erosion of trust in governmental and medical authorities ensued. Most social scientists would say that, beyond consideration of study-participant costs and benefits, special safeguards are needed; minimally those include informed consent, protection from deception except in extremely narrow circumstances, and safeguards of privacy.

Informed Consent

Faden and Beauchamp (1986: 54) give a particularly clear definition of informed consent as "encompass(ing) all discussions and arrangements between professional and patient or subject: (1) a patient or subject must *agree* to an intervention based on an *understanding* of (usually disclosed) relevant *information*, (2) consent must not be controlled by influences that would engineer the outcome, and (3) the consent just involves the intentional giving of *permission* for an intervention." Our modern conception of informed consent is alien to origins of human experimentation in ancient Greece. The Hippocratic Oath, which was the first Western source on medical professional conduct, bluntly advises physicians of the wisdom of "concealing most things from the patient." Faden and Beauchamp (p. 74) conclude that informed consent "as a practice of *respecting autonomy* has *never* had a sure foothold in medical practice." It came into use during the last 150 years, more as a practical expedient by professions concerned with the politics of regulation, the competition presented by quacks and sects, and public image over professional standards of care.

Informed consent would clearly have prevented some of the abuses of the

Tuskegee syphilis study. In the eyes of many persons, it is the most important means of research regulation. This doctrine first developed out of two principles in law: the duty of disclosure in a fiduciary relationship (that is, attorney or other professional and client), and the right of a person of sound mind to decide what will happen to his or her body. Its application to experimentation was defined in the post-World War II Nazi Germany "crimes against humanity" trials that resulted in the famous Nuremburg Code of 1947.

> The voluntary consent of the human subject is absolutely essential. This means that the person involved should have legal capacity to give consent, should be so situated as to be able to exercise free power of choice without the intervention of any element of force, fraud, deceit, duress, overreaching, or other ulterior form of constraint or coercion; and should have sufficient knowledge and comprehension of the elements of the subject matter involved as to enable him to make an understanding and enlightened decision. This latter element requires that before the acceptance of an affirmative decision by the experimental subject there should be made known to him the nature, duration, and purpose of the experiment; the method and means by which it is to be conducted; all inconveniences and hazards reasonably to be expected; and the effects upon his health or person which may possibly come from his participation in the experiment.

The Nuremberg Code presents an absolute ethical position on such things as informed consent. However, social life presents numerous obstacles to ethical absolutism. Consent and refusals are actions that nonautonomous persons— for example, a newborn child or illiterate immigrant—do not possess. Some social positions give more or less power and authority, which influences the degree of autonomy one may have.

Perhaps the most potent obstacle to informed consent comes from professionals of extremely high status. For example, Barber (1980) notes that American physicians see themselves, and are seen by others, as the supreme arbiters on matters of health. The exalted status of physicians results in compliant and dependent research subjects. The power and authority of medical officials, as represented in the Tuskegee syphilis study, can too easily override consent; informed consent requires individuals to make competent, reflective decisions. Choice by patients or research subjects implies not only information on risks, benefits, and alternatives but de facto encouragement to think for oneself. If at the crucial point of decision, the individual simply caves in to higher authority, all the signed consent forms collected in the name of the U.S. Department of Health, Education, and Welfare will not add up to free choice.

The power imbalance between researcher and study participants become grave when the participants are extremely poor, illiterate, or totally unaccustomed to challenging authority. Again, the Tuskegee syphilis study provides a classic illustration. Even if the investigators followed current informed consent guidelines, serious questions abound: Would the participants have understood the medical risks at stake? Would they have caved into the pressures of professional authority? Barber (1980) persuasively argues that not all individuals or groups require the same degree of protection. He points out that the poorly educated, and economic and racial minorities are most vulnerable to exploitation; they need more elaborate warnings and explanations than more educated, wealthier persons. Many researchers would include children, prisoners, Third World nationals, immigrants, and the mentally infirm as needing stronger than average safeguards from potential exploitation.

Consent should be obtained, whenever practicable, from the participants themselves. But when the subject group will include individuals who are not legally or physically capable of giving informed consent, because of age, mental incapacity, or inability to communicate, the researcher should consider the legality of consent by next of kin, legal guardians, or by other qualified third parties representing the participants' interests. In such instances, careful consideration should be given not only to whether these third parties can be presumed to have the necessary depth of interest and concern with the participants' rights and welfare, but also to whether these third parties will be legally authorized to expose the participants to the risks involved.

Informed consent is the major issue for research participant advocates because researchers must juxtapose protection of participants against (1) serving their profession by obtaining the best possible information, (2) serving science by increasing knowledge, and (3) possibly serving future generations by taking part in evolving "better" social policies. Therefore, the researcher is far from impartial and—many people argue—should be monitored by independent groups. Barber (1980: 28) asserts that "For the longest part of their history, professional codes have been paternalistically nonegalitarian:" From the Hippocratic Oath until the 1960s, the guiding assumption of medical ethics was that doctors alone should decide what is best for their patients, but do so responsibly.

By extension, in this world view, informed consent for research participants is superfluous. Even today, in spite of the burgeoning wake of malpractice lawsuits, there is no solid and independent basis for the principle of informed consent. Most professionals prop up such paternalistic views with their individualistic values. Researchers often profess that they alone should be responsible for dealing with subjects, and stoutly resist formal controls from the outside; nor are they keen on regulation from within their professions. Although institutional review boards have had some success as guardians of informed consent—perhaps because they are not dominated by any single groups—state licensing boards and professional associations have provided much weaker support.

The success or failure of informed consent regulation hinges on its social context. For some of the American scientific community, it has come to symbolize another obstacle the beleaguered scholar must pass before obtaining research clearance; procedures hindering the analysis of more important issues; a commodity that the researcher "gets" from the participant, rather than a condition that the participant attains through the researcher. But "informed consent" is much richer in meaning. It raises timeless questions of freedom and determinism, liberty, and equality. Who should know what? Are humans able to choose at all? If so, when is choice really voluntary? Are some people such as the educated and affluent more free to choose than others? How does power, authority, and influence interplay with choice?

The discussion of informed consent, so far, has emphasized the participant's position. From the researcher's viewpoint, an important question is: Does informed consent or choice affect the quality of research data? Studies of variations in informed consent procedures indicate that researchers may have unnecessary worries concerning deleterious effects of informed consent. Singer and Frankel (1982) varied both information about the content of an interview, and information about its purpose in an experimental study of informed consent in interviews. They found that neither factor significantly affected either the overall rate or response rates to individual items, nor quality of responses.

Social experimentation, by contrast, has many known problems with informed consent. A Brookings Institute (Rivlin & Timpane 1975: 78) conference on social experimentation went out of their way to suggest that "there should be no ethical responsibility to inform subjects in analytical detail about the intent of the research." The conferees generally argued that research procedures and purposes should be disclosed only insofar as the information is material to the participant's understanding of whether and how he or she is at risk, and therefore to his or her decision process on whether to participate in an experiment. The conferees agreed that to disclose the purpose of the research may jeopardize the scientific validity of the results (p. 78): "This is certainly true in social research, because it is concerned with the behavior of subjects. . . .This behavior may be influenced not only by the pure treatment, but by . . . the subject's perception of the experimenter's expectations."

Two realistic examples may clarify their position. First, consider a child who is the subject of unobtrusive research on educational performance. If the child is told that he or she will be watched through a one-way mirror, his or her behavior may not be spontaneous. Second, the major purpose of an income maintenance experiment is to observe whether participants quit work after receiving an experimental cash benefit. If the participants are aware of this purpose, conferees feared the participants' propensities to work might be affected by the awareness, rather than the cash benefit.

The reasonableness of this type of argument has led to government recognition that informed consent may sometimes impose unreasonably burdensome requirements on investigators or subjects in some kinds of research. Consider observational studies of controversial, illegal, or dangerous activities such as the one by Adler (1985) conducted to understand drug dealing on the West Coast. The very existence of signed consent forms in such situations would be more dangerous to the study participants and researchers than anything we can imagine the researchers doing. Likewise, the 1990s are likely to produce much social, political, and psychological research on Acquired Immuno Deficiency Syndrome. AIDS may well be the most politicized of diseases in the way it has been perceived and financed. It was identified in the U.S.A. at a time of heightened political conservatism, moral traditionalism, and fiscal constraints. It is easy to imagine how established informed consent is complicated by this highly socially stigmatizing disease. Social researchers studying AIDS (Feldman & Johnson 1986) have expressed fears over protecting AIDS victims from unintentional stigmatization and reaffirmation of the outcast status of some populations as at-risk groups, especially homosexual men. The problem stems from public misperception of AIDS as uniquely linked to homosexuality and drug abuse. Because of the highly charged atmosphere surrounding AIDS, researchers must grapple with thorny issues for which we do not have easy answers: Is an AIDS patient who is desperate for treatment at almost any cost able to give true informed consent? Would informed consent in such cases further stigmatize the victim? Should the researcher tell patients they have AIDS when the research is not about AIDS, but some other issues?

Finally, in some cases, a good argument can be made that requiring documentation of informed consent is clearly inappropriate. An anthropology department chairman wrote an amusing letter to an HEW official (see Tropp 1982: 407–408) summarizing this position:

> Signed consent forms are meaningful only to Americans (and in fact, not all of them). Elsewhere, people who are illiterate, people who are only required to sign forms when the government is getting ready to exploit them, and people who have no concept of Western law and judicially protected rights find consent form totally meaningless . . . (Therefore) signed consent forms in nonliterate or semiliterate societies are analogous to the proclamations read by Columbus to New World natives, converting them to subjects of Spain, subject to its laws. No one listening knew who Spain was, what a king was, or what the laws were that were involved.

Additionally, researchers (Lueptow 1976; Turner & Martin 1984) have documented that requiring disclosure of all research procedures and purposes inevitably skews survey and interview data, including drops in survey response rates, drops in timeliness of response, significantly increasing cost per completed interview, and diminished representativeness of samples and reliability of data.

Deception

Deception implies willful lack of choice or a purposeful impairment of a person's capacity to make decisions. As such, it raises serious questions concerning the proper justification of moral conclusions. As with informed consent, the issue of deception is usually discussed in terms of individual autonomy. This issue was first formulated by the great moral philosopher Kant, who believed any set of basic morals required that people be treated as ends in themselves, and never solely as a means to the ends of others.

Deception is usually perceived as a tangible form of invasion of privacy. Some ethical absolutists dogmatically condemn the use of deception; they sometimes argue that it is suitable only for a society of equals. Wax (1982: 55) counters that we live in a society of gross inequality, in which the lives of the poor are far more open to social researchers than are the lives of the more affluent and powerful. Like Galliher, he takes a more relativist position; he observes that without the use of deception, we would not have the classic works on white racism in the American south, as well as increasing public accountability. It is naive to treat research participants as if they are isolated individuals. Individuals occupy positions in the larger social stratification system that affect their personal freedom. Therefore, Wax concludes that allowing for deception in research on the powerful is important to such equal-rights movements as affirmative action in employment and progressive income tax laws.

Some researchers believe that the moral wrong entailed by deception can never be justified by appeals to the beneficial consequences of research; others believe that the potential harm and justification of deceptive practices is the issue. Humphreys' (1970) study of homosexual practices in public bathrooms provides a classic case study of particular projects that have generated moral controversy in the debate for and against deception. Humphreys found it necessary to conceal his identity as a social researcher by playing the established role of "watchqueen." This role requires someone to look out for intruders while men are engaged in acts of fellatio. He also surreptitiously recorded the license plate numbers of the persons he observed, used that information to obtain their place of residence through police registers and phone company records, and a year later (after changing his hair style and attire) interviewed these men as part of an ostensibly anonymous public health survey. Humphreys defended his methods by appealing to the beneficial consequences of his results: After all, he convincingly characterized the men as neither deviant (most were married with children) nor potentially dangerous to their communities (they engaged in homosexual behavior only with other consenting adults like themselves).

Warwick (1980) provides one of the best arguments for not using such types of deceptive practices. At the societal level, Warwick notes that such deceptive methods undermine the fundamental institution of trust necessary for society to function, through an increasingly cavalier attitude toward invasion of citizen privacy. But at the personal level of research participants, critics have also claimed that Humphreys' methods of identifying his subjects, regardless of the pains to which he went to protect his information, exposed them to serious risks of economic harm, damage to reputation, and legal jeopardy.

Field researchers who claimed the need to use deception, rather than claim a "cavalier attitude" toward their position, usually report a heavy burden of guilt and ethical turmoil over their actions. Adler (1985: 25–27) writes sensitively about these types of problems. She mentions ethical dilemmas at all stages of her study of a drug dealing and smuggling community on the West Coast. Drug-dealer informants confided things that "she had to pretend not to know when interacting with their close associates. This sometimes meant that [my husband and I] had to lie or build elaborate stories for some people (p. 25)." These lies spilled over into the final stage of writing, where she had to face the problem of using details that would support the integrity of her study, but which might blow particular informants' covers. The use of covert participant-observer roles made her fear her informants would, once her research was published, feel she had been simply exploiting their friendships. She ended up feeling like she had been "whoring for data."

Much of her ethical dilemma resulted from the nature of the organization she was studying: Drug dealing is structured around "secrecy, danger, hidden alliances, misrepresentations, and unpredictable changes of intent . . ." (p. 27). She is probably right in concluding that it is impossible, much less dangerous, to study criminals or deviants in their natural habitat without protecting one's own identity and commitment to the scientific community. But the psychological costs of feeling trapped between the norms of openness of the scientific and normal lay communities and deception necessary in a deviant community to minimize the risk of public exposure does take its toll eventually. The researcher typically starts to feel the consequences of the mistrust and disrespect inherent in his or her covert role.

Some writers have argued that researchers should feel no qualms about deceiving such groups as the Ku Klux Klan or the American Nazi Party (Galliher 1973), on the grounds that such groups are essentially dishonorable, morally outrageous, and destructive enterprises. But Macklin (1982: 206) points out that such arguments beg the question: "What is not morally perturbing to this writer may seem morally outrageous to another . . ." In other words, *who* is doing the judging, and what right does one have to presume one's judgments are more moral or just than others? Nothing in the professional training of social scientists makes them special experts in such matters. Nor is it certain that deception will yield significant social data—the justification normally given for using deception.

Social and psychological experimentalists also have a long history of justifying deception, on the grounds that the experimental conditions ought to be as lifelike as possible, and the participant's mind should be diverted from the true purpose of the experiment. Although little direct harm has ever come to participants in academic social experimentation involving deception, experimenters normally employ at least two guidelines when deception is used: (1) an explicit option to withdraw at any time during an experiment as a sort of "ongoing informed consent" procedure; and (2) a debriefing period immediately following the experiment, where participants are given a sense of the value of their participation, the researcher can restore a climate of honesty, and unpleasant emotional experiences can be discussed and diffused. Indeed, such debriefings can be viewed as refreshing signs of the experimentalist's ethical standards, when compared to the vast amount of deception that takes place in everyday life.

To deceive or not to deceive may not be the real issue. Elms (1982) gives one of the most literate middle-ground positions for arguing the need to look at the consequences of deception, rather than simply take an all-or-nothing ethical absolutist or relativist stance; the absolutist position closes off argumentation, while the relativist position can degenerate into a Nazi eugenicist mentality. But Elms (p. 244) argues that the dialogue between the two sides is a useful one, because it has led to a debate "*out in the open*, where [deception's] practitioners are continually forced to present their justifications to others and where their critics must resort to reason rather than coercion."

Privacy

According to Barrington Moore (1966:123):

> Now, in an ideal society there is by definition no need for a private sphere to which the individual can retreat. If social institutions work perfectly, and there is in place an educational system that grinds out new personalities suited to the perfect social order, why should there be any need for privacy? *Instead, privacy begins to look like a cover for evasion of ethical and social obligations.* (This is the usual attitude even now among revolutionary perfectionists and many enthusiastic reformers.) (italics added)

Of course, the world we live in is not an ideal society with institutions that work perfectly, such as that described by Moore, but more like that described by Goffman (1974:178) in his description of total institutions (prisons, hospitals, religious orders):

> Beginning with admission, a kind of contaminative exposure occurs. On the outside, the individual can hold objects of self- feeling—such as his body, his immediate actions, his thoughts, and some of his possessions—clear of contact with alien and contaminating things. But in total institutions, these territories of the self are violated; the boundary that the individual places between his being and the environment is invaded, and the embodiments of self profaned.

The ability to destroy our privacy can destroy our notions of personhood, personal identity, and selfhood. For this reason, all societies make provisions for some protection of individual privacy. By the right to privacy, we usually mean the right to control what is known by others about oneself and control over some spheres of one's personal life. Privacy is often an umbrella term for such notions as liberty, freedom, ownership, autonomy, and justice.

Those individuals with less power usually end up with less protection of their rights to privacy. We live in a world in which, in the past, social scientists were in a position of power vis-à-vis the weak subjects of their research—in sociology, the poor; in anthropology, the natives; in psychology, the individual students. But the balance of power has changed and the social investigator—whether census taker, survey researcher, experimentalist, or participant-observer—has to take into account not only the subject's reaction but that of other parties. Social inquiry is a process of negotiation among scientists, sponsors, gatekeepers, and citizens, parties who have differential power, and different perceptions of the objectives and likely outcomes of inquiry.

Before World War II, when scientists and citizens were socially and analytically unequal, social scientists modeled themselves after natural scientists. New knowledge was viewed as a source of enlightenment for the elite. However, since World War II, the powers and knowledge of citizens, research sponsors, and gatekeepers have become more democratized. Citizens have increasingly come to perceive knowledge as a kind of private property (Bulmer 1980). The result is that the social scientist can be caught in a pincer between genuine public concern to perserve individual privacy and autonomy on the one hand, and self-interested restrictions on the other. The right to privacy involves balancing the scientist's need to know, against the citizen's interest in protecting individual privacy.

It also involves consideration of particular social conditions. Galliher (1973) believes that no right to privacy should be applied to research on persons involved in roles accountable to the public. He makes a cogent argument for protection of private roles (father, lover), but not publicly accountable roles (business executive, governmental head), on the grounds that a democratic society has a moral duty to hold individuals accountable in their organizational and occupational roles. Hence, he feels subterfuge may be an acceptable and ethical researcher tactic, in studies of public roles where the individual(s) studied would not knowingly permit the data to be collected. The dilemma is to protect the private component of public roles.

The flow of information in modern information-based societies also grossly affects privacy. Meyrowitz (1985) showed how electronic media have fostered a blurring of many formerly distinct social roles, and the distinction between private selves and public roles. The information revolution, of which new electronic media are one manifestation, radically muddles the litmus test for what information is a private matter versus public concern. Advances in the use of information technology by researchers, therefore, raise new ethical questions. Consider such seemingly innocuous recently introduced technology as check-approval machines, electronic bar-coded foods, and bar-code reading cash registers. While they certainly rationalize the process of shopping, they make for much easier breach of privacy. Marketing researchers can easily misuse social research techniques to match up the electronic information provided by each of those technologies to trace down individuals, note what they spend their money on, how much money they spend, etc.

In fact, marketing firms are using such methods to target individuals for specifically marketed "junk mail" and phone or home sales solicitations. Similarly, utility companies are switching over to pocket-size, computerized meter reading devices that record the exact times of meter readings, etc. Such devices make organizational efficiency studies more reliable and accurate, but meter readers have complained that they introduce "Big Brother" into their pockets, because these devices can be used to show exactly how long any specific meter reader has worked, the number of meters read in a specified time period, and whether or not the worker was "gold bricking." The Congressional Office of Technological Assessment (1987) reports an Orwellian increase in "electronic sweatshop" practices in which the American clerical work force—predominantly composed of female and minority workers—must do boring, repetitive, fast-paced work that requires constant alertness and attention to detail, where the supervisor isn't even human, but an unwinking computer taskmaster.

Clearly, those who know how to obtain and use information in a society based on electronic media of any form have a powerfully new advantage; those who do not understand this information revolution are put to a disadvantage. Pushed to its logical extreme, an individual's sense of private space is significantly narrowed. Individuals have less ability to participate in decisions that grossly affect them personally: they can be pushed to be "better consumers," "more efficient workers," or whatever, without participating in the unfolding of their own futures.

The flip side of this ethical debate is that social researchers can contribute to equalization of information by studying the new information brokers and aiding public accountability through advocacy. But advocacy itself raises ethical issues. Since the early 1950s, anthropologists have acted as advocates on behalf of indigenous peoples. Other social scientists could profit from the scientific and professional difficulties that have resulted. When a researcher sheds the role of "objective observer," ethical issues crop up: (1) To whom does the researcher owe social responsibility? (2) Is advocacy simply a form of paternalism that will hinder the quest for self-empowerment? (3) What affects does advocacy have on research quality? and (4) Will professional difficulties result from advocacy? These are difficult questions that cannot be answered here. But it is important to recognize that a rich literature exists (Rubinstein 1987) that can serve as a resource to help those newly encountering the problems raised.

One way in which the researcher offers protection to study participants is to extend confidentiality. What affect does confidentiality of information have on the quality of social data? The Panel on Privacy and Confidentiality as Factors in Survey Response of the National Academy of Sciences (1979) studied differences in interviewer refusal rates for the U.S. Bureau of the Census and the University of Michigan's Survey Research Center (SRC). One of the few differences between the two organizations was an SRC refusal rate twice that of the U.S. Census Bureau. The only substantive difference contributing to this result was identification of the survey organization. Apparently, many more people believed the U.S. Census Bureau offers better protection of their privacy. Still, only 5% of the respondents believed that the Census Bureau would be able to protect the confidentiality of individually identifiable records against other agencies, if those agencies "really tried" to get access, and 18% believed these records were open to public examination, although in reality neither of these beliefs are substantiated. The U.S. Bureau of the Census has had a consistent record of successfully fighting such agencies as the Internal Revenue Service for its 200 years of existence.

The National Research Council panel also performed an interesting experiment to ascertain how respondents' behavior was affected by whatever was promised them about the confidentiality of their responses. The U.S. Bureau of the Census gave an assurance of confidentiality by random assignment at one of five levels: confidentiality in perpetuity, for 75 years, or for 25 years; unmentioned; or the statement that replies "may be given to other agencies and to the public." A promise of perpetuity gave the lowest refusal rate of 1.8%; an assurance of confidentiality for 75 years raised the refusal rate only one-tenth of a percent and a promise of 25 years added four-tenths of a percent to that. The highest rate of refusals was among the 2.8% of respondents who indicated that such data could not be given to other agencies and the public. The report concluded that assurance of a high level of confidentiality is apparently not essential for low refusal rates. The evidence suggests public receptivity to release of Census records for legitimate research use without long delay.

Nevertheless, certain types of information and research methods have potential for invasion of privacy. Boruch (1982) has been a leading developer of solutions to privacy problems in social science, without compromising the ability to do good research. Some social scientists have been increasingly pressing for a National Data Center that would facilitate statistical analysis for social research and end part of the duplication of effort by private survey organizations. While such a repository might provide a valuable information resource for social science, it also poses special threats to individual privacy. Because no such central data center exists, social scientists have turned to methods of linking individual data from various existing files, without compromising the identity of particular individuals. Baruch helped devise a "link file" system for insuring data security and respondent anonymity for some types of data.

Essentially a *link-file system* requires that researchers or bureaucrats create two separate files—one file containing the person's research data and an arbitrary identification code, the second file containing the person's name, address, and the same identification code. At a later date, when the data need to be matched up with other agency records or a new data collected at a second time period, a third file will be created—the "link-file"—which contains only the identification codes for each data set by a custodial intermediary. Identifying information can then be destroyed after file match-up. This type of match-up makes possible the linking of records from such independent sources as health records, school records, police records, and survey records, without disclosing identities.

One of the major legal problems faced by the researcher is that—unlike doctors and clergy—a pledge of confidentiality has little legal support. Subpoenas currently have legal priority over researcher pledges of confidentiality. Until such time as the judicial and congressional system gives a privileged information status to all social science research, it may be necessary in some cases for the scientist to deposit a link-file at a computer or other research-type facility located in a foreign country.

Of course, no system is foolproof from *deductive disclosure*; that is, sensitive data on individuals, organizations, or cities may become unintentionally vulnerable to exposure through simple logic. Kruskal (1981: 513) gives a classic example that has long been known and appreciated. Assume you are perusing a table that gives average incomes of physicians by field of specialization and county. If you knew that Dr. Zeuss was the only pediatrician in Lake Wobegon County, then you would know his income. Using this logic, Gibbons (1975) merely scanned census reports on cities to show how easily someone could deduce that criminal justice research in a city "disguised" as "Prairie City" was Decatur, Illinois. Anytime a researcher studies a relatively rare phenomenon—for example, rapes that result in pregnancy, towns devastated by tornadoes in a particular year, or hemophiliac AIDS cases—deductive disclosure becomes a potential threat to privacy that requires extra consideration on the part of the researcher.

Protecting Researchers from Required Disclosure

The problem of confidentiality is joined to the constitutional amendments protecting freedom of speech and freedom of the press. However, interpretation of those amendments is not a settled issue. The American Civil Liberties Union (ACLU) fights a constant battle against governmental attempts to gain rights to reporters' information sources. Both the mass media and professional social-science associations contend that freedom of the press requires the protection of confidential sources of information. They contend that such sources will dry up, if the sources feel they cannot give information with the confidence that they will be protected from governmental repression.

During the 1970s, the American Anthropological Association, the American Political Science Association, and the American Sociological Association presented an amicus (friend of the court) brief to the Supreme Court, in a case involving Professor Samuel L. Popkin of Harvard. The associations asked for a decision that the First Amendment to the Constitution protect the confidentiality essential in scholarly and scientific research. Social scientists noted that it is difficult to gain confidential access to many kinds of data, particularly data concerning deviant or criminal behavior, with adequate protective legislative, executive, and judicial protection. Governmental response has been limited and piecemeal. For example, seven acts of research immunity were passed during the 1970s. While all of them offered protection from prosecution for protecting the confidentiality of individual research data, only five of them offered automatic immunity from prosecution for the researcher who refused to disclose research records; five were offered automatic immunity from judicial inquiry; and four from legislative inquiry. Each act was limited to such narrowly defined areas of research interests as alcohol and psychoactive drugs, controlled substances, and drug abuse.

During the late 1970s, then-President Carter introduced several broader bills for congressional consideration intended to provide much broader coverage of privacy of research records and confidentiality of statistical records, but which never received enough congressional interest to pass. The succeeding Reagan administration showed even less concern with these issues during the 1980s. Until broader coverage is given to researchers, the situation looks bleak. In the event a subpoenaed researcher has promised confidentiality to informants, this is likely to mean unnecessary jailings of researchers for failure to divulge information sources and the avoidance of "sensitive" research areas to avoid legal hassles.

Without more omnibus legislation at the Federal level, researchers must depend more on state and local laws. Only a few states have actively supported the necessity for such legislation. Boruch (1982:306) gives a pointed example from a New York statute that extends protection to respondents in roadside interviews, concerning drunken driving and vehicle accidents to assure cooperation. Because accident victims often are reluctant to provide information about their accident, this statute provides that "the special investigative units shall not be required to produce their records on identifiable respondents or evidence contained in them in any legal action or other proceeding." Boruch notes that numerous discoveries about the role of alcohol and mechanical automotive defects in vehicular accidents would not have been recorded without this law.

The Scientist-Citizen Dilemma

Suppose you are experimenting with some new educational technique. By what authority can you justify better educating one group (the experimental group) than another (the control group)? Or suppose you are studying organized teenage shoplifting. What justification do you have for not reporting this activity to the authorities? As a third example, what if you were studying hemophiliacs, and happen to discover someone with Acquired Immunological Deficiency Syndrome. Should you or should you not bend to pressures from those parts of the community who demand your information? One final example: What if you have assessed elementary school children's self-esteem with some standard measure. Should you or should you not report low self-esteem to teachers? On one hand, the teacher might use this information beneficially, by singling the student out as needing more confidence bolstering through positive reinforcement of classroom efforts. On the other hand, you risk initiating a self-fulfilling prophecy, by reporting this, because the teacher may then knowingly or unconsciously treat the student in psychologically damaging ways.

Researchers cannot really cop out by "doing nothing." No choice *is* a choice. Researchers, implicitly or explicitly, have responsibility for inducing or denying change to study participants. Researchers, like any professionals, also have corporate obligations of good citizenship beyond the participants in their research: important dilemmas over mediocre practice, overcommitment of time, and, perhaps most importantly, the distribution of effort and priorities toward long-term societal needs and goals. Shils (1965) reasoned that the professions take their shape from a series of socially defined problems of order which their knowledge permits them to control, and professional practice is focused upon the control of central social problems. Indeed, this ability to control enhances professional status. Abbott (1983:879) emphasizes the status-enhancing effects of controlling ethical dilemmas when he states, "If one is ready for (the confrontation), there is something noble and charismatic in deciding who gets the scarce treatment, in weighing the rights of state and individual, in deciding to blow the whistle on the laundered data."

Scientists and scientific communities are not islands unto themselves; they are part of the larger societal fabric. As such, they have obligations to their communities and society. Although individuals are the atoms of larger groups, we conduct social and organizational studies that potentially hold more macroscopic perils and promise than research on single individuals. Let us consider the example of discrimination research. Although discrimination is felt by individuals, and one may discriminate against someone on personal grounds alone, it is most dangerous in its social form where individual distinctions are lost. In 1962, Eliot (1987) commenced performing what has become a quite notorious exercise in teaching the effects of discrimination. Eliot divided up her class of white, middle-class American elementary school students according to eye color; she arbitrarily treated those with blue eyes as inferior students, and those with brown eyes as superior students. Her results were powerful: Within 15 minutes of this treatment, she observed classic signs of racial and ethic discrimination: some of the "blue eyes" became withdrawn and passive, others became belligerent, rebellious, angry, and others broke down into fits of crying. "Brown eyes" began throwing classic racial epithets at the "blue eyes."

In the intervening decades, Eliot traced down her former students and found lasting effects of her experiment. The blunt experience of harsh discrimination for only one day remains a vivid memory among her former students. Indeed, their teachers in high school reported that they were less bigoted and more socially conscious of their actions than other students without this experience. Today, Eliot continues using this type of exercise in discrimination in adult workshops; she feels it is her duty as a good citizen to fight the battle against institutionalized bigotry. However, she is alarmed by the misuse of her study by teachers who may be well-meaning, but are socially ignorant. For example, Eliot reports that some teachers have used her study design in racially mixed schools. Eliot sharply points out that members of racial and ethnic minorities that have grown up in a culture of discrimination certainly should not have it reinforced. It is one thing to use such powerful exercises on majority groups; quite another, however unwitting, to impose more discrimination on groups who already suffer from it.

"To whom does one owe allegiance?" does not always have easy answers. Perhaps the most celebrated case of the dilemma of conflicting allegiances during the 1980s is the Steven Mosher case (Lewin 1987). Mosher was the first non-Chinese allowed by Chinese authorities to do social studies in their country since the isolationist "cultural revolution" period under Mao Tse Tung. What Mosher observed so shocked him that he found it difficult to be dispassionate. Chinese officials in the rural village where he was permitted to work were practicing infanticide as part of governmental policy to control population. Mosher took pictures documenting his field notes, then published an article accompanied by his photos in a Taiwanese journal soon after leaving China. What transpired since his departure is disquieting. The Chinese government accused him of gross improprieties during his field research of rural family-planning practices, and the political atmosphere became so inflamed that other social scientists complained of barriers to any politically sensitive research in China. Stanford University, upset by the Chinese allegations of "unethical conduct," has refused to permit him the PhD Mosher feels he is rightfully due. Because neither Stanford University nor the Chinese government has released substantial portions of the story, the allegations are difficult to challenge.

However, from the pieces available, it is possible to conclude that inherently conflicting allegiances partly led to the unfortunate set of events that transpired. Mosher's belief that infanticide is a moral abomination led him to expose the practice. The Chinese government, by contrast, is unwilling to let

its population continue to grow; its rationale is that it is immoral to let the world's largest population grow uncontrolled. Furthermore, Chinese authorities contend that the means of exposure was highly unethical: photos used in the journal article were left undoctored, which they consider an invasion of privacy; and the article was politically embarassing, because it was published in the journal of a country those officials believe purposefully seeks information that would destabilize their legitimacy. In the United States, both State Department and Stanford officials appear to have been swayed more by the political embarassment and chilling effects on U.S. relations with China than Mosher's ethics per se.

The Mosher case demonstrates most clearly how politically threatening research complicates the roles of researcher and citizen. Social scientists have not always been quick to realize that their observations may have huge impact beyond that of the individuals they study. Even when they act in transparently ethical ways, they need to consider the larger ramifications of their actions for other social scientists, communities, organizations, and their own and other governments. Does the researcher have an obligation to reveal confidential information if there is evidence of a group's threat to it members' civil liberties? Is a potential threat to the well-being of a nation more important than risks of exposure of the privacy of individuals or of research files? Is human life or national security worth more than research money or having an article or book published? Clearly, one's ethical choices hinge on one's own role concepts as citizen and as professional sociologist. But the roles may create moral and ethical dilemmas for the researcher because each may invite actions that may be logically in conflict.

Application-of-Knowledge Dilemma

The ideal in science is what the famous philosopher J. S. Mill (1978) called the "free marketplace of ideas." Mills held that open intellectual debate among scientists is crucial to scientific advancement; in the long run, truthful ideas crush false and fraudulent ones because scientists cross-check the veracity of each other's work in an essentially public arena. In conjunction with the ethics of protecting truthful information, the scientific community holds that it is essential to open all aspects of individual research to scrutiny to protect against fraud. Researchers know that truth can best be protected by this method.

Fraud

In 1961, the eminent British psychologist Cyril Burt published a paper "Intelligence and Social Mobility," in which he attempted to substantiate that intelligence is the genetic inheritance of the social upper crust of society. The paper came to be regarded as a classic, and led to his becoming the first psychologist ever knighted. This title was frequently cited by white supremacists as "proof" that whites inherently are more intelligent than blacks. In 1976, Kamin publicly stated that this paper contained several "extremely improbable statistics." Then, in 1978, *Science* published statistical evidence by Dorfman deducing how Burt must have concocted his "data."

The Burt fraud case shows institutionalized scientific ethical safeguards at their best. Scientists protect their knowledge through an open contest of each other's theories, methods, and data. For example, the leading sociology journals hold an official policy that data published in their pages must be made public to other scientists. For instance, Alwin (1986) reanalyzed classic survey research by Lenski (1963) on the religious factor in child rearing. In spite of the fact that Lenski did not have modern electronic means of coding and analyzing his data, Alwin found less than 2% differences between his tabular analysis and Lenski's.

However, some types of research are more difficult to challenge; unlike laboratory experiments and much survey research, participant observation is difficult to replicate. Social scientists must take on truth the research presented in their participant observation colleagues' work to a larger extent than other types of research. During the 1970s, Carlos Castaneda wrote a series of books that became enormously popular. Ostensibly, these books were based on extensive field research Castaneda did for his PhD dissertation. This cycle of "Don Juan" narratives attracted a large group of aficionados, despite negative reviews by authorities on the Yaqui culture of Mexico—the subjects of the series. Murray (1978) summarized the body of evidence attesting to the fraudulent basis of the books, and analyzed the books' scientific reception. His study recounted persuasive evidence that Castaneda did not do fieldwork among the Yaqui, but conducted library research in the UCLA library. The authenticity of Castaneda's data was also found wanting because of illogical sequencing of events in several of the books, failure to specify Spanish and Indian translations of key concepts, and the lack of cultural or ethnographic documentation.

Why did not eminent anthropologists—who believed this work to be a hoax—publish their judgments? Barnes (1972) points out that scientific communities usually use informal communication channels to notify each other of suspect work. This means that such informal communication channels are invisible to scholars in other disciplines and to the general public. A sociologist, Marcello Truzzi (1977), called upon UCLA to consider revoking Castaneda's doctorate and on the American Anthropological Association to investigate the case. Murray (1978) believes that fraud of this type is particularly serious because it is almost impossible to replicate. The proportion of scientists who create such hoaxes is probably quite small. But they emphasize the need for scientists to protect scientific knowledge in better ways from the costs of worthless data accumulations and public distrust of science.

Secrecy

The practice of Mill's free marketplace of ideas is absolutely essential to the detection of falsity and fraud but events in the outside world grossly temper its practice, raising new ethical dilemmas. Since the late 1930s, when governments in the United States, Germany, the U.S.S.R., and Japan independently commenced secret research into atomic warfare, the international scientific community has become less free to freely exchange scientific data and ideas under the guise of "national security." However, current governmental policy to close off scientific channels of communication goes beyond protecting classified research and the export of militarily critical technologies. Raloff (1987) reports that NASA has compiled a list of U.S. academics—for example, a social scientist who is Northwestern University's Center for the Interdisciplinary Study of Science and Technology director—who are declined subscriptions to unclassified federal publications. Also, the Department of Energy discourages scientists at national laboratories from sharing unclassified research data, and teams of "national security agents" have intimidated businesses engaged in vending unclassified information stored in electronic data-retrieval systems—for example, census tapes and survey data—from selling them to foreign nationals.

These programs share a "chilling effect" on the free flow of nonclassified scientific information necessary, ironically, to the vitality of our own scientific programs. While the main target of these programs has been outside the social science community, social scientists are increasingly employed by national scientific laboratories and private businesses engaged in selling or using social information data bases and technology exchange. Furthermore, academic social scientists routinely study such organizations as part of the sociology of science. Therefore, the difficulty in measuring the extent to which such governmental strictures on scientific exchange exist is disquieting. It raises the classic ethical question: Knowledge for whom? The present governmental response to this question is inconsistent with democratic principles and law as well as scientific advancement.

Probably we only see the tip of the iceberg. The policy is reminiscent of attempts back in the 1960s in certain quarters of the federal government to conceal the famous "Coleman" report on education, because of its implications for school desegregation and busing. This report was finally brought to public attention only because of the persistent efforts of sociologist James Coleman and others. The unanswered question is: How many other social scientists have been affected by governmental withholding of unclassified information with national policy implications under the guise of "national security"?

Values and Social Activism

Science is increasingly under public scrutiny; ethical and moral implications of its procedures, and its immediate and long-range consequences are subject to vigorous debate. Difficult questions are posed in this debate: Are there moral limits to scientific inquiry? Should social or political restraints be placed on research? Is some research so risky, so reprehensible, or so threatening to nonscientific values that it should not be done at all? Whether or not scientists like it, their research is embedded in, and constrained by, its cultural and political context. Genetic engineers have created a piglike creature by introducing cells from cattle gene into pigs in the hopes of producing an animal with more meat and less fat. This raises ethical concerns over our ability to create "designer" people. But social scientists engaged in social activism and applied social science also work on "designer" social systems that raise as many, if not more, questions of "unethical tampering" with the human condition.

In the political wake of the Korean War stalemate, the U.S. Air Force funded a scholar (Kecskemeti 1958) to study the conditions under which "strategic surrender" is ever an appropriate political response. Congress, rankled by his conclusion that an expectation of unconditional surrender is unrealistic in the modern international political context, explicitly limited future research with the use of public funds for any research into U.S. military surrender. Similar questions about the political acceptability of military-sponsored research arose concerning the infamous Department of Defense-sponsored Project Camelot. This project was not only conceived by a primarily social science-oriented agency, but also had dramatic effects on the conduct of American social science research outside of the United States. It had a mammoth budget of 6 million dollars financed by the U.S. Department of Defense. The ostensible focus of the study was to collect data on the nature and causes of revolutions in underdeveloped countries. More interesting yet, from the point of ethical commitments, was its aim of developing "insurgency prophylaxis" to prevent Latin revolutions.

Camelot was conceived in late 1963. The project never got off the ground. Ironically, a country not involved in the study provided the impetus for stopping Camelot. In 1965, the Chilean Senate and press released a statement by John Galtung, an eminent Norwegian sociologist, denouncing the project. This Chilean political pressure caused immediate halting of the project by concerned members of Congress and State Department officials, and eventual termination of the project directly by then President Lyndon Johnson. A major consequence of the affair was a new policy set down by President Johnson, stating that governmental sponsorship of foreign-area research could not be undertaken if the Secretary of State judged it to affect adversely United States foreign relations (Horowitz 1965:47–48).

There were several value biases running through the entire history of the project. First, the primary question asked was: How can revolutions be prevented? No apparent concern was given to revolution as a beneficial or productive force. Second, the project social scientists let the Department of Defense assume virtually complete responsibility for defining what problems would be of researchable interest to the project. Thus the nagging questions: Did the Defense Department, with the implicit help of project social scientists, actually set out to determine project outcomes, or did it determine project goals?

Several unfortunate ethical precedents were established with the demise of Project Camelot. One was that of social scientists as "hired help," so that the client came to determine project outcomes tailored to the client's needs without regard to the professional's scientific needs. As summarized by Irving Horowitz (1965: 47).

> (The) Project Camelot . . . cancellation came as an act of Government censorship, and an expression of the contempt for social science so prevalent among those who need it most. . . .We must be careful not to allow social science projects with which we may vociferously disagree on political and ideological grounds to be decimated by Government fiat.

That is, because Camelot was cut short due to its politically threatening nature rather than its lack of scientific merit, research of much greater scientific and ethical merit may likewise suffer the same fate as Camelot.

Use and Misuse of Research Findings

"Should the public be protected against 'dangerous' or 'threatening' ideas?" is a recurring question in the ethical arena. That science is often perceived as a threat to values is classically illustrated in the attempt by certain fundamentalist religious groups during the late 1970s and early 1980s to forbid a government-funded course taught in some elementary schools called "Man: A Course of Study" or MACOS. The message underlying this course was unacceptable to certain religious groups—that our beliefs, values, and behavior must be understood in their social, historical, and cultural context. The course material used cross-cultural and cross-animal comparisons of aggression, religion, infant nurturance, and social relations that some groups found highly objectionable. Nelkin (1982:167) reports that such groups "contended that MACOS undermined traditional interpretations of reality, violated sacred assumptions (for example, about the uniqueness of man), and fostered pernicious arguments about cultural relativity." In spite of the fact that numerous social scientists defended the academic integrity and educational worth of MACOS, these religious minority groups successfully pressured the withdrawal of federal support.

Knowledge is not neutral; it can be used and misused. Attitude-change research can be used to decrease prejudice or to convince people to buy things they do not need. Data on management-employee relations might be used to control employees or to substantiate a union's demands. Control of criminal behavior can be viewed as a way to bring recalcitrant individuals into a more "normal" and productive life, or as a means to maintain order at enormous cost to those who do not conform to establishment expectations. Accordingly, numerous sociologists have assumed ethical responsibility for speaking out on important issues. Charles Moskos, an expert on military sociology has appeared before congressional committees to communicate social-science research findings about the military draft. James Coleman has testified before congressional committees on school desegregation policy. James Laue has lobbied before Congress for a U.S. Peace Academy for training citizens in social techniques of conflict resolution and peace negotiation. The ethics of such applications of social science should be guided by two questions (Diener & Crandall 1978:212): Will they be used to limit people's freedom in an unjustified and dangerous way? Will only the powerful or elite profit from the application of such research? Responsible social scientists such as Moskos, Coleman, and Laue have been careful to be vigilant on both dangers.

Summary

According to Mark Twain, an ethical man is a Christian holding four aces. However cynical his definition is, it does rightly allude to the structural problems inherent in ethics: Although the words "ethics" and "morals" originally derive from a concern with individual character, they have broader social connotations, as evidenced in Durkheim's conception of collective conscience. Collective enforcement of professional ethics paradoxically helps the larger profession control individual researchers at the same time that it shelters individual researchers from outside opposition to their scientific quest and helps protect researcher status. This appendix has outlined major ethical dilemmas that are structurally inherent in the social sciences, offered some current thinking on how to provide researchers with more advantageous ethical "aces," and raised many ethical questions that researchers ought to consider before, during, and after completion or research. Kelman (1982: 46) gives a clear, although somewhat different classification of ethical issues in social research which nicely highlights the topics discussed. He breaks down individual rights and welfare into three broad issue areas of harm and benefit, privacy and confidentiality, and informed consent and deception, and then adds a fourth issue of social control that raises more macroscopic social issues. Kelman then adds a fourth issue of social control that raises more macroscopic social issues. Kelman then cross-classifies those four issues by three types of impact on research, ranging from concrete interests of individual participants through more socially oriented impacts of quality of interpersonal relationships and wider social values. Each of Kelman's resulting twelve cross-classifications (Table A-1) have been discussed in this appendix. For example, although the obligation to consider harm and benefit was discussed in terms of cost-benefit ratios, social researchers know that it is an exercise fraught with uncertainty. For this reason committees called institutional review boards (IRBs) usually spend the majority of their time hypothesizing the potential risk-benefits of individual research projects as representatives of the larger community and societal values.

A major means of protecting human subjects from harm is informed consent. From the perspective of literate persons who have a share of democratic power, "informed consent" seems reasonable; but it is a virtually new social invention of the latter half of our century that has little application outside literate, Western societies. Even within such societies as our own, it is a concept that is easily subverted by power and authority, raising issues over how otherwise to reduce the researcher-study participant power imbalance to insure freedom of human participants from exploitation while protecting scientific freedom and insuring high-quality scientific findings that may advance the quality of human life.

Table A-1 *A Classification of Ethical Issues in Social Science Research*

	Types of Impact of the Research		
Issue Areas	*Concrete Interests of Participants*	*Quality of Interpersonal Relationships*	*Wider Social Values*
Harm and benefit	Injury (physical, psychological, material) feelings of inadequacy, inequity	Stress and indignity (discomfort, embarrassment)	Diffuse harm (perversion of political process, manipulation, arbitrariness)
Privacy and confidentiality	Public exposure	Reduced control over self-presentation	Reduction of private space
Informed consent and deception	Impaired capacity for decision making	Deprivation of respect (lack of candor, choice, reciprocity)	Erosion of trust (cynicism, anomie)

Source: Kelman (1982:46)

Whether to deceive or not to deceive is another thorny issue in much research that is intimately related to the issue of informed consent. In both cases, researchers worry that disclosure of the true purposes of their research may change the participants' behaviors, jeopardizing scientific validity. But to deceive participants raises classical issues of individual rights of autonomy. But it also raises larger issues of the erosion of public trust. There is little excuse for disguising one's observations of others in the name of science. One's identity as a social scientist implies that participants be informed about what information the investigator will collect, and how it will be used in order to give group members the right to conceal what they consider private. It also protects the researcher's own consciousness which is likely to become burdened from the mistrust and disrespect inherent in a covert role. There may be some exceptions to this rule, but those exceptions are fairly narrowly defined to such things as studies of the powerful, of public behavior, or roles that are accountable to the public.

The line between public and private roles is increasingly blurred by advances in electronic media that have several ethical effects. First, it aids researchers more easily to control the data collection and analysis stages of research. Second, it increases the power advantage of those who understand this technological revolution, which can lead to individual alienation. This increases the need for social responsibility on the part of researchers to work toward aiding those groups and individuals that are disenfranchised. One such important step in social responsibility is protection of the confidentiality of data. Some types of information such as survey data do not always need such protective measures, but when it does researchers have developed such systems as "link file" methods to protect confidentiality.

Social researchers have long fought for better legal protection for confidentiality of their data. Various acts of Congress have offered limited immunity from prosecution, but all of these acts have been too narrowly defined. Social

Table A-2 *Major Ethical Issues Confronting Different Types of Social Research*

Types of Research	Types of Impact of the Research		
	Concrete Interests of Participants	Quality of Interpersonal Relationships	Wider Social Values
Experimental manipulation			
Laboratory experiments and simulations	Impaired capacity for decision making	Stress and indignity	Erosion of trust
Field experiments	Impaired capacity for decision making	Reduced control over self-presentation	Erosion of trust
Organizational and social experiments	Risk of material injury	Deprivation of respect	Inequity
Questioning of respondents			
Questionnaires and tests	Public exposure	Deprivation of respect	Inequality
Surveys and interview studies	Public exposure	Reduced control over self-presentation	Perversion of political respect
Records and secondary analysis	Public exposure	Deprivation of respect	Reduction of private space
Direct Observation			
Structured observation	Impaired capacity for decision making	Stress and indignity	Reduction of private space
Unobtrusive (public) observation	Impaired capacity for decision making	Reduced control over self-presentation	Reduction in private space

Participation observation	Public exposure	Deprivation	Erosion of trust

Source: Kelman (1982:69)

scientists continue their lobbying efforts to protect their research interests from legal inquiries that chill the process of discovery.

This process of discovery points to another potential ethical dilemma: the obligation to do good research versus being a good citizen. Scientific discovery does affect communities, organizations, and societies. The effects of research on quality of social life, therefore, is an important part of social scientific ethics: It raises the questions: To whom does the researcher owe allegiance? What are the larger social ramifications of particular research? One of those ramifications concerns the question: How will this research be applied?

Some ethical issues are more narrowly of professional concern. One important one is: How can the truth be protected? Fraud and honesty are problems that are solveable only in the long run, through an open contest of scientific theories, methods, and ideas. This means that scientists must give extremely accurate depictions of what they did methodologically, so that other scientists can replicate their research. Secrecy is an anathema to this process and social scientists, like other scientists, have become increasingly alarmed by governmental attempts to prevent free exchange of scientific data and ideas. Some of these attempts at preventing free exchange raise ethical issues over policy implications of research rather than "national security." Policy implications of social research create dilemmas over the desirability of "tampering with the human condition" that arise out of different societal values of competing interests groups within any heterogeneous society. It also raises issues of whether or not social science threatens the existing social order and individual freedom. A free society is swayed by public opinion, and the public must weigh the trade-offs. Social scientific and technological advancement can exact a significant cost; in this case, society, not individual researchers, must ultimately decide if the price is too high.

Kelman (1982:69) presents a tabular summary (Table A-2) of how specific types of social research are affected by various ethical issues. Although this appendix has not systematically explored all types of research, this table does summarize many of the ethical problems that have been met in this and the other chapters. Although it is an important summary of ethical dilemmas for the entire text, keep in mind that it is not a complete list, because it focuses mostly on individual participants of research. As we have seen, many ethical issues have much broader social scope.

APPENDIX

Reporting Research

Simple English is no one's mother tongue. It has to be worked for.[1]

I feel lucky if I write two pages of double-spaced typed shit each day.[2]

Key Terms

Active voice	Passive voice
Antonyms	Readability
Audience	Revision
Dangling participle	Sentence complexity
Draft	Split infinitive
Jargon	Style sheets
Negation	Synonyms
Outline	Thesaurus

[1]Attributed to Jacques Barzun.
[2]Attributed to Ernest Hemingway.

Study Guide Questions

1. Explain the six routines presented for shaping ideas into good writing.

2. How does the process of drafting aid good writing?

3. Discuss the value of paying attention to (a) audiences and (b) generalities. How does readability affect good writing?

4. Why is the active voice generally preferred to the passive voice? Give an example of each in your answer.

5. How does sentence length and complexity affect reading comprehension?

6. How does jargon and negation affect reading comprehension.

Reporting well cannot be learned from a book. The most you can expect from any book is help in considering how to express your thoughts, because truly effective communication is learned through practice. This appendix is provided to give you direction based on others' experiences, and it will focus on some essentially basic areas: how to get ideas, choice of words, the shape of thought-building, developing ideas, the art of quantitative display of information and relations, communicating data, and the relationship between writers and their audiences.

Scientific prose and illustration need not be literary novocain. The earliest scientists wrote with stylistic beauty that we ought all admire. Leonardo DaVinci and Galileo peppered their prose with detailed illustrations, Darwin frankly discussed problems he encountered in his scientific adventures including puzzling exceptions to his theory, and Benjamin Franklin's lively expository style sparked great lay interest in scientific applications. These, and other, early scientific writers used a lively, accurate form of narration that has degenerated into the passive voice, and conceals more than it reveals. The open discussion of difficulties and negative experiments in scientific journals has regrettably become nearly obsolete. Sophisticated mathematics and clear prose used to coexist on the same page, but rarely do so today.

The rhetorical habits of scientific writers and editors have degenerated during the last century. Happily, some of our most respected journal editors are starting to demand standards reminiscent of this earlier age of scientific prose. Abraham Pais (1986:4) writes with a model preciseness and dedication scientific writers would do well to mimic: "Since it is my principal purpose to describe how ideas evolved, I shall need to discuss . . . how false leads, incorrect improvisations, and dead ends are interspersed between one advance and the next. The omission of such episodes would anaesthetize the story." The revival of the nearly dead patient from anaesthetic overdose of bad writing is a worthy goal of all scientific writing.

The Shape of Ideas

In Chapter 3, I suggested that you start doing research by choosing a topic of interest to you. If a topic bores you, you probably will not be able to motivate yourself to follow a boring task through to completion, you will undoubtedly reveal your lack of interest through a sloppy and (for your reader) uninteresting presentation. Generally, a topic that interests you will make the routine of shaping ideas much less painful. Readable and sensible shaping of those ideas may be made easier by the following suggestions.

First, you should keep a research file as suggested and outlined in Chapters 3 and 8 (Field Research). Play "52-card pickup" with your file. That is, mix up your file folders, index cards, and any other file materials. Then, review your newly ordered materials. For example, although I save journals, books, and other materials for a book such as this one and write notes on my personal copies that suggest for which chapters and purposes, I believe they might prove fruitful, I purposively do not order these materials on my bookshelves by the chapters for which I have saved them. Instead, I force myself to rummage haphazardly through these materials from one end to the other, as a means of considering alternative means of using the materials. Many of a writer's best ideas evolved through the unforeseen linkages that one finds between ideas. Although it might be more "efficient" for me to order the materials I am considering using by chapter or subchapter divisions, I prefer the slower, serendipitous element because it allows me opportunities for reconsideration of alternative usage I might otherwise not consider. If you are fortunate enough to work with a personal computer, you can enhance the speed of this process with sorting, searching, and indexing routines.

Second, play with synonyms and antonyms of your key terms and phrases. Break down higher concepts into several components. This helps you clarify and make your research problem more precise. Also, play around with making your statements more abstract. The idea is to track every possible nuance by working back and forth between levels of abstraction. A good thesaurus comes in handy at this stage; after all, the word "thesaurus" originally meant a "treasure." An ordinary dictionary arranged in alphabetical order is not very helpful for purposes of searching for idiomatic combinations peculiar to words. For example, under Roget's *International Thesaurus*, you can track, from more to less abstract: voluntary action, intersocial volition, ex-prisoner, and to serve time. Similarly, "criminality" has four shades of meaning in Roget's: wrongdoing, guilt, vice, and lawlessness. The columnist William F. Buckley claims that using an electronic thesaurus changed his life. Whether you use a standard or electronic thesaurus, you must be wary of sabotaging your prose with obscure or pretentious terms. However, a thesaurus can sometimes lead you out of a minor writer's block or jog your memory, giving your sentences the forgotten term that fits exactly.

Third, develop habits of searching for new classifications of your ideas. Do not be content with existing classifications. Make your classifications as systematic and explicit as possible. If you are interested in conflict, you ought to consider references to cooperation and peace; acts of deviance are informed by knowledge of conformity. In ongoing research into incest that leads to abortions I have played around with numerous classifications to cull out the existing literature: Incest conjures up such key terms as blood relationships and family; it also is a traumatic event that suggests looking at the larger literature on social and physical stress.

Fourth, think in terms of opposites and extremes. If you are interested in revolution, then you might profit by studying periods of political stability. The process of contrast and comparison helps focus ideas. It also leads to a consideration of the effects of greater variation. Consider the banality of the sentence "The crook cheated the judge." What if we were to change that to "The judge cheated the crook"? Although it may seem absurd to do so, reflection on why we consider it absurd leads to some interesting questions: Why do we think that judges are less likely to cheat crooks than the reverse? Under what conditions might a judge be likely to cheat a crook, or a crook *not* likely to cheat a judge? Are some forms of cheating worse than others? Is it worse for a judge to cheat a crook or a crook to cheat a judge? Why or why not?

Fifth, Mills suggests that you "deliberately invert your sense of proportion. If somethings seems very minute, imagine it to be simply enormous . . ." (1959:215). Incongruity often helps focus ideas. Try to imagine the effects of complete illiteracy on political stability, or the effects of mass starvation on literacy. Or, returning to crooks and judges cheating, try to conjure up the effects of a completely corrupt judicial system, in which the judges cheat innocent victims. Sometimes, the apparent absurdity of such thought experiments turns out to be not so ridiculous: Remember that the classic work on cognitive dissonance theory suggested that people who were offered one dollar were considerably more likely than those offered twenty dollars to say they believed in something that was apparently inconsistent with their preexperimental beliefs.

Sixth, a comparative analysis also tends to aid the contrast and comparison of ideas. Do bureaucracies have the same effects in Japan as in Western Europe? Do they have the same effects today as forty years ago? Once again, this principle helps us to release our imaginations and aids us in making sense of our ideas.

Getting a First Draft

At some point you must face the most difficult of tasks: actually putting your thoughts down on paper. Hemingway, in this chapter's opening, quote gives the best advice I know of when he suggests simply getting some specified small chunk written down, however unsatisfactory it may seem at the start. If I regarded this book as an approximately 800–page monolith, I would never write another word. Instead, I follow Hemingway's model by working toward a minimum of two pages of double-spaced draft each day. It is much easier to rework an imperfect working draft than to attempt to create a perfect final draft the first time; and it is less anxiety provoking to work on smaller two-page chunks at a time than consider a totally finished product from the start.

Howard Becker (1986b) astutely notes that part of the difficulty in learning how to write can be traced to the difficulty in observing the writing process. Readers normally see only the final, polished product in print; what they do not see are the numerous drafts that a finished manuscript likely proceeds through, and they are even less likely to observe the process of creating those drafts. In the pre-electronic media days, I kept every major draft of my work. In the modern age of drafting on a word processor, keeping track of drafts becomes harder, because cutting, pasting, and editing becomes much easier, but a book such as this one will go through three or four major redrafts before it reaches press.

I used to think that this redrafting was a personal fault because I could not "get it right" the first time. I was relieved to discover that even two of my English-language heroes of wordsmithery, grammar, and syntax—John Barth and William Gass—could not claim to write perfect copy the first time either. Both of them, in print, give thanks to good editors for helping them improve their already superb writing, and both of them work hard at redrafting! The problem with great writers is that their final product seems so effortless that we all are easily seduced into believing they did not put their blood, sweat, or tears into the final product. Such beliefs are fallacious. Writing is largely a masochistic process. I believe that any writer who says that he or she *enjoys* writing means only that they enjoy the *final product*, but not the actual nitty gritty process of wrestling with putting imperfectly formed thoughts down on to paper.

Part of the masochism inherent in the writing process is due to the fact that the writer risks exposing his or her soul for others to see. Indeed, out of fear of lack of control over such barings of our souls, we often go to great lengths *not* to write. Becker (1986b:2) observes many of our nonwriting routines: Men who will nervously sharpen and resharpen twenty pencils before sitting down to write; women who first ritualistically clean house—both sexes using different "magic rituals," out of fear of producing an unsuccessful, messy result. All writers fear having "nothing to say" or "nothing worthwhile to say." But the irony is that until we write something down, we do not know what or how much we have to say.

Students often express the belief that a 20–page paper seems lengthy. But if one breaks up a writing project into small, manageable chunks one often discovers ironically that much of the problem is the reverse: narrowing one's ideas. If a topic interests you, you will at some point find it necessary to limit it to keep it to a manageable size. Conciseness and economy of thought is a virtue. Federal grant guidelines normally have 15– to 20–page limits. Many journals have similar page restrictions. One of my own interests over the last decade was the short-lived Citizen's Band, or CB, radio craze. I could have well spent considerable time collecting information on the history of CBs, the relationship of the Federal Communication Commission's (FCC) control over CB broadcasting, and the flagrant abuse of FCC rules by CBers. But, to make my study easier to wield, I chose to narrow my interests to the CB handle (nickname) as a reflection of CBers' presentation of self (Smith 1980).

A distinctive feature of most good writers is that they read voraciously, yet discriminatingly. Benjamin Franklin claimed to have learned how to write well by scrutinizing the published works of authors who wrote well. He started out by painstakingly copying over good writing. Franklin then mimicked good style until he developed his own. This is not plagarism. After all, Franklin never took credit for the writing of others; nor did he publish the writing of others. He simply copied out good writing from his own private desire to develop good habits. This is similar to athletes who study old film clippage of classic home-run hitters, power-tennis serves, or long-distance golf swings: The purpose is to look for characteristics that are worth mimicking in developing one's own style.

Another good practice in first-drafting is to start with an outline. Schopenhauer once said that we should write the way an architect builds—"who first drafts his plan and designs every detail." A good outline provides the structural base upon which to fill in details; a bad outline, as with any poorly laid out foundation, will quickly develop faults. Happily for the novice scientific writer, most science journals specify a fairly rigid outline shell that includes the following details:

1. TITLE: The subject of the research. A subtitle is sometimes appropriate.

2. STATEMENT OF THE PROBLEM AND A BRIEF DESCRIPTION OF IT: What is the purpose and significance of this study? Why is it necessary or advisable? This description is normally brief and succinct.

3. REVIEW OF THE LITERATURE: Summarize briefly the work already done, emphasizing any significant contributions. Refer freely here to your bibliography.

4. THE QUESTION AT ISSUE: State the hypothesis or hypotheses that you will test, or the information you expect from the study. What are you trying to discover that is not already known? How does it differ from previous studies in the area?

5. METHOD AND PROCEDURE: What are the important characteristics of the research participants? What were the sampling procedures? Make a list of the steps involved in the procedures and methods in direct, simple, easily understood language including:
   a. Specification of the sample;
   b. Means of evaluating the hypotheses or concepts;
   c. Tests or procedures used and data on their reliability and validity; and
   d. Other methods.

6. FINDINGS: Present the analysis of data collected. Your evidence is presented here with statistical or other means of evaluation.

7. DISCUSSION: Usually researchers evaluate the findings of the previous section, and discuss plausible explanations and implications of the findings in this section.

8. SUMMARY AND CONCLUSIONS: The statement of your problem and this section are extremely important. First and last impressions of research reports are somewhat like first and last impressions of people; they are remembered longer and more deeply. Remember that everything written is meant to please or to instruct and that it is difficult to achieve the second objective without attending to the first. The American Psychological Association (1984) publishes a manual that gives excellent advice and examples on all aspects of writing, which ought to be on the bookshelf of any serious social-science writer.

Outlines often help you get your pencil moving or your fingers typing. Polished style does not emerge at first stroke. Effective writers make rough outlines of ideas at the start, fill in gaps, and then polish them off. Before word processing became practical, I used to take a yellow pad and note ideas I wanted to include in my work, then played with means of organizing those ideas into conceptually similar patterns and logical flow of ideas. Then I attempted to make a rough draft, crossing out ideas as I covered them. Word processing has grossly sped up this process. The extremely prolific writer Isaac Asimov keeps three word processors active at the same time, so that he can quickly move between manuscripts at different stages of progress. A word processor will not make you a better writer, but it can aid in more efficient outlining, writing, and revising when used properly. Many word processors now have built-in spelling and grammar checkers. One popular grammar checker notes such grammatical and punctuation errors as redundancies, lack of paired sets of quotation marks, run-on sentences, passive voice, and split infinitives, and then suggests alternatives. Some of them will grade your writing for readability by counting sentence length, or providing difficulty of word information.

Still others have an electronic "post-it note" feature that allows for pasting the notes anywhere on an outline or document. Becker (1986b:153) notes that "Rewriting destroys your neatness." Upon reflection, this may be one of the reasons we hate to rewrite. Ugly, "bandaged" revisions are not easy to make or to look at. But word processing cut and paste commands quickly doctor a manuscript back into neatness.

On the one hand, much of the routine drudgery can be taken out of writing. On the other, although most of us can think much faster than we can word process—because we can word process much faster than we can type, and can type much faster than we can write in longhand—electronic technology can help get thoughts down with less likelihood of forgetting. Remember the fundamental principle of fieldwork note taking works for any kind of writing: If you do not get it written down, it does not exist. Much of the frustration of writing first drafts is forgetting what you want to say next after you have completed what you are in process of laboriously writing out.

In the final analysis, get it down in rough form and worry about polish later. Hemingway was right: Most of the time our problem is not "getting it right," but "getting it out." Once we have gotten the clutter in our minds down in black and white, we can rearrange, cut and paste, or slash our ideas into a more disciplined, lean, clear, and graceful whole. Forster (1927:152) summarizes this view succinctly through the rhetorical statement: "How can I tell what I think 'til I see what I say?"

The modern word processor can aid and abet the writing process, but only if the writer is willing to use if efficiently. Many students use the computer only as a word *producer*. They may go so far as to use a typewriter or yellow pad and pen to produce something that they will then key into a computer, simply because they want a neat and clear hardcopy. This practice ignores word-processing possibilities. English instructors who have incorporated word processors into freshman English composition programs (Balestri 1988) emphasize the importance of convincing students to forget the printer, and try writing directly to the screen: Hardcopy simply preserves current thought, not the development of thought. Balestri teaches the use of the computer screen to produce "softcopy" superior to hardcopy uses, because it describes the importance of text-in-process over text-as-product. The nonlinear advantages of softcopy writing are easily subverted by the printing of hard copy. The softcopy approach to writing encourages an iterative and recursive process of adjustment and improvement at the levels of both substance and style; experimentation with writing; rapid generation of text; and strategies of comparing, organizing, and outlining. The writer who uses a word processor simply to produce hard copy betrays all of these advantages.

Polishing Your Ideas

Writing requires some arrogance on the part of the writer, because writing presupposes an assertion that one has something to say, and it is worthy of the attention of the reader. Certainly, after you have put on paper what you want to say it is worthwhile pondering whether you have said everything you meant and meant everything you said—to paraphrase an old adage. The list of do's and don't's is probably infinite, but a few major common problems need constant vigilance.

Audiences

The basic problem in writing is that there is no direct feedback from your audience. Feedback means that behavior is scanned for its results, and that the success or failure of this result modifies future behavior. Writing well requires us to "see" our invisible audience as we write. We must imagine how they will behave, what they like and dislike, whether they need more or less information on some topic. The famous German philosopher Goethe (pronounced "Ger-ta") once said that "everyone hears but what he understands." No word means exactly the same thing to different people. The basic problem with most novice writers is that they have not learned that many of those who read their writing will incorrectly understand it. The art of interesting and understandable writing is predicting what your reader needs to hear.

One useful technique is to form a reciprocal relationship with a friend, on the understanding that each of you read the other's writing with an eye to what it is and is not communicating. Most successful writers have "friendly critics," people they trust to tell them what is wrong with their writing *before* it goes to a publisher. If your friends aren't being critical of your writing, they're not your friends. Once you get a poor grade for a paper because it did not communicate what you intended, it is too late. Much better that you find a friendly critic to tell you what needs improvement before the paper is turned in.

Another technique that many writers use is lecture or discussion groups. Many writers belong to literary criticism groups that meet regularly to listen to and discuss each other's latest writing. Similarly, scientists normally read from their latest work in progress at professional meetings to get a sense of professional reaction to their latest efforts. They, then return to the drawing board to revise their work for publication. This technique is valuable for students and professional alike for various reasons. First, it sets deadlines for completion of work that might easily be shoved aside unwritten. Second, it provides necessary feedback from a real audience. Third, the process of oral delivery often aids the writer to consider how better to express thoughts that did not get expressed in print. Fourth, when we reread our own work, we are all likely to read in what we intended to say but did not say; others are more likely to catch such incompletely or poorly expressed thoughts.

"For whom are you writing?" is the first question I ask of any colleague who asks me to read a draft of work intended for publication. A manuscript intended for professional sociologists should not be written with a lay audience in mind. Even for different audiences of professional sociologists, different vocabularies need be employed: Fieldworkers rarely write like or for statisticians. Similarly, students need to learn the difficult task of viewing their work from the perspective of particular others.

Becker (1986b:18) notes that the greatest obstacle to following the above suggestions is fear of being ridiculed for poor expression. It is true that many writers do not show drafts of their work to friends and colleagues out of such fears. A good audience can help the shy writer, by making constructive suggestions for reworking his or her writing. Those of us fortunate enough to have experienced model copy editing know this: We can all learn much from the professional copy editor who does not write or say such things as "This sentence is poorly written," but who instead rewrites a sentence with a tactful note of "Does this express better what you mean?" None of our egos will withstand for long the ruthless editorial work of a "hatchet man."

Good audiences and good writing go together; after all, there is no need for writers without readers. Selvin and Wilson (1984:207) suggest practicing the art of writing from the view point of George Herbert Mead when they state that "Meanings, then, are shaped by others' responses, and others respond not only to the content, but also to the form of transmission." Writers who do not attend to their intended readers' reactions delude themselves concerning the importance of audience reaction: The readers' motivations to struggle with a writer's intended meaning is less than the writer's to communicate it. Good writers start writing because they do not know what they think until they read what they have written, but they finish by taking the role of their readers—of imagining and anticipating their reader's reactions.

Generalities

Science strives for generalities. Clearly, generalities may add order and understanding. But generalities need translation into concrete, specific facts and illustrations. Flesch (1954:100) said that "concreteness isn't something you sprinkle on your words like Parmesan cheese. It's internal." There is nothing wrong per se with such statements as "Propinquity continues to foster solidarity, resisting the centrifugal effects of urbanization." Certainly that may indicate what some people take to be sociologese or socspeak. But such statements cry for the basic rule of "Specify!" The task of communication reminds us of the necessity to be concrete. It stimulates us to mention names, dates, places; to be exact; to spell out details; to use images, cases, illustrations.

The rule of thumb for the amount of concreteness needed to explain adequately one's generalities is to continually ask oneself "What does my intended reader need to understand my message?" Although one always prefers to assume that one's readers are reasonably intelligent and motivated, one may be wrong in judging those readers' reactions. Therefore, good writers actively seek the reactions of their audience; they realize that their audience is the final judge of their clarity, precision, and articulateness.

Readability

Scientists are often accused of being unreadable, abstruse, or ungraceful writers. Although there is some truth to such charges, we ought to distinguish between those language usages that are an inevitable result of scientific ways of looking at things and those that are the result of lazy writing. After all, science is the practice of looking for particular forms of abstractions. Social scientists do not study such concretely observed things as individuals but such useful abstracts as social routines, interpersonal conflict, and intergroup cooperation. Let us lay the blame for our irritation at the doorstep of all bad writing: lack of attention to revision. In this section, I discuss some common problems endemic to scientific writers who do not pay close attention to how they write.

Active versus the passive voice

The most common form of a passive voice is recognized by prefixing some form of the copula *be (is, are, was, were,* etc.) or *get* or *become* to the past participle: The group *was* watched. The experiment *got* completed. The community activists have *become* stalemated. The passive voice is the weakest part of the English language because it is circumlocutious, lacks brevity and clarity of subject, hides accountability for actions, and it confuses direction of causality compared to the active voice which indicates a subject that does something, or is, or is becoming something. Compare the following sentence starts:

Passive:	*Active:*
It was stated by him that . . .	Jones stated that . . .
It was found that . . .	He found that . . .
The respondents were observed objecting to . . .	Respondents objected to . . .
The findings are supportive of . . .	The findings support . . .
A more adequate test will be attempted . . .	We will attempt . . .
The deviants were labeled.	The politician labeled the group "deviants."

My favorite junior-high-school grammar teacher used to demonstrate the liveliness, directness, brevity, and clarity of accountability for causality of the active voice with classroom antics. When a student was daydreaming, she might throw a piece of chalk at the student while saying "The chalk was thrown." To a more attentive student she would say "I am throwing chalk at you!" Her point was simple: The passive voice is not only deadening, it is inefficient and irritating. Mitchell (1979:52–53) gives perhaps the most damning indictment of the passive voice:

> Among the better class of Grammarians [this] construction is known as the Divine Passive. It [suggests] that neither the writer nor anyone else through whose head you might like to hammer a blunt wooden spike can be held accountable for anything in any way. Like an earthquake or a volcanic eruption, [the passive voice] must be accepted [as revealing] an act of God. God may well be keeping count of the appearances of the Divine Passive.

Mitchell's (p. 11) disgust for the indiscriminant use of the passive voice shows in an earlier section of his book, where he cogently indicates that the "atrophy of the active and the compensatory dominance of the passive" is comparable to the compensatory means used by three-legged dogs to walk, adding that "the language of the typical administrator is not very different from the gait of the three-legged dog . . ." Psychological experiments support clear differences in meaning between the passive and active voice. Pryor and Kriss (1977) presented research participants with a series of statements in either active ("John likes the car") or passive voice ("The car is liked by John.") The grammatical structure of each type of sentence influenced both memory and inference: Persons were relatively more salient, and perceived as more causal, than objects when the sentence was in the active rather than the passive voice.

You should only rarely employ the passive voice; for instance, in cases where you do not know who the subject is, or if you can make a good case that the action of the verb genuinely affects the subject. But when you know *who* did something, the passive voice obscures information important to scientific evaluation. Like Mitchell's archetypical timid administrator, willful avoidance of the active voice implies fear of commitment.

Sentence length and complexity

In several chapters, I have argued that survey questions (Chapter 7) and attitude statement length (Chapter 13) should not run over 20 words if at all possible. Gustave Flaubert is reputed to have said, "Whenever you can shorten a sentence, do. And one always can. The best sentence? The shortest." Reading comprehension is clearly related to sentence length. Sentence lengths of 21 to 24 words are *fairly difficult* to comprehend for the average reader. Those of 25 to 38 words are, generally speaking, *difficult* to read. Those over 28 words are *very difficult* for the average reader to understand. Inexpensive, easy-to-use, and fast word-count programs exist for personal computers which makes inattention to sentence length and reading comprehensibility inexcusable.

Furthermore, sentence length is associated with sentence complexity. Most complex sentences can be broken down into several distinct thoughts. Compound sentences (those with *ands* and *buts*) do not usually cause too much trouble for writer and reader. Complex sentences that use such words as *if, because*, and *as* are the ones that may need to be split up. Novice writers often make the mistake of presuming that the complex thought or word is synonymous with elegance of thought. This is not true. We admire such writers as Hemingway because of their simplicity and economy of thought. Although scientists generally reserve the word "parsimonious" to describe model scientific theorizing, it is a word that also well describes beautiful writing style. In college, my advanced expository writing instructor used to muse out loud over the shape of Beauty. His conclusion was that classic beauty—whether we find it in dress attire, art, or writing—is always found in economy of expression, rather than in unnecessary frills. Most professional writers would agree.

Vocabulary and jargon

Words exist for reasons. One of the strengths of the English language is precisely its adaptability to the expression of new ideas. It is foolish to think that difficult, many-syllable words are necessarily pretentious and jargonish. Why say "a first-year college student" when that may be simply stated as "freshman"?

The problem occurs when our writing and speaking becomes affected. Perhaps the best measure of affection in communication is a paraphrase of the famous French philosopher Rousseau. He felt it unfortunate that we should have more words than ideas; that we should be able to say more than we think. Unaffected communication, then, occurs when we have more ideas than words; when we think more than we communicate; when we do not thoroughly grasp our ideas. If you do not let your words outstrip your ideas, you will find it much easier to communicate your ideas. Words usage should cherish reality, not rape it.

Negation

Much has been written about the double negative; so much so that little more need be said about it. Less has been written about the use of the simple negation. Communication of negative thoughts is more difficult to understand. Consider the following examples:

> *Negation*: I don't really enjoy my work.
> *Positive*: I dislike my work.

While both sentences are understandable, psychological research indicates it takes much longer to understand and comprehend negatively expressed ideas. Furthermore, the first sentence is much weaker than the second one; just because I don't enjoy my work doesn't mean I dislike it—I might feel neutral toward it. It is better practice to state your thoughts forthrightly than to leave them ambiguously hidden behind a negation.

Detail and preciseness

In the same manner that you want to rely on active constructions to make your writing more effective, you will find that detail and precision help your style. To paraphrase Mark Twain, the difference between precision and vagueness is the difference between lightning and a lightning bug. Lewis Carroll's Humpty Dumpty may say that a word means nothing more nor nothing less than whatever he wants it to mean, but such tautological imprecision does not go far in effective writing. Effective writing requires a love of words; my favorite wordsmith, the late poet John Ciardi, wrote a number of books on the crafting of words, and their meanings and origins that are both entertaining and educational for the novice writer. I recommend that you start with a good thesaurus and dictionary to help search for more precise words, and finish with such knowledgeable sources as Ciardi on the details of words.

Compare the differences in the following pairs of sentences for detail and precision:

> *General/Vague*: Lawson found men and women perceive unusual names differently from usual names.
> *Detailed/Precise*: Lawson found men and women perceive unusual names as less desirable, weaker, and more passive than usual names.
> *General/Vague*: CB handles were coded independently.
> *Detailed/Precise*: Two coders independently content analyzed and coded CB handles.

The first of each pair of sentences is much easier to understand. Nevertheless, although "less desirable, weaker, and more passive" aids clarification of the word "different" in the top sentence, we might still work toward more precision of "usual" and "unusual"; for example, is an unusual name one that is weird, unfamiliar, novel, or what?

Revision

Effective writers are constantly searching for alternative ways to state their case. Wordiness is a sin in our pressure-cooker world. Three general rules of thumb may help you. First, run a pen through every other word you have written. Second, underline words you think are essential to a complex sentence, arrange these in a sensible way, and then add whatever words you need to make a decent sentence. Third, test the essentiality of each word, by deleting it and listening for the sound of the sentence without it.

Copy editors spend much of their time doing exactly these things. They delete words from manuscripts and shift those that are left. Box B–1 shows this process for a later draft of my last text. Become your own editor. The volume of words you like so well probably can be cut in half and rearranged to make your point clearer. At least a dozen great writers have been said to have written: "I apologize for this long letter; I didn't have enough time to shorten it."

Special reporting styles

Advice given to this juncture has been applicable to writing in general. However, scientific writing often has special requirements. Some professional societies have published guidelines on writing: the American Psychological Association's *Publication Manual*, Modern Language Association's *MLA Guide*, and the University of Chicago's *Handbook of English*. Unfortunately, although there has been much talk about standardizing research-reporting conventions and style in sociology, the American Sociological Association has not yet published a guide. However at least once a year both of the two major journals in the field, the *American Sociological Review* and the *American Journal of Sociology* publish a short guide for contributors with information on margins, quotations, references, headings, and abbreviations. You may find these style guides of help in writing research reports. I also recommend that you copy a model article from any journal in which you are interested and examine its particular style. Feinstein (1960: 408) humorously proposes 12 basic rules of English the humor of which you would be well to review and understand:

1. Don't use no double negatives.
2. Make each pronoun agree with their antecedent.
3. Join clauses good, like a conjunction should.
4. About them sentence fragments.
5. When dangling, watch them participles.
6. Verbs has to agree with their subject.

Box B-1 *An Example of a Revised Paragraph*

The ancient Greeks ~~had a~~ word <u>zetetic</u>, meaning <u>inquiring skeptic</u>, ~~which~~ fits the posture of good science. Skepticism is not, despite popular misconceptions, a point of view. ~~It is~~ an essential component of intellectual inquiry, a method of determining the facts whatever they may be and wherever they may lead. It is part of the way science works ~~All who are~~ Anybody interested in the search for knowledge and the advancement of understanding ˄ support critical inquiry of this nature.   must

Source: Final draft of Smith (1987:2)

7. Just between you and I, case is important, too.
8. Don't write run-on sentences they are hard to read.
9. Don't use commas, that are not necessary.
10. Try to not ever split infinitives.
11. Its important to use your apostrophe's correctly.
12. Proofread your writing to see if you any words out.

Here's to better sounding words in your ear!

Summary

The point of good writing is accurate communication of information. Good communication is essential to the scientific research report. First, this requires that you have an ear for the audience with whom you are communicating. The audience should dictate what you say and how you say it. Effective writing and graphics read painlessly. (That's an excellent sign that it was a pain to accomplish.) Expect to struggle with the shaping and polishing of your ideas.

For your writing, this usually means paying attention to such technical details as (1) checking for the active voice, (2) breaking up complex and lengthy thoughts, (3) not taking vocabulary and jargon for granted, (4) avoiding negations, (5) striving for detail and precision, and (6) assuming that what you have created can be better stated through revision. I cannot overemphasize the revision process. Although technical details are important, a rough outline and drafts are necessary first steps, because without them, you have nothing to shape into a more polished product. The shape of the final product is best achieved through careful imagining and anticipation of one's audiences, making generalities come alive with specific details, and attention to readability.

A P P E N D I X

The Proper Display of Data

By orthodox methods, numerical data limit what the mind can encompass or a computer digest and present in reasonable time. However, more data can be comprehended if the information is converted from numbers into an image (three dimensions) in motion (time, a fourth). The computer's use of color makes it five dimensions from which the eye extracts information.[1]

Key Terms

Analytic graphic

Bar chart

Box plot

Dot chart

Innumeracy

Masking

Pie chart

Probability plot

Presentational graphic

Quantile-quantile plot

Three-dimensional scatterplot

---

[1]Cromie, W. J. (1988) Computer images in five dimensions. *Mosaic, 19*, p. 17.

Study Guide Questions

1. Defend the statement that a picture is worth a thousand words.

2. What are the basic differences between presentational and analytic graphics?

3. Why isn't the pie chart normally an effective way to convey percentages?

4. What perceptional limitations does the simple bar chart share with the pie chart?

5. How do the box plot and dot chart improve on visual clarity?

6. How can quantile-quantile plots improve upon traditional scatterplots? The probability plot upon bar graphs?

7. What techniques aid clarification of three-dimensional scatterplots? How?

8. Is color normally recommended for visual clarity in graphics? Why or why not?

9. Use figure C-7 to illustrate why tables may need more graphic replacements.

10. What are the main problems and advantages of scientific use of photographs?

11. List and explain the six fundamental errors of scientific graphing that Cleveland found.

All visual displays should encourage the viewer to think about the substance of research. Although to say "A picture is worth a thousand words" is a worn expression, there is much truth to this statement. Visual representations may aid understanding where words fail to describe adequately. Nevertheless, some journals and scientific disciplines devote little attention to graphic display of data. Cleveland and McGill (1984) surveyed 57 journals in 14 disciplines, and found that the publication with the most graphics was the *Journal of Geophysical Research* which devoted a third of its space to graphs. The journal with the least graphs in the group was the *Journal of Social Psychology*, which devoted only 0.001% of its space to graphs. The median amount of space given over to graphs was 10% in physical-science journals, 5% in mathematics and statistics journals, and 4% in the social-science journals he reviewed.

Until the 1980s, there was remarkably infrequent research into how to prepare good visual representations of data with a goal of understanding by highly heterogeneous audiences. However, as with written presentation, visual representation requires care and attention. Cleveland and McGill carefully examined 377 graphs from the most prestigious American journal, *Science*. They report that 30% of those graphs contained at least one error. Their survey led them to ask what it is that makes some graphs better than others in displaying data, and to devise guidelines for more effective use of graphs. Their method was to sit and look at graphs, and think very hard about what exactly are the elements that contain quantitative information. Then they asked study participants from such diverse groups as high-school students, housewives, and scientists to look at those graphs. Finally, they asked their viewers questions that forced them to focus on such very basic perceptual tasks as judging slopes of lines and areas. Out of such studies, two academicians (Cleveland 1985; Tufte 1983) have written landmark analyses of how scientists, journalists, and others often inadequately display quantitative data in scientific publications, and each has suggested simple means of improvement.

This section focuses upon principles for clear presentation of data that such researchers as Cleveland and Tufte have discovered. Just as a writer has responsibility for clarifying written ideas, a researcher ought to consider how to clarify data with such visual aids as graphs, charts, tabulations, diagrams, or photographs. Kruskal (1981:513) cogently argues that graphics and tabulations are the unshod Cinderellas of statistics. This section is based upon ideas for separating the Cinderellas of data presentation from their ugly sisters.

Graphics

According to an old saying, there are lies, damned lies, and statistics. But even when statistics do not "lie," they may be hard for readers to interpret. The purposes of graphic presentation should be to help uncover trends, summarize large blocks of data, and aid in interpreting data to others. However, mindless or careless use of graphics may obscure the attainment of such goals. Just as some writing is illiterate, some data display may be innumerate (numeric illiteracy). I have witnessed laypersons struggle with graphs and tables drawn up by supposedly professional social scientists who used such inconsistent "syntax" and poor layout, that those tables were nearly impossible to read. The clear presentation of data must follow rules of construction, just as good written expression does, if it is to turn dry statistics into clear analytical displays and strong presentations. Cleveland's main thesis is well taken: Scientists should not ask their audience to put up with inaccurate graphs or graphs whose data are nearly impossible to understand.

Presentational Graphics

The first decision the researcher needs to make is which of two basic graphic purposes his or her results will follow: presentational or analytical. Presentational graphics are used for communicating simple—usually univariate and categorical—results to others. Businessmen, for example, like to use simple bar charts and pie graphs, but such techniques are not analytical tools—they are used to persuade people.

If you want to use presentational graphics to persuade others, you ought to consider that the type of graphics most used by business—the pie chart—is *not* usually an effective way to convey percentages. Data are encoded on a pie chart as wedges with larger wedges representing larger percentages, but Cleveland (1985) has shown that visual perceptions of relative wedge sizes are consistently inaccurate unless the wedge differences (see Figure C–1) are grossly disproportionate; comparing the sizes of angles, areas, or wedges in a pie chart is not a particularly easy task when the differences are slight to moderate. In other words, Cleveland discovered that any graphic presentation that requires the reader to estimate area or angle size is difficult to read, especially if the differences are small.

Newspapers, magazines, and business presentations often use other equally demanding graphics. For example, maps of the United States with circles drawn in proportion to the amount of population of cities (large circles for large cities; small circles for small cities). Cleveland, Harris, and McGill (1982) have shown that circle size on maps are not perceived on a linear scale. Other types of graphics that tax perceptions are the area of stack graphs. Compare the three graphs in Figure C–2 with the less perceptually demanding graph in Figure C–3: The pie chart needs the percentages for the viewer to make accurate comparisons, leading us to believe we could just as well give only a percentage table and not use a pie chart. For example, the visual difference between the 26.74% and 28.7% wedges is indistinguishable. Furthermore, several narrow wedges, such as the one shown in the 10% pie wedge in Figure C–1, are difficult to label. The area and stack graphs share these same problems as well as having one final major problem: They do not have easy baselines for comparing areas. As with other psychological stimuli, seeing may be deceiving. The

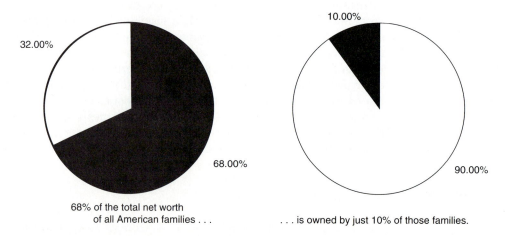

68% of the total net worth
of all American families . . .   . . . is owned by just 10% of those families.

Figure C-1.   Pie chart of the distribution of American wealth.

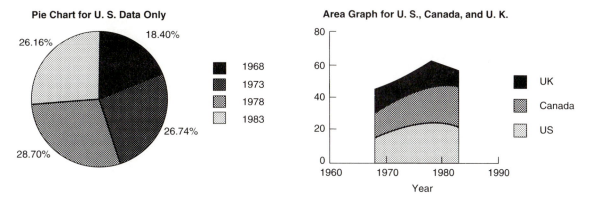

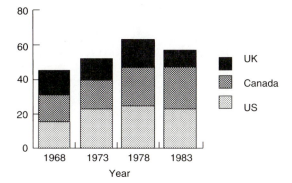

Figure C-2. Pie, area, and stack graphs for some hypothetical data (expressed in percentages).

solutions to these presentational graphic demands are simple: Pick a form of representation the viewer can perceive accurately, and do not try to graph too much. Happily, professional scientists rarely make graphs requiring estimates of areas.

Simple bar charts are somewhat less prone to perceptual error than pie, or other areal-type, charts. But they share other limitations along with pie charts: they can display only a relatively small amount of univariate and categorical data. Bars or pie wedges that number more than five place increasingly heavy demands on perceptual comparisons. They also place demands on accurate readings of percentages—to verify these problems try reading Figure C–2 without using the accompanying percentages (displayed in Figure C–3). Further, neither method allows for easy comparison of two or more variables, yet science is ultimately interested in the *relationships* between variables for which simple bar charts or pie charts will not do.

The advent of personal computers allows the generation of a wide selection of graphs of statistical data, many of which far outstrip the visual clarity of the traditionally popular pie charts and bar charts. Cleveland (1985) and Tufte (1983) give relatively complete lists and examples of numerous graphical inventions. Following are only two examples that can accurately display quan-

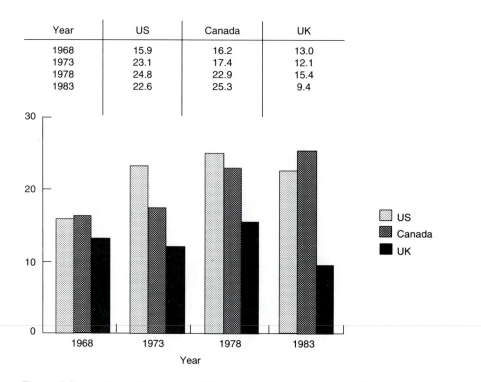

Year	US	Canada	UK
1968	15.9	16.2	13.0
1973	23.1	17.4	12.1
1978	24.8	22.9	15.4
1983	22.6	25.3	9.4

Figure C-3. A simple bar graph and hypothetical raw data used in Figure C-2 (expressed in percentages).

titative information visually—the dot chart and the box plot—to whet your appetite for exploring Cleveland's and Tufte's classic work on graphics.

The *dot chart* is constructed with two intersecting lines perpendicular to one another. The horizontal line or axis is the scale for data. The vertical line lists names for each object to be compared. Corresponding with each object named is a filled circle drawn along the horizontal axis at the appropriate numeric level. A dotted line connects each circle to the corresponding category named on the vertical axis. The dot chart makes category labeling easy, and quantitative data are shown on a single common scale which aids clarity. One final advantage is worth noting: A dot plot, unlike a bar chart, makes sense when the left-hand end of the horizontal axis is not zero.

Part of Figure C–4 illustrates a dot chart for some of the world-crisis data supplied to you through your instructor's teaching package; it plots the annual population increase for selected areas of the world. Note that East African countries are growing at 3.6% each year, which means it will take roughly only 20 years for them to double their population at that rate; at the other extreme are Northern European countries, with virtually no population growth.

Although differences and similarities in average rates are clearly shown in a dot graph, it might be more informative if we could compare regions by various measures of variation. The multiple box plot does precisely that. The

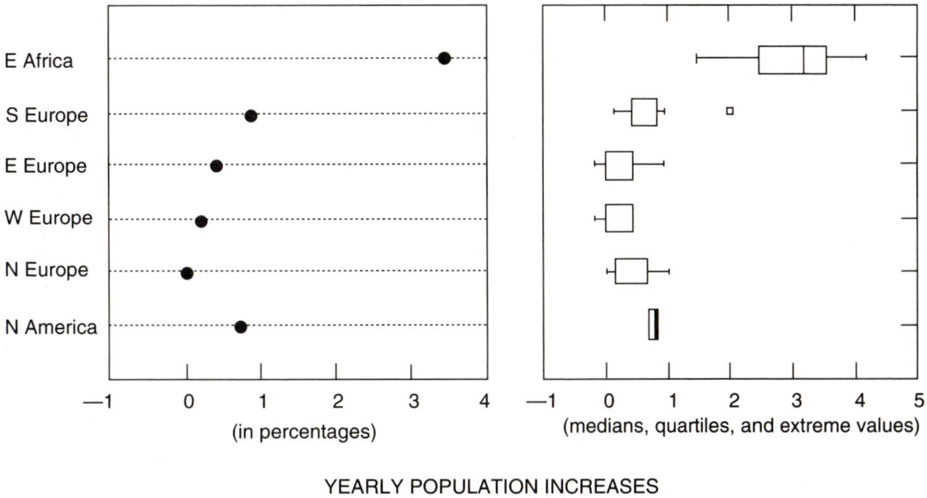

Figure C-4. A dot graph (left) and grouped box plot (right) comparison of annual population growth rates by selected regions of the world.

multiple box plot is a powerful way of comparatively displaying distributions: The vertical lines in the middle of each box plots medians (half the values lie above and below this point), the ends of each box represent the interquartile values (which splits each half of the values again), and the end "fences" represent the lowest and highest points of "normal" values. Two types of *outliers* (extreme values) are plotted: those outside the inner fences with asterisks, and values outside the outer fences with empty circles.

The multiple *box plot* shown in Figure C–4 is much more interesting than the accompanying dot graphs. For instance, the outlier (representing Albania) on the right side of Southern Europe must draw the mean value—displayed as 1% on the dot graph—considerably out from other Southern European countries, which have a median growth rate of just one-half of a percentage point each year. Note also that Eastern African states not only have the highest median growth rate, but they also have an enormous range of annual population increase—from 1.5% to 4.2%. The visual display of range in this box plot is much more informative, and so, is more interesting than the mean display shown in the dot graph.

Analytic Graphics

Analytic graphics are scientific: Nearly all such graphs use multivariate data sets which contain numerous data points. Unlike presentational graphics, which normally only display categorical data for one variable, analytic graphics can depict relationships between categorically or continuously distributed data for two or more variables. The analyst's objective is to reduce visual complexity and to clarify visual the *relationships* among variables without distorting the data's story.

Most laypersons have been introduced to simple *scatterplots* that show the relationship of each pair of values for two variables. A simple scatterplot may visualize the relative association between two variables. For good reasons, two-dimensional scatterplots are the method of choice to check data for the presence or absence of unusual and not so unusual features such as outliers, clusters, and nonlinearity.

Better yet, researchers may employ some simple statistical transformations in a scattergram-like graphic known as a *quantile-quantile plot* to compare distributions of two sets of measurements. The idea is extremely simple. For example, in a true experiment, one might administer a treatment to some group of subjects and a placebo to a control group. Then one would administer some posttest. In a traditional test for effects, one would end by comparing the average posttest scores for each group. However, with a quantile-quantile plot, the researcher depicts a display of all the aspects of the distribution of both sets of measurements.

The idea is to take the median of one of the group's posttest scores, and plot it against the median of the other group's. Then plot the 75 percentile of one group against the 75th percentile of the other group, then the 25th percentile of one against the other and so on. In the end, the investigator will pick out a variety of different percentiles and, in each case plot one group's value against that of the other group. The way the resulting data behave reveals much about the data. If the points lie along the line x = y, then the two populations are identical. As the data depart from that line, additional information comes to light. For example, if the points lie along a straight line with slope of 1.6, then the high values in one group are always 60% greater than the high values in the other group, the low values in that group are also 60% greater and, in fact, the whole distribution of values in that group are 60% greater than in the other group. We could conclude that the experimental treatment caused this increase.

Figure C–5 illustrates the above principles for nonexperimental data: the annual population growth of all United Nations-member countries by an index of human suffering that measures ten variables including such variables as rates of infant mortality, inflation, adult literacy, and access to clean drinking water. This scattergram plot shows a very high correlation (r = .83) between population growth and the human suffering index. Also note that the line of best prediction and .95% confidence intervals are drawn for all 130 nations. The line of best fit for predicting human suffering from the yearly population increase (SUFFERNG = 12.33 + 19.17 * (YRPOPINC)) also adds information of importance: Every percentage point added to the annual birth rate increases the 100-point human suffering index by slightly over 19 points!

The quantile-quantile plot adds the visual confirmation that both variables come from data with similar distributions, because it is remarkably straight. The slope for this data plot is .83; that is, the distribution of points for the standardized yearly population index are 17% less than those for the standardized human suffering. Therefore, we conclude that the relationship be-

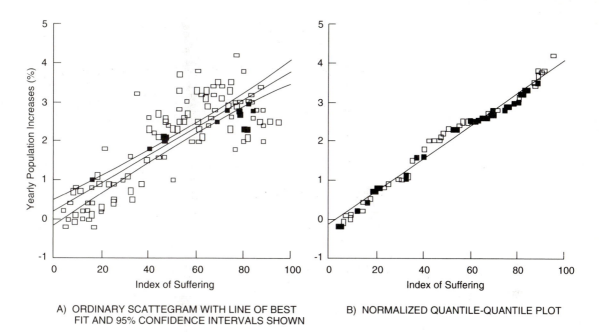

A) ORDINARY SCATTEGRAM WITH LINE OF BEST
FIT AND 95% CONFIDENCE INTERVALS SHOWN

B) NORMALIZED QUANTILE-QUANTILE PLOT

Figure C-5. An ordinary scattergram versus a quantile-quantile plot of yearly population increases (in percentages) of United Nations-member countries by an index of human suffering.

tween each variable is linear, and the human suffering increases roughly one-sixth faster than does the yearly population increase on a standardized scale.

Researchers often use histograms (a continuous variable version of the bar graph) to visualize whether the data is normally distributed. However, histograms are poor means of judging how normally distributed data are. Instead of the traditional histogram, some statisticians recommend an informative variation of the quantile-quantile plot known as a *probability plot*. A probability plot displays the raw values of a variable against corresponding percentage points of a standard normal distribution. The idea is quite simple and clever: If the joint values of the data variable plotted against the normal distribution lie on a straight line, then the researcher may feel comfortable that the actual data are normally distributed; if not, the converse is true.

Figure C–6 illustrates one final example of the possibilities of the new graphics technology: *three-dimensional scatterplots* of multivariate relationships. Three-dimensional scatterplots are a good way of data representation, because as they are transparent, and the front parts do not hide the back parts they may assist in visualizing higher-dimensional structures. However, these types of graphics are so simple to make with present graphics software technology that it is easy to get carried away and overwhelm the reader's perceptual skills with graphic clutter. Therefore, three-dimensional plots need much more careful construction. Indeed, quite often the researcher might better use one or more clear two-dimensional plots rather than a more complicated multidimensional one to illustrate his or her case.

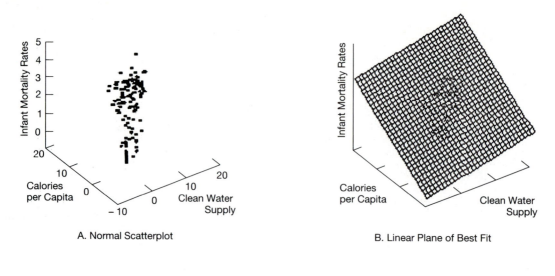

A. Normal Scatterplot

B. Linear Plane of Best Fit

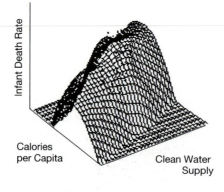

C. Nonlinear Function Plot

C-6

Figure C-6.   Three-dimensional plots of infant mortality rates per 1,000 live births by daily per capita calorie supply as percent of requirement and percent of population with access to clean drinking water: (a) normal plot; (b) linear plane of best fit; and (c) nonlinear function.

As with two-dimensional scatterplots three-dimensional ones may aid the quick identification of outliers and clusters or other unusual structures. How-ever, the raw presentation of data in a three-dimensional plot can furnish dis-tracting cues to our visual system; loading more information into a single plot than we can handle simultaneously can be counterproductive. One aid is to rotate the viewing angle until one can see the whole structure better. Because we are dealing with three-dimensional structures plotted on a two-dimensional space, this is equivalent to walking around the object to take in each side.

Nevertheless, one tends to view a three-dimensional point cloud in relation to itself rather than in relation to coordinate axes. Throughout this text, I have stressed the interaction of variables. Three-dimensional plots are good at illustrating interaction of variables only if one can rotate the graph until one obtains a clear three-dimensional view. Huber (1987:451) has listed some nice tricks for clearer visualization of a cloud of points in a three-dimensional scatterplot. First, he suggests that to use *masking*—moving a hyperplane through the data space, extinguishing (or illuminating) points when they are hit by a plane—is not helpful. However, Huber suggest *slicing*—illuminating all points between two hyperplanes—which adds sorting out categories on a black-and-white screen and helps find empty regions in a scatterplot. Second, switching back and forth between two related views may give helpful comparisons. Third, such *enhancements* as lines, symbols, text, and colors are more important to three-dimensional plots than their two-dimensional relatives.

I have plotted infant mortality rates in Figure C–6 by the daily per capita calorie supply as a percent of requirement and the percent of each nation's population with access to clean drinking water. The normal three-dimensional plot is difficult to read, as one would expect, but it does show a fairly narrow range of scatter over the two horizontal axes (Calories per Capita and Clean Water Supply) and a much broader scatter for the vertical (Infant Death Rate). The plane of best fit plot clarifies the effects of caloric needs and clean water supply on infant death rates. Note how the angle for Clean Water Supply is almost twice as steep as that for Calories per Capita. This suggests that, although both contribute to infant mortality, lack of access to clean water affects infant mortality rates almost twice as much as lack of adequate nutrients. Indeed, this accords with UNESCO data indicating that some 80% of morbidity (disease) and mortality (death) rates are directly attributable to waterborne carriers.

Finally, the third portion of Figure C–6 shows a locally smoothed nonlinear portrayal of the relationship between Infant Death Rate, Calories per Capita, and Clean Water Supply, to illustrate the power of nonlinear computing for enhancing the study of natural phenomena on their own beguiling nonlinear terms. The father of modern computations, von Neumann, emphasized that only a few phenomena can be described by a linear model, one in which a given input produces a proportionate output. Von Neumann's argument is shown quite clearly in this third part, which visually shows the more complex, tentlike nature of the influence of calories and water supply on infant death rates than does a plane of best fit.

Nevertheless, this type of graph raises at least as many questions as it answers. For example, the "mesh floor" of the tent would appear to represent values of water and caloric supply that have no influence on infant death rates while the "ceiling" area might represent average combined effects of caloric and water supply on infant deaths. But the ceiling ridge for all three variables rises which is counterintuitive; that is, why would infant death rates rise with a rise in both caloric and water supply unless maldistribution problems occur in wealthier countries? Indeed, the plane of best fit graphic seems much more intuitively appealing than the nonlinear one in this particular case. But the nonlinear one still better represents the complex interaction of all three variables.

In sum, these types of methods may help us understand depth and complex structure, because of the huge amount of data that can be visually represented. A billion numbers is not comprehensible in tabular form; graphics are needed to extract a meaningful pattern from them. But the researcher using graphics needs to carefully determine which form produces the clearest picture to better extract meaning.

Tabulations

Although tables are by far the most common form of quantitative data presentation in the social sciences, they are to some extent an ugly sister of Cinderella. Consider for a moment the workhorse of tabulations known as the percentage table. With only two variables—religion (divided into Catholic, Protestant, Jewish, and other) and race (black, white, other), there are already a total of 12 cells. If we wished to break that table down by a third variable, sex of respondent, we now must consider various comparisons between 24 cells. When we add new variables, the number of cells grows multiplicatively, so that even experts have difficulty managing tabular analysis. For this reason, statisticians grapple with discovering new ways to present tabular analysis, or to ransack tables for the meanings inherent in them. Some methods of tabular analysis are quite simple: One simply uses some agreed upon measure of association to reduce the complexity within the table to a single summary figure. Other methods are complex beyond the scope of an introductory text, and involve relatively esoteric approaches and require advanced statistical work.

Whatever the approach used in analysis, the purpose is always to reveal patterns in data. Ironically, many of the newer, more esoteric, approaches to data analysis end up with difficult-to-interpret solutions. Part of the problem is that many forms of tabular analysis, while having the virtue of presenting many numbers in a small space, do not efficiently make large data sets coherent, encourage the eye to compare different pieces of data, or reveal the data at different levels of detail. Anscombe (1973) presents an interesting tabular paradox of four data sets that illustrates the above tabular problem. Each of the following four sets of data has the same number of values, x, a, c, and e mean values are all equal to 9.0, y, b, d, and e mean values are all 7.5, the lines of prediction for each right-hand variable from each left-hand one is $Y = 3 = 0.5X$, and all four correlation coefficients are .82. Nevertheless, they differ markedly in ways that can best be described with simple scatterplots shown in Figure C–7. The moral is that we ought sometimes to consider other means than tabular analysis to more clearly present data.

	I		II	III			IV
x	y	a	b	c	d	e	f
10.0	8.04	10.0	9.14	10.0	7.46	8.0	6.58
8.0	6.95	8.0	8.14	8.0	6.77	8.0	5.76
13.0	7.58	13.0	8.74	13.0	12.74	8.0	7.71
9.0	8.81	9.0	8.77	9.0	7.11	8.0	8.84
11.0	8.33	11.0	9.26	11.0	7.81	8.0	8.47
14.0	9.96	14.0	8.10	14.0	8.84	8.0	7.04
6.0	7.24	6.0	6.13	6.0	6.08	8.0	5.25
4.0	4.26	4.0	3.10	4.0	5.39	19.0	12.50
12.0	10.84	12.0·	9.13	12.0	8.15	8.0	5.56
7.0	4.82	7.0	7.26	7.0	6.42	8.0	7.91
5.0	5.68	5.0	4.74	5.0	5.73	8.0	6.89

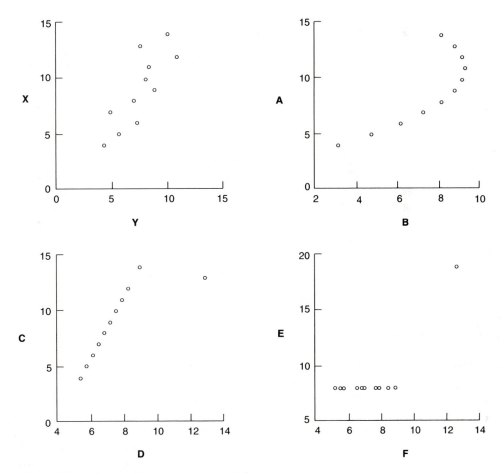

Figure C-7. Graphic Display of Anscombe's Quartet.

Source: Adapted from Anscombe (1973:17–21)

Photographs and Line Drawings

During the formative stages of sociology, sociologists use many more line drawings and photographs than they do presently. Becker (1986a) found that *American Journal of Sociology* articles from the 1890s through the 1910s typically used photographs to accompany articles, but this practice quickly died out as sociologists became concerned about the "scientific nature" of their discipline. This concern was clearly unfounded: Such respected journals as *Science* have long used photographs extensively to clarify data.

Becker (1986a) and Goffman (1976) have been instrumental in bringing photographs back into social-scientific analysis. One of the fascinating accounts Becker gives of this process is that of Margaret Mead and her then-husband Gregory Bateson's photographic essay on Balinese culture. Because neither of them could agree on what they ought to focus on, they each focused their cameras on quite different social phenomena. The result was a richer view of Balinese culture than we would otherwise have, but it raises questions concerning what the researcher ought to record.

The main problem with scientific use of photographs resides in their subjective nature. Photographs do not stand by themselves; they need interpretation. Just as with other visual presentation techniques, photographs need clear captions that clue the viewer into the photo's context. The editors of *Science* use a different scientific photograph without caption on each issue's weekly cover; but they also include a caption on the accompanying title page. Subscribers often write in to express their delight at being fooled by photos they thought they understood—until they read the caption. Viewers beware: Photographs do not speak for themselves. As with other graphics, photographs need attention to clear, precise, unabbreviated, but short explanations.

Whether one uses photographs or line drawings to illustrate data, their purpose is to assist the reader in comprehension of concepts that are difficult or impossible to express with words. Poizner, Klima, and Bellugi (1987) use the line drawing below to differentiate left-hemisphere damaged and right-hemisphere damaged patients. Although it is possible without such diagrams to express that right-hemisphere damaged patients have the kinds and severity of problems, this type of visual information is highly informative in ways that words can not express.

Some Basic Rules

Cleveland (1985) darkly concluded, from his study of scientific graphics in *Science*, that on the whole, scientists make at least *six fundamental errors* in their choice of graphs and in their techniques of graphic display. First, over 15% of the graphs he studied *left out needed explanatory materials*. Whether we consider such qualitative graphics as photographs or quantitative graphics like scatterplots, the data do not speak for themselves. We need to pay attention to providing material that aids the reader in interpreting our display of data. Second, in over 10% of the graphs, *either the graphic design or size interfered with*

GG's DRAWING
WITHOUT MODEL

MODEL

GG's DRAWING
WITH MODEL

Illustration.   Poizner et al. 1987 Right-lesioned Gilbert G.'s drawings with and without a model. Gilbert G.'s drawings do not show the same degree of impairment as those of the other right-lesioned signers.

visual discrimination of data or symbols displayed. The desire to provide too much visual information is too small a space is a common problem. Techniques for reducing visual clutter are needed to reduce perceptual demands. Third, *mistakes in graphic construction*—incorrectly spaced tick marks, mislabeled items, omitted items, wrong scales—contributed another 6% of errors. Fourth, *poor reproduction of graphs or partially missing graphics* contributed another 6% of errors that Cleveland noted. Each of these four errors are technical problems that simple guidelines, paralleling those for writing syntax, can eliminate. In fact, some popular computer software, such as the one used to produce many of the graphics in this appendix, all but eliminate these errors. For example, many of these graphics programs include intelligent scaling, positioning, and plotting routines that will not permit variable labels to collide or overlap with each other when large numbers of categories are plotted, because the programs automatically chose cutpoints and plotting scales. More importantly, such programs make it easy for the user to create such graphs as three-dimensional pie charts and perspective bar graphs, without distorting information and eliciting well-known visual illusions.

More serious, however, are the final two problems Cleveland uncovered: *poorly chosen graphical form or quantitative information.* Too often, graphics users have allowed themselves to be seduced by popular or traditional methods of data presentation, rather than searching for graphic forms that best reveal data. After all, *the primary function of graphics is to visually clarify* rather than obscure data. The diligent data analyst, as with the assiduous writer, unflaggingly toys with better means of explaining data. Such electronic media as personal computers with graphic capabilities, laser printers, and pen plotters have made high-quality graphic images affordable and easy to use, even for individuals without graphics experience. The data analyst may explore numerous alternative methods for displaying data with relatively little time and effort.

Statistical graphic programs are becoming more interactive. It is possible to sit in front of a computer terminal and flip through tens or hundreds of images until you find the one that works. This component of the information revolution makes possible graphs that, while too tedious to draw by hand, reveal data as they have never before been revealed. A well-designed graphic that reveals data will get much more attention than one that is difficult to comprehend. Indeed, the explosion of graphic capacity may produce new problems if users are not careful. It is easy to forget that high resolution and clarity of data are important, while color and flair are not. As with good writing, graphical aesthetics searches for simplicity.

Summary

There are two generic types of graphics: presentational and analytic. Whichever type you chose, clear graphics may aid your communication process: They may reveal data through presenting many numbers in a small space, encouraging comparison of different data, or expressing patterns difficult to describe with words. As with good writing, which pays attention to the reader's ear, good graphics pays attention to the viewer's eye. Seek graphic designs that clearly and accurately reduce complexity for your viewer.

Poorly designed graphics make it harder rather than easier for the viewer to understand. Particularly troublesome are graphics that require the viewer to make judgments of size of area, particularly where differences are small, or judgments without standard scale. Many older graphic techniques, such as the pie chart and bar chart, make unnecessary demands on the viewer's perceptions of areal size, while ordinary scatterplots and histograms lack useful scale information. Such graphic inventions as the dot chart, stem-and-leaf diagrams, and quantile-quantile plots often overcome such problems. In the final analysis, just as writers must play with words, sentences, and paragraphs to arrive at clearer presentation of their ideas, researchers need to play with their graphic presentations until the form of their data becomes most clearly apparent.

If you work at these basic principles, the more special conventions of reporting and research style will simply be ornaments on a diamond. Once you have established that you have something to say or to display, and established that you can do so clearly, the battle is largely won. This is not to discredit standardized reporting conventions, because they are important. But they can easily be checked against the style sheets of various professions and journals. You can either memorize or refer to them. There are no ten commandments for effective communication. That comes only from honest blood, sweat, and tears; but then, effective communication cures indigestion of the mind.

A P P E N D I X

MYSTAT ®

MYSTAT Version 2.1

An instructional version of SYSTAT

SYSTAT, Inc.
1800 Sherman Avenue
Evanston, IL 60201
Tel. 708.**864.5670**
FAX 708.**492.3567**

Introduction

This is a real statistics program—it is not just a demonstration. You can use MYSTAT to enter, transform, and save data, and to perform a wide range of statistical evaluations. Please use MYSTAT to solve *real* problems.

MYSTAT is a fully operational subset of SYSTAT, our premier statistics package. We've geared MYSTAT especially for teaching, with descriptive statistics, cross-tabulation, Pearson and Spearman correlation coefficients, regression, ANOVA, nonparametric tests, and graphics all in a single, easy-to-use package.

An instructional business version of MYSTAT is also available. MYSTAT has special forecasting and time series routines in addition to most of the regular MYSTAT features.

Both versions of MYSTAT are available in Macintosh, IBM-PC/compatible, and VAX/VMS versions. Copies are available at a nominal cost.

For more information about SYSTAT, SYGRAPH, and our other top-rated professional statistics and graphics packages, please call or write.

655

Installation MYSTAT requires 256K of RAM and a floppy or hard disk drive. It can handle up to 50 variables and up to 32,000 cases.

Your MYSTAT disk contains three files: MYSTAT.EXE (the program), MYSTAT.HLP (a file with information for on-line help), and DEMO.CMD (a demonstration that creates a data file and demonstrates some of MYSTAT's features).

Hard disk ### *Set up the CONFIG.SYS file*
The CONFIG.SYS file in your root directory must have a line that says FILES=20. If you don't have a CONFIG.SYS file, you can create one with the COPY CON command:

```
>CD \
>COPY CON CONFIG.SYS
FILES=20
[F6]
```

Press the Enter key after each line to tell the computer to start working. Nothing happens until you press Enter. (On some keyboards, the key is marked Return or with a ⏎ symbol.)

After typing "FILES=20" and pressing Enter, press the F6 key and then press Enter. F6 signals the computer that you are done writing to CONFIG.SYS, so you get another DOS prompt (>).

Set up the AUTOEXEC.BAT file
The AUTOEXEC.BAT file in the root directory must have the following PATH line. You can create an AUTOEXEC.BAT file with the following commands. Remember to press Enter at the end of each line.

```
>COPY CON AUTOEXEC.BAT
PATH=C:\;C:\SYSTAT
[F6]
```

Reboot your machine

Copy the files on the MYSTAT disk into a \SYSTAT directory
Now, make a \SYSTAT directory, insert the MYSTAT disk in drive A, and copy the MYSTAT files into the directory. (You must have the help file in the same directory as MYSTAT.EXE. If you put MYSTAT.EXE in a directory other than \SYSTAT, the help file MYSTATB.HLP must be either in that directory or the \SYSTAT directory.)

```
>MD \SYSTAT
>CD \SYSTAT
>COPY A:*.*
```

You are now ready to begin using MYSTAT. From now on, all you need to do to get ready to use MYSTAT is boot and move (CD) into the \SYSTAT directory. Save your MYSTAT master disk as a back up copy.

Floppy disk **Boot your machine**
Insert a "boot disk" into drive A. Close the door of the disk drive and turn on the machine.

Set up a CONFIG.SYS file on your boot disk
The boot disk must contain a file named CONFIG.SYS with a line FILES=20. If you don't have such a file, type the following lines when you get a DOS prompt (>).

```
>COPY CON CONFIG.SYS
FILES=20
[F6]
```

Press the Enter key at the end of every line to tell the computer to start working. Nothing happens until you press Enter. (On some keyboards this key is marked Return or with a ↵ symbol.)

After typing "FILES=20" and pressing Enter, press the F6 key and then press Enter. F6 signals the computer that you are done writing to CONFIG.SYS, so you get another DOS prompt (>).

Set up an AUTOEXEC.BAT file on your boot disk
The boot disk must also contain a file named AUTOEXEC.BAT with a line PATH=A:\;B:\. You can create one as follows:

```
>COPY CON AUTOEXEC.BAT
PATH=A:\;B:\
[F6]
```

Reboot your machine

Make a copy of the MYSTAT disk
When you get a DOS prompt (>), remove the boot disk. Put the MYSTAT disk in drive A and a blank, formatted disk in drive B and type the COPY command at the prompt:

```
>COPY A:*.* B:
```

Remove the master disk from drive A and store it. If anything happens to your working copy, use the master to make a new copy.

Use MYSTAT
Now, switch your working copy into drive A. If necessary, make drive A the "logged" drive (the drive your machine reads from) by issuing the command A: at the DOS prompt (>).

MYSTAT reads and writes its temporary work files to the currently logged drive. Since there is limited room on the MYSTAT disk, you should read and write all your data, output, and command files from a data disk in drive B.

From now on, all you need to do to use MYSTAT is boot, insert your working copy, and log the A drive.

Getting started

To start, type MYSTAT and press Enter.

```
>MYSTAT
```

When you see the MYSTAT logo, press Enter. You'll see a command menu listing all the commands you can use in MYSTAT.

Command menu

The command menu shows a list of all the commands that are available for MYSTAT. The commands are divided into six groups: information, file handling, miscellaneous, graphics, statistics, and forecasting.

```
MYSTAT --- An Instructional Version of SYSTAT
```

DEMO	EDIT	MENU	PLOT	STATS	MODEL
HELP		NAMES	BOX	TABULATE	CATEGORY
SYSTAT	USE	LIST	HISTOGRAM	TTEST	ANOVA
	SAVE	FORMAT	STEM	PEARSON	COVARIATE
	PUT	NOTE	TPLOT		ESTIMATE
	SUBMIT				
QUIT	OUTPUT	SORT	CHARSET	SIGN	
		RANK		WILCOXON	
		WEIGHT		FRIEDMAN	

As you become more experienced with MYSTAT, you might want to turn the menu off. You can use the MENU command to turn it on and off.

```
>MENU
```

Data Editor

MYSTAT has a built-in Data Editor with its own set of commands. To enter the Editor, use the EDIT command.

```
>EDIT
```

Inside the Editor, you can enter, view, edit, and transform data. When you are done with the Editor, type QUIT to get out of the Editor and back to MYSTAT, where you can do statistical and graphical analyses. To quit MYSTAT itself, type QUIT again.

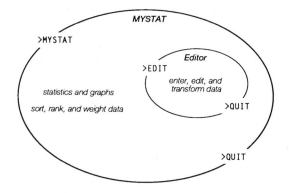

The Data Editor is an independent program inside MYSTAT and has its own commands. Five commands—USE, SAVE, HELP, QUIT, and FORMAT—appear both inside *and* outside the Editor.

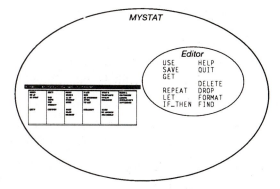

Demo
To see an on-line demonstration of MYSTAT, use the DEMO·command. (Remember to press Enter after you type the command.)

```
>DEMO
```

When the demonstration is finished, MYSTAT returns you to the command menu. After you've seen the demo, you might want to remove the DEMO.CMD file and the CITIES.SYS data file that it creates to save disk space.

Help
The HELP command provides instructions for any command—inside *or* outside the Editor. HELP lists all the commands with brief descriptions.

```
>HELP
```

You can get help for any specific command . For example:

```
>HELP EDIT
EDIT starts the MYSTAT full screen editor.

EDIT [filename]

EDIT     (edit a new file)
EDIT CITIES   (edit CITIES.SYS)

For further information, type EDIT [Enter], [ESC], and then type
HELP [Enter] inside the data editor.
```

The second line shows *a* summary of the command. You see that any EDIT command must begin with the command word EDIT. The brackets indicate that specifying a file is optional. Anything in lowercase, like "filename," is just a placeholder—you should type a real file name (or a real variable name, or whatever).

Customizing DEMO and HELP
All help information is stored in the text file MYSTATB.HLP. You can use a text editor to customize your help information. Similarly, teachers can design special demonstrations by editing the file DEMO.CMD.

Information about SYSTAT
For information about SYSTAT and how to order it, use the SYSTAT command.

Data Editor

The MYSTAT Data Editor lets you enter and edit data, view data, and transform variables. First, we enter data; later, we show you how to use commands.

To use the Editor to create a new file, type EDIT and press Enter. If you already have a MYSTAT data file that you want to edit, specify a filename with the EDIT command.

```
>EDIT [<filename>]
```

If you do not specify a filename, you get an empty Editor like the one above. MYSTAT stores data in a rectangular worksheet. *Variables* fill vertical columns and each horizontal row represents a *case*.

Entering data

First enter variable names in the top row. Variable names *must* be surrounded by single or double quotation marks, must begin with a letter, and can be no longer than 8 characters.

Character variables (those whose values are words and letters) must have names ending with a dollar sign ($). The quotation marks and dollar sign do not count toward the eight character limit.

Numeric variables (those whose values are numbers) can be named with subscripts; e.g., ITEM(3). Subscripts are useful because they allow you to specify a range of variables for analyses. For example, STATS ITEM(1-3) does descriptive statistics on the first three ITEM(*i*) variables.

The cursor is already positioned in the first cell in the top row of the worksheet. Type 'CITY$' or "CITY$" and then press Enter.

MYSTAT enters variable names in upper-case whether you enter them in lower- or upper-case.

The cursor automatically moves to the second column. You are no ready to name the rest of the variables, pressing Enter to store each name in the worksheet.

```
'STATE$'
"POP"
'RAINFALL'
```

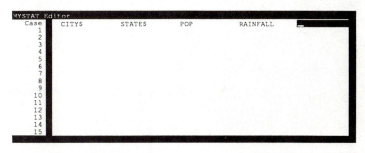

Now you can enter values. Move the cursor to the first blank cell under CITY$ by pressing Home. (On most machines, Home is the 7 key on the numeric keypad. If pressing the 7 key types a 7 rather than moving the cursor, press the NumLock key and try again.)

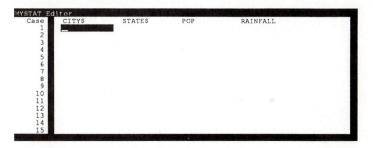

When the cell under CITY$ is selected, enter the first data value:

```
'New York'
```

When you press Enter, MYSTAT accepts the value and moves the cursor to the right. You can also use the cursor arrow keys to move the cursor.

Character values can be no longer than twelve characters. Like variable names, character values must be surrounded by single or double quotation marks. Unlike variable names, character values are case sensitive—upper-case is not the same as lower-case (for example, 'TREE' is not the same as 'tree' or 'Tree'). Enter a blank space surrounded by quotation marks for missing character values. To use single or double quotation marks as part of a value, surround the whole value with the opposite marks.

Numeric values can be up to 10^{35} in absolute magnitude. Scientific notation is used for long numbers; e.g., .000000000015 is equivalent to 1.5E–11. Enter a decimal (.) for missing numeric values.

Enter the first few cases: type a value, press Enter, and type the next value. The cursor automatically moves to the beginning of the next case when a row is filled.

```
   "New York"     "NY"     7164742        57.03
"Los Angeles"     "CA"     3096721         7.81
    "Chicago"     "IL"     2992472        34
(etc.)
```

```
SYSTAT Editor
Case   CITY$         STATE$     POP          RAINFALL
  1    New York        NY     7164742.000      57.030
  2    Los Angeles     CA     3096721.000       7.810
  3    Chicago         IL     2992472.000      34.000
  4    Dallas          TX      974234.000      33.890
  5    Phoenix         AZ      853266.000      14.910
  6    Miami           FL      346865.000      60.020
  7    Washington      DC      638432.000      37.730
  8    Kansas City     MO      448159.000      38.770
  9
 10
 11
 12
 13
 14
 15
```

Moving around

Use the cursor keys on the numeric keypad to move around in the Editor.

Esc		toggle between Editor and command prompt (>)
Home	7	move to first cell in worksheet
↑	8	move upward one cell
PgUp	9	scroll screen up
←	4	move left one cell
→	6	move right one cell
End	1	move to last case in worksheet
↓	2	move down one cell
PgDn	3	scroll screen down

If these keys type numbers rather than move the cursor, press the NumLock key which toggles the keypad back and forth between typing numbers and performing the special functions. (If your computer does not have a NumLock key or something similar, consult the manual that came with your machine.)

Editing data

To change a value or variable name move to the cell you want, type the new value, and press Enter. Remember to enclose character values and variable names in quotation marks.

Data Editor commands

When you have entered your data, press the Esc key to move the cursor to the prompt (>) below the worksheet. You can enter editor commands at this prompt. Commands can be typed in upper- or lower-case. Items in <angle brackets> are placeholders; for instance, you should type a specific filename in place of <filename>.

DELETE and DROP	DELETE lets you remove an entire case (row) from the dataset in the Editor. You can specify a range or list of cases to be deleted. The following are valid DELETE commands.

```
DELETE 3              Deletes third case from dataset.
DELETE 3-10           Deletes cases 3 through 10.
DELETE 3, 5-8, 10     Deletes cases 3, 5, 6, 7, 8, and 10.
```

DROP removes variables from the dataset in the Editor. You can specify several variables or a range of subscripted variables.

```
DROP RAINFALL         Drops RAINFALL from dataset.
DROP X(1-3)           Drops subscripted variables X(1-3).
DROP X(1-3), GROUP$   Drops X(1-3) and GROUP$.
```

Saving files	The SAVE command saves the data in the Editor to a MYSTAT data file. You must save data in a data file before you can analyze them with statistical and graphic commands.

```
SAVE <filename>       Saves data in a MYSTAT file.
  /DOUBLE | SINGLE    Choose single or double precision.
```

MYSTAT filenames can be up to 8 characters long and must begin with a letter. MYSTAT adds a ".SYS" extension that labels the file as a MYSTAT data file. To specify a path name for a file, enclose the entire file name, including the file extension, in single or double quotation marks.

MYSTAT stores data in double-precision by default. You can choose single precision with the SINGLE option if you prefer: add /SINGLE to the end of the command. Always type a slash before command options.

```
SAVE CITIES/SINGLE    Saves CITIES.SYS in single precision
```

Single precision requires approximately half as much disk space as double precision and is accurate to about 9 decimal places. The storage option (single or double precision) does not affect computations, which always use double precision arithmetic (accurate to about 15 places).

```
SAVE CITIES           Creates data file CITIES.SYS.
SAVE b:new            Creates file NEW.SYS on B drive.
SAVE 'C:\DATA\FIL.SYS'  Creates FIL.SYS in \DATA directory of C.
```

You can save data in text files for exporting to other programs with the PUT command. PUT is not an Editor command, though. First QUIT the Editor, USE the data file, and PUT the data to a text file.

Reading files	USE reads a MYSTAT data file into the Editor.

```
USE [<filename>]      Reads data from MYSTAT data file.
```

Starting new data files	Use the NEW command to clear the worksheet and start editing a new data file.

Importing data from other programs

You can import data from other programs through plain text (ASCII) file. ASCII files contain only plain text and numbers—they have no special characters or formatting commands.

Start the program and save your data in a plain ASCII file according to the instructions given by that program's manual. The ASCII file must have a ".DAT" extension, data values must be separated by blanks or commas, and each case must begin on a new line.

Then, start MYSTAT. Use EDIT to get an empty worksheet, and enter variable names in the worksheet for each variable in the ASCII file. Next, use GET to read the text file. Finally, SAVE the data in a MYSTAT file.

```
GET [<filename>]
```
Reads data from ASCII text file.

Finding a case

FIND searches through the Editor starting from the current cursor position, and moves the cursor to the first value that meets the condition you specify. Try this:

```
>FIND POP<1000000
```

This moves the cursor to case 4. After MYSTAT finds a value, use the FIND command without an argument (that is, "FIND" is the entire command) to find the next case meeting the same condition. All functions, relations, and operators listed above are available.

Some valid FIND commands:

```
>FIND AGE>45 AND SEX$='MALE'
>FIND INCOME<10000 AND STATE$='NY'
>FIND (TEST1+TEST2+TEST3)>90
```

Decimal places in the Editor

The FORMAT command specifies the number (0–9) of decimal places to be shown in the Editor. The default is 3. Numbers are stored the way you enter them regardless of the FORMAT setting; FORMAT affects the Editor display only.

```
FORMAT=<#>
    /UNDERFLOW
```
Sets number of decimal places to <#>.
Displays tiny numbers in scientific notation.

For example, to set a two-place display with scientific notation for tiny numbers use the command:

```
>FORMAT=2/UNDERFLOW
```

Transforming variables

Use LET and IF...THEN to transform variables or create new ones.

```
LET <var>=<exprn>
IF <exprn> THEN LET
   <var>=<exprn>
```
Transforms <var> according to <exprn>.
Transforms <var> conditionally according to <exprn>.

For example, we can use LET to create a variable LOGPOP from POP:

```
>LET LOGPOP=LOG(POP)
```

```
MYSTAT Editor
  Case    CITYS        STATES      POP       RAINFALL   LOGPOP
    1      New York      NY     7164742.000    57.030    15.785
    2    Los Angeles     CA     3096721.000     7.810    14.946
    3      Chicago       IL     2992472.000    34.000    14.912
    4       Dallas       TX      974234.000    33.890    13.789
    5      Phoenix       AZ      853266.000    14.910    13.657
    6       Miami        FL      346865.000    60.020    12.757
    7    Washington      DC      638432.000    37.730    13.367
    8    Kansas City     MO      448159.000    38.770    13.013
    9
   10
   11
   12
   13
   14
   15
```

LET labels the last column of the worksheet LOGPOP and sets the values to the natural logs of the POP values. (If LOGPOP had already existed, its values would have been replaced.)

Use IF...THEN for *conditional* transformations. For example:

```
>IF POP>1000000 THEN LET SIZE$='BIG'
```

creates a new character variable, SIZE$, and assigns the value BIG for every city that has population greater than one million.

For both LET and IF...THEN, character values must be enclosed in quotation marks and are case sensitive (i.e., "MALE" is not the same as "male"). Use a period to indicate missing values.

Some valid LET and IF-THEN commands:

```
>LET ALPHA$='abcdef'
>LET LOGIT1=1/(1+EXP(A+B*X))
>LET TRENDY=INCOME>40000 AND CAR$='BMW'
>IF SEX$='Male' THEN LET GROUP=1
>IF group>2 THEN LET NEWGROUP=2
>IF A=-9 AND B<10 OR B>20 THEN LET C=LOG(D)*SQR(E)
```

Functions, relations, and operators for FIND, LET, and IF...THEN			
+	addition	SQR	square root
-	subtraction	ABS	absolute value
*	multiplication	CASE	current case number
/	division	INT	integer truncation
^	exponentiation		
<	less than	URN	uniform random number
<=	less than or equal to	ZRN	normal random number
=	equal to	ZCF	standard normal CDF
<>	not equal to	ZIF	inverse normal CDF
>=	greater than or equal		
>	greater than	SIN	sine (argument in radians)
		COS	cosine
AND	logical and	TAN	tangent
OR	logical or	ASN	arcsine
		ACS	arccosine
LOG	natural log	ATN	arctangent
EXP	exponential function	ATH	hyperbolic arctangent

Logical expressions

Logical expressions evaluate to one if true and to zero if false. For example, for LET CHILD=AGE<12, a variable AGE would be filled with ones for those cases where AGE is less than 12 and zeros whenever AGE is 12 or greater.

Random data

You can generate random numbers using the REPEAT, LET, and SAVE commands in the Editor. First, enter variable names. Press Esc to move the cursor to the command line. Then, use REPEAT to fill cases with missing values and LET to redefine the values.

```
REPEAT 20          Fills 20 cases with missing values.
LET A=URN          Fills A with uniform random data.
LET B=ZRN          Fills B with normal random data.
SAVE RANDOM        Saves data in file RANDOM.SYS.
```

Leaving the
Data Editor

Use the QUIT command to leave the Editor and return to the main MYSTAT menu.

```
>QUIT
```

**General
MYSTAT
commands**

Once your data are in a MYSTAT data file, you can use MYSTAT's statistical and graphics routines to examine them.

Open a data file
First, you must open the file containing the data you want to analyze:

```
USE <filename>                          reads the data in <filename>
```

To analyze the data we entered earlier, type:

```
>USE CITIES
```

MYSTAT responds by listing the variables in the file.

```
VARIABLES IN MYSTAT FILE ARE:
     CITY$      STATE$      POP      RAINFALL   LOGPOP
```

See variable names and data values
The NAMES command shows the variable names in the current file.

```
>NAMES
VARIABLES IN MYSTAT FILE ARE:
     CITY$      STATE$      POP      RAINFALL   LOGPOP
```

The LIST command displays the values of variables you specify. If you specify no variables, all variables are shown.

```
>LIST CITY$
                        CITY$

CASE    1           New York
CASE    2        Los Angeles
CASE    3            Chicago
CASE    4             Dallas
CASE    5            Phoenix
CASE    6              Miami
CASE    7         Washington
CASE    8        Kansas City

   8 CASES AND   5 VARIABLES PROCESSED
```

Decimal places
Use the FORMAT command to specify the number of digits to be displayed after the decimal in statistical output. This FORMAT command has the same syntax and works the same as in the Editor:

```
FORMAT=<#>              Sets number of decimal places to <#>.
   /UNDERFLOW           Uses scientific notation for tiny numbers.
```

<table>
<tr><td>

Sorting and
ranking data

</td><td>

SORT reorders the cases in a file in ascending order according to the variables you specify. You can specify up to ten numeric or character variables for nested sorts. Use a SAVE command after the USE command to save the sorted data into a MYSTAT file. Then, USE the sorted file to do analysis.

```
>USE MYDATA
>SAVE SORTED
>SORT CITY$ POP
>USE SORTED
```

RANK replaces each value of a variable with its rank order within that variable. Specify an output file before ranking.

```
>USE MYDATA
>SAVE RANKED
>RANK RAINFALL
>USE RANKED
```

</td></tr>
<tr><td>

Weighting
data

</td><td>

WEIGHT replicates cases according to the integer parts of the values of the weighting variable you specify.

```
WEIGHT <variable>
```
Weights according to variable specified.

To turn weighting off, use WEIGHT without an argument.

```
>WEIGHT
```

</td></tr>
<tr><td>

Quitting

</td><td>

When you are done with your analyses, you can end your session with the QUIT command. Remember that the Data Editor also has a QUIT. To quit MYSTAT from the Editor, enter QUIT twice.

```
>QUIT
```

</td></tr>
</table>

Notation used in command summaries

Any item in angled brackets (< >) is representative—insert an actual value or variable in its place. Replace <var> with a variable name, replace <#> with a number, <var$> with a character variable, and <gvar> with a numeric or character grouping variable.

Some commands have *options* you can use to change the type of output you get. Place a slash / before listing any options for your command. You only need one slash before the option list, no matter how many options you use.

A vertical line (|) means "or." Items in brackets ([ ]) are optional. Commas and spaces are interchangeable, except that *you must use a comma at the end of the line when a command continues to a second line.*

You can abbreviate commands and options to the first two or three characters. You may use upper- and lower-case interchangeably.

Most commands allow you to specify particular variables. If you don't specify variables, MYSTAT uses its defaults (usually the first numeric variable or all numeric variables, depending on the command).

Statistics
Descriptive
statistics

STATS produces basic descriptive statistics. Here we use STATS with the POP, RAINFALL, and LOGPOP variables of the dataset we entered earlier.

```
>STATS
TOTAL OBSERVATIONS:  8

                        POP      RAINFALL  LOGPOP

N OF CASES              8           8         8
MINIMUM         346865.000       7.810    12.757
MAXIMUM        7164742.000      60.020    15.785
MEAN           2064361.375      35.520    14.028
STANDARD DEV   2335788.226      18.032     1.068
```

Here is a summary of the STATS command. The box on the facing page describes the notation we use for command summaries in this manual.

```
STATS <var1> <var2>…        Statistics for the variables specified.
  MEAN SD SKEWNESS, KURTOSIS  Choose which statistics you want.
    MINIMUM, MAXIMUM RANGE
    SUM, SEM
  /BY <gvar>                 Statistics for each group defined by the group-
                               ing variable <gvar>. The data must first be
                               SORTed on the grouping variable.
```

For example, you can get the mean, standard deviation, and range for RAINFALL with the following command.

```
>STATS RAINFALL / MEAN SD RANGE
 TOTAL OBSERVATIONS:  8

                 RAINFALL

N OF CASES           8
MEAN            35.520
STANDARD DEV    18.032
RANGE           52.210
```

Tabulation

TABULATE provides one-way and multi-way frequency tables. For two-way tables, MYSTAT provides the Pearson chi-square statistic. You can produce a table of frequencies, percents, row percents, or column percents. You can tell MYSTAT to ignore missing data with the MISS option.

```
TAB <var1>*<var2>…            Tabulates the variables you specify
  /LIST                      Special list format table.
  FREQUENCY PERCENT ROWPCT   Different types of tables
    COLPCT MISS
TABULATE                     Frequency tables of all numeric variables.
TABULATE AGE/LIST            Frequency table of AGE in list format.
TAB AGE*SEX                  Two-way table with chi-square.
TAB AGE*SEX$*STATE$/ROWPCT   Three-way row percent table.
TAB A,AGE*SEX/FREQ, PERC     Two two-way frequency and cell percent
                               tables (A*SEX and AGE*SEX).
TAB AGE*SEX/MISS             Two-way table excluding missing values.
```

One-way frequency tables show the number of times a distinct value appears in a variable. Two-way and multi-way tables count the appearances of each unique combination of values. Multi-way tables count the appearances of a value in each subgroup. Percent tables convert the frequencies to percentages of the total count; row percent tables show percentages of the total for each row; and column percent tables show percentages of the total for each column.

T-tests

TTEST does dependent and independent t-tests. A dependent (paired samples) t-test tests whether the means of two continuous variables differ. An independent test tests whether the means of two groups of a single variable differ.

To request an independent (two-sample) t-test, specify one or more continuous variables and one grouping variable. Separate the continuous variable(s) from the grouping variable with an asterisk. The grouping variable must have only two values.

To request a dependent (paired) t-test, specify two or more continuous variables. MYSTAT does separate dependent t-tests for each possible pairing of the variables.

```
TTEST <var1>…[*<gvar>]      Does t-tests of the variables you specify.
TTEST A B                   Dependent (paired) t-test of A and B.
TTEST A B C                 Paired tests of A and B, A and C, B and C.
TTEST A*SEX$                Independent test.
TTEST A B C*SEX             Three independent tests.
```

You can also do a one-sample test by adding a variable to your data file that has a constant value corresponding to the population mean of your null hypothesis. Then do a dependent t-test on this variable and your data variable.

Correlation

PEARSON computes Pearson product moment correlation coefficients for the variables you specify (or all numerical variables). You can select pairwise or listwise deletion of missing data; pairwise is the default. RANK the variables before correlating to compute Spearman rank-order correlations.

```
PEARSON <var1> ...          Pearson correlation matrix.
 /PAIRWISE | LISTWISE       Pairwise or listwise deletion of missing values.
PEARSON                     Correlation matrix of all numeric variables.
CORR HEIGHT IQ AGE          Matrix of three variables.
PEARSON /LISTWISE           Listwise deletion rather than pairwise.
```

Correlation measures the strength of linear association between two variables. A value of 1 or –1 indicates a perfect linear relationship; a value of 0 indicates that neither variable can be linearly predicted from the other.

Regression
and ANOVA

MYSTAT computes simple and multiple regression and balanced or unbalanced ANOVA designs. For unbalanced designs, MYSTAT uses the method of weighted squares of means.

The MODEL and ESTIMATE commands provide linear regression. MODEL specifies the regression equation and ESTIMATE tells MYSTAT to start working. Your MODEL should almost always include a CONSTANT term.

```
>MODEL Y=CONSTANT+X
>ESTIMATE
```
Simple linear regression.

```
>MODEL Y=CONSTANT+X+Z
>ESTIMATE
```
Multiple linear regression.

Use CATEGORY and ANOVA commands for fully factorial ANOVA. CATEGORY specifies the number of categories (levels) for one or more variables used as categorical predictors (factors). ANOVA specifies the dependent variable and produces a fully-factorial design from the factors given by CATEGORY.

All CATEGORY variables must have integer values from 1 to k, where k is the number of categories.

```
>CATEGORY SEX=2
>ANOVA SALARY
>ESTIMATE
```
One-way design with independent variable SALARY and one factor (SEX) with 2 levels

```
>CATEGORY A=2,B=3
>ANOVA Y
>ESTIMATE
```
Two-by-three ANOVA

Use COVARIATE to specify covariates in a fully factorial design.

```
>CATEGORY A=2 B=3
>COVARIATE X
>ANOVA Y
>ESTIMATE
```
This ANOCOVA includes factor (A,B) by covariate (X) interactions, which test the assumption of homogeneity of regression slopes.

Saving residuals

Use a SAVE command before MODEL or ANOVA to save residuals in a file. MYSTAT saves model variables, estimated values, residuals, and standard error of prediction as the variables ESTIMATE, RESIDUAL, and SEPRED. When you use SAVE with a linear model, MYSTAT lists cases with extreme studentized residuals or leverage values and prints the Durbin-Watson and autocorrelation statistics.

```
>SAVE RESIDS
>MODEL Y=CONSTANT+X+Z
>ESTIMATE
```

```
>SAVE RESID2
>CATEGORY SEX=2
>ANOVA SALARY
>ESTIMATE
```

You can USE the residuals file to analyze your residuals with MYSTAT's statistical and graphic routines.

Non-
parametric
tests

SIGN computes a sign test on all pairs of specified variables, omitting zero differences.

`SIGN <varlist>`	Sign tests on each pairing of the variables specified.
`SIGN`	Sign tests on all pairs of numeric variables in the file.
`SIGN A B C`	Sign tests on A and B, A and C, and B and C.

WILCOXON calculates a Wilcoxon signed-rank test on all pairs of specified variables, omitting zero differences and averaging ties.

`WILCOXON <varlist>`	Wilcoxon signed-rank tests on each pairing of the variables specified.
`SIGN`	Wilcoxon signed-rank tests on all pairs of numeric variables in the file.
`SIGN A B C`	Wilcoxon signed-rank tests on A and B, A and C, and B and C.

FRIEDMAN computes a two-way Friedman nonparametric analysis of variance, averaging tied ranks.

`FRIEDMAN <varlist>`	Friedman tests on each pairing of the variables specified.
`SIGN`	Friedman tests on all pairs of numeric variables in the file.
`SIGN A B C`	Friedman tests on A and B, A and C, and B and C.

Graphics

Use the CHARSET command to choose the type of graphic characters to be used for printing and screen display. If you have IBM screen or printer graphic characters, use GRAPHICS; if not, use GENERIC. The GENERIC setting uses characters like +, –, and |.

```
CHARSET GRAPHICS          For IBM graphic characters.
CHARSET GENERIC           For any screen or printer.
```

Scatterplots

PLOT draws a two-way scatterplot of one or more Y variables on a vertical scale against an X variable on a horizontal scale. Use different plotting symbols to distinguish Y variables.

```
PLOT <yvar1>…*<xvar>        Plots <yvar(s)> against <xvar>.
  /SYMBOL=<var$> | '<char>'  Use character variable values or character
                               string as plotting symbol.
  YMAX=<#> YMIN=<#> XMAX=<#> Specify range of X and Y values.
    XMIN=<#>
  LINES=<#>                  Specify number of screen lines for graph.
PLOT A*B/SYMBOL='*'          Uses asterisk as plotting symbol.
PLOT A*B/SYMBOL=SEX$         Uses SEX$ values for plotting symbol.
PL Y1 Y2*X/SY='1','2'        Plot Y1 points as 1 and Y2 points as 2.
PLOT A*B/LINES=40           Limits graph size to 40 lines on screen.
```

For example, we can plot LOGPOP against RAINFALL using the first letter of the values of CITY$ for plotting symbols.

```
>PLOT LOGPOP*RAINFALL/SYMBOL=CITY$
```

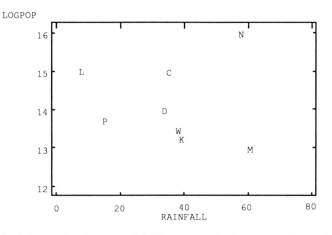

The SYMBOL option is powerful. If you are plotting several Y variables, you can label each variable by specifying its own plotting symbol.

```
>PLOT Y1 Y2*X/SYMBOL='1','2'
```

Or, you can name a character variable to plot each point with the first letter of the variable's value for the corresponding case:

```
>PLOT WEIGHT*AGE/SYMBOL=SEX$
```

Box-and-whisker plots

BOX produces box-and-whisker plots. Include an asterisk and a grouping variable for grouped box plots.

```
BOX <var1>...[*<gvar>]          [Grouped] box plots of the variables.
  /GROUPS=<#>,                  Show only the first <#> groups.
  MIN=<#> MAX=<#>               Specify scale limits.
BOX                             Box plots of every numeric variable.
BOX SALARY                      Box plot of SALARY only.
BOX SALARY*RANK                 Grouped box plots of SALARY by RANK
BOX INCOME*STATE$/GR=10         Box plots of first 10 groups only
```

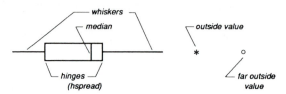

The center line of the box marks the *median*. The edges of the box show the upper and lower *hinges*. The median splits the ordered batch of numbers in half and the hinges split these halves in half again. The distance between the hinges is called the *Hspread*. The *whiskers* show the range of points within 1.5 Hspreads of the hinges. Points outside this range are marked by asterisks and those more than 3 Hspreads from the hinges are marked with circles.

Histograms

HISTOGRAM displays histograms for one or more variables.

```
HISTOGRAM <var1> ...            Histograms of variables specified
  /BARS=<#>                     Limits the number of bars used.
  SCALE,                        Forces round cutpoints between bars.
  MIN=<#> MAX=<#>               Specifies scale limits.
HISTOGRAM                       Histograms of every numeric variable.
HISTOGRAM A B/BARS=18           Forces 18 bars for histograms of A and B.
HIST A/MIN=0 MAX=10             Histogram of A with scale from 0 to 20.
```

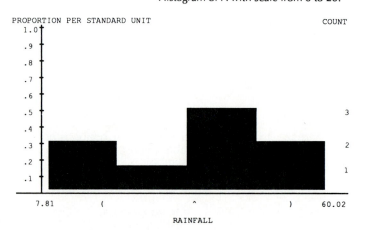

A histogram shows the *distribution* of a variable. The data are divided into equal-sized intervals along the horizontal axis. The number of values in each interval is represented by a vertical bar. The height of each bar is measured two ways: the right axis shows the number of cases, and the left axis shows the proportions per standard unit.

Stem-and-leaf diagrams

STEM plots a stem-and-leaf diagram.

```
STEM <var1>..              Diagrams of variables specified.
  /LINES=<#>               Specify number of lines in diagram.
STEM                       Stem-and-leaf of every numeric variable.
STEM TAX                   Stem-and-leaf of TAX.
STEM TAX/LINES=20          Stem-and-leaf with 20 lines.
```

The numbers on the left side are *stems* (the most significant digits in which variation occurs) . The *leaves* (the subsequent digits) are printed on the right. For example, in the following plot, the stems are 10's digits and the leaves are 1's digits.

```
        STEM AND LEAF PLOT OF VARIABLE: RAINFALL, N =    48

MINIMUM IS:          7.000
LOWER HINGE IS:         26.500
MEDIAN IS:       36.000
UPPER HINGE IS:         43.000
MAXIMUM IS:      60.000

              0    78
              1    0114
              1    55556
              2
              2 H 588
              3    00113333
              3 M 5557999
              4 H 001123333
              4    55567999
              5    0
              5    9
              6    0
```

(We added 40 more cases to the dataset for this plot. You will get a different plot if you try this example with the CITIES.SYS data file.)

Hinges are defined under "Box-and-whisker plots," above.

Time series plots

TPLOT produces time series plots, which plot a variable against Case (time). TPLOT's STANDARDIZE option removes the series mean from each value and divides each by the standard deviation. MYSTAT uses the first fifteen cases unless you specify otherwise with the LAG option.

```
TPLOT <var>               Case plot of variable specified.
  /LAG=<#>                Plots first <#> cases.
  STANDARDIZE,            Standardizes before plotting.
  MIN=<#>,MAX=<#>         Sets scale limits.
TPLOT                     Case plot of first numeric variable.
TPLOT PRICE/LAG=10        First 10 cases of PRICE.
TPLOT PRICE/STAN          Standardizes before plotting.
```

Submitting files of commands

You can operate MYSTAT in batch mode, where MYSTAT executes a series of commands from a file and you sit back and watch. (You've already seen a command file in action: the DEMO demonstration uses a file of commands, DEMO.CMD.)

The SUBMIT command reads commands from a file and executes the commands as though they were typed from the keyboard. Command files must have a ".CMD" file extension.

Use a word processor to create a file of commands—one command per line, with no extraneous characters. Save the file as a text (ASCII) file. (Use the command "COPY CON BATCH.CMD" and [F6] to type commands into a file if you have no word processor.)

```
SUBMIT <filename>        Submits file of commands.
SUBMIT COMMANDS          Reads commands from COMMANDS.CMD.
SUBMIT B:NEWJOB          Reads commands from file on drive B.
```

Redirecting output

Ordinarily, MYSTAT sends its results to the screen. OUTPUT routes *subsequent* output to an ASCII file or a printer.

```
OUTPUT *                 Sends output to the screen only
OUTPUT @                 Sends output to the screen and the printer.
OUTPUT <filename>        Sends output to the screen and a text file.
```

MYSTAT adds a .DAT suffix to ASCII files produced by OUTPUT. You must use OUTPUT *or QUIT the program to stop redirecting.

Printing and saving analysis results

To print analysis results, use OUTPUT @ before doing the analysis or analyses. Use OUTPUT <filename> to save analysis results in a file. Use OUTPUT * to turn saving or printing off when you are finished.

Printing data or variable names

You can print your data by using OUTPUT @ and then using the LIST command. Use LIST <var1>... to print only certain variables. Don't forget to turn printing off when you are done.

You can print your variable names by using OUTPUT @ and then NAMES. Don't forget to turn printing off when you are done.

Putting comments in output

NOTE allows you to write comments in your output. Surround each line with quotation marks, and issue another NOTE command for additional lines:

```
>NOTE 'Following are descriptive statistics for the POP'
>NOTE "and RAINFALL variables of the CITIES dataset."
>STATS POP RAINFALL
TOTAL OBSERVATIONS:  8

                        POP       RAINFALL

N OF CASES               8          8
MINIMUM           346865.000       7.810
MAXIMUM          7164742.000      60.020
MEAN             2064361.375      35.520
STANDARD DEV     2335788.226      18.032
>NOTE "Note that the average annual rainfall for these"
>NOTE 'cities is 35.52 inches.'
```

Saving data in text files

You can save datasets to ASCII text files with the PUT command. PUT saves the current dataset in a plain text file suitable for use with most other programs. Text files have a .DAT extension.

```
USE <filename>          Opens the dataset to be exported
PUT <filename>          Saves the dataset as a text file
```

Note that the PUT command is *not* an Editor command. To save a newly created dataset in a plain text file, you must QUIT from the Editor, USE the datafile, and finally PUT the data in an ASCII file.

```
>EDIT
[editing session here]
 >SAVE A:NEWSTUFF
 >QUIT
>USE A:NEWSTUFF
>PUT A:NEWTEXT
```

The above commands would create a plain ASCII file called NEWTEXT.DAT on the A disk.

Index of commands

This index lists all of MYSTAT's commands and the Editor commands, describes each briefly, and shows where to look for a description in this booklet.

Editor commands			
DELETE	9	delete a row (case)
DROP	9	drop a column (variable)
Esc key	8	toggle between command line and worksheet
FIND	10, 11	find a particular data value
FORMAT	4, 10	set number of decimal places in Editor
GET	10	read data from an ASCII file
HELP	4, 5	get help for Editor commands
IF...THEN	10–11	conditionally transform or create a variable
LET	10–12	transform or create a variable
NEW	9	create a new data file
QUIT	4, 12, 14	quit the Editor and return to MYSTAT
REPEAT	12	fill cases with missing values
SAVE	4, 9, 10, 12	save data in a data file
USE	4, 9	read a data file into Editor

MYSTAT commands			
ANOVA	17	analysis of variance
BOX	20	box-and-whisker plot
CATEGORY	17	specify factors for ANOVA
CHARSET	19	choose type of characters for graphs
COVARIATE	17	specify covariate term for ANOCOVA
DEMO	5	demonstration of MYSTAT
EDIT	4, 5, 6	edit a new or existing data file
ESTIMATE	17	start computations for regression
FORMAT	13	set number of decimal places in output
FRIEDMAN	18	Friedman nonparametric analysis of variance
HELP	4, 5	get help for MYSTAT commands
HISTOGRAM	20	draw histogram
LIST	13	display data values
MENU	4	turn the command menu on/off
MODEL	17	specify a regression model
NAMES	13	display variable names
NOTE	23	put comment in output
OUTPUT	22	redirect output to printer or text file
PEARSON	16	Pearson correlation matrix
PLOT	19	scatterplot (X-Y plot)
PUT	9, 23	save data in text file
QUIT	23	quit the MYSTAT program
RANK	14	rank data
SAVE	14, 17	save results in a file
SIGN	18	sign test
SORT	14	sort data
STATS	15	descriptive statistics
STEM	21	stem-and-leaf diagram
SUBMIT	22	submit a batch file of commands
SYSTAT	5	get information about SYSTAT
TABULATE	15	one-way or multi-way tables
TPLOT	21	case plot
TTEST	16	independent and dependent t-tests
USE	13, 14, 17, 23	read a data file for analysis
WEIGHT	14	weight data
WILCOXON	18	Wilcoxon signed-rank test

Glossary

Abstract A library reference work that carries short (often less than 200–word) synopses of scholarly and scientific articles.

Accountability A political means of looking back to assign praise or blame. Sunshine laws (requiring open public meetings) and "freedom of information" acts are examples.

Accretion measure Signs of material deposit which have been largely borrowed from archeology.

Acquiescence bias Refers to individuals who accept all or most statements ("yeasayers") or reject all or most statements ("naysayers").

Active voice A verb that indicates a subject that does something, or is, or is becoming something.

Additive effect The independent effects of two or more independent variables on a dependent variable.

Aggregative analysis The accumulations of individual characteristics, such as in demographic studies.

Algorithm A procedure that must be followed to solve a problem, or a set of instructions to be implemented in a given order.

Analogy Presumptive reasoning based upon the assumption that if things have some similar attributes, their other attributes are similar.

Analytic graphics Scientific graphs which use multivariate data sets containing numerous data points.

Analytic memo Notes which elaborate on or tie together theoretical notes in the fieldworker's ethnographic account.

Antecedent variable Exists when the original relationship disappears when controlled on the test factor, simply because X and Y are related due to the dependence of both on a common independent variable.

Antonym A word of opposite meaning.

Archival record Testimonial document which purports to record information about things that happened.

Artificial intelligence The attempt of cognitive experts to try and understand human intelligence; usually refers to programming machines which use symbolic logic to simulate deductive processes.

Association (statistical)   The link between two variables; a necessary but not sufficient step in deducing causation, involving the regular cooccurrence of two variables or events.

Asymmetric relationship   One-way causation of the sort that x can cause y but y cannot cause x.

Audience   The particular group for whom something is written should dictate what you say and how you say it when you write.

Backstage behavior   An analogy from the theater in which the "objective self" represents analytic perspective, using attitudes of skepticism, cynicism, and introspection.

Backup   The practice of keeping separate copies of electronically encoded data.

Backward reasoning   A form of intelligence whereby one works from the finished product or goal to the original state.

Bar chart   A histogram for nominal data which displays separate and distinct bars for each category.

Best-first searching   A form of intelligence in which one generates a series of possible solutions in rapid succession and quickly discards those that lead nowhere, leading to a prioritizing of solutions.

Beta weight   Measures the predicted linear unit change in values of the dependent variable, based on knowledge of the independent variable values.

Bidirectional reasoning   Uses both forward and backward rules of knowing. The goal of bidirectional reasoning is to compare logic paths to discover which one is the shortest, or to find out whether the forward and backward paths diverge or are the same.

Biased sampling   Does not accurately or fairly represent the working universe.

Bibliography   The list of works referred to in a text or consulted by the author.

Big Science   Refers to the increasing need for massive financial investments, full-time employees in research laboratories, and large numbers of scientists working in collaboration for coordination of cross-national verification.

Bivariate analysis   Analysis of two-variable relationships in the search for statistical association.

Blind treatment   The elimination of participant awareness of treatment conditions and dependent variable measurements.

Blind-experimental condition   A double-blind state in which neither the observer nor the participant know who receives what treatment or placebo, or triple-blind when even the researcher doesn't know; used to control for observer, participant, and researcher influences.

Boolean search   A strategy for efficiently locating some materials. The Boolean search allows efficient searches for two or more things at once—two authors; an author and subject, etc.

Boolean truth tables   Use Boolean algebra to deal with logical concepts and true-false statements.

Boomerang effect   An unintended effect of an evaluation program which has an undesirable or unwanted effect.

Bootstrap sampling   Involves drawing a large number of samples (perhaps as high as 100) from the original sample and computing the average (mean) value of those sample means to estimate the true population value.

Box plot   A powerful way of comparatively displaying distributions: The vertical lines in the middle of each box plots medians (half the values lie above and below this point), the ends of each box represent the interquartile values (which splits each half of the value again), and the end "fences" represent the lowest and highest points of "normal" values. Two types of outliers (extreme values) are plotted: those outside the inner fences with asterisks, and values outside the outer fences with empty circles.

Brute-force searching   The simplest form of artificial intelligence, which is also totally undiscriminating. The program must generate each branch of a logic tree and explore each in turn. An expert knows that all knowledge is not equal, but this type of rule ignores that wisdom.

Campbell-bipolar scale   A cross between Likert and forced-choice formats: The researcher gives the respondent sets of two items that are at opposite ends of a continuum (hence, bipolar). The items, however, are scored in Likert style.

Card catalog   A complete enumeration of items arranged systematically with descriptive details usually by either the Dewey decimal or the Library of Congress system.

Card list   A list given to the respondent if the question has more than three alternatives, so that the respondent's answer is not based on just those responses he or she has not forgotten.

Cardinal scale   Employs the "natural" or fundamental numbers 1, 2, 3, . . . n to answer the question: How many?

Case-study approach   Treats each case as incomparable and peculiar. For the social scientist, this practice is usually not very interesting; social scientists are trained to look for regularities, not peculiarities.

Casing   The only means by which the researcher can attempt to be systematic in organizing field operations. It is used to gain a picture of the parameters and complexity of the universe to be observed and its components.

Category-rank scale   A number of items rank ordered by the items according to some single criteria.

Causation   An inference that one variable influences or produces an effect on another variable.

Central limit theorem   Posits that one can infer the unknown population mean μ (the Greek letter mu) and its standard deviation σ (sigma) regardless of the shape of the population—if one repeatedly draws large enough simple random samples of size N.

Central tendency bias   Occurs when the observer arbitrarily chooses a less affective code over a more affective code.

Chunking   A psychological concept referring to the fact that human intelligence operates by grouping by phrases or units of meaning, rather than abstract strings of letters or words.

Citation   The act of quoting, excerpting, or mentioning as example, authority, or proof.

Cliometrics   Born from a marriage of economics and history which refers to quantification in historic research.

Closed-ended questions   Subdivide into two-way questions and multiple-choice questions. They restrict choice of responses by forcing the respondent to answer in terms of given categories or alternatives.

Cluster sampling   Units chosen because of close spatial proximity, such as counties from which the researcher either samples all, or a subdivision, of the units within those designated spatial areas.

Codebook   A data record-keeping device which minimally specifies the meaning of each numeric code; it also indicates the column in which each variable is located, and where more than one line of data is needed, on which line the data are to be found.

Coding   A data management means for putting data into numeric forms. For some forms of data, conventional precoding systems already exist or are easily developed. For open-ended questions, questions with multiple answers, and qualitative data, the process is much more challenging.

Coding relativism   The coding of more recent behaviors compared to past behaviors.

Cohort   A set of people who are born within the same time interval.

Column percentages   Analysis of tables is read by reading across rows.

Comparative-historic method   Falls into four generic camps: individualizers, universalizers, encompassers, and variation-finders.

Complete observer   A systematic and detached eavesdropping and reconnaissance fieldworker role. It is little used in later stages of field research, because the complete observer has virtually no contact at all with those in the field.

Complete participant   A fieldworker role which conceals the observer role from those observed, and remains a covert or "in disguise."

Component variable   An element of a global independent variable which is responsible for effects on some dependent variable.

Computer-assisted telephone survey (CATI)   A relatively new technique used to reduce problems of costs, and human errors in coding and sampling of interviewing.

Concept   Classification by definition of some phenomenon, which may or may not be a variable.

Concurrent data analysis   Simultaneously occurring observations which normally require the use of permanent records (film strips, videotapes), and viewing of those sources numerous times to analyze the increased complexity of such situations.

Concurrent validity   A technique in which the researcher locates known groups or judges—as opposed to variables—who experts agree are defined as high or low on the variable in question to judge validity.

Conditional test factor   Exists when (1) all three bivariate relationships (*XY, XT, and YT*) show statistical association; (2) after controlling on the antecedent variable (*T*), the independent-dependent relationship does *not* vanish; and (3) after controlling on the independent variable (*X*), the antecedent-dependent relationship *does* disappear.

Conditional cleaning   A means of checking the veracity of data employed when a code for one variable is dependent on previous variable codes.

Confidence limit   Specification of the risks or betting odds for a particular tolerance limit. A probability of a probability which estimates the chance that the tolerance limit is correct.

Constant comparative method   Starts out by coding each incident in the data in as many categories of analysis as possible. After a few codings, the fieldworker may find a conflict in how or why to code some instance that will call for logically reconciling recordings.

Construct validity   The degree to which certain explanatory concepts (known as constructs) account for performance on a measurement. Researchers do studies of construct validity to confirm the conceptual relationships underlying some theory. It is always based on multiple measures or theoretical predictions.

Content validity   Asks the question: Is the measure appropriate to the content area claimed for the measure? The most primitive form of testing for validity, because it uses a simple social consensus on what defines a particular content area.

Contextual comparisons   Within-culture comparisons made for several cultures, with the objective of looking for similarities and differences in those patterns.

Contingent acceptance field entry   The researcher asks the head of the organization only that he himself agree to the project, and that he agree to have the question put before the next level in the organization, and on down the hierarchy. This procedure has risks of rejection by particular echelons, but it provides cooperation and information if followed through successfully.

Control group   The group which does not receive the experimental treatment. Randomization of units into two groups makes both subsamples as nearly alike as is possible in the original condition before pretesting. To insure that both groups are initially equivalent, the experimenter measures similarity of the two groups on the dependent variable during the pretest. After pretesting, the experimenter introduces the presumed causal factor (independent or "treatment" variable) into the experimental subsample but withholds it from the control subsample.

Cooling out   Field relations tactic in preparation for ending the study. The researcher often finds it useful during this stage to spend most of the time interpreting and reviewing the study findings with the study group.

Correlation   Pearson's *r*, is the usual measure of correlation which mathematically is a special type of mean average score between two variables; it varies from -1.0 if the two variables have a perfect negative correlation to 0 indicating no association to $+1.0$, indicating a perfect positive correlation.

Cost-benefit analysis   An attempt to rationalize evaluation of programs through weighing ratios of costs to benefits. It is premised on the efficient and effective application of those resources. Evaluators have come to understand that social programs often have complex and subtle costs and benefits, and that what is a "cost" or a "benefit" is a valuation.

Cost-effectiveness analysis   Because it is often difficult to construct cost-benefit calculations, some evaluators advocate measuring the costs of alternative treatments or programs as cost information is usually easier to uncover than benefit information.

Counterrate   100% minus the actual rate standardizes the relative frequency of occurrence of some event by dividing the number of occurrences of some event by the size of the total group in which that event might take place.

Croce's problem   Either one is uncertain of the data when only a limited body exists, or uncertain of the sample when so much exists that selection is necessary.

Cross-sectional survey   A primitive study design based on one point in time.

Cultural analysis   The association of norms, values, practices, traditions, ideologies, technologic objects, and other artifacts of culture.

Cynicism   An essential attitude of the fieldworker, which asks "Can I believe that?"

Dangling participle   A part of a sentence without clear connection to other parts.

Data cleaning   A means of verifying data entry comparable to proofing one's written work for errors.

Data entry   Entering the data onto an electronic diskette or magnetic tape via a computer.

Data transformation   A convenient way for mathematically converting highly skewed data or data that has huge variation.

Database program   A convenient tool for entering data into electronically analyzable form.

Debriefing   A postexperimental interview to probe the participant's reaction to the experiment and to see if the experimental procedures worked, and if they work, how the participant perceived them.

Deception   Fraud, double-dealing, subterfuge, and trickery are among the types. As a general rule, deception in research is counterproductive in the long run.

Decisional method   Some combination of means by which the investigator uses such relatively eclectic methods as case studies collected in an anthropological or journalistic manner.

Deductive disclosure   Exposure through simple logic of sensitive data on individuals, organizations, or cities.

Deduction   General principles are used to derive specific testable hypotheses.

Dependent variable   A variable for which the researcher asserts the variation is an effect of some other variable (or variables) known as an independent variable.

Depth interview   Uses no "prepared script" (interview schedule) on which to fall back, but depends on the development of special interpersonal skills that permit the interviewer, rather than the respondent, to structure the interview.

Derecruitment   The issue of when to leave a particular site because the study is coming to an end.

Direct cost   Costs needed to provide specific mandated services.

Distorter variable   A test factor that actually reverses the original *XY* relationship. The sign of the original relationship changes from positive to negative (or negative to positive).

Dot chart   Constructed with two intersecting lines perpendicular to one another. The horizontal line or axis is the scale for data. The vertical line lists names for each object to be compared. Corresponding with each object named is a filled circle drawn along the horizontal axis at the appropriate numeric level. A dotted line connects each circle to the corresponding category named on the vertical axis.

Double negative   A difficult-to-understand sentence form that should be avoided.

Double-barreled question Presents more than one stimuli to the respondent. The problem with this is that the analyst will not know to which stimuli the respondent is actually answering. Such questions need to be broken down into separate questions.

Draft A preliminary sketch, outline, or version in the writing process.

Dummy variable A completely arbitrary convention for using dichotomized nominal classification (e.g., "0" for males and "1" for females) that is necessary for some types of sophisticated computerized statistical analyses.

Ecological analysis Concerns the interaction of humans and their environment.

Ecological correlation Occurs when measures of association increase with increasing aggregation of any kind of data. This implies that correlations based on aggregated data may give spuriously inflated measures.

Effort variables Activity variables are input variables because they measure what the program is doing or how it is doing it rather than program outcomes.

Electronic data processing (EDP) A means of analyzing data by modern, computerized form.

Erosion measures Primary sources including archaeological physical traces caused by the wearing away of materials. They provide useful records of incidence or frequency.

Ethical absolutism Assumes an unbending moral authority without exception.

Ethical relativism Assumes moral authority may have exceptions depending on the situation.

Ethics Deals with what is good and bad and with principles of moral duty and obligation.

Ethnocentrism Fieldworker interpretations may be incomplete, or inaccurate interpretations of the relevant respondent and informant interviews through the belief in the superiority of the values of one's own group.

Ethnography A manner of observing and recording the rush of ongoing events in some setting used in fieldwork.

Event sampling Uses samples based on the occurrence of human behavior or its by-products, rather than the individuals who perform particular actions.

Ex post facto interpretation A theoretical after-the-fact analysis, which is not normally recommended as a strong means of analysis.

Experimental realism The extent to which the experiment is realistic to participants, involves them, and forces them to take it seriously.

Expert choice sampling Depends on judgments of an expert(s) to choose "typical" individuals, "representative" cities, or to postulate the parent universe of a sample that the researcher has already taken.

Expert-system shell Bare bones of knowledge domains to which the purchaser can add. The shells are no better than the means by which they allow such reasoning processes to be incorporated into their structure.

Explanation One of the two primary functions of science is to elaborate causal relationships.

Exploratory data analysis Requires deductive methods for looking at data in as many ways as possible and actually thinking out the implications of emerging patterns by considering "what if" scenarios.

External criticism Involves painstaking care needed in scrutinizing historical documents with the following questions: Is the document authentic? When, where, and by whom was the document written? Why was it written?

Extralinguistic observations Include vocal, temporal, interactional continuity, and verbal-stylistic dimensions.

Extraneous variable A variable which has a spurious effect on another variable.

Extremity biases Include tendencies to check (or avoid) the extremes of answer categories—for instance, the tendency to check (or to avoid checking) "1's" and "7's" on a seven-point scale.

Facility-equipment cost   Costs such as word processors, fax machines, office supplies, vehicles, fuel, and office footage needed to run a program.

Factorial design   Elaborates on the *number* of experimental and control samples. There are two reasons for elaboration: First, the experimenter is usually ignorant which, out of the infinite possible independent variables, may ultimately prove to be the most important; second, the experimenter usually has no knowledge that any one independent variable will exert its effects independently of all others. Therefore, factorial designs set up each possible combination of two or more independent variables in classical or posttest-only form.

Fallacy of the wrong level of analysis   The error of inferring that the study of human or social behavior at one level gives information at other levels. For example, individual behavior may tell little about social relationships.

False-negative error   Rejecting a decision that is actually true. Also known as Type I error.

False-positive error   Type II error or "false positive": Accepting a decision that is actually false.

Falsification   To guard against untruths, one tries to disprove alternative hypotheses, rather than prove the actual hypothesis, through setting up what is termed a null hypothesis.

Field diary   A self-debriefing exercise to protect against memory decay, whereby the fieldworker re-reads and "free associates" from raw data to reconstruct the field events, and thereby uncovers observations not noted earlier; and to note changes in field relations for similar reasons.

Field research   A number of techniques aimed at producing direct observations of what people say and do, which focuses on habits and routines.

Forced-choice scale   Requires the respondent to choose which of several equally repulsive attitudinal statements is most true of him- or herself.

Forward reasoning   If a problem has only one starting state but many alternative solutions, this is a highly appropriate method of problem solving.

Frame of reference   Refers to the fact that most words may be interpreted from different points of view or perspectives, and that question design must take this problem into account.

Frontstage behavior   Implies that one avoids actually asking the host: "Is that really what is happening?" or "Can I believe that?" Rather, one asks questions that help the host express true opinions and concerns. (See backstage behavior.)

Fraud   Intentional perversion of truth; the act of deceiving or misrepresenting.

Fuzzy logic   Reasoning based on uncertainty and vagueness.

Galton's problem   Suggests that because of cultural borrowing, cultural units may not be independent of one another. Therefore, apparent similarities between cultures may not be independent of geographical closeness and cultural diffusion.

General universe   The abstract, theoretical population to which the researcher wishes to generalize study findings.

Going native   Becoming too immersed in and part of the culture the fieldworker is part of, so that sympathies make objectivity nearly impossible.

Grounded theory   An ideal process in which the fieldworker constantly compares emerging hypotheses and field data. This comparison aids reexamination of data in the light of emerging theory, and thus leads to analysis which of necessity goes beyond description.

Guttman scale   Based on two assumptions: (1) a set of items can be ordered along a continuum of difficulty or magnitude, and (2) such a set of items measures a unidimensional variable.

Haphazard sampling   The least purposive of any sampling technique, because it simply uses samples of convenience that fortuitously present themselves for study.

Heterogeneous sampling   Divisible into (1) representative samples, and (2) quota samples.

Heterogeneous samples   Considers the broadest possible spectrum of any particular variable.

Heuristic knowledge   Consists of the complex and normally fuzzy set of problem-solving strategies we use. We often use a few vague rules of thumb to make the multitude of choices confronting us more manageable. Heuristic knowledge also includes our intuitions, associations, judgments, rules, pet theories, and general inference-making procedures.

Histogram   Graphic display of the sample density and distribution of a continuous numerical variable.

History effects   All those possible independent variables (causes), other than the one(s) for which one wishes to study the effects on some dependent variable(s).

Homogeneous sampling   Two types exist: (1) extreme case samples represent only the boundaries of variable values, and (2) rare element samples which represent (or overrepresent) variable values of low frequencies.

Hypothesis   Describes the relationship between at least two variables such that we can say "as x increases, y increases (or decreases)." It consists of two or more variables linked by some relationship.

Hypothesis generation   After-the-fact theorizing in fieldwork, used to generate serendipitous data and new theory.

Implied alternative question   Does not clearly spell out all possible responses.

Independent variable   A variable that the researcher presumes causes change.

Index   A bibliographic list of citations to a body of literature arranged in alphabetical order of some specified datum like author, subject, keyword.

Indice   One single operational indictor of the research variable.

Indirect cost   Monies needed to support the program outside of any specific services.

Indirect measure   A procedure which provides disguised appraisals such as projective tests.

Individual autonomy   A moral principle that requires that people be treated as ends in themselves, and never solely as a means to the ends of others.

Individual risk   Typical risks include injury, undesired public exposure, stress, loss of control over self-presentation and loss of privacy, which should be weighed against personal and social benefits in ethical research.

Induction   Begins with specific observations from which one determines a general principle.

Inference engine   An AI routine that performs the actual logical operations (inference building) that reaches conclusions. The inference engine controls the program—it controls what the program does next.

Innumeracy   Numeric illiteracy.

Institutional analysis   Compares relationships within and across the legal, political, economic, or familial institutions of society.

Interitem correlation reliability   Associates each item in a scale against every other item, and obtains the average intercorrelation for the entire set of correlations or associations.

Interaction effect   A nonadditive effect of two or more variables, which suggests that the variables are not independent of each other in their effects.

Interactive analysis   Equivalent to relational analysis, in which the focus is on interaction between individuals.

Interlibrary loan   Cooperative local, state, regional, national, or international networks, built upon joint agreements to avoid the expense of duplication of rarely used materials, to encourage reciprocal borrowing and lending of materials, and to allow for greater freedom of access to information.

Internal analysis   Accomplished by separating participants into two groups (those upon whom the manipulation seemed to work and those upon whom it did not), to check for the success of the treatment manipulation.

Interrupted time-series design   In between the periodic measurement of some group or set of individuals, 0_1 to 0_8, the treatment (X) occurs. The researcher assumes that any discontinuity in recorded measurements is an indicator of the effects of the treatment.

Intervening variable   Suggests that a third variable, T, mediates the original XY relationship.

Interview   Subdivided into those which are relatively structured, with preset questions, responses, and question order—and unstructured, which give only enough direction to the interviewer that he or she knows what topics ought to be covered.

Introspective skepticism   A fieldworker attitude of vigilance, in which one asks "Is that really what is happening?"

Invisible college   Denotes the informal collectives of closely interacting scientists, generally limited to a size that can be handled by interpersonal relationships. Invisible colleges are significant social and cognitive formations that advance the research frontiers of science, beyond the physical universities and research laboratories to which scientists are formally attached.

Jacknife sampling   By taking one case at a time out of the original sample for n-1 samples and computing the mean of these n-1 samples, one derives an estimate of the true mean.

Jargon   Obscure and pretentious language marked by circumlocutions and long words.

Keypunching   An old-fashioned method of inputing data by hand into machine-readable form with a keyboard-like machine which has been virtually supplanted by more efficient means.

Keyword search   Uses meaningful, standardized, and thesaurus-based terms for on-line computer searches of library holdings.

Knowledge base   Consists of a structured collection of facts and rules with which to communicate knowledge or expertise in intelligence-amplification software.

Latitude of acceptance   The respondent's most acceptable attitudinal positions. Positions the respondent accepts.

Latitude of noncommitment   Attitudinal positions the respondent neither accepts nor rejects.

Latitude of rejection   The respondent's most unacceptable attitudinal positions.

Leading question   Lures the respondent's answers toward the wishes of the researcher.

Life-history method   Combines data gleaned from autobiographies, letters, and diaries, where available, and to supplement these sources with unstructured interviews and structured questionnaires for a more systematic coverage of gaps in the life history.

Likert-summated rating scale   The most popular method of scaling subjective phenomena. Generally, the scale design permits only five responses: (1) strongly agree, (2) agree, (3) uncertain, (4) disagree, and (5) strongly disagree; sometimes, researchers modify this rule to four, six, or seven response categories.

Line of best fit   Also known as the regression line, this is the line of most accurate prediction for x from y or y from x. If one took all of the actual scores and the predicted scores (those along the regression line), and squared the differences between actual and predicted scores, the sum of these squared deviations around the regression line would be smaller than for any other straight line.

Linguistic observation   The development and use of systematic verbal techniques of observation.

Link-file system   Aids data security and respondent anonymity for some types of data. It requires that researchers or bureaucrats create two separate files—one file containing the person's research data and an arbitrary identification code, the second file containing the person's name, address, and the same identification code. At a later date, when the data need to be matched up with other agency records or new data collected at a second time period, a third file will be created—the "link file"—which contains only the identification codes for each data set by a custodial intermediary. Identifying information can then be destroyed after file match-up.

Literature reviews   The "genealogy" of established scholarship, which are used to show how the work of other researchers extend, modify, support, or challenge one's own work.

Logarithmic transformation   Uses a different base from simple numeric analysis; for example, a base 10 logarithm of 100 is 2.0 because $10^{2.0}$ is 100, log of $10^{3.0}$ equals 1000, log of $10^{4.0}$ equals 10,000 and so on. Because the logs 1, 2, 3, 4 . . . correspond to the numbers 10, 100, 1000, 10000 . . . , logarithms become a convenient way for transforming highly skewed data or data that has huge variation.

Longitudinal studies   Employs data on many periods of time but only one (or a few) variables.

Machine-readable data   Data that can be manipulated by computers. Usually this means inputting with a numeric system of some type.

Main effect   The independent effects of the independent variables in an experimental study.

Marginal   A term used to describe the subtotals of cell rows or columns or totals for an entire table.

Masking   Creates the illusion of three-dimensional space by moving a hyperplane through the data space, extinguishing (or illuminating) points when they are hit by the plane.

Matching   A nonrandomization method of insuring that the same number of some class of objects are in each of two groups. It is used to control for some alternative hypotheses, although it is not as powerful as randomization.

Maturation effect   Relatively microchanges in the internal conditions of the sample or population that are separate from the study's independent and dependent variables.

Mean   The arithmetic mean is defined as the sum of all data values divided by the number of such values.

Median   Measured by collecting all the values and ordering them by increasing value. Half of the values in the sample will fall below and above the median value. The median value is highly appropriate when the data are not bimodal and when the data are highly skewed.

Metaphor   Refers to a particular set of linguistic processes whereby aspects of one object are "carried over" or transferred to another object, so that one speaks of the second object as if it were the first.

Method of agreement   Examines several cases that share crucial similarities that imply common causal factors.

Method of disagreement   Examines several positive and negative cases lead to a crude implication of causation of the variation.

Methodological note   The field researcher's self-observational notes or concern about the methodological process.

Mixed-motive game   Combines features of both zero-sum and nonzero-sum strategies. Mixed-motive strategies are most common in everyday life, but they lead to relatively complex outcomes that are challenging to understand.

Mode   Simply the value that occurs most frequently.

Model   A distillation of reality to highlight important processes; the more distilled, the more likely the model loses generality or external validity.

Morals   Principles of right and wrong behavior.

Multicollinearity   If two independent variables are highly correlated, the high correlation can make the computation of the effects of each independent variable on the dependent variable highly unreliable.

Multiple (alternate) forms validity   Alternate forms of identical measuring devices for the same sample. A high association between measures is a criteria for high reliability. Researchers say that multiple-form measures of reliability provide a measure of equivalence of forms.

Multiple r squared   Is used in regression analysis. A measure of the combined effects of all the independent variables.

Multiple time-series design   Provides a comparison group (though *without* randomization of treatment); the researcher can use this design to give some indication of comparative, shared historical trends.

Multiple-choice question   One with more than two alternative responses.

Multistage sampling   Employs at least two stages. Usually, these designs combine various types of sampling methods to take advantage of the positive features of each. In actual practice, sampling experts recommend that multistage sampling designs utilize cluster sampling.

Mundane realism   Whether or not the events that occur in the experimental setting are part of the realm of everyday experiences.

Narrative account   A primary goal of fieldwork is a written product of what went on in the sequence in which various actions occurred. It is meant to assist memory in recording events for analysis, because memory is always selective and distorted.

Necessary condition   Refers to a state of affairs that must exist for another state to exist.

Negation   Less desirable than positive statements, because the communication of negative thoughts is always more difficult to understand.

Nominal classification   Something that can only be differentiated as alike or unalike.

Nonexperimental design   Design in which one is unable to randomize individuals into different groups and has no control over the introduction of the treatment.

Nonrecursive relationship   Reciprocal causal relationships which are forbidden in ordinary regression analysis.

Nonzero-sum game   Strategies in which there may be more than one winner or loser.

Nondirective probes   Include a variety of neutral techniques for obtaining more complete information from respondents.

Nonequivalent control group design   Equivalent to the classical design, except for the crucial factor of the researcher's inability to randomize subjects into treatments.

Nonsequential analysis   Totals of absolute or relative (percentage) frequencies of observational forms or analysis of duration of behaviors.

Nonverbal observation   Communicates important information, but that information is highly restricted to emotional content. It says little or nothing about other important factors, such as what the person is thinking or intends to do.

Note taking   The process of keeping a file in which one records ideas, personal notes, excerpts from books, bibliographic items, and outlines of projects; a crucial tool in field research.

Nuremberg Code   Grew out of the Nazi war crime trials and presented an absolute ethical position on such things as informed consent.

Observational note   The field researcher's statements of who said or did what, when, where, and how in an ethnography.

Observer self-interview schedule   Uses a structured interview-like format which the observer fills out during, or immediately following, each observational transaction.

Observer-as-participant   A fieldworker role whereby one engages in telling him- or herself what he or she is seeing as opposed to understanding action from the point of view of the participants.

On-line catalogue   A computerized display of a library's card catalog.

On-line database search   "On-line" refers to direct communication with a computer. A "database" is a machine-readable record on which indexes, abstracts, catalogs, or other data are stored.

Open-ended question   Leaves the respondent free to respond in an unrestricted manner.

Operationalization   The precise means of measurement used to detail as explicitly as possible the ways in which variables are measured in a study, so that other scientists may judge how accurately and adequately those measurements test the study hypotheses and measure the evidence for or against some theory.

Optically scanned data (OpScan)   An efficient form of data entry using sheets of paper with entry spots marked with special pencils such as are widely used in mass educational testing.

Oral history   Traces back to the life history method which has come to represent groups of people who have paltry written records. Oral historians pride themselves on doing "grass roots history," or the history of the nonelite, or the history of ordinary people leading ordinary lives.

Ordinal scale   Allows for the rank ordering of some phenomena in terms of fixed greater or lesser amounts.

Organizational analysis   Employs such variables as bureaucratization, criteria (universalistic versus particularistic), rigidity of rules, and type of organizational control (public versus private, sectarian versus nonsectarian, decentralized versus centralized).

Outlier   A value which is extremely far from the mean; usually defined as more than three standard deviations.

Outline   Provides a structural base upon which to fill in details for effective writing.

Panel study   Usually involves a large number of variables from a single sample followed over a small number of times.

Paradigms   A special type of intellectual puzzle. Different scientific communities share specific constellations of beliefs, values, and techniques for deciding what questions are interesting or not, how one should break down an interesting question into solvable parts, and how to interpret the relationships of those parts to the answers.

Parsimony   The logic that the scientist assume no more causes or forces than are necessary to account for all the facts. In practice, this means that when faced with two theories with equal explanatory value, the scientist should chose the simpler one.

Participant observation   Includes watching and being a part of the events under study, and maintaining stable relationships in a host group. The goal is to experience a social setting from the participant's point of view; it provides insights into routinized and habitual actions often hidden even from the participant; and it can create an understanding of groups and experiences about which outsiders may know little or nothing.

Participant-as-observer   A fieldworker role which depends on more time participating than observing, and those observed are generally aware of his or her role, but the building of rapport presents the danger of informants overidentifying with the fieldworker and his or her role.

Passive voice   Recognized by prefixing some form of the copula *be* (*is, are, was, were,* etc.) or *get* or *become* to the past participle. The passive voice is the weakest part of the English language, because it is circumlocutory, lacks brevity and clarity of subject, hides accountability for actions, and it confuses direction of causality.

Path analysis   An extension of multiple regression, much used in the social sciences, which uses variations on multiple regression to examine theoretical models. The objective is to examine the fit of the model to the data. The most interesting use of path analysis is in the tracing of indirect relationships of the type x → y → z, where *x* only indirectly influences *z* through *y*.

Pearson's correlation coefficient (*r*)   The most used measure of correlation between two variables. (See correlation.)

Percentage table   Standardizes raw data which is cross-classified on either the row subtotals, column subtotals, or total of all scores.

Performance variables   Measures program output in terms of policy objectives.

Personnel cost   In addition to salaries, there are a wealth of less visible costs: employer contributions to dental, medical, and disability insurance, retirement plans and social security.

Phenomenology   Holds that humans cannot know reality, but rather, humans construct reality by virtue of what goes on inside their minds. Phenomenologists maintain that it is impossible to know an object external to the self, without considering how the mind influences perceptions of the outside world.

Physical traces   Fall into two classes: (1) erosion measures, or signs of selective wearing of some material; and (2) accretion measures, or signs of material deposit.

Pie chart   A nonscientific, presentational graphic which uses a circle with pie wedges representing different nominal categories.

Placebo   Includes any innocuous treatment that can serve as a control, because participants believe they are receiving a real treatment when in fact they are not.

Postcoding   Coding of data after they have been collected.

Posttest   Measurement of a control and treatment group after the introduction of a treatment to test for effects of the treatment.

Precoding   Those situations where the researcher decides before starting data collection what symbols to assign for any particular variable.

Prediction   Estimates of how things will work in the future.

Predictive validity   Associates the operationalization with some variable of theoretical interest.

Presentational graphic   Used for communicating simple—usually univariate and categorical—nonscientific results to others.

Pretest   A measurement taken on an experimental and control group, before a treatment is introduced; used to insure that they are equivalent.

Primary data sources   Original sources as opposed to secondhand and thirdhand sources.

Primary sampling unit (PSU)   Imagine a listing of all counties in the United States stratified according to size of population. Within each list, one samples from the stratified clusters of counties as a first stage. In the second stage, one samples clusters of city blocks. Within these sampling units, one draws a simple random sample of dwelling units termed primary sampling units.

Primary source   Based on direct experience rather than secondhand information.

Prisoner's dilemma   A much used game for studying conflict and cooperation, which by definition, is a mixed-motive game in which the temptation to defect (T) must be of greater value than the reward for mutual cooperation (C), which must be of greater value than the punishment for mutual defection (D), which must be of greater value still than the sucker's payoff (S); and (2) the combination of the temptation (T) and sucker's payoff (S) divide by two must be smaller than (preferable to) the reward for mutual cooperation (C).

Privacy   Freedom from unauthorized intrusion.

Probability plot   An informative variation of the quantile-quantile plot, which displays the raw values of a variable against corresponding percentage points of a standard normal distribution.

Probability proportionate to size (PPS)   Takes into account the varying sizes of clusters. The statistician wishes to select a city block according to its size. Within each block, the statistician chooses the same number of households, so that each household always has the same chance of selection. The PPS strategy, therefore, calculates probability of selection as a three-stage process.

Probability sampling   Occurs when every unit, whether sampled or not, has a known chance of selection which is greater than 0 and less than 1.

Probability scale   Presumes only the likelihood that a phenomenon exists, as opposed to cardinal scales which measure actual existence.

Program inputs   Effort or activity variables that measure what the evaluation program is doing or how it is doing.

Program outputs   Measures in evaluation studies that focus on performance on policy objectives and efficiency of program costs.

Project goals   Operationalized as "outputs" or "outcomes" of evaluation programs.

Project objectives   Formulations of project goals, which depend in large measure on whose values the evaluator considers and who the intended user of the results is thought to be.

Provisionalizing   The earliest stage of field research, when the investigator knows little about the group or organization, which is normally spent in simple selection of problems, concepts, indices, and their definitions.

Proximics   The study of man's need to lay claim to an organized territory, as well as to maintain a pattern of discrete distances from one's fellows.

Purposive sampling   Lacks at least one of the characteristics of a probability sample; a purposive sample has units with a known selection chance equal to 0% or 100% or, as is much more likely, where the chance of selection is unknown.

Qualitative typology   Nominal classifications used because the qualitative nature of most field data obviates the possibility of rigor of ordinal-, cardinal-, or ratio-scaled measures.

Quantile-quantile plot   Uses the median of one of the group's posttest scores, and plots it against the median of the other group's, then plots the 75th percentile of one group against the 75th percentile of the other group, then the 25th percentile of one against the other and so on. In the end, the investigator will pick out a variety of different percentiles and, in each case plot one group's value against that of the other group.

Quartile   Divides the ordered data into quarters.

Quasi-experimental design   Controls the *when* and *to whom* of *measurement* but not of subject assignment.

Questionnaire   A self-administered interview which requires particularly clear self-explanatory instructions and question design.

Quick analysis   Entails the active and rapid employment of a gross outline of what is known about some problem or policy to figure out the logical implications of general courses of action.

Quintamentional design   A fivefold organization of questions, which can increase the reliability and validity of subjective phenomena measurement: an open-ended knowledge question taps *awareness* of the attitude object; another open-ended question helps ascertain *general attitudes* toward the same object; a closed-ended question then measures *specific attitudes*; fourth, another open-ended question taps *reasons* for holding this attitude; and finally, a closed-ended exploration of *intensity* of feeling.

Quota sampling   A special case of representative samples, in which the variable representation is made *proportionate* to the working universe.

Randomization   A technique used in experimentation which divides all units into two groups, then making both subsamples as nearly alike as is possible in the original condition before pretesting.

Randomized response technique   A method of protecting individual privacy for any type of sensitive behavior or attitude in which the respondent flips a coin (or similarly manipulates some other randomizing device) just after the interviewer has asked a sensitive two-way question. Because only the respondent knows the outcome of the coin toss, only the respondent will know whether his or her succeeding answer is a response to the coin toss or the question.

Randomness   Involves empirical answers to three important questions: How much uncertainty exists in the initial conditions? How quickly—after how many iterations (computational repetitions) or trials—is a little bit of uncertainty in the initial conditions magnified? How close is the system to random after a certain number of iterations?

Rare element sampling   Represents (or overrepresents) variable values of low frequencies.

Rate   Standardization of the relative frequency of occurrence of some event, by dividing the number of occurrences of some event by the size of the total group in which that event might take place.

Ratio   Standardization of population size for purposes of comparison.

Ratio scale   Based on the relationship between two quantities.

Raw frequency distribution   Displays the number of cases for each category of a variable.

Reactive effect   A problem of external validity which asks how broadly applicable the results of the study are; that is, it questions how the process of measurement may *change* that which the researcher is measuring.

Readability   Some formula exist for judging grade level of reading which are widely used to judge ability of respondents to understand questions.

Readability formula   Some quantitative means of judging the educational grade level of a particular piece of written work.

Ready-reference   For short, quick answers to basic questions, the researcher may turn to standard reference works: dictionaries, encyclopedias, almanacs, yearbooks, and the like.

Reciprocal relationship   Exists when *both* of two variables influence one another.

Recoding   The coding of data which needs further coding through new coding schemes or reduced, increased, or more precise categorization.

Recursive relationship   The path analysis requirement that the influence of one variable on another must be asymmetrical.

Reference source   Something used for consultation containing useful information or facts such as an encyclopedia, that capsulizes and organizes accumulated knowledge alphabetically by subject for scholarly purposes.

Regression analysis   Breaks down the effects of the analysis into the net effects of each independent variable and the total effect of all independent variables.

Reification   The mistaking of theoretical abstraction for reality.

Reliability   Measures whether or not different measures produce similar responses.

Replication   The systematic duplication of research, or reproduction of results. Answers the question: What *chance* is there that the results were due to chance?

Reputational method   A study in which the researcher asks panels of "judges" to identify community leaders.

Research method   Provides ways to organize scientific inquiries into knowledge by adhering to particular rules and principles of logic.

Retrospective observation   A reiterative process of running through the considerable number of field notes collected to redirect and reconceptualize the observation.

Revision   The act of looking over written work to improve and correct it.

Robust   Statistical analysis which holds up when different tests or assumptions are used.

Routine mapping   The production of a *narrative account* of what went on in the sequence in which various actions occurred.

Row percentage   A form of tabular analysis, in which the raw cell totals are first added across rows and used to divide into each raw cell frequency to standardize the data.

Rule-based knowledge   Begins with a set of premises, and the goal is another statement known as the theorem. The logician combines and modifies premises through a half-dozen rules of inference until the manipulation applied in the right order produces the theorem.

Sampling frame The concrete list of sampling units from which a probability sample is selected.

Scale Consists of *more than two* indices that have been combined into a single measurement through some procedural rule or rules.

Scatterplot A two-dimension plot similar to the two-variable tables in that the researcher charts one variable on the vertical axis and the other on the horizontal axis, just as in tabular analysis, where one variable goes along the rows and the other along the columns.

Schedule, Survey A highly structured interview technique which is based on the desire to present all respondents with the same stimuli so that they respond to the same research instrument.

Science Involves methods of knowledge, as opposed to belief or opinion. Over time, the word "science" has come to denote particular branches of knowledge, and ways of knowing.

Scientific anomaly An observation that is incompatible with an hypotheses or that is not deducible from established theories, and which contradicts the accepted approach.

Scientific revolution Changes in fundamental rules which lead to new sciences or disciplines.

Secondary data sources Are citations from primary sources. Textbooks, encyclopedias, handbooks, annual reviews, newspaper articles, and television reports typically quote or cite from original research or writing. In historical research, it refers to archival records.

Secrecy The state of being hidden or concealed. In the ethics of social research, it is normally self-defeating in the long run, leading to lack of trust.

Semantic differential scale Distinguishes between the *connotations*, or meanings, of words using three major connotational dimensions: *Evaluation, Potency*, and *Activity* known by the acronym EPA.

Sensitizing concept Qualitative variables that refer only to *what* will be observed, as opposed to the more quantitative variables that refer to *how* it will be observed.

Sentence complexity Consisting of a main clause and one or more subordinate clauses.

Sentence-syntax bias Systematic sources of bias rooted in linguistic context of three types: sentence complexity, voice, and direction.

Separate-sample pretest-posttest design Similar to both the nonequivalent control group design and the classical design, but the researcher has no assurance that the control group did not receive the experimental treatment. This design is especially useful in studying *large* social units.

Sequential analysis Analysis of streams of antecedent-consequent behaviors.

Serendipity Looking for one thing, but unexpectedly finding another.

Serial A publication issued as one of a consecutively numbered and indefinitely continuing series.

Simple random sampling (s.r.s.) A sample from a working universe in which every unit, whether sampled or not, has the same chance of selection.

Simulation The exercise of a flexible imitation of processes and outcomes for the purpose of clarifying or explaining the underlying mechanisms involved. A simulation, therefore, is a symbolic abstraction, simplification, or substitution for some system. In other words, a simulation is a theoretical model of the elements, relationships, and processes that may reasonably symbolize some system.

Situational variables Variables that are not subject to project control, but which might be plausible candidates as independent variables.

Skepticism The obligation to demonstrate the truth of theories. Ideally, scientists operate by following stringent rules for demonstrating claims, rather than accepting authority and social convention.

Sleeper questions Mislead all respondents to catch the few who mislead the researcher by asking fake questions.

Slope Describes the effect of x on y in a linear equation of the form $y = a + bx$ where b is the slope. The larger the slope, the greater the effect of x on y.

Snowball sampling Uses those persons (or things) suggested by the researcher's first wave of respondents to suggest new persons to study in a second wave, and so on, until the researcher exhausts all persons from which to sample.

Social audit Provides a means of tracing resource inputs throughout the life course of a program to find out whether inputs actually reached intended recipients and, if so, whether they were effective.

Social benefit Used in cost-benefit analysis as a means of measuring trade-offs of those things that promote well-being.

Social desirability bias Choice of an answer because it makes a person appear well-adjusted, unprejudiced, rational, open-minded, or democratic.

Social network The study of clusters of individuals joined by a variety of links that transmit goods, services, information, influence, or affect.

Societal analysis Involves such macroscopic indicators as degree of urbanization, industrialization, education, gross national product, and distributions of political wealth and power.

Sociogram A visual representation of social choice, communication, and interaction in groups in which the analyst asks individuals such questions as: With whom would you like most (or least) to work?

Sociological calendar A device for condensing and analyzing data about social processes. In constructing a sociological calendar, the fieldworker attempts to work out the *latent* units of time in a social organization, by contrast to manifest units such as days, weeks, and months.

Sociometric measures Based on subjective reports (or even actual observations) the investigator represents individuals by simple points or numbers and network relations between individuals with directed lines or with matrices.

Solomon four-group design This design combines the classical and posttest-only designs to determine (and thus control for) any reactive effects of testing (pretest measurement or observation).

Spatial observation Studies how humans use and perceive space.

Spearman's rho A commonly used measure of association between variables used only with rank-order (ordinal) data.

Split infinitive An infinitive with *to* having a modifier between the *to* and the verbal as in "to actually do."

Split-ballot technique Randomly splits a population of respondents into two groups. The researcher compares different versions of a question for each group. The survey designer can reasonably attribute any differences in responses elicited by the questions to question wording.

Split-half reliability Requires the researcher to measure the variation in *differences* between measurements of the two half-tests (σ^2_c) and the variation in total (unsplit test) scores (σ^2_T).

Spreadsheet Visualizes data as a rectangular spreadsheet with cases down rows and variables across columns.

Spurious association A false association. In practice, one introduces some third variable to judge whether it has an influence on the original relationship. If the original relationship no longer exists, it is said to be spurious.

Standard deviation When the data are approximately normally distributed, the measures of choice are two special types of mean averages known as the variance and standard deviation. The variance is simply the mean of squared deviations of scores from the arithmetic mean. The standard deviation is the square root of the variance.

Standardized beta weight A measure of the *net* effect of an independent variable.

Statistical control Tests correlations and tabular associations for spuriousness. The researcher accomplishes this task through the introduction of a third test factor. The idea is that if the original bivariate relationship stays essentially the same after the introduction of the test factor, then it is a robust relationship.

Statistical elaboration Introduction of test factors into tables to test for spurious and true causal relationships.

Statistical interaction The combined effects of two independent variables which are not additive.

Statistical regression Occurs when quantitative measurements taken at two points in time are subject to misinterpretation, if participants were either initially selected or are compared on the basis of the *extremity* of their scores.

Stem-and-leaf plot Looks like a sideways histogram or tally, but is a more accurate visual representation of univariate data. The stems are on the left side of the display, and indicate the most significant digits in which variation occurs. The leaves are on the right side, and represent the next decimal digit after each stem for each case.

Strategic informant sampling The researcher seeks out persons occupying leadership roles to obtain an organizational picture from "the top down"; or they can use informants of lower rank to more fully comprehend the view from "the bottom up." Sometimes deviant or marginal (from the organization's point of view) informants provide distinctively strategic observations about the system's workings. Two subtypes of strategic informant samples are (1) snowball sampling, and (2) expert choice samples.

Stratified sampling Involves at least two stages. First, the researcher divides the working universe into homogeneous subparts technically known as "strata": a list of people might allow for division into men and women; a list of cities might be ordered by size of population. Second, the researcher then draws a series of random samples; one from each strata.

Structural sampling Unlike purposive samples, these are selected because of such specific *relational properties* as positions in a dominance hierarchy, communication chains, or social networks.

Style sheet A short guide for contributors with information on margins, quotations, references, headings, and abbreviations which is helpful in writing research reports.

Sufficient condition A state that assures the existence of another state.

Suppressor variable A test factor that acts to overpower the "true" strength of some variable relationship. The actual strength of the *XY* relationship becomes apparent only after controlling for the test factor.

Survey Several meanings are appropriate to its specialized use in social research: To examine or ascertain some situation, condition, or value; to determine the form, extent, or shape of some thing; and to examine some phenomenon with care.

Symbolic logic Begins with a set of premises, and the goal is another statement know as the theorem. The logician combines and modifies premises through a half-dozen rules of inference until the manipulation applied in the right order produces the theorem.

Synonym One or more words or phrases that have the same or nearly the same meaning.

Systematic observation The sustained, explicit, methodological observing and paraphrasing of social situations.

Systematic response bias Extraneous determinants of the participant's responses that undermine the scale's validity.

Systematic sampling Involves taking every *n*th unit after a randomly chosen starting unit equal or less than *n*.

Tautology Circular reasoning, involving absurdity of the repetition of a statement as its own reason, or referring to the meaninglessness of the identification of cause and effect.

Test factor A means of examining the relationship of independent and dependent variables through use of a third variable.

Test-retest reliability Take two measurements on the same population with the same instrument at different times. The higher the agreement between these measurements, the higher the reliability.

Testable question   Sets true theory apart from simple opinion; the art of construction of variables from concepts to make falsifiable predictions.

Theoretical abstraction   How grounded in concreteness one's theories are.

Theoretical notes   Inferential declarations; they are the field researcher's interpretations, inferences, hypotheses, and conjectures of observational meaning.

Theoretical Scope   Pertains to the universality of the theory.

Theory   Reserved for referring to the systematic relationships between two or more hypotheses. These are minimal definitions because mature theories and hypotheses often relate more than two hypotheses and variables. However, in any case, scientists do not use "theory" or "hypothesis" in the way laypersons do to mean a simple personal opinion or belief. The coherent set of hypothetical, conceptual, and pragmatic principles forming the general frame of reference for a field of inquiry.

Thesaurus   A book of words and their synonyms.

Three-dimensional scatterplot   Visualizes the association between three variables in a two-dimensional space.

Thurstone scale   A laborious method for measuring social consensus concerning a set of beliefs. To achieve this end, the researcher first collects a huge pool of statements that cover the entire range of valued beliefs. Second, independent judges evaluate the favorableness or unfavorableness of each *pair* of items in the scale. Third, the researcher chooses ten items that represent the full range of subjective feelings. Finally, the researcher asks the actual respondents to choose the statements that best or least express their own feelings.

Time sample   Selection of elements spread across time rather than space.

Tolerance limit   The degree of variation in precision that a researcher (or client) will willingly bear.

Treatment group   In a true experiment, this is the group randomized into the condition that receives introduction of the independent variable.

Treatment variable   The independent variable in a true experiment.

Trend study   Analyzes a small number of variables over a large number of points in time. The main problem in such studies is to control for all variables extraneous to the variables of interest, because the researcher wishes to study the "pure" effects of the variables of interest, not the confounding effects of extraneous variables.

Triangulation   The use of a variety of methods, techniques, tools, and theories to arrive at a closer approximation of the truth.

Turing test   An imaginary test for true knowledge, consisting of an interrogator communicating via teleprinters with a human and a computer, in which it would be the interrogator's job to determine which is which via conversation over the communication links.

Turnover   The mover-stayer patterns in special tables that measure change (or turnover) from one period of time to another.

Two-way question   Has only two possible responses.

Univariate analysis   Simple one-variable analysis, such as computations of measures of central tendency or variation for a single variable.

Validity   Whether or not a measurement really represents that which it is suppose to measure.

Variable   A particular type of concept, namely, a classification into two or more mutually exclusive and totally inclusive categories that explicitly undergoes change in degree.

Variable relationship   Scientific hypotheses relating two or more variables in the form "as *x* varies, *y* varies . . ."

Variance   The mean of squared deviations of scores from the arithmetic mean. It is useful as a descriptive measure when the data are relatively normally distributed.

Verification   Strictly speaking does not exist as a method of science. (See falsification.)

Working universe   The concrete operationalization of a general universe; it is a practical approximation of the ideal general universe. In probability sampling, it is identical with the sampling frame.

World-systems theory   Proposes one single world economic empire dominated by one strong center and many weak periphery states. Core states amass wealth and promote global accumulation through a system in which core countries promise weak, peripheral ones eventual wealth, as long as they stick by the rules of liberal capitalism and allow themselves to be exploited. This all-encompassing system is generated and sustained in Wallerstein's theory, by rivalry and competition between core powers, inadequate demand, wage pressures, and the search for cheap raw materials.

Zero sum game   Outcomes in which if one player wins, the other must lose, because resources are fixed.

Bibliography

Aaron, H. J. (1981) Policy implication: A progress report. Pp. 67–112 in K. L. Bradbury & A. Downs (eds.), *Do housing allowances work?* Washington, D.C.: The Brookings Institution.

Abbott, A. (1983) Professional ethics. *American Journal of Sociology, 88*, 855–885.

Abelson, R. P. (1968) Simulation of social behavior. In G. Lindzey & E. Aronson (eds.), *Handbook of social psychology, vol. II*, Reading, MS: Addison-Wesley.

Abercrombie, N., Hill, S., & Turner, B. S. (eds.) (1988) *The Penguin dictionary of sociology.* (2nd ed.) London: Penguin.

Abrams, P. (1982) *Historical Sociology.* Ithaca, New York: Cornell University Press.

Aby, S. H. (1987) *Sociology: A guide to reference and information sources.* Littleton CO: Libraries Limited.

Achen, C. H. (1987) *The statistical analysis of quasi-experiments.* Berkeley and Los Angeles: University of California Press.

Adler, P. (1985) *Wheeling and dealing: An ethnography of an upper-level drug dealing and smuggling community.* New York: Columbia University Press.

Agar, M. H. (1980) *The professional stranger: An informal introduction to ethnography.* New York: Academic Press.

Agar, M. H. (1986) *Speaking of ethnography.* Beverly Hills, CA: Sage.

Alexander, C. N. Jr., & Rudd, J. (1984) Predicting behaviors from situated identities. *Social Psychology Quarterly, 47*, 172–177.

Allen, M. (1988, January 25) When jurors are ordered to ignore testimony, they ignore the order. *The Wall Street Journal*, p. 31.

Alwin, D. (1986) Religion and parental child-rearing orientations: Evidence of a Catholic-Protestant convergence. *American Journal of Sociology, 92*, 412–440.

Ambert, A. M. (1988) Relationship between ex-spouses: Individual and dyadic perspectives. *Journal of Social and Personal Relationships, 5*, 329–346.

American Association of University Professors (1981) Regulations governing research on human subjects: Academic freedom and the institutional review board. *Academe*, xx: 358–370.

American Psychological Association (1984) *Publication manual of the American Psychological Association*. (3rd ed.) Washington, D.C.: American Psychological Association.

American Sociological Association Committee on Professional Ethics (1989) *Code of ethics*. Washington, D.C.: American Sociological Association.

American Sociological Association Council (1986) *The Cameron case*. Council report at the annual meeting of the American Sociological Association, New York.

Anderson, B. A., & Silver, B. D. (1987) The validity of survey responses: Insights from interviews of married couples in a survey of Soviet emigrants. *Social Forces, 66*, 537–554.

Anscombe, F. J. (1973) Graphs in statistical analysis. *American Statistician, 27*, 17–21.

Aronson, E., Brewer, M., & Carlsmith, J. M. (1985) Experimentation in social psychology. Pp. 441–486 in G. Lindzey & E. Aronson (eds.), *Handbook of social psychology, vol. II* (2nd ed.). Hillsdale, NJ: Lawrence Erlbaum Associates.

Aronson, E., & Carlsmith, J. M. (1968) Experimentation in social psychology. Pp. 1–79 in G. Lindzey & E. Aronson (eds.), *Handbook of social psychology, vol. II* (2nd ed.). Reading MA: Addison-Wesley.

Axelrod, R. (1984) *The evolution of cooperation*. New York: Basic.

Aydelotte, W. O. (1969) Quantification in history. Pp. 1–14 in D. K. Rowney & J. Q. Graham, Jr. (eds.), *Quantitative history: Selected readings in the quantitative analysis of historical data*. Homewood IL: The Dorsey Press.

Bahr, H. M., Caplow, T., & Chadwick, B. A. (1983) Middletown III: Problems of replication, longitudinal measurement, and triangulation. *Annual Review of Sociology, 9*, 243–264.

Bales, R. F. (1970) *Personality and interpersonal behavior*. New York: Holt, Rinehart, & Winston.

Balestri, D. P. (1988) Softcopy and hard: Wordprocessing and writing process. *Academic Computing, 2*, 14–17, 41–45.

Banaka, W. (1971) *Training in depth interviewing*. New York: Harper & Row, Pub.

Barber, B. (1980) *Informed consent in medical therapy and research*. New Brunswick: Rutgers University Press.

Barker, E. (1984) *The making of a Moonie: Brainwashing or choice?* New York: Basil Blackwell.

Barnes, S. D. (1972) On the reception of scientific beliefs. Pp. 269–291 in B. Barnes (ed.), *Sociology of science*. Baltimore: Penguin.

Barry, H., Child, I., & Bacon, M. (1959) A cross-cultural survey of some sex differences in socialization. *Journal of Abnormal Social Psychology, 55*, 327–332.

Barton, A. H., & Lazarsfeld, P. F. (1955) Some functions of qualitative analysis in social research. *Frankfurter Beiträge zur Sociologie, 1*, 321–361.

Barzun, J., & Graff, H. F. (1970) *The modern researcher*. New York: Harcourt, Brace & World, Inc.

Baum, W. K. (1977) *Transcribing and editing oral history*. Nashville TN: American Association for State and Local History.

Becker, H. S. (1963) *Oursiders*. London: Free Press.

Becker, H. S. (1970) *Sociological work: Methods and substance*. Chicago: Aldine.

Becker, H. S. (1985) Software for sociologists: Finding facts and mastering data. *Contemporary Sociology: A Journal of Reviews, 14*, 450–451.

Becker, H. S. (1986a) Photographing the social landscape. Pp. 15–18 in J. S. Tucker (ed.), *Landscape perspectives: Photographic studies*. St. Louis: University of Missouri-St. Louis.

Becker, H. S. (1986b) *Writing for social scientists: How to start and finish your thesis, book, or article.* Chicago: University of Chicago Press.

Belson, W. A. (1981) *The design and understanding of survey questions.* Aldershot, Hants., England: Gower.

Benbow, C., & Stanley, J. C. (1983) *Academic precocity: Aspects of its development.* Baltimore: Johns Hopkins.

Bendix, R. (1963) Concepts and generalizations in comparative sociological studies. *American Sociological Review, 28,* 532–539.

Bendix, R. (1984) *Force, fate, and freedom.* Berkeley: University of California Press.

Bennett, J. M. (1960) Individual perspective in fieldwork: An experimental training course. Pp. 431–442 in R. N. Adams & J. J. Preiss (eds.), *Human organization research.* Homewood, Ill.: Dorsey.

Bennett, N., & Bloom, D. (1985, May) *Black and white marriage patterns: Why so different?* Presented at the annual meeting of the Population Association of America, Boston, MA.

Bentler, P. M., & Bonett, D. C. (1980) Significance tests and goodness of fit in the analysis of covariance structures. *Psychological Bulletin, 88,* 588–606.

Berger, J., Rosenholtz, S., & Zelditch, M. (1980) Status organizing processes. *Annual Review of Sociology, 6,* 479–508.

Birdwhistell, R. (1970) *Kinesics and context.* Philadelphia: University of Pennsylvania Press.

Blalock, H. M., Jr. (1968) The measurement problem: A gap between the language of theory and research. Pp. 5–27 in H. M. Blalock, Jr. and A. B. Blalock (eds.), *Methodology in social research.* New York: McGraw-Hill.

Blau, P. M. (1964) The research process in the study of *The dynamics of bureaucracy.* Pp. 18–57 in P. E. Hammond (ed.), *Sociologists at work.* Garden City, NY: Doubleday.

Blau, P. M., & Duncan, O. D. (1967) *The American occupational structure.* New York: John Wiley.

Blumstein, A., & Cohen, J. (1987) Characterizing criminal careers. *Science, 237,* 985–991.

Bloom, D. E. & Carliner, G. (1988) The economic impact of AIDS in the United States. *Science, 239,* 604–610.

Bohrnstedt, G. W. (1970) Reliability and validity assessment in attitude measurement. Pp. 80–99 in G. F. Summers (ed.), *Attitude measurement.* Chicago: Rand McNally.

Borgatta, E. F. (1961) Toward a methodological codification: The shotgun and the saltshaker. *Sociometry, 24,* 432–435.

Borgatta, E. F., & Evans, R. R. (1969) *Smoking, health and behavior.* Chicago: Aldine.

Boring, E. G. (1953) The role of theory in experimental psychology. *American Journal of Psychology, 66,* 169–184.

Boritch, H., & Hagan, J. (1987) Crime and the changing forms of class control: Policing public order in "Toronto the Good," 1859–1955. *Social Forces, 66,* 307–335.

Boruch, R. F. (1982) Methods for resolving privacy problems in social research. Pp. 292–314 in T. L. Beauchamp, R. R. Faden, R. J. Wallace, Jr., and L. Walters (eds.), *Ethical issues in social science research.* Baltimore: The Johns Hopkins Press.

Boruch, R. F., McSweeny, A. J., & Soderstrom, E. J. (1978) Randomized field experiments for program planning, development, and evaluation: An illustrative bibliograph. *Evaluation Quarterly, 2,* 655–695.

Bourguignon, E. (1977) Altered states of consciousness, myths, and rituals. Pp. 7–23 in B. M. Du Toit (ed.), *Drugs, rituals and altered states of consciousness.* Rotterdam: A.A. Balkema.

Bower, B. (1987, October 31) How effective are bulimia treatments? *Science News, 132* p. 2178.

Bradburn, N. M., Rips, L. J., & Shevell, S. K. (1987) Answering autobiographical questions: The impact of memory and inference on surveys. *Science, 236*, 157–161.

Brazleton, T. B. (1988) *To listen to a child*. Reading, MA: Addison-Wesley.

Brent, E. (1987) *EX-SAMPLE* [IBM–PC compatible program] Columbia, MO: The Idea Works, Inc.

Bridges, W. P., & Villemez, W. J. (1986) Informal hiring and income in the labor market. *American Sociological Review, 51*, 574–582.

Briggs, V. M. Jr. (1987) The growth and composition of the U. S. labor force. *Science, 238*, 176–180.

Broadbent, J. (1989) Environmental politics in Japan: An integrated structural approach. *Sociological Forum, 4*, 179–202.

Brooks, M. P. (1965) The community action program as a setting for applied research. *Journal of Social Issues, 21*, 29–40.

Brown, J. A., & Gilmartin, B.G. (1969) Sociology today: Lacunae, emphasis and surfeits. *American Sociologist, 4*, 283–291.

Bruner, J. S., & Postman, L. (1949) On the perception of incongruity: A paradigm. *Journal of Personality, 18*, 206–223.

Buchanan, B. G., & Shortliffe, E. H. (eds.) (1985) *Rule-based expert systems: The MYCIN experiments of the Stanford heuristic programming project*. Menlo Park, CA: Addison-Wesley.

Bulmer, J. A. (1980) *Who should know what? Social science, privacy and ethics*. New York: Cambridge University Press.

Burke, P. (1980) *Sociology and history*. London: George Allen & Unwin.

Button, G. (1987) Answers as interactional products: Two sequential practices used in interviews. *Social Psychology Quarterly, 50*, 160–171.

Caldwell, P. (1983) *The Puritan conversion narrative*. New York: Cambridge University Press.

Camic, C. (1986) The matter of habit. *American Journal of Sociology, 91*, 1039–1087.

Campbell, D. T. (1958) Common fate, similarity and other indices of the status of aggregates of persons as social entities. *Behavioral Science, 3*, 14–25.

Campbell, D. T. (1968) Likert versus bipolar formats: A comparison of strengths and weakness. Unpublished paper, Northwestern University.

Campbell, D. T. (1969) Reforms as experiments. *American Psychologist, 24*, 409–429.

Campbell, D. T. (1972) Methods for the experimenting society. *American Psychologist, 27*, 810–818.

Campbell, D. T., & Fiske, D. W. (1959) Convergent and discriminant validation by the multitrait-multimethod matrix. *Psychological Bulletin, 56*, 81–105.

Campbell, D. T., & Stanley, J. C. (1963) *Experimental and quasi-experimental designs for research*. Chicago: Rand McNally.

Cannell, C. F., & Kahn, R. L. (1968) Interviewing. Pp. 526–595 in G. Lindzey & E. Aronson (eds.), *Handbook of social psychology, vol. II* (2nd ed.). Reading, MA: Addison-Wesley.

Caplow, T. (1983) Response to the comment by Miller and Cisin—"Avoiding bias in 'derivative samples': A neglected issue in family studies." *American Sociological Review, 48*, 878.

Caplow, T., & McGee, R. J. (1958) *The academic marketplace*. New York: Academic.

Carroll, L. (1960) *The annotated Alice*. (M. Gardner, ed.). New York: Clarkson M. Potter. (Original work published 1865).

Case, D. O. (1986) Office bookshelf spatial differences among academics *Journal of Information Science, 12*, 97–104.

Center for Disease Control Vietnamese Study (1987) Post-service mortality among Vietnamese veterans. *Journal of the American Medical Association, 257*, 790–795.

Chapple, E. D. (1949) The interaction chronograph: Its evaluation and present application. *Personnel, 25*: 295–307.

Chirot, D., & Hall, T. D. (1982) World-system theory. *Annual Review of Sociology, 8*, 81–106.

Christie, R., & Geis, F. L. (eds.). (1970). *Studies in Machiavellianism*. New York: Academic Press.

Chun, K., Barnowe, J. T., Wykowski, K., Cobb, S., & French, J. R. (1972) Selection of psychological measures: Quality or convenience? *American Psychological Association Proceedings, 1*, 15–16.

Cleary, P. (1987) Compulsory premarital screening for the human immunodeficiency virus. *Journal of the American Medical Association, 258*, 1757–1783.

Cleveland, W. S. (1985) *The elements of graphing data*. Belmont, CA: Wadsworth.

Cleveland, W. S., Harris, C. S., & McGill, R. (1982) Judgments of circle sizes on statistical maps. *Journal of the American Statistical Association, 77*, 541–547.

Cleveland, W. S., & McGill, R. (1984) Graphical perception: Theory, experiments, and the application to the development of graphical methods. *Journal of the American Statistical Association, 79*, 531–554.

Cobb, R. (December 3, 1971) Historians in white coats. *Times Literary Supplement*, Pp. 1527–1528.

Cohen, I. B. (1985) *Revolution in science*. Cambridge, MS: Belknap Press.

Cohen, J. (1977) *Statistical power analysis for the behavioral sciences* (Rev. ed.). New York: Academic.

Cohen, L. E., & Land, K. C. (1987) Age structure and crime: Symmetry versus asymmetry and the projection of crime rates through the 1990s. *American Sociological Review, 52*, 170–183.

Cole, S. (1979) Age and scientific performance. *American Journal of Sociology, 84*, 958–977.

Coleman, J. S. (1964) Mathematical models and computer simulation. Pp. 1027–1062 in R. E. L. Faris (ed.), *Handbook of modern sociology*. Chicago: Rand McNally.

Coleman, J. S. (1966) In defense of games. *American Behavioral Scientist, 10*, 3–4.

Coleman, J. S. (1972) *Policy research in social science*. Morristown, N. J.: General Learning Press.

Coleman, J. S., Katz, E., & Menzel, H. (1957) The diffusion of an innovation among physicians. *Sociometry, 20*, 253–270.

Collins, B. J. (1987) Compound random number generators. *Journal of the American Statistical Association, 82*, 525–527.

Committee on the Status of Women in Sociology (1988) *The treatment of gender in research*. Washington, DC: American Sociological Association.

Congressional Office of Technology Assessment (1987) *The electronic supervisor*. Washington, DC: U. S. Government Printing Office.

Conklin, G. H. (1982) CLEAR 5: Social Inequality (IBM-PC & APPLE II + software). New York: Holt, Rinehart, & Winston.

Converse, P. E., & Traugott, M. W. (1986) Assessing the accuracy of polls and surveys. *Science, 234*, 1094–1098.

Cook, T. D., & Campbell, D. T. (1979) *Quasi-experimentation: Design and analysis issues for field settings*. Chicago: Rand McNally.

Coombs, C. (1953) *Research methods in the behavioral sciences*. New York: John Wiley.

Crane, D. M. (1972) *Invisible colleges: Diffusion of knowledge in scientific communities*. Chicago: University of Chicago Press.

Cronbach, L. J. (1980) *Toward reform of program evaluation*. San Francisco: Jossey-Bass.

Dalby, L. C. (1985) *Geisha*. New York: Vintage Books.

Dalton, M. (1964) Preconceptions and methods in *Men Who Manage*. Pp. 58–110 in P. E. Hammond (ed.), *Sociologists at Work*. Garden City, N.Y.: Doubleday/Anchor.

Darley, J. M., & Bateson, C. D. (1973) From Jerusalem to Jericho: A study of situational and dispositional variables in helping behavior. *Journal of Personality and Social Behavior, 27*, 100–108.

Davies, M., & Kandel, D. B. (1981) Parental and peer influences on adolescents' education plans: Some further evidence. *American Journal of Sociology, 87*, 363–387.

Davis, C., Back, K., & MacLean, K. (1977) *Oral history: From tape to type*. Nashville TN: American Association for State and Local History.

Davis, J. A. (1970) *Elementary survey analysis*. Englewood Cliffs, NJ: Prentice-Hall.

Davis, K. (1978) Methods for studying informal communication. *Journal of Communication, 90*, 112–116.

Davis, M. (1983) *Game theory: A nontechnical introduction*. New York: Basic. (Originally published in 1970.)

Dawes, T. L., & Smith, R. M. (1985) Attitude and opinion measurement. Pp. 509–566 in G. Lindsey & E. Aronson (eds.), *Handbook of social psychology, vol. 1: Theory and method* (3rd ed.). Hillsdale, NJ: Erlbaum.

Dean, J. P., Eichhorn, R. L. & Dean, L. P. (1967) Observations and interviewing. (Pp. 274–304 in J. P. Doby (ed.), *An introduction to social research* (2nd ed.). New York: Appleton-Century-Crofts.

Dennett, D. C. (1984) The role of the computer metaphor in understanding the mind. Pp. 266–276 in H. R. Pagels (ed.), *Computer culture: The scientific, intellectual, and social impact of the computer*. New York: New York Academy of Sciences.

Denzin, N. K. (1970) *The research act*. Chicago: Aldine.

Devine, J. A., Sheley, J. F., & Smith, M. D. (1988) Macroeconomic and social-control policy influences on crime rate changes, 1948–1985. *American Sociological Review, 53*, 407–420.

Dexter, L. (1970) *Elite and specialized interviewing*. Evanston, IL: Northwestern University Press.

Diaconis, P. (1986, April) Interview on *All things considered* with Persi Diaconis, Professor of Statistics at Stanford University. Washington, D. C.: National Public Radio.

Diaconis, P. & Engel, E. (1986) "Some statistical applications of Poisson's work" by I. J. Good. Comment. *Statistical Science, 1*, 171–174.

Dibble, V. K. (1963) Four types of inference from documents to events. *Theory and History, 3*, 203–221.

Diener, E., & Crandall, R. (1978) *Ethics in social and behavioral research*. Chicago: University of Chicago Press.

Dodd, S. C. (1947) Standards for surveying agencies. *Public Opinion Quarterly, 11*, 115–130.

Dorfman, D. D. (1978) The Cyril Burt question: New findings. *Science, 201*, 1177–1186.

Dreeban, R., & Gamoran, A. (1986) Race, instruction, and learning. *American Sociological Review, 51*, 660–669.

Duncan, O. D. (1984) *Notes on social measurement*. New York: Russell Sage Foundation.

Durkheim, E. (1958) *Professional ethics and civic morals*. Glencoe, IL: Free Press.

Efron, B. (1987) Better bootstrap confidence intervals. *Journal of the American Statistical Association, 82*, 171–186.

Efron, B., & Thisted, R. (1976) Estimating the number of unseen species: How many words did Shakespeare know? *Biometrika, 63*, 435–447.

Ekman, P. (1985) *Telling lies. Clues to deceit in the marketplace, politics, and marriage*. New York: Norton.

Eliot, J. (1987) *A class divided: Then and now*. New Haven, CT: Yale University Press.

Elms, A. C. (1982) Keeping deception honest: Justifying conditions for social scientific research stratagems. Pp. 232–245 in T. L. Beauchamp, R. Faden, R. J. Wallace, Jr., & L. Walters (eds.), *Ethical issues in social science research.* Baltimore: The Johns Hopkins Press.

Erikson, K. T. (1966) *Wayward Puritans: A study in the sociology of deviance.* New York: Wiley.

Erikson, K. T. (1970) Sociology and the historical perspective. *The American Sociologist, 5*, 331–338.

Evans, G. (1979) On-line networking: A bibliographic essay. *Bulletin of the American Society for Information Science, 5*, 11–14.

Faden, R. R., & Beauchamp, T. L. (1986) *A history and theory of informed consent.* New York: Oxford University Press.

Farber, H. S. (1987) The recent decline of unionization in the U. S. *Science, 915*, 915–920.

Farquharson, R. (1969) *Theory of voting.* New Haven, CT: Yale University Press.

Feinstein, G. W. (1960) Letter from a triple-threat grammarian. *College English, 21*, 408.

Feldman, D. A., & Johnson, T. M. (eds.). (1986) *The social dimensions of AIDS: Method and theory.* New York: Praeger.

Fialka, J. J. (1987, December 31) Maybe you thought they didn't produce wine in England. *Wall Street Journal*, Pp. 1,10.

Finke, R., & Stark, R. (1988) Religious economies and sacred canopies: Religious mobilization in American cities, 1906. *American Sociological Review, 53*, 41–50.

Fiorentine, R. (1987) Men, women, and the premed persistence gap: A normative alternative approach. *American Journal of Sociology, 92*: 1118–1139.

Firebaugh, G. (1978) A rule for inferring individual-level relationships from aggregate data. *American Sociological Review, 43*, 557–572.

Fischer, D. H. (1970) *Historian's fallacies: Toward a logic of historical thought.* New York: Harper & Row.

Fishbein, M. (1980) A theory of reasoned action: Some applications and implications. *Nebraska Symposium on Motivation, 1979, 27*: 65–116.

Flesch, R. (1954) *How to make sense.* New York: Harper & Row.

Form, W. (1987) Editor's comments. American Sociological Review, *52*, vi.

Forster, E. M. (1927) *Aspects of the novel.* New York: Harcourt Brace.

Forsyth, E., & Katz, L. (1946) A matrix approach to the analysis of sociometric data. *Sociometry, 9*, 340–347.

Freedman, D. (1983) *Margaret Mead and Samoa: The making and unmaking of an anthropological myth.* Cambridge: Harvard University Press.

Freeman, J., Carroll, G. R., & Hannan, M. T. (1983) The liability of newness: Age dependence in organizational death rates. *American Sociological Review, 48*, 692–710.

Freilich, M. (1970) Mohawk heroes and Trinidadian peasants. In M. Freilich (ed.), *Marginal natives: Anthropologists at work.* New York: Harper & Row.

Freud, S. (1959) Fragment of an analysis of a case of hysteria. *Collected papers.* (Vol. 3) New York: Basic Books. (Original work published 1905.)

Friedman, D. (1986) *Price theory: An intermediate text.* Cincinnati, OH: SouthWestern Publishing Co.

Friedrichs, R. W. (1970) *A sociology of sociology.* New York: Free Press.

Galliher, J. F. (1973) The protection of human subjects: A reexamination of the professional code of ethics. *American Sociologist, 8*, 93–100.

Gallup, G. (1947) The quintamentional plan of question design. *Public Opinion Quarterly, 11*, 385–393.

Galton, F. (1885) Regression towards mediocrity in hereditary stature. *Journal of the Anthropological Institute, 15*, 246–263.

Galtung, J. (1967) *Theory and methods of social research*. New York: Columbia University Press.

Gamson, W. A. (1978) *SIMSOC: A participant's manual and related readings* (2nd ed.). New York: Free Press.

Gardner, R. J., & Zelevansky, L. (1975) The ten commandments for library customers. *Special Libraries, 66*, 326.

Garson, G. D. (1987) The role of inductive expert systems generators in the social science research process. *Social Science Microcomputer Review, 5*, 11–24.

Garson, G. D. (1986) On-line bibliographic searching: A brief tutorial using dialog. *Social Science Microcomputer Review, 4*, 67–74.

Gibbons, D. C. (1975) Unidentified research sites and fictitious names. *American Sociologist, 10*, 32–36.

Gilbert, G. N. (1981) *Modeling society: An introduction to loglinear analysis for social researchers*. London: George Allen & Unwin.

Glazer, B. G. (1965) The constant comparative method of qualitative analysis. *Social Problems, 12*: 436–445.

Glazer, B., & Strauss, A. (1967) *The discovery of grounded theory*. Chicago: Aldine Press.

Glazer, E. M., Abelson, H. H., & Garrison, K. N. (1983) *Putting knowledge to use: Facilitating the diffusion of knowledge and the implementation of planned change*. San Francisco: Jossey-Bass.

Gleick, J. (1987) *Chaos: Making a new science*. New York: Viking.

Goffman, E. (1974) *Frame analysis: An essay on the organization of experience*. Cambridge, MA: Harvard University Press.

Goffman, E. (1976) *Gender advertisements*. New York: Harper, Colophon.

Gourman, J. (1985) *The Gourman report: A rating of graduate and professional programs in American and international universities*. Los Angeles: National Education Standards.

Goyder, J. C. (1982) Further evidence on factors affecting response rates to mailed questionnaires. *American Sociological Review, 47*, 550–553.

Granberg, D. (1982) Family size preferences and sexual permissiveness as factors differentiating abortion activists. *Social Psychology Quarterly, 45*, 15–23.

Granovetter, M. (1974) *Getting a job*. Cambridge: Harvard University Press.

Green, M. (1988) After 1,500 years a trireme tries its water wings. *Smithsonian, 18*, 75–83.

Greenberg, J. (1987, May 23) Advances reported in predicting violence. *Science News, 131*, 324–325.

Greene, B., Bailey, J., & Barber, F. (1981) An analysis and reductive of disruptive behavior on school buses. *Journal of Applied Behavior Analysis, 14*, 177–192.

Greenhalgh, S., & Bongaarts, J. (1987) Fertility policy in China: Future options. *Science, 235*: 1167–1172.

Grobman, A. (1983) University of Missouri-St. Louis: Its status and the aspirations of its chancellor. Unpublished paper, St. Louis: University of Missouri.

Guttentag, M., & Secord, P. F. (1983) *Too many women? The sex ratio question*. Beverly Hills, CA: Sage.

Hage, G. (1972) *Techniques and problems of theory construction in sociology*. New York: John Wiley.

Hall, E. T. (1963) A system for the notation of proxemic behavior. *American Anthropologist, 65*, 1003–1026.

Hamilton, R. F. (1982) *Who voted for Hitler*? Princeton, NJ: Princeton University Press.

Hammersley, M., & Atkinson, P. (1983) *Ethnography, principles in practice*. London: Tavistock.

Haney, C., Banks, W. C., & Zimbardo, P. (1973) Interpersonal dynamics in a simulated prison. *International Journal of Criminology and Penology, 1*, 69–97.

Hastings, D. W., & Berry, L. G. (1979) *Cohort analysis: A collection of interdisciplinary readings*. Oxford, OH: Scripps Foundation.

Hauser, R. M. (1987) Sharing data: It's time for ASA journals to follow the folkways of a scientific sociology. *American Sociological Review, 52*, vi–viii.

Hawkins, J. D., & Nederhood, B. (1986) *Staff/Team Evaluation of Prevention Programs: STEPP Handbook*. Washington, D.C.: National Institute of Drug Abuse.

Heise, D. (1979) *Understanding events: Affect and the construction of social action*. New York: Cambridge University Press.

Heise, D. (1986) *ETHNO: Documentation: Guide, Reference, Tutorial* [IBM–PC computer program] Raleigh, N.C.: National Collegiate Software Clearinghouse.

Heise, D. (1988) Modeling event structures. *Journal of Mathematical Sociology, 13*, 138–168.

Heise, D., & Lewis, E. (1988) *Introduction to INTERACT* [IBM-PC computer program] Raleigh, N.C.: National Collegiate Software Clearinghouse.

Hendershot, G. E., & Placek, P. J. (1981) *Predicting fertility*. Lexington, KY: Heath.

Heyneman, S. P., & Loxley, W. A. (1983) The effect of primary-school quality on academic achievement across twenty-nine high- and low-income countries. *American Journal of Sociology, 88*, 1162–1194.

Hindelang, M. J. (1978) Race and involvement in common law personal crimes. *American Sociological Review, 43*, 93–109.

Hite, S. (1987) *Women and love*. New York: Knopf.

Hofstadter, D. (1979) *Gödel, escher, bach*. New York: Basic Books.

Holmes, T. H., & Rahe, R. H. (1967) The social readjustment rating scale. *Journal of Psychosomatic Research, 11*, 213–218.

Homans, G. C. (1950) *The human group*. Harcourt, Brace, & Jovanovich.

Hopkins, T. (1982a) The study of the capitalist world-economy: Some introductory consideration. Pp. 9–38 in T. K. Hopkins & I. Wallerstein, (eds.), *World-system analysis: Theory and methodology*. Beverly Hills: Sage.

Hopkins, T. (1982b) World-systems analysis: Methodological issues. Pp. 145–158 in T. K. Hopkins & I. Wallerstein, (eds.), *World-system analysis: Theory and methodology*. Beverly Hills: Sage.

Horowitz, I. L. (1965) The life and death of project Camelot. *Transaction, 3*, 44–48.

Hovde, H. T. (1936) Recent trends in the development of market research. *American Marketing Journal, 3*, 3.

Hovland, C. I. (1959) Reconciling conflicting results derived from experimental and survey studies of attitude change. *American Psychologist, 14*: 8–17.

Huber, P. J. (1987) Experience with three-dimensional scatterplots. *Journal of the American Statistical Association, 82*, 448–453.

Humphreys, L. (1970) *Tearoom trade: Impersonal sex in public places*. Chicago: Aldine Publishing Co.

Inbar, M, & Stoll, C. S. (eds.) (1972) *Simulation and gaming in social science*. New York: Free Press.

Isen, A. M., & Simmonds, S. (1978) The effect of feeling good on a helping task that is incompatible with good mood. *Social Psychology Quarterly, 41*, 346–349.

Janes, R. W. (1961) A note on phases of the community role of the participant observer. *American Sociological Review, 26*: 446–450.

Jasso, G. (1978) On the justice of earnings: A new specification of the justice evaluation function. *American Journal of Sociology, 83*, 1398–1419.

Jefferson, G. (1984) On stepwise transition from talk about a trouble to inappropriately ex-positioned matters. Pp. 191–222 in J. M. Atkinson, & J. Heritage (eds.), *Structures of social action*. Cambridge: Cambridge University Press.

Jennings, C. (1978) Have the samaritans lowered the suicide rate? A controlled study. *Psychological Medicine, 8*, 413–422.

Jones, R. B., & Moberg, D. P. (1988) Correlates of smokeless tobacco use in a male adolescent population. *American Journal of Public Health, 78*, 61–63.

Kain, J. F. (1981) A universal housing allowance program Pp. 339–373 in K. L. Bradbury & A. Downs (eds.), *Do housing allowances work?* Washington, D.C.: The Brookings Institution.

Kahn, R. L., & Mann, F. (1952) Developing research partnerships. *Journal of Social Issues, 8*, 4–10.

Kalton, G. (1983) *Compensating for missing survey data*. Ann Arbor, MI: University of Michigan, Institute for Social Research, Survey Research Center.

Kamin, L. (1976) *The science and politics of IQ*. Potomac, MD: Erlbaum.

Kass, R. (1977) Recent changes in male income. *The Sociological Quarterly, 18*, 357–377.

Katz, W. A. (1982a) *Introduction to reference work*. (Vol. I: Basic information sources.) New York: McGraw-Hill.

Katz, W. A. (1982b) *Introduction to reference work*. (Vol. II: Reference services and reference processes.) New York: McGraw-Hill.

Kearney, H. (1975) Personal involvement and communication context in social judgment of a controversial social issue. (Doctoral Dissertation, Pennsylvania State University, 1975) *Dissertation Abstracts International, 36*, 4756–B.

Kecskemeti, P. (1958) *Strategic surrender*. Palo Alto: Stanford University Press.

Kelly, J. R., & McGrath, J. E. (1988) *On time and method*. Newbury Park CA: Sage.

Kelman, H. (1980) The role of action in attitude change. *Nebraska Symposium on Motivation, 179, 27*, 117–196.

Kelman, H. (1982) Ethical issues in different social science methods Pp. 40–100 in T. L. Beauchamp, R. R. Faden, R. J. Wallace, Jr., & L. Walters (eds.), *Ethical issues in social science research*. Baltimore: The Johns Hopkins Press.

Kemper, T. D. (1987) How many emotions are there? Wedding the social and autonomic components. *American Journal of Sociology, 93*, 263–289.

Kerbo, H. R., & Fave, L. R. D. (1979) The empirical side of the power elite debate: An assessment and critique of recent research. *The Sociological Quarterly, 20*, 5–22.

Kidder, L., & Campbell, D. T. (1970) The indirect testing of social attitudes. Pp. 333–385 in G. F. Summers (ed.), *Attitude measurement*. Chicago: Rand McNally.

Kinsey, A. C., Pomeroy, W. B., & Martin, C. E. (1948) *Sexual behavior in the human male*. Philadelphia: Saunders.

Kish, L. (1965) *Survey sampling*. New York: John Wiley.

Kish, L. (1987) *Statistical design for research*. New York: John Wiley.

Kneale, D., & Barnes, P. W. (1987, December 28) For Saturday–morning kids' shows the "people meter" verdict is grim. *The Wall Street Journal*, p. 13.

Knoke, D., & Burke, P. J. (1980) *Log-Linear Models*. Beverly Hills CA: Sage Publications.

Kohn, M. L. (1987) Cross-national research as an analytic strategy. *American Sociological Review, 52*, 713–731.

Kohn, M. L., & Schooler, C. (1978) The reciprocal effects of the substantive complexity of work and intellectual flexibility: A longitudinal assessment. *American Journal of Sociology, 84*, 24–52.

Kolata, G. (1986) Shakespeare's new poem: An ode to statistics. *Science, 231*, 335–336.

Kortarba, J. A. (1984) One more for the road: The subversion of labeling within the tavern subculture. Pp. 152–160 in J. D. Douglas (ed.), *The sociology of deviance*. Boston: Allyn and Bacon.

Koshland, D. E. (1987) Retroactive prophets. *Science, 238*, 727.

Koslowsky, M., Pratt, G. L., & Wintrob, R. M. (1976) The application of guttman scale analysis to physicians' attitudes regarding abortion. *Journal of Applied Psychology, 61*, 301–304.

Kraemer, H. C., & Thiemann, S. (1987) *How many subjects? Statistical power analysis in research.* Newbury Park CA: Sage.

Kruskal, W. (1981) Statistics in society: Problems unsolved and unformulated. *Journal of the American Statistical Association, 76*, 505–515.

Kruttschnitt, C, Ward, D., & Sheble, M. A. (1987) Abuse-resistant youth: Some factors that may inhibit violent criminal behavior. *Social Forces 66*, 501–519.

Kuhn, T. (1970) *The structure of scientific revolutions.* (2nd ed. enl.) Chicago: University of Chicago Press.

Kuroda, Y., Hayashi, C., & Suzuki, T. (1986) The role of language in cross-national surveys: American and Japanese respondents. *Applied Stochastic Models and Data Analysis, 2*, 43–59.

LaFree, G. D. (1980) The effect of sexual stratification by race on official reaction to rape. *American Sociological Review, 45*, 842–854.

Laing, R. D. (1970) *Knots.* New York: Pantheon.

Lakoff, R. T. (1975) *Language and women's place.* New York: Harper, Colophone Books.

Lavrakas, P. J. (1987) *Telephone survey methods: Sampling, selection and supervision.* Beverly Hills, CA: Sage.

Lazarsfeld, P. F. (1972) The problem of measuring turnover. Pp. 358–362 in P.F. Lazarsfeld, A. Pasanella, & M. Rosenberg (eds.), *Continuities in the language of social research.* New York: Free Press.

Lehman, D. R., Wortman, C. B., & Williams, A. E. (1987) Long-term effects of losing a spouse or child in a motor vehicle accident. *Journal of Personality and Social Psychology, 52*, 218–231.

Lenski, G. (1963) *The religious factor.* New York: Doubleday.

Lenski, G. (1988) Rethinking macrosociological theory. *American Sociological Review, 53*, 163–171.

LeVine, R. A. (1966) Towards a psychology of populations: The cross-cultural study of personality. *Human Development, 9*, 30–46.

Lewin, R. (1987) Science on the roof of the world. *Science, 236*, 910–912.

Lewis, O. (1951) *Life in a mexican village: Tepoztlan revisited.* Urbana, IL: University of Illinois Press.

Lieberson, S. (1985) *Making it count.* Berkeley and Los Angeles: University of California Press.

Liebow, E. (1967) *Tally's corner.* Boston: Little, Brown.

Light, D., Jr. (1975) The sociological calendar: An analytic tool for fieldwork applied to medical and psychiatric training. *American Journal of Sociology, 80*, 1145–1164.

Lin, N., & Wie, W. (1987) Occupational prestige in urban China. *American Journal of Sociology, 93*, 793–832.

Lipsitz, L. (1965) Working-class authoritarianism: A re-evaluation. *American Sociological Review, 30*, 106–108.

Lofland, J. (1966) *Doomsday cult: A study of conversion, proselytization and maintenance of faith.* Englewood Cliffs, NJ: Prentice-Hall.

Long, G. L. (1987) Organizations and identity: Obituaries 1856–1972. *Social Forces, 65*, 964–1001.

Lord, F. M., & Novick, M. R. (1968) *Statistical theories of mental test scores.* Reading, MA: Addison-Wesley.

Lustig, M. W. (1987) Bales's interpersonal rating forms: Reliability and dimensionality. *Small Group Behavior, 18*, 99–107.

Lynch, F. R. (1977) Field research and future history: Problems posed for ethnographic sociologists by the "doomsday cult" making good. *The American Sociologist, 12,* 80–88.

Lueptow, L. B. (1976) *Bias and non-response resulting from informed consent procedures in survey research on high school seniors.* Washington, DC: Unpublished report to the Office of the Assistant Secretary for Planning and Evaluation of HEW.

McCall, G. J. (1969a) Data quality control in participant observation: Pp. 126–141 in G. J. McCall & J. L. Simmons (eds.), *Issues in participant observation: A text and reader.* London: Addison-Wesley.

McCall, G. J. (1969b) The problem of indicators in participant observation research. Pp. 230–238 in G. J. McCall & J. L. Simmons (eds.), *Issues in participant observation: A text and reader.* London: Addison-Wesley.

McCall, G. J. (1984) Systematic field observation. *Annual Review of Sociology, 10,* 263–282.

McCall, G. J., McCall, M., Denzin, N. K., Suttles, G. D., & Kurth, S. B. (1970) *Social relationships.* Chicago: Aldine.

McCloskey, D. (1985) Economical writing. *Economic Inquiry, 24,* 187–222.

McCall, G. J., & Simmons, J. L. (eds.) (1969) *Issues in participant observation: A text and reader.* London: Addison-Wesley.

McMillan, P., & Kennedy, J. R. (1981) *Library research guide to sociology.* Ann Arbor MI: Pierian Press.

McPhail, C., & R. T. Wohstein. (1989) Collective locomotion as collective behavior, *American Sociological Review,* 56: 447–463.

Machiavelli, N. (1989) *The Prince.* Russell Price (ed.) New York: Cambridge University Press.

Mack, R. W. (1969) Theoretical and substantive biases in sociological research. Pp. 52–64 in M. Sherif & C. Sherif (eds.), *Interdisciplinary relationships in the social sciences.* Chicago: Aldine.

Macklin, R. (1982) The problem of adequate disclosure in social science research. Pp. 193–214 in T. L. Beauchamp, R. R. Faden, R. J. Wallace, Jr., & L. Walters (eds.), *Ethical issues in social science research.* Baltimore: The Johns Hopkins Press.

Maines, D. R. (1987) The significance of temporality for the development of sociological theory. *The Sociological Quarterly, 28,* 303–311.

Marble, D. E., Calkins, H. W., & Peuquet, D. T. (1984) *Basic readings in geographic information systems.* Williamsville, NY: SPAD Systems.

Margenau, H. (1959) Philosophical problems concerning the meaning of measurement in physics. Pp. 160–171 in C. W. Churchman & P. Ratoosh (eds.), *Measurement definitions and theories.* New York: John Wiley.

Marsaglia, G. (1984) The exact-approximation method for generating random variables in a computer. *Journal of the American Statistical Association, 79,* 218–221.

Marsh, R. (1961) The bearing of comparative analysis on sociological theory. *Social Forces, 43,* 188–196.

Massey, D. S. (1987) Understanding Mexican migration to the United States. *American Journal of Sociology, 92,* 1372–1403.

Merton, R. K. (1965) *On the shoulders of giants: A Shandean postscript.* New York: Free Press.

Merton, R.K. (1967) *On theoretical sociology.* New York: The Free Press.

Meyrowitz, J. (1985) *No sense of place: The impact of electronic media on social behavior.* New York: Oxford University Press.

Michotte, A. (1963) *Perception of causality.* New York: Basic.

Micklin, M., & Durbin, M. (1969) Syntactic dimensions of attitude scale techniques: Sources of variation and bias. *Sociometry, 32,* 194–205.

Milgram, S. (1963) Behavioral studies of obedience. *Journal of Abnormal and Social Psychology, 67*, 371–378.

Milligan, J. D. (1979) The treatment of an historical source. *Theory and History, 18*, 177–196.

Mill, J. S. (1950) *Philosophy of scientific method*. (E. Nagel, ed.) New York: Hafner. (Originally published in 1881)

Mill, J. S. (1978) *On liberty*. (E. Rapaport, ed.). Toronto: University of Toronto Press.

Mills, C. W. (1959) *The sociological imagination*. New York: Academic Press.

Mitchell, R. (1979) *Less than words can say*. Boston: Little, Brown.

Mohr, H. (1987) *How to talk Minnesotan*. New York: Viking Penguin.

Monkkonen, E. H. (1981) *Police in urban America, 1860–1920*. New York: Cambridge University Press.

Moore, B., Jr. (1966) *Social origins of dictatorship and democracy*. Boston: Beacon Press.

Morehead, J. (1983) *Introduction to United States public documents*. (3rd ed.). Littleton, CO: Libraries Unlimited, inc.

Moorman, J. E. (1987, May) *The relationship between education and marriage*. Paper presented at the annual meeting of the Population Association of American, Chicago, IL.

Morgan, R. K., & Heise, D. (1988) Structure of emotions. *Social Psychology Quarterly, 51*, 19–31.

Moskos, C. C. Jr. (1976) *Peace soldiers: The sociology of a United Nations military force*. Chicago: University of Chicago.

Moure, R., & Sugimoto, Y. (1986) *Images of Japanese society: A study in the structure of social reality*. London: KPI.

Murray, S. O. (1978) The scientific reception of Castaneda. *Contemporary Sociology, 8*, 189–192.

Mura, D. (1987, September) *Japanese and Japanese influence in Minnesota*. Paper presented at the meeting of the Midwest Council on Asian Affairs, Northfield, MN.

Nagel, E. (1961) *The structure of science*. Princeton: Princeton University Press.

Nakamura, T. (1986) Bayesian cohort models for general cohort table analysis. *Annals of the Institute of Statistical Mathematics, 38*, 352–370.

Naroll, R. (1968) Some thoughts on comparative methods in cultural anthropology. Pp. 236–277 in H. M. Blalock & A. B. Blalock (eds.), *Methodology in social research*. New York: McGraw-Hill.

Nelkin, D. (1982) Intellectual property: The control of scientific information. *Science, 216*: 704–708.

Nelson, J. F. (1980) Multiple victimization in American cities: A statistical analysis of rare events. *American Journal of Sociology, 85*, 870–891.

Newell, A. (in press) *A unified theory of cognition*. Cambridge MS: Harvard University Press.

Newell, A., & Simon, H. A. (1972) *Human problem solving*. Englewood Cliffs, NJ: Prentice-Hall.

Newport, F. (1979) The religious switcher in the United States. *American Sociological Review, 44*, 528–552.

Nunnally, J. C. (1967) *Psychometric theory*. New York: McGraw-Hill.

O'Barr, W., and Atkins, B. (1978) "Women's language" or "powerless language"? Pp. 93–110 in R. Borker, N. Furman, & S. McConnell-Ginet (eds.), *Language in women's lives: Literature, culture, and society*. New York: McGraw-Hill.

Orback, E. (1979) Simulation games and motivation for learning. *Simulation and Games, 10*, 3–14.

Osgood, C. E., Sugi, G. J., & Tannebaum, P. H. (1957) *The measurement of meaning*. Urbana: University of Illinois Press.

Osgood, C. E. (1960) Some effects of motivation on style of encoding. Pp. 293–306 in T. A. Sebeok (ed.), *Style in language*. Cambridge, MA: M.I.T. Press.

Otis, L. L. (1985) *Prostitution in medieval society: The history of an urban institution in languedoc*. Chicago: University of Chicago Press.

Pais, A. (1986) *Inward bound: of matter and forces in the physical world*. Oxford: Oxford University Press.

Panel on Privacy and Confidentiality as Factors in Survey Response. (1979) *Privacy and confidentiality as factors in survey response*. Washington, D.C.: National Academy of Sciences.

Parke, R. D. (1978) Parent-infant interaction: Progress, paradigms, and problems. Pp. 69–94 in G. P. Sackett (Ed.), *Observing behavior volume 1: Theory and applications in mental retardation*. Baltimore: University Park Press.

Patterson, G. R., & Moore, D. (1979) Interactive patterns as units of behavior. Pp. 77–96 in M. E. Lamb, S. J. Suomi, & G. R. Stephenson (eds.), *Social interaction analysis: Methodological issues*. Madison: University of Wisconsin Press.

Patton, C. V., & Sawicki, D. S. (1986) *Basic methods of policy analysis and planning*. Englewood Cliffs: Prentice-Hall.

Payne, D. E. (1978) Cross-national diffusion: Effects of Canadian TV on rural Minnesota viewers. *American Sociological Review, 43*, 740–756.

Payne, D. E., & Peake, C. A. (1977) Cultural diffusion: The role of U.S. TV in Iceland. *Journalism Quarterly, 54*, 523–531.

Payne, S. L. (1951) *The art of asking questions*. Princeton: Princeton University Press.

Pescosolido, B.A., & Georgianna, S. (1989) Durkheim, suicide, and religion: Toward a network theory of suicide. *American Sociological Review, 54*, 34–48.

Petty, R., Ostrom, T., & Brock, T. (1981) Historical foundations of the cognitive response approach to attitudes and persuasion. Pp. 5–28 in R. Petty, T. Ostrom, & T. Brock (ed.), *Cognitive responses in persuasion*. Hillsdale, N. J.: Lawrence Erlbaum Associations.

Plank, M. (1949) *Scientific autobiography and other papers*. (F. Gaynor, trans.) New York: Philosophical Library.

Platt, J. (1981) Evidence and proof in documentary research I: Some specific problems of documentary research, *Sociological Review, 27*, 31–52.

Poggie, J. J. Jr. (1972) Toward quality control in key informant data. *Human Organization, 31*, 23–30.

Poincaré, H. (1921) *Science and method*. (G.E. Halsted, trans.) Garrison, N.Y.: The Science Press.

Poizner, H., Klima, E. S., & Bellugi, U. (1987) *What the hands reveal about the brain*. Cambridge, MA: MIT Books.

Polsby, N. (1969) "Pluralism" in the study of community power, or, *erkläring* before *verkäring* in *wissenssoziologie*. *American Sociologist*, 4: 118–122.

Pope, W. (1976) *Durkheim's Suicide: A classic analyzed*. Chicago: University of Chicago Press.

Powers, D. E., and Alderman, D. L. (1979) Practical techniques for implementing true experimental designs. *Evaluation Quarterly, 3*, 89–96.

Price, D. J. D. (1986) *Little science, big science . . . and beyond*. New York: Columbia University Press.

Primoff, E. H. (1987, October 3) Mind-crushing tests. *Science News, 132*, 211.

Pryor, J. B., & Kriss, M. (1977) The cognitive dynamics of salience in the attribution process. *Journal of Personality and Social Psychology, 35*, 49–55.

Punch, M. (1986) *The politics and ethics of fieldwork*. Beverly Hills, CA: Sage.

Putt, A. D., & Springer, J. F. (1989) *Policy research: Methods and applications*. Englewood Cliffs, N. J.: Prentice-Hall.

Quine, W. V. (1987) *Quiddities: An intermittently philosophical dictionary*. Cambridge, MS: Belkap Press of Harvard University.

Ragin, C. C. (1987) *The comparative method: Moving beyond qualitative and quantitative strategies*. Berkeley: University of California Press.

Ragland, D. R., & Brand, R. J. (1988) Type A behavior and mortality from coronary heart disease. *New England Journal of Medicine, 318*, 65–69.

Raloff, J. (1987, May 16) Coming: The big chill? *Science News, 132*, 314–315.

Redfield, R. (1930) *Tepoztlan: A Mexican village*. Chicago: University of Chicago Press.

Reiss, A. J. Jr. (1968) Police brutality—answers to key questions. *Transaction, 5*, 10–19.

Reiss, A. J. Jr. (1971) Systematic observation of natural social phenomena. Pp. 3–33 in H. L. Costner (ed.), *Sociological methodology, 1971*. San Francisco: Jossey-Bass.

Rice, J. (1988) Serendipity and holism: The beauty of opacs. *Library Journal, 113*, 138–141.

Richardson, L. (1988) Secrecy and status: The social construction of forbidden relationships. *American Sociological Review, 53*, 209–219.

Rivlin, A. M., & Timpane, P. M. (eds.) (1975) *Ethical and legal issues of social experimentation*. Washington, D C: Brookings Institution.

Roberts, S. K. (1981, September) Artificial intelligence. *Byte*, 164–178.

Robinson, J. P., & Meadow, R. (1982) *Polls apart*. Cabin John, MD: Seven Locks Press.

Robinson, W. S. (1950) Ecological correlations and the behavior of individuals. *American Sociological Review, 15*, 351–357.

Rodman, H., and Kolodny, R. (1972) Organizational strains in the researcher-practitioner relationship. Pp. 117–135 in F. Caro (ed.), *Readings in evaluation research*. New York: Russell Sage Foundation.

Rogers, E., & Kincaid, D. (1981) *Communication networks: Toward a new paradigm of research*. New York: Free Press.

Rokeach, M., & Cochrane, R. (1972) Self-confrontation and confrontation with another as determinants of long-term value change. *Journal of Applied Social Psychology, 2*, 283–293.

Rosenberg, M. (1965) *Society and the adolescent self-image*. Princeton: Princeton University Press.

Rosenberg, M. (1968) *The logic of survey analysis*. New York: Basic Books.

Rosenthal, R. (1966) *Experimenter effects in behavioral research*. New York: Appleton-Century-Crofts.

Rossi, A. S. (1977) A biosocial perspective on parenting. *Daedalus, 106*, 1–31.

Rossi, P. H., & Wright, J. D. (1984) Evaluation research: An assessment. *Annual Review of Sociology, 10*, 331–352.

Rubinstein, R. A. (1987) Anthropology and advocacy. *Science, 236*, 823.

Sakiey, E., & Fry, E. (1984) *3,000 instant words*. Providence, RI: Jamestown Publications.

Savage, D. (1988) *A User's Guide to SocialScene and SocialTrend* [IBM-PC computer programs] New York: Holt, Rinehart, & Winston.

Schatzman, L., & Strauss, A. L. (1973) *Field research: Strategies for a natural sociology*. Englewood Cliffs, NJ: Prentice-Hall.

Schooler, C., & Naoi, N. (1988) The psychological effects of traditional and of economically peripheral job settings in Japan. *American Journal of Sociology, 94*, 335–355.

Schubert, G. (1962) The 1960 term: A psychological analysis. *American Political Science Review, 56*, 90–107.

Schuerman, J. R. (1987) Expert consulting systems in social welfare. *Social Work Research and Abstracts, 23*, 14–17.

Schuman, H., & Presser, S. (1979) The assessment of "no opinion" in attitude surveys.

Pp 241–275 in K. Schuessler (ed.), *Sociological methodology, 1979*. San Francisco: Jossey-Bass.

Schuman, H., & Presser, S. (1981) *Questions and answers in attitude surveys: Experiments on question form, wording, and context*. New York: Academic Press.

Schwartz, H., & Jacobs, J. (1979) *Qualitative sociology: A method to the madness*. New York: The Free Press.

Schwartz, M. S., & Schwartz, C. G. (1956) Problems in participant observation. *American Journal of Sociology, 60*, 343–354.

Selvin, H. C., & Wilson, E. K. (1984) On sharpening sociologists' prose. *The Sociological Quarterly, 25*, 205–222.

Sewell, W. H. (1985) *Structure and mobility: The men and women of Marseille, 1820–1870*. Cambridge: Cambridge University Press.

Sewell, W. H., Haller, A. O., & Ohlendorf, G. W. (1970) The educational and early occupational status attainment process: Replication and revision. *American Sociological Review, 35*, 1014–1027.

Shangraw, R. F., Jr. (1987) Knowledge acquisition, expert systems, and public management decisions. *Social Science Microcomputer Review, 5*, 163–173.

Shepelak, N. J. (1987) The role of self-explanations and self-evaluations in legitimating inequality. *American Sociological Review, 52*, 495–503.

Sherif, C. (1980) Social views, attitudes and involvement of the self. *Nebraska Symposium on Motivation, 1979, 27*, 1–64.

Shils, E. (1975) *The intellectuals and the powers and other essays: Selected essays of Edward Shils*. Chicago: University of Chicago Press.

Sieber, S. D. (1973) The integration of fieldwork and survey methods. *American Journal of Sociology, 78*, 1335–1359.

Sieber, S. D. (1981) *Fatal remedies: The ironies of social intervention*. New York: Plenum.

Simon, A., & E. G. Boyer (1974) *Mirrors for behavior III: An anthology of observation instruments*. Wyncote, Pa.: Communication Materials Center.

Singer, E., & Frankel, M. R. (1982) Informed consent procedures in telephone interviews. *American Sociological Review, 47*, 416–427.

Sjoberg, G., & Nett, R. (1968) *A methodology for social research*. New York: Harper & Row, Pub.

Skocpol, T. (1979) *States and social revolution: A comparative analysis of France, Russia, and China* Cambridge: Cambridge University Press.

Skocpol, T. (1984a) Sociology's historical imagination. Pp 1–21 in T. Skocpol (ed.), *Vision and method in historical sociology*. New York: Cambridge University Press.

Skocpol, T. (1984b) Emerging agendas and recurrent strategies in historical sociology. Pp. 356–391 in T. Skocpol (ed.), *Vision and method in historical sociology*. New York: Cambridge University Press.

Smith, H. W. (1978) Effects of sex on subject's interpretation of placebo marijuana's effects. *Social Science and Medicine, 12*, 107–109.

Smith, H. W. (1980) The CB handle: An announcement of adult identity. *Symbolic Interaction, 3*, 95–105.

Smith, H. W. (1982) Improving the quality of field research training. *Human Relations, 35*, 605–619.

Smith, H. W. (1983) Predictions of same-sex and cross-sex observational recognition effects in visual accuracy of action. *Perceptual and Motor Skills, 57*, 380–382.

Smith, H. W. (1985) Pretest, treatment and pretest-treatment interaction effects on observational accuracy. *Communications: The European Journal of Communication, 3*, 119–129.

Smith, H. W. (1987) *An introduction to social psychology*. Englewood Cliffs, NJ: Prentice-Hall.

Smith, H. W. (1990) The politics of abortion: Husband notification legislation, self-disclosure, and marital bargaining. *The Sociological Quarterly, 4*, 585–596.

Smith, H. W. (unpublished) Rape ending in abortion. University of Missouri-St. Louis.

Smith, L. W. (1988) Microcomputer-based bibliographic searching. *Nursing Outlook, 37*, 125–127.

Smith, M. D. (1979) Increases in youth violence: age, period or cohort effect. Presented at the Meetings of the American Sociological Association. Boston.

Smith, T. W. (1980b) *A compendium of trends on general social survey questions*. (NORC Report No. 129) Chicago: National Opinion Research Center.

Smith, V. L., Suchanek, G. L., & Williams, A. W. (1988) Bubbles, crashes and endogenous expectations in experimental asset markets. *Econometrica, 56*, 1119–1151.

Smith-Lovin, L. (1979) Behavior settings and impressions formed from social scenarios. *Social Psychology Quarterly, 42*, 31–43.

Smith-Lovin, L., & Heise, D. R. (1988) (eds.) *Analyzing social interaction: Advances in affect control theory*. New York: Gordon & Breach Science Publishers.

Snow, D. A., & Anderson, L. (1987) Identity work among the homeless: The verbal construction and avowal of personal identities. *American Journal of Sociology, 92*, 1336–1371.

Snow, D. A., Zurcher, L. A., Jr., & Ekland-Olson, S. (1980) Social networks and social movements. A microstructural apporach to differential recruitment. *American Journal of Sociology, 45*, 787–801.

Sorokin, P. (1956) *Fads and foibles in modern sociology and related sciences*. Chicago: Regnery.

Soskin, W. F., & Kauffman, P. E. (1961) Judgment of emotion in word-free voice samples. *Journal of Communication, 11*, 73–80.

South, S. J., & Messner, S. F. (1987) The sex ratio and women's involvement in crime: A cross-national analysis. *The Sociological Quarterly, 28*, 171–188.

Spanier, G. B. (1976) Measuring dyadic adjustment: New scales for assessing the quality of marriage and the family. *Journal of Marriage and the Family, 38*, 15–28.

Stack, S. (1987) Publicized executions and homicide, 1950–1980. *American Sociological Review, 52*, 532–540.

Stang, D. J., & Wrightsman, L. S. (1981) *Dictionary of social behavior and social research methods*. Monterey CA: Brooks/Cole Publishing Co.

Star, S. L., & Gerson, E. M. (1986) The management and dynamics of anomalies in scientific work. *The Sociological Quarterly, 28*, 147–170.

Stark, R. (1987) *SHOWCASE for introduction to sociology*. [IBM-PC compatible program] Belmont, CA: Wadsworth.

Starr, L. (1984) Oral history. Pp. 3–26 in D. K. Dunaway & W. K. Baum (eds.), *Oral history: An interdisciplinary anthology*. Nashville, TN: American Association for State and Local History.

Starr, P. (1982) *The social transformation of American medicine*. New York: Basic Books.

Stein, M. (1990) *The Ethnography of an Adult Bookstore: Private Scenes in Public Places*. Edwin Mellen Press.

Stevens, S. S. (1975) *Psychophysics*. New York: Wiley.

Stevenson, H. W., Lee, S., & Stigler, R. (1986) Mathematics achievement of Chinese, Japanese, and American children. *Science, 231*, 693–699.

Stinchcombe, A. L. (1968) *Constructing social theories*. New York: Harcourt, Brace, & World.

Strauss, A., Schatzman, L., Bucher, L., Ehrlick, D., & Sabshin, M. (1964) *Psychiatric ideologies and institutions*. New York: Free Press.

Suchman, E. A. (1969) *Evaluative research: Principles and practice in public service and social action programs*. New York: Russell Sage Foundation.

Sudman, S. (1976) *Applied sampling*. New York: Academic Press.

Sudman, S., & Bradburn, N. M. (1982) *Asking questions: A practical guide to questionnaire design*. San Francisco: Jossey-Bass, Inc.

Szasz, T. S. (1987) *Insanity: The idea and its consequences*. New York: Wiley.

Szent-Gyorgyi, A. (1972) Dionysians and appollonians. *Science, 175*, 966.

Thibaut, J., & Kelly, H. (1959) *The social psychology of groups*. New York: Wiley.

Thomas, D. S., & Nishimoto, R. S. (1946) *The Spoilage*. Berkeley: University of California Press.

Thomas, W. L., & Znaniecki, F. (1927) *The Polish peasant in America*. New York: Knopf.

Thompson, M. S. (1980) *Benefit-cost analysis for program evaluation*. Beverly Hills, CA: Sage.

Thurstone, L., & Chave, E. (1929) *The measurement of attitude*. Chicago: University of Chicago Press.

Tilly, C. (1978) *From mobilization to revolution*. Reading MA: Addison-Wesley.

Tilly, C. (1981) *As sociology meets history*. New York: Academic Press.

Tilly, C. (1984) *Big structures, large processes, huge comparisons*. New York: Russell Sage Foundation.

Touchstone Applied Science Associates, Inc. (1985) *Readability report in DRP units*. (7th edition) New York: College Entrance Examination Board.

Tracy, P. E., & Dawes, J. A. (1981) The validity of randomized response for sensitive measurements. *American Sociological Review, 46*, 187–200.

Triandis, H. C. (1964) Exploratory factor analysis of the behavioral component of social attitudes. *Journal of Abnormal and Social Psychology, 68*, 420–430.

Tropp, R. A. (1982) A regulatory perspective on social science research. Pp. 391–416 in T. Beauchamp, R. Faden, R. Wallace, & L. Walters (eds.), *Ethical issues in social science research*. Baltimore: The John Hopkins University Press.

Truzzi, M. (1977) Review of Castaneda's journey. *The Zetetic*, 1: 88–98.

Tuchman, B. (1984) Distinguishing the significant from the insignificant. Pp. 3–26 in D. K. Dunaway & W. K. Baum (eds.), *Oral History: An interdisciplinary anthology*. Nashville, TN: American Association for State and Local History.

Tufte, E. R. (1983) *The visual display of quantitative information*. Santa Monica, CA: Graphics Press.

Tukey, J. (1977) *Exploratory data analysis*. Reading, MS: Addison-Wesley Publishing Co.

Tuma, N. B., Hannan, M. T., & Groeneveld, L. P. (1979) Dynamic analysis of event histories. *American Journal of Sociology, 84*, 820–854.

Turing, A. M. (1936) On computable numbers, with an application to the entscheidungsproblem, *Proceedings of the London Mathematics Society*, Series 2, 42: 230–266.

Turner, C. F., & Martin, E. (eds.). (1984) *Surveying subjective phenomena*. (vol. 1). New York: Russell Sage Foundation.

United Nations (1985) *Demographic yearbook*. New York: United Nations.

U.S. Department of Health, Education and Welfare (1971) *The institutional guide to DHEW policy on protection of human subjects*. Washington, DC: U.S. Government Printing Office.

Vallier, I. (1971) Empirical comparisons of social structure: Leads and lags. Pp. 203–266 in I. Vallier (ed.), *Comparative methods in sociology*. Berkeley: University of California Press.

van der Sprinkel, O. (1963) Max weber on China. *Theory and History, 3*, 348–370.

Vidich, A., & Bensman, J. (1968) *Small town in mass society*. Princeton: Princeton University Press.

Vietze, P. E., Abernathy, S. R., Ashe, M. L., & Faulstich, G. (1978) Contingency interaction between mothers and their developmentally delayed infants. Pp. 115–134 in G. P. Sackett (ed.), *Observing behavior volume 1: Theory and applications in mental retardation*. Baltimore: University Press.

von Neumann, J. (1963) *Collected works*. New York: Pergamon Press.

Wallace, W. (1971) *The logic of science in sociology*. Chicago: Aldine.

Wallerstein, I. (1974) *The modern world-system*. 2 vols. New York: Academic Press.

Ward, L. (1906) *Applied sociology*. New York: Greenwood Press.

Warwick, D. (1982) *Bitter pills; Population policies and their implementation in 8 countries*. Cambridge: Cambridge University Press.

Watts, H. W., & Rees, A. (1977) (Eds.) *The New Jersey income maintenance experiments, vol. 2: Labor-supply responses*. New York: Academic.

Wax, M. (1982) Researcher reciprocity rather than informed consent in fieldwork. Pp. 33–48 in J. E. Sieber (ed.), *The ethics of social research: Fieldwork, regulation, and publication*. New York: Springer-Verlag.

Webb, E. J., Campbell, D. T., Schwartz, R. D., & Sechrest, L. (1966) *Unobstrusive measures: Nonreactive research in the social sciences*. Chicago: Rand McNally.

Weick, K. E. (1985) Systematic observational methods. Pp. 567–634 in G. Lindsey & E. Aronson (eds.), *Handbook of social psychology, vol. 1: Theory and method* (3rd ed.). Hillsdale, NJ: Erlbaum.

Weisenbaum, J. (1976) *Computer power and human reason*. San Francisco: Freeman.

Weiss, C. (1972) *Evaluation research: Methods of assessing program effectiveness*. Englewood Cliffs, N. J.: Prentice-Hall.

Westie, F. R. (1957) Towards closer relations between theory and research: A procedure and an example. *American Sociological Review, 22*, 149–154.

Whitehead, A. N. (1947) *Essays in science and philosophy*. London: Greenwood.

Whiting, J. W. M. (1968) Methods and problems in cross-cultural research. Pp. 693–728 in G. Lindzey & E. Aronson (eds.) *Handbook of social psychology, vol. II* (2nd ed.). London: Addison-Wesley.

Wiggins, J. A. (1968) Hypothesis validity and experimental laboratory methods. Pp. 390–427 in H. M. Blalock & A. B. Blalock (eds.) *Methodology in social research*. New York: McGraw-Hill.

Wilcox, D. L. (1984) World crises: *The fate of civilization, a computer simulation of the quality of human life during the next century*. [Apple II software] New York: Saunders Publishing Co.

Williams, K. R., & Flewelling, R. L. (1988) The social production of criminal homicide: A comparative study of disaggregated rates in American cities. *American Sociological Review, 53*, 421–431.

Williams, W. (1971) *Social policy research and analysis: The experience in the federal agencies*. New York: American Elsevier.

Winklestein, W., Samuel, M., Padian, N. S., Wiley, J. A., Lang, W., Anderson, R. E., & Levy, J. A. (1987) The San Francisco men's health study: III. Reduction in human immunodeficiency virus transmission among homosexual/bisexual men, 1982–86, *American Journal of Public Health, 76*, 685–689.

Wintrob, R. M. (1969) An inward focus: A consideration of psychological stress in fieldwork. Pp. 63–76 in F. Henry & S. Saberwal (eds.), *Stress and response in fieldwork*. New York: Holt, Rinehart & Winston.

Woods, P. (1981) Understanding through talk. In C. Adelman (ed.) *Uttering, muttering:*

Collecting, using and reporting talk for social and educational research. London: Grant McIntyre.

World Medical Association. (1964, August 22) Declaration of Helsinki. *Medical Journal of Australia.*

Wylie, R. (1979) *The self-concept* (rev. ed., vol. 2). Lincoln: University of Nebraska Press.

Yalow, R. S. (1979) Peer review and scientific revolutions. *Biological Psychiatry, 21,* 1–2.

Yamagishi, T., Gillmore, M. R., & Cook, K. S. (1988) Network connections and the distribution of power in exchange networks. *American Journal of Sociology, 93,* 833–851.

Yarrow, M. R., Campbell, J. D., & Burton, R. G. (1964) Reliability of maternal retrospection: A preliminary report. *Family Process, 3,* 207–218.

Yoder, S. K. (1987, October 14) Native son's nobel award is Japan's loss. *The Wall Street Journal,* p. 30.

Yule, G. U., & Kendall, M. G. (1950) *An introduction to the theory of statistics.* London: Charles Griffin.

Zelditch, M., Jr. (1962) Some methodological problems of field studies. *American Journal of Sociology, 67,* 566–576.

Zuckerman, H. (1977) *Scientific elite: Nobel laureates in the United States.* NY: Free Press.

Author Index

Subject Index